. . . . . . . . . . . . . . . . . .

# Contexts and Communities

# CONTEXTS
## AND
# COMMUNITIES
## Rhetorical Approaches to Reading, Writing, and Research

### Ruth B. Greenberg
Jefferson Community College

### Joseph J. Comprone
Arizona State University West

Macmillan College Publishing Company

New York

Editor: Timothy Julet
Production Supervisor: P.M. Gordon Associates, Inc.
Production Manager: Aliza Greenblatt
Text Designer: Eileen Burke
Cover Designer: Curtis Towe Graphics
Cover art: Ralph Fasanella, "Washington Square Park"


This book was set in Century Old Style by Carlisle Communications
and was printed and bound by Arcata Graphics.
The cover was printed by New England Book Components.

Macmillan College Publishing Company
866 Third Avenue, New York, New York 10022

Macmillan College Publishing Company is part of
the Maxwell Communication Group of Companies.

Maxwell College Macmillan Canada, Inc.
1200 Eglinton Avenue East
Suite 200
Don Mills, Ontario M3C 3N1


Library of Congress Cataloging-in-Publication Data

Greenberg, Ruth B.
    Contexts and communities : rhetorical approaches to reading, writing, and research /
    Ruth B. Greenberg, Joseph J. Comprone.
        p.   cm.
    ISBN 0-02-346645-6
    1. English language–Rhetoric.   2. Interdisciplinary approach in
education.   I. Comprone, Joseph J.   II. Title.
PE1408.G78   1994                                                    93–27465
808′.042—dc20                                                        CIP

Printing: 1 2 3 4 5 6 7        Year: 4 5 6 7 8 9 0

To our families—for their help, encouragement,
and most of all, for their patience.

# Preface

*Contexts and Communities (C&C)* provides students and teachers with a new kind of resource for the freshman writing course. The book is new because it brings together in innovative fashion two recent developments in freshman English courses: an interest in writing beyond the boundaries of literature and the humanities, including writing in the sciences and more technical professions, and a need to use rhetoric as the means of helping students learn to write for a broad range of purposes and audiences. In *Contexts and Communities,* rhetoric becomes the means for learning to understand writing situations as they occur across the academic curriculum and through different professional fields.

## WHAT ARE THE MAIN FEATURES OF CONTEXTS AND COMMUNITIES?

### Functional Organization and Format

*Contexts and Communities* is divided into three major sections, sequenced in a manner that will help students learn in a more natural fashion.

The first section introduces both the skills and concepts behind the critical reading and writing processes. It also introduces students to the basic college essay form and to the basics of doing college-level research. Combined, the chapters in this first section provide students with a general background for the specific readings and assignments that follow in Section Two. These chapters can be read in their entirety before students read and write their way through chapters in Section Two, or they can be read in part as students move from one chapter in Section Two to another.

The second section of *C&C* is devoted to accomplishing two course goals: first, in a natural and integrated fashion, it provides a basic understanding of rhetorical analysis that will help students define the situations within which they read and write; second, it provides readings that will both introduce students to a range of curricular and professional content and provide them with contexts for their writing.

*Contexts and Communities* concludes with two useful sections: a rhetorical glossary and a research appendix. The glossary supplements the rhetorical discussions that appear throughout the earlier parts of the book. The research appendix works as an extension of the earlier chapter on using research to inform the writing process.

Overall, we believe that *C&C* more effectively integrates reading, writing, rhetoric, and research than does any other freshman textbook in the field. It provides flexibility for teachers as they arrange their writing courses; it also provides students with the opportunity to learn reading and writing skills and concepts as they consider a range of interesting and accessible ideas.

## A Rhetorical Approach to Writing Across the Curriculum

Many composition books have begun to emphasize writing across the college curriculum. This one does it in a new way. It links reading in different fields with rhetorical analyses of those fields. The rhetorical analysis, however, is not deadly dull, but is integrated into each reading chapter in a natural and efficient way. In each chapter, readings are introduced through a general rhetorical analysis of the theme and readings of the entire chapter. Collaborative activities are suggested. Then, pre- and post-reading questions help students explore more specifically the rhetorical situation of each reading in the chapter. Writing tips and assignment ideas are also explored along the way, as readings are introduced and examined.

This integration of rhetoric with reading and writing activities enables students to learn writing skills within a natural inquiry process. Learning to write occurs within the larger process of learning to think critically, interpret, and belong to larger communities of educated people.

## A Full Treatment of the Reading Process

*Contexts and Communities* provides full coverage of the basic skills and concepts necessary for effective critical reading. It also ties in those skills and concepts with each stage in the writing process. Section One includes a chapter in which skills such as summarizing and paraphrasing are presented as parts of the process of building written interpretations. Each reading in Section Two is then surrounded by pre- and post-reading questions that help students enter into and figure out the contexts within which a reading appears; these questions also prepare students to construct and analyze the contexts in which their own writings will function.

*Contexts and Communities* also presents a wide range of academic writing, including writing in the sciences, the professional fields, and the humanities. For those courses in which writing is treated in its realities across the disciplines and professional fields, *C&C* presents a useful and interesting selection of cross-curricular readings; it also provides strategies useful for critical reading in those fields.

## Accessible and Wide-Ranging Content

*Contexts and Communities* brings together the best of the thematic and cross-disciplinary approaches to writing. Most of the readings represented are of mid-range difficulty. They reflect the complexity of recent work in a variety of fields, yet they are usually written by journalists or nonspecialists for general audiences. The content of these fields is thus not oversimplified; the writing, however, in all cases, is accessible to nonspecialist readers. In the process of reading selections from various chapters, students will also develop a general understanding of how knowledge is subdivided into different academic fields, preparing them in the process for later, more advanced work in areas of those fields that might interest them.

*Contexts and Communities,* through its thematic organization, also helps students refine and develop their approaches to the issues that are raised in the readings. Each chapter in Section Two begins with readings that introduce common problems in a field; other readings then are organized into clusters that relate back to the central thematic issue of the chapter. As students work through reading selections, they are helped by study questions to find and limit individual perspectives on chapter themes and to carry those perspectives into their writing. The chapter themes in Section Two, then, provide interesting content as well as defined perspectives for students' writing. Every chapter in Section Two closes with a list of optional assignments, all related in one way or another to the theme developed in the chapter's readings.

## An Integrated Approach to Research and Writing

In addition to stressing writing across the curriculum, most beginning college writing courses now require at least one researched essay or report. Beginning with Chapter 4 in Section One, *Contexts and Communities* covers the entire research process, ranging from initial searching and outlining to using appropriate documentation and editing effectively. Each stage in the research process is integrated with an appropriate stage in the writing process. *Contexts and Communities* will fit nicely into those college writing courses that emphasize the fact that "effective writing is informed writing." Yet, it will make gathering information through library and field research a natural part of student composing processes, not an afterthought to be superimposed on texts long after they have been planned and drafted. *Contexts and Communities* also provides an approach to research that will work for students as they write short essays including brief references to only one or two outside sources or longer, more fully researched papers and reports.

· · · · · · · · · · · ·

## HOW DOES *CONTEXTS AND COMMUNITIES* FIT INTO THE UNIVERSITY CURRICULUM?

Most freshman writing courses serve general education and skill functions in the university curriculum. *Contexts and Communities* addresses both those functions in a way that is accessible and useful to students. Its wide-ranging selection of readings will introduce students to interesting and significant themes in today's world. Its practical discussions of reading, writing, rhetoric, and research will engage students in active learning of critical reading and writing skills. In other words, *C&C* will help teachers and students accomplish the more general goals of writing across the curriculum while it provides a sound background in basic skills.

· · · · · · · · · · ·

## ACKNOWLEDGMENTS

As co-authors, we recognize the collaborative nature of writing and the enormous debt we owe to those individuals who, knowingly and often unknowingly, supported and contributed to this textbook. We thank those students who responded to this book at various stages of its development and those who allowed us to reproduce their writing in it. We are grateful to our editor, Barbara Heinssen, who provided a framework for our own writing processes and offered support and suggestions. Sharon Gibson, who team taught the class in which this textbook originated, played an important role in *C&C*'s early development. We thank the following reviewers, who offered valuable suggestions that prompted us to "re-see" our work: Cora Agatucci, Central Oregon Community College; Lydia Blanchard, Southwest Texas State

University; Marlene Clarke, University of California–Davis; Joe Law, Texas Christian University; Judith Levine, Eastern Kentucky University; Kay Limburg, Montgomery College; Donna Hickey, University of Richmond; Elizabeth Hodges, Virginia Commonwealth University; and Chris Thaiss, George Mason University. And, of course, we thank our families, whose good humor and understanding sustained us and this project. Finally, we thank one another for support, friendship, and commitment during innumerable composing crises and their inevitable resolutions.

# Contents

· · · · · · · · · · · · · · SECTION ONE · · · · · · · · · · · · ·

**1**
· · · · · · · · · · · · · · · · ·
**BECOMING PART OF A CRITICAL
READING COMMUNITY   3**

**2**
· · · · · · · · · · · · · · · · ·
**WRITING AS A LEARNING TOOL   29**

# 3
. . . . . . . . . . . . . . . .
## SHAPING AN ACADEMIC ESSAY   60

**4**

. . . . . . . . . . . . . . . .

## USING RESEARCH TOOLS TO BROADEN YOUR PERSPECTIVE    74

. . . . . . . . . . . . **SECTION TWO** . . . . . . . . . . . . .

**5**

. . . . . . . . . . . . . . . .

## PERSPECTIVES ON INTELLIGENCE    101

# 6
## PERSPECTIVES ON ANIMAL
## AND HUMAN COMMUNITIES   183

# 7
. . . . . . . . . . . . . . . .
## THE POWER AND LIMITS OF LANGUAGE 240

# 8
. . . . . . . . . . . . . . . .
## PERSPECTIVES ON HEALTHCARE ETHICS
## AND SOCIETY 327

# 9
. . . . . . . . . . . . . . . .
## WOMEN AND THE
## CORPORATE WORKPLACE      402

## 10
. . . . . . . . . . . . . . .
## CONSUMERISM    471

# 12

· · · · · · · · · · · · · · · · ·

## PERSPECTIVES ON CENSORSHIP   653

· · · · · · · · · · · · · · · ·

## GLOSSARY OF RHETORICAL TERMS   727

. . . . . . . . . . . . . . . .
## RESEARCH APPENDIX:
## USING RESEARCH TOOLS   735

. . . . . . . . . . . . . . . .
## INDEX OF AUTHORS AND TITLES   819

# SECTION
# ONE

# 1

# Becoming Part of a Critical Reading Community

How do readers construct meaning in what they read?
Why do reading processes differ? What is critical reading?
How do critical readers use skimming and annotating
strategies?
Why is critical reading so important to success in college?

## 1
## THE READING PROCESS

Why does this college writing textbook begin with a section about reading? Reading and writing are interconnected processes. In many college courses, teachers expect students to write about course and related readings. More important, teachers expect students to write critically: to use writing to demonstrate not only that they understand what they have read but that they are able to interpret, evaluate, and respond to it. Writing is connected to the reading process in other ways. Both writers and readers construct meaning in texts. Writers read as they generate ideas for, draft, and review and revise texts. Readers write as they predict what texts will mean, confirm and revise those predictions, and then respond to those meanings.

## Generating, Confirming, and Revising Predictions
## While Reading

To construct meaning in a text, readers generate, confirm, or revise predictions about what they read, whether the text is a journal article, a newspaper article, or a poem. The ability to make predictions depends, in part, on the reader's familiarity with the content, organization, and style of particular kinds of texts. This is similar to a college student's ability to predict what particular college courses will be like, which depends, in part, on experiences with previous college courses. Students entering college for the first time bring past experiences with education and particular subjects, as well as some general expectations about college life, with them. After spending some time in college, however, they become more knowledgeable about college life and college courses. This acquired knowledge prompts revision of some original predictions and helps students predict more successfully what courses will be like. Readers also use past experiences and expectations to make predictions about a text, match those predictions to what actually occurs, and then use what has been learned to generate new predictions.

Reading begins with comprehension: the ability to recognize and interpret another person's words, symbols, and signs. Comprehension means being able to summarize accurately, to follow specific words and sentences through to a general idea. Here is the beginning of an interview published in *Psychology Today,* in which James Ellison, an editor at the magazine, questions research psychologist Howard Gardner about his theories on intelligence and IQ testing (Gardner believes that intelligence cannot be quantified; see Chapter 5 for the complete interview.).

> *Ellison: Frames of Mind* embraces a theory of multiple intelligences. Can you explain that theory in relatively simple terms?

What predictions may readers make while reading this excerpt that would lead to comprehension?

Most readers would focus on the words "explain," "theory," and "simple terms" to predict what information will follow. Also, their understanding of "multiple" and "intelligence" would determine the kind of meaning constructed for the phrase "multiple intelligences." However, other cues can also guide readers' efforts to comprehend. The italicized "Ellison" and the colon after his name let readers know that this article is based on an interview. A reader who has read other articles like this will recognize this cue and be able to make predictions about the article's organization. Similarly, by italicizing *Frames of Mind,* Ellison lets readers know that the interview will focus on a book Gardner has written. Ellison's language choices also help readers make predictions about his tone, perspective, and intended readers. Ellison is direct, reporter-like, and aware that his readers may need some information about the subject of Gardner's book and theory.

Even the punctuation and the order of words in sentences guide readers as they predict, revise, and confirm meanings in what they read. Beginning the sentence with "Can you explain" instead of "You can explain" provides a cue that is confirmed when readers arrive at the end of the sentence and find the question mark.

This reading process of predicting, confirming, and revising to construct meaning is not, however, straightforward. Even though readers move through a sentence from beginning to end, they are constantly predicting, confirming, and revising, although they are not usually conscious of these processes. Readers do not make meaning after reading, but while reading. They generate expectations about what the text will contain; those expectations are then fulfilled or revised. If a sentence begins with "The colors of the American flag are . . . ," most readers would probably predict that the sentence will end with "red, white, and blue." If readers don't find "red, white, and blue" in the sentence, they will probably return to the beginning of the sentence and try again (The sentence could have ended with ". . . found in everything from tablecloths to t-shirts on July 4," for example.). Readers also make different kinds of predictions. For example, a student reading a novel may make predictions about plot, character, and theme, which, like the predictions discussed earlier, are revised and confirmed throughout the reading process.

Sometimes readers experience difficulty in predicting meanings. How many times have you stopped in the middle of a sentence or a paragraph and returned to the beginning to reread it? How many times have you skipped a word you did not understand, hoping the next sentence would contain a clue that would help you? All readers do this. Therefore, when readers make predictions that do not work out or when they cannot make any prediction at all, the reading process is jolted. Only when readers can produce predictions that are confirmed by the words and symbols on the page does comprehension occur. Every time a reader moans, "I can't make any sense out of this chapter" or "I can't read this poem," it is because he or she is having difficulty predicting, revising, and confirming expectations.

Here is a sentence from journalist Susan Gilbert's article about creativity workshops in industry (see Chapter 5 for the complete article):

The popular notion that creativity springs from the right side of the brain is a canard.

To understand the point Gilbert is making about the connection between creativity and the right side of the brain, readers must construct a meaning for the word "canard." How might that happen? Readers who know that "canard" means a rumor or untruth unconsciously predict that Gilbert plans to discredit the idea that the right side of the brain controls creativity; and that prediction is confirmed. But what about readers who are unfamiliar with the word? Some readers might use cues in the sentence, such as Gilbert's word order—beginning the sentence with "The popular notion that"—to predict that Gilbert plans to discredit the idea. Other readers might stop reading and check a dictionary, or continue to read, hoping the next sentence contains confirming cues. In that case, the word "misrepresentation" in the next sentence provides a clue to the word's meaning:

> It is a *misrepresentation* of research by Nobel laureate neurobiologist Roger Sperry and others that suggests that the left hemisphere is most active when we speak, write and puzzle out problems with logic and that the right hemisphere takes over to recognize faces and understand spatial relations

Remember, these processes usually occur unconsciously. Most readers are unaware of their predicting behaviors; only when these predicting behaviors are stymied would readers become aware of how they construct meaning while reading.

Because predicting meaning is so important to constructing meaning, readers who have limited experience with the subject discussed in a text or with its specialized vocabulary or jargon often experience frustration and anxiety as they attempt to make sense of the ideas in that text. The unfamiliar names, concepts, and terms make predicting meanings more difficult. And, when readers find predicting meanings difficult, they often slow down the reading process or reread portions of a text in an effort to understand. This frustration occurs because what readers bring to the reading process is a critical factor affecting particular reading contexts or situations.

### Analyzing Your Own Reading Processes: A Writing Exercise

What role does reading play in your life right now? How much time do you spend reading? What kinds of texts do you read? Do you prefer certain kinds of texts? What kinds? How might the role reading plays in your life change after college? How would you describe your own reading processes? How would you rate your ability to construct meaning? Are some texts more difficult to comprehend than others? Do you adapt your reading processes to the kinds of texts you read? Are there aspects of your reading process that you would like to work on changing? Take a few minutes to consider your answers to these questions, then write a paragraph describing how you feel about reading, how you approach reading experiences, and how you might go about changing some aspects of your reading process.

# 2
· · · · · · · · · · · · · · ·
# THE READING CONTEXT

Although readers always predict, revise, and confirm to construct meaning, how that process plays itself out depends on the particular reading context or situation. Readers may read parts of a text or the entire text; they may read quickly or slowly, only once or more than once, easily or with difficulty. Readers may read aloud or silently, with or without a highlighter in hand, taking notes or not. These differences in reading behaviors occur because reading contexts differ and because readers and their reading strategies differ. In particular, two factors that contribute to differences among reading contexts are the reader's purpose or purposes for reading and what the reader brings to the reading process. Consciously or unconsciously, readers and their reading purposes affect reading contexts.

Consider first how reading purpose affects the reading process. College students reading a chapter in a psychology textbook seek to understand and learn the new ideas in the chapter; they also need to prepare for class discussions, future study sessions, and possible quizzes by identifying the most important ideas in the chapter. To accomplish those purposes, they read slowly and take notes or high-light main points as they read. They may also reread sentences or paragraphs when predicting and confirming meaning become difficult. But those students' teacher will read the same chapter with a different purpose, perhaps to review its contents for a lecture or to generate questions for a pop quiz. To accomplish this purpose, the teacher may concentrate on the chapter's headings, generate a list of key terms, and make notes detailing how to explain and elaborate on them during a lecture.

Similarly, experiences with a subject define reading contexts and affect reading processes. For example, because teachers bring exten-sive experience and highly specialized knowledge to the reading process, their reading contexts differ from their students', who are probably reading without benefit of such specialized knowledge and experience. The psychology teacher reading a psychology textbook reads "down" because it is written in less specialized ways than are the journal articles that other specialists like themselves produce and read. She may read quickly, with few backward glances to revise predictions. In contrast, students reading the same textbook read "up" because it is more specialized than the information they bring to the reading process. Their reading may involve much rereading before they comprehend the text's ideas. These differences in what the teacher and student bring to the reading process contribute to differences in predicting, confirming, and revising; they represent powerful contextual forces affecting how readers construct meaning.

You, too, will need to adapt your reading processes to the reading contexts you confront in college. For example, you would approach writing a chapter summary somewhat differently from a critique or an evaluation of a journal or magazine article. Your writing purpose influences your approach to reading. To write a summary, you concentrate your reading efforts on identifying the writer's main points; to write a critique, you concentrate on identifying main points *and* analyzing strengths and weaknesses in the writer's approach to communicating those main points. Your familiarity with what you are reading also affects your reading. If you are reading about a subject you already know well, you construct meaning and respond to ideas in the text differently from when you are reading about a subject you know little about.

Because what readers bring to reading plays such an important role in achieving reading purposes, "making meaning" sometimes presents quite a challenge for college students. College students use reading primarily to learn about fields of study *new* to them. Thus, reading a journal article assigned by the sociology professor may be quite difficult for students unfamiliar with the article's subject and vocabulary. Even when students feel they understand what they are reading, they may experience difficulties achieving specific reading purposes. For example, a student seeking to analyze and evaluate the reasoning in an essay about health-care reform may reread that essay several times if he is unfamiliar with its reasoning patterns and types of evidence, and he may not achieve his goal at all. For this student, discussing his reading with classmates or his teacher may help. Such discussions create opportunities for students to share their ideas about what a text means *and* to learn from one another. One student may say something that causes another student to consider the reading in another light. Another student may ask a question and her classmate's answer leads to a better understanding of the kind of reasoning the author uses to achieve his writing purpose. This kind of active discussion goes on in learning communities inside and outside of college classrooms.

Understanding the reading process and how particular reading contexts affect that process provides a good starting point for successful college reading. The next sections in this chapter cover strategies that help readers achieve those purposes.

# 3
· · · · · · · · · · · · · ·
# CRITICAL READING PURPOSES

All readers must be able to recognize the words, symbols, and signs on a page; combine them into sentences and paragraphs; and comprehend or produce units of meaning from those combinations. Sometimes a reader's sole purpose for reading is to comprehend. But reading need not end with comprehension. Some readers move beyond comprehension to *critical reading*. Critical readers use comprehension as a starting point and then summarize, analyze, and evaluate the ideas in the text. Critical readers read to understand not only what a piece of writing says, but what it is supposed to accomplish and whether it succeeds.

College students must often read critically, moving beyond comprehension to analysis, response, and interpretation. This does not mean they are expected to find fault with everything they read; it does mean that they must produce personal interpretations of what they read. Critical readers have several reading purposes: to understand what is written, to analyze the author's purpose for writing and how it is achieved, to evaluate how successfully the author achieves that purpose, and to respond personally and analytically to the text's contents. In other words, critical reading involves more than just reading for information; it involves interacting with that information by summarizing, analyzing, or evaluating. And it also involves considering what a text says in relation to the reader's own experience and prior knowledge.

Critical reading demands a great deal from a reader. Unlike most everyday reading (newspapers, menus, etc.), critical reading is often time-consuming and challenging. Constructing meaning and responding to it can be quite difficult, especially when material is unfamiliar, highly detailed, or specialized. Nonetheless, most college teachers expect students to read critically. Teachers may ask students to *analyze* a writer's argument in an essay or to *evaluate* the kinds of evidence used to support that argument; to *respond critically* to the conclusions discussed in a field report written by a team of sociologists or to *summarize* the methods described in a report of research conducted by a team of physicians; or to *respond personally* to a character or theme in a short story. All of these writing assignments require critical reading to a greater or lesser degree.

Effective and efficient critical readers use two helpful strategies to achieve their critical reading purposes: they *skim* or preview a text before reading it and they *annotate* or interact with it while reading.

These critical reading strategies prepare them for writing purposes such as those described above. Guidelines for practicing skimming and annotating are outlined in the next section.

# 4
· · · · · · · · · · · ·
# CRITICAL READING STRATEGIES

Before and during reading, critical readers use two reading tools:

> Critical readers *skim* a text before reading it.
> Critical readers *annotate* a text while reading it.

After reading, critical readers use their annotations to write. They may summarize a piece of writing, critique what an author says, or synthesize what several authors say. The review of these two basic critical reading strategies that follows will prepare you for the reading you will do in this course and in your other college courses.

## Skimming

Skimming involves quickly previewing a book, a chapter, or an article to seek clues to main ideas and topics covered. Skimming also helps readers analyze a text's contents in terms of its difficulty and usefulness, as well as the writer's purposes in terms of perspective or "angle" and tone (how writers feel about their subject and readers). Here are some suggestions for skimming before reading.

---

1. Scan internal textual features.
2. Read the introduction and conclusion.
3. Read topic sentences.
4. Scan supporting textual features.

---

*1. Scan internal textual features.* The title, headings, illustrations, and italicized or highlighted portions of a text contain textual clues to key points.

For example, the title of science writer Signe Hammer's article in the chapter on intelligence (Chapter 5) is "Stalking Intelligence: IQ Isn't the End of the Line; You Can Be Smarter." What clues to the article's contents are contained in the title? For example, will Hammer be suggesting that intelligence never changes or that people can become more intelligent over time? (Other readings in this textbook contain tables and graphs; see, for example, "Women and the Labor Market: The Link Grows Stronger" in Chapter 9.) This quick skimming of textual features sets up general expectations that give readers something to work with as specific sentences are read.

These textual clues also help readers assess the difficulty of the text and the writer's perspective on a subject. For example, what does the word "stalking" in the title suggest about this article? Would a writer use this word in a title geared to specialist or non-specialist readers? What does the language in the title suggest about the difficulty of the article's contents?

*2. Read the introduction and conclusion.* The introduction and conclusion of a chapter, an article, or a book often indicate an author's main ideas or purpose. They serve as a "frame" for a piece of writing; the "picture" inside depends on the frame for definition.

Here are the first and the last two paragraphs of Hammer's article on intelligence. What do they suggest about the article's contents?

*Paragraph 1 (Introduction)* When Bob Sternberg stands at the head of a seminar table, looking down at his notes, he seems grown-up and serious enough to be a tenured professor at Yale. You can believe the gray flecks in his otherwise black hair. Then he sits down, scrunches up in his chair and smiles, and suddenly he looks like Woody Allen—or your cousin from New Jersey. The one who's always smiling a little apologetically, to show off the carefully orthodontured, precisely regimented remains of a serious overbite. Sternberg is talking about Diet Chocolate Fudge Soda.

*Paragraphs 40 and 41 (Conclusion)* Above all, Sternberg's is a pragmatic theory. He sees intelligence as a source of individual differences, but he also believes that most people, including himself, don't work anywhere near their potential. His is a theory for our time, when more people believe they can succeed than ever before. Sternberg will soon be training businessmen and women to be smarter: telling them about those essential processes, guiding them through examples, as he did the Yale undergraduates in his seminar room, and putting them through cases so they can put their executive processes to work on their newly acquired tacit knowledge.

"Let's take these processes and see if they can help us lead better lives, or at least not make the same mistakes over and over again," he says. "That's the ultimate test, isn't it—whether it makes any difference to your life? If it doesn't, who the hell cares?"

Reading these framing paragraphs prepares readers for what the entire article will say. What does a quick reading of Hammer's introduction and conclusion suggest about this article? These paragraphs tell readers that Sternberg teaches at Yale University and that the article is about his theory of intelligence. They also tell readers that Sternberg believes people can become more intelligent and that he has developed strategies he believes teach people to act more intelligently. On the basis of what the framing paragraphs say, readers might reasonably expect the body of the article to describe Sternberg's theory in detail, its development, and his methods for teaching individuals to behave more intelligently.

The introduction and conclusion also give readers a chance to assess the text's difficulty and the writer's purpose and perspective. If readers understand the introduction and conclusion, for example, they can expect to have little difficulty constructing meaning from the entire article. Similarly, Hammer's humorous, personal description of Sternberg's teaching approach and her use of the phrase "a theory for our time" provide readers with clues to her angle or approach to the subject, to her tone, and to how she feels about Sternberg's theory. These insights add to the reader's understanding.

*3. Read topic sentences.* The paragraphs that support a writer's main points usually contain topic sentences. These sentences (often the paragraph's first sentence, but sometimes another sentence or an implied idea) also provide clues to a text's main ideas. Here are some sample topic sentences from the Hammer article:

> *Paragraph 6*  Robert Sternberg is a major figure in intelligence theory.

> *Paragraph 7*  In the hot field of cognitive science, people in half a dozen disciplines—psychology, artificial intelligence, philosophy, anthropology, linguistics, and neurosciences—are all trying to figure out what goes on in our heads when we bring our intelligence to bear on our behavior.

> *Paragraph 8*  Cognitive psychologists are looking at behavior—how people solve problems—and analyzing the mental steps involved.

Just as skimming the introductory and concluding paragraphs produces helpful insight into a text, skimming the topic sentences outlines how the ideas in the introduction will be developed and previews what sub-topics or themes the writer will cover. By skimming the first and last paragraphs as well as the topic sentences of body paragraphs, critical readers construct a sense of the entire reading package—the subject, the main point or points, and the order in which those points are discussed.

What information do the sample topic sentences from the Hammer article contain that would add to a reader's developing sense of what this article is about? The phrase "major figure" suggests that Hammer provides details about Sternberg's prominence in his field. The reader can also expect to learn more about how different cognitive scientists are studying the relationships between intelligence and behavior— particularly how people solve problems. When skimming topic sentences, readers find focusing on verbs and nouns very helpful, because they provide excellent clues to a paragraph's contents. Although these three first sentences foreshadow the ideas contained only in these paragraphs, they demonstrate how skimming adds to a reader's ability to predict the contents of a piece of writing.

The sample topic sentences from Hammer's article provide other helpful information for readers. For example, the vocabulary provides clues to the entire article's level of difficulty. Readers skimming these topic sentences can decide whether the article is generally within their level of comprehension or not. These topic sentences also suggest how detailed the article is and what Hammer's perspective is. For example, do these topic sentences suggest a neutral or biased approach to Hammer's ideas? Do they suggest a serious or humorous tone?

*4. Scan supporting textual features.*   Some texts contain additional sections or features that critical readers skim before reading. For example, readers often check a book's table of contents before reading because it previews the major topics covered in the book. This book's table of contents, for example, identifies all of the reading, writing, and researching strategies covered and lists each reading theme and the individual readings. Readers may scan a book's index to find out if it contains information on a particular topic. A quick look at a book's index will also reveal how specialized and detailed its content and vocabulary are. Scanning portions of a book that provide information about its contents provides critical readers with yet another previewing tool that helps them predict meanings and build interpretations.

All of the skimming strategies discussed in this section allow readers to determine a text's level of difficulty. Knowing how readable a text is is crucial to assessing a particular reading context and to functioning successfully as a critical reader. For instance, readers who cannot understand a text's introduction and conclusion because of highly specialized vocabulary have produced a valuable piece of previewing information. These readers know that understanding the text may take several readings or the help of a specialized dictionary or a glossary of terms (often found at the end of a book). If the text is an assigned reading, these readers could now schedule extra reading time. On the other hand, if the text is not assigned but is being considered as a possible source for a researched essay or report, those readers finding the text too difficult would most likely reject it as a source and search for one containing less specialized terminology.

Time spent skimming a text is productive because it helps readers identify a text's main points, level of difficulty, and usefulness in a relatively short period of time. By producing this general map of the territory to be covered while reading, they have prepared themselves for careful, critical engagement with a text.

## Annotating

Critical readers react to and annotate what they read. They highlight main points and write summary notes, questions, and explanatory or evaluative comments. These annotations help readers construct meaning, respond to it, and remember it. Annotating allows readers to carry on a conversation with an author; thus it creates *active* readers. Whatever reading purposes drive readers, the interaction that occurs when readers annotate a piece of writing leads to comprehension and provides a foundation for interpretation, the ultimate critical reading goal.

Annotating can be time-consuming because it is a multi-purpose reading activity. Readers annotate to identify main ideas; to analyze an author's perspective, purpose, and argument; and to record their personal responses. Annotating also prepares readers to apply ideas in readings to their experiences.

Like all readers, critical readers adapt annotating strategies to particular reading contexts. They may read and annotate a text once or more than once, depending on their background knowledge and the text's level of difficulty. Highly specialized texts may take more time to annotate; non-specialist readers may need to read and annotate specialized or technical texts several times, while specialist readers may read and annotate these same texts only once.

Critical readers also adapt annotating strategies to their reading purposes. Some readers may annotate only to identify main ideas, others to connect ideas in a text to their personal experiences or to other texts they have read, still others to analyze how a writer organizes a text or what kinds of evidence a writer uses to develop an argument. Critical readers may first read to identify main ideas, then reread to analyze and respond to ideas. All critical readers adapt their annotating strategies to particular contexts.

Look over the passages that follow. They are excerpts from Susan Gilbert's article on creativity (Chapter 5) and were completed by college writing students who had never annotated a text before. What do the students' notes and underlinings suggest about the meanings they constructed as they read and about their personal responses to those meanings? How do their annotations differ? What factors account for those differences? For example, how might their prior experiences with the intelligence topic or their lack of experience annotating texts have affected their annotating behaviors? Take a minute to think about the notes and underlinings you would have produced while annotating this portion of the Gilbert article. Would they have been the same? Different? Why?

## Sample Student Annotation #1

The popular notion that creativity springs from the right side of the brain is a (canard.) It is a misinterpretation of research by Nobel laureate neurobiologist Roger Sperry and others that suggests that the left hemisphere is most active when we speak, write and puzzle out problems with logic and that the right hemisphere takes over to recognize faces and understand spatial relations. "There is zero evidence from EEGs or any other studies that creative thinking comes from a particular region of the brain," says psychobiologist Jerre Levy of the University of Chicago, who was once a student of Sperry's and who has continued to investigate the specialties of the brain's hemispheres.

"Creativity is a function of an unusual level of inter-hemispheric communication," Levy says – a trait she claims can be developed in children by, for example, reading. The right hemisphere visually decodes the letters and the left hemisphere deciphers their meaning. "This indicates," says Levy, "that it's not just genes but experience that fosters interhemispheric communication."

Sample Student Annotation #2

The popular notion that <u>creativity springs from</u> the <u>right</u> →false
side of the brain is a (canard.) It is a misinterpretation of statement
research by Nobel laureate neurobiologist <u>Roger Sperry</u>
and others that <u>suggests that the left hemisphere is most
active when we speak,</u> write and puzzle out <u>problems with
logic and that the right hemisphere takes over to recognize faces and understand spatial relations.</u> "There is <u>zero
evidence</u> from EEGs or any other studies <u>that creative
thinking comes from a particular region of the brain,</u>" says
psychobiologist Jerre Levy of the University of Chicago,
who was once a student of Sperry's and who has continued to investigate the specialties of the brain's hemispheres.

*Where* "Creativity is a function of an unusual level of <u>inter-
*does* hemispheric communication,</u>" Levy says—a trait she claims
*creativity* can be developed in children by, for example, reading. The
*come* right hemisphere visually decodes the letters and the left
*from?* hemisphere deciphers their meaning. "This indicates," says
Levy, "that it's <u>not just genes but experience that fosters
interhemispheric communication.</u>"

　　Although both students were annotating the same portion of Susan
Gilbert's article about creativity workshops in business settings, their
annotations are slightly different. Both students, for example, were
unfamiliar with the word *canard,* yet only one used a dictionary to
check the meaning. What similarities in their backgrounds might
explain their unfamiliarity with the word? What differences in their
reading experiences might explain the differences in their response to
not knowing this word?
　　Also, one student underlined more of the text than did the other.
What does this difference suggest about their reading processes?
About the usefulness of these underlined portions of text? And their
personal reactions to the text differ as well. Although both jotted down

questions in the margin, the questions differ. The first student's question seems to challenge Gilbert's claims about creativity, while the second student's question seems to suggest possible discussion or research. The first student's question indicates some misunderstanding about what Gilbert is saying in these paragraphs (Gilbert is not disagreeing with a Nobel Prize winner but saying that his findings have been misinterpreted.). The differences in the two students' annotations resulted from the differences in the two students, in particular the background knowledge about this subject that they brought to the annotating process and their understanding of what it means to annotate a text.

This is why annotating is such an important critical reading tool. It forces readers to interact with a text in ways that other forms of reading do not and it produces the kinds of responses that lead to understanding and interpretation that critical readers must produce to become critical writers. However, these two examples also serve as a reminder that annotating does not always produce instant insight into a text and its writer's intentions. For this reason, students often discuss their annotations with other readers. Used as a basis for a discussion, their annotations represent an initial conversation between reader and writer that, when shared with other critical readers, creates additional insights, revised interpretations, and further interactions—the ultimate critical reading purposes.

The guidelines that follow will help you annotate the texts you must read critically. Remember that the goal of annotating is not only to understand what the author is saying, but to contribute to your own interpretations as well.

---

1. Identify main ideas.
2. Summarize main ideas.
3. React personally to main ideas.
4. Analyze the writer's purpose, strategies for achieving purpose, and perspective.
5. Evaluate the writer's success.

---

*1. Identify main ideas.* Highlight or underline parts of the text that contain main ideas, key terms, or summaries of ideas. Look for sentences in which details are used to support and reveal the writer's attitude. Be selective. An over-highlighted text is *not* very helpful to the critical reader.

Here is how a student highlighted the main points in a paragraph in Robert Sokolowksi's article about natural and artificial intelligence (The complete article is in Chapter 5.):

One of the first things that must be clarified is the ambiguous word artificial. This adjective can be used in two senses, and it is important to determine which one applies in the term artificial intelligence. The word artifi- cial is used in one sense when it is applied, say, to flowers, and in another sense when it is applied to light. In both cases something is called artificial because it is fabricated. But in the first usage artificial means that the thing seems to be, but really is not, what it looks like. The artificial is the merely apparent; it just shows how something else looks. Artificial flowers are only paper, not flowers at all; anyone who takes them to be flowers is mistaken. But artificial light is light and it does illuminate. It is fabricated as a substitute for natural light, but once fabricated it is what it seems to be. In this sense the artificial is not the merely apparent, not simply an imitation of something else. The appearance of the thing reveals what it is, not how something else looks.

Notice how this student has highlighted phrases that define two different meanings for the adjective *artificial:* "seems to be, but really is not" and "it is what it seems to be." However, the student has not highlighted the examples Sokolowski uses to explain the differences between the two meanings because those examples do not convey Sokolowski's main ideas.

*2. Summarize Main Ideas* While reading or during a second reading, review highlighted or underlined sections and write short marginal notes that restate those ideas *in your own words.* Writing these summary notes helps you understand and remember what a text says and prepares you to react to it.

Here is the same paragraph from the Sokolowski article, this time with the student's summary notes. Notice how the student, in just a few words, is able to capture the gist of this paragraph. The student has tried not to use Sokolowski's exact words in these summary notes. The act of writing summary notes not only helps the student *understand* and *learn* these ideas, but prepares the student for discussions and writing assignments based on them.

*[handwritten margin notes: artificial. intell. defined 2 ways = ① sub. for intell (it is intell) ② just seems to be intell (it isn't intell)]*

One of the first things that must be clarified is the ambiguous word artificial. This adjective can be used in two senses, and it is important to determine which one applies in the term artificial intelligence. The word artificial is used in one sense when it is applied, say, to flowers, and in another sense when it is applied to light. In both cases something is called artificial because it is fabricated. But in the first usage artificial means that the thing seems to be, but really is not, what it looks like. The artificial is the merely apparent; it just shows how something else looks. Artificial flowers are only paper, not flowers at all; anyone who takes them to be flowers is mistaken. But artificial light is light and it does illuminate. It is fabricated as a substitute for natural light, but once fabricated it is what it seems to be. In this sense the artificial is not the merely apparent, not simply an imitation of something else. The appearance of the thing reveals what it is, not how something else looks.

*3. React Personally to Main Ideas* Critical readers react personally to an author's ideas, using their past experiences and knowledge (or lack of it) to engage themselves with the author. Put question marks in the margins when the text is confusing and circle words that must be checked in a dictionary. Consider connections between the ideas in the text and what you know and feel about the subject. For example, something you read in an article about intelligence may remind you of a test or classroom discussion in high school. Write a marginal note indicating this comparison or connection. Consider also whether you agree or disagree with the author's ideas, and use the margins to write your personal responses to those ideas. Remember that one of the important goals of annotating is to bring your own ideas and opinions out in the open and compare them with the author's.

Here are two students' personal annotated responses to a small portion of the Gilbert article.

## Sample Student Annotation #1

*Stupid statement. How many geniuses are there?*

Although normal or above-normal intelligence is necessary to creativity, genius is not. Given enough intelligence to function professionally in a field, Gardner says, slight variations either higher or lower have no significant effect on creative achievement. "Genius in the sense of dramatic talent may simply foster highly skilled performance, as with a gifted violin virtuoso who does not compose nor offer innovative interpretations," wrote David Perkins, codirector of Project Zero, in a paper he delivered at the 1984 Symposium on Creativity in Science. Nonetheless, he

*Society does, but individuals sometimes don't. we In h.s. I thought the creative some were weird. kids were weird.*

added, we persist in making creativity "the crown jewel of human achievement which most of us will never touch." Learning to be creative requires that we shift our perception of creativity from the gift of creativity to the product of process.

## Student Sample Annotation #2

*Is this proven? What about a person with sub-normal intel?*

Although normal or above-normal intelligence is necessary to creativity, genius is not. Given enough intelligence to function professionally in a field, Gardner says, slight variations either higher or lower have no significant effect on creative achievement. "Genius in the sense of dramatic talent may simply foster highly skilled performance, as with a gifted violin virtuoso who does not compose nor offer innovative interpretations," wrote David Perkins, codirector of Project Zero, in a paper he delivered at the

1984 Symposium on Creativity in Science. Nonetheless, he

*Creativity is a product of process* added, we persist in making creativity "the crown jewel of human achievement which most of us will never touch." Learning to be creative requires that we shift our perception of creativity from the gift of genius to the product of process.

Notice how the students' personal responses compare. Both students reacted differently to the same portions of the text. Both question Gilbert's statement explaining connections between intelligence, creativity, and genius, but each student focuses on a different aspect of the statement, presenting a different challenge in question form. Similarly, both students react to an expert's statement that society should pay less attention to "the gift of genius" and more to the "product of process," but one student writes a summary note while the other writes about a personal experience. What accounts for the differences in the two students' annotations? Personal reactions to ideas in texts are just that—personal. They reflect readers' prior experiences and so vary from one reader to another. These two students' responses differ because their personal experience, or lack of experience, with this particular topic differs. How would you have reacted to the ideas in this paragraph? What personal experiences and viewpoints would have shaped your reaction?

These students' reactions, like your own, are neither static nor etched in stone. Their reactions are subject to change when they encounter new experiences. For example, the students' experiences reading and annotating Gilbert's article represent one experience with the topic of intelligence. If they share their reactions with other students, these discussions represent another experience with this topic and create an opportunity for them to reconsider their reactions in light of what the other students say. In this sense, critical readers use annotating as a foundation for constructing interpretations that, like all ideas, are subject to revision and reconsideration as new experiences with a topic occur.

*4. Analyze Writer's Purpose, Strategies for Achieving Purpose, and Perspective* Critical readers analyze what they annotate, dissecting or taking a text apart. Having figured out what an author is saying and how they feel personally about it, readers then consider the author's purpose and how that purpose is achieved. Consider one or all of the questions that follow while analyzing what you read.

*What is the writer's purpose?* A writer always has one or more purposes or reasons for writing: to explain, to persuade, to entertain, to criticize. When you know what the writer's purpose is, write a marginal note to help you remember.

Here is the introductory paragraph in Sokolowski's article on artificial intelligence. The student who annotated this article identified Sokolowski's statement of purpose and noted this purpose in the margin. Writing this marginal note helped the student connect the ideas that appear later in the article to the purpose stated in the introduction.

*Purpose analyze issue- Is art intell. same as real intell?*

In <u>this essay</u> we will not attempt to decide whether artificial intelligence is the same as natural intelligence. Instead we will examine some of the <u>issues and terms</u> that must be clarified before that question can be resolved. We will discuss how the question about the <u>relationship between natural and artificial intelligence</u> can be formulated.

Writers don't always directly state their purpose. Here is the introductory paragraph in William Golding's personal essay "Thinking as a Hobby" (Chapter 5). Although the student who annotated this essay did not find Golding's purpose directly stated, the marginal note indicates that the student is making a prediction about Golding's implied purpose. The note suggests that the student has already figured out part of Golding's purpose: to provide an explanation of what he thinks are the three basic ways of thinking.

*Will explain 3 kinds of thinking-not all alike?*

While I was still a boy, I came to the <u>conclusion</u> that there were (three) <u>grades of thinking</u>; and since I was later to claim thinking as my hobby, I came to an even stranger conclusion—namely, that I myself could not think at all.

*How does the writer achieve purpose?* Writers use different kinds of information or evidence to achieve their purposes: examples, expert testimony, personal experiences, results of controlled laboratory experiments or field work, stories, or combinations of these kinds of evidence. Depending on their purpose, writers may use more of one kind of evidence than another. They also organize their texts to achieve their purposes. One writer may begin with the main point and then offer evidence to explain that point; another may offer evidence first and then conclude with the main point. Some writers organize ideas from least important to most important, some the other way around. Others organize ideas chronologically or by causes or effects. They may use headings to separate main points, or they may use a format required by a particular journal or profession (as many scientists do). These decisions about evidence and organization reflect a writer's assumptions about what will most effectively persuade particular readers. As you read, make marginal notes that will help you remember what kinds of evidence the writer is using and how that evidence is organized.

Here are two paragraphs from Stephen J. Gould's essay on booby birds (Chapter 5). The student's annotations indicate that she has analyzed the kinds of evidence Gould uses to support his claim that animals make yes/no decisions in response to signals. She recognizes that Gould moves from the general category of animals to the example of a specific classification of animals: birds. She also notes that W. H. Thorpe is an "expert," indicating she understands that Gould is using Thorpe's finding to generalize about the specific behavior detailed in his bird example. (Note, too, that the student has reacted to Gould's support by asking a question based on her personal experience and has highlighted one of Gould's main points.)

Yet this inflexible model does represent the style of intelligence followed with great success by most other animals. The decisions of animals are usually unambiguous yeses or noes triggered by definite signals, not subtle choices based upon the assessment of a complex gestalt.

*bird example - what is in nest vs. outside nest*

Many birds, for example, do not recognize their own young and act instead according to the rule: care for what is inside the nest; ignore what is outside. British ethologist

*expert agrees*

W. H. Thorpe writes: "Most birds, while they may be very attentive to their young in the nest, are completely callous and unresponsive to those same young when, as a result of some accident, they are outside the nest or the immediate nest territory."

*What is the writer's perspective?* The question "Where are you coming from?" suggests what teachers mean when they discuss perspective. Writers always communicate to readers their perspective or way of treating their subject. Writers may strive to create a neutral perspective—like a reporter—about their subject, or they may take a position—either pro or con—about the subject. Writers may adopt a group's point of view, that of a political party or a special interest group, for example. Think of perspective as the writer's angle. Just as photographers change or adjust their lenses to view something from a different angle, writers can examine subjects from different perspectives. Determining a writer's perspective may be difficult because writers often imply their perspective rather than state it directly.

The language writers use may provide clues to how they feel about their subject and audience. Just as speakers can be serious, humorous, or sarcastic about the subjects they discuss, writers also project a tone. For example, writers who include many personal anecdotes in an article usually sound more informal and personally involved than writers who rely only on facts and statistics. Writers who use specialized vocabulary without defining terms or providing examples may sound more formal and distant than writers who provide definitions. A writer's decisions about language, evidence, and organization provide clues to tone and perspective. As you read, write marginal notes describing the author's perspective and relate those notes to specific words, phrases, and structures.

Here is another annotated paragraph from Golding's essay on thinking. In it he recalls his childhood and adult views on "grade-three" thinking ("full of unconscious prejudice, ignorance and hypocrisy").

*Golding doesn't like grade-3 thinkers*

True, often there is a kind of innocence in prejudices, but in those days <u>I viewed grade-three thinking with an intolerant contempt</u> and an incautious mockery. I (de-lighted) to confront a (pious lady) who hated the Germans with the proposition that we should love our enemies. She taught me a great truth in dealing with grade-three thinkers; because of her, I no longer dismiss lightly a mental process which for <u>nine-tenths of the population is the nearest they will ever get to thought.</u> They have *Is he being sarcastic?* immense solidarity. <u>We had better respect them,</u> for we are outnumbered and surrounded. A crowd of grade-three

*Should this go us keep warm?*

thinkers, all shouting the same thing, all <u>warming their hands at the fire of their own prejudices,</u> will not thank you for pointing out the contradictions in their beliefs.

Man is a gregarious animal, and enjoys agreement as

cows will <u>graze</u> all the same way on the side of a hill.
            *man = Contented cow*
        *Worship "the golden calf"?*

The student's annotations not only note Golding's main point about grade-three thinking, but analyze Golding's perspective. Her note about Golding's comparison of grade-three thinkers to cows indicates that she sees a connection between Golding's language and his feelings toward individuals whose prejudices are encouraged by the reinforcement provided by others. She recognizes that Golding's choice of words creates a particular tone, which reveals his perspective. In turn, his perspective reveals his attitude toward the entire subject of thinking.

*5. Evaluate Writer's Success*   Once critical readers have identified an author's purpose and analyzed how the author strives to achieve that purpose, they can consider how successful the author is. Using their experiences and knowledge of the subject, and their analysis of the writer's purpose and strategies for achieving it, critical readers strive for an informed judgment.

While annotating, write marginal notes that sum up your evaluation of the writer's success. If a writer uses inappropriate kinds of evidence or insufficient evidence of a particular kind, note that in the margin. For example, a writer using only personal experiences with his own pets to convince readers that animals are just as intelligent as humans may not achieve his writing purpose. The critical reader might write "the writer's love for pets interferes with reasoning" in the margin. A writer who quotes only experts on one side of an issue will probably not convince readers that the controversy has been explained adequately. The critical reader may write "fails to give equal time to opposition" in the margin. If a writer omits an important argument, cause, or piece of information, the critical reader may write a marginal note indicating that omission.

Here is how one student evaluated Gardner's claim that each of the seven types of intelligence he identifies is associated with a different portion of the brain. What weakness has the student identified in Gardner's evidence?

*Ellison:* I assume from *Frames of Mind* that the neural organization of the brain determines the strength of various intelligences.

*Gardner:* As you know, when somebody has a stroke or an injury to the head, not all skills break down equally.

Instead, certain abilities can be significantly impaired while others are spared. A lesion in the middle areas of the left hemisphere will impair somebody's linguistic abilities while leaving musical, spatial, and interpersonal skills largely undamaged. Conversely, a large lesion in the right hemisphere will compromise spatial and musical abilities, leaving linguistic abilities relatively intact. Probably the unique feature of my list of intelligences, compared with those of other researchers, is that I claim independent existences for the intelligences in the human neural system. And my chief source of information is how they function following brain damage. There is impressive evidence that each of the seven intelligences has its own special neurological organization.

*What about evidence from healthy brains?*

*What is this evidence? Should we just believe it exists?*

Below is another example of a student annotating a text to evaluate the writer's success. These paragraphs are from Gould's essay on the booby bird. This student cannot accept Gould's expert testimony (the reference to Konrad Lorenz) without more information about who Lorenz is or where he made the statement. The student also notes that Gould's claim about animal intelligence is unsubstantiated. Both marginal notes reflect the student's efforts to evaluate how well Gould achieves his writing purpose.

After all, the essence of human intelligence is creative flexibility, our skill in grasping new and complex contexts—in short, our ability to make (as we call them) judgments, rather than to act by the dictates of rigid, preset rules. We are, as Konrad Lorenz has stated, "specialists in nonspecialization." We do not behave as machines with simple yes-no switches, invariably triggered by definite bits of information present in our immediate

*Don't we? Society is pretty set.*

*where does he state it? who is he?*

environments. Our enlightened sailor, no matter how successful at combating rust or avoiding the brig, is not following a human style of intelligence.

Yet this inflexible model does represent the style of *How does he know?* intelligence followed with great success by most other animals. The decisions of animals are usually unambiguous yeses or noes triggered by definite signals, not subtle choices based upon the assessment of a complex gestalt.

Many birds, for example, do not recognize their own young and act instead according to the rule: care for what is inside the nest; ignore what is outside.

All of the annotating strategies discussed in this section contribute to a critical reader's personal response and interpretation of an author's ideas. However, annotating also helps critical readers evaluate how they can use the information in a text in their own essays, although they may wait to do this until they have a clear sense of their own writing purposes. For example, critical readers may write marginal notes about statistics in an article or draw arrows to highlight quotations that would work well in an introduction or conclusion of an essay in progress. Readers can be struck by an example a writer uses or some expert testimony. These marginal "good example" or "use in introduction" notes become helpful when student writers draft their own essays.

# 5
· · · · · · · · · · · · ·
# THE CRITICAL READING "HABIT"

The annotations critical readers make become the basis for personal responses and interpretations, as well as for planning decisions about how those interpretations may fit their own writing purposes. That is why it is so important that students develop the critical reading "habit." As we noted earlier, annotating does not always provide instant insight. Students' underlinings and marginal notes may reflect misreadings and missed connections produced while annotating. Such missed connections may occur because students are still developing annotating skills or because a text is difficult or unfamiliar. However, the more practice students have reading, annotating, and sharing their annotations with other students, the more highly developed their critical reading skills become.

Many college students find highlighting main ideas less difficult than writing marginal notes that react, analyze, and evaluate those ideas. Engaging in a conversation with a writer's ideas takes practice and time. But most professionals believe that annotating what they read is important to their success as readers and writers. Students usually find that annotating feels more natural once they have familiarized themselves with the kinds of questions critical readers ask as they read.

# 6
## • • • • • • • • • • • •
# CHAPTER SUMMARY

Not every reading situation or context is the same, nor are all readers the same. Readers interact with a text within a particular reading context. Two factors contributing to differences among reading contexts are the reader's purpose and the text being read. Readers also bring to any reading situation prior reading experiences, which affect their success as readers and provide a foundation for future reading experiences. When readers read, they are honing their reading skills—using skills they already have developed and practicing ones they have not yet mastered.

As readers interact with the words on a page, they are continually predicting, confirming, and revising their understanding of another person's words, symbols, and signs. This interaction enables readers to follow specific words and sentences through to general ideas and comprehension.

But not all reading ends with comprehension. Critical readers go beyond comprehension, using analysis and evaluation to build personal interpretations of the ideas in a text. Experienced readers use skimming and annotating to understand and to produce their own interpretations of what they read.

# 2

# Writing as a Learning Tool

What is the writing process? How are writing processes
adapted to particular writing situations? How do writing
situations differ? What is academic writing? How do writers
use summaries and critiques to achieve their writing purposes?

## 1
### THE WRITING PROCESS

Writing is a complex process that involves conscious and unconscious
planning, drafting, and reviewing activities that occur both sequentially
and simultaneously. Most people associate writing with the act of
putting words on a page or keying them into a computer or word
processor; actually, what writers do before drafting a text is as much a
part of the writing process as the written words themselves. In many
personal and job situations, writing is as much a way of managing
information as it is of putting words on paper.

### Planning, Drafting, and Reviewing Activities

Planning, drafting, and reviewing occur before, during, and after writers
put words on a page.
  *Planning* includes everything writers do to produce a draft of a piece
of writing—thinking, discussing, reading, researching, or pre-writing.

29

College students use a variety of planning strategies. A conference with a teacher may help a student narrow a topic for an assigned research paper, while a discussion with classmates may produce suggestions of possible library sources for a persuasive essay on a current social issue. Time spent thinking about tentative ideas may help a student organize ideas; journal entries may lead to a clearer perspective on a subject. A classmate's response to a draft helps a student plan a second draft. Notes taken during chemistry lab provide the basis for a written lab report, while those taken during a sociology lecture later become the basis for an answer on the mid-term exam. A five-minute break in the middle of a drafting session provides a writer with time to plan the rest of the draft. These are just some of the planning behaviors identified with the writing process.

*Drafting* occurs when writers produce a text. Whatever the tool— legal pad, word processor, or typewriter—drafting a text, whether it is a complete version with beginning, middle, and end or just one section, gives a writer something to work with as the writing process proceeds. Just as there are various planning strategies, there are various ways to draft a piece of writing. For example, some college students produce several drafts before they are satisfied with a text, while others are satisfied with the first draft. Some students focus on *what* they want to communicate in their first draft, concentrating on expressing their ideas as fully and completely as possible. Then, in later drafts, they shift their focus to *how* they communicate those ideas, concentrating on style, tone, and correctness. This shift in attention from what is written to how it is written often signals a shift from writer-based drafts (those written from the writer's perspective) to reader-based drafts (those written from the reader's perspective). And, as we mentioned above, some students write a complete draft in one sitting, while others compose one section at a time.

*Reviewing* refers to writers' efforts to "re-see" or evaluate what they have planned or written as they work toward producing a final draft. Writers may *revise*—add, delete, rearrange, and rewrite their plans or drafts. Many writers seek advice from outside readers, who are often more detached from the text and can identify areas in a piece of writing that are underdeveloped, unclear, or unorganized. Students, too, seek feedback about their plans and drafts—from other students, from teachers, or from writing instructors. These "outside responders" often play a critical role in helping students reshape their writing. A question from a reader about why a particular example was used or how a piece of information from a source relates to the main idea may cause a student to add a sentence or reorganize a paragraph. When reviewing a draft, writers may also *edit*—check for grammatical and mechanical correctness, and *proofread* for typographical errors. Writers may ask outside readers to edit or proofread, or they may use a computer program. Some writers even test a draft on a group of readers. Technical writers, for example, often ask volunteers to test an instruction manual before signing off on a final draft. Most students test their drafts on friends, classmates, or teachers, asking them to make suggestions about style, language choices, content, and correctness. Remember: reviewing involves not only editing and proofreading for correctness, but revising words, sentences, and paragraphs until a text achieves a writer's purposes. And, in the end, all writers, including college students, are ultimately responsible for their final drafts.

## How Composing Processes Interact

Like reading, writing is a complex activity, one that researchers continue to investigate. We know, for example, that when writers compose, they do not simply plan, then draft, then review. Instead, they move back and forth among these processes, although they may be consciously focusing on only one.

For example, during the early stages of the writing process, a student probably expends most energy generating ideas and planning, conducting research at the college library, developing a questionnaire, or asking the teacher for guidance. These activities help narrow a focus, produce evidence to support ideas, and plan how to present those ideas to readers. These same activities, whether consciously or unconsciously, also help the student review goals and plans for the writing assignment. For instance, after reading a few articles in the library, the student decides to narrow the focus and, after conferring with the teacher, to interview someone with specialized knowledge on the subject. This student is consciously focusing on planning strategies as well as using reviewing strategies to develop those plans.

Similarly, during a drafting stage, a student is likely to focus on getting the ideas down on paper but may stop in the middle of a sentence or paragraph to review what has been written or to plan what will be written next. Or a student may decide to consider an alternative solution to a problem or a new piece of evidence suggested by a fellow student, a teacher, or a friend. Understood this way, the planning, drafting, and reviewing behaviors identified with the writing process are as much recursive or repeated processes as they are straightforward ones.

Consider how planning, drafting, and reviewing strategies interact when a college student writes an essay about intelligence. The teacher has asked students to develop a *thesis* (a statement that expresses the writer's main point or idea) about intelligence that in some way is connected to one of the readings about intelligence in this textbook (Chapter 5). A student begins to plan the essay. Her reading of Gould's essay on booby birds motivates her to focus on animal intelligence. ( In this essay, Gould explains that animals respond to signals, and then uses the booby bird as an example. These birds care for what is inside of their marked territory and ignore what is outside, even if what is outside is one of their own family.) After reviewing her journal entries and discussing the article with classmates, she develops an initial approach to the essay. She decides to compare the instinctive yes-no type of intelligence booby birds exhibit with other kinds of animal intelligence that she observed during the three summers she worked at the zoo in her community.

After reading one or two library articles on animal intelligence, speaking with the curator at the zoo, and reviewing her plans with her teacher, she revises her initial plan. She decides that instead of comparing booby birds with the animals she has observed, she will try to persuade her readers that booby bird intelligence is not instinctive, but learned. She will combine her knowledge about how alligators at her zoo were taught to turn on heat lamps to warm themselves with information provided by the curator. This student's essay-planning process, therefore, is not completely straightforward. She is actually planning and reviewing while she generates her essay plans.

During the drafting stage, the student might sit at her word processor with her outline, her journal notes, the Gould article, and some notes taken from a library article. Although she focuses most of her mental energy on drafting this essay, she is also reviewing what she has planned and written as she drafts, and sometimes she finds herself planning in her mind what she will write in the next sentence or paragraph. Once again, planning, drafting, and reviewing interact as she writes. She also decides on word changes and smoother ways of writing particular sentences as she produces a first draft. Even though these changes might be replaced by others later, she develops a "feel" for the style she wants to create, even in these early activities.

After drafting, she shares her draft with two or three classmates during a collaborative revising session. At this session, students who have read her draft ask questions about what she has written and share their reactions and suggestions, pointing out statements or ideas that are misleading, unclear, or perhaps underdeveloped. Then, using those suggestions, she pencils in revisions and writes another draft. She reviews this draft several times, revising and editing each time. Finally, the night before the essay is due, she runs a spellcheck and prints a final draft on the word processor. During this reviewing session, she focuses mainly on editing and proofreading, perhaps consulting a writing handbook to clarify grammatical points. At the same time, however, her reviewing also consists of planning and drafting as she polishes the final draft to assure that she puts her best foot forward for readers.

The final draft that she turns in to the teacher for a grade has been planned, drafted, and reviewed over a three-week period. However, her planning, drafting, and reviewing were, at the same time, straightforward and recursive. Like all other effective writers, this student's process involved continuous planning, drafting, and reviewing—in her mind and on the page.

## How Writers' Composing Processes Differ

No two writers have identical writing processes. Planning, drafting, and reviewing behaviors vary among writers. One writer may spend a great deal of time thinking about what to write before a single sentence is written; another may sit down and begin without spending more than a few minutes planning, but then spend hours reviewing and making changes. Some writers compose in spurts—one part at a time—while others complete an entire draft in one sitting.

Writers review their texts differently, too. Some produce several drafts before they are satisfied, while others revise and edit only once. Some writers use computers to revise and edit; others rely on colleagues, personal friends, or professional editors as they move closer to a finished piece of writing.

### Analyzing Your Own Composing Processes:
### A Writing Exercise

How would you describe your own writing process? How much time do you spend planning, drafting, and reviewing what you write? Is one part of the writing process more difficult for you than others? Are there aspects of your writing process that you would like to work on changing? Take a few minutes to consider your answers to these questions; this will help you understand how you write and how you can improve.

If you keep a writing journal, use it to manage your writing process. Begin by doing a one- or two-page entry in which you describe your writing process as you produced a particular piece of writing in a previous class. Then, reread your first entry and list what you now think were the strengths and weaknesses of that process. Did you do enough reviewing and revising? Would your process have produced a better result if you had consulted peers about content or form? Did you wait too long to get started? Did you revise too much and lose a good, early idea as a result? Should you have spent more or less time editing your final draft? Finish this journal exercise by writing a paragraph in which you describe two or three changes that you will make in your writing process. Keep a record in your journal of your subsequent efforts to include these changes in your writing of essays for this course.

# 2
· · · · · · · · · · · · · ·
## THE WRITING SITUATION

Writing processes are influenced by individual writers' differences and preferences. Writers themselves are an important component of what is called the *writing situation*—factors affecting writers as they plan, draft, and review. But many other factors define particular writing situations. Because writing situations vary, effective writers analyze a writing situation's requirements before they begin composing. Here are some examples of typical writing situations undergraduate college students face: lab reports, research papers, summaries, critiques, pop quizzes, essays, requests for reference letters, essays on mid-term and final exams.

Have you ever been around students who were discussing their grades on the first written assignment in a course and heard one of the students say to the group, "I'll do much better on the next paper. Now I understand what the teacher meant"? Or perhaps you have heard classmates say they thought they would earn a higher grade on a final exam because sitting for the mid-term had helped them develop a better fix on the kinds of questions the teacher would ask and had given them practice dealing with the difficult time constraints that mid-term and final exams create.

Although the students described above did not say they were learning to analyze writing situations, their statements indicate that they were considering how words must be shaped to achieve writing purposes for particular readers. Their statements also demonstrate another important point about analyzing writing situations: it is a writing strategy that requires practice and develops slowly. Furthermore, new writing situations require more analysis than familiar ones, which explains why students, who face many new writing situations in college, often spend lots of time analyzing why and for whom they are writing until they become familiar with what will work in different writing situations. This book emphasizes using *rhetoric* (the study of how language works in specific situations) as a means of fitting writing processes to the needs created by particular academic situations.

Students writing lab reports for the first time may have an excellent understanding of what occurred in the lab; however, without analyzing what written lab reports are supposed to accomplish for the researcher or what readers of lab reports expect to find in them, they cannot draft the report. These students must take time to analyze writing purpose and readers' needs and expectations before drafting the report. Likewise, those students who feel they will do better on a second written assignment or on a final exam are learning to analyze writing situations by figuring out how to write essay answers and how to analyze a teacher's goals and preferences.

## Analyzing Writing Situations: An Example

How do college students learn to analyze particular writing situations? Most of them learn by doing it, both consciously and unconsciously. Courses such as this one, as well as increased familiarity with what college professors expect, teach students about differences among writing situations. The more college students analyze particular writing situations and use those analyses to generate their writing plans, the easier it becomes to connect new writing situations to old, even when the writing situations are different. Students who write two or three lab reports in Chemistry I develop writing and analyzing skills that are helpful when lab reports must be written in Biology I. And students who have had difficulty writing essays for a previous semester's final exams may find writing exams easier the next semester because they are better able to decide quickly what the teacher is asking them to do, even when the exam covers different subject matter. When writers are able to make choices based on analyses of particular writing situations, they have developed what is called the *rhetorical approach* to writing.

How did the student discussed earlier in this chapter develop a rhetorical approach to writing an essay connected to one of the readings on intelligence? In the essay, she had to develop a thesis (main point) about intelligence. During the planning stage, she decided that her purpose would be to convince readers (her classmates) that booby bird behavior might not be instinctive, but learned. This clear sense of purpose then enabled her to decide what she had to do in the essay to explain the point she was making about booby bird intelligence. She began to consider carefully the kinds of information needed to persuade her readers. She decided to include examples of animals whose behavior seems instinctive but is actually learned, quotations from her interview with the zoo curator, and information from the magazine article she read in the library. She considered explaining how booby bird behavior might be viewed as learned. What is important about her analysis of the writing situation is that her efforts to understand what was required led to the development of a clear sense of purpose. In turn, this decision-making process helped her determine what she needed to do in the essay to accomplish her purpose.

This student's efforts to develop a writing purpose were also guided by considerations of who would read her essay. One reader she considered was her teacher. Any statements the teacher made about expectations for the essay were important to her understanding of the writing situation. Since the teacher had asked students to consider class-mates as the primary readers for the essay on intelligence, the student chose her information in terms of what she believed would be most convincing to her classmates. To analyze her readers' needs and expectations, she considered whether she would need to summarize Gould's main points for her classmates. She also had to decide when her class-mates would need a term defined and how detailed her examples should be. And she asked herself whether her readers would be convinced by her experiences at the zoo. Deciding that they would, she then had to determine how much about those experiences she should include.

This student's essay on intelligence was based on a careful analysis of her writing situation, in particular her purpose and readers. Considering readers and purpose (and any other factors that may affect your writing plans) before you begin to draft a text and, of course, while you draft and review will help you make the right choices as you write.

## Analyzing Writing Situations: Purposes and Readers

Here are some questions useful for analyzing writing situations. The answers you produce about your purposes and your readers will provide a basis for making choices about what and how you write. (Section 4 in this chapter, "The Rhetorical Approach to Academic Writing," provides additional guidelines for making some of these choices.) Answer those questions that seem most helpful for each writing situation you analyze; after using them several times, you should develop the ability to analyze your purpose and readers without referring to the list of questions each time. Remember: the better you understand a particular writing situation, the more effective your rhetorical approach to composing a piece of writing will be.

---

### Questions About Writing Purposes

1. What information has my teacher provided that will help me develop a sense of purpose?
2. What have my discussions with classmates contributed to my sense of purpose?
3. What other factors might affect my writing purpose? (deadlines, requirements for using library sources, personal experiences with the subject)
4. Is my purpose realistic? (too broad? too narrow?)
5. Can I clearly state my purpose in a sentence or two?

**Questions About Readers**

1. What do I know about my readers? (my teacher, my classmates, an outside reader)
2. What can I infer about my readers?
3. What is my current relationship with my readers?
4. What relationship do I want to establish with my readers?
5. What do my readers know about my subject?
6. How do my readers feel about my subject?
7. What questions will my readers have about my subject?
8. What biases do my readers hold for or against my subject?

We have emphasized the role of audience and purpose in analyzing particular writing situations. But there are other aspects of writing situations that often must be analyzed by writers. For example, college students, like professional writers, face deadlines for writing assignments. Deadlines provide a framework for planning, drafting, and reviewing strategies. Also, requirements concerning length, format, organization, and content may warrant consideration. One writing situation might require that the writer include a list of sources at the end; another might require that the writer use particular headings. Still another might require charts, graphs, or tables. Finally, writers themselves are an important part of the writing situation. Their knowledge of a subject, personal experiences, and writing experience must be considered as they develop a rhetorical approach or writing strategy. The student who owns and cares for a dog, for example, brings that background to the writing situation and may decide to include an anecdote about that pet to make a point in an essay on animal intelligence. This option would not be available to the student who has never had a pet. Similarly, the student who has worked in a pet store brings those experiences to the writing situation and could incorporate them in an essay. Successful writers consider who they are as they analyze what particular writing situations require.

Because each writing situation is different, successful writers continuously adapt planning, drafting, and reviewing strategies, particularly with regard to purpose and readers. The ability to recognize and adapt to elements of particular writing situations develops over time and requires practice. College seniors often have less difficulty than college freshmen completing writing tasks because they have developed the skills necessary to analyze and respond successfully to various writing situations. Informal rhetorical analysis has made them more effective writers.

The writing strategies described later in this chapter will help you use your analyses of particular writing situations to complete writing assignments. The readings in Part II, along with the pre- and post-reading questions, will provide opportunities to analyze writing situations other writers have faced. Evaluating how professional writers have responded to writing situations is good practice for analyzing your own writing situations.

## Writing Situations as Rhetorical Contexts

*Rhetoric* is the study of how language works in specific situations. We have emphasized the relationship between analyzing writing situations and composing effective pieces of writing in order to introduce the concept that writing is a *rhetorical act.* Because writers shape written language, their writing process is a rhetorical act: writers are rhetoricians. Take this idea one step further and writing situations can be viewed as *rhetorical contexts.*

A key to succeeding as a writer in school or at work is learning to become part of a rhetorical context. You are part of such a learning process as you use this book. You and your peers will be learning how to bring three elements together into your sense of rhetorical context. First, you will consider a chapter topic from the viewpoint of your *personal experience.* You will also *work together with others* to hear and consider their views, and they will listen and respond to yours. Third, you will *read, discuss, and analyze the readings* gathered under each chapter topic. This kind of learning will help you in many college courses, and it will carry over into team and group communication situations that many of you will later experience on your jobs.

What distinguishes these academic situations from other rhetorical contexts is scope. The college writing situations used in this textbook as examples are quite specific and localized. They are the kinds of rhetorical situations created primarily in college classes. But the communities of writers created each semester in college courses have a short life span, usually no more than sixteen weeks, so the writing situations created within these classes are localized and limited as well. In addition, college writing assignments are usually intended for readers students actually know: a teacher, classmates, or college students in general. Members of the writing community usually communicate with each other directly and are available to one another for questions and discussion as rhetorical decisions about shaping language are made.

In contrast, some rhetorical contexts may be less physically and more globally defined. For example, a physician writing a medical article is part of an international rhetorical context, one with a long history and a particular perspective on a very highly specialized field of knowledge, but without physical borders. This particular rhetorical context continues to exist long after the physician stops writing, just as it has existed long before the physician began to write. Similarly, the novelist works within a global rhetorical context that shares conventions that, in turn, guide decisions about plot and character development.

Understanding rhetorical situations as part of larger rhetorical contexts is especially important as you learn to write academic essays because universities and colleges are divided into fields of study. Each field functions as a separate learning community. Each community, in turn, has its own rules, forms, and common knowledge. These learning communities provide the rhetorical contexts for the writing situations students encounter.

# 3
• • • • • • • • • • • • •
## ACADEMIC WRITING

How do academic fields function as rhetorical contexts? College teachers are scholars whose professional life consists of teaching, studying, and contributing to the knowledge base of a subject area or discipline. Research and writing play primary roles in academic life. Scholars use writing to plan and conduct research and to generate new disciplinary knowledge. They also use writing to share the results of that research with other members of their discipline, usually in the form of papers presented at regional or national conferences or in journal articles. This writing and research is guided by commonly held beliefs, knowledge, and writing behaviors.

Academicians rely on writing to share ideas with one another because they have few opportunities to get together and discuss their very specialized fields of study. Depending on a college's size, a Department of English or a Department of Biology may have only a few teachers, and each teacher may research a different aspect of the department's field of study. One English teacher might study nineteenth-century poetry while another studies only scientific writing. Writing, usually in the form of professional journal articles, allows teachers who share specialized research interests within the same discipline but who are physically scattered around the world to communicate. Each journal article represents one scholar's attempt to participate in the ongoing conversation about disciplinary ideas and issues.

Like all writers, scholars writing journal articles compose in
response to particular rhetorical contexts. Unlike most college writing
contexts in which students compose for readers they interact with
frequently, academic writing contexts are usually not physically
defined. Journal articles are composed for other scholars with whom
the writers rarely interact in person. However, this lack of physical
contact does not mean that the writers do not have a highly developed
sense of their readers. In fact, most academicians know a great deal
about their readers. They know, for example, that their readers share a
knowledge base and ways to study, discuss, and write about a subject,
even though they may never discuss these shared ways together.
These agreed-upon ways of researching and writing are sometimes
referred to as *conventions*. Conventions dictate standards for the way
an article is organized, the way headings are used, or the way sources
are identified. These conventions may also guide the scholar's choices
about language, sentence length, and illustrations. Although conventions are often unstated and unwritten, they are important aspects of
any academic rhetorical context.

For example, college writing teachers who write articles for *Research in the Teaching of English* or *College Composition and Communication* expect their readers to share a specialized vocabulary for
discussing college writing and college writing research and to recognize names of leading researchers and theorists as well as important
research studies that have become part of the discipline's knowledge
base. They know their readers will expect them to support their ideas
with appropriate forms of evidence and to identify their sources of
information in a particular way. Both readers and writers share conventions for writing and reading these journal articles.

Professors in science fields share conventions that are different
from those English professors share. They put what they call "literature
reviews" into the introductions of their articles; they develop research
questions based on hypotheses; they use very precisely defined methods of investigation that are described in a separate section of an
article. These conventions of science writing exist because scientists
have decided to use them to organize their work, and they provide the
larger rhetorical context for all science writers.

Take a few minutes to skim and then read the two journal article
introductions below. What visual clues suggest differences in
conventions followed by the articles' authors? What differences exist
in their content, organization, and writing style? What do these
differences suggest about some of the conventions valued by the two
authors' particular academic communities? What similarities can you
identify between the two introductions? What might explain these
similarities?

# KENNETH BURKE AND THE TEACHING OF WRITING

## Joseph Comprone

Does Kenneth Burke's eclecticism, his pluralistic approach to rhetoric as it applies to human motivation and action in language, really have any potentially substantive contribution to make to the writing classroom? A positive answer is best grounded in those theoretical areas in which the word *process* functions as a key term. The connections between Burkean theory and teaching composition can be made more specific by pointing out where research and practice in teaching writing seems most compatible with Burkean rhetorical pluralism.

Despite the many recent claims for reductive methods of teaching composition solely in functional and pragmatic contexts, a large and convincing body of research has been building in an area almost diametrically opposed to any of these reductive methodologies, whether rooted in simplistic approaches to grammar or to rhetoric. Composition researchers and theorists have drawn from other disciplines–particularly psychology, philosophy, linguistics, and rhetoric–to expand upon their understanding of what writers do, behaviorally and cognitively, as they compose. This research has included research into the creative process of professional writers, whether imaginative or expository, and it has included close scrutiny of how successful student-writers compose. Still others have written on their own writing habits and their implications for teaching others to write.[1]

All this usually high-quality research and theory can be summarized by saying that informed teachers are now considering writing as a complex act including a wide range of stages or sequences, most of which do not follow one upon the other in linear fashion. The traditional pedagogical assumptions are rapidly becoming suspect: one cannot teach writing by beginning with words, working through sentences and paragraphs, and moving finally through essays and longer papers; nor can one teach writing by having students learn skills one by one as if they could be expected to magically coalesce at some final examination; nor can one expect students to learn to write when writing is taught totally as product, as words on a page to be corrected and adapted to conform to the standards the public and its professions think they uphold every day; nor can one teach writing as if it were not intrinsically related to a

---

[1]See Janet Emig, *The Composing Process of Twelfth-Graders* (Urbana, Illinois: NCTE, 1971) for a seminal examination of student composing; see Peter Elbow, *Writing Without Teachers* (New York: Oxford University Press, 1973) for a seminal examination by a professional writer of his own composing, with a thorough discussion of its implications for the writing classroom.

student's habits of perceiving, thinking, and expressing. Writing, in other words, is very much a part of anyone's general experience with language.

## THE INFLUENCE OF SEX AND VIOLENCE ON THE APPEAL OF ROCK MUSIC VIDEOS

### Christine Hall Hansen
### Ranald D. Hansen

*Two experiments examined the effects of sex and violence in rock music videos on viewers' judgments of the appeal of the music and visuals and emotional responses to the videos. The effects of videos with high, moderate, or low visual sex content were compared in Experiment 1. Positive emotions and the appeal of both the music and visuals were found to be positively related to the level of sexual content. In Experiment 2, the effects of videos with high, moderate, and low levels of visual violence content indicated that negative emotional responses and reduced appeal of both the music and the visuals were related to the level of violence. Evidence was obtained from both experiments that the combination of sex and violence also decreased appeal. In addition, music arousal was found to have an effect on appeal. More arousing music was positively related to appeal and positive emotions in sexy videos, but its influence was found to be independent of visual sex. In violent videos, however, music arousal was associated with decreased appeal and negative emotions and appeared to result from the "transfer" of excitation from the arousing music to the violence of the visual content.*

A generation is coming of age while watching sex and violence on [1] television (Gerbner, Gross, Morgan, & Signiorelli, 1986; Singer & Singer, 1980). Rock music videos, in particular, have been the target of public criticism (Gore, 1987; Steinem, 1988). The National Coalition on Television Violence (1984), for example, has argued that the sexual and violent content of rock music videos makes them unwholesome viewing for young people. A similar opinion has been voiced by the American Academy of Pediatrics (Strasburger, 1988). Rock music videos hold a sizable share of the young television-viewing audience (Zimmerman, 1984), and content analyses have documented the presence of significant sexual and violent content (Brown & Campbell, 1986; Hansen & Hansen, 1989; Sherman & Dominick, 1986; Waite & Paludi, 1987). Yet, if only because the popularity and prevalence of rock music videos is relatively recent, little research has been conducted to test their effects on the viewer (Greeson & Williams, 1986; Hansen, in press; Hansen, C.H. & Hansen, R.D., 1988, in press). But, the effects of this sex and violence per se are not at issue here. Rather, our research was constructed to bear on another, related, question—why is the sex and violence there in the first place?

## Academic Writing Contexts: An Example

To close this discussion of academic writing contexts, consider the topic of intelligence and how different scholars representing different academic contexts might study the same topic. One academic community may investigate intelligence in controlled laboratory settings because scholars in this field agree that to produce new knowledge about intelligence, claims should be verified by observations made in strictly controlled laboratory environments. This research method also is appropriate for questions these types of scholars raise about intelligence: What is intelligence? How does it work?

A second group of scholars may study intelligence in school classrooms. Their research method reflects a different perspective on knowledge production; these scholars value the observations of intelligence gathered in the field or natural settings. Their research strategy also reflects the question they are asking about intelligence: How do perceptions about intelligence affect relationships in a classroom?

A third group of scholars may study intelligence using historical documents, their research method reflecting another perspective on scholarship. These scholars value the kinds of interpretation produced by careful examination of textual evidence. Their research method also reflects the question they are asking about intelligence: How does intelligence or the lack of it affect quality of life?

These field perspectives are like camera lenses. Each academic field uses a different lens—just as photographers do—to investigate a particular subject from a particular angle. One field's lens is not better than another's; each lens simply allows the viewer to examine a subject from a different perspective.

The different perspectives on investigating intelligence described above represent three ways to study intelligence, but there are other ways. These examples simply illustrate how field perspectives, research, and writing are interconnected. We also want to stress that, although academic writing contexts differ, all scholars share a common desire to participate in their field's conversation about new theories and new ideas. Writing is the medium that makes this conversation possible; the academic writing context controls the conversation as it progresses.

## Becoming an Academic Writer

How do most college teachers become academic writers? For most of them, the process takes place over several years. It usually begins when they are undergraduates, soon after they identify a particular college subject as their major. Their undergraduate teachers provide an introduction to the discipline's conventions by requiring them to read journal articles and write papers in which they follow the conventions they learned from those journal articles.

The learning process continues when they pursue graduate degrees in their discipline. As graduate students, they conduct their own research, probably under the guidance of a more experienced member of the discipline, and compose their own articles to submit to journals. By the time they become college teachers, they have learned not only the specialized knowledge identified with a particular field of study, but how to discuss, read, and write about that knowledge using conventions shared by others in the same field. Increased participation over time enables them to make the transition from student-observer to neophyte-imitator to teacher-representative of a specialized group of scholars. They belong to a scholarly community that is part of a larger rhetorical context.

Although most college teachers do not expect you to write the kinds of scholarly articles they do, they will expect you to understand what academic writing is and how writers respond to academic contexts successfully. Many rhetorical strategies teachers use to compose journal articles are explained later in this chapter and can be applied to student writing situations.

# 4
. . . . . . . . . . . . .
# THE RHETORICAL APPROACH
# TO ACADEMIC WRITING

To become effective academic writers in college, students need to become good rhetoricians. That means learning how to fit what they have to say on subjects into frameworks provided by social groups, particular situations, previous discussions, and history in general. Although this process sounds complicated, students can learn efficient strategies to handle rhetoric, whether they are writing, speaking, or analyzing a television show—strategies that allow them to figure out the situations within which they write and speak.

This book contains many opportunities to analyze, practice, and develop rhetorical strategies. It also provides subject matter for writing essays in the form of readings organized around interesting topics and issues. This section stresses the relationship between developing a rhetorical approach and making choices. It also explains some of the important rhetorical choices writers must make and how you can train yourself to make the right choices each time you develop a rhetorical approach for a piece of writing.

## Making Choices

Developing a rhetorical approach to writing means making complex choices at almost every point along the way to producing a final essay. At first, many students feel the choices are impossible to make, partly because there are so many and partly because the choices are new to them. Most students find that making these choices becomes easier with each writing assignment they tackle; the decisions they must make become more familiar, and the decision-making process takes less time. Eventually, developing a rhetorical approach through decision making seems a natural part of their composing process.

Each reading in this book creates an opportunity to make choices and develop a rhetorical approach. Initially, you may need to use the questions that follow the readings to guide the rhetorical choices you make. Then, as you become more familiar with the decisions writers make to develop a rhetorical approach, you will rely less and less on these questions and more on your own developing instincts and skills as an academic writer. Remember, every course that includes writing assignments will require that you make rhetorical choices. Learning to make those choices as you compose essays and reports will help you respond effectively and appropriately to different rhetorical situations.

## Using Reading, Writing, and Discussions
## to Make Choices

The choices you must make in this course will be based on the reading, writing, and discussion you experience inside and outside of the classroom. Because the chapter essays you write will grow out of these reading, writing, and discussion experiences, you must take advantage of the decision-making opportunities they offer you as an academic writer.

You will probably begin reading with personal opinions on the chapter's topic and issues in mind; then you will have those opinions challenged and built on by what you read and hear in the way of response from others. Gradually you will build a thesis for your chapter essay out of this mixed group of sources. To make this process work, you will need to have your rhetorical sensitivities on alert. That will mean careful critical reading of all chapter readings assigned. That will also mean discussing readings and draft writings not simply for pleasure or because the course requires it, but to gather carefully ideas and responses that will later become the substance of your chapter essay. In other words, maximizing the decision-making opportunities created by these unit activities will help you analyze writing situations and develop a rhetorical approach to your writing.

Maximizing reading, writing, and discussion experiences to develop a rhetorical approach also means that you will need to make decisions about weaving these experiences together. Developing a rhetorical approach means writing your drafts with other students in mind. What would they think about your ideas? Did they respond to a particular reading as you did, or were their responses very different? What reasons were behind these differences? Has your past experience in regard to a chapter's theme been similar to or different from those of other students? How are your own ideas changing as you work through readings, discussions, and writings? Keeping these questions in mind throughout the writing process will help you develop the clear sense of audience and purpose that is at the heart of the rhetorical approach to writing. The following sections describe the kinds of decisions you will need to make to develop a rhetorical approach to essay writing. Chapter 3 focuses on how essays are structured once these decisions have been made.

## Developing a Thesis

One choice you must make concerns your thesis or main point. To develop a thesis for an essay, you must manage ideas and information, usually in response to the reading, writing, and discussions that define a particular writing situation. Thesis development is a *narrowing or limiting process*. Reading about and discussing aspects of the intelligence topic may lead to a decision to write an essay about standardized achievement tests. This decision, in turn, would lead to further exploration of the narrowed topic and the development of a tentative thesis such as "Standardized achievement tests often ignore certain kinds of intelligence." Then, during a review of a first draft, this tentative thesis might be narrowed down to "Standardized tests do not measure creativity." You do not want to tie yourself to a thesis that is too broad to defend in a short essay or that you will be unable to support in a brief period of time. You may find yourself *qualifying* your initial thesis to accommodate useful ideas from a reading or a class workshop. Sometimes that may simply entail adding a limiting word to a thesis statement: "*Most* standardized tests do not measure creativity." It may require a more substantive revision of a thesis: "With only minor changes, standardized tests could begin to test creative as well as traditional abstract intelligence." By the time you begin to write the second draft of your chapter essay, you should have a revised and concise statement of your thesis in front of you as you write, and you should be checking back to see that you have stuck to that thesis after writing every paragraph. The optional assignments at the end of each chapter will help you develop a thesis.

## Rhetorical Context: Readers, Purposes, Evidence, Organization

Developing a thesis is only one of the steps in developing a rhetorical approach to writing an academic essay. All writers must decide not only what their main point will be, but how they will support that point and how they will shape that support to meet their writing purposes for particular readers. That process also begins with rhetorical considerations, in this case, of readers, purposes, evidence, and organization.

*Readers.* Writers use different strategies for approaching different audiences. Writers who know that particular audiences are hostile to their views might appeal to common interests before getting into controversial issues. Writers who know that they are addressing an audience that shares their convictions might use certain key or buzz words to remind an audience of common beliefs and to achieve greater emotional appeal. On the other hand, writers who know little about their readers must base decisions on inferences about readers. In this course you may be asked to write essays with your classmates as intended readers. When writing for your classmates, you must realize they are likely to represent diverse backgrounds and viewpoints. That will mean that you will not be able to assume agreement on questions of value and opinion. That, obviously, will be a disadvantage. On the other hand, you will have the opportunity to get to know your fellow students much more intimately than most writers do. You will hear their ideas in discussions and workshops and together you will argue and develop ideas on a common topic. If you listen carefully, discuss with an open but critical mind, and include your classmates' responses in your own thinking, you will have internalized a sense of audience by the time you write your chapter essays.

You can sharpen your understanding of readers by considering the strategies used by the professional writers of these essays. Most of these essays and articles have been written for educated general audiences. The assumption is that intelligent readers want to know more about recent work on important subjects. These essays provide new information to readers. In every case, the professional writers must learn about work that has been done in specialized fields and translate the results of that work into ideas and examples accessible to educated non-specialists. They cannot ignore technicalities in describing specialized work, but they also cannot get bogged down in highly technical or abstract discussions. Their examples and illustrations have to be clear to general readers; these professional writers often have to *create* interest in the details of a problem that might be so technical as to be inaccessible to general readers.

You will be using their reports to develop an informative and interesting thesis of your own. If your classmates are your intended readers, the following questions will help you develop a sense of audience as you work through each chapter theme. (If you are keeping a journal, you might want to build answers to the following questions into your journal writing habit.) They will serve as a record of your ongoing audience considerations and provide very useful reading when you begin writing your chapter essay.

How are your classmates responding to what they read? Are their responses similar to or different from yours? Where are they most at odds with each other, where in most agreement? How are your fellow students responding to your ideas on the theme? Which ones are they in agreement with? Which ones are they opposed to? What reasons and assumptions lie behind their agreement or opposition? How will you create identification with your audience? (They are in many ways different from you. But they *are* all students enrolled in the same institution and course.) What possibilities of audience appeal do those similarities between you and your audience provide?

Of course, these questions will sharpen your sense of audience for any group of readers you are considering. Your task as writer is to determine what you know for certain and what you can infer about your intended readers through a question-answer process.

*Purpose.* Your readers' responses are influenced by *why* you are writing. Will you be providing a straightforward account of a topic, or will you try to persuade readers to hold a particular view on that topic? Will you be writing a personal narrative to make a point, or will you be narrating simply to illustrate an aspect of the topic? These are the kinds of questions you will need to answer before you write the final draft. These questions, like the ones about readers, must be answered gradually, by listening to the reactions of fellow students, by reading closely and critically, and by revising your ideas as you read, write, and interact with others. The driving question is, "Why am I writing this essay, and what do I want my readers to get out of it?"

*Evidence.* Your decisions about readers and purpose will lead you to consider evidence. Here the central question is, "How will I support my thesis?" Will you use personal experience? Why? Will you use direct quotations, paraphrases, or summaries of what others have said? Why? Will you interview fellow students or faculty? Why? How will you combine evidence, and why will you combine it in that way? Are you choosing evidence with readers in mind? What will they think of your evidence? Will they find it engaging, boring, convincing? Why? How much background information will your readers need to understand your evidence? How can you best supply that background while keeping to your main point?

*Organization.* A final set of decisions concerns organization. In what order will you present your ideas and evidence? You will need to consider your subject, readers, and evidence as you decide on an organizational strategy. Will you create better rapport with your audience if you begin with an anecdote that introduces your thesis indirectly, or would you be better off starting out with a direct statement of your thesis? Should you stay with a standard *beginning* (introduce your thesis), *middle* (develop that thesis with evidence), and *end* (conclude with a statement of the significance of your thesis), or should you change that structure to fit your purpose and audience? If, for example, you are writing an essay on a particular theory of intelligence, should you begin with an illustration of how that theory would explain a situation in real life, or should you begin simply by describing that theory in abstract terms? Which approach would have greater appeal to your readers? Which would be easier to follow? And which of these last two questions is more important in this situation?

# 5
. . . . . . . . . . . . .
# ACADEMIC WRITING SKILLS AND STRATEGIES

Analyzing a writing situation to develop a rhetorical approach is the foundation for writing an academic essay. Writers also use particular skills to develop a rhetorical approach.

Two academic writing strategies—*summarizing* and *critiquing*—form the starting point for most scholarly writing, regardless of the particular writing situation. Although college students are not full-fledged members of specialized fields of study, they, too, depend on these critical writing strategies to compose academic texts appropriate for college writing situations.

*Summaries* (brief restatements of a text's main ideas) and *critiques* (organized reports of critical reading interpretations) serve several purposes for college writers. First, they produce a record of college reading for students to use when reviewing or studying. Second, students write summaries to complete assignments, to record information in library sources, or to help them learn and remember a writer's main points. Third, they include summaries in other pieces of writing, for example, critiques or research reports. Students write critiques to complete assignments or to record their responses to a writer's ideas. Often students combine summary and critique in one piece of writing.

The guidelines that follow will help you develop the writing skills needed to summarize and critique the readings in this book and in your other classes. These guidelines will also prepare you for the kinds of writing you will do in this and other college classes.

## Writing a Summary

Summaries (short, concise versions of parts or all of a piece of writing) rely on a reader's ability to identify and express the main points in a text. Teachers ask students to write summaries to demonstrate that they have a clear understanding of what they have read. Summary writing also helps students learn and remember a writer's ideas because the writing process itself reinforces the ideas in the text being summarized. Finally, summaries create a foundation for other writing assignments. They serve as starting points for analyzing, evaluating, and responding.

The academic community as a whole has developed conventions for writing summaries. These conventions reflect what readers expect to find when they read a summary. The descriptions that follow explain the conventions summary writers observe.

---

**Conventions for Summary Writing**

1. Be brief.
2. Use your own words.
3. Adopt a neutral point of view.

---

*1. Be brief.*   Readers expect summaries to be significantly shorter than the original. The length of a summary depends on the writing context, in particular the length and complexity of the original text and the reader's expectations. A teacher may request a one-page or one-paragraph summary, or a student may decide that one- or two-sentence summaries of textbook chapters are sufficient to prepare for an exam. A highly complex, technical text may require a longer summary than a less technical one. Regardless of the adaptations summary writers make in response to writing contexts, they always seek to produce a "no frills" version of the text, one which contains clear, specific language and communicates the main ideas in a minimum number of words.

*2. Use your own words.*   Readers expect a summary to "sound" like the writer of the summary, not the writer of the original text. Therefore, summaries contain few, if any, quotations. Teachers are especially firm about this convention because they assign summaries to test students' understanding of reading assignments. If students quote the main ideas, they are demonstrating that they can copy information from a text, not that they understand and can express its contents in their own words.

*3. Adopt a neutral point of view.* Readers expect to find only the ideas from the original text in a summary, not the ideas of the summary writer. Opinions about the ideas contained in a text or evaluations of how those ideas are presented are inappropriate. Phrases like "The writer presents an *excellent* argument for . . ." or "*In my opinion,* this writer's views are *biased* . . ." express judgments about writers or their ideas that have no place in summaries. Like other summary conventions, the neutral perspective is a response to the writing context. Readers use summaries to learn what the original writer said; they do not read summaries to learn how the summary writer has evaluated that text.

Understanding what readers value, however, is only the first step in developing effective summary writing skills. Here are the steps you should follow to complete a summary.

---

### The Summary Writing Process

1. Read and annotate the text.
2. Compose a first draft.
3. Revise the draft.
4. Edit and proofread.
5. Complete a final draft.

---

*1. Read and annotate the text.* Before you can express a text's main ideas, you must understand them. This process begins when you read the text (and reread it, if necessary) carefully and actively. As you read, write brief summary notes in the margins and underline or highlight main ideas and key terms. Choose the ideas to highlight carefully; overhighlighting makes observing conventions for brevity and conciseness difficult. (See pages 18 to 19 for an explanation of how to write summary notes.) Discussions with classmates about your summary notes will also provide an opportunity to test your understanding of a text's main ideas.

Do not begin to draft a summary until you feel you understand the material you must summarize. If you cannot reproduce the text's main points in your own mind, you will not be able to express those ideas in writing.

*2. Compose a first draft.*   Begin your draft with a *thesis statement*—a sentence that identifies the text being summarized (by title, author, or both) and states its main idea. Remember this thesis statement should communicate to your readers the gist of the text. To help you generate this thesis, imagine that you are permitted only one sentence to tell someone what the text says. Or you may find a sentence in the text that states the main point. In that case, simply restate that sentence using your own words.

Once you have written the thesis of your summary, you will need to compose summary sentences based on your reading notes and highlightings. These summary sentences should focus only on the text's main points, not details (unless you believe they are important to understanding the main ideas). Remember to write these summary sentences as concisely as possible and in your own words. Do not repeat ideas. You should also present the ideas in the summary in the same order in which they are presented in the original.

*3. Revise the draft.*   Compare what you have written to the original text. These questions will help you evaluate what you have written:

- Does the summary highlight only the text's main ideas, free of detail?
- Does the summary begin with a thesis that identifies the writer and expresses the text's main point?
- Does your summary contain only the author's ideas, not your own?
- Is the summary as brief and concise as possible without omitting main ideas?
- Is the summary's organization consistent with the organization of the original?
- Does the draft sound like you or like the writer of the original?

The answers to these questions determine what should be added, deleted, or replaced. Once you make these revisions, you will need to add transitional words or phrases to identify the relationships you are establishing between sentences or paragraphs and to help create coherence in the summary. For example, *in addition, also, moreover,* and *furthermore* are used when writers add information to ideas presented in the preceding sentence. Consistent use of pronouns, parallelism, and repetition of key words or phrases also makes a summary more coherent. These coherence strategies help to guide readers of the summary.

*4. Edit and proofread.*   Finally, you should edit and proofread your summary to correct punctuation, spelling, and typing errors. If possible, ask a peer to compare your summary and the text you are summarizing for accuracy and concision. This reader could also make revising and editing suggestions.

*5. Complete a final draft.* After you have revised and edited your summary, compose a final draft, being certain you have responded to all contextual requirements. If formal documentation is required, be sure you have cited the original text properly. (Documentation systems are reviewed in the Research Appendix at the end of this book.)

Here is a student's one-paragraph summary of "Conversation with Howard Gardner/Seven Frames of Mind" (see Chapter 5). Use the conventions discussed earlier in this section and the review questions on page 52 to evaluate the success of this student's summary.

### Student Summary

```
    In an interview with James Ellison, Howard Gardner dis-
cusses his book, The Seven Frames of Mind. These frames are
the linguistic, logical-mathematical, spatial, musical,
bodily-kinesthetic, interpersonal, and intrapersonal intel-
ligences. Gardner argues that there are many more forms of
intelligence than reading or being mathematically inclined,
and that these other forms are often ignored in standard
intelligence tests. He also believes that different people
and cultures use and need different intelligences. Gardner
closes by proposing a nonquantitative experiment to test
his theories in grading preschool-aged children.
```

## Writing a Critique

*Critiques*—formal reports of a writer's analysis, evaluation and response to a text—represent writers' efforts to add something to an ongoing academic discussion. This discussion focuses on critiques of written texts; however, it is important to keep in mind that writers critique other kinds of "texts"—films, plays, paintings, or sculptures, for example. Critiques are the specific beginnings of larger acts of interpretation. Teachers ask students to critique texts as part of the larger process of responding critically to what they read and experience. Only when writers are able to write critiques of what they read can they begin the larger task of interpretation.

Writing a critique can be quite challenging, more challenging than a summary, because it requires writers to move beyond comprehension to interpretation and evaluation. Critique writers make an investment in a text; they stake an interpretive claim that they hope readers will invest in as well. And the claims made in a critique must be supported—by references to the text itself and by reasoned statements that reflect thoughtful and careful analysis, evaluation, and response.

Students writing critiques must follow the conventions laid down by academic writers. Understanding what these conventions are and what academic values they reflect will help you to respond to any critical writing context that you may face in college. The following points summarize the essentials in critique writing.

---

**Conventions for Critique Writing**

1. Represent the original writer's ideas fairly and accurately.
2. Provide adequate support for your claims.

---

*1. Represent the original writer's ideas fairly and accurately.* Regardless of whether your judgment of a text is positive, negative, or both, you must not slant or distort the ideas in the original text. If a writer claims that a particular event—passage of a new state law, for example—*may* have a negative impact on American economics, you could not distort that statement by telling readers that this writer believes passage of this law *would* have a negative impact. This would be stretching what your source has said. Academic readers evaluate the claims and evidence of critique writers in terms of what they are told about the original text; for this reason, they expect all references to the original text to be accurate. Do not interpret when you should describe.

*2. Provide adequate support for your claims.* Many students have difficulty writing critiques. They focus more on reporting a writer's main ideas than on assessing those ideas, probably because reporting is easier than analyzing and evaluating. Summarizing ideas in a text is only part of the critiquing process; the bulk of a critique must discuss the writer's analysis and interpretation of the source text.

How are interpretations best supported? Most writers simply use carefully developed reasons for each idea in their critique. For example, a critique writer who says that the source text fails to establish a basis for the claim that corporations are ignoring environmental laws must at least show where in the source text that claim could have been supported. A critique writer who asserts that a source text is unfair in its judgment of a particular artwork needs to provide convincing support that the art critic has distorted or omitted important information.

Readers expect some of the support for a critique's assessment to come from the text itself. If a writer critiques a film, aspects of the film (special effects, acting, cinematography) must be analyzed and connected to the judgment of the critique. When writers critique written texts, elements of the text (language, logic, organization, claims) must be analyzed and connected to the judgment of the critique.

Knowing what academic readers value in a critique is the first step to learning how to write one. The guidelines that follow will provide a framework for your critique writing process.

---

**The Critique Writing Process**

1. Read and annotate the text critically.
2. Share the results of your critical reading.
3. Compose a first draft.
4. Revise the draft.
5. Edit and proofread the draft.
6. Complete a final draft.

---

*1. Read and annotate the text critically.*  A strong, convincing critique begins with careful, and often repeated, critical reading. To read critically, annotate as you read, concentrating first on understanding the text. Consider reading the text first to be sure you understand what the writer is saying, then again to analyze, evaluate, and respond to what is being said. As a critical reader, you need to consider the writer's purpose, how it is accomplished, and whether you agree with the ideas, assumptions (stated and implied beliefs and values), and evidence (examples, facts, statistics, expert testimony). (See pages 14 to 27 for a discussion of annotating guidelines.)

Use the questions that follow to guide your critical reading process. These questions will keep you focused on your critical reading objectives. Answer as many of the questions as you can, making annotations in the text's margins as you read.

Questions for Analysis

- What is the writer's purpose?
- How does the writer divide the text into sections?
- What kinds of evidence does the writer use to support interpretations?
- What are the writer's assumptions?
- Who are the intended readers?
- What kind of style, language, and tone does the writer use?

Questions for Response

- What is my reaction to this text?
- What assumptions do I bring to this reading?
- What personal experiences affect my reading?

- How does my knowledge about this topic affect my reading?
- What else influences my reaction to this text?

Questions for Evaluation

- How convincing is the writer's evidence?
- How sound is the writer's reasoning?
- Has the writer omitted or overlooked any evidence?
- How persuasive is the writer's style?

*2. Share the results of your critical reading.*   Critical reading and annotating help you begin to interpret or assess the text you are critiquing. However, sharing your assessment with other students who have read the text helps you probe the assumptions behind your interpretation and the evidence you use to support it. Hearing others respond to your ideas allows you to identify the strengths and weaknesses of your interpretation. This information then guides your efforts to review and revise your critique as you develop a thesis for it. The reason for discussing your interpretation with others is to create an opportunity to test and assess your interpretation and to develop new insights.

*3. Compose a first draft.*   The first draft should reflect your analysis of the critical reading and your understanding of what is valued in a critique. Your purpose is to add something to the ongoing discussion in your classroom community about this text—a new insight, a new interpretation, or a new assessment. The content and organization of your critique depend on your reading of the text and your writing context.

Academic readers have certain expectations about critiques. These expectations can be understood in terms of the questions they ask each time they read a critique. Of course, individual readers may have different or additional questions. The following basic questions will help you write a first draft. Answer them in the order they are presented and make changes when you review the draft. Keep in mind that the bulk of the critique is support for your thesis.

- What are you critiquing? (Identify the text as thoroughly as your writing situation requires.)
- What background information about the text or its author does the reader need to follow your ideas and reasoning? (Provide background information on the topic, biographical information, or whatever you think readers need to create a reading context.)
- What is your purpose? (State your thesis.)
- What are the writer's main points? (Provide a summary.)
- What is the basis for your thesis? (Offer your support.)
- What do you want readers to gain from this critique? (Close by restating your interpretation.)

*4. Revise the draft.* Review what you have written using the conventions for critiquing as a guide. Share your draft with a fellow student. The questions below will be helpful as you, or whoever is responding to your draft, review it.

- Are the source writer's ideas represented fairly and accurately?
- Does the critique contain appropriate, sufficient support for the interpretation it presents?
- Does the critique offer a "new" perspective on the text?
- Does the critique demonstrate your ability to summarize, analyze, evaluate, and respond to the text's ideas?
- Is the organization of the critique clear to the reader?
- Does the critique include just enough summary to provide the reader with a context for understanding the points you are making?
- Does the critique analyze both the assumptions behind your views and those of the writer of the original text?

The answers to these questions will help you decide what should be added, deleted, or replaced in your first draft.

*5. Edit and proofread the draft.* Edit the first draft for correctness, coherence, and style. Have you provided transitional words and phrases so that your readers will be able to follow the flow of your ideas? How well have you defined terms? Have you correctly identified source materials, if documentation is required? Carefully check your draft for grammar, punctuation, spelling, and typographical errors.

*6. Complete a final draft.* After you have revised and edited your critique, incorporate your revisions into the draft, check that the text reads smoothly, and produce a final draft.

Here are the first few paragraphs of a student's critique of the Gardner interview included in Chapter 5. Use the questions above as a checklist to evaluate how well the student has responded to academic conventions for writing a critique.

## Student Critique

Howard Gardner believes that American society's views about intelligence are undemocratic. In an interview with Ellison, he discussed his views on multiple intelligences, his theory that there are different kinds of intelligence and that they should all be equally respected. Although his goal is a very noble one, his theory seems impractical and even illogical for several reasons.

Basically, Gardner believes that we place too much emphasis on certain kinds of intelligence like math ability and thinking skills. He believes that because we only test for these kinds of intelligences, children get labeled dumb or smart. These labels affect how kids feel about themselves and then the kinds of decisions they make. They also affect the choices they have to make. Gardner says if we would value his kinds of intelligence and test kids for them all, we could help kids choose careers they are best suited for. Then everyone would be living up to their potential and no one would think they were better than someone else.

I question Gardner's claim that all intelligences are equal. He bases that claim on the fact that other cultures value different kinds of intelligence. He says, for example, that in some cultures people are considered intelligent if they can navigate the seas using just the stars and their instincts. Doesn't Gardner realize that in that culture, those who can navigate better are probably respected more, just as smarter people are respected more in our society. In that sense, they're no better than we are. They have established a hierarchy based on intelligence like ours; only the steps on the ladder to respect are different. Their hierarchy is based on different abilities. Their system is just as unequal as ours is, so arguing that their system gives us a reason to see all intelligences as equal is illogical.

Gardner also claims that scientific theories and literary theories are equal in status. They are not. Maybe they are in an ideal world, but not in the real world. Some scientific theories change the world for everyone on the planet, while a literary theory may affect only a few scholars. Society values certain kinds of intelligence for a good reason. And that's not going to change.

I also question the kinds of behaviors Gardner calls intelligences. . . .

Before concluding this section on critical writing strategies, we need to restate the important connection between the writing context and the critical reading strategies we have outlined. Although we have discussed summary and critique strategies separately, many college writing situations require that students use summary and critique in the same piece of writing. Indeed, effective critiques must contain a summary of the ideas in the source text. But there are situations where a summary or critique is not the final goal, but the means to achieve that goal. Students often write summaries and critiques of library sources they are considering for a research paper. They also use summary and critique writing skills when they take lecture notes and study, using these strategies to capture the main points in a professor's lecture or to develop interpretations and connections among ideas in different lectures. In other words, these writing strategies are a part of their daily college writing routines.

Students may also integrate summaries and critiques within a single piece of writing. For example, a student writing the introduction for a report of field research in a sociology class could combine information from several articles on a topic (using summary writing strategies) and then analyze and evaluate some of the ideas in those articles (using critique writing strategies). Or a student writing a research paper for a history course may incorporate summaries of parts of several sources, critiques of the ideas in some of those sources, and examples of personal experiences. This student draws on summary and critique writing skills to complete a writing assignment. (See pages 92 to 94 for a discussion of synthesis strategies.)

Critique and summary are tools for writers. They help them respond to writing contexts successfully. And, as with any tools, their helpfulness depends on their nature and the skill of the user. That is why teachers encourage the practice of summary and critique writing. They are the most important writing tools used to connect what you read to what you write.

# 6
· · · · · · · · · · · · · ·
## CHAPTER SUMMARY

We have covered a great deal of ground in this chapter. We began it with a description of the writing process, emphasizing that writers adapt their planning, drafting, and reviewing processes to particular writing situations or contexts. When writers produce a text, they consider why they are writing (purpose) and who will read their text (audience). Their analysis of the writing context influences how they plan, draft, and review.

Academic writers (scholars who compose primarily for other scholars with highly developed expertise in a particular field of study) learn to respond to their particular writing contexts during a lengthy socialization process that begins in college and continues in and after graduate school. Although conventions vary from one field to another, all scholars use writing to learn more about their subjects and to communicate this knowledge to their peers.

College students learn to be academic writers themselves. In many college courses, students are required to compose texts to demonstrate that they can use strategies academic scholars use to read, write, and conduct research. Summary and critique are basic tools on which college students build successful academic writing careers.

# 3

# Shaping an Academic Essay

How are academic essays structured? What are the reasons
for that structure? How does reading fit into the process of
writing an academic essay? How can a writer *focus* an
academic essay? What is a thesis? How can an academic
essay be built around a thesis? How do writers effectively
begin and end an academic essay?

## 1
## FROM READING TO WRITING

An essay, simply defined, is a writer's attempt to provide an organized
written response to a complex issue. In a college course, essays are
most often assigned by teachers to help students develop their own
approaches to the issues raised in course readings, lectures, and
demonstrations. Essays help students learn course content; they also
contribute to a student's ability to communicate effectively. This chapter
focuses on planning and drafting strategies for essays developed in
response to course readings; however, these strategies may also be
applied to other college writing situations.

### Using Journals and Notes to
### Prepare for Writing Essays

Writers often take notes and make journal entries to help develop
theses (main points) for essays. Here is one method for using a journal
to develop your own theses. As you read in preparation for writing,

write brief reactions before and after reading sessions. To help you develop a focused thesis, however, your reactions should contain the following:

Pre-Reading Statements

- A sentence describing your current feelings or position about the topic or issue.
- A second sentence predicting how this text could affect your position.

Post-Reading Statements

- A sentence describing the author's main point.
- A second sentence describing the author's main support for that point.
- A third sentence describing your response to the author's point.

Every time you are assigned a new essay to read, go back and read the pre- and post-reading statements you wrote for earlier reading assignments. Then, write new reaction statements *before* and *after* reading the new assignment. Initially, these written reactions provide a basis for classroom discussions about the readings. Then, as you develop your essay plans, your reaction statements allow you to organize responses into focused thesis statements.

Keeping your reaction statements in a journal will make it easier for you to review all your reading reactions at once (along with the other writing you have done during the unit, such as free writings, tentative outlines, and brainstorming lists) just before you plan your own essay. If you are not keeping such a journal, however, write your reactions on separate pieces of paper and keep them in one place to review before reading, planning, and drafting sessions.

Keep in mind that when writing an essay based on reading, the reading *you* do is the starting point for the ideas you develop. First, *retain* ideas from your reading, but also *organize* those ideas to develop your own for your essay. (This strategy also applies when you are reading library sources for information to include in an essay.) Connecting ideas from reading and personal experience in an organized way provides the basis for the standard college essay's structure.

## How Is an Academic Essay Structured?
## What Are the Reasons for that Structure?

The most efficient way to approach writing an essay is to understand that the assignment of an essay or academic paper is a contract between you (the writer) and your readers. Say to yourself: "By adopting a structure we all recognize, I will communicate successfully my ideas to my readers." Like any contract, this one stipulates a shared set of expectations concerning any academic essay. One expectation your teacher and other readers share concerns structure: they expect the various parts of your essay to take on different but related functions. Most academic essays follow a basic *introduction–body–conclusion* structure in which the introduction identifies the focus of the essay; the body provides evidence (logical reasoning, illustration, personal experience) that develops the focus; and the conclusion draws out the significance of the ideas developed in the body. Differences among writers, writing purposes and decisions about how to shape an introduction, body, and conclusion are what prevent all essays from sounding alike. Twenty students writing about prenatal testing, for example, would produce 20 different essays, even though they all used the basic structure discussed above.

Some experienced writers depart from the traditional introduction–body–conclusion structure. A well-reasoned essay can deviate from these general expectations. Such original essays, however, succeed because their writers know the structure that is expected and deliberately depart from it only when their analysis of a particular writing situation suggests that such a rhetorical approach will be successful.

One effective way to remember the function of the general form of the academic essay is to keep in mind the following mental sketch of the purpose of each part of that structure. This sketch of readers' expectations is called the **GSG.**

| | |
|---|---|
| General | So What's the Problem? What's Your Approach to It? = Introduction |
| Specific | So What's the Evidence? = Body |
| General | So Why Is Your Point Important? = Conclusion |

## How Does Reading Fit into the Writing of an Academic Essay?

What you read and your personal experience provide the evidence—in the form of experiences, reasons, and examples—for the point you make in your essay. For most writers, building an essay's central idea out of support developed while reading, thinking about, and discussing personal experiences represents a two-way process. While you read, you will be taking in ideas one by one and building them into a main point for your essay. When you move on to writing, you will be taking this main point and looking back at your reading and your personal experience to find support for that point. Your reading moves you forward toward a general idea; your writing moves you back toward specifics.

# 2
. . . . . . . . . . . . . .
# FOCUSING: DEVELOPING THESES AND SUPPORT

## What Is a Thesis?

Your readers *will* expect your essay to have a thesis or main point, and they will expect your entire essay to develop that point. That does not mean that they want to be beaten over the head with that point. But they want you to keep that point in front of them, to show them how a single piece of evidence reinforces or explains that point, and to remind them at the end how your support and thesis work together.

## How Does a Thesis Work?

This question demands two answers. First, it must be answered from the writer's perspective. Then, it must be answered from the reader's perspective.

You ought to be able to express the thesis of your essay in a simple sentence. Only then will you be able to check the various parts of your essay against that thesis to ensure that it and your support for it hang together. It is important, however, to remember that your thesis will develop *while* you read, think, discuss, and draft your essay; it will not pop into your head all at once. Thunderbolts may strike trees and light instant fires; theses seldom strike writers and light fires in essays. *If* you keep a reading notebook or journal with summaries and reactions to each reading, and *if* you review those journal entries every time you read a new essay, and *if* you participate actively in classroom discussions about those readings, and *if* you begin the drafting process by turning your journal entries into more and more specific thesis statements, *then* you will have a succinct thesis sentence as you write your final draft. Developing a unified, workable thesis for the final draft of your essay will take patience and hard work. It will entail looking ahead as you read and looking back as you write drafts.

How does a thesis work for readers? Readers begin academic reading expecting to find a point, wherever that point might appear in the essay itself. And they expect that point to be supported—by examples, statistics, logic, case studies, anecdotes, whatever the writer can come up with from reading, personal experience, and discussion. Every word, beginning with the title, that the writer composes reshapes the reader's initial expectations. If an essay begins with a story, readers will look for the point of that story. Sometimes the point is directly expressed; at other times it is indirectly expressed. In either instance, however, it should answer the question, "Why did the writer include this story?" If an essay begins with a position statement, then readers will expect to find reasons supporting that position and statements that acknowledge and refute opposing arguments.

## How Can an Academic Essay Be Built Around a Thesis?

Because we read essays line by line and page by page, we often mistakenly think that essays are structured by writers in the same way that they appear to us as we read. In actuality, essays are usually structured around theses in ways that are better represented by a visual diagram than they are by linear or line-by-line outlines. Take a moment to study the diagram of the idea-structure that is embedded in most essays (Figure 3–1).

### The Hub and Spokes of the Essay Wheel

Once you have developed a thesis through careful reading and thinking and by hearing the responses of others in your writing class, you are ready to make that thesis into the *hub* or central idea around which every sentence in your essay revolves. The hub of an essay can be considered the core of a writer's rhetorical approach. It develops in response to a particular writing situation, then is supported by evidence the writer considers appropriate and effective in that context. In many cases, the best time to clarify your thesis in a final way is *after* you have read and reacted, considered personal experiences and others' responses, and written a first draft. This approach is especially useful when you have given yourself forty-five minutes to an hour to compose a first draft by writing without stopping. Immediately after finishing that first draft, reread what you have written and write one sentence describing the purpose of your essay. Address the sentence to another member of your class whom you can assume has considered some of the same readings. Tell that person what you are saying and how you will say it in your essay.

Once the thesis has been written, the hub diagram can guide your revision of the first draft. The purpose of this revision is to ensure that every part of your essay clearly develops the thesis and is consistent with your planned rhetorical approach. Every revision decision that you make (adding, deleting, or substituting words, sentences, and paragraphs) should be connected to the thesis. The questions in Figure 3–1 will help you check your first draft and write a second draft in which each part does indeed develop your thesis.

*How is the* **thesis** *introduced?* Have you presented your thesis in your first paragraph so that your readers know where they are

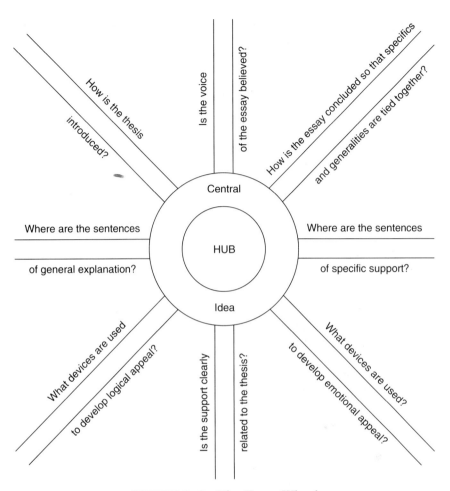

How is the thesis introduced?

Is the voice of the essay believed?

How is the essay concluded so that specifics and generalities are tied together?

Central

Where are the sentences

HUB

Where are the sentences

of general explanation?

of specific support?

Idea

What devices are used to develop logical appeal?

Is the support clearly related to the thesis?

What devices are used to develop emotional appeal?

FIGURE 3–1   The Essay Wheel

going from the start? If you chose *not* to do that, where in the essay will you clarify your thesis for your readers? Why have you chosen not to present your thesis up front? Are you building up to a dramatic statement of your thesis in the concluding paragraph? Or have you decided that repeating your thesis several times throughout the body of the essay provides the emphasis you seek?

*Where are the sentences of* **general explanation?** Usually, you will devote some sentences to general discussion of the significance of your thesis. These sentences should be placed in a way that helps readers understand how your thesis and support are related. Most writers place sentences of general significance at the beginnings of the essay's major support or body paragraphs.

Often, these sentences are called the **topic sentences** of these body paragraphs. They function within the overall essay structure to tie together the thesis and its specific support. They also serve to connect paragraphs with the thesis and each other. For example, a student making the point that Saturday morning television cartoons contain several kinds of positive female role models might begin each support paragraph with a sentence announcing a particular kind of positive female cartoon character.

*Where are the sentences of* **specific support?** Before you begin your second draft, you should have a clear idea of how you will specifically support your thesis. The major paragraphs of the body of your essay should contain at least two kinds of sentences: a sentence or two in which you describe the paragraph's topic and connect it with the thesis of the essay (general explanation sentences); several specific support sentences in which you provide evidence for that topic. That evidence should come in the form of examples, analysis, comparisons, statistics, or stories—all the strategies you have decided to use in this particular essay. As you make decisions about the kinds of specific support you will use, you must also consider how much support to include and whether that support is appropriate to your writing purposes and your particular readers.

*Is the evidence clearly related to the thesis?* The material in the support sentences of the body paragraphs of your essay must clearly relate to your topic sentence. Most writers signal the connections between their evidence and thesis by using common *transitional devices,* repeated key words, synonyms, and connection words, such as subordinating and coordinating conjunctions. One effective way of checking on these connections is to ask another student to point out how a piece of support is related to your thesis. If the student has trouble doing that, re-evaluate the support you have offered: How well does it establish logical connections between the thesis and topic sentences? How clearly have you signaled these connections?

*What devices are used to develop* **logical appeal?** Logical appeal describes the reasoning in your essay. How are your support sentences logically related to your thesis? Are you arguing that something is wrong because it breaks a law? If so, what have you written to convince readers that a law has been violated? Are you arguing that something is wrong because it is an inappropriate response to a particular situation? What have you done to convince readers to accept your definition of *inappropriate.* If you are telling a story to illustrate how particular groups respond to an issue or a politician, are you suggesting that response can stand for many responses? If you are, what have you done to persuade your readers that your claim of broader application is warranted? Academic essays require good reasons for their claims.

*What devices are used to develop* **emotional appeal?** Writers often use stories, extended examples, and emotionally charged language to build emotion in their essays. In academic contexts, emotion must always be balanced with reason. A poignant story will often need to be interpreted rationally. The opposite is also true. Rational arguments need to be balanced with some kind of emotional appeal to be convincing. After all, most readers respond to essays with both their brains and their hearts.

*How is the essay* **concluded** *so that specifics and generalities are tied together?* In academic essays, conclusions are usually meant to tie together loose ends. Before you write your conclusion, go back and read your thesis statement. Should you repeat or rephrase it in your conclusion? If your essay makes a complex argument, should you remind your readers of the major points and the main lines of support for those points? What can you say about the general significance of your thesis that will help your readers keep your essay in focus?

*Are the essay's* **perspective** *and* **language** *appropriate?* Do you sound convincing, given the angle you have chosen for your essay? If you are making a serious ethical argument, your voice should be appropriately serious, straightforward, and logical. If you are making an ironic or satiric appeal, your voice should be suited to that appeal. Are your language choices appropriate to the perspective you have chosen? Do your words imply a bias or an overly technical approach to your subject?

# 3
. . . . . . . . . . . . . .
# BEGINNINGS AND ENDINGS

Strategies for beginning and ending essays vary according to purpose and audience. Introductions should pique a reader's interest and provide a context for the essay. Writers use a variety of strategies to accomplish these goals—brief anecdotes, startling facts or statistics, background information, or quotations from experts or well-known individuals, which are all related in some way to the essay's topic and thesis. Conclusions should give readers a sense of closure and completeness. Writers use a variety of strategies to provide closure—summaries of key points, statements of implications suggested by a thesis, or predictions about the future, for example. Despite the various strategies for beginning and ending essays, however, there is a very basic structure that all writers of informative, critical essays (the kind usually required in college courses) follow. Beginnings and endings always work together to form a *frame* for the essay's ideas. This frame may work in the way that is represented in Figure 3–2.

This diagram clarifies how you should organize your essay. You must pull the main points, subpoints, and evidence together into a coherent whole. On a general level, you do this by providing a clear-cut frame for the picture that your essay will give its readers. As you move to the final drafting stage, you will need to use the questions in Figure 3–2 to check your essay's organization. As you make final revisions, you will need to keep your readers in mind. You are writing to convince them, not yourself; therefore, your organizational strategies need to be directed to those who do *not* know your subject as well as you do.

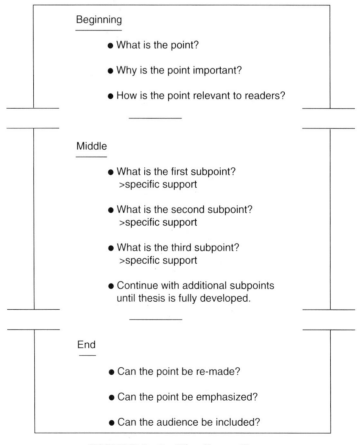

Beginning
- What is the point?
- Why is the point important?
- How is the point relevant to readers?

Middle
- What is the first subpoint?
  >specific support
- What is the second subpoint?
  >specific support
- What is the third subpoint?
  >specific support
- Continue with additional subpoints until thesis is fully developed.

End
- Can the point be re-made?
- Can the point be emphasized?
- Can the audience be included?

FIGURE 3–2   The Essay Frame

**4**

· · · · · · · · · · · · · ·
# STUDENT ESSAY: AN EXAMPLE

The student essay reprinted below was written to complete a writing assignment in a college writing course. Mike Meyer, the student, was asked to develop a critical response to one of the ideas Neil Postman presents in *Amusing Ourselves to Death,* a book that argues that many education problems are caused by television. To write his essay, Mike used the rhetorical decision-making processes and the essay framework described in this chapter.

Read Mike Meyer's essay, using the study questions below to guide your analysis of how he fulfills the requirements of this particular writing situation and his writing purpose. In completing your analysis, you will be describing how Mike Meyer used the essay-writing framework described in this chapter to develop his response to Postman's book.

## Study Questions

1. How effective is the essay's opening? Does that opening clarify the essay's thesis? Does it state the significance of that thesis? Does it clearly address its audience? How does the introduction attempt to pique the reader's interest? How successful is it?
2. How well does the body of this essay relate to the essay's thesis? Are the subpoints related to parts of the thesis? Is the specific evidence clearly related to those subpoints? Is there sufficient use of transitional devices to ensure sentence-to-sentence coherence? Does the middle of the essay relate to both the beginning and the end? How is that backward-and-forward connection achieved?
3. How well does the end of the essay combine the main points, subpoints, and evidence into a coherent package? Is the thesis restated in new ways? Is the significance of the thesis clearly established? Are the essay's readers included in the final appeal of this essay? How are they included?

```
          Television: Its Current Misuse and Its Potential
                          by Mike Meyer
                 Michigan Technological University

     Ask any personnel manager what he looks for in his pro-     1
spective employees and his or her answer, regardless of the
field he or she works in, will be ''communication skills.''
Many businessmen, engineers, scientists, and researchers
```

are returning to school to attain these skills--the most
valuable available to people in our technological world.
Ironically, while the value of communication skills has increased, the American communication media have decreased in
value, often stooping to triviality in their treatment of
American viewers. In his book Amusing Ourselves to Death,
Neil Postman argues that the current decline in communication skills among high school and college graduates can be
attributed to television's intrinsic inferiority as a medium. Postman idealizes writing, describing it as the more
informative and complex medium, while he denigrates television as a potential source of communication power. He
fails, however, to see the limitations of print media, and
he fails to acknowledge the potential strengths of television. Since I am a child of the image-based society that
Postman denigrates, however, I do not agree. Rather, I see
the degradation of communication in America as a result of
the misuse of both writing and television.

    Writing has simply been the central intellectual medium    2
of communication much longer than television; perhaps that
is why it has established itself as a serious form of communication without its even seeming that pervasive. Many
historians agree that prehistoric people invented writing
as a means of describing their world. Most written languages were in their origins at least partially pictorial;
as the phonetic alphabet came into use, however, societies
began to organize themselves around languages made up of
words that represented sounds rather than physical objects.
Phonetic writing, although it gave people more control over
what they described, also sacrificed a great deal of visual
impact and immediacy because it did not ''look like'' what
it described.

    Today writing to describe has become every high school    3
writer's nightmare. English teachers find great joy in
watching students struggle to ''describe a tree as if you
have never seen one . . . as if you had just gotten here
from Mars.'' Inevitably these descriptions end up dripping
with instructor criticisms like ''more detail!'' or ''show
. . . don't tell!'' But these criticisms are not fairly
aimed at students. Written language is idea rather than image oriented, and the connotations, abstract meanings, and
resulting ambiguities of words do not allow for the completely accurate descriptions of physical objects. Images
exist in infinite detail; they are never completely captured in writing. Professional writers can create the illu-

sion of complete reality, but they can never truly re-create that reality itself. In other words, only the most talented of writers can re-instill the feeling of substance itself that any physical object possesses simply by being what it is.

Words, for example, often reduce the complexity of phys-   4
ical substances. Color and size provide the best illustra-tions. If I write that something is <u>green</u>, I have conveyed to readers only one primary property that can actually ex-ist in several thousand shades (<u>forest</u>, <u>lime</u>, <u>emerald</u>, <u>dark</u>, or many other ''greens'') and be used for many dif-ferent purposes (to indicate ''go'' on a street corner or the infield area of a baseball field, to name just two). If I decide to say that the object that I am describing is ''large,'' then I will need to establish what I, as writer, think is large. Is a large dog ''large'' compared to a small elephant or oversized flea? Even trying to show and not tell is a matter of finding what you and your readers share as far as preconceived notions of an object are. To an Eskimo snow is many-faceted. To a Floridian it may be a simple white substance the comes in only one shape and color.

What, then, should writers do? Should they embellish in   5
order to entertain and beautify? Or should they restrain themselves and the language in order to be more accurate? Writing is probably a far more powerful medium for describ-ing concepts than physical reality; photographs and films do a much better job at capturing visual detail. A writer can address a universal question such as ''What Is Human Nature?'' with greater confidence than he or she can ad-dress the problem of describing the petal of a flower. Ideas are best expressed through selective use of detail in writing; feelings and emotions may be best expressed through direct visual representation.

Neil Postman, however, oversimplifies the difference be-   6
tween the verbal and visual media when he argues that writ-ing is by definition better able to express a definite or precise meaning than visual imagery. Actually, writing, be-cause it is so selective, is apt to produce a meaning that is more in the writer's mind than it is in the object it-self. It effectively communicates abstract ideas, but it does not reproduce objects any more accurately than does film, television, or other types of visual imagery. In ac-tuality, meaning cannot be any more accurately transferred in any one medium; all media transform reality in one way

or another. Visual images are selected and presented according to the writer's intentions as well.

Postman would argue that careful word choice by writers            7
cuts down the ambiguity and subjectivity of written communication. To a degree, when writers are skilled, this is true. But even the most skilled writers fail to stabilize meanings entirely, and they never achieve complete descriptions of the objects they describe. Written words are limited by different kinds of constraints than are visual images, but the limitations are there nonetheless. There is no word that can perfectly describe my view of love to a reader and to invent a new word would eventually entail in its process of definition all the old connotations of love. This vicious circle makes writing just as imperfect a means of communication as visual imagery, or any other medium for that matter.

I would argue, then, that visual imagery better communi-      8
cates the concrete and sensory world than writing, at least as far as accuracy and completeness are concerned. This argument is further supported by the fact that we all live in an image-saturated world. We have as viewers many hours of experience as consumers of visual imagery. This extensive experience enables us to complete the visual images we see on television, in the movies, or in magazines, with references to the other contexts within which we have seen those images. The result is a more complete communication transaction, although that transaction may not allow for as much abstract interpretation as does writing.

In fact, it may well be television's success in communi-       9
cating visual images that lessens its impact when it comes to communicating ideas. On this point, I agree with Postman. But, with careful treatment, television can, to a degree, overcome its inherent weakness in communicating interpretations. When it does, it uses images to convey themes. Any good television drama will employ repetition of imagery, for example, to get across important ideas. In other words, television imagery does not have to be mass-produced; it can, with hard work and craft, become a medium in which visual images are artfully presented so as to question our conventional ways of seeing things.

When Postman criticizes the fast-paced consumerism of         10
television he is actually focusing on the misuse, not the artful use of television imagery. Written language can be misused as well, and has often been. Why not exploit both writing's ability to communicate abstract ideas and television's ability to convey powerful visual images? As far as

television is concerned, this could be done by limiting the
control of commercial interests on the medium, which encourages producers of shows to exploit the sensational
rather than the thoughtful use of visual imagery.

Perfect communication is not achievable. But we can do
the best we can to communicate both abstract ideas and powerful imagery in all our communications. Neil Postman, in
Amusing Ourselves to Death, seems to stack the cards for
writing and against television in an unfair way. Both television and writing can be misused. Both can be well-used. I
think we should avoid the former and pursue the latter.

# 5
· · · · · · · · · · · · ·
# CHAPTER SUMMARY

An academic essay represents a writer's attempt to provide an organized written response to a complex issue. To produce these written
responses, students generally use the introduction–body–conclusion
structure that has been developed for essay writing.

When college students write essays, reading plays an integral part
in their composing processes. What they read, as well as their personal
experiences before, during, and after reading, provide the evidence that
supports the main point or thesis they develop. Generating a thesis out
of ideas and responses to what is read and personal experiences is a
two-way process. While reading, a writer takes in ideas and builds them
into a main idea for an essay. While writing, a writer takes the main idea
and looks back at what has been read and experienced in order to
support that point. Your essay writing process will follow this same
pattern.

A thesis becomes the hub or center of an essay, around which
every sentence revolves. These connections are not always completely
developed until a writer has written several drafts of an essay. Each
draft represents an attempt to fit thesis and evidence into the essay
framework to achieve writing purposes for particular readers. Your own
efforts to write academic essays will be guided both by this essay
structure and by the needs of particular writing situations. When you
write an academic essay, however, you need to assess how well your
thesis is supported and how well you have presented this support in
ways that readers will find appropriate, effective, and convincing.
Remember, the best reason for having a framework for structuring an
essay is not to restrict your writing efforts, but to support and enhance
them.

# 4

## Using Research Tools to Broaden Your Perspective

What is research? Why add research to the writing process? How is research done? How can you synthesize your research and your own ideas? How can you avoid plagiarism?

### 1
#### WHAT IS RESEARCH?

*Research* describes that part of the writing process in which writers *look back* at their work asking the following question: What additional information would help strengthen the argument I intend to make in this essay? This is the point in the writing process (usually during the early stages—analysis of the writing situation and development of the rhetorical approach, or when the first draft has been written) at which writers need to devise specific research questions. These research questions help to limit and direct research.

The following examples demonstrate how research questions can help focus additional information for an essay:

Example #1

Suppose you were writing an essay on intelligence. You have written an exploratory draft in which you have argued that animals are just as intelligent as human beings, but that their intelligence is different from that of human beings. You have provided several examples of animal intelligence drawn from readings in the intelligence chapter of this book. You have also included some of your own experience with animals and some ideas and experience taken from others in your class to support your argument. You have re-read your draft and decided that a few outside references would make your argument more persuasive. You then look back over your draft and come up with the following questions to limit and direct your research.

Research Questions

- Where can I get information about one or two experiments dealing with the question of animal intelligence? (You could summarize these experiments and tie them into an argument for understanding animal intelligence to be different from human intelligence. The explanation of the Social Science Index and Social Science Abstracts in the "Using Library Research Tools" section of the Research Appendix identify the basic sources you need to answer this research question.)
- Could I interview someone in the local community—an animal breeder, a pet owner, or an experimental psychologist on campus—to provide first-hand reports on animal intelligence? (You could summarize this interview and relate it to your developing argument on animal intelligence. The information on interviewing in the Research Appendix prepares you to answer this question.)

## Example #2

Suppose you were writing an essay on communication. In your first draft, you have argued that animals learn languages much as humans do. You re-read your draft and conclude that your introduction would be more effective if you could include the number of animal language studies conducted during the past few years, simply to demonstrate that this is an important topic in recent scientific literature.

Research Questions

- Where would I find out how many animal language studies were conducted at research universities and institutes over the past three years? (Begin by reading the "Using Library Research Tools" section in the Research Appendix, particularly those parts

describing research abstracts. Choose and duplicate those abstracts pertaining to this question.)
- If these abstracts contain enough evidence that animal language research projects have increased in number, or that their number remains consistently high, could I then summarize the percentage of increase or total number of studies and include those figures in my introduction to make my essay more persuasive and my introduction more interesting?

These examples show why beginning the research process with specific and relevant research questions is very important. Without these questions, you will spend a great deal of time going through information that does not directly apply to your argument. You may have to examine several different research tools before finding the one you need most. With specific, appropriate research questions, however, you will be able to use the Research Appendix to make the most of your research efforts. Developing your research questions with your readers and your writing purposes in mind helps to manage your research better, as will discussing those tentative questions with fellow classmates, your teacher, and a research librarian. Remember that research questions may be revised in light of research findings. Writers must keep an open mind when they explore a subject, even after they have begun writing.

Several potential problems may arise as you move from planning to conducting and using the results of research in your essays. First, you must leave yourself enough time to carry out your research plans and to write your essay in a complete and systematic way. Poor time management can weaken even the most thorough and intelligent student's term paper or essay. Start as soon as possible and plan ahead. Consider how to conduct research most efficiently. If you have decided to conduct library research, for example, ask a reference librarian whether computers are available to help you identify library sources. Before making decisions about which library sources you will use, determine whether certain print sources would be inappropriate or unacceptable because of their sensationalism or superficiality. Check with professors or librarians to determine if the magazines, journals, and books you plan to cite are suitable for use in an academic essay. And, as you locate and choose sources, consider whether you have selected a broad enough group of sources to represent your subject adequately, especially if the subject involves controversy. If you have decided to conduct an interview, make sure that you schedule your interview early enough to allow time for interpreting results and scheduling a second interview, if necessary.

When you are ready to begin writing, plan carefully how to synthesize your thesis, the results of your research, and your own ideas and support. First, decide where you will put the different parts of your research results. Think about how to relate quotations, paraphrases, and summaries of research results to your main points. Include enough of your own analysis and ideas to enable your readers to understand clearly how the sources support your main ideas. You cannot expect readers to make those connections without guidance and explanation. Even in essays that incorporate researched information, *your* voice must be the dominant one, and your essay should not be simply a report of others' ideas. When preparing a final draft, check once again that your readers can follow your train of development from the main point in your introduction to subpoints and evidence in supporting paragraphs. Also, check that you have clearly explained the connections between your research and your own ideas. Your fellow classmates or other readers can provide helpful feedback as you complete the drafting process. (The review of "How Can an Academic Essay Be Built Around a Thesis?" in Chapter 3 is helpful.)

Other problems to consider to ensure that your final draft is effective concern how accurately you present the results of your research. Publication information for written sources must be recorded carefully so that you can document smoothly and accurately. Information from sources that are too highly specialized or too difficult to be understood by your audience may need to be summarized in less technical language or eliminated. (See the Research Appendix for specific guidelines on how to use particular documentation systems.)

To summarize, research provides information that you, as writer, are not able to provide yourself, either from your own experience or from course reading and discussion. Research gives your writing authority; it combines with the power of your own voice to produce persuasive writing. Research also connects what you have to say on a topic to what others—experts and generalists—have said. It broadens your appeal to readers. However, like all other aspects of the writing process, research requires making choices that consider your readers and purposes.

## 2
. . . . . . . . . . . . . .
## WHY ADD RESEARCH TO THE WRITING PROCESS?

The essays that you write in this course will be informed by the professional readings included in this book, by your own experience and ideas, and by the discussions you have with others. In some essays, however, you may need to add to these sources of information. Experienced writers know that information is power. Essays are far more persuasive if they include some outside information that supports the writer's main ideas. In this course, this will not necessarily mean that the major part of your essays will be based on research; it simply means that you will add some researched information to what you take from your reading, personal experience, and discussion. Some facts and statistics concerning the numbers of people who do well on standardized intelligence tests might, for example, add important support to an argument for or against such tests. A statement from an important psychologist who has investigated animal communication adds powerful testimony to an argument that animals use symbols to communicate. Research adds power and persuasiveness to your arguments.

This book includes two sections that will help you add research to your writing process. This chapter defines research and provides an overview of the research process. The Research Appendix at the end of the book contains more detailed information on the different kinds of research and on different documentation styles. Reading this chapter before you write essays will help you understand when and how writers add research to the writing process. It will also help you develop effective research questions that clearly relate to the main ideas in your essays, and it will give you an overview of where to find the information you need to answer those research questions. Once you have decided on the particular research strategy, and once your teacher has indicated which documentation style you must use in a particular essay, you will need to consult the Research Appendix. If, for example, you have decided to use field research—perhaps an interview or two with key sources of local information on a subject—read the section on field research in the Research Appendix. If your teacher requires the American Psychological Association documentation style in a particular essay, refer to that section of the Research Appendix to learn the conventions of that documentation style. The sample student essays in the Research Appendix also provide some examples of how students apply the research-related strategies described in this chapter to their writing.

# 3
· · · · · · · · · · · · · ·
## HOW IS RESEARCH DONE?

The key to writing successful essays that include research is integrating the results of your research carefully and coherently. The idea is not simply to tack on information but to use it to support main points in your argument. Research begins with looking back and developing questions concerning what to look for and where. It continues with the processes of *finding, recording, and documenting* information. It closes with the process of weaving information and documentation into your essay. We have already discussed the first stage. Now we need to take a general view of the second stage: finding, recording, and documenting the results of your research.

## Finding: The First Stage of Research

The *finding* stage of the research process begins with careful consideration of research questions. This consideration involves analyzing research questions to reveal clues that direct your library or field research. To illustrate, reconsider one of the research questions discussed in a previous section of this chapter. This question evolved from a student's intention to add authority to an introduction in an essay about animal intelligence: Where would I find out how many animal language studies were conducted at research universities and institutes over the past three years? Because the student wants to learn "how many" animal language studies were conducted, field research would not answer this research question because it would produce only a partial picture of animal language research, not a total figure. For example, a survey or direct observations provide information about only *some* animal research studies, and an expert may not have the total number of studies readily available during an interview. On the other hand, a journal article could provide the answer to her question, if she could identify the appropriate article. This kind of consideration leads to a focused search for answers. (See details about types of library sources and instructions for conducting your own field research in the Research Appendix.)

## Library Research

How would the student discussed above know how to identify a helpful library source? At this point in the research process, she should first examine the sections in the Research Appendix that describe the social science and psychology indexes and abstracts. How would she know to do this? A close examination of the research question, either on her own or with the help of a teacher, librarian, or classmates, would reveal that animal language research is most likely conducted by social scientists in general and experimental psychologists in particular. Having located the fields to be surveyed, she could use the Research Appendix section on library research to find explanations of the tools needed to survey those fields. A reference librarian could tell her whether the indexes and abstracts needed could be surveyed using computers or print forms.

## Field Research

When should a student use field research to answer a research question? Consider this research question: Do researchers choose an animal for laboratory experiments on the basis of intelligence? The word "researchers" suggests at least one possible type of field research. If a student asking this question had access to a professor who conducted such research, an interview could provide a first-hand, expert answer to this question. But how would this student know that an interview could provide that answer, and what would he need to know in order to arrange for and conduct an interview? First, he would need to read the Research Appendix section that explains the different types of field research—interviews, surveys, and direct observation. Then he would need to look closely at his research question to decide which, if any, type of field research would answer his question and whether he could successfully conduct it. Here, too, his teacher and fellow students could help him decide on a particular type of research.

Some research questions may be answered by more than one type of field research. Once again we can consider a research question discussed earlier in this chapter: Where could I obtain first-hand reports of animal intelligence? Would it be useful to observe the behavior of a pet or an animal that frequents your campus or neighborhood? Would it be useful to interview a psychologist who has conducted animal language research on your campus or to interview three or four students who have worked closely with animals—perhaps horse owners or local animal shelter personnel? Would a survey of pet owners concerning animal communication be useful? Which of these possibilities best support the thesis? The answer to this question will be determined by analysis of readers and writing purposes, as well as consideration of other aspects of the writing situation, such as availability of specialists or time constraints. The section in the Research Appendix that reviews the different possibilities for field research is helpful in narrowing the process to one or two kinds of field research.

## Recording: The Second Stage of Research

The *recording stage* of the research process includes the different strategies used to record the results of research. Chapter 1 explains different strategies for recording ideas and facts as you read—in particular, annotating and summarizing. These strategies help to record ideas, facts, and responses from your library sources as well, particularly when you are using duplicated copies of library sources on which you can write without penalty. If you are working directly from one or several library sources or conducting field research, you may need a more systematic way of recording your research findings. What follows is a description of several different methods of recording the results of both library and field research. These methods provide the kind of running account of extended research that annotation and summary used by themselves do not produce.

## Notecard Format

Notecards create a record of the most important data gathered from library sources. You should put on notecards only condensed information that has immediate relevance to your topic. *Direct quotations* that have a high probability of being cited in your essay should be carefully recorded on notecards so that you can ensure accuracy without having to return to a source a second time. *Summaries* of important data and ideas should be carefully written out on notecards for incorporation into your essay draft. You should also record your own personal responses to the ideas in sources on notecards immediately after you have recorded direct citations and summaries. Put square brackets ([]) around these personal responses to remind yourself that they are your ideas, not ideas contained in the source. The sample notecard in Figure 4–1 and the guidelines for using notecards that follow will help you develop the recording skills so important to the research process.

---

- Write with pen or ink.
- Record complete bibliographic data.
- Write notes on only one side of a notecard.
- Record only what is relevant to your topic and writing purposes.
- Use square brackets to indicate your personal reactions and how you will use source notes in your essay.

---

- *Write with pen or ink.* Pencil smudges can be hard to read after notecards have been lying in stacks for several days.
- *Record complete bibliographic data.* Put an abbreviated form of the source title or topic at the top of each card, on the left or right side. When you have finished recording your note, turn the card over and record *complete* bibliographic data: author, title, volume and edition number (if these apply), place and date of publication, page numbers, and any other relevant publication

~~Medical Ethics~~ "Painful Decisions"                                    p. 53

While mainly dealing with urban patients, the Einstein Hospitals are still committed to bioethical programs.

"It is paradoxically surprising and logical that these overburdened hospitals have made such a commitment to a program of bioethics."

[This might go against the notion, ~~and~~ and show that, hospitals really do care about patients.]

Back of card:

Bouton, Katherine. "Painful Decisions: The Role of the Medical Ethicist." New York Times Magazine. August 5, 1990. pp 24-25, 53, 62-64.

~~MEDICAL ETHICS~~ "Painful Decisions"                                    p. 25

Dr. Ruth Macklin — Bioethicist at Einstein Hospital in New York. She sees her job not as solving Doctors dilemma, but bringing clarity:

"The ability to structure a set of moral principles that gives us a way to discuss the issues."

[Great definition of a bioethicist. This will work well with my other ethics card.]

FIGURE 4–1   Sample Notecards

"Painful Decisions"                                    p 25

▇▇ Some issues of bioethics include the right
to die, withholding or withdrawing treatments
for adults, right to confidentiality and
treatment of a severely handicapped newborn.

"...study how traditional philosophical tenets
might be applied to the emerging issues"

⌐ [good for introduction]

Back of card:

Bouton, Katherine. "Painful Decisions"
New York Times Magazine August 5, 1990
pp. 24 - 25, 53, 62 - 64.

FIGURE 4-1 *Continued*

information. When you have finished taking notes, stack all
cards from the same source together.

- *Write notes on only one side of a notecard.* If notes from a single
source run to more than one side of a notecard, you should
continue the note on the front side of a second card. Then, you
will need to number consecutively the front sides of each card
containing notes from the same source. If you record notes from
more than one page on the front of a single card, put a page
number next to each note. (Record complete bibliographic
information on the back of the first card and an abbreviated
citation on all other cards containing notes from that source so
that you are sure of the source of every note you take.)

- *Record only what is relevant to your topic and writing purposes.* You
must condense and rewrite. Simply copying material verbatim
from a source or writing rambling summaries will not produce
helpful, relevant essay materials.

- *Use square brackets to indicate your personal reactions and how
you will use source notes in your essay.* Conclude a notecard entry
with a brief statement describing your response and why and
where you plan to use the note.

## Journal Formats

**Logbooks.**   Logbooks are commonly used by social and natural scientists, usually to record data derived from direct observation and other kinds of field research. Entries in logbooks are usually chronologically organized; each time researchers observe the subject being studied, they take detailed notes describing what is happening. Most social and natural science researchers attempt to avoid having their own emotions or preconceptions interfere with their observations; they also record their observations in as neutral a language as possible, avoiding obvious metaphor or biased language as far as possible.

Often, social scientists use two-columned logbook formats to help them distinguish between their actual observation notes and their response or interpretation notes. In such two-columned logbooks, direct observations are recorded in neutral language on one side of the page and interpretations and personal responses on the other. This distinction is helpful later when writer-researchers are required by their professional communities to distinguish between objective observations and interpretations.

**Laboratory Notebooks.**   Laboratory notebooks are used by natural and social scientists to record the results of laboratory experiments. These notebooks also follow, in the initial stage, a chronologic format. The writer describes and records the results of an experiment carried out according to established procedures in the field in which the experiment is conducted. In almost every case, these experiments have the following underlying format:

- First, the experimenter provides an *introduction* to the subject being demonstrated—what is already known about the subject and why it is analyzed in a certain way.
- Second, the experimenter describes the procedures or *methods* used to do the experiment. (Usually these procedures are ones conventionally accepted by the scientific field in which the experiment is being done.)
- Third, the experimenter records the *results* of the experiment. During this stage, the experimenter is careful not to let extraneous or irrelevant elements interject into the experimental situation.
- Fourth, the experimenter *discusses* the general implications of the results of the experiment.

Laboratory notebooks are most useful if they follow this introduction–methods–results–discussion format. The most effective way to accomplish this reorganization of laboratory notes is first to take notes during the experiment and then to rework those notes under these four essential categories.

Laboratory notebooks often include diagrams, tables, and charts that were either produced during the experiment or distributed by a laboratory supervisor before the experiment was conducted. These visual aids are always used to support particular parts of the text; they are never simply added on at the end of the discussion section. If a visual diagram is not clearly relevant to a particular part of your notebook description, do not include it.

The purpose of a laboratory notebook is first to define the context of the experiment and then to describe accurately what actually happened during the experiment. Accuracy is of foremost importance because other scientists and students will want to duplicate the experiment. Finally, the significance of the experiment to scientific research in general is addressed in the discussion section. This discussion section usually details what effects this research might have on society in general. You must be careful not to confuse your analysis of the specific results of a particular experiment with the exploration of general significance in the discussion section.

You will not be asked to keep a laboratory notebook in most writing courses. You may, however, want to use the results of a laboratory experiment in another course to support the ideas in an essay. In that case, transferring your notes into the laboratory format described above should make it easier to incorporate the results of your experiment into your essay.

**The Personal Journal.** Keeping a personal journal is a less structured way of recording the results of research. The personal journal encourages the writer to include imaginative and original responses to the subjects observed. Many professional writers keep journals. A science journalist may record plans for interviews with scientists, random observations from scientific publications, personal reactions to current issues in science, and reactions to science television programming; a fiction writer may record overheard conversation, specific pieces of interesting language, descriptions of everyday scenes, ideas for plots and characters drawn from everyday experience, and beginning paragraphs for possible stories; and a technical writer working in a corporation might record notes on developing projects, comments evolving from conversations with engineers, reactions to particular corporate publications, and notes on daily newspaper items that are related to corporate life.

In all these cases, personal journal writers are much less restricted by the object being observed than writers of logbooks or laboratory notebooks. They are free to combine objective and personal response. In fact, writers often assert that one of the significant advantages of keeping a personal journal is this freedom to combine the personal and the objective into original perspectives.

Personal journals also offer writers greater freedom with language. Keepers of logbooks and laboratory notebooks strive to record their subjects in concrete, specific language. They must keep their language as neutral as possible, to ensure that the subjects they describe are not distorted by language. Journal writers, in contrast, play with different language options; they may experiment with several different ways of describing the same object or experience. They often use figurative language (metaphors, plays on words, varying tones and styles) to record their experiences.

How does journal writing fit into the research process? A personal journal can become a useful alternate strategy for recording experiences that are peripheral to a research subject. Suppose you have decided to research and write about the subject of everyday intelligence. You have arrived at this subject by, first, reading about special kinds of intelligence—creative, mathematical, and scientific, for example. Then, you discussed the subject with fellow students and decided that not enough attention in the literature on intelligence had been given to everyday, functional kinds of intelligence. Once you arrived at this subject, you decided to keep a journal in which you record your own responses to people in everyday situations exhibiting this functional or everyday intelligence. You record samples of mealtime conversations, of scenes in classes or at sports events, of family life, of experiences represented on television or in movies. As you record, you keep your eye on your purpose, but also allow yourself free range to comment, play with imaginative responses, and be ironic or humorous.

If you have two or three weeks to research and write your essay, you will probably have at least ten to fifteen pages of journal writing to reread and consider at the end of that period. Go back over your journal entries to get a general impression of your subject—in this case, functional or everyday intelligence—and to select passages that support the thesis of your essay. In most cases, you should combine material in your journal with ideas from your reading and other kinds of research, to provide balanced support for your thesis.

These three recording tools—the logbook, the laboratory notebook, and the personal journal—demonstrate the options writers have in research. The logbook and laboratory notebook are more precise and scientific research tools. They provide writers with formats to record research results precisely and systematically. The personal journal provides a less systematic format to encourage imaginative recording of research processes and ideas. All three tools can be balanced in an integrated approach to writing from research. (The research notebook, described in the Research Appendix, provides yet another tool for managing the research process.) We need at this point to describe a tool for managing the entire research process—the outline.

## Outline Format

Formal outlines are usually not very useful in managing writing and research processes. Research indicates that most professional writers do not have the time or inclination to produce extended, formal outlines. That same research suggests, however, that effective writers do engage in considerable planning, although it is often of a more informal and less complete kind than that found in formal outlines. Planning also occurs throughout the writing process, rather than simply before writing begins.

An informal outline can help you manage the research process. When considering how to add research to the writing process, you may find it helpful to produce an outline before composing a rough draft; however, many writers delay outlining until after they have written a rough draft. At that point, you can reread your draft, consider the responses of your teacher and fellow students, and then complete an informal, topical outline. A topical outline is limited to listing the thesis and main ideas of your essay. This outline will help you re-order the material from your first draft into a more logical and persuasive order. It will provide you with the occasion for deciding what kind of research you wish to add to each item in your outline. The topical outline will also help you decide where in your essay you need to add the results of your research. Your draft and outline will then become the basis for further planning in later drafts and revisions. You may want to use the following template to direct your outlining process.

Outline Template

**Thesis:**
   **Topic Idea Number 1:**
      Supporting Research
   **Topic Idea Number 2:**
      Supporting Research
   **Topic Idea Number 3:**
      Supporting Research
   **Topic Idea Number 4:** (continue until all main ideas are covered)
      Supporting Research
**Synthesizing Conclusion**

# Documenting: The Third Stage of Research

Because much research involves reading source materials (books, journals, periodicals, newspaper and magazine articles, and government documents) and then using ideas from those materials to support ideas in essays, you need to know the academic conventions for acknowledging outside information. In this introductory research chapter, we describe the basics of documenting your research: how to use *direct citation, paraphrase,* and *summary* as you integrate outside sources into your essays. This chapter also covers strategies for integrating source material into essays and for avoiding plagiarism. You will find specific information on particular documentation styles relevant to different academic fields in the Research Appendix. In the Appendix, you will also find information on in-text citation, on when and how to use footnotes and endnotes, and on how to cite special sources, such as newspaper articles, television programs, and congressional records.

## Direct Citation, Paraphrase, Summary

*Direct citations or quotations* include words, phrases, sentences or paragraphs from sources, reproduced *exactly* as they appear in a source. Quotations are most useful when they are short and pointed and directly support in a concise fashion one of your main ideas. Analyze citations immediately after you use them. *You must acknowledge all quotations through parenthetical notes, endnotes, or footnotes.* If you copy information from a source exactly as it appears but omit quotation marks, you are plagiarizing.

Each documentation system has its own conventions for integrating quotations into the body of an essay. For example, writers using MLA (Modern Language Association) rules for documenting must enclose all direct quotations of less than five lines in quotation marks; longer quotations of five or more lines (you will usually not use longer quotations in short essays) are indented ten spaces from the left-hand margin and transcribed *without* quotation marks. Also, direct quotations are usually incorporated into a sentence with introductory phrases such as "According to" or "Recent polls indicate that."

Inexperienced writers sometimes overuse quotations, particularly in short essays. A useful rule of thumb is to avoid using long quotations or an excessive number of quotations (no more than four or five short ones in a three or four page essay). Every quotation that you put into an essay should be followed by your own analysis and interpretation; you are also responsible for showing your readers how the quotation supports your main ideas.

*Paraphrase* occurs when you use your own words to describe source material. Paraphrase reproduces the meaning, length, and general organization of your source, but in your own writing style. Unless a direct quotation would lose its original meaning or effectiveness when restated in your own words, paraphrase usually is a more efficient way to represent your sources. Because paraphrase involves rewriting information in sources, it also demonstrates to readers that you understand the source. Finally, paraphrase lets you rewrite in words that relate directly to the ideas in your essay, which improves the coherence of your writing.

However, you must not change or misrepresent the ideas in a source. Another danger of paraphrase is plagiarism, the unacknowledged rewording of your source's ideas. (A section defining and offering an example of plagiarism is included at the end of this chapter.) *You must acknowledge all paraphrases with parenthetical notes, endnotes, or footnotes.*

Consider this illustration of the use of paraphrase. Here is a passage from "Before They're Born," included in Chapter 8:

> Although the American College of Obstetricians and Gynecologists does not actually recommend ultrasound as a routine test in a normal untroubled pregnancy, more and more doctors seem to be doing routine ultrasounds on more and more women. Some of this probably grows out of the parents' desire to be assured that all is well with the fetus; some grows out of the doctor's desire to guard against lawsuits by doing every test.

A paraphrase of the first sentence of the passage follows:

> Perri Klass, a pediatrician and writer, indicates that many doctors are requiring ultrasound tests in perfectly normal pregnancies, even though this test is not considered necessary by the American College of Obstetricians and Gynecologists for trouble-free pregnancies.

Keep in mind that any paraphrase used in an essay must be documented.

*Summaries* condense particular passages from your sources. The purpose of summarizing is to capture the gist or central idea of a source passage and to relate that idea to the reasoning in your own essay. Summaries save space by highlighting particular ideas and facts. Too much summary, however, can make essays seem too general, lacking the substance provided by specific ideas, language, and facts. Summaries are most effectively used when they are combined with paraphrase and direct citation. Like quotations and paraphrased passages, *summaries must be acknowledged through parenthetical notes, endnotes, or footnotes.*

An example of summary follows; it is based on the same excerpt from "Before They're Born" as the previous example of paraphrase.

> Perri Klass, a pediatrician and writer, explains that more doctors are using ultrasound tests even when pregnancies are perfectly normal, because patients like the reassurance that tests provide, and doctors want to avoid malpractice suits.

Here, too, you need to document the source of the information.

Once you have decided when to use direct citation, paraphrase, and summary, how do you actually represent your sources in your essay? Several methods exist for documenting sources. Here are two examples of documented sentences in which the student accurately acknowledges source information.

### MLA Documentation

> In "The Intelligence Transplant," Marvin Minsky explains that one of the challenges facing artificial intelligence experts is teaching computers to learn on their own (58).

### APA Documentation

> In "The Intelligence Transplant," Minsky (1982) explains that one of the challenges facing artificial intelligence experts is teaching computers to learn on their own (p. 58).

By including the exact title of the source and the author's name along with a summary of what that author said, these writers were able to benefit from the authority of the source while retaining their own meaning and style. They simply needed to include the appropriate publication information in parentheses, which depends on the documentation system being used. Then, they include the complete publication information on a separate page at the end of the essay, which lists all sources used. Information about MLA and APA documentation conventions and about producing this bibliographic page or pages is included in the Research Appendix at the end of this book.

## Why Document?

Writers document sources for two general reasons. The first is that documenting provides readers with a trail to follow as they retrace the writer's research. A researcher in one department at a Midwestern university may be working on the same cell research as a colleague at a California university. As these two scholars read their academic field's journals, they want to learn about each other's work, and they want to know what previous research influenced their respective studies. Other biologists working on similar problems want to know the same things about these scientists' work as they do of each other. Careful documentation of sources ensures that such academic community readers have full access to the sources of each other's work; it also ensures that the larger academic community represented by these scientists will continue to share its efforts. In this way, new discoveries come to influence everyone, rather than a select few. By asking you to follow the same conventions of documentation, your teacher is helping you to understand and experience the work of academic communities.

The second reason for learning to document is simple honesty. Many people in modern society make their livings through intellectual work—writers, scientists, industrial researchers, marketing analysts, computer programmers, to name a few. They work long and hard to develop and design new medicines, to improve ways of reading and doing mathematics, to produce novels and software programs. People who work primarily with their minds want to protect their ideas as much as any inventor would want to protect a physical invention. Documenting the sources of ideas in written material is simply an extension of that desire to protect one's intellectual work from theft. Also, it is impossible to distinguish your own thinking from that of another without acknowledging sources carefully.

## What Will You Be Expected to Document?

As a general rule, you must document all information from sources that your readers would not consider "common knowledge." You are not required to document the statement that Stephen Jay Gould is a natural scientist who often discusses evolution. Gould writes a regular column in a popular science magazine and has published several books dealing with evolution, so this information is known by most educated readers. On the other hand, you are required to document the statement that Gould tells us that the blue-footed booby bird lays its eggs on the ground and does not build nests. It is likely that only a specialist would know this. Educated readers expect to have such information documented.

Although information in encyclopedias and newspapers is often considered common knowledge, we recommend that you take a very conservative approach to documentation. Sometimes even these general sources contain very specialized information. It is probably a good idea to document any specifics in these types of sources. Do not provide documentation for the date of Abraham Lincoln's birth, but do provide documentation for the fact that he spent a certain number of years in his native state of Illinois.

# 4
. . . . . . . . . . . . .
## HOW CAN YOU SYNTHESIZE YOUR RESEARCH AND YOUR OWN IDEAS?

### Learning to Synthesize

So far, we have been discussing the mechanics of research: directing the search for sources; reporting research through direct citation, paraphrase, and summary; and documenting sources through in-text citation. *Synthesizing,* the most challenging part of the research process, is difficult because it requires integrating sources and methods of reporting sources into a coherent essay. In the final stages of revising your essay draft, reconsider these three questions:

- Have you used and represented sources in places in your essay where they clearly support main ideas?
- Have you analyzed and explained the relevance of each citation in terms of your essay thesis?
- Does your final essay draft *flow*? In other words, does it weave citations and your own analysis and explanation together into a coherent package? Will your readers be able to move from one citation and related analysis to the next without rereading?

The first two questions were addressed in the discussion of direct citation, paraphrase, and summary. The third question can be effectively addressed by looking closely at how a student writing about scientific communities has handled the problem of synthesizing sources.

Look at how this student has synthesized a passage from one of her primary sources:

```
Beecher argues that scientists are ''objective'' only be-
cause they agree to follow certain procedures of investiga-
tion and reporting, not because they are any closer than
others who study nature to direct apprehension of physical
reality (Source: ''What Scientists Really Do,'' Science as
Social Reality).
```

Notice how this writer captures two main ideas in the source in one sentence; how a key word in the source is put in quotation marks for

emphasis and authority; and how, in the following sentence, the student
relates the paraphrase of Beecher to her thesis:

```
Scientific objectivity, then, is as much a result of social
convention as it is the single, right way to study nature.
```

Later in her essay, this student further strengthens the coherence of
her text by integrating a brief direct citation into a sentence in which
she summarizes a source's description of one scientific community's
reliance on social conventions:

```
''[E]ven Einstein depended on others in developing his the-
ories,'' says Werner Heisenberg; in ''Tradition in Sci-
ence,'' a lecture delivered several decades ago, Heisenberg
described Einstein and other scientist's dependency on one
another (Source: ''Tradition in Science'').
```

After discussing how this scientific collaboration between Einstein and
others occurred, she relates this example of scientific community
collaboration to her own thesis in the following sentence:

```
Here again we have an example in Einstein's community of
how science constructs knowledge by working through social
processes to theories that explain nature.
```

This student weaves together direct citation, paraphrase, summary and
her own interpretation in ways that are easy for readers to follow. She
does this by keeping her thesis clearly in focus, by assuring that
whatever she cites is clearly related to that focus, and by using
transitional words ("then," "here again") that signal to readers the
kinds of relationships and connections she is establishing between
source ideas and her thesis. Notice how direct citation, paraphrase,
summary, and interpretation are merged in this paragraph, which leads
to her conclusion:

```
Many of us believe that scientists work alone in laborato-
ries, or as aloof observers and interviewers in the field.
Science seems such an individual endeavor. Yet many sociol-
ogists who study scientific communities, and many scien-
tists themselves, feel differently. They argue that ''even
when working alone'' most scientists are heavily influenced
by what other scientists have thought and done, and by the
methods they use to do it (Beecher 132). Heisenberg ex-
plains how even world-renowned physicists such as Einstein
and Max Planck often relied upon each other for discoveries
```

and insights (219-20). What does this suggest about our
common notions of individuality and social influence?

This paragraph begins by stating the problem, proceeds by summarizing expert research on the topic, and concludes by relating the problem
and the summary to a question that introduces the writer's thesis. That
thesis then appears as the first sentence in the next paragraph, which is
also the final paragraph of the essay. This kind of synthesis by the
writer makes reading more efficient and worthwhile (for a checklist of
questions for reviewing documentation, see Section 10 in the Research
Appendix).

## 5
. . . . . . . . . . . . . .
## HOW CAN YOU AVOID PLAGIARISM?

Plagiarism is using others' words or ideas without acknowledging
them, whether intentionally or accidentally. In fact, most student
plagiarism occurs because of inefficient research rather than intentional
dishonesty. It results from the writer's failure to integrate source
information into his or her own thinking. In turn, this general failure
evolves from inefficient note taking, careless recording of citation
information, and faulty incorporation of sources into the final draft of an
essay.

The following passage comes from an article by an academic writer
who addresses the topic of popular science writing (Greg Myers, "The
Social Construction of Two Biologists' Proposals"). Read the passage
closely, then compare it to the student plagiarism in the passage that
follows. The plagiarized material is underlined in the student sample.

Original

The researchers I studied are, in some respects, representative
of biologists at large universities: they both supervise laboratories and have published many articles, and they both have
received grants in the past and reviewed grant applications
themselves. But I chose to work with them partly because they
were atypical: they were presenting work based on new models
that put them between two well-established subspecialties of
research. Judging by the response to articles presenting these
models, their work is controversial. The fact that they assumed
resistance to their proposals may have made them more
self-conscious about their writing processes, and certainly
made the rhetorical features of their proposals more apparent

to a non-specialist. In the proposals I am studying, they faced quite different rhetorical problems: one was taking his well-known and respected research in a new theoretical direction; the other was entering a new field in which he was unknown.

## Plagiarized Version

When <u>entering a new field</u> or <u>taking well-known and respected research in a new theoretical direction,</u> many scientists seem to write differently. They do this because they are trying to meet the demands put on them by their new co-workers in these new fields or theoretical areas. Also, because these situations create <u>different rhetorical problems,</u> scientists <u>assume resistance to their proposals</u> and become <u>more self-conscious about their writing processes.</u> Their past experiences as science writers enable them to meet the demands of these new rhetorical situations.

This student has actually done a good job of summarizing several of his source's points. He fails, however, to acknowledge the source of those points, either within the sentences or parenthetically. Furthermore, he does a good job of relating what his source has to say to his own thesis (that experienced scientists know how to write in a way that satisfies fellow scientists, even when they propose new theories or use new models). But he also fails to use quotation marks to indicate that he has used some of his source's exact wording to support that thesis. These failures to acknowledge and document his source make what otherwise would be a well-synthesized paragraph into an example of plagiarism.

## Guidelines for Avoiding Plagiarism

Here are several guidelines for avoiding plagiarism:

*1. Begin the research process with a plan that will ensure that you can distinguish between your own and others' thinking.* This chapter has provided several specific strategies for making that distinction. You will need to adapt those strategies to your own ends.

*2. Keep to a reasonable schedule when you plan to integrate research into an essay.* Often, plagiarism will occur when you are rushing to meet a deadline. It is too easy at such times to simply use your source's words or to leave a paraphrase unacknowledged.

*3. Choose and develop topics that you sincerely want to tell others about.* Avoid simply fulfilling an assignment. When you think that you have something to add to a topic, you are less apt to rely solely on others' ideas; you also want to distinguish between your source ideas and your own.

*4. Summarize and paraphrase your sources; do not overuse direct citation.*  When you do summarize and paraphrase, push yourself to use your own words, not the words of your sources. This guideline applies to note taking and to actual writing.

*5. Before you write a final draft, review your notes and be sure that you know exactly where they will go in your essay.*  Also, be sure that you have clear in your mind where your source materials end and your interpretations begin.

*6. Document carefully and correctly.*  When you incorporate information from sources into your essay, document them immediately. If you are unfamiliar with the requirements of the particular documentation system you are using, refer to the appropriate section in the Research Appendix. Remember that you must document *all* of your paraphrased, summarized, and quoted statements.

## 6
## • • • • • • • • • • • •
## CHAPTER SUMMARY

Research provides writers with information they are not able to provide themselves. This researched information allows writers to connect their ideas to what others have said and makes writing more persuasive. The research process begins when writers develop research questions that must be answered to achieve their writing purposes. These questions are generated early in the writing process, usually when writers are developing a thesis and a plan for supporting that thesis to convince their particular readers. Additional research questions may develop at any time during the writing process. Once questions have been generated, writers make rhetorical choices about the kinds of sources that provide answers to those questions. Library sources provide researchers with a written record of what other writers have said about a topic, while field research—interviews, surveys, and direct observation—and controlled laboratory research create opportunities for researchers to produce new information about a topic.

When writers conduct research, they carefully record the results of their efforts. Taking care to reproduce the results of research appropriately and accurately, they use a variety of record-keeping formats: notecards, laboratory notebooks, logbooks, and personal notebooks. The recording system chosen by a particular writer depends usually on the kind of research conducted. Whatever recording system is used, however, all researchers always indicate the sources for their research question answers.

Because readers expect to be able to reproduce the writer's research process, and because the ideas contained in sources are considered the property of the original writer, researchers always acknowledge or document their research sources, although particular documentation styles or systems vary from one academic field to another. Careful documentation prevents plagiarism. Writers incorporate information gathered from research into their texts by using quotation, paraphrase, and summary. Each of these integrating strategies provides writers with a different and efficient way to use what someone else has said or done.

The final task of the researcher is to carefully synthesize the information gathered from source materials and his own ideas. This is accomplished by balancing paraphrase, summary, and quotation, and by providing statements that clearly indicate connections between the incorporated source materials and the thesis being developed.

# SECTION TWO

# 5

# Perspectives on Intelligence

What is intelligence? How is it studied?
Are there different kinds?

## 1
## DEVELOPING A RHETORICAL APPROACH

Scientists and humanists in the academic and professional world have been studying and discussing intelligence for many years. Some experts argue that many different types of intelligence exist and that no one kind of intelligence is by definition better than any other. Other experts argue that a universal or standard type of intelligence exists, one that we are only beginning to understand. Still others debate about how to measure and reinforce intelligence. Recently, journalists and popular science writers have begun to write about intelligence, often picking up the same issues that have been the focus of expert discussions. The readings in this chapter provide perspectives from expert and popular writers. They do not provide a comprehensive perspective on intelligence, but they do provide a varied and well-documented group of sources out of which to fashion a *rhetorical community,* a group of people who share knowledge and ways of writing and talking about a topic.

No matter what definitions of intelligence particular writers reflect, they all are interested in how these different perspectives actually affect our daily lives. If multiple kinds of intelligence exist, should we look for different kinds of intelligence in the workplace or at school? If creative intelligence can be learned, how can we encourage it at school or in the workplace? If animals do indeed display intelligence, is that intelligence different from or similar to human intelligence? If it *is* different, how can we learn from it?

These are the types of questions suggested by this chapter. You will be constructing from your interaction with fellow students a clearer sense of the *purpose* (Why do I want to write this essay) and *audience* (For whom do I want to write this essay?) for the essay on intelligence that you will write at the end of this chapter.

## 2
## GENERATING IDEAS ABOUT INTELLIGENCE BEFORE READING

Learning to write includes learning to carry out some preliminary thinking activities. Very few experienced writers start to think about a subject only at the point of picking up a pen or sitting down at the computer. The same is true of reading. Effective readers start thinking about a topic *before* they begin reading. The following activities will help you develop ideas that will enrich your responses to what you read and to your own ideas as they develop on paper. These activities are presented in the sequence described above: first, probe your personal experiences, then consider the reactions of other students, and, finally, respond in a preliminary way to the topic covered by the readings in this chapter.

### Probing Personal Experience

Write short, informal answers to the following questions. If you are keeping a course journal, write your answers there. Whatever you do, be sure to put your written responses in a form that can be used in class.

1. How would you describe the ideal kind of intelligence? What are its characteristics? What might this ideal intelligence enable someone to do?
2. Do you think there are different kinds of intelligence or only one kind? If there are different kinds, what are they? If you think there is only one kind, how would you describe or measure it?
3. Describe an intelligent person you know who is either a failure and ineffective, or a success and effective. Why are

some intelligent people unsuccessful and ineffective and others the reverse?

4. Can intelligence be measured? Why, or why not? If your answer is positive, *how* can intelligence be measured? Do schools measure intelligence effectively or accurately?

5. What types of thinking might a computer do more effectively than human beings? What types of thinking might a computer do less effectively? What reasons lie behind these distinctions? Can you describe examples?

6. Describe an example of what you would call "intelligent" animal behavior. What was the animal doing and what made that behavior intelligent?

7. Give two or three examples of popular movies in which a character with a scientific or technical mind, or a computer with non-human intelligence, played a major part in the story. What response did you have to these characters? What were the reasons behind your responses? Did you feel that the movie encouraged this response? If so, how?

8. Describe a friend or acquaintance whom you feel was or is "creative" but not extraordinarily intelligent. How is it that you respond to this person in this way? What in his or her behavior causes this complex response?

9. Describe and respond to an experience that you have had with some kind of intelligence test. Did you think that your true intelligence had been tested? Why, or why not?

10. Is group or social intelligence different from individual intelligence? If so, how? If not, why not? What do people mean when they say things such as "She doesn't know how to work with people" or "He's a people person?"

## Freewriting to Capture Personal Experience

Freewriting is an effective way to transfer your preliminary thinking on a topic to paper, where it can become the subject of response and revision. Freewriting includes non-stop writing for a set period (usually 10 or 20 minutes) on either any topic that comes to mind or on a pre-set topic. Because this book is organized around pre-set topics, we encourage freewriting on those topics. It is important to remember that freewriting is unstructured—when freewriting, do not worry about correctness or polish; it is acceptable to digress even if you started out with a focus on one topic.

Begin with the first idea or experience that comes to mind. Keep writing without stopping to think. If you get stuck and cannot think of anything else to say, write the topic word, or a synonym for it, as many times as you need to get the process going again. The key point is to write quickly so that mental blocks and distractions do not interfere with what may be a rich idea.

After a freewriting session, read over what you have written, perhaps aloud. Mark with an X those places in your text where a new or particularly good idea occurs. Also mark those places where you think you can add to a potentially good idea, perhaps by providing an example or more detail, or by making a revealing comparison. This technique usually makes a writer more comfortable about writing in general; it also draws attention to topics to which a writer might not have given much thought.

The following is a list of topics related to intelligence that you can write about in ten-minute sessions. (If you are keeping a journal, do your freewriting there.)

Animal Intelligence
Genius
Smart and Intelligent People: Is There a Difference?
IQ Testing
Artificial (Computer) Intelligence
An Intelligent Person Whom I Have Known
Gender and Intelligence

How can you most effectively capitalize on your freewriting experience? Many writers follow their freewritings with this sequence: **Re**read, **F**ocus, **R**ewrite (**RFR**). To begin this sequence, freewrite for ten minutes on a focused topic. Then reread and discuss your text with another student or friend. Then refocus by writing a one-sentence response to your first freewriting, and use that focus to start your second freewriting.

Remember, freewriting gets you going and prepares you to respond to a topic with a richer and deeper array of ideas. By following the **RFR** process, you will enter classroom reading, writing, and discussion situations with much more to say than you ever thought possible.

# 3
· · · · · · · · · · · · ·
## DEVELOPING RHETORICAL CONTEXT
## THROUGH GROUP ACTIVITIES

Collaboration, or working with others in groups on course-related topics, is another good way to create ideas on a topic. But collaboration also helps in a second way. It helps create a sense of classroom community that, later, will help you decide on an audience and purpose for your formal essay.

Talking with others about a common topic in which you are mutually interested is one of the most effective ways of learning how to approach others in your writing. These conversations will help you understand how others feel and think about the topic and your responses to it. Such useful collaborations, however, do not happen without planning.

Collaborative groups vary in size, depending on a teacher's goals for a particular group session. Usually groups of three or four persons work best, because each person gets the opportunity to contribute and to listen and respond in a thirty- to forty-minute group session. Groups of two usually work best for activities such as editing the final draft of an essay, or developing a particular perspective on a larger topic. Good participation and a successful final product should be the goals that affect decisions about how to structure and direct a group. A list of several specific rules or conventions to live by when working in groups follows:

Conventions Guiding Group Work

1. Groups need to work in long enough periods of time to allow each member time to contribute.

2. Every group member should assume a responsibility for every group discussion session. Usually, these jobs should be varied, with each member taking on a different one each time the group meets. Responsibilities should include chairs or group discussion mediators or leaders, group presenters, group respondents, group recorders (who report to the whole class or to the teacher), and, when necessary, group researchers (who help the group by looking up useful information for subsequent group meetings).

3. Groups are usually most efficient when they have clearly defined tasks. Often, these tasks need to be broken down into sequential steps that groups can use to organize their activities. Sometimes the teacher provides these tasks and lists; at other times they are constructed by the groups themselves.

4. Group work must be purposeful. All group tasks should be clearly related to the topic of the chapter under discussion; most group sessions should produce materials that individual students can use as they write essays on the topic under consideration.

## A Group Activity

The following group activities will help your class develop both a set of ideas and a sense of community based on the topic of intelligence.

Brainstorming

- Brainstorm with your group about one of the following topics: animal intelligence, genius, smart and intelligent people, intelligence tests, computers and intelligence, the smartest person that you have ever known. Brainstorming, like freewriting, is a mental limbering-up exercise. It will help you and others jog your memory and generate new ideas. You begin to brainstorm by listing, as quickly as possible, words and phrases that are the first to come to mind in a group session. The best way to operate such a session is to have one person record notes as group members call out their associative responses. First, these responses should focus on the topic itself; as the session continues, they should be cumulative, with one response coming in response to the previous one. Every few minutes the group should pause in order to review what has been produced. The process itself should continue until every group member has contributed at least one idea. The process should close with a summary session in which main ideas and supporting examples and reasons are listed. The summary session is the point at which the group's thinking should be related to the process of developing theses for the essay to be written at the end of this chapter.

    It is useful to go a step further in the brainstorming process by having each brainstorming group review its list to identify related words and phrases—to find patterns among the groups' responses. These patterns can usually be turned into material for essay theses.
- You and your group can also organize group responses under key word pairs, such as *intelligent* and *unintelligent, shrewd* and *intelligent, methodical* and *sharp,* and others. Once a word-pair list has been filled out, members of the group can work on producing sentences that explain the pattern behind the key word list. Key word lists and their explanatory sentences can then be discussed as potential essay topics.

# 4
· · · · · · · · · · · · ·
## USING READINGS TO DEVELOP
## A RHETORICAL COMMUNITY

In a writing course, reading is treated as a central part of the composing process. Sharing reading with other members of your class creates common ground from which to write essays. This common ground also enables you to find out what others think about a common topic. Understood this way, sharing reading will help you develop and respond to a rhetorical community by providing the resources you will need to define purposes and audiences for your essays.

## The Readings in This Chapter

The readings on intelligence introduce subjects such as human compared to animal intelligence, universal or multiple intelligences, creativity and intelligence, the social implications of intelligence, and the relationship between school and practical intelligence. They will elicit very different reactions from you and your peers. These reactions may sometimes reinforce your own responses, sometimes contradict them, sometimes cause you to change your initial reactions, and at other times may make you firmer than ever in supporting your own views. Whatever someone's particular views on the topic, entering this kind of public discussion on intelligence, or any significant topic, for that matter, creates an opportunity for an individual to participate in building public knowledge and understanding.

William Golding, an internationally praised novelist and writer of essays (you may have read his *Lord of the Flies* in high school), provides a personal description of different kinds of human thinking. As he describes these types of thinking, mostly through autobiographical examples, Golding also evaluates: he places balanced and open intelligence at the top of his human-intelligence scale.

How intelligent are animals? Stephen Jay Gould, an evolutionary biologist, raises this question in all its complexity when he focuses on one of the so-called "dumbest" of animals (in this case, the booby bird). He shows that this bird, in its nesting and feeding habits, exhibits intelligence of a very definite kind, but an intelligence that is very different from that of humans and higher-order animals. Gould's essay concludes by raising a second question, implied by his description and analysis of the booby bird—what *is* intelligence?

The third piece in this chapter, journalist Signe Hammer's journalistic treatment of recent psychological research on intelligence, picks up where Gould leaves off. Hammer directly addresses the question of how we define intelligence. She compares the work of Howard Gardner and Robert Sternberg on the question of multiple or universal definitions of intelligence. Hammer's article is complemented by James Ellison's interview of Howard Gardner, whose concept of "frames" of intelligence is one of the most important ideas supporting multiple definitions of intelligence. Hammer and Ellison do their journalistic best to address the question of whether one kind of intelligence exists that is adaptable to many different contexts, or many different intelligences (artistic, mathematical, scientific, verbal, for example) that different people exhibit in different situations.

Susan Gilbert, also a science journalist, shows readers how recent work on creative thinking and problem solving has been brought into the workplace through workshops and seminars conducted by psychologists. Her article, which raises questions about the kinds of intelligence needed to solve on-the-job problems, is complemented by Edward Sokolowski's more academic essay, which compares artificial and natural intelligences and describes a possible future for artificial intelligence. Both essays raise questions regarding the usefulness of different kinds of artificial and natural intelligence.

Finally, Sheila Tobias' article is directed to professors, students, and the general public and concerns the anxiety many students feel when they attempt to learn mathematics. Tobias describes what she considers the source of the difficulties American students have with mathematics and suggests some solutions. As you read her essay, you will again face the questions raised in this chapter about intelligence: Are some people without the aptitude for high-level mathematics, or do they simply need to be taught mathematics (and science and philosophy, for that matter) in different ways? Is the problem of dealing with the intelligence question more social and educational in origin than it is mental or physiological?

These are tough questions. They can be answered only provisionally, and only if you listen to others, examine your own thinking in an open way, and read critically from the experts. If you engage in these activities, you will become part of a serious academic community. You will learn to probe that community for useful ideas and strategies for writing. You will evolve a sense of purpose and audience that can make writing your essay on intelligence a much more interesting job than it would otherwise be.

# 5
· · · · · · · · · · · · ·
## READINGS ON INTELLIGENCE

# WILLIAM GOLDING ON THINKING

### Pre-Reading Questions

1.  Do you think that most people take thinking seriously? Or are most of us willing to substitute our own feelings and prejudices for "thought"? Think of some examples of "good" and "bad" thinking. What was wrong with the "bad" thinking, and what was right about the "good" thinking?

2.  Teachers are supposed to be paradigms of good thinking. Yet, in the essay that follows, William Golding provides several examples of

teachers in his schooling who were third-rate thinkers. How do the
teachers in your own background stack up against your definition of
intelligence, or of good thinking?

3. Golding thinks that intelligent people have more difficult lives than
those who are more average. Do you agree or disagree? Why?

# THINKING AS A HOBBY
## William Golding

While I was still a boy, I came to the conclusion that there were three  1
grades of thinking; and since I was later to claim thinking as my hobby,
I came to an even stranger conclusion—namely, that I myself could not
think at all.

I must have been an unsatisfactory child for grownups to deal with.  2
I remember how incomprehensible they appeared to me at first, but not,
of course, how I appeared to them. It was the headmaster of my
grammar school who first brought the subject of thinking before
me—though neither in the way, nor with the result he intended. He had
some statuettes in his study. They stood on a high cupboard behind his
desk. One was a lady wearing nothing but a bath towel. She seemed
frozen in an eternal panic lest the bath towel slip down any farther; and
since she had no arms, she was in an unfortunate position to pull the
towel up again. Next to her, crouched the statuette of a leopard, ready to
spring down at the top drawer of a filing cabinet labeled A–AH. My
innocence interpreted this as the victim's last, despairing cry. Beyond the
leopard was a naked, muscular gentleman, who sat, looking down, with
his chin on his fist and his elbow on his knee. He seemed utterly
miserable.

Some time later, I learned about these statuettes. The headmaster  3
had placed them where they would face delinquent children, because
they symbolized to him the whole of life. The naked lady was the Venus
of Milo. She was Love. She was not worried about the towel. She was
just busy being beautiful. The leopard was Nature, and he was being
natural. The naked, muscular gentleman was not miserable. He was
Rodin's Thinker, an image of pure thought. It is easy to buy small plaster
models of what you think life is like.

I had better explain that I was a frequent visitor to the headmaster's  4
study, because of the latest thing I had done or left undone. As we now
say, I was not integrated. I was, if anything, disintegrated; and I was
puzzled. Grownups never made sense. Whenever I found myself in a
penal position before the headmaster's desk, with the statuettes glimmering whitely above him, I would sink my head, clasp my hands behind my
back and writhe one shoe over the other.

The headmaster would look opaquely at me through flashing  5
spectacles.

"What are we going to do with you?"

Well, what *were* they going to do with me? I would writhe my shoe  6
some more and stare down at the worn rug.

"Look up, boy! Can't you look up?"                                  7

Then I would look up at the cupboard, where the naked lady was  8
frozen in her panic and the muscular gentleman contemplated the
hindquarters of the leopard in endless gloom. I had nothing to say to the
headmaster. His spectacles caught the light so that you could see nothing
human behind them. There was no possibility of communication.

"Don't you ever think at all?"                                   9

No, I didn't think, wasn't thinking, couldn't think—I was simply
waiting in anguish for the interview to stop.

"Then you'd better learn—hadn't you?"                       10

On one occasion the headmaster leaped to his feet, reached up and
plonked Rodin's masterpiece on the desk before me.

"That's what a man looks like when he's really thinking."         11

I surveyed the gentleman without interest or comprehension.

"Go back to your class."

Clearly there was something missing in me. Nature had endowed the  12
rest of the human race with a sixth sense and left me out. This must be
so, I mused, on my way back to the class, since whether I had broken a
window, or failed to remember Boyle's Law, or been late for school, my
teachers produced me one, adult answer: "Why can't you think?"

As I saw the case, I had broken the window because I had tried to hit  13
Jack Arney with a cricket ball and missed him; I could not remember
Boyle's Law because I had never bothered to learn it; and I was late for
school because I preferred looking over the bridge into the river. In fact,
I was wicked. Were my teachers, perhaps, so good that they could not
understand the depths of my depravity? Were they clear, untormented
people who could direct their every action by this mysterious business of
thinking? The whole thing was incomprehensible. In my earlier years, I
found even the statuette of the Thinker confusing. I did not believe any
of my teachers were naked, ever. Like someone born deaf, but bitterly
determined to find out about sound, I watched my teachers to find out
about thought.

There was Mr. Houghton. He was always telling me to think. With a  14
modest satisfaction, he would tell me that he had thought a bit himself.
Then why did he spend so much time drinking? Or was there more sense
in drinking than there appeared to be? But if not, and if drinking were in
fact ruinous to health—and Mr. Houghton was ruined, there was no
doubt about that—why was he always talking about the clean life and the
virtues of fresh air? He would spread his arms wide with the action of a
man who habitually spent his time striding along mountain ridges.

"Open air does me good, boys—I know it!"                                15

Sometimes, exalted by his own oratory, he would leap from his desk and hustle us outside into a hideous wind.

"Now boys! Deep breaths! Feel it right down inside you—huge  16 draughts of God's good air!"

He would stand before us, rejoicing in his perfect health, an open-air  17 man. He would put his hands on his waist and take a tremendous breath. You could hear the wind, trapped in the cavern of his chest and struggling with all the unnatural impediments. His body would reel with shock and his ruined face go white at the unaccustomed visitation. He would stagger back to his desk and collapse there, useless for the rest of the morning.

Mr. Houghton was given to high-minded monologues about the  18 good life, sexless and full of duty. Yet in the middle of one of these monologues, if a girl passed the window, tapping along on her neat little feet, he would interrupt his discourse, his neck would turn of itself and he would watch her out of sight. In this instance, he seemed to me ruled not by thought but by an invisible and irresistible spring in his nape.

His neck was an object of great interest to me. Normally it bulged a  19 bit over his collar. But Mr. Houghton had fought in the First World War alongside both Americans and French, and had come—by who knows what illogic?—to a settled detestation of both countries. If either country happened to be prominent in current affairs, no argument could make Mr. Houghton think well of it. He would bang the desk, his neck would bulge still further and go red. "You can say what you like," he would cry, "but I've thought about this—and I know what I think!"

Mr. Houghton thought with his neck.                                    20

There was Miss Parsons. She assured us that her dearest wish was our welfare, but I knew even then, with the mysterious clairvoyance of childhood, that what she wanted most was the husband she never got. There was Mr. Hands—and so on.

I have dealt at length with my teachers because this was my  21 introduction to the nature of what is commonly called thought. Through them I discovered that thought is often full of unconscious prejudice, ignorance and hypocrisy. It will lecture on disinterested purity while its neck is being remorselessly twisted toward a skirt. Technically, it is about as proficient as most businessmen's golf, as honest as most politicians' intentions, or—to come near my own preoccupation—as coherent as most books that get written. It is what I came to call grade-three thinking, though more properly, it is feeling, rather than thought.

True, often there is a kind of innocence in prejudices, but in those  22 days I viewed grade-three thinking with an intolerant contempt and an incautious mockery. I delighted to confront a pious lady who hated the Germans with the proposition that we should love our enemies. She taught me a great truth in dealing with grade-three thinkers; because of her, I no longer dismiss lightly a mental process which for nine-tenths of the population is the nearest they will ever get to thought. They have immense solidarity. We had better respect them, for we are outnumbered and surrounded. A crowd of grade-three thinkers, all shouting the same thing, all warming their hands at the fire of their own prejudices, will not thank you for pointing out the contradictions in their beliefs. Man is a gregarious animal, and enjoys agreement as cows will graze all the same way on the side of a hill.

Grade-two thinking is the detection of contradictions. I reached 23 grade two when I trapped the poor, pious lady. Grade-two thinkers do not stampede easily, though often they fall into the other fault and lag behind. Grade-two thinking is a withdrawal, with eyes and ears open. It became my hobby and brought satisfaction and loneliness in either hand. For grade-two thinking destroys without having the power to create. It set me watching the crowds cheering His Majesty the King and asking myself what all the fuss was about, without giving me anything positive to put in the place of that heady patriotism. But there were compensa-tions. To hear people justify their habit of hunting foxes and tearing them to pieces by claiming that the foxes liked it. To hear our Prime Minister talk about the great benefit we conferred on India by jailing people like Pandit Nehru and Gandhi. To hear American politicians talk about peace in one sentence and refuse to join the League of Nations in the next. Yes, there were moments of delight.

But I was growing toward adolescence and had to admit that Mr. 24 Houghton was not the only one with an irresistible spring in his neck. I, too, felt the compulsive hand of nature and began to find that pointing out contradiction could be costly as well as fun. There was Ruth, for example, a serious and attractive girl. I was an atheist at the time. Grade-two thinking is a menace to religion and knocks down sects like skittles. I put myself in a position to be converted by her with an hypocrisy worthy of grade three. She was a Methodist—or at least, her parents were, and Ruth had to follow suit. But, alas, instead of relying on the Holy Spirit to convert me, Ruth was foolish enough to open her pretty mouth in argument. She claimed that the Bible (King James Version) was literally inspired. I countered by saying that the Catholics believed in the literal inspiration of Saint Jerome's *Vulgate,* and the two books were different. Argument flagged.

At last she remarked that there were an awful lot of Methodists, and 25 they couldn't be wrong, could they—not all those millions? That was too easy, said I restively (for the nearer you were to Ruth, the nicer she was to be near to) since there were more Roman Catholics than Methodists anyway; and they couldn't be wrong, could they—not all those hundreds of millions? An awful flicker of doubt appeared in her eyes. I slid my arm round her waist and murmured breathlessly that if we were counting heads, the Buddhists were the boys for my money. But Ruth had *really* wanted to do me good, because I was so nice. She fled. The combination of my arm and those countless Buddhists was too much for her.

That night her father visited my father and left, red-cheeked and indignant. I was given the third degree to find out what had happened. It was lucky we were both of us only fourteen. I lost Ruth and gained an undeserved reputation as a potential libertine. 26

So grade-two thinking could be dangerous. It was in this knowledge, at the age of fifteen, that I remember making a comment from the heights of grade two, on the limitations of grade three. One evening I found myself alone in the schoolhall, preparing it for a party. The door of the headmaster's study was open. I went in. The headmaster had ceased to thump Rodin's Thinker down on the desk as an example to the young. Perhaps he had not found any more candidates, but the statuettes were still there, glimmering and gathering dust on top of the cupboard. I stood on a chair and rearranged them. I stood Venus in her bath towel on the filing cabinet, so that now the top drawer caught its breath in a gasp of sexy excitement. "A-ah!" The portentous Thinker I placed on the edge of the cupboard so that he looked down at the bath towel and waited for it to slip. 27

Grade-two thinking, though it filled life with fun and excitement, did not make for content. To find out the deficiencies of our elders bolsters the young ego but does not make for personal security. I found that grade two was not only the power to point out contradictions. It took the swimmer some distance from the shore and left him there, out of his depth. I decided that Pontius Pilate was a typical grade-two thinker. "What is truth?" he said, a very common grade-two thought, but one that is used always as the end of an argument instead of the beginning. There is a still higher grade of thought which says, "What is truth?" and sets out to find it. 28

But these grade-one thinkers were few and far between. They did not visit my grammar school in the flesh though they were there in books. I aspired to them, partly because I was ambitious and partly because I now saw my hobby as an unsatisfactory thing if it went no further. If you set out to climb a mountain, however high you climb, you have failed if you cannot reach the top. 29

I *did* meet an undeniably grade-one thinker in my first year at Oxford. I was looking over a small bridge in Magdalen Deer Park, and a tiny mustached and hatted figure came and stood by my side. He was a German who had just fled from the Nazis to Oxford as a temporary refuge. His name was Einstein. 30

But Professor Einstein knew no English at that time and I knew only two words of German. I beamed at him, trying wordlessly to convey by my bearing all the affection and respect that the English felt for him. It is possible—and I have to make the admission—that I felt here were two grade-one thinkers standing side by side; yet I doubt if my face conveyed 31 more than a formless awe. I would have given my Greek and Latin and French and a good slice of my English for enough German to communicate. But we were divided; he was as inscrutable as my headmaster. For perhaps five minutes we stood together on the bridge, undeniable grade-one thinker and breathless aspirant. With true greatness, Professor Einstein realized that any contact was better than none. He pointed to a trout wavering in midstream.

He spoke: *"Fisch."* 32

My brain reeled. Here I was, mingling with the great, and yet helpless as the veriest grade-three thinker. Desperately I sought for some sign by which I might convey that I, too, revered pure reason. I nodded vehemently. In a brilliant flash I used up half of my German vocabulary. *"Fisch. Ja. Ja."*

For perhaps another five minutes we stood side by side. Then 33 Professor Einstein, his whole figure still conveying good will and amiability, drifted away out of sight.

I, too, would be a grade-one thinker. I was irreverent at the best of 34 times. Political and religious systems, social customs, loyalties and traditions, they all came tumbling down like so many rotten apples off a tree. This was a fine hobby and a sensible substitute for cricket, since you could play it all the year round. I came up in the end with what must always remain the justification for grade-one thinking, its sign, seal and charter. I devised a coherent system for living. It was a moral system, which was wholly logical. Of course, as I readily admitted, conversion of the world to my way of thinking might be difficult, since my system did away with a number of trifles, such as big business, centralized government, armies, marriage. . . .

It was Ruth all over again. I had some very good friends who stood 35 by me, and still do. But my acquaintances vanished, taking the girls with them. Young women seemed oddly contented with the world as it was. They valued the meaningless ceremony with a ring. Young men, while willing to concede the chaining sordidness of marriage, were hesitant about abandoning the organizations which they hoped would give them a career. A young man on the first rung of the Royal Navy, while perfectly agreeable to doing away with big business and marriage, got as red-necked as Mr. Houghton when I proposed a world without any battleships in it.

Had the game gone too far? Was it a game any longer? In those 36 prewar days, I stood to lose a great deal, for the sake of a hobby.

Now you are expecting me to describe how I saw the folly of my 37 ways and came back to the warm nest, where prejudices are so often called loyalties, where pointless actions are hallowed into custom by repetition, where we are content to say we think when all we do is feel.

But you would be wrong. I dropped my hobby and turned 38 professional.

If I were to go back to the headmaster's study and find the dusty 39
statuettes still there, I would arrange them differently. I would dust
Venus and put her aside, for I have come to love her and know her for
the fair thing she is. But I would put the Thinker, sunk in his desperate
thought, where there were shadows before him—and at his back, I
would put the leopard, crouched and ready to spring.

## Post-Reading Questions

1.  Describe the kind of evidence that Golding uses in this essay. Would
    it appeal to a reader looking for scientific evidence? Why, or why not?
    To what kind of readers would Golding's evidence appeal?
2.  Summarize the three kinds of thinking defined by Golding. Would
    you categorize different kinds of thinking in the same way that
    Golding does? What categories would you add to his list of three?
    Do you disagree with any of his categories? Why, or why not?
3.  Irony exists when authors suggest something other than what they
    are actually saying. Golding uses irony when he describes the bust of
    Rodin's "The Thinker" in his headmaster's office. In what ways is
    this description ironic? What does it tell us about the headmaster,
    and about Golding's attitude toward the headmaster? Can you find
    other examples of irony in this essay? Would you agree that Gold-
    ing's overall attitude is ironic?
4.  *Tone* is a term used to describe the way in which authors address
    readers. Describe Golding's tone in this essay. Is he friendly, pushy,
    distant? What evidence from the essay itself would you use to
    support your description of his tone?

# STEPHEN JAY GOULD ON
# ANIMAL INTELLIGENCE

## Pre-Reading Questions

1.  Describe several ways in which animals demonstrate intelligence. Is
    that intelligence (or intelligence*s*) different from or similar to human
    intelligence (or intelligence*s*)?
2.  Define the difference between "programmed" and "natural" intel-
    ligence. Is one more creative and flexible than the other? Compare
    the disadvantages and advantages of both intelligences.
3.  Stephen Jay Gould teaches biology, geology, and the history of
    science at Harvard University. He is, in other words, an academic
    scientist. Knowing that, what are your expectations concerning the
    style and structure of the following article before you actually read it?
    Why do you have those expectations? What are the sources of those
    expectations?

# THE GUANO RING
## Stephen Jay Gould

When I first went to sea as a petrified urbanite who had never ridden  1
anything larger than a rowboat, an old sailor (and Navy man) told me
that I could chart my way through this *aqua incognita* if I remembered
but one simple rule for life and work aboard a ship: if it moves, salute it;
if it doesn't move, paint it.

If we analyze why such a statement counts as a joke (albeit a feeble  2
one) in our culture, we must cite the incongruity of placing such a
"mindless" model for making decisions inside a human skull. After all,
the essence of human intelligence is creative flexibility, our skill in
grasping new and complex contexts—in short, our ability to make (as we
call them) judgments, rather than to act by the dictates of rigid, preset
rules. We are, as Konrad Lorenz has stated, "specialists in nonspecialization." We do not behave as machines with simple yes-no switches,
invariably triggered by definite bits of information present in our
immediate environments. Our enlightened sailor, no matter how successful at combating rust or avoiding the brig, is not following a human style
of intelligence.

Yet this inflexible model does represent the style of intelligence fol-  3
lowed with great success by most other animals. The decisions of animals
are usually unambiguous yeses or noes triggered by definite signals, not
subtle choices based upon the assessment of a complex gestalt.

Many birds, for example, do not recognize their own young and act  4
instead according to the rule: care for what is inside the nest; ignore what
is outside. British ethologist W. H. Thorpe writes: "Most birds, while
they may be very attentive to their young in the nest, are completely
callous and unresponsive to those same young when, as a result of some
accident, they are outside the nest or the immediate nest territory."

This rule rarely poses evolutionary dilemmas for birds, since the  5
objects in their nests are usually their own young (carrying their
Darwinian heritage of shared genes). But this inflexible style of intelligence can be exploited and commandeered to a nefarious purpose by
other species. Cuckoos, for example, lay their eggs in the nests of other
birds. A cuckoo hatchling, usually larger and more vigorous than the
rightful inhabitants, often expels its legitimate nest mates, which will die,
frantically begging for food, when their parents follow the rule, ignore
them for their inappropriate location, and feed the young cuckoo
instead. We can intellectualize our anthropomorphism away, but we
cannot expunge it from our aesthetic reactions. I must confess that no
scene of organic activity makes me angrier about the world's injustice
than the sight of a foster parent, its own young killed by a cuckoo,
solicitously feeding a begging parasite that may be up to five times its

own size (for cuckoos may choose much smaller birds as their hosts, and the fledglings are often much larger than the foster parents).

This summer, while in the Galápagos Islands, I encountered another, 6 and interestingly different, example of birds that exploit this common rule, twisting it to different uses. But this time, both the victim and benefactor are true siblings and the end result, although condemning weaker siblings to death, is evolutionary advantage for family lines.

The boobies (along with their cousins, the gannets) form a small 7 (nine species) but widespread family of seabirds, the Sulidae. (Everything, and more, that you will ever want to know about sulids you will find in J. Bryan Nelson's magnificent monograph: *The Sulidae: Gannets and Boobies,* 1978.) Earliest references in the Oxford English Dictionary indicate that boobies received their unflattering name, not for the distinctive waddling walk of one major display, big feet out and head held high in a behavior called "sky pointing," but for their remarkable tameness, which allowed sailors (bent only on destruction) to catch them so easily.

Three species of sulids inhabit the Galápagos Islands: the red-footed, 8 the blue-footed, and the masked booby. The red-footed booby lays a single egg in a conventional nest built near the tops and edges of trees and bushes. By contrast, its cousin of markedly different natural pedicure, the blue-footed booby, lays its eggs on the ground and builds no true nest at all. Instead, it delimits the nesting area in a remarkable and efficient way: it squirts guano (bird excrement to nonornithologists who have not read *Doctor No*) in all directions around itself, thus producing a symmetrical white ring as a symbolic marker of its nest.

Within this ring, the female blue-foot lays, not one (as in many 9 bobbies), but from one to three eggs. In his most impressive discovery, Nelson has explained much about the breeding behavior and general ecology of boobies by linking the production of eggs and young to the quality and style of feeding in parents. Boobies such as the red-foot, which travel long distances (up to 300 miles) to locate scarce sources of food, tend to lay but a single large egg, hatching into a resilient chick that can survive long intervals between parental feedings. On the other hand, when food sources are rich, dependable, and near shore, more eggs are laid and more young reared. At the extreme of this tendency lies the Peruvian booby, with its clutch of two to four eggs (averaging three) and its ability to raise all chicks to adulthood. Peruvian boobies feed on the teeming anchovies of their local waters, fish that may be almost as densely packed in the ocean as in the sardine cans that may become their posthumous home.

The blue-foot lies between these two tendencies. It is a nearshore 10 feeder, but its sources have neither the richness nor the predictability of swarming anchovies. Consequently, conditions vary drastically from generation to generation. The blue-foot has therefore evolved a flexible

strategy based on the exploitation by older siblings of their parents'
intellectual style: yes-no decisions triggered by simple signals. In good
times, parents may lay up to three eggs and successfully fledge all three
chicks; in poor years, they may still lay two or three eggs and hatch all
their chicks, but only one can survive. The death of nest (or, rather, ring)
mates is not the haphazard result of a losing struggle to feed all chicks
with insufficient food but a highly systematic affair based on indirect
murder by the oldest sibling.

I was reminded of the quip about painting and saluting while 11
observing blue-footed boobies on Hood Island in the Galápagos. Their
guano rings cover the volcanic surface in many places, often blocking the
narrow paths that visitors must tread in these islands. Parents sit on their
eggs and young chicks, apparently oblivious to groups of visitors who
gawk, gesticulate, and point cameras within inches of their territory. Yet
I noticed, at first by accident, that any intrusion into a guano ring would
alter the behavior of adult birds—from blissful ignorance to directed
aggression. A single toe across the ring elicited an immediate barrage of
squawking, posturing, and pecking. A few casual experiments led me to
the tentative conclusion that the boundary is an invisible circle right in
the middle of the ring. I could cautiously advance my toe across the
outer boundary with no effect; but as I moved it forward, as slowly and
as unobtrusively as possible, I invariably passed a central point that
brought on the pronounced parental reaction all at once.

Three hours later, I learned from our excellent guides and from 12
Bryan Nelson's popular book (*Galápagos: Islands of Birds*, 1968) how
older siblings exploit this parental behavior. And, anthropomorphic as we
all must be, it sent a shiver of wonder and disgust up my spine. (Science,
to a large extent, consists of enhancing the first reaction and suppressing
the second.) The female blue-foot lays her eggs several days apart, and
they hatch in the same order. The firstborn sibling is thus larger and
considerably stronger than its one or two ring mates. When food is
abundant, parents feed all chicks adequately and the firstborn does not
molest its younger siblings. But when food is scarce and only one chick
can survive, the actions of younger sibs evoke (how, we do not know) a
different behavior by big sister or brother. The oldest simply pushes its
younger siblings outside the guano ring. As human mammals, our first
reaction might be: so what? The younger sibs are not physically hurt and
they end up but a few inches from the ring, where parents will surely
notice their plaintive sounds and struggling motions and gather them
quickly back.

But a parental booby does no such thing, for it operates like our 13
proverbial sailor who made an either-or judgment by invoking the single
criterion of movement. Parental boobies must work by the rule: if a chick
is inside the ring, care for it; if it is outside, ignore it. Even if the chick

should flop, by happenstance, upon the ring, it will be rejected with all the vehemence applied to my transgressing foot.

We saw a chick on Hood Island struggling just a foot outside the ring 14 in plain sight of the parent within, sitting (in an attitude that we tend to read as maternal affection) upon the triumphant older sibling (which did not, however, seem to be smirking). Every mother's son and daughter among us longed to replace the small chick, but a belief in noninterference must be respected even when it hurts. For if we understand this system aright, such a slaughter of the innocents is a hecatomb for success of the lineages practicing it. Older chicks only expel their siblings when food cannot be secured to raise them all. A parental struggle to raise three on food for one would probably lead to the death of all.

The rule of "nurture within, ignore or reject outside" cannot 15 represent all the complexity of social behavior in nesting boobies. After all, most birds are noted "egalitarians" in their division of labor between sexes, and male boobies spend almost as much time incubating eggs and chicks as do the females. Since these stints last on the order of a day or so, boobies must permit their mates to transgress the sanctity of the guano ring when exchanging roles of care and provision. Still, the basic rule remains in force; it is not flouted but rather overridden by specific and recognized signals that act as a ticket of admission. K.E.L. Simmons, working on Ascension Island with the related brown booby (a species that does not inhabit the Galápagos), described the extensive series of calls and landing rituals that returning mates use to gain admission to their territory. But when adults trespass upon the unattended territory of an unrelated bird (as they often do to scrounge nest material on the cheap), they enter as "silently and as inconspicuously as possible."

If chicks could perform the overriding behaviors, they too could win 16 readmission to the ring. Indeed, they learn these signals as they age, as well they must, for older chicks begin to wander from the ring as they gain sufficient mobility for such travels at about four to five weeks of age. (Nelson argues that they wander primarily to seek shade when both parents are foraging; overheating is a primary cause of death in booby chicks.) Yet hatchling boobies display only a few behaviors—little more than food begging and bill hiding (appeasement) gestures, as Nelson demonstrates—and the overriding signals for entrance into the ring are not among them.

The third species of the Galápagos, the white, or masked, booby, 17 works on a more rigid system, but follows the same rules as its blue-footed cousin. Masked boobies are distant foragers, feeding primarily on flying fish. By Nelson's maxim, they should be able to raise but one chick. Sometimes, masked boobies lay only one egg, but usually they provision each nesting site with two. In this case, "brood reduction" (to use the somewhat euphemistic jargon) is obligatory. The older chick always pushes its younger sibling outside the nest (or occasionally stomps it to death within). This system seems, at first, to make no sense. The blue-foots, whatever our negative, if inappropriate, emotional reactions, at least use sibling murder as a device to match the number of chicks to a fluctuating supply of available food.

By what perverse logic should masked boobies produce two eggs, yet 18 never rear more than one chick invariably branded with the mark of Cain? Nelson argues forcefully that clutches of two eggs represent an adaptation for greatly increased success in raising *one* chick. The causes of death in eggs and young hatchlings are numerous—siblings intent upon murder being only one of many dangers to which booby flesh is heir. Eggs crack or roll from the nest; tiny hatchlings easily overheat. The second egg may represent insurance against death of the first chick. A healthy first chick cancels the policy directly, but the added investment may benefit parents as a hedge worth the expense of producing another egg (they will, after all, never need to expend much energy in feeding an unnecessary second chick). At Kure Atoll in the Hawaiian Archipelago, for example, clutches of two eggs successfully fledged one chick in 68 percent of nests examined during three years. But clutches of one egg fledged their single chick only 32 percent of the time.

Evolutionary biologists, by long training and ingrained habit, tend to 19 discuss such phenomena as the siblicide of boobies in the language of adaptation: how does a behavior that seems, at first sight, harmful and irrational really represent an adaptation finely honed by natural selection for the benefit of struggling individuals? Indeed, I have (and somewhat uncharacteristically for me) used the conventional language in this essay, for Nelson's work persuades me that siblicide is a Darwinian adaptation for maximizing the success of parents in rearing the largest number of chicks permitted by prevailing abundances of food.

But I am most uncomfortable in attributing the whole behavioral 20 system, of which siblicide is but a specific manifestation, only to adaptation, although this too is usually done. I speak here of the basic style of intelligence that permits siblicide to work: the sailor's system (of my opening paragraph) based on yes-no decisions triggered by definite signals. John Alcock, for example, in a leading contemporary text (*Animal Behavior: An Evolutionary Approach,* 1975) argues over and over again that this common intellectual style is, in itself and in general, an adaptation directly fashioned by natural selection for optimal responses in prevailing environments: "Programmed responses are widespread," he writes, "because animals that base their behavior on relatively simple signals provided by important objects in their environment are likely to do the biologically proper thing."

(On the overwhelming power of natural selection, no less a person- 21 age than H.R.H. Prince Philip, duke of Edinburgh, has written in the preface to Nelson's popular book on birds of the Galápagos: "The process of natural selection has controlled the very minutest detail of every feature of the whole individual and the group to which it belongs." I do not cite this passage facetiously to win an argument by saddling a position I do not accept with a mock seal of royal approval but rather to indicate how widely the language of strict adaptation has moved beyond professional circles into the writing of well-informed amateurs.)

As I argued for siblicide and guano rings, I am prepared to view any 22 specific manifestation of my sailor's intellectual style as an adaptation. But I cannot, as Alcock claims, view the style itself as no more than the optimized product of unconstrained natural selection. The smaller brain and more limited neural circuitry of nonhuman animals must impose, or at least encourage, intellectual styles different from our own. (Notice that I say different, not inferior.) These smaller brains may not be viewed as direct adaptations to any prevailing condition. They represent, rather, inherited structural constraints that limit the range of specific adaptations fashioned within their orbit. The sailor's style is a constraint that permits boobies to reduce their broods by exploiting a behavioral repertoire based on inflexible rules and simple triggers. Such a system would not work in humans, for parents will not cease to recognize their babies after a small and simple change in location. In human societies that practice infanticide (for ecological reasons that may be quite similar to those inducing siblicide in boobies), explicit social rules or venerated religious traditions—rather than mere duplicity by removal—must force or persuade parental action.

Birds may have originally developed their brain of characteristic size 23 as an adaptation to life in an ancestral lineage more than 200 million years ago; the sailor's style of intelligence may be a nonadaptive consequence of this inherited design. Yet this style has set the boundaries of behavior ever since. Each individual behavior may be a lovely adaptation, but it must be fashioned within a prevailing constraint. Which is more important: the beauty of the adaptation or the constraint that limits it to a permissible path? We cannot and need not choose, for both factors define an essential tension that regulates all evolution.

The sources of organic form and behavior are manifold and include 24 at least three primary categories. We have just discussed two of them: immediate adaptations fashioned by natural selection (exploitation by older booby siblings of a parental style of intelligence, leading to easy dispatch of nest mates); and potentially nonadaptive consequences of basic structural designs acting as constraints upon the pathways of adaptation (the intellectual style of yes-no decisions based on simple triggers).

In a third category, we find definite ancestral adaptations now used 25 by descendants in different ways. Nelson has shown, for example, that boobies reinforce the pair-bond between male and female through a complex series of highly ritualized behaviors involving the gathering of objects and their presentation to mates. In boobies that lay their eggs upon the ground, these behaviors are clearly relics of actions that once served to gather material for ancestral nests—for some of the detailed motions that still build nests in related species are followed, while others have been lost. The egg-laying areas of masked boobies are strewn with appropriate bits of twigs and other nesting materials that adults gather for their mutual displays and then must sweep out of the egg-laying area to lie unused upon the ground. I have emphasized these curious changes in function in several previous columns, for they are the primary proof of evolution—forms and actions that only make sense in the light of a previous, inherited history.

When I wonder how three such disparate sources can lead to the 26 harmonious structures that organisms embody, I temper my amazement by remembering the history of languages. Consider the amalgam that English represents—vestiges, borrowings, fusions. Yet poets continue to create things of beauty with it. Historical pathways and current uses are different aspects of a common subject. The pathways are intricate beyond all imagining, but only the hearty travelers remain with us.

## Post-Reading Questions

1. Define the following terms, using a biological dictionary (which you can find at almost any library Reference Desk), and the context within which the words appear in Gould's essay.
   **parasite**
   **natural selection**
   **evolution**
   **ecology**
   **adaptation**
2. Gould often mixes jokes and interesting bits of information into his essay (see paragraphs 1, 8, 11, and 14). What does this technique suggest about the kind of audience Gould has in mind? Do you find these asides distracting or effective? Why?
3. Why is it important that some adult boobies are able to move in and out of guano rings, while booby chicks are unable to re-enter a guano ring once they have been pushed out by a sibling?
4. What connection does Gould make between the food-gathering, egg-laying, and nesting behaviors (particularly the rejection of chicks by mother boobies) of the booby bird? What do these three sets of behavior tell us about natural selection and evolution?
5. What important distinction in intelligence lies behind Gould's description of booby bird behavior? What is the implied comparison between this form of animal intelligence and human intelligence? Is one by definition better than the other?

# SIGNE HAMMER ON INTELLIGENCE RESEARCH

## Pre-Reading Questions

1. Do you think that intelligence is mostly an inherited quality? Explain the reasons behind your answer.
2. Can people improve their intelligence quotients (IQ)? Why, or why not?
3. Is there one kind of intelligence, or many? Does academic success have a direct relationship to intelligence? What other factors influence academic success?
4. In your experience, how do schools reward intelligence? What else could schools reward? When would a teacher or school official respond negatively to intelligent behavior? Provide examples for each of these situations.
5. What does it mean to say that intelligent people lack common or practical sense? Give an example to support your answer.

## STALKING INTELLIGENCE
### Signe Hammer

When Bob Sternberg stands at the head of a seminar table, looking down 1 at his notes, he seems grown-up and serious enough to be a tenured professor at Yale. You can believe the gray flecks in his otherwise black hair. Then he sits down, scrunches up in his chair and smiles, and suddenly he looks like Woody Allen—or your cousin from New Jersey. The one who's always smiling a little apologetically, to show off the carefully orthodontured, precisely regimented remains of a serious overbite. Sternberg is talking about Diet Chocolate Fudge Soda.

"I was grossed out when I found out it was a best-seller," he is 2 saying. "I mean, somehow, it can't be the true stuff if it doesn't have the calories, you know?"

Is this any way for a full professor of psychology to talk? The students 3 who have come to his class to participate in an "experiment" aren't sure. We are sitting in a room with leaded-glass windows and oak paneling, on the third floor of the clean-lined, 1920s-Gothic tower that houses part of Yale's psychology department. The student volunteers don't know it, but Sternberg is teaching them to increase their intelligence.

He segues smoothly from diet soda to a hypothetical chain of weight 4 watchers' restaurants that failed. "I guess what they did is misrecognize the problem," he says. "They viewed it as, 'People are on diets so they'll run to this restaurant'; they didn't look at it from the standpoint of who goes to restaurants. You go because you want to have a nice evening and get served good food, not to have the same junky stuff you eat when you get home."

Sternberg is demonstrating the second metacomponent in the inter- 5
nal, or "componential," part of his triarchic theory of intelligence: recognizing the nature of the problem. It's no accident that the demonstration is in the context of a more or less real-life situation. Sternberg thinks that real life is where intelligence operates. What's more, he believes that since intelligence is essentially mental activity, a *process* and not simply some sort of built-in, inherited thing you either have or don't, it can be trained. You can learn to be smarter.

Robert Sternberg is a major figure in intelligence theory. He aims at 6
nothing less than a kind of grand synthesis of ideas that for others are mutually contradictory. His three-part theory accommodates both the traditional view that intelligence is general, the same from one culture to another, and the countertraditionalist view that environment—whether classroom or inner-city streets—shapes intelligence to different but equally valid ends. And, like the physicist who is comfortable with the knowledge that light is both a particle and a wave, Sternberg can look at intelligence as a set of components, "a wide array of cognitive and other skills," which are at the same time strongly unified by what he calls executive processes.

In the hot field of cognitive science, people in half a dozen different 7
disciplines—psychology, artificial intelligence, philosophy, anthropology, linguistics and the neurosciences—are all trying to figure out what goes on in our heads when we bring our intelligence to bear on our behavior. Or, to define the problem cognitively, we want to know how we process information. Models of the mind in action are essential if computer scientists working on artificial intelligence are to develop the so-called fifth generation of smarter computers. Neuroscientists have been analyz-ing the actual activity of the brain on the basic level of neuron and synapse and are preparing to test theories about the brain's operations in terms of larger processing units or circuits of neurons.

Cognitive psychologists are looking at behavior—how people actu- 8
ally solve problems—and analyzing the mental steps involved. But as Sternberg points out, the problems on which most psychological information-processing theories are based have largely been of the type—verbal-analogy, sequence-completion and spatial-orientation—familiar to anyone who has come up through American schools taking intelligence tests, aptitude tests and achievement tests, from elementary school right through to the College Boards and the GREs (Graduate Record Examinations).

In everyday life, though, as Sternberg writes in his recent book, 9
*Beyond IQ: A Triarchic Theory of Human Intelligence,* "people no more

go around solving testlike analogies . . . than they go around pressing buttons in response to lights or sounds."

IQ, or intelligence quotient, is a figure constructed statistically by 10 converting a percentile score on a series of tests to a number. Percentile scores are arrived at by "norming" a test—giving it to a representative sample of people and finding out what score represents the fiftieth percentile; this is the median and, quite arbitrarily, represents an IQ of 100.

The tradition of intelligence testing belongs to the psychometric 11 branch of psychology, which originated 80 years ago in France when the government commissioned psychologist Alfred Binet to develop a way to identify children who might need special help. According to evolutionary biologist Stephen Jay Gould in *The Mismeasure of Man,* Binet regarded the number he arrived at as a "rough empirical guide constructed for a limited, practical purpose." But American psychometricians enthusiastically applied the measurement to nearly 2 million soldiers in World War I and subsequently to millions of schoolchildren. IQ came to be seen as a measure of something real—something fixed, innate and inheritable—that was, in fact, intelligence. This interpretation continues to be held by such psychologists as Arthur Jensen, whose 1969 article questioning the value of compensatory schooling for black children set off a dispute that has influenced a generation of cognitive psychologists.

In addition to questions that demand the kind of school-oriented 12 cognitive processes needed to solve analogies, many IQ tests include those that require specific knowledge, such as "Who wrote the *Iliad*?" As Sternberg and others have pointed out, IQ tests really measure intelligence as a child's achievement in school. In both psychometrics and information processing, the domain of intelligence has been what Ulric Neisser of Emory University, who in 1967 wrote *Cognitive Psychology*—the book that defined the field—and who is now highly critical of the discipline, calls "academic."

Properly used, Sternberg writes, IQ is "moderately correlated"— 13 from 0.4 to 0.7, where a perfect correlation would be 1.0—with school achievement. But doing well in school isn't necessarily the same thing as doing well in life. "Typical correlations between IQ test scores and measures of actual occupational performance generally fall at about the 0.2 level," writes Sternberg. "Employment tests typically do no better," since they are often constructed of the same kinds of questions.

"I started off as an information-processing psychologist," Sternberg 14 says, "and then I realized, well, it's not that this stuff is wrong, it's only answering a subset of interesting questions. It doesn't deal with how business executives function in their jobs. It doesn't say anything about why my best student is the one with the relatively low GRE scores, while people with high seven hundreds, even eight hundreds, sometimes come to Yale and flop."

In response to such questions, Sternberg's triarchic theory of intel- 15
ligence evolved. A triarchy is a government by three—a triumvirate.
Sternberg sees three areas in which intelligence is exercised: the external,
or contextual, the experiential and the internal. (Intelligence is always
mental activity, but each part of the theory considers it in relation to a
different domain.)

The context is, simply, the environment in which intelligence func- 16
tions, whether classroom, office or squash court. The same person may
use his intelligence in each environment in a different way. Experience is
the domain in which people face new situations, and in which intuition,
insight and creativity—nonrational processes that simply don't come into
the usual information-processing picture—operate. Mental mechanisms,
by which intelligence relates to the internal world of the individual, are
brought to bear on intelligence through experience.

In short, Sternberg's triarchic theory is intended to get at the kind of 17
intelligence that counts in real life—what Neisser calls general and
Sternberg calls practical. Along with a number of other psychologists,
many of whom disagree with him on almost everything else, Sternberg
aims to change the way we think about intelligence. Ultimately, he hopes
to revise intelligence testing to take practical intelligence into account.

One thing that makes some of his less academically successful 18
students more successful in graduate school, Sternberg decided, is their
ability to become aware of, to learn and to apply tacit knowledge—"the
things you need to know to succeed on the job that you're never
explicitly taught and that often aren't even verbalized. You have to pick
this stuff up on your own, and it matters: Whether you get promoted, or
get raises, or can move to another company or another school is going to
depend in part on how well you pick it up."

Tacit knowledge includes things like knowing how to prioritize tasks 19
and allocate your time and other resources; how to manage the people
who work for you; and how to establish and enhance a reputation in your
career, by convincing your boss of the value of your work, for instance.
All this has to do with contextual intelligence, "mental activity directed
toward purposive adaptation to, and selection and shaping of, real-world
environments relevant to one's life."

Sternberg is an excellent example of his own definition of intelli- 20
gence. He has adapted himself perfectly to the requirements for success
in the world of academic psychology: He publishes, widely and well, the
results of research that is at once innovative and respectful of the
traditions in his field. One colleague calls his rate of output frightening;
in 1984 Sternberg published 25 papers as sole or senior author, two as
junior author and two anthologies. He is in demand at conferences and
colloquiums. At 35, he is director of graduate studies in the department
of psychology at Yale, from which he graduated, summa cum laude and
Phi Beta Kappa, in 1972.

The real-world environment of cognitive psychology is extremely 21 relevant to his life. "I think I have a real edge over a lot of people in the intelligence field," he says. "When I was a little kid, I was utterly test-anxious, and I was a real bomb on IQ tests. So I've been there. I was this overachiever, but when I was in sixth grade I was sent back to take the fifth-grade IQ test. The absurdity of that situation helped me get over the test anxiety; I said, 'I can handle this.' "

As a result, Sternberg got very interested in IQ tests. "When I was in 22 junior high school I ordered a lot of them, and I made my own test, the STOMA, or Sternberg Test of Mental Ability. Then I gave a lot of kids the Stanford-Binet, and I really got into trouble with the school psychologist, who threatened that if I ever brought the book into school again, he'd burn it. And that doesn't work with me." Sternberg laughs. "When I won that APA early career award [in 1981 he was awarded the American Psychological Association's Distinguished Scientific Award for Early Career Contribution to Psychology], I was very tempted to send this jerk a copy of it. To some extent I think it's better if you have personal motivations."

Sternberg has also selected another academic field, love, in which to 23 experiment and originate theory. He has even selected a second environment that seems to suit him as well as academia: the popular media. His article "The Measure of Love" appeared in the April issue of *Science Digest;* later this year, Harcourt Brace Jovanovich will publish his *Understanding and Increasing Your Intelligence,* a "how to" version of his theory for a general audience. Love landed him a Valentine's Day spot on the *Today Show,* and last December he appeared in *Science Digest* as one of America's Top 100 Young Scientists.

To learn something about the role of tacit knowledge, Sternberg and 24 a colleague, Richard K. Wagner, studied the differences between the performances of experts and novices in business. Psychologists have examined such differences in fields ranging from physics and chess to horserace handicapping. In chess, for example, William Chase and Herbert Simon of Carnegie-Mellon University in Pittsburgh found in 1973 that experts had a much better memory than novices for game positions they had glimpsed only briefly. They "chunked" more game pieces together in familiar configurations—recognizable as single units—and so were able to remember where most of the pieces were. The experts' advantage disappeared when the chess pieces were randomly set on the board. Their edge, then, lay in knowledge of the game, not in any innate superiority of memory.

Sternberg and Wagner asked successful, experienced business man- 25 agers to describe typical on-the-job situations and how they had reacted to them. Once the researchers had assembled sets of work-related situations with possible responses and had identified key responses statistically, they used these to compare the reactions of novices and

experts. The experts were a group of 54 business managers, 19 of whom
came from companies in the top 20 of the *Fortune* 500 list and the rest
from non-*Fortune* 500 companies. The novices were a group of 51
graduate students from five different business schools and a separate
group of 22 Yale undergraduates.

A work-related situation might be something like the following: "It 26
is your second year as a mid-level manager. . . . Your goal is rapid
promotion to the top of the company." The object was for the test taker
to rate the importance of each item in a list of possible actions that might
help distinguish him from the other mid-level managers: "Get rid of the
'deadwood' among your assistants"; "Find ways to make your superiors
aware of your accomplishments"; "Become involved in a public-service
organization"; and so forth.

Not surprisingly, the managers scored higher in tacit knowledge than 27
the business graduate students, who scored higher than the undergraduates. More interesting, for the managers tacit knowledge turned out to
be related to "indicators of success," including, Sternberg writes,
"whether or not the company was from among the top companies on the
*Fortune* 500 list," salary and years of schooling beyond high school. It
was not related to "years of management experience, level of title or
number of employees supervised."

In another study, Sternberg asked philosophers, business people, 28
artists and physicists how they perceived intelligence, wisdom and
creativity. "Business was the only field in which creativity and wisdom
were seen as negatively correlated," Sternberg says. "I've seen the
squeeze put on the creative people, because they don't tend to fit in. One
of the reasons I think IBM has succeeded is that it's run by people who
you hope are wise, but just when you think the company is getting so
staid that it'll never survive, it will have this group of creative people go
off to Florida and come up with the PC."

Intuition, insight and creativity are the nonrational, the stuff that is 29
often assumed can't really be measured. But Sternberg believes these
operations can be analyzed to some extent. Through them, intelligence
relates to experience, especially when there is something new to be dealt
with. They are important in applying tacit knowledge: "A lot of getting
ahead is knowing when to come up with the right theory or when to get
into a certain area," Sternberg says. "You know, there are areas that are
hot at a certain time and then two years later are as cold as ice. Knowing
when to get into them is definitely not luck." (See page 126 for
Sternberg's analysis of insight processes.)

The mental mechanisms through which intelligence relates to the 30
internal world of the individual operate in the real world through his
responses to experience. Executive processes, or metacomponents, are
crucial. They involve recognizing the existence of a problem, deciding
what it is and how to deal with it. They also include the "how am I
doing?" processes, used to monitor progress and respond to feedback.

## Insight: A Demonstration

Insight involves **selective encoding,** in which relevant information is extracted from a mass of undifferentiated material; **selective combination,** in which apparently isolated or random bits of information are integrated into a whole; and **selective comparison,** in which newly acquired information is related to that already acquired.

Combining these three insight skills, read the following problem and compare your solution with the one below.

2Dr. Smith was reading an article called "Plants Have Feelings, Too." It reported that a scientist had conducted an experiment to see whether plants expressed feelings, not by smiles or frowns but by electromagnetic waves. To test this theory, he connected the plants to machines that measured the waves, and had different people approach the plants and talk to them. The scientist was pleased to discover that Person A, who spoke kindly to the plants, registered one way on the machine, whereas Person B, who abused the plants, registered in a different way. He concluded that plants responded to human actions in different ways.

Dr. Smith wanted to test this theory. He repeated the experiment, but this time he attached the machine to plants and to empty plastic cups. He was surprised. Sure enough, the plants responded to different people in different ways. But so did the cups!

Dr. Smith was mystified, but slowly, an incredible idea began to form in his mind. "I can't believe this discovery," he said, "I've ... I've learned that plastic cups have feelings!"

Unfortunately, he had drawn the wrong conclusion. What conclusion would you draw?

ANSWER: When Dr. Smith's cups registered on the machine, he should have known that something other than the plants was causing vibrations. Instead, he misinterpreted the evidence offered by the "control" condition. The machine registered for irrelevant reasons.

Executive processes make it possible to apply tacit knowledge and change strategies when something doesn't work.

"To me, part of intelligence is recognizing your blind spots," says 31 Sternberg. "When I give talks, I get feedback; someone may say, 'Your theory doesn't deal with this' or 'That doesn't seem quite right.' That makes me more aware of my blind spots."

The big problem with teaching tacit knowledge, he finds, is that 32 "people can be surprisingly resistant to acting on it. You need to apply some of those metacomponents to context; you have to recognize things for yourself."

Sternberg thinks the mental mechanisms are a domain of intelligence 33
that holds good from one context or culture to another. The problems
confronting an urban American and a bush-dwelling African may be
totally different, but both have to recognize problems and figure out
how to resolve them. If the American and the African are presented with
the same problems, their solutions may also be completely different, in
keeping with their different cultures, but they may use the same mental
mechanisms in arriving at a solution. The same could be said of a lawyer
and a farmer.

The contextual view of intelligence is one of the legacies of the 34
heredity-versus-environment battles of the 1970s, when Sternberg was
still in school. Opposing those who said that the low IQ scores of
minority children were the result of an inherited deficiency in intelligence
were those who said that intelligence is a response to a cultural context
and that, in a nonschool setting, it may not show up on IQ scores.
Among those who hold the latter view are many information-processing
theorists. Today, most cognitive psychologists agree that heredity will
inevitably account for some degree of intelligence; the nature-versus-
nurture debate is no longer interesting. "The hot question of the
eighties," Sternberg says, "is 'What's the whole domain here, and what
isn't?' "

One of Sternberg's chief critics locates the domain of intelligence in 35
several places. In his 1983 book, *Frames of Mind: The Theory of Multiple
Intelligences,* psychologist Howard Gardner of Harvard University theorizes in favor of the existence of several different, "relatively autonomous
human intellectual competencies," or intelligences, a number of which
are not "intellectual" in the sense that Sternberg's intelligence is.
Gardner thinks that our Western tradition of focusing on the mind, and
particularly on rationalism, is limiting. In his argument for a "bodily-
kinesthetic intelligence," for instance, he points out that "skilled use of
one's body has been important in the history of the species for thousands, if not millions, of years." He also asserts that each of the
intelligences (in addition to the bodily-kinesthetic, his list includes
linguistic, musical, logical-mathematical, spatial and two personal intelligences) can be isolated or absent in particular populations and highly
developed in particular people or cultures.

Gardner also thinks that the intelligences are characterized by "the 36
existence of one or more basic information-processing operations or
mechanisms. . . . One might go so far as to define a human intelligence as
a neural mechanism or computational system." As an associate professor
of neurology at the Boston University School of Medicine, he has had
many opportunities to observe the effects of damage to the brain on
specific areas of ability. He is critical of Sternberg's model because it is
not rooted in the physical brain: It is, he says, "a computational model."

To this, Sternberg replies, "Some biologically based models use 37 biology metaphorically rather than being truly based on the biology of the brain." He also thinks that "there are different levels at which you can theorize, and no one has really succeeded in being good at all of them. I think your best bet is to try to find out what you're good at and then to make the most of that." He chuckles, and adds, "That relates to my theory of intelligence." Sternberg thinks some of Gardner's multiple intelligences aren't, properly speaking, intelligences at all. "Would you really want to say that someone who is tone-deaf, lacking in an important aspect of musical intelligence, is mentally retarded?" he asks. "I don't think so."

Eventually, information processing will probably be understood both 38 as observable behavior and as brain activity. In the meantime, the argument over whether there is a central "intelligence" or many different intelligences—and where the one or the many operate—continues to occupy theorists.

Sternberg thinks that if we get rid of the word *intelligence* we will 39 promptly reinvent it. People *notice* that some people do better than others. "Gardner's theory appeals," he says, "because we want everyone to be gifted, and it's true that everyone has some talent. When you look at IQ, it constrains your vision of the world. And everyone thinks he or she is above average. We did a study in which we asked people to rate their own intelligence on a scale of one to nine. Everyone was a six or seven. Gardner allows you to think, 'Well, if I don't win on IQ, I've got six other intelligences left to try.' "

Above all, Sternberg's is a pragmatic theory. He sees intelligence as a 40 source of individual differences, but he also believes that most people, including himself, don't work anywhere near their potential. His is a theory for our time, when more people believe they can succeed than ever before. Sternberg will soon be training businessmen and -women to be smarter: telling them about those essential processes, guiding them through examples, as he did the Yale undergraduates in his seminar room, and putting them through cases so they can put their executive processes to work on their newly acquired tacit knowledge.

"Let's take these processes and see if they can help us lead better 41 lives, or at least not make the same mistakes over and over again," he says. "That's the ultimate test, isn't it—whether it makes any difference to your life? If it doesn't, who the hell cares?"

## Post-Reading Questions

The following questions may be answered individually or collaboratively. In either case, be prepared to share your responses with your classmates.

1.  Define the terms listed below by referring to a psychological diction-
    ary (available at most library Reference Desks) and by analyzing the
    context within which the terms appear in this essay.
    **tacit knowledge**
    **mental mechanisms**
    **multiple intelligences**
    **executive processes**
    **central intelligence**
    **triarchic theory**
    **IQ test**
2.  Why does this article begin with a physical description of Robert
    Sternberg? What does that beginning suggest to you concerning the
    audience and purpose of this article? Define that audience and
    purpose.
3.  How does Robert Sternberg's triarchic method differ from the more
    traditional ways of measuring intelligence, such as the Stanford-Binet
    test and other more mathematical methods? What advantages and
    disadvantages does it have when compared to these methods?
4.  Describe an occasion in which your "tacit knowledge" helped you
    solve a problem. Use this description to explain how tacit knowledge
    works.
5.  Signe Hammer is a science journalist and reports the latest develop-
    ments in science. Does she do a good job of capturing the technical
    aspects of her subject while getting her audience interested in her
    subject? If you think she does, use several paragraphs to explain how
    she accomplishes this difficult goal. If you think she fails, use several
    paragraphs to explain why.

# HOWARD GARDNER ON INTELLIGENCE

### Pre-Reading Questions

Before you read the following interview, you need to know a bit more
about Howard Gardner and his book *Frames of Mind,* which has
become a ground-breaking classic in intelligence studies. Gardner
argues that the idea of universal intelligence, as tested by standard IQ
tests, is reductive and dangerous and must be replaced by a more
flexible concept. This more flexible concept Gardner calls "multiple
intelligence." His research supports his belief that at least seven kinds
of intelligence exist and that different people possess different degrees
and combinations of these intelligences. Like Sternberg (who was
profiled in the previous reading in this chapter), Gardner argues that
intelligences can be increased through learning and experience. He
disagrees, however, with Sternberg, who continues to argue that there

are universal elements to intelligence. But both are critical of traditional intelligence tests.

1. Describe two or three people you know who demonstrate different kinds of intelligence. Are these different kinds of intelligence recognized by others? Are they valued by those in authority in schools or in the workplace? Why, or why not?
2. Describe the intelligence of a person who is involved in an activity—such as athletics or performing arts—that is not usually considered to require a large degree of intelligence. Do you disagree with the conventional line on these activities, or do you simply think they require a different kind of intelligence?
3. Do you think that the environment has a great deal to do with a person's intelligence? Give a few examples to support your answer.

## THE SEVEN FRAMES OF MIND
### Howard Gardner

Since receiving his doctoral degree in social psychology from Harvard 13 years ago, Howard Gardner has been a fulltime research psychologist, dividing his time among three research sites. He conducts neuropsychological research with aphasic patients and other victims of brain disease at the Boston Veterans Administration Medical Center, codirects Harvard Project Zero, where he and his colleagues study the development of artistic skills in normal and gifted children, and is an associate professor at the Boston University School of Medicine. In the past decade Gardner has written seven books, and in 1981 he was awarded a MacArthur Foundation prize fellowship.

*Frames of Mind,* Gardner's most recent book, was written in response to a request from the Bernard Van Leer Foundation of the Netherlands. The foundation asked Gardner, among others, to prepare a series of books on the nature and realization of human potential. Gardner chose to focus on human cognitive potentials. Although he was trained as a Piagetian,* his research and reading had undermined his belief in general intellectual structures. His work on children's cognition and on the results of brain disease suggested to him that humans were capable of a set of different and often unrelated intellectual capacities or "intelligences." The book gave Gardner an opportunity to synthesize these findings and, at the same time, to offer a critique of current notions of intelligence and IQ testing. As he notes: "Many people realize our contemporary notions of intelligence are

*Piagetian:* Piaget (1896–1980) was a Swiss psychologist who outlined distinct stages of intellectual development.

inadequate, but until we come up with a new and better theory, we'll
continue to be stuck with talk about intelligence and with IQ tests."
                                                          —James Ellison

*Ellison:* *Frames of Mind* embraces a theory of multiple intelligences.  1
Can you explain that theory in relatively simple terms?

*Gardner:* Most people in our society, even if they know better, talk as if  2
individuals could be assessed in terms of one dimension, namely how
smart or dumb they are. This is deeply ingrained in us. I became
convinced some time ago that such a narrow assessment was wrong
in scientific terms and had seriously damaging social consequences.
In *Frames of Mind,* I describe seven ways of viewing the world; I
believe they're equally important ways, and if they don't exhaust all
possible forms of knowing, they at least give us a more comprehensive picture than we've had until now.

*Ellison:* Linguistic and logical-mathematical intelligence are the two we  3
all know about.

*Gardner:* Most intelligence tests assess the individual's abilities in those  4
two areas. But my list also includes spatial intelligence. The core
ability there is being able to find your way around an environment,
to form mental images and to transform them readily. Musical
intelligence is concerned with the ability to perceive and create pitch
patterns and rhythmic patterns. The gift of fine motor movement, as
you might see in a surgeon or a dancer, is a root component of
bodily-kinesthetic intelligence.

*Ellison:* That leaves the interpersonal and intrapersonal, which would  5
seem to be controversial categories.

*Gardner:* They are. But then my entire theory breeds controversy,  6
particularly among those who have a narrow, largely Western conception of what intelligence is.

*Ellison:* How would you define the interpersonal and intrapersonal as  7
intelligences?

*Gardner:* Interpersonal involves understanding others—how they feel,  8
what motivates them, how they interact with one another. Intrapersonal intelligence centers on the individual's ability to be acquainted
with himself or herself, to have a developed sense of identity.

*Ellison:* I can see where your critics would grant that language and logic  9
are intelligences, and they'd probably throw in spatial, grudgingly.
But they might balk at your other four measures as not being strictly
mental activities.

*Gardner:* What right does anyone have to determine *a priori* what the  10
realm of the mind is and is not? Some of my critics claim that I'm
really talking about talents, not intelligences, to which I say fine, if
you'll agree that language and logical-mathematical thinking are

talents, too. I'm trying to knock language and logic off a pedestal, to democratize the range of human faculties.

*Ellison:* Democratize?                                                                    11

*Gardner:* Forget about Western technological society for a moment and 12 think about other societies. In the Caroline Islands of Micronesia, sailors navigate among hundreds of islands, using only the stars in the sky and their bodily feelings as they go over the waves. To that society, this ability is much more important than solving a quadratic equation or writing a sonnet. If intelligence testers had lived among the Micronesians, they would have come up with an entirely differ- ent set of testing methods and a wholly distinct list of intelligences.

*Ellison:* And reading would have been low on the totem pole for these 13 people.

*Gardner:* Five hundred years ago in the West, a tester would have 14 emphasized linguistic memory because printed books weren't readily available. Five hundred years from now, when computers are carrying out all reasoning, there may be no need for logical-mathematical thinking and again the list of desirable intelligences would shift. What I object to is this: Decisions made about 80 years ago in France by Alfred Binet, who was interested in predicting who would fail in school, and later by a few Army testers in the United States during World War I, now exercise a tyrannical hold on who is labeled as bright or not bright. These labels affect both people's conceptions of themselves and the life options available to them.

*Ellison:* Isn't it true that high SAT and IQ scores predict superior social 15 and economic results?

*Gardner:* In the short run, these tests have decent predictive value, at 16 least in schools. Children who do well in the tests tend to get good grades in school, for schools also reward quick responses to short- answer questions. Interestingly, though, the tests don't have a good predictive value for what happens beyond school.

*Ellison:* Are there statistics in support of that condition?                              17

*Gardner:* Well, the best studies I know of were done by sociology 18 professor Christopher Jencks of Northwestern University. He and his associates have shown that IQ tests have only a modest correlation with success in professions.

*Ellison:* How can you possibly test something like interpersonal 19 intelligence?

*Gardner:* You can't, in the usual sense of testing. But let me tell you 20 about a plan that some colleagues and I would like to get funded. We're interested in monitoring intellectual capacity in the preschool years. We want to set up what we call an enriched environment, filled with materials that children can interact with freely on their own. How children interact with these materials over a period of time would serve as a much better indicator of their strengths than any short-term measure.

Let's say we're looking in the area of spatial intelligence. One of 21 the things we would want to do is to give children blocks of various sorts and observe what and how they build. We would show them games involving more complex structures and see if they pick up principles of construction. In the area of music we would give them Montessori bells and simple computer toys that allow children to create their own melody. Schools can be equipped with these aids. To assess personal intelligences, we'll have the children enact different roles in play or work cooperatively on the project. The point is that, in a few weeks or months, you could see the developmental steps children go through, as well as the richness and depth of their play.

*Ellison:* I take it you feel this is a better method to use than standard 22 testing.

*Gardner:* Yes. First of all, it relates much more to children's natural way 23 of doing things, which is exploring, testing themselves with materials. Second, if a child had an off day or didn't like the experimenter, we would simply go on to the next day. A child would be monitored for six months or a year, and at the end of the year we would come up with a profile of intellectual propensities somewhere between an IQ score and an annotated report card. We would observe intelligences and combinations of intelligences for a year. Then we would have descriptions a page or two long that say in plain English what the child's strengths and interests are, along with his areas of weakness and how they could be strengthened.

*Ellison:* Evidently, then, you still feel that some kind of score is 24 necessary.

*Gardner:* It is efficient for the professional to be able to quantify, but 25 I'm ambivalent about sharing scores with nonspecialists. We actually hope to develop four kinds of tests. One we call a test of core ability. For example, in the area of music we would look at the child's pitch and rhythm ability. But rather than assess sensitivity to pitches in isolation (as in traditional musical tests), we would teach children a song and code how quickly they learn it and how accurate the pitch and rhythm are. The second test is developmental. We would provide children with materials and give them ample opportunity to explore, to get deeper and deeper into the process, to invent their own product.

The third test, a multiple-intelligence measure, involves taking 26 children to a movie, a museum, perhaps a zoo. Afterwards, children would be asked to recreate the experience, talk about it, sing it, draw it. We would look at how children choose to encode the experience, whether in their recreations, they focus on spatial, musical, linguistic or some combination.

*Ellison:*  You mentioned a fourth test.                                                    27

*Gardner:*  Yes, an incidental-learning measure. We would supply some-     28
thing in the environment that children have no idea they're ever
going to be asked about. We want to see what they would pick up
spontaneously, without ever attending explicitly.

*Ellison:*  Can you give an example?                                                        29

*Gardner:*  Say the child enters a classroom and there's a certain song     30
playing, each day the same song. One day we simply say to the child,
"Can you sing the song you hear in the morning?" This is how you
discover what kids pick up incidentally. It has a lot to do with how
intelligences work. A person does not have a high intelligence
because he works very hard at something. On the contrary, having a
high intelligence means that you naturally, without effort, pick up
certain kinds of things.

*Ellison:*  What about the practicality of administering these sorts of tests?   31
It obviously would involve a tremendous amount of time and energy.

*Gardner:*  First, you have to decide if the whole thing is feasible. If it is,   32
we move to the question of practicality. Clearly, to be done adequately would involve several hours of monitoring spread out
through the year. But if you take into account the amount of time a
teacher spends determining the grades for a report card, the monitoring wouldn't take that much more time. And most important,
when you consider the social value of assessing an individual's
talents, the costs become trivial. A relatively small amount of time
and money can make a huge difference for the person and for the
society.

*Ellison:*  Do you think there is a chance of changing the way testing is     33
used in the United States today?

*Gardner:*  Once people appreciate the perils, change will follow. There's   34
treachery in labeling and overquantifying. This is true of IQ tests and
also applies to SAT scores. SATs, after all, are basically IQ tests. More
people probably know their SAT scores than their own Social
Security numbers. I'm delighted that some of the best universities
are now questioning the need for an SAT, and I'll do whatever I can
to come up with a more humane and pluralistic way of assessing
humankind.

*Ellison:*  A way that spans the seven intelligences.                                 35

*Gardner:*  Let me put this in personal terms for a moment. I've certainly   36
gotten ahead by virtue of some of those intelligences that are valued
in society. Moreover, I learned early in life to use those intelligences
to supplement things that I couldn't do so well. For example, I'm
not particularly gifted in the spatial area, but if I'm given a spatial
test, I can usually use logical means to figure out the right answers.
Also, I think I was "saved" because I've always been very interested
in the arts. They are every bit as serious and cognitive as the sciences,

and yet because of various prejudices in our society, the arts are considered to be mainly emotional and mysterious. Our culture confuses being a scientist with being smart and serious. I came to realize that we really had to rethink the whole notion of what cognition is all about.

*Ellison:*  In school, the science kids have always been marked as the 37 intellectual whizzes, haven't they? Evidently the attitude that science kids grow up to be our intellectual elite persists in the general adult culture.

*Gardner:*  They are the high priests. And yet the cognitive complexity of 38 Henry James's or Proust's structure of knowledge is every bit as involved and sophisticated as the structural complexities of a physics theory: Granted, it's a different kind of complexity, but I think it's worth noting that someone can be incredibly good as a scientist and have no sense of what's going on in a Henry James novel.

*Ellison:*  Once these various intelligences are identified, how can they be 39 translated into a cohesive educational experience?

*Gardner:*  Let's say you have a child with strong spatial abilities, as 40 assessed by block play or by finding the way around a new environment. And let's say the school doesn't have teachers who work in that area. There certainly are other people in the community with those kinds of gifts, and it should be the school's role to help children and parents find them. I'm in favor of dissolving the boundaries between school and the rest of the community. I think it has to happen in this country, and I'm convinced it will happen.

Also, the apprenticeship system should be reconstituted. The 41 child who's gifted in the spatial area ought to be working in an architect's office or in mapmaking. Apprenticeship ensures the transmissions of skills to individuals in a position to use them. We need to motivate people toward things they're good at. Those who are gifted in math like doing it because it provides a lot of satisfaction and they make a lot of progress. But why stop with math? Apprentice the musical kind to a piano tuner. God knows, we need good piano tuners.

*Ellison:*  Are you saying we shouldn't invest energy in areas where our 42 aptitude isn't high?

*Gardner:*  I believe that, up to a point. But still, an effort to understand 43 other subjects has to be made.

*Ellison:*  But why? The students who are whizzes in English and can't 44 solve a geometric problem on pain of death—why should they keep trying?

*Gardner:*  One of the major things that prompted my work was recog- 45 nition that in the real world people have different abilities and disabilities. Take someone with a good prognosis in the spatial area. What should we do? I think it's crucial to try to diagnose that early because everything we know from neuroscience suggests that the earlier an individual has a chance to work intensely with the relevant materials, the more rapidly he or she will develop in that area. And it makes no difference how meager their potential is, it should be developed.

*Ellison:* Then in a sense you disagree with my idea that we should 46 ignore areas of low aptitude.

*Gardner:* Areas of low aptitude should be detected early in life and they 47 can be bolstered by what we might call prostheses for an intelligence. Let's assume I have poor visual memory and can't remember forms. Today we have all sorts of aids to make the forms perfectly visible. What if I can't transform an image in my mind? We now have a simple computer program that transforms it for me on demand. Culture, you see, can create instruments to supplement lacks in intelligences.

*Ellison:* How well do we understand these lacks in others, though? Can 48 the skilled linguist who can't carry a tune appreciate the world of the jazz trombonist who can barely read the newspaper?

*Gardner:* I think the theory of multiple intelligences helps you to 49 understand how people relate, and fail to relate, to one another. We all know that sometimes opposites attract. And if you think about this not in terms of hair color but of intelligences, it's quite intriguing. Often somebody who can't do music worth a damn is attracted to somebody who thinks well musically but has no personal skills and admires the person who's gifted interpersonally. However, problems may arise. One person thinks very spatially but has trouble trying to describe how to get somewhere. The spouse has no spatial ability or has to think of everything linguistically. This can cause considerable conflict, with each person thinking the other stupid, whereas, in fact, their minds are simply working in different ways, displaying contrasting intelligence.

*Ellison:* Let's move to the personal intelligences. Can you really teach 50 someone to interact well with others? Isn't that an art, a gift, in a sense, inborn?

*Gardner:* It can be taught. I think a lot can be done through different 51 kinds of media. For example, you can tell stories to children and see what they understand about the motivations of different characters. Or let them act the characters. Show them films and have them look closely at the interactions of characters in the films. We must always be alert for settings in which children can develop in productive ways. It is harmful to put children who are shy and afraid of other people in an environment where everyone is much older and much more sophisticated. But put them in a game room with younger children, and you'll enhance their interpersonal understanding.

*Ellison:* Sometimes individuals are blocked for psychodynamic reasons. 52
Do you see therapy as a possible teaching tool, as a way to promote
the personal intelligences?

*Gardner:* Therapy is our society's way of helping individuals use what- 53
ever intrapersonal knowledge they have in a more effective way. In
the East you have Hindu, yoga and other kinds of religious philosophies that develop their own sense of what it means to be
knowledgeable about the self.

*Ellison:* Wouldn't you say that the intra- and interpersonal intelligences 54
communicate with each other constantly?

*Gardner:* Certainly they enhance each other. The more you understand 55
about other people, the more potential you have for understanding
yourself and vice versa. Nonetheless, there are people highly skilled
in understanding other people and manipulating them—certain
politicians and celebrities come to mind—and they show no particular intrapersonal understanding. By the same token, there are
people in the artistic areas who seem to understand themselves while
routinely missing cues in other people. An important part of my
theory is that each intelligence has its own operation, and one can be
strong in one intelligence while weak in others.

Still, there are many activities that involve blends of intelligences, 56
where, as you put it, they communicate. If you look at a society
where certain activities use a combination of intelligences, each
intelligence will tend to buoy the other. Take those with strong
logical-mathematical intelligence. Once they begin to study science,
they discover that if they can't write about their findings, they aren't
really scientists. They have to be able to publish. That often means
finding a collaborator who writes well. As a result of such collaborations, many scientists go from being wretched writers to becoming
decent ones.

*Ellison:* I assume from *Frames of Mind* that the neural organization of 57
the brain determines the strength of the various intelligences.

*Gardner:* As you know, when somebody has a stroke or an injury to the 58
head, not all skills break down equally. Instead, certain abilities can
be significantly impaired while others are spared. A lesion in the
middle areas of the left hemisphere will impair somebody's linguistic
abilities while leaving musical, spatial, and interpersonal skills largely
undamaged. Conversely, a large lesion in the right hemisphere will
compromise spatial and musical abilities, leaving linguistic abilities
relatively intact. Probably the unique feature of my list of intelligences, compared with those of other researchers, is that I claim
independent existences for the intelligences in the human neural
system. And my chief source of information is how they function
following brian damage. There is impressive evidence that each of
the seven intelligences has its own special neurological organization.

*Ellison:*  If *Frames of Mind* were to leave the reader with one point, what  59
one would you choose?

*Gardner:*  Nothing would make me happier than if society were to stop  60
measuring people in terms of some unitary dimension called "intelligence." Instead, I would like us to think in terms of intellectual
strengths. I'd like to get rid of numbers entirely and simply say that
an individual is, let's say, relatively stronger in language than in logic,
even though he or she might be well above the norm in both.
Because after all, the norm is irrelevant. If you manage to change the
way people talk about things, parents and teachers may begin to
think and talk about intellectual proclivities rather than just how
"smart" a child is. And if we begin to accept these new terms, we can
stop labeling one another as smart or dumb.

## Post-Reading Questions

1.  What does Gardner say about the role of environment in developing
    intelligence?
2.  Do you find what Gardner has to say about cultural influences on
    intelligence convincing? Explain why you agree or disagree; analyze
    at least one of his examples to support your answer.
3.  What kinds of intelligence tests would Gardner substitute for the
    traditional tests? What do you think of these tests? Would they be
    difficult to implement? Why, or why not?
4.  How well does Gardner explain his approaches to testing and
    developing the different intelligences? What techniques does he use
    and why are they successful or unsuccessful?
5.  If you were writing an essay criticizing traditional, standardized tests
    of intelligence, how would you use Gardner to help make your case?

# SUSAN GILBERT ON CREATIVITY

## Pre-Reading Questions

1.  Describe a situation in which you had a mental block when trying to
    solve a problem. What did you do to get rid of the block? Were you
    successful? Why, or why not.
2.  Would you rather think a problem through alone or with others?
    What do you think are the advantages and disadvantages of each
    approach to problem solving?
3.  Think of one of the most creative moments in your life. First,
    provide some background; then, list some of the things you did that
    were creative. Is this kind of behavior exceptional or normal for you?
4.  Explain why you think that creativity can or cannot be taught. If you
    think it can, describe how.

# PROFITING FROM CREATIVITY
## Susan Gilbert

"The winner got eleven million dollars, the loser lost ten million, and in 1 the middle there were people who made or lost about three million," says Roy Fitzwater, group leader of product development at Anderson Clayton Foods. Fitzwater is smiling, even though he was the loser. He is referring to a computer game he and 14 other research and development managers played the day before in which the challenge was to bring a new product, a printing plate, to market. With profit and loss still uppermost in their mind, these people turn to the next phase of their leadership seminar: a workshop on creativity.

Product development one day, product invention the next—these are 2 the ingredients of a five-day seminar at the Center for Creative Leadership in Greensboro, North Carolina. It is one of at least six schools in the country that teach business people how to be creative—that is, how to generate novel ideas and do something with them. Based on some recent investigations, many behavioral scientists are now convinced that this rare and envied ability can be taught.

Research indicates that creative people are made, not born. "Some 3 people might be born with a greater tolerance for stress or tension, which comes with creativity," says psychologist Howard Gardner, one of the codirectors of Harvard's Project Zero, an ongoing research program on creativity and intelligence. "But to be creative, you have to be willing to take risks, to work alone and to want to be distinctive, not to run with the pack. Modeling is important. If you spend five years around risk takers, chances are you may be willing to take risks, too."

The popular notion that creativity springs from the right side of the 4 brain is a canard. It is a misinterpretation of research by Nobel laureate neurobiologist Roger Sperry and others that suggests that the left hemisphere is most active when we speak, write and puzzle out problems with logic and that the right hemisphere takes over to recognize faces and understand spatial relations. "There is zero evidence from EEGs or any other studies that creative thinking comes from a particular region of the brain," says psychobiologist Jerre Levy of the University of Chicago, who was once a student of Sperry's and who has continued to investigate the specialties of the brain's hemispheres.

"Creativity is a function of an unusual level of interhemispheric 5 communication," Levy says—a trait she claims can be developed in children by, for example, reading. The right hemisphere visually decodes the letters and the left hemisphere deciphers their meaning. "This indicates," says Levy, "that it's not just genes but experience that fosters interhemispheric communication."

Although normal or above-normal intelligence is necessary to cre- 6 ativity, genius is not. Given enough intelligence to function professionally in a field, Gardner says, slight variations either higher or lower have no significant effect on creative achievement. "Genius in the sense of dramatic talent may simply foster highly skilled performance, as with a gifted violin virtuoso who does not compose nor offer innovative interpretations," wrote David Perkins, codirector of Project Zero, in a paper he delivered at the 1984 Symposium on Creativity in Science. Nonetheless, he added, we persist in making creativity "the crown jewel of human achievement which most of us will never touch." Learning to be creative requires that we shift our perception of creativity from the gift of genius to the product of process.

Disarming the creative process is what the creativity workshops do    7
best. Some accomplish this by pushing participants to fly kites and build junk sculptures. Others present a more businesslike environment with computer terminals and problem-solving exercises. Whatever their style, these workshops don't come cheap; corporations such as IBM, Mead and Kodak pay from about $250 a head for a day-long seminar to more than $1,000 for five days. But with companies plunging more than $45 billion a year into research and development, any course that teaches some shortcuts and surefire strategies for generating high-quality ideas should eventually pay for itself in profitable new products.

On day two at the Center for Creative Leadership, three groups of    8
five people, mostly men, are seated at round tables in small, boxy rooms with beige walls and one-way internal-viewing windows. The setting seems more appropriate to an experiment involving laboratory rats darting through a maze than to one with humans generating ideas. Large newsprint pads hang on the walls, and pencils and paper are placed at each table. Each group is told to conceive as many novel solutions as possible to a different problem. Fitzwater's group must figure out what can be made with felt left over from the manufacture of tennis balls.

The exercise is designed to show the difference between the ideas    9
generated by individuals and those that come from a group. For 15 minutes the group members work alone, writing down as many ideas as they can. This is called brainwriting. For the next 15 minutes, they all brainstorm, calling out ideas. The rule of fruitful brainstorming, everyone is told, is to refrain from passing judgment on any suggestion. With the pep of a young schoolteacher, Sharon Sensabaugh, a cognitive psychologist at the center, moves from one one-way window to another.

Psychologists studying creativity disagree as to whether the most    10
novel and useful ideas come from individuals or from groups. Some researchers argue in favor of individuals, seeing groups as mediators of uniform thinking. Others think groups produce better ideas, reasoning that groups contain more information and that group discussion can lead to conflict and resolution and therefore to innovative solution.

In this morning's exercise, brainwriting yields predictable sugges-    11
tions about what to do with the surplus felt: furniture stuffing, novelty

toys, pads to place under lamps and trophies. By contrast, the ideas derived from brainstorming are imaginative: a two-sided adhesive, filters for sound boxes, wicks, felt tips for markers and material for absorbing oil spills.

"The creativity techniques you use impact on the kinds of solutions 12 you get," Sensabaugh says in a lecture following the exercise. "Research shows that brainwriting is best for short-term solutions that will be implemented within a year." This is because the brainwriting ideas, being relatively conventional, are least likely to meet with resistance in the corporation. "Brainstorming is good for ideas usable one to three years in the future."

Studies also show that a third class of techniques—called excursion— 13 are most effective for long-term planning. One technique involves getting a group together to look at images that evoke emotional responses: a view of Earth taken from a satellite, two Bloody Marys, an apple blossom twig against a blurred background. The images should make people perceive whatever problem they're working on in a new way and thereby lead them to come up with creative solutions.

At the Norfolk Southern Corporation in Norfolk, Virginia, training 14 officer Joseph Gelmini and colleagues used another excursion technique— fantasy—to jog their imagination as they searched for solutions to a problem the railroad industry has been grappling with: how to extend the life of hardwood cross ties. Gelmini fantasized about ways that dead trees could be made to grow. Then he thought of biotechnology and wondered if it could be used to make the improved wood preservative he was seeking. "We don't have any usable products yet," he says. But Norfolk Southern's Research and Technical Center may explore the feasibility of a bioengineered preservative.

Just before lunch, the participants at the Center for Creative Lead- 15 ership sit around a U-shaped table in a large, spare room with beige wallpaper that looks like cloth. Two long strings hang from the ceiling. Sensabaugh enters the room and instructs the group to "make the strings meet." People quickly learn that the ends are too far apart to be tied. One person suggests tying weights to the strings to make them longer. Someone else wants to lengthen the strings by wetting them. Another idea is to move the strings closer together. One man removes his belt and ties it to the ends of both strings.

The way a problem is defined greatly influences the way it is solved, 16 says Sensabaugh. Some people define problems adaptively; that is, they accept a set of limitations: The strings don't meet, so extend them in some way. More innovative people redefine the problem: The strings are too far apart, so why not move them closer together.

Innovators are not necessarily more creative than adapters, according 17 to Sensabaugh, but their "creative style" is different. Her point is, when building a creative team, it's desirable to have a mix of adapters and innovators, because they will define and redefine the problem in many ways. From this diversity comes a willingness to play with the problem and find the unusual connections that spark creative ideas.

The insight that it's not only acceptable but actually advantageous to 18 redefine a problem led Dick Wright, vice-president of research and development at the Mead Imaging Division of the Mead Corporation in Dayton, Ohio, and his staff of scientists to "break the mold" and develop a new kind of color-copying paper that is due on the market in 1988. "The Mead Imaging Division began as a small R&D group that was formed to make a copying process in which the light source was included in the copy paper," Wright says. "We hired the Center for Creative Leadership to give a series of seminars. As a result of our training, we went beyond the original idea and developed a silverless process to make high-quality color prints cheaply."

It seems doubtful that creativity exists in a vacuum; we can only be 19 creative at something. "You have to have a mastery of a field," says Gardner. "You can't be a creative composer without knowing music. But merely mastering all the techniques won't make you a creative composer." What sets the technical virtuosos apart from the creative composers, Gardner believes, are factors of personality and temperament.

On a gut level, innovative business people have known this all along. 20 Computer engineers at Data General Corporation looked for exceptional inner drive in the "microkids" they hired for the computer project described in Tracy Kidder's Pulitzer prizewinning book, *The Soul of a New Machine*. The idea was to get engineers fresh out of graduate school who were willing to accept a low salary and work nights and weekends just for the chance to build a better computer. It worked.

Managers can foster the intrinsic motivation necessary to their staff's 21 creativity, according to psychologist Teresa Amabile of Brandeis University. Work environment was cited as the most important stimulant or obstacle to creativity in a study conducted by Amabile in collaboration with the Center for Creative Leadership. She asked 120 managers of R&D labs to describe examples of high and low creativity in their work experience. The obstacle cited most frequently was constraint on their work—being told precisely what to do and how to do it. The most important stimulant was freedom, meaning the opportunity to discuss and develop their ideas.

Kodak established its office of innovation in Rochester, New York, 22 seven years ago to encourage all employees to propose ideas for new products. At that time, it was the first department of its kind at any American corporation. "A chemist whose regular job is to make emulsions may come up with an idea to improve one of our cameras or may suggest a new business opportunity for the company," says Robert Rosenfeld, head of innovation-network development and founder of the office of innovation.

Hundreds of ideas for new products and business ventures that 23
otherwise would not come to the company's attention are submitted
each year, and 3 to 4 percent go all the way to implementation—"a very
high percentage," Rosenfeld says. Over the past few years, the office has
helped Kodak diversify by nurturing new businesses like Eastman Communications, a data communications company. Rosenfeld says 40 percent
of the new ideas fall outside the photography field.

No one has studied the effectiveness of the creativity courses being 24
given to business people. But there's indication that workshops using real
business problems are more effective than those that administer abstract
exercises like "How many uses can you think of for a brick?" "The
research shows that real-world creativity does not correlate very well with
the performance on ideational fluency instruments," writes Harvard's
David Perkins.

He and colleague Catalina Laserna developed a series of lessons on 25
inventive thinking, part of a course on thinking skills that was given for
one year to seventh-grade students in Venezuela. The training involved
analyzing, evaluating, improving and designing everyday objects. When
asked to design a table for a small apartment, the trained students
performed far better than students in a control group, generating nearly
twice as many ideas for overcoming the space constrictions and describing and sketching their designs in greater detail.

On their last day at the Center for Creative Leadership, the partici- 26
pants have a second crack at the computer simulation of new product
development. Although the game requires no idea generation, Fitzwater
says his creativity training shows: It helps him make better "people"
decisions—for example, in staffing and in knowing when to rely on
group consensus and when on personal judgment. His group wins $43
million.

## Post-Reading Questions

1. What does "interhemispheric communication" mean (see paragraphs 4 and 5)? Explain what it is and how it works.
2. This article begins with a brief anecdote. What is the purpose of that
   anecdote? What does this type of opening technique tell you about
   the intended audience and purpose of this article?
3. Describe Gilbert's style in a few sentences. Do you think it is
   effectively aimed at the intended audience of this article? Support
   your answer with at least two or three references to the language of
   the article.
4. What are the three creative thinking techniques used by the Center
   for Creative Leadership? Do they sound innovative to you, or do you
   think the Center is making a big issue out of the obvious? Explain
   the reasons for your answer.

5. Why is the word *play* used in such a positive way in paragraph 17? What does this emphasis suggest to you about the business executives who usually attend these conferences? Why would they need to be encouraged to loosen up in order to become more creative?

# SHEILA TOBIAS ON MATH ANXIETY

### Pre-Reading Questions

1. Describe an experience from your past school life that indicates why you had a difficult time learning a particular subject. Be prepared to read your story aloud to the class or your workshop group.
2. When you had difficulty with a school subject, do you think the cause was inside you or in the way you were taught or treated by teachers, parents, friends, or others? Were there other causes? Give specific reasons for your answer.
3. Do your experiences in math classes support or refute the often expressed belief that women find learning math more difficult than men? Describe some specific experiences that explain your answer. Do you believe young women are expected by society to do as well in math as men? Again, describe some specific experiences that explain your answer.

## THE NATURE OF MATH ANXIETY
### Sheila Tobias

A warm man never knows how a cold man feels.
                                        —Alexander Solzhenitsyn

### SYMPTOMS OF MATH ANXIETY

The first thing people remember about failing at math is that it felt like 1
sudden death. Whether it happened while learning word problems in sixth grade, coping with equations in high school, or first confronting calculus and statistics in college, failure was sudden and very frightening. An idea or a new operation was not just difficult, it was impossible! And instead of asking questions or taking the lesson slowly, assuming that in a month or so they would be able to digest it, people remember the feeling, as certain as it was sudden, that they would *never* go any further in mathematics. If we assume, as we must, that the curriculum was reasonable and that the new idea was merely the next in a series of learnable concepts, that feeling of utter defeat was simply not rational;

and in fact, the autobiographies of math anxious college students and adults reveal that no matter how much the teacher reassured them, they sensed that from that moment on, as far as math was concerned, they were through.

The sameness of that sudden death experience is evident in the very metaphors people use to describe it. Whether it occurred in elementary school, high school, or college, victims felt that a curtain had been drawn, one they would never see behind; or that there was an impenetrable wall ahead; or that they were at the edge of a cliff, ready to fall off. The most extreme reaction came from a math graduate student. Beginning her dissertation research, she suddenly felt that not only could she never solve her research problem (not unusual in higher mathematics), but that she had never understood advanced math at all. She, too, felt her failure as sudden death.

Paranoia comes quickly on the heels of the anxiety attack. "Everyone knows," the victim believes, "that I don't understand this. The teacher knows. Friends know. I'd better not make it worse by asking questions. Then everyone will find out how dumb I really am." This paranoid reaction is particularly disabling because fear of exposure keeps us from constructive action. We feel guilty and ashamed, not only because our minds seem to have deserted us but because we believe that our failure to comprehend this one new idea is proof that we have been "faking math" for years.

In a fine analysis of mathophobia, Mitchell Lazarus explains why we feel like frauds. Math failure, he says, passes through a "latency stage" before becoming obvious either to our teachers or to us. It may in fact take some time for us to realize that we have been left behind. Lazarus outlines the plight of the high school student who has always relied on the memorize-what-to-do approach. "Because his grades have been satisfactory, his problem may not be apparent to anyone, including himself. But when his grades finally drop, as they must, even his teachers are unlikely to realize that his problem is not something new, but has been in the making for years."[1]

It is not hard to figure out why failure to understand mathematics can be hidden for so long. Math is usually taught in discrete bits by teachers who were themselves taught this way; students are tested, bit by bit, as they go along. Some of us never get a chance to integrate all these pieces of information, or even to realize what we are not able to do. We are aware of a lack, but though the problem has been building up for years, the first time we are asked to use our knowledge in a new way, it feels like sudden death. It is not so easy to explain, however, why we take such personal responsibility for having "cheated" our teachers and why so many of us believe that we are frauds. Would we feel the same way if we were floored by irregular verbs in French?

One thing that may contribute to a student's passivity is a common myth about mathematical ability. Most of us believe that people either have or do not have a mathematical mind. It may well be that mathematical imagination and some kind of special intuitive grasp of mathematical principles are needed for advanced research, but surely people who can do college-level work in other subjects should be able to do college-level math as well. Rates of learning may vary. Competence under time pressure may differ. Certainly low self-esteem will interfere. But is there any evidence that a student needs to have a mathematical mind in order to succeed at *learning math*? 6

Leaving aside for the moment the sources of this myth, consider its effects. Since only a few people are supposed to have this mathematical mind, part of our passive reaction to difficulties in learning mathematics is that we suspect we may not be one of "them" and are waiting for our nonmathematical mind to be exposed. It is only a matter of time before our limit will be reached, so there is not much point in our being methodical or in attending to detail. We are grateful when we survive fractions, word problems, or geometry. If that certain moment of failure hasn't struck yet, then it is only temporarily postponed. 7

Sometimes the math teacher contributes to this myth. If the teacher claims an entirely happy history of learning mathematics, she may contribute to the idea that some people—specifically her—are gifted in mathematics and others—the students—are not. A good teacher, to allay this myth, brings in the scratch paper he used in working out the problem to share with the class the many false starts he had to make before solving it. 8

Parents, especially parents of girls, often expect their children to be nonmathematical. If the parents are poor at math, they had their own sudden death experience; if math was easy for them, they do not know how it feels to be slow. In either case, they will unwittingly foster the idea that a mathematical mind is something one either has or does not have. 9

Interestingly, the myth is peculiar to math. A teacher of history, for example, is not very likely to tell students that they write poor exams or do badly on papers because they do not have a historical mind. Although we might say that some people have a "feel" for history, the notion that one is *either* historical or nonhistorical is patently absurd. Yet, because even the experts still do not know how mathematics is learned, we tend to think of math ability as mystical and to attribute the talent for it to genetic factors. This belief, though undemonstrable, is very clearly communicated to us all. 10

These considerations help explain why failure to comprehend a difficult concept may seem like sudden death. We were kept alive so long only by good fortune. Since we were never truly mathematical, we had to memorize things we could not understand, and by memorizing we got 11 through. Since we obviously do not have a mathematical mind, we will make no progress, ever. Our act is over. The curtain down.

## AMBIGUITY, REAL AND IMAGINED

> What is a satisfactory definition? For the philosopher or the scholar, a definition is satisfactory if it applies to those things and only those things that are being defined; this is what logic demands. But in teaching, this will not do: a definition is satisfactory only if the students understand it.
>
> —H. Poincaré

Mathematics autobiographies show that for the beginning student 12 the language of mathematics is full of ambiguity. Though mathematics is supposed to have a very precise language, more precise than our everyday use (this is why math uses symbols), it is true that mathematical terms are never wholly free of the connotations we bring to words, and these layers of meaning may get in the way. The problem is not that there is anything wrong with math; it is that we are not properly initiated into its vocabulary and rules of grammar.

Some math disabled adults will remember, after fifteen to thirty 13 years, that the word "multiply" as used for fractions never made sense to them. "Multiply," they remember wistfully, always meant "to increase." That is the way the word was used in the Bible, in other contexts, and surely the way it worked with whole numbers. (Three times six always produced something larger than either three or six.) But with fractions (except the improper fractions), multiplication always results in something of smaller value. One-third times one-fourth equals one-twelfth, and one-twelfth is considerably smaller than either one-third or one-fourth.

Many words like "multiply" mean one thing (like "increase rapidly") 14 when first introduced. But in the larger context (in this case all rational numbers), the apparently simple meaning becomes confusing. Since students are not warned that "multiplying" has very different effects on fractions, they find themselves searching among the meanings of the word to find out what to do. Simple logic, corresponding to the words they know and trust, seems not to apply.

A related difficulty for many math anxious people is the word "of" as 15 applied to fractions. In general usage, "of" can imply division, as in "a portion of." Yet, with fractions, one-third *of* one-fourth requires multiplication. We can only remember this by suspending our prior associations with the word "of," or by memorizing the rule. Or, take the word "cancel" as used carelessly with fractions. We are told to "cancel" numerators and denominators of fractions. Yet nothing is being "cancelled" in the sense of being removed for all time. The same holds true for negative numbers. Once we have learned to associate the minus sign with subtraction, it takes an explicit lesson to unlearn the old meaning of minus; or, as a mathematician would put it, to learn its meaning as applied to a new kind of number.

Knowles Dougherty, a skilled teacher of mathematics, notes:          16

> It is no wonder that children have trouble learning arithmetic. If you ask an obedient child in first grade, "What is Zero," the child will call out loudly and with certainty, "Zero is nothing." By third grade, he had better have memorized that "Zero is a place-holder." And by fifth grade, if he believes that zero is a number that can be added, subtracted, multiplied by and divided by, he is in for trouble.[2]

People also recall having problems with shapes, never being sure for 17 example whether the word "circle" meant the line around the circle or the space within. Students who had such difficulties felt they were just dumber than everyone else, but in fact the word "circle" needs a far more precise definition. It is in fact neither the circumference nor the area but rather "the locus of points in the plane equidistant from a center" (Fig. 1).*

A mind that is bothered by ambiguity—actual or perceived—is not 18 usually a weak mind, but a strong one. This point is important because mathematicians argue that it is not the subject that is fuzzy but the learner who is imprecise. This may be, but as mathematics is often taught to amateurs differences in meaning between common language and mathematical language need to be discussed. Besides, even if mathematical language is unambiguous, there is no way into it except through our spoken language, in which words are loaded with content and associations. We cannot help but think "increase" when we hear the word "multiply" because of all the other times we have used that word. We have been coloring circles for years before we get to one we have to measure. No wonder we are unsure of what "circle" means. People who do a little better in mathematics than the rest of us are not as bothered by all this. We shall consider the possible reasons for this later on.

Meanwhile, the mathematicians withhold information. Mathemati- 19 cians depend heavily upon customary notation. They have a prior association with almost every letter in the Roman and Greek alphabets, which they don't always tell us about. We think that our teachers are

*One student, learning to find the "least common denominator," took the phrase "least common" to mean "most unusual" and hunted around for the "most unusual denominator" she could find. Instead of finding the smallest common denominator, then, she found a very large one and was appropriately chastised by her teacher for misunderstanding the question.

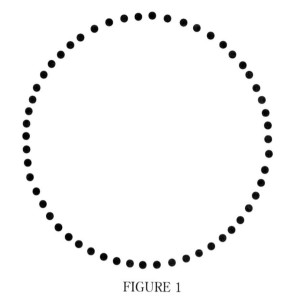

FIGURE 1

choosing $X$ or $a$ or delta ($\Delta$) arbitrarily. Not so. Ever since Descartes, the letters at the end of the alphabet have been used to designate unknowns, the letters at the beginning of the alphabet usually to signify constants, and in math, economics, and physics generally $\Delta$ means "change" or "difference." Though these symbols appear to us to be chosen randomly, the letters are loaded with meaning for "them."

In more advanced algebra, the student's search for meaning is made 20 even more difficult because it is almost impossible to visualize complex mathematical relationships. For me, the fateful moment struck when I was confronted by an operation I could neither visualize nor translate into meaningful words. The expression $X^{-2} = 1/X^2$ did me in. I had dutifully learned that exponents such as $^2$ and $^3$ were shorthand notations for multiplication: a number or a letter squared or cubed was simply multiplied by itself twice or three times. Trying to translate math into words, I considered the possibility that $X^{-2}$ meant something like "$X$ not multiplied by itself" or "multiplied by not-itself." What words or images could convey to me what $X^{-2}$ really meant? To all these questions—and I have asked them many times since—the answer is that $X^{-2}=1/X^2$ is a definition consistent with what has gone before. I have been shown several demonstrations that this definition is indeed consistent with what has gone before.* But at the time I did not want a demonstration or a proof. I wanted an explanation!

I dwell on the $X^{-2}$ example because I have often asked competent 21 mathematicians to recall for me how they felt the first time they were told $X^{-2} = 1/X^2$. Many remember merely believing what they were told in math class, or that they soon found the equivalency useful. Unlike me, they were satisfied with a proof and an illustration that the system works. Why some people should be more distrustful about such matters and less willing to play games of internal consistency than others is a question we shall return to later.

Willing suspension of disbelief is a phrase that comes not from 22 mathematics or science but from literature. A reader must give the narrator an opportunity to create images and associations and to "enter" these into our mind (the way we "enter" information into a computer) in order to carry us along in the story or poem. The very student who can accept the symbolic use of language in poetry where "birds are hushed by the moon," or the disorienting treatment of time in books by Thomas Mann and James Joyce, may balk when mathematics employs familiar words in an unfamiliar way. If willingness to suspend disbelief is specific to some tasks and not to others, perhaps it is related to trust. One counsellor explains math phobia by saying, "If you don't feel safe, you won't take risks." People who don't trust math may be too wary of math to take risks.

A person's ability to accept the counter-intuitive use of time in 23 Thomas Mann's work and not the new meaning of the negative exponent does not imply that there are two kinds of minds, the verbal and the mathematical. I do not subscribe to the simple-minded notion that we are one or the other and that ability in one area leads inevitably to disability in the other. Rather, I think that verbal people feel comfortable with language early in life, perhaps because they enjoyed success at talking and reading. When mathematics contradicts assumptions acquired in other subjects, such people need special reassurance before they will venture on.

Conflicts between mathematical language and common language 24 may also account for students' distrust of their intuition. If several

---

*While interviewing for this book, I have finally found out that negative two is a different kind of number from positive two and that it was naïve of me to think that it would have the same or similar effect on $X$. And it does work. If you divide $X^3$ by $X^5$ (remember you subtract exponents when you divide) you end up with $1/X^2$. See the following:

$$X^{-2} \equiv \frac{X^3}{X^5} = \frac{XXX}{XXXXX} = \frac{1}{XX} = \frac{1}{X^2}$$

associated meanings are floating around in someone's head and the text considers only one, the learner will, at the very least, feel alone. Until someone tries to get inside the learner's head or the learner figures out a way to search among the various meanings of the word for the one that is called for, communication will break down, too. This problem is not unique to mathematics, but when people already feel insecure about math, linguistic confusion increases their sense of being out of control. And so long as teachers continue to argue, as they have to me, that words like "multiply" and "of," the negative exponents, and the "circles" or "disks" are not ambiguous at all but perfectly consistent with their definitions, then students will continue to feel that math is simply not for them.

Some mathematics texts solve the problem of ambiguity by virtually 25 eliminating language. College-level math textbooks are even more laconic than elementary texts. One reason may be the difficulty of expressing mathematical ideas in language that is easily agreed upon. Another is the assumption that by the time students get to college they should be able to read symbols. But for some number of students (we cannot know how many since they do not take college-level math) proofs, symbolic formulations, and examples are not enough. After I had finally learned that $X^{-2}$ must equal $1/X^2$ because it was consistent with the rule that when dividing numbers with exponents we subtract the exponents, I looked up "negative exponents" in a new high school algebra text. There I found the following paragraph.

### Negative and Zero Exponents

The set of numbers used as exponents in our discussion so far has been the set of positive integers. This is the only set which can be used when exponents are defined as they were in Chapter One. In this section, however, we would like to expand this set to include all integers (positive, negative and zero) as exponents. This will, of course, require further definitions. These new definitions must be consistent with the system and we will expect all of the laws of exponents as well as all previously known facts to still be true.[3]

Although this paragraph is very clear in setting the stage to explain 26 negative exponents through definitions which are presumably forthcoming, it does not provide a lot of explanation. No wonder people who need words to make sense of things give up.

## THE DROPPED STITCH

"The day they introduced fractions, I had the measles." Or the 27 teacher was out for a month, the family moved, there were more snow days that year than ever before (or since). People who use events like these to account for their failure at math did, nevertheless, learn how to spell. True, math is especially cumulative. A missing link can damage understanding much as a dropped stitch ruins a knitted sleeve. But being sick or in transit or just too far behind to learn the next new idea is not reason enough for doing poorly at math forever after. It is unlikely that one missing link can abort the whole process of learning elementary arithmetic.

In fact, mathematical ideas that are rather difficult to learn at age 28 seven or eight are much easier to comprehend one, two, or five years later if we try again. As we grow older, our facility with language improves; we have many more mathematical concepts in our minds, developed from everyday living; we can ask more and better questions. Why, then, do we let ourselves remain permanently ignorant of fractions or decimals or graphs? Something more is at work than a missed class.

It is of course comforting to have an excuse for doing poorly at 29 math, better than having to concede that one does not have a mathematical mind. Still, the dropped stitch concept is often used by math anxious people to excuse their failure. It does not explain, however, why in later years they did not take the trouble to unravel the sweater and pick up where they left off.

Say they did try a review book. Chances are it would not be helpful. 30 Few texts on arithmetic are written for adults.* How insulting to go back to a "Run, Spot, run!" level of elementary arithmetic, when arithmetic can be infinitely clearer and more interesting if it is discussed at an adult level.

Moreover, when most of us learned math we learned dependence as 31 well. We needed the teacher to explain, the textbook to drill us, the back of the book to tell us the right answers. Many people say that they never mastered the multiplication table, but I have encountered only one person so far who carries a multiplication table in his wallet. He may have no more skills than the others, but at least he is trying to make himself autonomous. The greatest value of using simple calculators in elementary school may, in the end, be to free pupils from dependence on something or someone beyond their control.

Adults can easily pick up those dropped stitches once they decide to 32 do something about them. In one math counselling session for educators and psychologists, the following arithmetic bugbears were exposed:

How do you get a percentage out of a fraction like $7/16$?
Where does "pi" come from?

---

*Deborah Hughes-Hallett is writing a book (W. W. Norton, 1978) for adults and college students that starts with arithmetic and brings the reader up to calculus, in two volumes.

> How do you do a problem like: Two men are painters. Each paints a room in a different time. How long does it take them to paint the room together?*

The issues were taken care of within half an hour.

This leads me to believe that people are anxious not because they dropped a stitch long ago but rather because they accepted an ideology that we must reject: *that if we haven't learned something so far it is probably because we can't.*

One of the reasons we did not ask enough questions when we were younger is that many of us were caught in a double bind between a fear of appearing too dumb in class and a fear of being too smart. Why anyone should be afraid of being too smart in math is hard to understand except for the prevailing notion that math whizzes are not normal. Boys who want to be popular can be hurt by this label. But it is even more difficult for girls to be smart in math. Matina Horner, in her survey of high-achieving college women's attitudes toward academic success, found that such women are especially nervous about competing with men on what they think of as men's turf.[4] Since many people perceive ability in mathematics as unfeminine, fear of success may well interfere with ability to learn math.

The young woman who is frightened of seeming too smart in math must be very careful about asking questions in class because she never knows when a question is a really good one. "My nightmare," one woman remembers, "was that one day in math class I would innocently ask a question and the teacher would say, 'Now that's a fascinating issue, one that mathematicians spent years trying to figure out.' And if that happened, I would surely have had to leave town, because my social life would have been ruined." This is an extreme case, probably exaggerated, but the feeling is typical. Mathematical precocity, asking interesting questions, meant risking exposure as someone unlike the rest of the gang.

It is not even so difficult to ask questions that gave the ancients trouble. When we remember that the Greeks had no notation for multi-digit numbers and that even Newton, the inventor of the calculus, would have been hard pressed to solve some of the equations given to beginning calculus students today, we can appreciate that young woman's trauma.

At the same time, a student who is too inhibited to ask questions may never get the clarification needed to go on. We will never know how many students developed fear of math and loss of self-confidence because

---

*Pi* can be derived by drawing many-sided polygons (like squares, pentagons, hexagons, etc.) and measuring the ratio between their diameters and their perimeters. Even if you do this roughly, the ratios will approach 3.14.

they could not ask questions in class. But the math anxious often refer to this kind of inhibition. In one case, a counsellor in a math clinic spent almost a semester persuading a student to ask her math teacher a question *after* class. She was a middling math student, with a B in linear algebra. She asked questions in her other courses, but could not or would not ask them in math. She did not entirely understand her inhibition, but with the aid of the counsellor, she came to believe it had something to do with a fear of appearing too smart.

There is much more to be said about women and mathematics. At 38 this point it is enough to note that some teachers and most pupils of both sexes believe that boys naturally do better in math than girls. Even bright girls believe this. When boys fail a math quiz their excuse is that they did not work hard enough. Girls who fail are three times more likely to attribute their lack of success to the belief that they "simply cannot do math."[5] Ironically, fear of being too smart may lead to such passivity in math class that eventually these girls also develop a feeling that they are dumb. It may also be that these women are not as low in self-esteem as they seem, but by failing at mathematics they resolve a conflict between the need to be competent and the need to be liked. The important thing is that until young women are encouraged to believe that they have the right to be smart in mathematics, no amount of supportive, nurturant teaching is likely to make much difference.

## DISTRUST OF INTUITION

Mathematicians use intuition, conjecture and guesswork all the time except when they are in the classroom.
                    —Joseph Warren, Mathematician

Thou shalt not guess.
                    —Sign in a high school math classroom

At the Math Clinic at Wesleyan University, there is always a word 39 problem to be solved. As soon as one is solved, another is put in its place. Everyone who walks into the clinic, whether a teacher, a math anxious person, a staff member, or just a visitor, has to give the word problem a try. Thus, we have stimulated numerous experiences with a variety of word problems and by debriefing *both* people who have solved these problems and people who have given up on them, we gain another insight into the nature of math anxiety.

One of the arithmetic word problems that was on the board for a 40 long time is the Tire Problem:

A car goes 20,000 miles on a long trip. To save wear, the five tires are rotated regularly. How many miles will each tire have gone by the end of the trip?

Most people readily acknowledge that a car has five tires and that four are in use at any one time. Poor math students who are not anxious or blocked will poke around at the problem for a while and then come up with the idea that four-fifths of 20,000, which is 16,000 miles, is the answer. They don't always know exactly why they decided to take four-fifths of 20,000. They sometimes say it "came" to them as they were thinking about the tires on the car and the tire in the trunk. The important thing is that they *tried* it and when it resulted in 16,000 miles, they gave 16,000 a "reasonableness test." Since 16,000 seemed reasonable (that is, less than 20,000 miles but not a whole lot less), they were pretty sure they were right.

The math anxious student responds very differently. The problem is 41 beyond her (or him). She cannot begin to fathom the information. She cannot even imagine how the five tires are used. She cannot come up with any strategy for solving it. She gives up. Later in the debriefing session, the counsellor may ask whether the fraction four-fifths occurred to her at all while she was thinking about the problem. Sometimes the answer will be yes. But if she is asked why she did not try out four-fifths of 20,000 (the only other number in the problem), the response will be—and we have heard this often enough to take it very seriously—"I figured that if it was in my head it had to be wrong."

The assumption that if it is in one's head it has to be wrong or, as 42 others put it, "If it's easy for me, it can't be math," is a revealing statement about the self. Math anxious people seem to have little or no faith in their own intuition. If an idea comes into their heads or a strategy appears to them in a flash they will assume it is wrong. They do not trust their intuition. Either they remember the "right formula" immediately or they give up.

Mathematicians, on the other hand, trust their intuition in solving 43 problems and readily admit that without it they would not be able to do much mathematics. The difference in attitude toward intuition, then, seems to be another tangible distinction between the math anxious and people who do well in math.

The distrust of intuition gives the math counsellor a place to begin to 44 ask questions: Why does intuition appear to us to be untrustworthy? When has it failed us in the past? How might we improve our intuitive grasp of mathematical principles? Has anyone ever tried to "educate" our intuition, improve our repertoire of ideas by teaching us strategies for solving problems? Math anxious people usually reply that intuition was not allowed as a tool in problem solving. Only the rational, computational parts of their brain belonged in math class. If a teacher or parent used intuition at all in solving problems he rarely admitted it, and when the student on occasion did guess right in class he was punished for not being able to reconstruct his method. Yet people who trust their intuition do not see it as "irrational" or "emotional" at all. They perceive intuition as flashes of insight into the rational mind. Victims of math anxiety need to understand this, too.


## THE CONFINEMENT OF EXACT ANSWERS

Computation involves going from a question to an answer. Mathematics involves going from an answer to a question.
                                        —Peter Hilton, Mathematician


Another source of self-distrust is that mathematics is taught as an 45 exact science. There is pressure to get an exact right answer, and when things do not turn out right, we panic. Yet people who regularly use mathematics in their work say that it is far more useful to be able to answer the question, "What is a little more than five multiplied by a little less than three?" than to know *only* that five times three equals 15.* Many math anxious adults recall with horror the timed tests they were subjected to in elementary, junior and senior high school with the emphasis on getting a unique right answer. They liked social studies and English better because there were so many "right answers," not just one. Others were frustrated at not being able to have discussions in math class. Somewhere they or their teachers got the wrong notion that there is an inherent contradiction between rigor and debate.

This emphasis on right answers has many psychological benefits. It 46 provides a way to do our own evaluation on the spot and to be judged fairly whether or not the teacher likes us. Emphasis on the right answer, however, may result in panic when that answer is not at hand and, even worse, lead to "premature closure" when it is. Consider the student who does get the right answer quickly and directly. If she closes the book and does not continue to reflect on the problem, she will not find other ways of solving it, and she will miss an opportunity to add to her array of problem-solving methods. In any case, getting the right answer does not necessarily imply that one has grasped the full significance of the problem. Thus, the right-answer emphasis may inhibit the learning potential of good students and poor students alike.

In altering the learning atmosphere for the math anxious the tutor or 47 counsellor needs to talk frankly about the difficulties of doing math. The tutor's scratch paper might be more useful to the students than a perfectly conceived solution. Doing problems afresh in class at the risk of making errors publicly can also link the tutor with the student in the

---

*A little more than five multiplied by a little less than three will produce a range between 12.5 and 16.5. Inequalities, of which this is one example, are common in more advanced math, as are equations that have more than one solution.

process of discovery. Inviting all students to put their answers, right or wrong, before the class will relieve some of the panic that comes when students fail to get the answer the teacher wants. And, as most teachers know, looking carefully at wrong answers can give them good clues to what is going on in students' heads.

Although an answer that checks can provide immediate positive feedback, which aids in learning, the right answer may come to signify authoritarianism (on the part of the teacher), competitiveness (with other students), and painful evaluation. None of these unpleasant experiences is usually intended, any more than the premature closure or panic, but for some students who are insecure about mathematics the right-answer emphasis breeds hostility as well as anxiety. Worst of all, the "right answer" isn't always the right one at all. It is only "right" in the context of the amount of mathematics one has learned so far. First graders, who are working only with whole numbers, are told they are "right" if they answer that five (apples) cannot be divided between two (friends). But later, when they work with fractions, they will find out that five *can* be equally divided by giving each friend two and one-half apples. In fact both answers are right. You cannot divide five one-dollar bills equally between two people without getting change. 48

The search for the right answer soon evolves into the search for the right formula. Some students cannot even put their minds to a complex problem or play with it for a while because they assume they are expected to know something they have forgotten. 49

Take this problem, for example, 50

> Amy Lowell goes out to buy cigars. She has 25 coins in her pocket, $7.15 in all. She has seven more dimes than nickels and she has quarters, too. How many dimes, nickels, and quarters does she have?

Most people who have done well in high school algebra will begin to call the number of nickels $X$, the number of dimes $X + 7$, and the number of quarters $7.15$ minus $(5X + 10X + 70)$ without realizing that Amy Lowell must have miscounted her change, because even if all 25 coins in her pocket were quarters (the largest coin she has), her change would total $6.25, not $7.15.*

This is a tricky problem, which is fair, as opposed to a trick problem which is not. But it also shows how searching for the right formula can cause us to miss an obviously impossible situation. The right formula may become a substitute for thinking, just as the right answer may replace consideration of other possibilities. Somehow students of math should learn that the power of mathematics lies not only in exactness but in the processing of information. 51

---

*I am indebted to Jean Smith for this example.

## SELF-DEFEATING SELF-TALK

One way to show people what is going on in their heads is to have them 52
keep a "math diary," a running commentary of their thoughts, both
mathematical and emotional, as they do their homework or go about
their daily lives. Sometimes a tape recorder can be used to get at the same
thing. The goal is twofold: to show the student and the instructor the
recurring mathematical errors that are getting in the way and to make the
student hear his own "self-talk." "Self-talk" is what we say to ourselves
when we are in trouble. Do we egg ourselves on with encouragement
and suggestions? Or do we engage in self-defeating behaviors that only
make things worse?

Inability to handle frustration contributes to math anxiety. When a 53
math anxious person sees that a problem is not going to be easy to solve,
he tends to quit right away, believing that no amount of time or
rereading or reformulation of the problem will make it any clearer.
Freezing and quitting may be as much the result of destructive self-talk as
of unfamiliarity with the problem. If we think we have no strategy with
which to begin work, we may never find one. But if we can talk ourselves
into feeling comfortable and secure, we may let in a good idea.

To find out how much we are talking ourselves into failure we have 54
to begin to listen to ourselves doing math. The tape recorder, the math
diary, the self-monitoring that some people can do silently are all
techniques for tuning in to ourselves. Most of us who handle frustration
very poorly in math handle it very well in other subjects. It is useful to
watch ourselves doing other things. What do we do there to keep going?
How can these strategies be applied to math?

At the very minimum this kind of tuning in may identify the 55
particular issue giving trouble. It is not very helpful to know that "math
makes me feel nervous and uncomfortable" or that "numbers make me
feel uneasy and confused," as some people say. But it may be quite useful
to realize that one kind of problem is more threatening than another.
One excerpt from a math diary is a case in point:

> Here I go again. I am always ready to give up when the equation looks as
> though it's too complicated to come out right. But the other week, an
> equation that started out looking like this one did turn out to be right, so I
> shouldn't be so depressed about it.

This is constructive self-talk. By keeping a diary or talking into a tape
recorder we can begin to recognize our own pattern of resistance and
with luck we may soon learn to control it. This particular person is
beginning to understand how and why she jumps to negative conclusions
about her work. She is learning to sort out the factual mistakes she makes
from the logical and even the psychological errors. Soon she will be able

to recognize the mistakes she makes *only* because she is anxious. Note that she has been encouraged to think and to talk about her feelings while doing mathematics. She is not ashamed or guilty about the most irrational of thoughts, not frightened to observe even the onset of depression in herself; she seems confident that her mind will not desert her.

    The diary or tape recorder technique has only been tried so far with 56 college-age students and adults. So far as we can tell, it is effective only when used in combination with other nonthreatening teaching devices, such as acceptance of discussion of feelings in class, psychological support outside of class, and an instructor willing to demystify mathematics. The goal in such a situation is not to get the right answer. The goal is to achieve mastery and above all autonomy in doing math. In the end, we can only learn when we feel in control.

## REFERENCES

This chapter is based primarily on interviews with and observations of math anxious students and adults. These people are not typical of those who are math incompetent. Most of them are very bright and enjoy school success in other subjects, but they avoid or openly fear mathematics.

1. Mitchell Lazarus, "Mathophobia: Some Personal Speculations," *The Principal,* January/February, 1974, p. 18.
2. Knowles Dougherty. Personal communication to the author.
3. J. Louis Nanney and John L. Cable, *Elementary Algebra: A Skills Approach,* Boston, Allyn and Bacon, Inc., 1974, p. 215.
4. Matina Horner, "Fear of Success," *Psychology Today,* November, 1969, p. 38ff.
5. Sanford Dornbusch, as quoted in John Ernest, "Mathematics and Sex," *American Mathematics Monthly,* Vol. 83, No. 8, October, 1976, p. 599.

### Post-Reading Questions

1. List the symptoms of math anxiety as defined by Tobias. What social and psychological reasons lie behind these symptoms? What events in a young person's life would cause these symptoms? What would reinforce them as the person grew older?
2. Tobias spends time explaining why the language associated with mathematics (see paragraphs 12 to 18) creates problems for many "math-anxious" people. What is Tobias suggesting about how this particular problem could be solved?
3. What does Tobias mean by the "dropped stitch" metaphor (see paragraphs 27 to 33)? Why does she think it is important to consider the phenomenon? What does the metaphor suggest are some of the reasons for math anxiety?

4.  Why does Tobias suggest keeping a math diary (see paragraph 54)? How would keeping a diary help someone suffering from math anxiety?
5.  What kinds of choices did Tobias have to make about the language she would use to discuss math anxiety? What do her decisions about language suggest about her intended readers? What specific language features led you to identify these intended readers?
6.  Do you think that Tobias would agree or disagree with Howard Gardner's idea of multiple intelligences? Why?
7.  Do you think Tobias would agree with Robert Sternberg's contention that intelligence is at least partially influenced by social conditions? Where in her essay does she seem to most directly support that contention?

# ROBERT SOKOLOWSKI ON ARTIFICIAL INTELLIGENCE

## Pre-Reading Questions

1.  Working in a group with other students, list the different kinds of reactions all members of the group have toward artificial intelligence. What are the emotional reactions, the rational arguments for and against, and the associations held toward artificial intelligence? What experiences and reasons explain these reactions?
2.  Work up your own draft definition of artificial intelligence before you read Sokolowski's essay. Later, you can compare your initial definition with the one you give after reading the essay and discussing the concept with others.
3.  Do machines such as calculators and computers actually think? Consider your own experiences with so-called "thinking machines"— calculators, bank-teller machines, and service computers of all kinds. Has your experience been positive or negative? Why?
4.  To what other forms of thinking—writing, mathematics, formal logic, the scientific method—is the thinking of machines similar? In what ways?

## NATURAL AND ARTIFICIAL INTELLIGENCE
### Robert Sokolowski

In this essay we will not attempt to decide whether artificial intelligence  1
is the same as natural intelligence. Instead we will examine some of the issues and terms that must be clarified before that question can be resolved. We will discuss how the question about the relationship between natural and artificial intelligence can be formulated.

One of the first things that must be clarified is the ambiguous word  2
*artificial*. This adjective can be used in two senses, and it is important to
determine which one applies in the term *artificial intelligence*. The word
*artificial* is used in one sense when it is applied, say, to flowers, and in
another sense when it is applied to light. In both cases something is
called artificial because it is fabricated. But in the first usage artificial
means that the thing seems to be, but really is not, what it looks like. The
artificial is the merely apparent; it just shows how something else looks.
Artificial flowers are only paper, not flowers at all; anyone who takes
them to be flowers is mistaken. But artificial light is light and it does
illuminate. It is fabricated as a substitute for natural light, but once
fabricated it is what it seems to be. In this sense the artificial is not the
merely apparent, not simply an imitation of something else. The appearance of the thing reveals what it is, not how something else looks.

The movement of an automobile is another example of something  3
that is artificial in the second sense of the word. An automobile moves
artificially; it moves only because human beings have constructed it to
move and have made it go by the release of stored energy. But it really
does move—it does not only seem to be moving. In contrast, the
artificial wood paneling in the car only seems to be wood; it burns,
bends, breaks, and decays as plastic, not wood. It also smells, sounds, and
feels like plastic, not wood. It seems to be wood only to vision and only
from a certain angle and in certain kinds of light.

In which sense do we use the word *artificial* when we speak of  4
artificial intelligence? Critics of artificial intelligence, those who disparage
the idea and say it has been overblown and oversold, would claim that
the term is used in the first sense, to mean the merely apparent. They
would say that artificial intelligence is really nothing but complex
mechanical structures and electrical processes that present an illusion (to
the gullible) of some sort of thinking. Supporters of the idea of artificial
intelligence, those who claim that the term names something genuine
and not merely apparent, would say that the word *artificial* is used in the
second of the senses we have distinguished. Obviously, they would say,
thinking machines are artifacts; obviously they are run by human beings;
but once made and set in motion, the machines do think. Their thinking
may be different from that of human beings in some ways, just as the
movement of a car is different from that of a rabbit and the flight of an
airplane is different from that of a bird, but it is a kind of genuine
thinking, just as there is genuine motion in the car and genuine flight in
the plane.

Suppose we were to claim that artificial intelligence is a genuine,  5
though constructed, intelligence. Must we then prove the truth of that
claim? Are we obliged to show that the machines really think, that they
do not only seem to possess intelligence? Perhaps not; no one has to
prove the fact that artificial light illuminates and that airplanes really fly.

We just see that they do. If thinking machines display the activity of thinking, why should we not admit that they truly are intelligent?

The problem is that thinking is not as visible and palpable as are illumination, motion, and flight; it is not as easy to say whether thinking is present or not. Even when we talk with another human being, we cannot always be sure if that person is speaking and acting thoughtfully or merely reciting by rote, behaving automatically. And there are cases in which machines only seem to think but really do not: the electronic calculator can do remarkable things, but only someone who is deceived by it—someone like the person who takes artificial flowers for real ones—would say that the calculator possesses its own intelligence. The calculator may reveal the intelligence of those who built and programmed it, but it does not originate its own thinking.

How is artificial intelligence different from the calculator? How is it different from numeric computing? What does it do that we can call its own machine thinking, its own activity that cannot be dissolved into the thinking of the people who made and programmed the machine? If we are to claim that the thinking machine, though an artifact, does exhibit intelligence, we must clarify what we mean by the "thinking" it is said to execute. This may not be a proof, but it is an explanation, and some such justification seems to be required to support our claim that machines think.

Alan Turing set down the principle that if a machine behaves intelligently, we must credit it with intelligence.[1] The behavior is the key. But the Turing test cannot stand by itself as the criterion for the intelligence of machines. Machine thinking will always reproduce only part of natural thinking; it may be limited, for instance, to the responses that are produced on a screen. In this respect our experience of the machine's thinking is like talking to someone on the telephone, not like being with that person and seeing him act, speak, and respond to new situations. How do we know that our partial view of the machine's intelligence is not like that angle of vision from which artificial flowers look real to us? How can we know that we are not being deceived if we are caught in the perspective from which a merely apparent intelligence looks very much like real intelligence? Some sort of argument has to be added to the Turing test to show that artificial intelligence is artificial in the second sense of the word and not in the first—that although it is constructed and partial, it is still genuine and not merely apparent. We need to say more about intelligence to show whether it really is there or not, and we need to clarify the difference between its natural and artificial forms.

I

In discussing the distinction between natural and artificial intelligence, we must be careful not to establish divisions that are abrupt and naive. If we formulate our question in terms of stark alternatives we may put our argument into a straitjacket and deprive it of the flexibility it needs. With this rigid approach we might set the computer in opposition to the brain, considering natural intelligence an activity carried on in the brain, artificial intelligence an activity carried on in computers. Here the brain, there the computer; here the natural intelligence, there the artificial intelligence. The activity is defined by the material in which it takes place.

This approach is blunt and naive because it neglects something that 10 bridges natural and artificial intelligence: the written word. Artificial intelligence does not simply mimic the brain and nervous system; it transforms, codifies, and manipulates written discourse. And natural intelligence is not just an organic activity that occurs in a functioning brain; it also is embodied in the words that are written on paper, inscribed in clay, painted on a billboard. Writing comes between the brain and the computer.

When thinking is embodied in the written word, there is something 11 artificial about it. Consider a flashing neon sign that says Hotel. People do not react to the sign as they would to a rock or a tree. They both read the sign and answer it. They behave toward it in a manner analogous to the way they would react to someone who told them that the building was a hotel and that they could get a room there. Furthermore, the person who put the sign where it is—the one who is stating something in the sign and can be held responsible for saying what the sign says—does not have to remain near it for the sign to have its effect. He can let the sign go; it works without him. It is an artifice, and one that manifests and communicates something to someone, inviting both an interpretation and a response.

Of course, artificial intelligence promises to do more than writing 12 can do, but it has a foothold in writing: it puts into motion the thinking that is embodied in writing. Our philosophical challenge is to clarify what sort of motion thinking is.[2] The continuity between writing and artificial intelligence should make us less apprehensive about being somehow replaced by thinking machines. In a way, we are already replaced by the written word. If I leave written instructions behind me, I do not have to be around for the instructions to take effect. But this does not cancel my thinking; it enhances it. If we find written records in the ruins of an ancient city, we do not think that the speakers in that city were obliterated as speakers by the documents or that their subjectivity was destroyed by them; we think that their speech was more vividly appreciated as speech in contrast with the written word. We also believe that their thinking was amplified by their writing, not muffled by it, because through the written word they are able to "speak" to us. Likewise, the codification of writing in artificial intelligence does not mean that we no longer have to think. Rather, our own thinking can be more vividly appreciated in contrast with what can be done by machines; the fact that some dimensions of thinking can be carried out mechanically makes us more vividly aware of those dimensions that we alone can perform. If artificial thinking can substitute for some of our thinking as artificial light can take over some of the functions of natural light, then the kinds of thinking for which no substitute is possible will surface more clearly as our own.

The gradual diffusion of writing into human affairs can serve as a 13 historical analogue for the seepage of artificial intelligence into human exchanges. Writing did not simply replace the linguistic activities that people carried out before there was writing; its major impact was to make new kinds of activity possible and to give a new shape to old kinds. It enlarged and differentiated economic, legal, political, and aesthetic activities, and it made history possible. It even allowed religion to take on a new form: it permitted the emergence of religions involving a book, with all the attendant issues of text, interpretation, and commentary. Writing did all this by amplifying intelligence. Printing accelerated the spread of the written word, but it did not change the nature of writing.

The question that can be put to artificial intelligence is whether it is 14 merely an extension of printing or a readjustment in the human enterprise that began when writing entered into human affairs. Word processing is clearly just a refinement of printing, a kind of glorified typing, but artificial intelligence appears to be more than that. It seems able to reform the embodiment of thought that was achieved in and by writing. What will artificial intelligence prove to be? Will it be just a postscript to writing, or will writing turn out to be a four-thousand-year prelude to artificial intelligence? Will writing's full impact lie in its being a preparation for mechanical thinking?

If artificial intelligence is indeed a transformation of writing, then it 15 is more like artificial light and less like artificial flowers: a genuine substitute for some forms of thought, not merely a superficial imitation. Thinking is shaped by writing; intelligence is modified when it takes on the written form; writing permits us to identify and differentiate things in ways that were not possible when we could speak but not write. If artificial intelligence can in turn transform writing, it may be able to embody a kind of intelligence that cannot occur in any other way, just as the automobile provides a kind of motion that was not available before the car was invented.

In the case of any new technology, the new is first understood within 16 the horizon set by the old. The earliest automobiles, for instance, looked very much like carriages. It takes time for truly new possibilities to assert themselves, to shape both themselves and the environment within which they must find their place. It took time for the automobile to generate highways and garages. The expert systems developed in the early stages of artificial intelligence are following this pattern.[3] They attempt to replace a rather prosaic form of thinking, a kind that seems ripe for replacement: the kind exercised by the man in the information booth or the pharmacist—

the person who knows a lot of facts and can coordinate them and draw out some of their implications. Expert systems are the horseless carriages of artificial intelligence. They are analogous to the early writings that just recorded the contents of the royal treasury or the distribution of the grain supply.

This is not to belittle expert systems. The initial, small, obvious 17 replacements for the old ways of doing things must settle in before the more distinctive accomplishments of a new intellectual form can take place—in this case, before the Dantes, Shakespeares, and Newtons, or the Jaguars, highways, and service stations of artificial intelligence can arise. And just as the people who experienced the beginning of writing could hardly imagine what Borges and Bohr could do, or what a national library or a medical research center or an insurance contract could be, so we—if artificial intelligence is indeed a renovation of writing—will find it hard to conceive what form the flowering of machine thinking may take.

Furthermore, there is a lot of human thinking that is rather mechan- 18 ical. It demands only that we be well informed and that we be able to register relationships and draw inferences within what we know. The extent to which such routine thinking permeates our intellectual activity may only be realized when artificial thinking succeeds in doing most of this work for us.[4] Large tracts of scientific data-gathering, measuring, and correlation, of planning strategies in taxation or insurance, of working out acceptable combinations of antibiotics and matching them with infections, of constructing networks and schedules for airline travel, of figuring out how to cope with laws and regulations, are tasks that can be codified and organized according to specifiable rules. Artificial intelligence will most readily be able to relieve us of such laborious thinking. But, since there are few unmixed blessings, it is also likely to introduce new routines and drudgeries and unwelcome complexities that would not have arisen if computers had not come into being.

We are quite properly astonished at how machines can store knowl- 19 edge and information, and at how they even seem to "think" with this knowledge and information. But these capabilities of machines should not blind us to something that is simpler but perhaps even more startling: the uncanny storage and representation that occurs when meaning is embodied in the written word. In artificial intelligence the embodiment changes, but the major difference is in the new kind of embodying material, not in embodiment as such. The neon light flashing the word Hotel engages many of the features found in thinking machines: a meaning is available, a course of behavior is indicated, inferences are legitimated. There seems to be no one who speaks or owns the meaning—the meaning seems to float—and yet it is somehow there in the sign. The meaning is available for everyone and seems to outlast any particular human speaker.

In artificial intelligence such meanings get embodied in materials 20
that permit extremely complex manipulations of a syntactic kind. Hence
the machine seems to reason, whereas the sign does not seem to reason
but only to state. Instead of simply comparing computers and brains, we
should also compare the "reasoning" of the machine with the "stating"
of the sign, and examine storage and representation as they occur in the
machine and in writing.

It is true that artificial intelligence may go beyond printouts into 21
artificially voiced speech. It may move beyond printing to the more
subtle embodiment of meaning that occurs in sounds. If it succeeds in
doing so, its "speech" will have been a transformation of its writing and
will bear the imprint of writing. Artificial intelligence will have moved in
a direction that is the reverse of that followed by natural thinking, which
went from voiced speech to the written word.

## II

The written word can serve as a broker between natural and artificial 22
intelligence. It straddles the two: natural intelligence is embodied and
modified in writing, yet writing is somewhat artificial, something of an
artifact. Let us investigate this mediating role of writing more closely.
How can writing serve as a bridge to artificial intelligence?

We will circle into this issue by asking a more general question about 23
the conditions necessary for the emergence of artificial intelligence: What
things are required to allow artificial intelligence to come into being? An
obvious answer is that certain computer languages, such as LISP and
Prolog, are necessary. Another is that the computers themselves, with the
appropriate hardware, architecture, and memory, are also required. Still
another answer is that the mathematical logic devised during the past
hundred years or so by Gottlob Frege, Giuseppe Peano, Bertrand Russell,
and others was necessary as a condition for both the software and the
hardware we now have. It is interesting that these advances in mathematics
and logic were carried on for purely theoretical reasons—to show, for
example, that arithmetic is a part of pure logic (Frege's goal)—and not to
prepare a language for thinking machines.[5] The technological application
took advantage of the opening provided by the theoretical achievement:
"The opportunity created the appetite, the supply the demand."[6]

All these prerequisites for artificial intelligence—computer lan- 24
guages, computer hardware, and formalized logics—have been made by
identifiable persons at definite times. We can give names and dates for
their invention. But there is another enabling condition that is of still
another nature. It is of much greater philosophical interest, and it is also
much more elusive; it is hard to say when it appeared on the scene and
who was responsible for bringing it about. But without it, neither

artificial intelligence nor any of its other prerequisites could have arisen. The condition in question is that we are able to take a linguistic sign in two ways. We can think about what the sign expresses, or we can think about the sign and the way it is composed.

To illustrate the distinction, consider two ways of translating.[7] Consider first the translator who works at international meetings and who translates speeches as they are being given. Such a translator thinks about the topic being discussed. If the speech is about ocean shipping, the translator thinks about ships, cargoes, laws, coastlines, and ocean currents. He talks along with the original speaker; he may anticipate some of the speaker's phrases or words, and might even sometimes speak ahead of the speaker. The translator can do this because he is guided by the things that are spoken about and presented in the speech; he does not focus on analyzing the speaker's words.

In contrast, consider someone who is learning Greek and trying to translate a Greek text. He inspects each word, notices the word endings, picks out which word must be the verb and which the subject, tries to figure out how this word results from certain elisions and contractions, tries to determine what it means and how it fits with the other words. Gradually he figures out a possible sense for the sentence. In this case what is expressed in the words does not guide the translation; rather, the thing meant comes last, only after the words have been the direct concern for quite some time. This translator could not anticipate the speaker's words because the translator is not being guided by the subjects discussed. In this case the things expressed are on the margin of attention while the words are the focus of thought, whereas in the first case the words are on the margin while the subject expressed is in focus.

We can shift from a focus on what is expressed to a focus on words, we can move back to the things expressed, and we can move back and forth again and again. When we are in one focus, the other always remains on the margin as a focus we can enter. And the two foci are not merely annexed to each other; each is what it is only in conjunction with the other. The focus on words as words is possible because it is played off against the focus on what the words express; the focus on the subject is what it is (for us as speakers) only as played off against a focus on what the subject is called or what it could be called. There are no words except as drawn into this double perspective; there are no words just "lying around."

Now artificial intelligence is possible because we can turn our attention quite decisively toward the word, and instead of analyzing its grammatical or phonemic composition, we can begin to codify the word—to replace its letters by a series of binary digits and its syntactical possibilities by computerized operations. We can alphabetize and grammatize the word in a new way. We can reduce it to strings of ones and zeros and rules of manipulation. But in doing so, we never cancel our appreciation that this is a word we are dealing with, and that it expresses a certain thing; we never cut away the margin in which the meaning is expressed. For this reason the final result of our codification and transformation continues to express something. For this reason we call the outcome of what we and the machine do an artificial *intelligence*—an understanding of something, not just a rearrangement of marks.

This is where the "intentionality" of computer programs should be 29 explored and understood: not by asking how the computer is like a brain, but by asking how the outputs of the computer are like written words, and how our shift of focus, between thinking about expressions and thinking about what is expressed, can still take place in regard to the "speech" that is delivered up to us by the processes going on in the thinking machine.[8]

It can even be misleading to say that the word must have a meaning, 30 because the meaning might then appear to be an entity of some sort that comes between the word and the thing it represents. In some theories about cognition, such a substantialized meaning gets located in the brain or in the mind, and an argument may follow as to whether this meaning is also to be found as some sort of representation in the computer and its program.[9] There is no need for such an entity. All we need to do is acknowledge the capacity that is in us to focus on the word while the thing it represents is in the margin, or to focus on the thing while the word that symbolizes it is in the margin. Nothing more is needed. The meaning is simply the thing as meant by the word.

We know that Frege devised his new logical notation in the years 31 prior to 1879, when his *Begriffsschrift* was published. But when did somebody realize that we can focus on words as words and that we can take words apart even while keeping in mind what they mean? There is no date for this; this goes way back. And who was the somebody who appreciated this? Artificial intelligence is greatly indebted to him, and so are we all, since we can hardly imagine ourselves without this ability. We could turn toward the word even if we were limited to voiced speech, but we can turn toward it much more explicitly and decisively and analytically once we have begun to write. But the ability we have to shift our focus precedes writing and makes writing possible, and it also precedes and enables the further codification of writing that occurs in artificial intelligence.

Our ability to shift our focus from, say, a tree to the word *tree*, helps 32 us explain how words are established as symbols and how things are established as being named by words or signified by symbols. But this ability to shift focus can also help us approach one of the most vexing problems associated with artificial and natural intelligence—the problem of how physiological events in the brain can present something that occurs in the world, the problem of how we are to describe mental representations or mental images or mental symbols. When I perceive this lamp, something occurs in my brain. Neural networks are activated. How is it that these activations are more than just an electrical storm or a chemical process in the brain? How is it that they serve to present or represent something beyond themselves and beyond the brain? How is it that they serve to present this lamp? How are we to describe the "brain-word," or the "brain-image," of the lamp?

Most writers who discuss this issue simply say that there is a mental symbol or representation that does the job, but they do not differentiate the "brain-symbol" from the kinds of symbols we normally deal with— those we find in sound, on paper, on canvas, in wood, in stone. A crucial difference between the brain-symbol and the normal, "public" symbol seems to be the following. In the case of the public symbol, we can focus either on the symbol or the thing it symbolizes: on *this lamp* or the lamp itself. But in the case of the brain-symbol, the individual cannot focus on the neural activation in his brain; he can only attend to the object presented, the lamp. The brain-symbol is essentially and necessarily transparent to him. But one who does focus on the brain-word—the neurologist, say, who examines the neural activations involved in seeing this lamp—cannot see these activations as a presentation of the lamp; he cannot intend the lamp through them (as he might marginally intend the lamp while focusing on the term *this lamp*). For the neurologist, the cerebral activations are essentially and necessarily opaque; they are a biological phenomenon in their own right. For him they are not symbolic, not even marginally so. He has to be told by the person he is examining that a lamp is being seen.

Thus the brain-word is not like the spoken word, but reflection on how we constitute the spoken word can help us clarify the perplexing nature of the brain-word. A person, in the case of the public symbol, can shift from the symbol to the thing; but in the case of the brain-symbol, he is fragmented into two persons: the one who sees the thing but not the brain-symbol, and the one who sees the brain-event but not the thing. These remarks, of course, are only the beginning of an analysis of mental representations, but they do indicate that one of the best ways we have of adapting our language to describe the brain properly is to contrast the brain-symbol with the public symbol and work out this contrast in all its details. Earlier in this essay we used the embodiment of meaning that occurs in writing as an aid in describing artificial intelligence; here we use the embodiment of meaning found in public symbols as an aid in understanding the representation that occurs in natural intelligence.

Let us leave the issue of mental representation and turn once again to the written word. We have taken it for granted that the writing in question is alphabetic writing, the kind familiar to speakers of English. But there is also ideogrammatic writing, and it would be interesting to compare alphabetic and ideogrammatic writing in regard to the shift of focus we have described—the shift between attending to the thing and attending to the word.

An ideograph, since it is something like a picture of the thing meant, 36 keeps that thing vividly in the mind even when one turns to the written word.[10] An alphabetic word, on the other hand, lets go of any image of the object and symbolizes the sounds of the spoken word. Ideogrammatic writing pulls us toward the thing, alphabetic writing pulls us toward the word, but neither can cut away the other of the two foci. It would no longer be writing if it did.

Artificial intelligence has worked primarily with alphabetic symbol- 37 ism. It is interesting to speculate whether some features of ideogrammatic script could find a place in artificial intelligence, to complement the alphabetic in some way. Ideogrammatic writing does away with inflections and brings the deep grammatical structures of sentences close to the surface[11]; these qualities might simplify the grammar and logic of narration and make narratives easier to codify. Ideogrammatic expression might not be useful for creating programming languages, but could be used to modify what programs print out for users of computers to read and interpret. An ideogrammatic influence on the language at the user-machine interface would make this language different from the one we normally speak—it might produce a kind of pidgin English, for example—but we should expect that.[12] Our natural language has developed quite apart from any involvement with thinking machines and is not adapted to them. It has served other purposes in other circumstances. Why should artificial intelligence be forced into all the constraints that would be required to make its output look like a speech in ordinary English? The thinking machine is a new presence, as writing once was. Our natural language, with its exuberant adaptability, will find ways to curl around it and into it, even if it has to stretch beyond its alphabetic form to do so.

## III

The kind of thinking that artificial intelligence is supposed to be able to 38 emulate is deductive inferential reasoning—drawing out conclusions once axioms and rules of derivation have been set down. Making deductions means reaching new truths on the basis of those we already know. It was this sort of reasoning that Frege wanted to formalize in his new logical notation, the forerunner of computer languages. Frege wanted to secure the accuracy of deductions by making each step in the deduction explicit and formally justified, and by keeping the derivations clear of any hidden premises. His notation was supposed to make such purity of reasoning possible.[13] The subsequent outcome of Frege's efforts have been logics and programs that make the deductions so explicit that they can be carried out mechanically; indeed, the part of an artificial intelligence program that draws out conclusions is sometimes called by the colorful name of "the inference engine."

But drawing inferences is not the only kind of intelligence; there are 39 other kinds as well. We will discuss quotation and making distinctions as two forms of intellectual activity that are not reducible to making inferences. We will also discuss the desire that moves us to think. These forms and aspects of natural intelligence—quotation, distinguishing, desire—are of interest to artificial intelligence in two ways. If artificial intelligence can somehow embody them, it will prove itself all the more successful in replacing natural intelligence. But if it becomes apparent that artificial intelligence cannot imitate these powers and activities, we will have discovered some of the borders of artificial thinking and will better understand the difference between natural and artificial intelligence.

Artificial intelligence depends on both engineering and phenomenol- 40 ogy. The engineering is the development of hardware and programs; the phenomenology is the analysis of natural cognition, the description of the forms of thinking that the engineering may either try to imitate and replace, or try to complement if it cannot replace them. Our present discussion is a contribution to the phenomenology of natural intelligence, carried out in the context set by the purposes and possibilities of artificial intelligence.


## QUOTATION

One of the essential characteristics of natural intelligence is that we as 41 speakers can quote one another. This does not just mean that we can repeat the words that someone else has said; it means that we can appreciate and state how things look to someone else. Our citation of someone else's words is merely the way we present to ourselves and others how the world seems to someone different from ourselves.[14] The ability to quote allows us to add perspectives to the things we experience and express. I see things not only from my own point of view, but as they seem to someone from another point of view, as they seem to someone who has a history different from mine, as they seem to someone with interests different from mine. It is a mark of greater intelligence to be able to appreciate things as they are experienced by others, a mark of lesser intelligence to be unable to do so: we are obtuse if we see things only one way, only our way.

We do not describe this ability properly if we call it the power to put 42 ourselves in someone else's place, as though the important thing were to share that person's moods and feelings, to sympathize with his subjective states. Even the feelings and moods we may want to share are a response to the way things look, and the way things look to someone can be captured in a quotation. Furthermore, there can be complex layers of quotation. I can, for example, cite not only how something seems to John, but also how its seeming to John seems to Mary. But no matter how complex the citation, I remain the one doing the quotations; I remain the citational center.

When we speak we always play off the way things seem to us against the way they seem to others. The way things seem to others influences the way they seem to us. This supplement of alternative viewpoints is neglected when we concentrate on straight-line deductive inferences. The logic of deduction is a logic for monologues—a cyclopic, one-eyed logic. All diversity of points of view is filtered out. Only what follows from our premises is admitted. And even in the formal logics that try to handle cases that are not covered by a specific set of axioms—even in nonmonotonic logics, which try to cope with situations and facts that do not follow from the premises that are set down in the system—we still remain limited to inferences executed from a single point of view. As Raymond Reiter has written, "All current nonmonotonic formalisms deal with single agent reasoners. However, it is clear that frequently agents must ascribe nonmonotonic inferences to other agents, for example, in cooperative planning or speech acts. Such multi-agent settings require appropriate formal theories which currently we are lacking."[15] 43

The restriction of logic to a single point of view is a legitimate and useful abstraction, but it should be seen as limited, as not providing a full picture of human thinking. In our natural thinking, the opinions of others exercise an influence on the opinions we hold. We do not derive our positions only from the axioms we accept as true. If artificial intelligence is to emulate natural thinking, it must develop programs that can handle alternative viewpoints and not just straight-line inferential reasoning. It must develop a logic that will somehow take the expectations and statements of an interlocutor into account and formalize a conversational argument, not just a monological one. Such an expansion of artificial thinking would certainly help in the simulation of strategies and competitive situations. On the other hand, if quotation is beyond artificial intelligence, then perhaps we alone can be the final citational centers in thinking; perhaps our thinking machines will always just be quoted by us, never able to quote us in return. 44

## MAKING DISTINCTIONS

Another kind of thinking different from inferential reasoning is the activity of making distinctions.[16] A computer program can make a distinction in the sense that it can select one item instead of another, but such an activity assumes that the terms of the distinction have been 45 programmed into the machine. A more elementary issue is whether a distinction can "dawn" on a machine. Can a machine originally establish the terms of a distinction?

In our natural thinking we do not infer distinctions. To recognize 46 that there are two distinct aspects to a situation is a more rudimentary act of thinking than is inference. It is also a mark of great intelligence, especially if the two terms of the distinction have not been previously established in the common notions stored in our language. For example, to appreciate that in a difficult situation there is something threatening and also something insidiously desirable, and to have a sense of the special flavor of both the threat and the attraction, is a raw act of insight. It is not derived from premises. This sort of thinking, this dawning of distinctions, is at the origin of the categories that make up our common knowledge. It is prior to the axioms from which our inferences are derived.

Similarly, the stock of rules and representations that make up a 47 computer program, a data base, and a knowledge base presumes that the various stored representations have been distinguished, one from the other. This store of distinctions has to have been built up by natural intelligence. And each representation, each idea in natural intelligence, is not just soaked up by the mind as a liquid is soaked up by a blotter; each idea must also be distinguished from its appropriate others.[17] Some thinking, some distinguishing, goes into every notion we have. The thoughtful installation of an idea always involves distinction. Is there any way that artificial intelligence can generate a distinction between kinds of things? Can distinctions dawn on a machine? Or is the thinking machine like a household pet, fed only what we choose to give it?

## DESIRE

Desire is involved with thinking in two ways. There is first the desire to 48 know more: the curiosity to learn more facts or the urge to understand more fully. But there is also the desire for other satisfactions such as nourishment, exercise, repose, and the like. Let us call these desires the passions. How is thinking related to passion?

A common way of expressing this relationship is to say that reason is 49 the slave of the passions.[18] In this view, the passions we are born with establish the ends we want to pursue, the satisfactions we seek; reason then comes into play to figure out how we can attain what the passions make us want. Desires provide the ends, thinking provides the means. In this view there is little room for rational discussion of goals because the goals are not established by reason.

Such an understanding of the relation between desire and reason fits 50 well with some presuppositions of artificial intelligence. It is easy to see

that the computer might help us determine how to get to a goal—
perhaps by using the General Problem Solver techniques initiated by
Allen Newell, Cliff Shaw, and Herbert A. Simon—but the computer has
to have the goals set down for it in advance, just as it needs to have its
axioms set down.[19] The computer helps us reach our goals by working
out inferences appropriate to the problem we face and the resources we
have. Thus, if natural intelligence is indeed the slave of the passions,
artificial intelligence may go far in replacing it.

But natural reason is not completely external to our desires. It is true 51
that as agents we begin with passions that precede thought, but before
long our thinking enters into our desires and articulates what we want, so
that we want in a thoughtful way. We desire not just nourishment but to
eat a dinner; we want not just shelter but a home. Our passions become
penetrated by intelligence. Furthermore, new kinds of desire arise that
only a thoughtful being could have. We can desire honor, retribution,
justice, forgiveness, valor, security against future dangers, political society. Our "rational desire" involves not only curiosity and the thoughtful
articulation of the passions but also the establishment of ways of wanting
that could not occur if we did not think.

Artificial intelligence might be able to do something with goals that 52
are set in advance, but can it emulate the mixture of desire and
intelligence that makes up so much of what we think and do? Can it
emulate curiosity? The thinking machine is moved by electrical energy,
but can there be any way of giving it the kind of origin of motion that we
call desire? Can its reasoning become a thoughtful desire? Or will all the
wanting be always our own?

.      .      .

Drawing inferences is an intellectual activity that is less radically our 53
own than are the three activities we have just examined. Once axioms and
rules of derivation have been set down, anyone can infer conclusions.
Even if we happen to be the ones who carry out the deductions, we need
not believe what we conclude. We need only say that these conclusions
follow from those premises. Inference can remain largely syntactic. But in
quotation we stand out more vividly on our own, since we distinguish
our point of view from that of someone else. In making a distinction we
also think more authentically, more independently, since we get behind
any axioms and premises that someone might set down for us and simply
allow one thing to distinguish itself from another. In thoughtful desire
we express the character we have developed and the way our emotions
have been formed by thinking. Quotation, distinction, and desire are
more genuine forms of thinking than inference. And although these
forms of thinking are more thoroughly our own, they do not become
merely subjective or relativistic. They express an objectivity and a truth

appropriate to the dimensions of thinking and being in which they are involved, dimensions that are neglected in inferential reasoning.[20]

If artificial intelligence were able to embody such forms of thinking 54 as quotation, distinction, and desire, it would seem much more like a genuine replacement for natural intelligence than a mere simulacrum of it. It would seem, in its artificiality, to be similar to artificial light. It would seem somehow capable of originating its own thinking, of doing something not resolvable into the reasoning and responsibility of those who make and use the thinking machines. But even if artificial intelligence cannot fully embody such activities, it can at least complement them, and precisely by complementing them it can help us to understand what they are. We can learn a lot about quotation, distinction, and desire by coming to see why they cannot be mechanically reproduced, if that does turn out to be the case. We can learn a lot about natural intelligence by distinguishing it from artificial intelligence. And if artificial intelligence helps us understand what thinking is—whether by emulation or by contrast—it will succeed in being not just a technology but part of the science of nature.

ENDNOTES

1. Alan Turing, "Computing Machinery and Intelligence," *Mind* 59 (1950): 434–60.
2. Frege speaks of a *Gedankenbewegung* as the process his notation is supposed to express. See "On the Scientific Justification of a Conceptual Notation," in *Conceptual Notation and Related Articles,* ed. T. Bynum (Oxford: Claredon, 1972), 85.
3. See Paul Harmon and David King, *Expert Systems in Business* (New York: John Wiley & Sons, 1985).
4. Jacques Arsac asks, "How many semantic activities of man can be represented by signs in an appropriate language, and treated 'informatically' [i.e., coded and syntactically manipulated]? Who, at this point in time, can determine the borders that this science will not be able to cross?" Arsac, *La science informatique* (Paris: Dunod, 1970), 45.
5. See G. P. Baker and P. M. S. Hacker, *Frege: Logical Excavations* (New York: Oxford University Press, 1984), 8: "Frege's avowed primary goal was to substantiate the logicist thesis that arithmetic is part of pure logic. Everything else he did was peripheral. Consequently *he* viewed what we judge to be his greatest achievement, i.e., his invention of concept-script, as altogether instrumental."
6. The phrase is from J. J. Scarisbrick, *The Reformation and The English People* (New York: Blackwell, 1984), 74.
7. I adapt these examples from Arsac, *La science informatique,* 34–47.
8. For a recent statement and survey of the problem of intentionality and computer science, see Kenneth M. Sayre, "Intentionality and Information Processing: An Alternative Model for Cognitive Science," *Behavioral and Brain Sciences* 9 (1986):121–65. On the importance of "intentionality" or

"representation," see the conclusion of Howard Gardner, *The Mind's New Science: A History of the Cognitive Revolution* (New York: Basic Books, 1985), 381–92.

9. In my opinion this "substantializing" of a "sense" occurs in some interpretations of Husserl's doctrine of the noema—those that take the noema as a mental representation that accounts for the intentional character of mental activity. I have commented on this issue, and given references to various positions and participants in this controversy, in "Intentional Analysis and The Noema," *Dialectica* 38 (1984):113–29, and in "Husserl and Frege," *The Journal of Philosophy* 84 (1987) (forthcoming). For an attempt to explain what meaning is without appealing to mental representations, or, as they are sometimes called, "abstract entities," see my essay "Exorcising Concepts," *Review of Metaphysics* 40 (1987):451–63.

10. See Ernest Fenollosa, *The Chinese Written Character as a Medium for Poetry,* ed. E. Pound (San Francisco: City Lights Books, 1936), esp. p. 9: "In reading Chinese we do not seem to be juggling mental counters, but to be watching *things* work out their own fate."

11. As David Diringer says about Chinese, "There is an extreme paucity of grammatical structure in Chinese; strictly speaking, there is no Chinese grammar, and hardly any syntax." *The Alphabet,* 3d ed. (New York: Funk and Wagnalls, 1968), vol. 1, 63.

12. If we tried to read aloud some of the formulas devised by C. A. R. Hoare we would find ourselves speaking something very much like pidgin English. See the formulas in *Communicating Sequential Processes* (Englewood Cliffs, NJ: Prentice-Hall, 1985), 27–30, 43, 47–49. Ideograms tend to express events rather than predicates, and Hoare's formalism is an attempt to capture events in a process; see p. 25. And Hoare is quite aware that he is symbolizing not words or names, but things and events. He begins his book as follows (p. 23): "Forget for a while about computers and computer programming, and think instead about objects in the world around us, which act and interact with us and with each other in accordance with some characteristic pattern of behavior. Think of clocks and counters and telephones and board games and vending machines. To describe their patterns of behavior, first decide what kinds of event or action will be of interest, and choose a different name for each kind."

13. See Baker and Hacker, *Frege: Logical Excavations,* p. 35: Frege's concept-script "was designed to give a perspicuous representation of inferences, to ensure that no tacit presuppositions remain hidden. . . . The heart of *Begriffsschrift* is then the elaboration of a notation for presenting inferences and the setting up of a formal system for rigorously testing their cogency. . . . He foreswore expressing in concept-script anything 'which is without importance for the chain of inference.' "

14. See Robert Sokolowski, "Quotation," *Review of Metaphysics* 37 (1984): 699–723.

15. Raymond Reiter, "Nonmonotonic Reasoning," *Annual Reviews of Computer Science* 2 (1987):183. I am grateful to John McCarthy for bringing this article to my attention.

16. See Robert Sokolowski, "Making Distinctions," *Review of Metaphysics* 32 (1979):639–76.

17. An interesting example of how one term can rest on several distinctions, and how the "activation" of one or another of the distinctions can modify the sense of an actual use of the term, is found in Pierre Jacob, "Remarks on the Language of Thought," in *The Mind and the Machine: Philosophical Aspects of Artificial Intelligence,* ed. S. Torrance (New York: John Wiley & Sons, 1984), 74: "For Bob's use of the predicate [black], something will count as black if it is not perceived as dark blue or any other color but black, whether or not it is dyed. For Joe's use of the predicate, something will count as black not only if it looks black but also if it turns out not to be dyed." The incident sense of "not black" makes a difference in the current sense of "black."

18. The phrase is, of course, from David Hume: "Reason is, and ought only to be the slave of the passions, and can never pretend to any other office than to serve and obey them." *A Treatise of Human Nature,* ed. L. A. Selby-Bigge (New York: Oxford University Press, 1960), vol. 3, 415.

19. For a summary of the General Problem Solver (GPS) and means-ends analysis, see John Haugeland, *Artificial Intelligence* (Cambridge: MIT Press, 1985), 178–83.

20. In *Artificial Intelligence,* Haugeland contrasts two models of thinking: the "Aristotelian," in which the mind is said to think by absorbing resemblances of things, and the "Hobbesian," in which thinking is said to be computation carried out on mental symbols. Haugeland calls Hobbes "the grandfather of AI" because of his computational understanding of reason (p. 23), but he concludes that we may need to invoke a theory of meaning that involves both resemblance and computation (p. 222). It seems to me that rich resources for such a theory can be found in the philosophy of Husserl, for whom all presentations are articulated and all mental articulations are presentational. For Husserl, syntax and semantics are essentially parts of a larger whole. As against Haugeland I would say, however, that the mind should not be conceived as absorbing resemblances of things but simply as presenting things in many different ways.

## Post-Reading Questions

1. In what ways does Sokolowski distinguish between artificial and natural intelligence? What does he do to provide readers with clear and useful definitions of artificial intelligence? Summarize Sokolowski's definition.

2. Why does Sokolowski devote so much space to describing writing as an early type of intelligence? How does this discussion of writing help Sokolowski make his point about how we should think about artificial intelligence?

3. Compare this discussion of artificial intelligence to one of the other discussions of intelligence in this chapter—animal, creative, mathematical, artistic, or traditional rational. What does the definition of intelligence produced in this essay suggest about the other kind of intelligence you chose?

4. What is the point of Sokolowski's discussion of the hotel sign in paragraphs 19 and 20? Explain that point and relate it to what

Sokolowski has to say about writing, artificial intelligence, and our attitudes toward artificial intelligence.

**6**
· · · · · · · · · · · · ·
## OPTIONAL WRITING ASSIGNMENTS FOCUSED ON INTELLIGENCE

The following list of assignments provides contexts within which you can develop essays on the topic of intelligence. Each option needs to be analyzed rhetorically as you plan, draft, and review your essay (see "The Rhetorical Approach to Academic Writing" in Chapter 2).

1. *You are a college freshman returning to your high school to address a group of college-bound juniors and seniors.* They are in the midst of applying to colleges and taking the necessary admissions tests. You have been asked by their teachers to talk about your experience with college entrance examinations and intelligence tests, and to provide the students with advice on the whole intelligence and admissions testing process.

You decide to discuss what you believe would be effective ways to prepare for and take these admission and intelligence tests. Drawing from your reading of articles on intelligence and intelligence testing in this chapter, and from your own and others' past experiences with such tests, make an argument for a particular approach to taking these tests. Tell the students what kind of attitude you think they should have toward such a test, what kinds of skills they need to do well in the test, what type of knowledge these tests measure, and how they can prepare for the tests.

You should make up the specific context for this assignment: Is the school small or large? Is the school urban, suburban, or rural? Are the students first-, second-, or third-generation college students? Do the students value a college education? Answers to these questions should help you choose the right style and approach for your audience and purpose. Remember that the teachers who invited you want you to take the assignment seriously, while the students will expect some friendliness and humor.

2. *Write a speech for delivery to a local group of college and high-school teachers.* These teachers want to know your attitude toward current methods of measuring intelligence. Use your own experience and articles that you have read in this chapter to explain what you believe are the strengths and weaknesses of existing intelligence tests. Be sure to adapt what you say to the situations of high-school teachers; they will be most interested in what effects these tests could have on their students. How do current tests affect those who are tested? Are tests flexible enough to account for different kinds of intelligence? What alternatives could be used?

3. *Choose an attitude toward intelligence that is widespread yet distasteful to you.* Write a letter to a friend in which you explain, in detail, why the attitude is wrong, offensive, or prejudicial and how you believe it could be changed for the better. Use readings and personal experience to support your main idea. Imagine a particular individual as the audience for this letter; direct your style and approach to that person.

4. *Write an argument defending or attacking Howard Gardner's notion of multiple intelligence.* Consider the pro and con arguments, and address what you have to say to an audience of college students. You may wish to focus your defense or attack by directing it toward what you think is a common belief concerning intelligence held by your audience. You may imagine your article being published in a national magazine read by college students, or appearing as a syndicated article in college newspapers across the country. Suit your style, organization, and evidence to such an audience.

5. *Write an essay defending the notion of animal intelligence.* Include some close description of intelligent animal behavior in your essay, drawn either from reading or direct observation. Imagine your essay addressed to an audience of skeptical scientists who believe that what you call animal "intelligence" is no more than imitative behavior and instinct, and that only human beings possess intelligent consciousness or reason. Direct your style, choice of evidence, and organization to this audience.

6. *Write a narrative in which you describe a conflict between two people possessing different types of intelligence.* You might choose to show an engineer with very systematic and logical intelligence in conflict with a creative thinker, or a sober mathematics teacher in conflict with a wise-cracking, friendly student. Frame your narrative with an informative introduction, in which you clarify the purpose of your contrast, and a conclusion, in which you say something about the significance of your contrast. Use plenty of detail to show your readers the differences between the two types of intelligence. Imagine yourself writing for an educated general audience.

7. *Conduct an experiment in which you test the intelligence of an animal—an insect, perhaps—or a human being confronted with a puzzle of some kind—a roommate or sibling, perhaps.* Plan your experiment beforehand. Keep the experiment simple, and be sure you know ahead of time what you want to find out. In other words, have what scientists call a "research question" clearly in mind before you begin the experiment. Take notes during the experiment; then, write a three- or four-page report, in which you describe the *purpose* of your experiment, how you carried the experiment out (or your *method*), and its *results*. Imagine your report addressed to an audience of fellow students interested in intelligence.

# 6

## Perspectives on Animal and Human Communities

What are communities? How do they function?
How do they differ?

### 1
#### DEVELOPING A RHETORICAL APPROACH

This chapter considers how different animal and human communities operate and what kinds of relationships develop between individuals and particular communities. Some of the readings contain illustrations of how scientists study communities of insects and animals, employing careful systematic observation over extended periods of time to show how these communities function. Other readings provide examples of humanists applying their interpretive tools to different human community issues.

Although these articles do not address all the issues raised by those who study animal and human communities, they do provide a varied group of sources out of which you and your classmates may develop a rhetorical community. They also provide a basis for examining your own experiences with these communities—as an observer and as a participant. These articles raise some important questions. How do communities control the behavior of their members? Do communities ever exert too much control over their members or other communities?

In what ways are communities dependent on one another? What are the responsibilities of humans toward animal communities?

By discussing possible answers to these questions and by generating your own questions, you will construct from your reading, writing, and discussing with fellow students a clearer sense of the *purpose* (Why do I want to write this essay?) and *audience* (For whom do I want to write this essay?) for the essay on community you will write at the end of this chapter.

**2**
. . . . . . . . . . . . .
## GENERATING IDEAS ABOUT ANIMAL AND HUMAN COMMUNITIES BEFORE READING

Your own experiences as a member of various human communities, your observations of animal communities, and your knowledge of these communities will be helpful tools for reading these articles. They will contribute to your understanding of the different perspectives on community and to the shared knowledge base developed from class discussions of these readings.

The following activities provide a framework for your reading and writing by helping you develop ideas with which to respond in more meaningful ways to what you read and to your ideas as they develop on paper.

### Probing Personal Experience

Write short, informal answers to the following questions. If you are keeping a course journal, write your answers there. Be sure that your written responses are in a form that can be used in class.

*1. What are communities?* Are they defined by the individuals who belong to them, by the values or principles that underlie them, by the kinds or quality of activities that are carried out in them, or by some combination of these factors?

*2. How many in number are required before a community exists?* Must all members of a community share the same goals, behaviors, tools, knowledge, and instruments?

*3. What are some of the symbols that identify particular communities?* What kinds of things about the community do these symbols reflect?

*4. In what ways do animal communities differ from human communities?* Use illustrations from communities you have observed, belong to, or know about to explain the differences.

*5. Describe a community to which you do* not *belong.* Who are the members of this community? Why do they belong? What do they do together? What values and beliefs do members share? What rituals and patterns of behavior do they observe? If the choice existed, would you join this community? Why or why not?

6. *On what basis and by whom should communities be evaluated?* Should they be evaluated by their memberships, activities, goals, values, or symbols? Should the well-being of individuals or the welfare of the group be paramount in evaluating a community? Or should these all be considered together? Should members or outsiders be responsible for evaluating them?

7. *In what ways could competition be viewed as a positive and negative force within communities?* Explain your answer using some experiences you have had with competition within communities.

### Freewriting to Capture Personal Experience

A list of topics related to animal and human communities about which you can freewrite in ten-minute sessions follows. If you keep a journal, do your freewriting there. (For an explanation of freewriting, see pages 103 to 104.)

Animal Communities
Evolution
Ecological Issues
Survival of the Fittest
The Melting Pot
Cultural Pluralism
Immigration
Competition vs. Cooperation
Homophobia

Freewriting is most effective when you follow this sequence: **Reread, Focus, Rewrite (RFR).** (For an explanation of RFR, see page 104.)

## 3
· · · · · · · · · · · · ·
## DEVELOPING RHETORICAL CONTEXT
## THROUGH GROUP ACTIVITIES

Each of the following collaborative activities asks you to work with other students to revise a freewriting. These collaborative revising activities will enable you to subject your freely expressed observations and opinions to the questions and responses of others who are working with you on the community theme. Their responses should help you develop and refine your ideas. The collaborative activities also help to define the ideas about community shared by students belonging to the rhetorical community developing around this theme. (If you are collaborating for the first time, read the description of strategies for effective collaboration on pages 104 to 105.)

- Exchange your freewriting with a partner. Write questions in the margins of drafts to help each other discover and define a larger purpose in writing about community. If, for example, you have described a community you belonged to in high school, then your partner should ask questions that will help you figure out *why* you wrote about that community. What interest motivated you to describe that particular community? Was it the kind of people who belonged to it? Or was it the goals to which the community claimed it aspired? Or perhaps you belonged because of its rituals or shared symbols?
- Work with a group of fellow students to produce a position paper, collectively written, defining the perspectives on community each member of your group has decided to take. Use each member's freewriting draft to develop this group statement. Each member of the group may read his or her draft aloud for comment and response before the group begins work on the position paper. Students can then use the group's position paper to develop their own chapter essay, although no student need feel bound to write such an essay. Alternatively, the group may plan, research, and write a collaborative essay on community; the group may also work together to revise and edit the drafts of the essay. (Groups need a teacher's approval for such an alternative.)

# 4
· · · · · · · · · · · · ·
## USING READINGS TO DEVELOP
## A RHETORICAL COMMUNITY

The readings on community introduce topics such as immigration and migration and their effects on existing animal and human communities; competition and cooperation within and among groups; differences and similarities in animal and human communities; cultural pluralism; homophobia; and shared ethnicity. They will elicit different reactions from you and your classmates. These reactions will cause you to make adjustments or become more firmly committed to your own perspective. Reading also creates opportunities for you to analyze how experienced writers respond to different rhetorical contexts when writing about the same topic.

Whatever occurs as a result of your reading, writing, and discussing, your experiences with the theme of animal and human communities will add to your understanding of issues related to this theme and provide opportunities to practice critical reading and writing strategies that will contribute to your development as an academic writer.

## The Readings in This Chapter

Three articles in this chapter explore aspects of animal communities. George Uetz, an ecologist, explains how particular spider communities work together to catch prey, build webs, and carry out other survival activities. Uetz suggests that these spiders, who seem to work together because of their physical environment, differ from most other spiders, who encourage only competition among one another. He also discusses possible factors affecting the development of sociability among spiders. John Wiens, a professor of biology, also deals with cooperation and competition in his article, which describes birds living in the same geographical space and their competition for food and shelter. In this case, individuals of each species seem to display a social need to share, even when resources are scarce. Should these studies, Wiens asks, cause us to question the Darwinian theories of survival of the fittest and competition of species? Elizabeth Royte, a journalist specializing in environmental subjects, focuses on E. O. Wilson, the world's leading authority on ants. She offers an in-depth report of his life and work. In doing so, she presents his perspective on some controversial issues related to the environment, biodiversity, and the survival of our planet.

These three articles provide a basis for developing a rhetorical community with a shared understanding of how scientists study animals and a framework for contrasting the natures of animal and human communities.

The other four articles in this chapter focus on human communities and consider how human beings and communities function and interact. Leon Bouvier, a senior research associate at the Population Reference Bureau in Washington, D.C., describes and interprets statistics on immigration and migration. He closes his article with some suggestions for dealing with controversial legal and ethical immigration issues. Ti-Hua Chang, a producer for ABC News, recounts a personal experience with two other Chinese New Yorkers. Although his narrative concerns his own personal experience, it raises broad societal issues related to shared ethnicity and how members of the same community treat one another. Under the pseudonym Bell Hooks, a college professor analyzes homophobia in black communities and addresses questions about how all communities treat members whose values or behaviors differ. Finally, Peter D. Salins, a professor of urban planning, discusses the importance of multiculturalism to New York City's survival as a major urban center.

# 5
· · · · · · · · · · · · ·
## READINGS ON ANIMAL
## AND HUMAN COMMUNITIES

# GEORGE W. UETZ
# ON SOCIABLE SPIDERS

## Pre-Reading Questions

1. What does an *entomologist* study? Why are the research findings of entomologists important to the quality of human life?
2. Describe your behavior toward insects. Would you step on an ant, observe it closely, or ignore it? Use some examples and personal experiences to analyze and explain your behavior.
3. What insects do you consider "sociable"? What would identify an insect as being sociable? Why do some insects exhibit sociability while others do not? Use some examples from your own experiences with insects to explain your answer.
4. What do you expect from a scientific report on spider behavior? As you read, compare the essay to your expectations.

## SOCIABLE SPIDERS
### George W. Uetz

The common image of a spider is that of a solitary predator, aggressive toward other spiders and even cannibalistic when hungry enough. Antisocial tendencies have certainly had a strong influence on spider evolution, as evidenced by the elaborate courtship rituals performed by male spiders attempting to convince females they are potential mates, not meals. Nonetheless, sociality occurs, as a rare but significant phenomenon, in about 35 of the world's 35,000 spider species. The social behavior of spiders is not nearly as advanced or as highly organized as that of the better-studied social insects (bees, wasps, ants, and termites), but it is no less fascinating.

My interest in social spiders began in 1975, when Wes Burgess, then 2 doing his doctoral research at North Carolina State University, asked me to accompany him on a research trip to Mexico. Several accounts by early naturalists and explorers, including Darwin, had mentioned the existence of communal web-building spiders in South and Central America, and Wes had become intrigued by reports of group-living spiders in Mexico. I was invited along to provide some insight as an ecologist and, as I later learned, to help drive over seemingly endless miles of Mexican highways. The research that began then continues today (although Wes has gone on to study fish schools and monkey troops) and is concerned with answering several basic questions: What kinds of social organization can be seen in spiders? How do individuals interact while living together? How does the social behavior of spiders enable them to "fit" into the environment? How could sociality evolve in such antisocial animals?

Depending on the species, social spiders live in groups whose 3 numbers may range from only a few individuals to thousands. Some small groups are made up simply of a mother and her offspring on a single web; these groups last until the young reach maturity and disperse to form colonies of their own. In other groups, each individual builds its own web within a communal framework, which, depending on the size of the group, may reach immense proportions. Spiders of still other, more socially complex species live in communal webs and nests, join together in prey capture and feeding, and share in the care of young.

This wide range of social behavior and organization is seen in spiders 4 from several unrelated families, suggesting that arachnid sociality has evolved independently several times. Despite their multiple origins, however, social spiders have some telling features in common. All, for example, are web builders. Several biologists have suggested that the importance of the web to the evolution of social behavior in spiders comes from its role as a dwelling that, under certain circumstances, can be attached to those of other spiders. But the spider's web is more than just a place to live; it is also a unique device to capture prey. Insects become entangled in the web's silk threads, and as they struggle to free themselves, they set up vibrations in the web, informing the spider of their whereabouts. Thus, other biologists have suggested that the ability of the web to transmit vibrations, which spiders commonly exploit as a means of communication during courtship, has provided a way of linking individuals in social groups. Both of these attributes of webs have probably contributed to the evolution of social grouping in spiders.

Social spiders also have in common their occurrence in tropical and 5 subtropical environments, where year-round warm climate and abundant moisture have fostered tremendous biotic diversity. This diversity has, in turn, resulted in ecosystems crowded with many species—especially insects and spiders. In such environments, sociality may give some species a competitive advantage over others, and it is probably no coincidence that most social spiders, as well as many species of social ants, bees, and termites, live in rain forests or subtropical grasslands where climates are moderate and productivity is high. This is a happy coincidence as far as I am concerned because it means that field research on these animals can be conducted in very pleasant places. During the past several years, I have made many trips to Mexico to study the ecology and behavior of two social spider species, whose very different kinds of social organization illustrate the range of social spider life styles.

Orb-weaving spiders of the family Araneidae are widely admired for their intricate and beautiful circular webs. Closer examination reveals these lovely geometric structures for what they really are: finely engineered death traps made of nearly invisible silk strung taut in an open space. Some species of orb weavers are solitary; in others—even within the same genus—the spiders string their webs together, creating a communal prey-catching network. Individuals of solitary species in the genus *Metepeira,* for example, build two-part webs: a sticky spiral orb for catching prey and, attached to the orb by a signal thread, a nonsticky, three-dimensional tangle of webbing, or space web, in which the spider lives in a silken retreat. In contrast, individuals of the Mexican species *Metepeira spinipes* construct similar composite webs but usually fasten them to the webs of other individuals in permanent social aggregations on agave, prickly pear, or other plants. 6

In this maze of webbing, dozens, hundreds, or even thousands of *M. spinipes* spiders share a living arrangement that has both territorial and communal characteristics. Individuals build and maintain their own webs and retreats and capture their own prey, defending their space and food with aggressive behavior. Yet aggregations remain together for long periods of time and will rebuild the communal web if it is destroyed. There is a high degree of tolerance among members of this species, and individuals taken from colonies hundreds of miles apart will build webs together. The social-grouping tendency, however, appears to be somewhat flexible: the size of groups and the distance between individuals within groups vary from place to place. This variability, and the combination of solitary and communal behavior exhibited, suggest that this species may represent an intermediate stage in the evolution of social behavior in spiders. 7

Within the communal web of *M. spinipes,* the spiders spend most of the day sitting motionless in their retreats. In this way they escape exposure to intense solar radiation, which is reflected by the dense white silk of their tentlike retreat. The eerie calm of this apparent siesta is deceptive because the spiders are constantly alert and will rush out onto the web in an instant to attack insects when the signal thread vibrates. In the late afternoon, rain falls, the temperature drops, and the spiders venture out on the hub to capture mosquitoes and other small flies that 8 become active as darkness falls. The spiders are active throughout the night, taking down and renewing the sticky orb and repairing any damage to the space web caused by wind, rain, or insects.

Just before dawn—the most active period of web construction—   9 aggressive interactions between spiders occur at the rate of one per spider per hour. These disputes spring up between the resident of a particular space in the communal framework and an intruder that has attempted to build a web in that space. They are usually settled by ritualized combat involving web plucking, web shaking, and grappling, where fangs are open, but biting and loss of life are rare. As a result of such conflicts, the location and orientation of spiders' webs within colonies may change from time to time. When dawn arrives, disputes are settled, work on the webs is finished, and the spiders return to their retreats. Thousands of hours of observation have shown that the behavior of solitary and communal individuals is essentially the same, with the exception of territorial encounters, which are usually limited to spiders in colonies.

Differences in the size of *M. spinipes* groups are related to habitat 10 differences. Where the environmental conditions are harsh and prey availability is low, such as at high-elevation mountainsides and desert grasslands, most individuals are solitary or live together only in small groups. In habitats of intermediate quality, where rainfall is seasonal, the spiders are more frequently found in aggregations. In moist tropical areas, where the climate is favorable year-round and insect abundance is great, spiders form immense aggregations. Some of the colonies in these areas consist of 6,000 to 10,000 individuals; we have recently found some that may contain up to 100,000.

This habitat gradient is also responsible in part for differences in the 11 spacing of individuals within colonies. Spiders in desert habitats are much farther apart from each other within the communal web than spiders in the tropical rain forest. Experimental field studies have demonstrated the importance of food availability in determining the distance at which these spiders will tolerate their closest neighbors. Spiders were moved from sites with abundant prey to prey-poor sites and monitored for several weeks. Within ten days the distance between spiders in these colonies had increased by two to three times, except in places where the food supply was supplemented by piling cow dung—to attract insects—around the transplanted colonies. Apparently, individuals of *M. spinipes* can tolerate other spiders at closer range in areas of higher prey availability. This finding is further supported by laboratory studies of spiders maintained in cages with different levels of prey.

The flexible social spacing of *M. spinipes* can shed light on how social 12 behavior in spiders might evolve, especially when this species is compared with others. Susan Riechert of the University of Tennessee has discovered that the solitary desert spider *Agelenopsis aperta*, found in Mexico and the southwestern United States, also shows habitat-specific differences in territory size related to food supply, but in this species, the differences are genetically based and fixed within each population. Spiders from prey-poor habitats defend larger territories even when provided with large amounts of prey. Genetically fixed levels of tolerance or territory size, based on the minimum rate at which food is available during "hard times," are adaptive in the harsh desert environment because they insure that each spider always has enough space to obtain sufficient food.

In certain other environments, such as the tropics, where prey is 13 superabundant, evolution of more advanced social behavior becomes possible. If spiders show higher levels of aggression when they are hungry and more tolerance when they are well fed, they will occur more closely together in habitants where prey are more abundant. In these places, natural selection will favor smaller territories and higher degrees of tolerance because aggressive behavior is costly—in terms of the energy expended—and wasteful under the circumstances. Over evolutionary time, barriers to tolerance may disappear, allowing spiders to build webs together—thus crossing the threshold from solitary existence to sociality. *M. spinipes,* with its mix of communal and territorial habits and its variable social-grouping tendency, has apparently recently crossed this threshold or may be in the midst of such a transition.

Simply having the evolutionary opportunity to make the transition, 14 of course, is not enough; the benefits to the individuals living in a group must exceed the costs. One obvious cost of communal living for spiders is the time and energy spent in frequent aggressive encounters. Another potential cost is greater vulnerability to predators and parasites caused by the increased visibility of the communal web.

Among the benefits of communal web building is safety in numbers. 15 Biologists have speculated that the mathematical probability of a single individual in a group falling victim to a predator is quite low. For *M. spinipes,* this advantage may be magnified by the vibration-transmission properties of webs, which seem to provide an early warning system against predators. I have seen many individuals, apparently alerted by vibrations, escape predation by wasps. Another benefit is the increased architectural stability of the communal web, which allows *M. spinipes* to build webs in large open spaces where solitary spiders could not.

In his book *Sociobiology,* E. O. Wilson quotes an old Ethiopian 16 proverb, "When spider webs unite, they can halt a lion." Although lions have never been observed in spider webs, the saying holds a critical element of truth: communal webs do enable spiders to capture more, and often larger, prey. Insects that strike a solitary web may escape, but those that run into a *M. spinipes* colony often escape from one web only to ricochet onto another until they become stuck. The result is that individuals in communal webs capture up to 20 percent more insects than do solitary spiders. Furthermore, since the prey captured after striking and escaping from several webs are generally larger insects, such as beetles and bees, spiders in communal webs may obtain as much as 30 percent more prey biomass. For *Metepeira,* at least, this increase may have tipped the balance in favor of communal living.

Since the sticky spiral of orb weavers like *Metepeira* can be built by 17 only one individual, the social evolution of these spiders is limited to communal groups in which spiders attach their webs together yet remain somewhat territorial. A higher level of social organization is found in another of the Mexican social spiders I am studying, *Mallos gregalis.* This species lives in colonies of thousands of individuals, and unlike *Metepeira,* it is not territorial, shows no intraspecific aggressive behavior, and even cooperates in prey capture and feeding.

*Mallos gregalis* spiders, which belong to the family Dictynidae, do 18 not weave orb webs. The tiny (5 mm) individuals live close together in a mass of webbing produced by the efforts of all colony members. This web resembles that of tent caterpillars—it enswathes the branches of small-leafed oak trees with sheets of dense silk and is honeycombed inside with tunnels and small communal retreats where the spiders live, often many individuals to one retreat. The web's surface is covered with sticky silk for capturing prey.

In some colonies, more than 20,000 individuals of both sexes and all 19 ages live together and join in colony activities. During the day, most spiders are inactive, staying in the interior of the web to avoid the heat, although they will come to the surface to capture prey. Activity is greatest at night, when many spiders emerge to spin silk and repair the surface. Web construction is, to some degree, cooperative—some individuals put down silk framework lines while others lay sticky silk upon them. However, there is no real organization of collective activities and no division of labor among individuals; jobs are performed by whichever spider happens to be in the location where work needs to be done. William Tietjen, of Lindenwood College in Missouri, has studied *Mallos* activity with a sophisticated computer-linked videoscan system, which permits analysis of the movements of numerous individuals. His work shows that while activity in a colony appears the same on a daily basis, it may not involve the same spiders since the activities of individual spiders are not synchronized to any great extent. Thus, *Mallos* colonies, although highly organized by spider standards, do not show the kind of social complexity found among ants and other social insects.

Communal brood care and nest cleaning are characteristic of many 20 social animals, but neither is seen in *Mallos gregalis.* Females lay eggs in individual chambers in the interior of the web and apparently leave them to hatch on their own, as happens in many solitary spider species. When they emerge, the tiny spiderlings join in colony activities like other spiders. The absence of nest-cleaning behavior in *Mallos* seems peculiar at first. Spiders meticulously avoid fouling the web interior by going to the surface to defecate, often positioning themselves so that fecal matter falls completely free of the web, but they leave prey carcasses behind to be incorporated into the web as new sheets of silk are laid down. Tietjen has found that there is some advantage to this seemingly unsanitary practice: mold colonizes the remains of prey and apparently gives off an odor that attracts more flies. The fly attraction and trapping properties of *Mallos* webs have been known for many years by the Indian residents of Michoacan, who named this spider *el mosquero*, the fly eater. Prior to the widespread use of insecticides, the Indians brought web-covered branches into their homes as flypaper.

The manner in which *Mallos gregalis* captures insects is truly remark- 21 able. When a fly lands on the surface of the communal web, only spiders nearby seem to note its presence. A few of them will orient toward the insect, but none approach until the fly has become ensnared in the sticky silk. A furious struggle is the only chance the fly has to escape at this point, but the vibrations produced by the buzzing insect may instead only serve to signal its doom. Burgess found that experimentally induced web vibrations in the same frequency range as those of the struggling fly were the most effective stimulus for eliciting attack by these spiders. Moreover, the communal web appears to transmit these vibrations more effectively than it does others.

The buzzing attracts the attention of a large number of spiders 22 throughout the web, and they rush to join in the attack. The first spiders to reach the fly, which is twice their size, grab its legs or wings and bite, inserting their fangs and injecting venom. As other spiders arrive, the fly is bitten in many places on its head, thorax, and abdomen. Four to eight spiders may join in the attack, but even in this onslaught, which requires split-second timing, the spiders themselves rarely get bitten. Once three or more spiders have contacted the fly, escape is impossible. The combined action of venom and restraint by several spiders will subdue a fly in less than thirty seconds. Cooperative prey capture in spiders such as *Mallos* has probably evolved because it improves efficiency and allows the spiders to go after larger prey.

An attack generally involves three to eight individuals, but as many as 23 twenty individuals may come to feast, feeding side by side and packed so tightly around the victim that only their posterior ends can be seen. One indication of the relatively high degree of cooperation and sharing among these spiders is that individuals that have not contributed to the attack are allowed to feed. The key to understanding how such behavior might evolve may lie in the nature of spider feeding. Spiders regurgitate digestive juices, then suck up their food as it is dissolved. My students and I have conducted feeding studies that show that *Mallos* spiders feeding in groups obtain more than single individuals can. This is surely due to the combined dissolving action of enzymes produced by several spiders feeding at one time.

Prey sharing may be especially important for juveniles, whose small 24
size prevents them from contributing in any significant way to the
capture of larger insects. Some of the individuals initially involved in the
attack may leave without feeding, thus allowing others to take their place
at the kill. Recent observations in my laboratory suggest that this species
even engages in some degree of feeding solicitation. Spiders may leave
the fly carcass before or after feeding and enter the web interior, where
they contact others, which then emerge to feed. The kind of information
exchanged during these encounters—perhaps tactile or chemical cues—is
not yet known.

Considering the advantages that group living must impart to social 25
spiders, one might well ask why there are so few of them. To answer this
question, we need to recall that the usual habit of spiders is to be solitary,
cannibalistic predators and that for most, tolerance of other spiders is
against their basic nature. The circumstances under which natural
selection favors tolerance, and thus sets the stage for the evolution of
sociality, occur seldom—only in certain environments where the conditions are right.

Studies of *Metepeira spinipes* and of *Mallos gregalis* have suggested 26
that moderate environments and an abundance of food resources allow
increased tolerance of neighbors and that cooperation and sharing
improve exploitation of those resources. These findings have given us
some new insight into the origins of sociality, suggesting how under the
appropriate circumstances, the rudiments of social behavior may
appear—even in the most unlikely of creatures.

## Post-Reading Questions

1. Define the terms *biotic density* and *biotic mass* using a biological
   dictionary (at almost any library Reference Desk), and describe the
   context in which the words appear in Uetz's article.
2. What is Uetz trying to accomplish in his first paragraph? Does he
   accomplish his purpose? How? How might he change his first
   paragraph if he were writing primarily for other ecologists?
3. What can you infer about the kinds of research naturalists and
   ecologists conduct from the information in paragraph two? Where
   else in the article does Uetz provide information about how his
   information about spiders was obtained?
4. What does the information that Uetz presents in paragraphs four and
   five tell you about Uetz's sense of who his readers are? What strategies
   does Uetz use to respond to his readers' needs and expectations?
5. Where in the article does Uetz inject his own feelings into his
   account of sociable spiders? Why do you think he does that?
6. Write a paragraph describing possible connections between what
   Uetz learned about sociable spiders and human communities. Do

the advantages of communal life he describes apply to human communities? If so, how? If not, why not? What about the disadvantages?

7. Try your hand at imitation. Write an introductory sentence for an essay on any group you choose that uses the following structure: The common image of a _____ is that of . . . What would your next sentence be?

# JOHN A. WIENS ON COMPETITION AMONG BIRDS

## Pre-Reading Questions

1. What does the term "survival of the fittest" mean to you? How is it applied to animal communities and to human communities?
2. Do you believe that competition among community members is healthy or destructive? Can it be both? Explain your opinion using your own experiences and observations of animal and/or human communities.
3. How does competition affect your family? In what ways do members of your family compete with one another? For what? How and where did you learn to compete?

## COMPETITION OR PEACEFUL COEXISTENCE?
### John A. Wiens

Examples of competition between species seem to abound in nature. A calliope hummingbird feeding at a nectar-rich flower in a mountain meadow is apt to be supplanted by a larger broad-tailed hummingbird, which, in turn, may be chased from the flower by a rufous hummingbird. Deer mice on islands that have no meadow mice seem to occupy a broader range of habitats and exploit more types of foods than do deer mice in adjacent mainland areas where meadow mice are present. As one travels up a mountainside in western North America, the scrub jays common at lower elevations may suddenly disappear, replaced by ecologically similar Steller's jays.

These kinds of observations have led many ecologists to conclude that competition between species is commonplace and that it determines, to a great extent, how natural communities are put together. According to this view, species are likely to compete if they require similar resources, such as food, habitat, or breeding sites, and if those resources are in limited supply. This competition will lead to the exclusion of one species by another or, over evolutionary time, to divergence in the species' use of resources until competition is minimized. Competition thus limits the number and kinds of species that may coexist in an environment.

These views are by no means new. To Charles Darwin, competition 3 between and within species was a fundamental component of the "struggle for existence." In *On the Origin of Species,* he noted: "We have reason to believe that species in a state of nature are limited in their ranges by the competition of other organic beings quite as much as, or more than, by adaptation to particular climates." Elsewhere in this work, Darwin provided examples of such competitive exclusion:

> The struggle will generally be more severe between species of the same genus, when they come into competition with each other, than between species of distinct genera. We see this in the recent extension over parts of the United States of one species of swallow having caused the decrease of another species. The recent increase of the missel-thrush in parts of Scotland has caused the decrease of the song-thrush. How frequently we hear of one species of rat taking the place of another species under the most different climates! In Russia the small Asiatic cockroach has everywhere driven before it its congener. One species of charlock will supplant another, and so in other cases. We can dimly see why this competition should be most severe between allied forms, but probably in no one case could we precisely say why one species has been victorious over another in the great battle of life.

In the early 1960s, interest in the role of competition was stimulated 4 by the development of mathematical theories of the ecology of communities. Numerical models attempted to describe the degree of difference needed between species to permit their coexistence, how resources might be subdivided between species, how the configuration of a habitat might affect the number of species present, how a species might expand its use of resources in the absence of a competitor, and so on. In part to make the mathematics tractable, such models contained the assumption that the communities they described were in equilibrium—that is, that the species making up a community were in balance with their resources and with one another. This theoretical work generated interesting questions and neat predictions about competition and communities and sent ecologists scurrying into the field and the laboratory to test the predictions and answer the questions.

Over the past decade, my student John Rotenberry (now on the 5 faculty at Bowling Green State University) and I have explored these ideas. We have concentrated on communities of breeding birds at a number of locations in western North America, scattered from the prairies of the Great Plains to the shrub-grass mixtures (shrubsteppe) of the Great Basin. We chose these environments for several reasons. First, they are open. Prairie grasses and shrubsteppe plants, such as sagebrush, rarely exceed knee height; shortgrass prairies often resemble a well-trimmed lawn. We can easily see what the birds are doing. Second, these environments generally support relatively few species of grasses or shrubs and their physical structure is simpler than that of a multilayered forest. Consequently, different species of birds should be compelled to compete for the same resources more often than in more complex habitats. Third, the production of plant material and insects is relatively low, which we believed was another reason the birds might often have to compete for food. Finally, the habitats support few breeding bird species (generally two to eight per twenty-five acres), and the possible pathways of interactions among the species should thus be much less complex and easier to study than in habitats with many species.

6    We fully expected either to find competition going on in these communities or to be able to document patterns confirming that competition had existed in the past. As the research progressed, however, these expectations proved to be naïve. We now think that direct, ongoing competition is infrequent in these systems and that it may have relatively little to do with the organization of the bird communities. But I am getting ahead of my story.

7    The communities of breeding songbirds in the grasslands and shrubsteppe of North America are dominated by a few characteristic species—eastern meadowlarks, dickcissels, and grasshopper sparrows in the lusher eastern grasslands; western meadowlarks, horned larks, and longspurs in the shortgrass prairies; and sage thrashers, sage sparrows, and Brewer's sparrows in the shrubsteppe. These and the other songbirds that are present are ecologically similar. All of them forage on the ground or in low vegetation and feed primarily upon insects and other arthropods during the breeding season. Most nest directly on the ground, in small flowering plants, or in shrubs, and males proclaim their territorial holdings by singing from exposed, elevated perches or in flight. Some, such as the meadowlarks and the dickcissel, mate polygamously, but most form monogamous pair bonds that are maintained through the breeding season. In the shrubsteppe of Oregon, where we have watched the birds closely for several years, adults seem to return to previous breeding locations for several successive years, but young birds apparently settle elsewhere to breed. This pattern is likely to hold in other shrubsteppe and grassland habitats as well.

8    Competition theory suggests that, such general similarities notwithstanding, these coexisting species must be adapted to grassland and shrubsteppe conditions in different ways. One way to accomplish this necessary separation among the species is through differences in diet. If, as is generally assumed, populations are normally limited by their food supplies, then the feeding habits of coexisting species should reveal something about their relationships, including possible competitive interactions. To test this prediction, we sampled the diets of breeding

species at four widely spaced locations for two, and in some cases three, successive years. Our sampling method involved collecting the birds and identifying food fragments in their stomachs. Unexpectedly, the patterns that emerged seemed muddled. Some of the coexisting species did differ substantially in the types of prey they consumed but often not consistently from year to year. At a South Dakota prairie, for example, both 17-gram grasshopper sparrows and 32-gram horned larks gleaned large numbers of moth and butterfly larvae from the vegetation one year. The following year, however, the larks switched to a diet composed largely of chenopod seeds, while grasshopper sparrows preyed almost entirely upon grasshoppers. Moreover, in some years the diets of grasshopper sparrows overlapped extensively with those of the substantially larger (110 grams) meadowlarks.

Neither insect taxonomy nor avian body size thus seems to be a good    9 measure of differences in diet among members of these communities. Because birds use their bills to obtain food, however, bill size might be more closely related to diet. Community theory, in fact, predicts that species should be evenly spaced along a bill-size gradient, each successively larger species having a bill about a third again as large as that of the next smaller species. Species with bill-size differences much smaller than this 1.3:1 ratio presumably will have extensively overlapping diets and will thus compete, leading to the elimination of one or the other. On the other hand, if two adjacent species on the gradient differ by a substantially greater amount, a third species, with an intermediate bill size, should be able to invade the community. The community should thus rapidly attain this even-spacing configuration, but the bird communities in grasslands and shrubsteppe do not. In these habitats, the spacing of species along a bill-size gradient is outrageously uneven, and there are substantial gaps in the sequence. In the South Dakota prairie, for example, grasshopper sparrows had a bill only 1.03 times longer than that of chestnut-collared longspurs. The bill of horned larks was 1.28 times the size of that of grasshopper sparrows (reasonably close to the predicted ratio), but the bill of the next and largest species in the sequence, the western meadowlark, was 2.26 times the length of a lark's bill. Other communities we looked at also seemed less consistently patterned and less fully packed with species than the theory led us to expect. Like body size, bill size failed to turn up clear evidence of differences caused by competition.

We also investigated the size of the food items eaten by the birds.   10 Although the kinds of insects or seeds eaten by different species overlapped, perhaps the sizes might not. Coexisting species could then diverge ecologically by specializing on prey of different sizes irrespective of taxon. One of our study sites, a west Texas shortgrass prairie, seemed to support this possibility. There, the breeding species (horned larks, grasshopper sparrows, and western meadowlarks) differed substantially in the sizes of the foods they consumed. Furthermore, they differed in strict accordance with their body- and bill-size rankings. Other locations, however, produced conflicting results. At our South Dakota location, the diets of all species included prey of various sizes and overlapped extensively. The birds in the southeastern Washington shrubsteppe ate food items of virtually identical sizes. At both sites, there were considerable differences in bill and body sizes among the birds.

Excited by these findings and wanting to learn what, if not bill or body size, was determining the birds' diets, Rotenberry subjected the Washington shrubsteppe birds to greater scrutiny. By sampling their food habits frequently, he demonstrated that each species changed its feeding habits dramatically through the breeding season and that the diets of the different species changed in tandem. For example, as the sage sparrows switched from a diet dominated by beetle larvae, grass seeds, weevils, and grasshoppers in April to one dominated by weevils and lepidopteran larvae in May, so did the larger horned larks. Overall, the species seemed to be responding opportunistically and similarly to seasonal changes in the availability of different types and sizes of food. This certainly is not the sort of pattern one would expect of a set of species locked in intense competition over food. 11

Important as food is, it is only one of the resources over which competition might occur. Habitat—a place to live—is equally vital. If the habitats of coexisting species differ consistently, even in subtle features, this might circumvent competition even among species with similar diets. After all, if the species obtain their food in different places, what does it matter if the prey are of the same types or sizes? 12

To determine the relations of birds to their habitats, ornithologists generally look at habitat in structural terms, measuring such features as vegetation height and density, understory coverage and stratification, grass cover, and litter accumulation. The low vegetation in shrubsteppe and grasslands makes such features easy to measure, and we recorded habitat structure in many locations. This information allowed us to ask, Are there clearly defined sets of co-occurring species that are closely related to features of habitat structure? If so, they might represent the groups of competitively adjusted species that theory leads us to expect. 13

The answer to the question turns out to be yes or no, depending on scale. When the entire spectrum of environments from midwestern tallgrass prairies to northwestern shrubsteppe is considered, well-defined groupings of co-occurring species do exist and are clearly related to large-scale variations in habitant structure. The distribution and abundance of dickcissels and grasshopper sparrows, for example, are tightly linked to tall vegetation, extensive grass cover, and a well-developed litter layer—features of tallgrass prairies. Sage sparrows and sage thrashers, on the other hand, avoid grassy areas and instead occupy habitats dominated by shrubs, where vegetation is patchily distributed and large areas of bare ground are common—typical shrubsteppe conditions. 14

On this large a scale, our findings offer little more than intuitive 15
associations of birds with certain habitats, which any practiced bird
watcher can make. To provide significant evidence that these sets of
species have been organized by competitive interactions, we would need
to discover the same bird–habitat relations when the focus is restricted to
small-scale variations within one habitat type, such as the shrubsteppe.
When we looked at a variety of shrubsteppe locations, however, we
detected no consistent sets of co-occurring species. The species, instead,
varied in abundance and were distributed independently of one another.
Moreover, at this scale we found that in most cases the associations
between individual species and features of habitat structure were weak at
best. Several methods of analysis indicated that, overall, less than 17
percent of the variation in the distribution and abundance of the birds in
these areas could be explained by habitat structure.

Clearer patterns of bird–habitat association emerged when we con- 16
sidered the species composition of the vegetation, instead of its structural
configuration. Within the shrubsteppe, the abundance of sage sparrows
clearly varied in accordance with the amount of big sagebrush present,
while sage thrashers and Brewer's sparrows varied independently of
sagebrush but seemingly avoided areas where small spiny shrubs, such as
hopsage or budsage, were common. These associations were not strong,
but they do indicate that the plant species composition of an area may be
more important to the birds than has been thought. Desert shrubs vary
in the chemical composition of their leaf tissues, and these chemical
differences may influence the abundance and variety of insects present on
different plant species. If this is so, some apparent associations of plants
and insect-eating birds may be reflections of the birds' food preferences.

In any case, the birds that breed in America's shrubsteppe and 17
grasslands exhibit little regard for the predictions of ecological theory.
Variations in the population size of one species in an area are largely
independent both of the presence or absence of other species and of
variations in habitat features. Coexisting species appear to use resources
more or less opportunistically. We find little evidence that they are
currently much concerned about competition with one another or that
competition in the past has led to an orderly community structure.

When observations of nature do not match the predictions of a 18
theory, we must ask why. In this case, one possibility is that the theory is
inappropriate for grassland and shrubsteppe bird communities. A basic
assumption of competition theory is that the communities one observes
in nature, like the mathematical community models one can create, are in
equilibrium. Is this assumption violated in our systems?

As any farmer or rancher will tell you, both midwestern grasslands 19
and western shrubsteppe are extremely variable and unpredictable environments. From one year to another, the weather can vary from deluge
to drought, and the effects on natural vegetation, as well as on croplands

and pastures, can be profound. The weather in these environments is certainly not in equilibrium, but are the bird communities? The answer hinges in part on how long it takes the birds to respond to changes in their environment. If they take much time to adjust, then the interactions between species may be altered and the effect of competition on the community will be diffused. If, however, the birds respond with no appreciable time lag, they might maintain a rough balance, or equilibrium, with resource levels. In that case, competition could still have a strong influence on community structure.

Our shrubsteppe studies included one of the driest years on record in the region, followed by two abnormally wet years. This provided an opportunity to observe how the vegetation and the birds reacted to such dramatic fluctuations. The response of the vegetation at our sites was clearcut: in the two wet years that followed the drought, annual plants and grasses flourished. The overall height of the vegetation and the extent of ground cover increased; the amount of bare ground and patchiness decreased. The bird populations also varied, but none of the species changed in a way that was clearly associated with changes in habitat structure.  [20]

Another alteration in habitat, this time a result of human activities rather than weather, provided some perspective on why the birds may not closely track such variations. At one of our sites in southeastern Oregon, state and federal agencies applied herbicides as part of a "range improvement" program. The following fall, the native shrub, sagebrush, was disked and an exotic bunch grass, crested wheatgrass, planted. Because we had monitored this site for three years before the application, we could record the response. The vegetation, of course, was decimated—sagebrush coverage decreased from more than 25 percent of the ground area to less than 2 percent, and no vegetation taller than eight inches remained. Despite this, sage sparrows, which had in past years shown a clear preference for sagebrush, returned to the site in about the same numbers as before the treatment. We think that these birds had previously bred on the site and that the urge to breed in a traditional location overrode the tendency to select an appropriate habitat. Our continuing studies should record a decline in sage sparrows as these adults die or give up and move elsewhere. This example indicates that time lags in the responses of individuals to environmental changes can complicate attempts to compare natural systems to ecological theory.  [21]

In variable environments, such as grassland and shrubsteppe, populations may often be out of phase with their resources. This may provide the setting for feast or famine situations: periods of benign environmental conditions, when resource supplies may far exceed demands, may be punctuated by periods of sharply reduced resource availability. During these ecological crunches, the supplies of resources may be so limited that competition among the species intensifies, leading to precisely the sorts of consequences predicted by theory. During the intercrunch  [22] intervals, however, the relative superabundance of resources may render competition unnecessary.

All of this suggests that competition is not the ubiquitous force that 23 many ecologists have believed. Certainly, it does occur in some situations. Careful studies of groups of hummingbirds feeding on nectar, for example, have clearly documented competition between the birds, as well as between the birds and bees. Competition may be more likely to exist and easier to perceive in stable environments. In unstable environments, however, population sizes may be unrelated to immediate resource conditions, and assemblages of species may often not express the relationships that theory says they should.

Upon reflection, these statements seem to make good sense. Why, 24 then, have ecologists since the time of Darwin been so preoccupied with competition, and why, in thinking about competition, have so many assumed that nature is more or less in equilibrium? Part of the answer is that we have used simplified theories in an attempt to gain some understanding of nature. But our views have also been influenced by their cultural context. Science does not develop in a vacuum but is a mixed product, influenced by previous findings and ideas in the discipline and by the prevailing world views of the society in which it grows and matures. The notion of equilibrium is deeply embedded in Western culture. It derives from Greek metaphysics, which portrayed the universe as ultimately ordered and balanced, and it is expressed in the commonly accepted notion of a "balance of nature." Competition also occupies a central position in Western culture—witness its expression in sports, economics, space exploration, international politics, or warfare. Little wonder, then, that community ecologists expected that the species they studied would be in balance with one another and with their resources, and that the primary factor organizing communities would be competition. After all, we have grown up immersed in such a world view. But now, the birds of grasslands and shrubsteppe seem to be telling us that nature may not always be this way. Darwin's "great battle of life" may be fought in skirmishes that are interspersed with periods of relative peace.

## Post-Reading Questions

1. According to Wiens, competition between species has always been considered common. Why?
2. In paragraph three, Wiens includes two quotations from Charles Darwin's writings. Summarize these quotations. Why did Wiens include these quotations? Why does he use different formats to present the two quotations?
3. What strategy does Wiens use in the first paragraph to introduce his topic? How effective is this strategy? How does this strategy tie in with what Wiens does in paragraph 2?

4. Explain Wiens' use of mathematical theories of ecology in this essay. What do those theories tell you about the species of birds Wiens is describing? Compare these mathematical theories to Wiens' descriptions.
5. Why does Wiens not identify his source of information on these mathematical theories? Why is a writer of an academic essay expected to cite a source for such information? Why might a student be required to identify the source?
6. What is Wiens' purpose in this article? Is it stated directly or implied? Where are the clues or statements that help readers understand his purpose?
7. Explain in your own words how the size of a bird's bill relates to differences in diet and "community theory." How does this same reasoning apply to human communities?
8. Why must Wiens conclude that his observations *suggest* that competition may not be as powerful a force as many ecologists have believed (paragraph 24)? What does his use of the word "suggests" tell us about the scientific method?
9. What is Wiens doing in the concluding paragraph that differs from what he has been doing in the body of the article? Why do you think he concludes with a reference to Darwin?

# ELIZABETH ROYTE ON E. O. WILSON

## Pre-Reading Questions

1. Look up sociobiology in the dictionary. How might sociobiology contribute to our understanding of human behavior?
2. E. O. Wilson has suggested that genetic make up may shape certain aspects of human nature. Why might such a theory create controversy? What particular groups might argue against such a theory? Why?
3. Describe your interest and involvement in the environmental movement. What are some of the issues that interest you? Have you made any changes in your lifestyle in response to environmental concerns? Why or why not?

## THE ANT MAN
### Elizabeth Royte

E. O. Wilson doesn't make a lot of headway hiking through the Panamanian rain forest. Invertebrates distract him. He stops to poke. A wasp is acting strangely—he must see why. A bee clamps its mandibles onto his hand—no problem. He'll just observe it for a while. He snaps off epiphytes—plants that grow in the lower forest canopy—looking for nesting ants. With a chisel he chips off some bark and discovers an embiopteran web spinner. "That's not too common," he says, impressed.

Ten minutes into his hike, Wilson—the steely-haired, 61-year-old  2 Frank B. Baird Jr. Professor of Science at Harvard, curator in entomology of its Museum of Comparative Zoology, controversial father of sociobiology, the world's leading authority on ants—sits down in the mud. He leans casually against a tree, oblivious to the possibility of disturbing a dread Paraponera clavata, a giant ant with a giant sting, and dumps a vacuum aspirator full of dirt and tiny Adelomyrmex ants onto his lap. After a 15-minute search he takes out a pair of tweezers and deposits a worker ant in a tiny vial of alcohol. He pockets the specimen and stands up, but he's not yet ready to turn for home.

"I want to set foot on the Wheeler trail," says Wilson, referring to  3 the path named for his academic predecessor, the entomologist William Morton Wheeler. Wilson is acutely conscious of his place in the evolution of his department, and ordinarily is reverent of the men who shaped him, but his success with the Adelomyrmex and the prospect of more riches ahead have leavened his usual sobriety. "I don't see what the big deal is," he continues. "The guy wasn't that good. Well, it helps to be dead." He brushes off his pants and laughs at his little joke, perhaps wondering if they'll name a path after him.

Wilson has come to Barro Colorado Island, a tropical rain forest in  4 the middle of Panama's Gatun Lake, to collect Pheidole, the largest ant genus in the world. He and his students at Harvard are in the process of "describing," or documenting the physical characteristics of, some 300 new Pheidole species.

The Barro Colorado Nature Monument on Barro Colorado Island is  5 the most-studied tropical rain forest of its size in the world. The Panamanian Government established it as a nature reserve in 1923, and the Smithsonian Institution has operated it as a research station since 1946. A walk through the forest shows the large, green hand of Biology omnipresent. Nets stand under giant trees to collect leaf litter; gauze covers fruits and flowers for pollination studies; metal tags mark each tree in a 123-acre plot. A sign in a lab announces a $10 reward for anyone who can produce the corpse of a howler monkey (the population has been recently stricken by disease). The island is the kind of place where youthful, chigger-bitten researchers in earnest conversation will suddenly snatch at the air, their interest caught by a passing moth, bee or Hemiptera, an insect order whose members are properly known as "bugs." In the mess hall, a plant physiologist nudges a beetle into a vial. "Oooh, where'd you get that?" a bat researcher asks. "On the cake," he answers, and they both smile. "My beetle friend in Peru is going to love it."

The profusion of animal and vegetable life on the island makes a  6 convenient text for Wilson, who will wind up his trip to Panama by preaching the gospel of biological diversity to an audience of his peers at the Smithsonian Tropical Research Institute in Panama City. This venture into public speaking marks a new phase in Wilson's career. One of the first and most prominent scientists to document the "biodiversity crisis"—the global decline in habitat that leads to the extinction of plant and animal species—he now brings his message to anyone who will listen. The role of planetary defender has been thrust upon him, but he performs it with passion. As Wilson sees it, the Earth's time is running out. He is, he says, like an art curator watching the Louvre burn down.

No matter the shape or direction of Wilson's career, his muse has 7 always been the ant. "The ants gave me everything," he has written, "and to them I will always return, like a shaman reconsecrating the tribal totem." He brings ant colonies to his home in Lexington, Mass.; he still studies them in his backyard. Ants dominate his office, in the annex to Harvard's Museum of Comparative Zoology. In large plastic tubs on slate counters, hundreds of thousands of Pheidole from Costa Rica, Barro Colorado Island and Peru nest in test tubes and forage for dead crickets. On the walls hang classical black-and-white photographs of Harvard's famed entomologists.

Down the hall in the laboratories of the museum, home to a million 8 ant specimens, Wilson throws open the doors to a ceiling-high steel cabinet and announces, not unlike a salesman in Better Suits, "The Pheidole Collection." Inside are stacks of drawers holding rows of straight pins, each supporting two or three different castes of ants glued to cardboard triangles. From a plastic tub near his desk, Wilson extracts a living leafcutter queen the size of a bumblebee. ("That's a beautiful ant," he says.) He had high hopes for one battle-ax of a matriarch, who, if she reached the record-breaking age of 18 years (about double the average), he and his students planned to honor with a bottle of champagne. Alas, she succumbed two years ago, five years shy.

Forty years of devotion to the ant reached a culmination in March, 9 when Wilson published "The Ants," the most complete work ever written on the subject—a profusely, sometimes frighteningly illustrated, 732-page volume dedicated to the world's most underrated species.

Wilson and his co-author, Bert Hölldobler, the Alexander Agassiz 10 Professor of Zoology at Harvard, intended the book as a guide and inspiration to future myrmecologists—ant scientists. Accordingly, "The Ants" contains keys to 11 ant subfamilies and 292 currently recognized genera, plus every ant fact known to man. But the book's clarity of style and literary tone helped it onto the front page of *The Los Angeles Times Book Review;* it got Wilson on "Good Morning America," the "Today" program and National Public Radio's "Morning Edition."

For Wilson and Hölldobler, ants are "the little creatures who run the 11 world." Ants, they write, "represent the culmination of insect evolution, in the same sense that human beings represent the summit of vertebrate evolution." Ants have been evolving 100 million years longer than humans, and it shows. Because all the ants in a colony are closely related—they have the same queen as a mother—they tend to act in the interest of the whole. Ants are altruistic: with chemical signals secreted from glands, they share information (where to find food or the enemy, which ants to feed). Some ants store food in giant, expanding stomachs to be regurgitated to others in times of need. Self-sacrificing ants explode in the face of an enemy, covering it with poison from a long gland that also summons recruits to battle, usually the oldest soldiers (younger ants are left behind to care for families).

Ants cooperate. Ants of the genus Atta bring leaf segments to the 12 nest, where smaller ants masticate them, then set the pulp down; on this spongy bed, even smaller ants cultivate a fungus that feeds the colony. (A typical colony of two million workers collects more vegetation each day than the average cow.) Weaver ants bend leaves into nests, making living chains of their bodies to pull and hold leaf edges together until they can be glued with the secreted silk of larvae, which are held gently in the mandibles of the workers like glue guns. Some ants care for the young of other species, such as aphids or mealybugs, in their own nests, then herd or carry the mature insects from one feeding site to another; in return they take the nourishing droplets of sugary fluid passed as excrement through their wards' bodies.

Ants may have brains the size of pinpoints, but they've evolved an 13 ability to communicate and carry out complex tasks, mostly by dividing the labor among various castes (foragers, soldiers, groomers, fungus gardeners, and so on). Wilson calls ant colonies superorganisms, larger than the sum of their parts, because evolution has worked on colonies as if they were single organisms, "made up not of individual animals but of genetically similar cells." Indeed, colonies can in some ways be compared to the human body: ants that specialize in carrying food or messages play the part of circulatory or nervous systems.

Ants cooperate so well because otherwise nothing would get done. 14 The older a colony, the more specialized the roles of the various castes, and the more interdependent the social relationships between individuals. At the colony's founding stage, a queen lays trophic, nonviable eggs for nourishment and eggs that will grow into nonreproducing workers, devoted to nest enlargement, food gathering and brood care (licking, feeding and relocating the larvae). As the workers increase in number, more specialized castes are added.

Once the colony becomes established, the queen's attention turns 15 entirely to reproduction. She produces small-brained males—their only function is to have sex, once, and die—and winged females capable of reproducing, known as virgin queens. As a rule, males and young queens depart the nest in a "nuptial flight," leaving in sex-segregated waves (the better to avoid incest) to mate with ants from other colonies. Once inseminated, a queen snaps off her wings, burrows a nest in the ground, and converts her now useless flight muscles into tissues needed to make eggs.

Somewhere along the way, ants have also developed behavior familiar 16 to anyone who works in a large, hierarchic organization. They spend a good deal of their time looking busy but not in fact doing much of anything. Despite their legendary reputation for hard work, they are known to loaf. Some species even sleep, curled up in the fetal position.

Apart from the pure pleasure of dining out on ant arcana, why 17 should we care? Wilson and Hölldobler point out that ants create soil and keep it fertile—good for plants, good for vertebrates. Together with termites, they make up a third of the animal biomass—the total weight of animal life—of the Amazon rain forest. Closer to home, ants disperse the seeds of nearly a third of New York's herbaceous plant species. If the 8,800 ant species and their several million invertebrate relatives were suddenly to disappear, the physical structure of the forest would degrade. Most of the fish, amphibian, reptile, bird and mammal populations would crash to extinction for lack of food. "The earth would rot," Wilson writes. "As dead vegetation piled up and dried out, narrowing and closing the channels of the nutrient cycles, other complex forms of vegetation would die off, and with them the last remnants of the vertebrates."

In the rain forest, however, the gloom and doom of species extinc- 18 tion is far from Wilson's mind. The jungle is hot, steamy, green and crawling with life, and the erudite professor—late of tweed jacket and sober tie, now resplendent in a stained Pierre Cardin short-sleeve shirt and khaki pants—is in his element. "Paradise regained," he exclaimed mildly when he first stepped off the boat onto the island's leafy shores. But if there is any place earthly that fits the phrase, that place probably lies close to childhood.

Edward Osborne Wilson grew up in rural, subtropical Alabama, the 19 only child of a Government accountant. His parents divorced when he was 6. Like most children, Wilson went through a bug phase, but he never grew out of his, never moved on to the larger creatures most naturalists drift toward. To use his own lingo, Wilson was preadapted for ant work. Poor hearing in the upper registers excluded birds from his study. When he was 7, he accidently jerked a fish fin into his right eye; the accident limited his ability to focus at distances but gave him exception- ally acute close-up vision in his left eye.

Work required his father to move frequently, and Wilson attended 16 20 schools in 11 years. He had few friends, but he could amuse himself. "Mainly what I liked was to put on rubber boots and wander the fields, following streams down through swamps," he says. "I was a devoted naturalist at the age of 9. I knew this was what I wanted to be, and I can't explain that exactly." A bit out of the social mainstream—he struggled to make the football team's third string at a time when the game and the Baptist Church were Alabama's twin verities—Wilson always knew he was different: "For one thing, well, I'll just say it, I was brighter."

As a boy, Wilson imagined his love of insects might some day win 21 him a job with the Department of Agriculture, and he'd get to drive around the countryside in a green pickup truck and talk to farmers about crop pests. Instead, Wilson took his bachelor's in biology at the University of Alabama in 1949, then a master's there the following year. At the suggestion of a friend at Harvard, he wrote full-length studies of dacetine and fire ants that so impressed the Cambridge entomologists that they ushered him up to Harvard, where he earned his Ph.D. at the age of 26.

"Anyone closely associated with Wilson, even from the beginning of 22 grad school, knew he was a hot scientist," says Thomas Eisner, a professor of biology at Cornell University, and a friend of 39 years. "The breadth of his knowledge—from behavioral ecology to paleontology to evolution—and the way he applied it to new areas, was overwhelming."

Wilson was also bold: he recognized early on that the dominant 23 theories of any behavior didn't go far enough. Many entomologists had suspected that ants were governed by chemical scents, such as nest odors, but it took Wilson to identify the source of those substances and their chemical nature. In 1959, he removed a venom gland from a fire ant, then crushed and smeared it across a glass plate. He was astonished to see worker ants pick up the chemical signal from within their test-tube nest and pour out to follow the artificial trail. The chemical from the sac, a pheromone, was "not just a guidepost, but the entire message," he wrote. It told the ants the location of the food, its quantity, when to get it, how many ants should go and how fast. Wilson went on to find that ants secrete telegraphic chemicals from 10 to 20 different glands.

During his next 20 years at Harvard, Wilson's fascination with the 24 tangled processes of evolutionary biology led him around the world. He studied ants, published scores of monographs, and developed the taxon cycle—the pattern in which species adapt and multiply as they spread throughout a habitat and extend their ranges to distant parts of the world. With the late Robert D. MacArthur, who taught at Princeton, he explored population biology, from genetics to the dynamics of growth and competition. In 1967 they came up with the theory of island biogeography, a mathematical formula increasingly used by park planners and conservationists to estimate the rate at which species decline as habitat disappears.

In 1971 Wilson brought together the vast and diffuse scholarship on 25 social insects—wasps, bees, termites and ants—in his book "The Insect Societies," all the while edging closer to a synthesis of theories on animal behavior that would result in his seminal work on sociobiology.

Wilson's 11 books reflect a wide-ranging intellect. They deal with 26 subjects from the mathematics of population biology to the evolutionary reasons behind man's affinity for the natural world. (Book No. 12, "Success and Dominance in Ecosystems," to be published this fall, will address biodiversity.) "Wilson has built a backyard venture of watching bugs into a rather impressive world view," says Howard Boyer, Wilson's editor at Harvard University Press. This year Wilson added to his dozens of scientific awards and honors the Crafoord Prize, the ecologists' equivalent of a Nobel.

A shy man, secretive about his personal life, Wilson reluctantly 27 assumes the spotlight. Most of his colleagues know little or nothing of him outside of work. Only after working for him 20 years did Wilson's secretary meet his wife. Wilson has no hobbies and few close friends. At the end of the day, he comes home and draws Pheidole. To use a biologist's word, the man appears hypertrophied, excessively developed in one area to the detriment of others. Being good at his job, Wilson says, requires "a capacity to absorb yourself in a group of organisms or an environment, to forget about daily life, and be away from people." Says Boyer: "If I ran into him at a movie, I'd be very surprised."

Yet the biodiversity crisis has given Wilson a new public prominence. 28 His phone rings constantly (he answers it himself): the press wants stats on rain forest destruction; a colleague wants advice on grants; a biologist congratulates him from overseas. In May he met with Prince Philip of Britain.

"I don't play the eco-hero role very well," Wilson says of his position 29 in the current clamor. "I don't particularly like to be in crowds or lead groups. And I had quite enough attention from the press back in the 70's, that's for sure."

Wilson's brush with notoriety came in 1975, when he published 30 "Sociobiology: The New Synthesis." Through 26 closely reasoned chapters he demonstrated the biological basis of social behavior in animals: how such things as dominance roles, methods of communication and control of population density evolved. So far, so good. In Chapter 27, however, Wilson extended his theory to human beings—and demonized himself into history. Wilson suggested that sexual divisions of labor may be an adaptive trait, and that genetically determined traits and worldly success may have a "loose correlation." Genetic imperatives, he said, not cultural upbringing, shape certain aspects of human nature.

Wilson's timing was off. Marxist influence at Harvard was at its peak: 31 when some academics, many of them associated with a group called Science for the People, read Wilson's text they smelled sexism, racism, determinism. Several students picketed his class and spread leaflets about the campus. In an angry letter to The New York Review of Books, 16 professors, doctors and students (including Wilson's colleagues Richard C. Lewontin and Stephen Jay Gould) condemned "Sociobiology" as providing "a genetic justification of the status quo and of existing privileges for certain groups according to class, race or sex." Wilson had no evidence for the existence of genes for behavior, the group said; he based his assertions on sexually biased ethnographic data; he selectively cited supporting evidence and ignored contradictory evidence.

The uproar came to a climax at a 1978 meeting of the American 32 Association for the Advancement of Science. A group of hecklers took the stage just before Wilson was to speak, and one of them read a five-minute speech denouncing him—while the subject paid most courteous attention. When the speaker concluded, "We think you're all wet," another heckler picked up a carafe of ice water and emptied it onto Wilson's head.

The media pounced. Scientists from the ivory tower mixing it up! 33 High jinks! Emotions! But Wilson refused to play. He dried his head, canceled a couple of speaking engagements (the controversy was distressing his wife and daughter) and got back to work. In his next book, "On Human Nature" (which won the Pulitzer Prize in 1979), he carefully argued that the danger of oppression lay not in sociobiological theory, but in uninformed views of man's evolution—in particular, the kind of genetic pseudo-science that led to restrictive immigration laws in this country and to the eugenic policies of Nazi Germany.

Though Wilson today calls the controversy "one of the most intense 34 and divisive disputes in the recent history of ideas," he diminishes the episode's effect on his life. "It was a small group of very angry, voluble opponents," he says, quietly. "It was not evenly matched, not the battle the media made it out to be. Most scientists and sociologists were on my side."

Although Wilson's work in sociobiology won him a National Medal 35 of Science in 1977, other academics are cautious about extrapolating his findings to human beings: to some, Chapter 27 remains as controversial as ever. "It may be taught and discussed," says Marcus W. Feldman, editor of The American Naturalist and a biology professor at Stanford University, "but it's not necessarily agreed with. . . . The book has had the biggest impact on the way animal behavior is studied." Gould maintains his original position: "There's been no more study since then, no data to prove Wilson's thesis," he says. "It's not subject to testing. How can it be?"

For Wilson, the controversy is history. "My role was to introduce 36 evolutionary biology in human development; now the ball is rolling and it's not my field. The social insects are my true love."

The sun emerges after Barro Colorado Island's daily downpour and 37 Wilson sets out through the steaming jungle. He says he's interested in mammals this afternoon, but after spotting a few coatimundi and several agoutis, the call of the ants is too hard to ignore. Wilson climbs a 125-foot tower to get a close look at the forest canopy. Arboreal ants, which never touch the forest floor, are now being studied for the first time as new rope-climbing techniques, cranes and chemical fogging devices bring the canopy frontier within reach.

Atop the tower, Wilson marvels nonstop at the forest's abundance. 38 "Get a load of that!" he says, as a giant blue morpho, a butterfly, flops by, its wings gently stirring the sodden air. "Isn't that outstanding?" he asks, rapt. He eagerly shares his passion, explaining, unbidden, the territorial dogfighting of certain treetop butterflies, and the desires of stingless bees (they may be covering your face, but all they want is salt).

"Why are there so many ants in the canopy?" he asks, somewhat 39 rhetorically, giving John E. Tobin, one of his doctoral students, an opportunity to test his myrmecology chops. Ants are generally considered predators, Tobin explains, and predators, higher on the food chain, should be much less abundant than the herbivores they feed on. But in Peru, for example, ants constitute 70 percent of the canopy's insects. Wilson and Tobin, among others, are trying to find out why.

At dinner, post-docs and research fellows, botanists and bat, bee, 40 bird and frog specialists share the day's adventures. But as the Atlas beers begin to flow, the true concern of these, our best and brightest bug jocks, comes to the fore. If their days are devoted to unraveling nature's secrets, evenings are spent sniping at molecular and cell biologists. They get so much *money*, and so much *publicity*, the conversation goes. They have such expensive *machines*. They hang around in troops, says Wilson, like *langur* monkeys. Plus, says one former student, they're no fun: "I think only 16 percent of biochemists have a sense of humor." Wilson can't resist this kind of thing. "I think it's 12 percent," he counters dryly.

The issue truly rankles. While the Government has committed $60 41 billion to Big Science projects in the coming decade—to the Hubble Telescope, the gene-mapping project and the superconducting supercollider—a National Science Board task force on which Wilson served proposed a budget of only $30 million for the study of the biodiversity crisis—its economic and social causes, consequences and remedies. No wonder the assembled company fantasize about a blockbuster adventure movie starring eco-heroes, a movie that might capture the public's imagination and elevate field biologists to their proper Olympian heights. Indiana Jones in search of cancer-curing bromeliad plants, pursued by columns of Eciton burchelli—army ants—would do.

More beer, some recidivism in the group, and only Wilson and two 42 former students remain to toast the social insects and the mighty myrmecologist. "Ant people are broader than other field biologists because ants figure in so many things," Wilson says. "People talk about how plush theories of biochemistry and astronomy are. But we have a blue-collar contempt of swells, the effete, the overfunded." Wilson is only half kidding, but he's fully amused with himself. His shoulders hunch forward in a tiny, unconscious hug. "Field biologists are a good deal more congenial. They have a great deal more 'gee whiz'—call it wonder. But isn't that what it's all about?"

Wilson and Hölldobler dedicated "The Ants" to the next generation 43
of myrmecologists. But the book is more than a vade mecum; it's a
response to the lack of detailed information about the thousands of
species in crisis today, threatened by diminishing habitat. "The Chinese
have a saying: the beginning of wisdom is getting things by their right
name," says Wilson. "The point I've been making in my little crusade is
that if you don't know what organisms are, you can't really figure out
what's going on. Each species has these intricate life cycles; they fit
together in ways that are largely unexplored and will be until we figure
out the biodiversity. Biodiversity is the key to it."

Whether it's desert plants threatened by motorcycle races or the red 44
squirrels of Arizona's Mount Graham threatened by the proposed
construction of an observatory, biodiversity matters because plants and
animals contain genetic material. A large gene pool provides the flexibility that natural systems need to reproduce and adapt over evolutionary
time. For those who prefer to see this in human terms, Wilson points out
that biodiversity is the reason man has pharmaceuticals, foods, fibers,
sources of oil and ways to regenerate soil. "To let one species go because
you want to clear another mile of road," Wilson says heatedly, "seems to
me obscene."

With 40 to 50 million acres of tropical rain forest disappearing each 45
year, Wilson estimates that, annually, as many as 100,000 species are also
being lost. When loggers cleared a mountaintop in Ecuador, 38 plant
species exclusive to that site disappeared, forever. In most cases, there is
no way of knowing what is being lost. Scientists have formally identified
1.4 million species of plants, animals and microorganisms, but recent
studies indicate there may be as many as 30 million kinds of insects alone.

Wilson is nearly evangelical in spreading the word of impending 46
catastrophe and proposing solutions. He's good at it, too. Asked what he
thinks Wilson will be remembered for, Thomas E. Lovejoy, assistant
secretary of internal affairs at the Smithsonian Institution and former vice
president of the World Wildlife Fund, says: "A few years ago I would
have said sociobiology, but what he's doing today is critical. Wilson is
one of the real leaders in evolutionary and behavioral biology. He's a
wonderful spokesperson because information that's unattainable and
mysterious he makes crystal clear. He really gets to people."

Wilson, like most of today's activist scientists, now focuses on 47
economics as a prime incentive for preserving biodiversity. The greatest
hope for biodiversity today, according to a recent report by the National
Science Foundation, lies in giving third-world countries, which contain
most of the world's tropical forests, an economic incentive to preserve
their natural environments.

For example, they could be encouraged to develop economies based 48
on new forest products that would not require vast clearing of land or

soil depletion. At least 50,000 plant species have edible parts, but man relies heavily on only about 20 of these. One plant with vast commercial potential, the winged bean of New Guinea, has been called a one-species supermarket: its roots, seeds, leaves, stems and flowers are all edible.

Besides bringing economic prosperity to developing countries, Wil- 49 son argues, an intact forest system would help mitigate the greenhouse effect. Trees that aren't burned to clear land for unsustainable agriculture would convert carbon dioxide to oxygen; moreover, trees saved would reduce present levels of heat-trapping gases in the atmosphere.

As for what Americans can do to save the rain forest, Wilson is 50 typically, perhaps naïvely, optimistic. He believes in the political system; that with proper encouragement, elected officials will do the right thing. "Support candidates with global environmental platforms," he says. He also suggests contributing money to conservation groups that target threatened habitats around the world, like Conservation International or the World Wildlife Fund, on whose board Wilson sits.

In his lectures and his books, Wilson strongly encourages young 51 biologists to consider working in systematics, the classification of biological organisms and the evaluation of their evolutionary history. How can we value these species, Wilson argues, if we can't even recognize them? To combat human overpopulation, a major reason for environmental degradation, he champions birth control, and he implores someone, anyone, to either "convert or silence" Carl Sagan. "He wants to go to Mars," Wilson told the Smithsonian audience in Panama City. "We haven't even landed on this planet yet. Let's put the money into research here."

In bits and pieces, the framework for preservation and recovery is 52 being put in place. Wilson and his colleagues at Harvard recently began developing a curriculum to combine biology with studies in economics, government and sociology. Harvard's new biodiversity studies program will address, says Wilson, with typical precision, "the study of the total diversity of life: the flora and fauna of the world, where they came from, how they are maintained, and how they can be managed, preserved and put to use for human benefit."

Wilson dreams about retiring to a place like Barro Colorado and 53 "basking in stimuli," but he's got too much to do. "We're in a make-or-break decade," he says. "Now is the time when you can probably have the most influence per hour spent. If you're a scientist, you've got the ear of the media, the ear of Congressmen."

So Wilson carries on, consulting for and lecturing to disparate groups 54 of policy makers and educators, developing his curriculum for a hybrid systematist-politician-economist who likes to put on rubber boots and wander the fields and streams.

The vision of a teeming forest, rich in diversity and stable in its 55 complexity, drives Wilson by day and haunts him by night. On the morning before he leaves Barro Colorado Island, Wilson tells a small gathering of his recurring nightmare: "I'm on some fabulous tropical island like New Caledonia, and my plane's about to leave. Suddenly, I realize I haven't collected any ants. So I get back in the car and I'm driving, driving. I know there's a great forest on the northern side of the island, but I can't seem to find it. It's getting later. So I start looking for some trees, but all I can find are subdivisions. The land has all been developed. I can't find a single ant."

## Post-Reading Questions

1. This article originally appeared as a feature article in *The New York Times Magazine,* published every Sunday with the newspaper. What kind of readers might journalist Royte have had in mind when she wrote this article? Make a list of some of the questions she felt her readers wanted answered.
2. What terms does Royte define for readers in the first few paragraphs? How? Why?
3. In your own words, explain the "gospel of biological diversity" and "biodiversity crisis." Why does Royte use the word *gospel*? What does it suggest about her and about E. O. Wilson?
4. Royte uses many direct quotations in this article. Examine several. How do they help Royte achieve her purpose? How do they relate to the journalistic perspective she has adopted?
5. What is Royte's attitude toward E. O. Wilson? Identify evidence in the article that supports your analysis.
6. Write a paragraph describing how ants behave. Then write a second paragraph analyzing how their behavior contrasts with human behavior.
7. What kinds of information about Wilson does Royte include that detail his personal self rather than his scientific self? Identify some examples. Why did she include this kind of information?
8. How does Royte organize her article? Can you identify three or four sections? What is the topic of each of these sections? Can you describe the thinking that led her to organize the article this way?
9. Why does Royte conclude the article with Wilson's dream? How does it connect to the introduction?

# LEON F. BOUVIER ON INTERNATIONAL MIGRATION PATTERNS

## Pre-Reading Questions

1. Describe someone you know who has moved to your community from another country or city. What kinds of adjustments did that person have to make? Describe any difficulties that person encountered. How long did it take to make the transition?

2.  How do you feel about immigration quotas? How do they affect the cultural make-up of America? Should quotas be larger or smaller? Should they exist at all? Refer to specific groups of immigrants to explain your feelings.
3.  Describe your own roots. What racial, ethnic, and religious groups are represented in your own family? How does membership in each of these groups affect your life or your family's life?

# HUMAN WAVES
### Leon F. Bouvier

When the problem of worldwide population growth is mentioned, attention is almost always focused on fertility rates. Yet another side of the population problem is causing mounting concern—the movement across national borders of millions of people in search of a better life. People have always dreamed of moving to greener pastures, but never in recorded history have migration levels approached those of today. The rising tide of migrants is raising legal and ethical questions that nations have not previously had to face.

Some thirty-five years ago, American sociologist-demographer Kingsley Davis wrote:

> Not only is the earth's total population increasing at the fastest rate ever known, but the increase is extremely unequal as between different regions. Generally the fastest growth is occurring in the poorest regions; the slowest growth in the richest. . . . Between the two kinds of areas the differences in level of living are fantastic. What is more natural than to expect the destitute masses of the underprivileged regions to swarm across international and continental boundaries into the better regions? . . . One wonders how long the inequities of growth between major regions can continue without an explosion that will somehow quickly restore the imbalance.

Davis's prediction is beginning to be realized. People do not move simply because they are crowded; they move because there is not enough food, jobs are scarce, and wages are low in their home countries. If population growth levels had been falling instead of rising during the 1950s and 1960s, conditions would be far less difficult in most countries. Unfortunately, nothing can be done about past demographic behavior. We are just now beginning to witness the impact of the decline in mortality that occurred during the 1950s and 1960s, particularly infant and child mortality, while fertility remained high. Those fifties and sixties babies are now entering adulthood, moving to cities, and forming their own households and families. That is why, in Mexico, for example, despite the decline in fertility among individual women, the country's current population of 75 million will surpass 175 million in less than fifty years. There, and in many other less developed countries, the sheer numbers of women entering reproductive age will keep the overall rate of natural increase high. So while we must reinforce our efforts to lower fertility, that will not solve the problem of millions upon millions of young adults seeking a better way of life now.

For years, many demographers saw the 3 percent rates of growth— 4 meaning a doubling of the population in less than twenty-five years—as problems only for underdeveloped nations. We expressed the opinion that such unprecedented growth could not continue for very long— death rates would soon climb as a rapidly growing population encountered a dwindling supply of resources. But now that the beneficiaries of declining infant and child mortality have come of age, the true impact of the population explosions in the developing countries is being felt not only in those countries but also in the advanced countries, as immigration levels swell.

In 1940, 65 percent of the people on the earth lived in developing 5 countries; today the number approaches 75 percent of the 4.6 billion world population. In a short seventeen years it will surpass 80 percent of some 6.1 billion people. Increasingly, residents of the poorest nations are making the decision to move across international borders in an attempt to improve their lives. But with the emergence of nation-states and political barriers, migration has become subject to control. To people facing the prospect of staggering poverty at home, the spectacular advances in communications and transportation have made the possibly dire consequences of migration seem less risky than staying put. This is becoming evident all over the planet as people move from Mexico and Central America to the United States; from Guinea to the Ivory Coast; from Colombia to Venezuela; even from such small islands as Saint Vincent and Saint Lucia to Barbados. Some are legal migrants whose decision to move results from considerable discussion and thought; some 13 million are refugees forced to abandon their homelands for political reasons; some are illegal migrants who enter a country surreptitiously and lead guarded lives for fear of apprehension. The effects of these movements across borders are awesome and differ substantially from one region to another.

When Third World countries exhibit rapid industrial growth, as some 6 OPEC nations have in recent years, they attract residents from less fortunate neighboring states. Thus in Kuwait and the United Arab Emirates, 75 to 80 percent of the population are immigrants—temporary residents who are not citizens and in all likelihood will never become citizens. Illegal immigrants from such impoverished countries as Colombia and Ghana have swarmed to Venezuela and Nigeria. The recent forced exodus of Ghanaians from Nigeria uncovered hundreds of thousands of illegal migrants. Some half a million Colombians may be living clandestinely in Venezuela. About 25 percent of the population of the Ivory Coast are foreigners, many having migrated from Upper Volta and other Sahelian countries.

What happens when the economic bubble bursts and there is no 7 longer any employment for foreign workers, when there is not even enough work for the native-born citizens of the country? Nigeria has provided one answer with its sudden mass expulsion of Ghanaians. The arbitrary and cyclical nature of economic differences between countries is pointed up by Ghana's expulsion in 1969 of all aliens without residential permits, forcing some 200,000 persons, mostly Nigerians, to leave. The recent massacres of Bangladeshis residing in Assam, a state of India, is still another example of what may happen when a large immigrant population competes with natives for insufficient land or jobs. Such solutions may well be repeated again and again in other parts of the world.

In the United States there is increasing concern with immigration 8 issues involving refugees and both legal and illegal immigrants. Since the mid-1970s we have accepted well over 100,000 refugees every year, and given the unstable political situation in many regions of the world, one can only speculate as to the demands in future years. Since 1980, legal immigrants to the United States have averaged more than 600,000 per year. To that we must add the untold hundreds of thousands of clandestine immigrants who enter the country without legal documents. Their number is simply not known. Some illegal immigrants return home each year so that estimates of net illegal migration range from as low as 100,000 to upward of 500,000 per year. In particular, the number of clandestine entrants across the 2,000-mile border between the United States and Mexico is increasing as economic and political conditions deteriorate in parts of Latin America.

The situation in Western Europe is somewhat different. In Switzer- 9 land, Sweden, West Germany, and France, the 1960s and early 1970s saw a growing need for unskilled workers from other countries. Between 1960 and 1974 every major country in Western Europe had a positive net migration of legal "guest workers." France accepted 3.8 million workers; West Germany, 6 million. The early movements tended to come from countries such as Spain and Italy, but by the late 1960s and early 1970s the sources of immigration had changed dramatically. Poorer countries such as Morocco, Tunisia, Turkey, Yugoslavia, and Portugal had become the main sources of workers for France. In West Germany, over the same period, the Yugoslav and the Turkish proportion of immigrants increased so that by the early 1970s, Turks accounted for 39 percent of net immigration. Many of these workers came without their families. After 1973, economic conditions worsened in Germany and elsewhere and the demand for labor lessened. Under these economic conditions, some nations attempted to repatriate "temporary" workers to their home countries. Those efforts usually took the form of financial incentives often made only on the condition of permanent exile. Such repatriation programs have not been very successful. Guest workers have become permanent legal residents, and European governments have allowed some family reunifications. Nevertheless, the question remains: What does a country do with the foreign workers already there, particularly in a depressed economic situation?

Another very touchy issue has arisen in the more developed nations. 10 Fertility has fallen to historical lows in almost every one of these countries. Women in West Germany are averaging 1.4 births; in Sweden 1.6; in Great Britain 1.7—all well below the level needed to replace the population. Without immigration the populations in these countries will soon begin to decline. Such a decline has already begun in West Germany, Denmark, and Sweden, and a number of other Western European countries are expected to begin losing population by the year 2000. With immigration, or at least with the higher fertility of the immigrants already there, the total populations may not decline, but within fifty to seventy-five years what were once homogeneous nations will hardly be recognizable. The Turks and Yugoslavs in Germany and Sweden, the Portuguese and North Africans in France, the West Indians in England, will all become significant minorities in these countries. This could result in new kinds of assimilation. More likely, however, rivalries between groups will become more intense and bitter, possibly leading to major disturbances.

In the United States, fertility has remained well below the population 11 replacement level for more than a decade. Without continued immigration the population would begin falling after the year 2020. If the current pattern of migration were to continue for a century, the former, so-called white non-Hispanic majority would make up less than 50 percent of the population. This country is a "nation of immigrants," and at the turn of the twentieth century it experienced major ethnic changes in its white population as the main source of immigration shifted from northwest Europe to southern and eastern Europe. As we approach the twenty-first century the nation is faced with a new challenge: accepting millions of newcomers, this time of predominantly Asian and Hispanic backgrounds. Whether orderly assimilation will take place or increased racial conflicts will occur remains to be seen. One thing is certain: in the emerging era of high international migration, the concept of the nation-state and its cultural identity will be called into question. Emerging trends are forcing upon us some difficult ethical questions for which there are no real historical precedents.

Does an independent nation have the right to block immigration or 12 to expel recent and not-so-recent immigrants if their presence is perceived as jeopardizing the economic well-being of the native inhabitants?

The overtly inhumane and violent measures taken in Nigeria and Assam are merely drastic examples of more extensive problems.

We have noted the repatriation attempts made by Western European 13 nations. In the United States more than one million apprehensions of those engaged in illegal entry occur every year. These people are sent back to their home countries, but many return again and again. The U.S. Congress is currently wrestling with the issue of amnesty. Should the millions of residents who have lived and worked here for years without documentation be granted the legal right to remain or should they be repatriated?

Many in the United States feel that numerical increase should come 14 to an end and be followed by an era of zero population growth at perhaps 275 or 300 million. Even with our very low fertility the population will, if immigration continues at recent rates, approach 350 million within a hundred years and will still be growing. Furthermore, the existing culture of the nation will be altered by the increasing proportion of immigrants and their descendants in the population. Thus ethical considerations are raised that go far beyond the matter of competition for jobs. Does a nation have a right to determine its own demographic and cultural characters?

The problems are not limited to countries with a long history of 15 receiving immigrants. Tiny Belize, with a population of fewer than 150,000 people and independent of Great Britain only since September 1981, is faced with massive refugee and immigrant movements from El Salvador, Guatemala, and Nicaragua. Predominantly black and English speaking, Belize could easily become Hispanic through immigration. Barbados, population 250,000 with fertility below replacement, is concerned about current immigration from neighboring, poorer islands; some Barbadians are worried that their nation's culture will be changed by the incursion of East Indians. Such agonizing issues face many nations. Is it proper for a nation to insist that its culture remain as it is? If the answer is yes, is this a subtle new form of racism or is it a laudable expression of cultural identity?

The Universal Declaration of Human Rights adopted by the United 16 Nations General Assembly in 1948 states unequivocally: "Everyone has the right to leave any country including his own and to return to that country." This "right" is hardly honored by many countries—witness the tragic plight of Jews trying to leave the Soviet Union. But even if all the members of the United Nations were to uphold the right of emigration, of what value would it be if no concomitant right of immigration had been agreed to? As a U.N. document reports, "There are few countries which have not placed restriction on the number of immigrants who may enter or upon the activities of the immigrants after arrival."

While there are no easy answers, I believe that action on a variety of 17 fronts might help to reduce the future political and social stresses that will be caused by international migration. For one thing, massive economic as well as family-planning assistance must be supplied to developing nations if both population growth and emigration are to be curtailed. Assistance that contributes to labor-intensive rather than capital-intensive industry and agriculture should be emphasized. As countries like the United States and Japan become increasingly techno-logically oriented, more assembly-line work should become available in developing countries. To the extent that residents of these nations are able to share in global economic growth without leaving their homes, migration pressures will be reduced.

I believe that the developed countries must be prepared to accept 18 changes in the age and ethnic composition of their populations. Even with increased economic and family-planning assistance to developing nations, any substantial reduction in the level of migration cannot be assumed for the near future. As a result, those of us in the developed countries must prepare for major changes in the composition of our future populations. We will be older societies simply because of our low fertility rates, and we will be more heterogeneous because of continued migration. Sweden may not be as Swedish in fifty years as it is today; West Germany may not be as German. The United States may be on its way to becoming a truly multiracial society, with no single population group constituting a majority. Such changes will occur, but they should not be allowed to come about so abruptly as to make a nation unrecognizable in a mere half century or even a century. Immigration must be limited to some reasonable level; nevertheless, it is important that the receiving nations consider innovative approaches to the acculturation of their newest residents.

The American people, while accepting continued immigration, must 19 decide if they prefer a multicultural, integrated society, with perhaps two or more working languages, or whether every effort should be made to assimilate the newest immigrants into what many have traditionally considered the American culture to be—an Anglo-Saxon umbrella cov-ering a limited variety of customs. Similarly, the heretofore homogeneous societies of Europe must decide whether they will assimilate their newest residents or maintain ethnic enclaves, where the residents, while inte-grated in some respects, will remain Turkish or Moroccan or whatever, and not become German or French.

Finally, the very size of international population movements of all 20 kinds begs for a reexamination at the global political level of the issues involved. No nation has an open-door policy today. Yet migration is bound to increase in the future into precisely those nations that now exercise restriction on how many and what kinds of people are to be permitted to enter. A thorough discussion of alternative solutions to the new challenges posed by migration must be on the agenda of future inter-national meetings, beginning with the United Nations World Population

Conference, to be held in 1984 in Mexico City. The international community must seek some agreed norms of conduct in a world that combines increased disparities with increased mobility. Conflict and suffering are inevitable, but we must do what we can to hold them to a minimum.

## Post-Reading Questions

1. What sentence in paragraph 1 might be called the *thesis* of Bouvier's article? How does the sentence forecast not only the point Bouvier seeks to make about international migration patterns, but the way he plans to organize the body of the article? In what paragraph does he shift focus as forecasted in the main idea sentence?
2. Why will efforts to lower fertility rates not solve problems caused by increased numbers of individuals seeking to relocate in search of a better life?
3. What purpose do the statistics in paragraph four serve for Bouvier? How effective are they as evidence? Why?
4. How are immigration and a country's economic conditions related?
5. What does Bouvier mean in paragraph 11 when he says that "the concept of the nation-state will be called into question" because of high international migration? What is the difference in saying "will be called into question" and "may be called into question"? Why does Bouvier use *will* here? Do you agree with his statement? Explain.
6. This article was written in 1983. How could you use the library to find out what Congress decided about granting amnesty to illegal residents (paragraph 13)? What other international situation mentioned in the article has changed?
7. Where does Bouvier shift from explaining information that could be termed factual to expressing his personal viewpoint? Explain your answer by referring to the words or phrases that signal this shift.
8. What immigrant groups are currently arriving in the United States in large numbers? How has this current immigration situation affected American life, the American economy, American attitudes toward immigration, and your own attitude?

# TI-HUA CHANG
# ON SHARED ETHNICITY

## Pre-Reading Questions

1. Do you think that group members who "make it" should be responsible for helping members of the group who are still struggling? Explain your answer by referring to specific groups.
2. What causes friction between members of a group? Supply a real or hypothetical situation to explain your answer. How does the nature

of the group affect the reasons for friction, or even whether or not friction occurs? Again, supply a real or hypothetical situation to explain your answer.

3. Describe an occasion when you felt embarrassed or hostile about your own group membership or a particular member of the group. What caused your feelings? How did you resolve them?

## DOWNTOWN COUSIN
### Ti-Hua Chang

I had just finished a spending spree for suits, a binge delayed for years, 1 when I hailed a taxi. I wanted to head uptown to buy a sing-along tape machine at a discount electronics store. The cabdriver, like me, was Chinese, and somewhere in our conversation about my good English and his tough life as an immigrant, he learned that I was heading for a midtown store. "Why you do that? You should go Chinatown! Much better than uptown, cousin. You know Chinatown cheaper. Much cheaper."

"You sure it will save me money?"                                             2

"Ah, ya! You save . . . one hundred dollars." In his enthusiasm he seemed to levitate briefly.

A small smile breached my lips. I liked him, this friendly, hustling 3 cabby, his breed rare among the muttering, angry men who cursed gasoline prices and scarce riders. I enjoyed his boisterous loudness; he appeared untamed by a nation that prided itself on being composed of immigrants, yet still regarded Asians as alien. He was not like me—a quiet Asian-American who avoids loud talk in public places, fearing attention from that one bigot who seemingly lurks in every crowd.

"Look, I got Chinese newspaper. We call before go. I no waste your 4 money."

"O.K. We can do that," I said, assuming he wanted to help a fellow 5 Asian. He pulled over to the curb a block from Radio City Music Hall and theatrically paged through a blue-and-red-bannered Chinese news-weekly.

"I can't find store ad. Ah, ya. Very good store," he said and told me 6 its name.

"You're sure they have sing-along machines? With a microphone, 7 and your voice is mixed with the background music?"

"Yeah, sure. I know they got!"                                                8

"Forget about calling, then. Just go. I trust you." I wanted to trust 9 him, to connect with this newfound buddy. But my fear of being conned lingered.

Flooring the accelerator, he cut the cab across Madison Avenue and 10 began a tortured route past the throngs at Union Square's outdoor clothing stands, the alcoholics on the Bowery and then the Chinese in Chinatown. I wondered why only here we looked like a serried mass of black-haired sheep, and instantly flushed with shame. Even I have been affected by movies about Fu Manchu, Charlie Chan and attacking hordes of yellow "gooks." How could I view myself this way—I, a television-news producer who once led student demonstrations against racism?

"This best store. You see." The cabby glanced down, adding as an aside, "13 dollar." This seemed excessive, but ethnic obligation and pleasure at the prospect of saving more money produced a rare $3 tip from me. 11

The door to the electronics store was wedged open with an egg carton. The salesmen were eating lunch with chopsticks out of Chinese takeout containers. No one spoke. The only sounds were the hum of a plastic fan and the slurping of lo mein. 12

One salesman, standing by the toaster ovens, was not eating. He ended his telephone conversation and smiled. He looked like the stereotype my father demanded I not be: skinny, with glasses and squinting eyes. 13

I noted with pride that I measured several inches taller and weighed 30 pounds more than he. I stood up straight, chest out. My father posed for every picture this way. Chest out, head up. "Chinese," he lectured my brother and me for years, "too stooped." 14

In one sepia photograph, frayed at the edges, my father stood straight with his head cocked back, chest out, a Thompson submachine gun cradled in his arms. This was during World War II, in Burma, where my father, a Chinese journalist, reported on the campaign against Japan. I, too, cocked my head. 15

"Do you sell sing-along machines?" 16
"What?" the salesman asked.
"Sing-along machines."
"What that?"
"The Japanese sing-along, karaoke machine."
"Oh, you mean ka-RA-oke."
"That's what I said."
"No, you say wrong, it ka-Ra-oke."
"Look, do you have them or not?"
"We got plenty. Over here." When he reached the one and only karaoke machine, he paused and turned as if setting up for a classroom lecture. With a heavy Chinese accent, he began a long discourse on the machine. He gesticulated expansively. Laser disk not tape, video not sound alone. All of which I knew meant expensive not cheap. I imagined carnival music and a barker in a red-striped jacket and straw hat sermonizing with a bamboo cane: "And here my friends you have your quadrasound, superturbo, nuclear-injected, atomic-powered machine."

With repressed sarcasm, I asked, "Can I change the pitch?" 17

Through a tight smile, the salesman said: "You must let me finish. 18
You start from end, I start from beginning."

Anger rising, I wanted to leave the store. I did not. Our shared 19
ethnicity prevented me, knowing that he undoubtedly struggled as my
parents had in a new country.

I noticed he rarely looked me in the eyes. Other salesmen were 20
listening, and he seemed to be putting on a show for them. I wondered
if he would try to cheat me because I was an American-born Chinese
who dressed, acted and spoke like a *beiren,* a white man. I wondered if he
hated me for my American upbringing, for my expensive new suits slung
over my shoulder. Was he angry at his stained plaid tie and red shirt? Did
he resent my luck at having been born here, at having had more chances
to succeed? Could he understand the poverty and racial slurs of *my*
childhood, growing up in Spanish Harlem, attending private school on
scholarship with rich kids?

He droned on, disingenuous grin never fading. Finally I asked again, 21
"Can I change the pitch?"

"You don't need pitch. Here, look this, this laser, don't need change 22
nothing, hah!" He smiled more broadly, turning to another salesman.

"That's all I need to know," I said as I turned and walked out, 23
incensed that he had wasted my time. He could have immediately
answered my question about the stupid machine. Fuming, I thought to
myself that from his accent he was from Hong Kong, having arrived in
the States probably five or six years ago, possibly within the last few years.
Hong Kong Chinese would cheat anyone, I thought. Chinese from that
quintessential free market cheated everyone. It was a malicious, intentional stereotyping. Angry at the salesman, I found myself debasing the
people of his region.

I decided not to ride the subway but to spend the extra money and 24
take a taxi home. I hoped the driver would not be Chinese, preferring an
unintelligible immigrant from some obscure country, one of those angry,
silent men from a place so foreign to me that I would not care. I threw
my arm up, stopped a cab and, wordlessly, pointed uptown.

## Post-Reading Questions

1. What kind of background information does Chang provide in
   paragraph one that is important to understanding the personal
   experience he narrates? How is narrating a personal experience
   different from reporting someone else's experiences? How is it
   different from reporting the results of your own research?

2. Chang narrates a brief personal experience to make a point, yet he
   never states that point directly. What is that point? How do you
   know? What evidence from his essay helps you understand the point
   he is making?

3. How does Chang want you to feel about him after you have read the essay? About the cabby? The salesman? How do Chang's feelings about himself change?

4. How might a psychologist or sociologist study shared ethnicity? How would their perspective differ from Chang's? How would it be alike?

5. How is Chang's response to the cabby similar to his response to the salesman? Why?

6. How do you think Chang feels about his own description of himself in paragraph four: "a quiet Asian-American who avoids loud talk in public places, fearing attention from that one bigot who seemingly lurks in every crowd." Is there one aspect of your own or a friend's personality that you can identify as a defense against societal prejudices or stereotypes? Explain, using a personal experience.

7. What issues about shared ethnicity does Chang's essay raise? How do you feel about these issues?

8. How does Chang make the cabby and salesman seem believable? Give examples from the essay to explain your answer. Should we accept Chang as a reliable story teller? Why or why not?

# BELL HOOKS ON HOMOPHOBIA IN BLACK COMMUNITIES

### Pre-Reading Questions

1. Describe your own feelings about homosexuality. How do you explain the origin of your feelings? How do your attitudes toward homosexuality compare and contrast with your family's and friends' attitudes?

2. Pick a medium (film, television, radio) and explain how it portrays homosexuality. Give a specific example. Do you believe media portrayals of homosexuality are accurate? Do they *reflect* or *create* societal attitudes toward homosexuality? Do they do both?

3. What is *homophobia*? What causes it in society? What causes it on a college campus? Does it exist on your college campus? Is it getting worse or better? Does it exist in your home or in your community? How can it be prevented or eliminated?

## HOMOPHOBIA IN BLACK COMMUNITIES
### Bell Hooks

Recently I was at my parents' home and heard teenage nieces and nephews expressing their hatred for homosexuals, saying that they could never like anybody who was homosexual. In response I told them,   1

"There are already people who you love and care about who are gay, so just come off it!" They wanted to know who. I said, "The who is not important. If they wanted you to know, they would tell you. But you need to think about the shit you've been saying and ask yourself where it's coming from."

Their vehement expression of hatred startled and frightened me, even more so when I contemplated the hurt that would have been experienced had our loved ones who are gay heard their words. When we were growing up, we would not have had the nerve to make such comments. We were not allowed to say negative, hateful comments about the people we knew who were gay. We knew their names, their sexual preference. They were our neighbors, our friends, our family. They were us—a part of our black community.

The gay people we knew then did not live in separate subcultures, not in the small, segregated black community where work was difficult to find, where many of us were poor. Poverty was important; it created a social context in which structures of dependence were important for everyday survival. Sheer economic necessity and fierce white racism, as well as the joy of being there with the black folks known and loved, compelled many gay blacks to live close to home and family. That meant however that gay people created a way to live out sexual preferences within the boundaries of circumstances that were rarely ideal no matter how affirming. In some cases, this meant a closeted sexual life. In other families, an individual could be openly expressive, quite out.

The homophobia expressed by my nieces and nephews coupled with the assumption in many feminist circles that black communities are somehow more homophobic than other communities in the United States, more opposed to gay rights, provided the stimulus for me to write this piece. Initially, I considered calling it "homophobia in the black community." Yet it is precisely the notion that there is a monolithic black community that must be challenged. Black communities vary—urban and rural experiences create diversity of culture and lifestyle.

I have talked with black folks who were raised in southern communities where gay people were openly expressive of their sexual preference and participated fully in the life of the community. I have also spoken with folks who say just the opposite.

In the particular black community where I was raised there was a real double standard. Black male homosexuals were often known, were talked about, were seen positively, and played important roles in community life, whereas lesbians were talked about solely in negative terms, and the women identified as lesbians were usually married. Often, acceptance of male homosexuality was mediated by material privilege—that is to say that homosexual men with money were part of the materially privileged ruling black group and were accorded the regard and respect given that group. They were influential people in the community. This was not the case with any women.

In those days homophobia directed at lesbians was rooted in deep 7 religious and moral belief that women defined their womanness through bearing children. The prevailing assumption was that to be a lesbian was "unnatural" because one would not be participating in child-bearing. There were no identified lesbian "parents" even though there were gay men known to be caretakers of other folks' children. I have talked with black folks who recall similar circumstances in their communities. Overall, a majority of older black people I spoke with, raised in small, tightly knit southern black communities, suggested there was tolerance and acceptance of different sexual practices and preferences. One black gay male I spoke with felt that it was more important for him to live within a supportive black community, where his sexual preferences were known but not acted out in an overt, public way, than to live away from a community in a gay subculture where this aspect of his identity could be openly expressed.

Recently, I talked with a black lesbian from New Orleans who 8 boasted that the black community has never had any "orange person like Anita Bryant running around trying to attack gay people." Her experience coming out to a black male roommate was positive and caring. But for every positive story one might hear about gay life in black communities, there are also negative ones. Yet these positive accounts call into question the assumption that black people and black communities are necessarily more homophobic than other groups of people in this society. They also compel us to recognize that there are diversities of black experience. Unfortunately, there are very few oral histories and autobiographies which explore the lives of black gay people in diverse black communities. This is a research project that must be carried out if we are to fully understand the complex experience of being black and gay in this white-supremacist, patriarchal, capitalist society. Often we hear more from black gay people who have chosen to live in predominantly white communities, whose choices may have been affected by undue harassment in black communities. We hear hardly anything from black gay people who live contentedly in black communities.

Black communities may be perceived as more homophobic than 9 other communities because there is a tendency for individuals in black communities to verbally express in an outspoken way anti-gay sentiments. I talked with a straight black male in a California community who acknowledged that though he has often made jokes poking fun at gays or expressing contempt, as a means of bonding in group settings, in his private life he was a central support person for a gay sister. Such contradictory behavior seems pervasive in black communities. It speaks to ambivalence about sexuality in general, about sex as a subject of conversation, and to ambivalent feelings and attitudes toward homosexuality. Various structures of emotional and economic dependence create gaps between attitudes and actions. Yet a distinction must be made between black people overtly expressing prejudice toward homosexuals and homophobic white people who never make homophobic comments but who have the power to actively exploit and oppress gay people in areas of housing, employment, etc. While both groups perpetuate and reinforce each other and this cannot be denied or downplayed, the truth is that the greatest threat to gay rights does not reside in black communities.

It is far more likely that homophobic attitudes can be altered or 10 changed in environments where they have not become rigidly institutionalized. Rather than suggesting that black communities are more homophobic than other communities, and dismissing them, it is important for feminist activists (especially black folks) to examine the nature of that homophobia, to challenge it in constructive ways that lead to change. Clearly religious beliefs and practices in many black communities promote and encourage homophobia. Many Christian blacks folks (like other Christians in this society) are taught in churches that it is a sin to be gay, ironically sometimes by ministers who are themselves gay or bisexual.

In the past year I talked with a black woman Baptist minister, who, 11 although concerned about feminist issues, expressed very negative attitudes about homosexuality, because, she explained, the Bible teaches that it is wrong. Yet in her daily life she is tremendously supportive and caring of gay friends. When I asked her to explain this contradiction, she argued that it was not a contradiction, that the Bible also teaches her to identify with those who are exploited and oppressed, and to demand that they be treated justly. To her way of thinking, committing a sin did not mean that one should be exploited or oppressed.

The contradictions, the homophobic attitudes that underlie her 12 attitudes, indicate that there is a great need for progressive black theologians to examine the role black churches play in encouraging persecution of gay people. Individual members of certain churches in black communities should protest when worship services become a platform for teaching anti-gay sentiments. Often individuals sit and listen to preachers raging against gay people and think the views expressed are amusing and outmoded, and dismiss them without challenge. But if homophobia is to be eradicated in black communities, such attitudes must be challenged.

Recently, especially as black people all over the United States discussed 13 the film version of Alice Walker's novel *The Color Purple,* as well as the book itself (which includes a positive portrayal of two black women being sexual with each other), the notion that homosexuality threatens the continuation of black families seems to have gained new momentum. In some cases, black males in prominent positions, especially those in media, have helped to perpetuate this notion. Tony Brown stated in one editorial, "No lesbian relationship can take the place of a positive love relationship between black women and black men." It is both a misreading of Walker's novel and an expression of homophobia for any reader to project into this work the idea that lesbian relationships exist as a competitive response to heterosexual encounters. Walker suggests quite the contrary.

Just a few weeks ago I sat with two black women friends eating 14 bagels as one of us expressed her intense belief that white people were encouraging black people to be homosexuals so as to further divide black folks. She was attributing the difficulties many professional heterosexual black women have finding lovers, companions, husbands, to homosexuality. We listened to her and then the other woman said, "Now you know we are not going to sit here and listen to this homophobic bull without challenging it."

We pointed to the reality that many black gay people are parents, 15 hence their sexual preference does not threaten the continuation of black families. We stressed that many black gay people have white lovers and that there is no guarantee that were they heterosexual they would be partnered with other black people. We argued that people should be able to choose and claim the sexual preference that best expresses their being, suggesting that while it is probably true that positive portrayals of gay people encourage people to see this as a viable sexual preference or lifestyle, it is equally true that compulsory heterosexuality is promoted to a far greater extent. We suggested that we should all be struggling to create a climate where there is freedom of sexual expression.

She was not immediately persuaded by our arguments, but at least 16 she had different perspectives to consider. Supporters of gay rights in black communities must recognize that education for critical consciousness that explains and critiques prevailing stereotypes is necessary for us to eradicate homophobia. A central myth that must be explored and addressed is the notion that homosexuality means genocide for black families. And in conjunction with discussions of this issue, black people must confront the reality of bisexuality and the extent to which the spread of AIDS in black communities is connected to bisexual transmission of the HIV virus.

To strengthen solidarity between black folks irrespective of our 17 sexual preferences, allegiance must be discussed. This is especially critical as more and more black gay people live outside black communities. Just as black women are often compelled to answer the question—which is more important: feminist movement or black liberation struggle?—women's rights or civil rights?—which are you first: black or female?—gay people face similar questions. Are you more identified with the political struggle of your race and ethnic group or gay rights struggle?

This question is not a simple one. For some people it is raised in such a way that they are compelled to choose one identity over another.

In one case, when a black family learned of their daughter's lesbianism, they did not question her sexual preference (saying they weren't stupid, they had known she was gay), but the racial identity of her lovers. Why white women and not black women? Her gayness, expressed exclusively in relationships with white women, was deemed threatening because it was perceived as estranging her from blackness. 18

Little is written about this struggle. Often black families who can acknowledge and accept gayness find inter-racial coupling harder to accept. Certainly among black lesbians, the issue of black women preferring solely white lovers is discussed but usually in private conversation. These relationships, like all cross-racial intimate relationships are informed by the dynamics of racism and white supremacy. Black lesbians have spoken about absence of acknowledgement of one another at social gatherings where the majority of black women present are with white women lovers. Unfortunately, such incidents reinforce the notion that one must choose between solidarity with one's ethnic group and solidarity with those with whom one shares sexual preference, irrespective of class and ethnic difference or differences in political perspective. 19

Black liberation struggle and gay liberation struggle are both undermined when these divisions are promoted and encouraged. Both gay and straight black people must work to resist the politics of domination as expressed in sexism and racism that lead people to think that supporting one liberation struggle diminishes one's support for another or stands one in opposition to another. As part of education for critical consciousness in black communities, it must be continually stressed that our struggle against racism, our struggle to recover from oppression and exploitation are inextricably linked to all struggles to resist domination—including gay liberation struggle. 20

Often black people, especially non-gay folks, become enraged when they hear a white person who is gay suggest that homosexuality is synonymous with the suffering people experience as a consequence of racial exploitation and oppression. The need to make gay experience and black experience of oppression synonymous seems to be one that surfaces much more in the minds of white people. Too often, it is seen as a way of minimizing or diminishing the particular problems people of color face in a white-supremacist society, especially the problems encountered because one does not have white skin. Many of us have been in discussions where a non-white person—a black person—struggles to explain to white folks that while we can acknowledge that gay people of all colors are harassed and suffer exploitation and domination, we also recognize that there is a significant difference that arises because of the visibility of dark skin. Often homophobic attacks on gay people occur in 21 situations where knowledge of sexual preference is indicated or established—outside of gay bars, for example. While it in no way lessens the severity of such suffering for gay people, or the fear that it causes, it does mean that in a given situation the apparatus of protection and survival may be simply not identifying as gay.

In contrast, most people of color have no choice. No one can hide, 22 change, or mask dark skin color. White people, gay and straight, could show greater understanding of the impact of racial oppression on people of color by not attempting to make these oppressions synonymous, but rather by showing the ways they are linked and yet differ. Concurrently, the attempt by white people to make synonymous experience of homophobic aggression with racial oppression deflects attention away from the particular dual dilemma that non-white gay people face, as individuals who confront both racism and homophobia.

Often black gay folk feel extremely isolated because there are 23 tensions in their relationships with the larger, predominately white gay community created by racism, and tensions within black communities around issues of homophobia. Sometimes, it is easier to respond to such tensions by simply withdrawing from both groups, by refusing to participate or identify oneself politically with any struggle to end domination. By affirming and supporting black people who are gay within our communities, as well as outside our communities, we can help reduce and change the pain of such isolation.

Significantly, attitudes toward sexuality and sexual preference are 24 changing. There is greater acknowledgement that people have different sexual preferences and diverse sexual practices. Given this reality, it is a waste of energy for anyone to assume that their condemnation will ensure that people do not express varied sexual preferences. Many gay people of all races, raised within this homophobic society, struggle to confront and accept themselves, to recover or gain the core of self-love and well-being that is constantly threatened and attacked both from within and without. This is particularly true for people of color who are gay. It is essential that non-gay black people recognize and respect the hardships, the difficulties gay black people experience, extending the love and understanding that is essential for the making of authentic black community. One way we show our care is by vigilant protest of homophobia. By acknowledging the union between black liberation struggle and gay liberation struggle, we strengthen our solidarity, enhance the scope and power of our allegiances, and further our resistance.

## Post-Reading Questions

1. Analyze what Hooks is doing in the first four paragraphs of her essay. What is her overall purpose? How does she organize these four paragraphs? What is she comparing? Why?

2.  What kinds of "evidence" does Hooks provide for her claims about homophobia? How convincing is her evidence? Why? What kinds of evidence would a sociologist provide that she does not provide? What would a sociologist omit that she includes?

3.  Although Hooks attacks feminists who believe black communities are more homophobic than other communities, she appears to have some sympathy for the feminist movement. Where in the essay does she reveal that sympathy? Be specific.

4.  How does Hooks use language to reveal her attitude toward white society? Point to specific words and phrases that suggest her feelings. What is her attitude toward whites?

5.  What, according to Hooks, causes the perception that black communities are more homophobic than other communities? In what other communities do these same causes exist? Can you provide an example? Do you believe that Hooks makes her case about homophobia? Why?

6.  Summarize in a few sentences Hooks' solution to the problem. Then evaluate her solution, providing reasons to support your evaluation.

# PETER D. SALINS ON NEW YORK'S ETHNIC FUTURE

## Pre-Reading Questions

1.  Describe the racial-ethnic make-up of the community within which you grew up. Would you describe your childhood neighborhood as diverse? Why or why not? What are some advantages of living in a diverse neighborhood? What are some disadvantages?

2.  What does the term *melting pot* mean to you? In what way is America viewed as a melting pot? Would you describe your college campus community as a melting pot? Why or why not? Be specific.

3.  Salins believes that ethnic pluralism may be New York City's salvation. What does *ethnic pluralism* mean to you?

4.  What expectations does Salins' title create?

## IN LIVING COLORS
### Peter D. Salins

New York City, America's premier metropolis and its only municipal candidate for "world class" status, is widely assumed to be in decline. Among the many emblems of the malaise—Wall Street in retreat, a rash of homicides, a replay of the fiscal crisis—one hovers just below the surface of polite discourse: New York's changing racial profile. The city's demographic range, which not so long ago seemed to run from Archie Bunker to Jacqueline Onassis, with a large cohort of smart, white yuppies in between, now appears dominated by poor minorities. The subtext of a lot of the grousing, that this growing minority population threatens New York's economy and its social fabric, is false on two counts. New York actually has a more balanced racial mix than most large U.S. cities. And the growing ethnic pluralism that characterizes the city may turn out to be its salvation rather than its downfall.

Since the end of World War II most older cities of the East and    2 Midwest have experienced a steady exodus of white residents moving to the suburbs. Until the 1970s their places were taken by a large influx of Southern blacks. From the 1970s on, the migration of native-born American blacks into the cities has dwindled even as white mobility has continued unabated. In most large cities east of the Mississippi this has resulted in dramatic population declines because the birth rate of their remaining residents hasn't been large enough to offset white flight.

New York has largely confounded this picture of big city "racial    3 succession" through its continuing influx of immigrants and in-migration of Americans from other places. With only 3 percent of the nation's population, the city now receives 15 percent of all legal immigrants. Although New York's current size is a matter of dispute, since 1950 the city's population has fallen at most by 6 percent. (In contrast, Chicago's has shrunk by 18 percent; Philadelphia's by 21 percent; Detroit's by 44 percent. Even Washington, D.C., despite the federal government's growth, has 23 percent fewer people today than in 1950.)

Thanks to immigration, New York's minorities are also far more    4 diverse than those of other U.S. cities, and becoming more so all the time. New York's population is more than 50 percent "minority," as are those of most other large American cities. But because of the number of ethnics, particularly Hispanics, who have moved to New York, the black share of New York's population is only 24 percent, the smallest of any large city east of the Rockies. And unlike the black proportion of most cities, New York's hasn't grown much over the past two decades: it was actually slightly smaller in 1987 than it was in 1980. New York now has nearly as many Hispanics as blacks. Only Los Angeles and San Antonio have large proportions of Hispanic residents. In absolute numbers, New York is the most Hispanic city in the nation, and its Hispanic citizens are uniquely diverse, with the majority coming from at least eight Spanish-speaking nations.

New York also has a rapidly growing Asian population. Although    5 Asian births accounted for only 5 percent of the total births in New York in 1987, Asians constituted more than 20 percent of all immigrants that year. At the same time, the much-celebrated influx of white yuppies from the suburbs and beyond has largely offset the traditional tide of suburban out-migration of the middle-aged middle class. European immigration too has experienced a dramatic revival. The ranks of European immigrants, who now account for 10 percent of the total, will swell even further with the growing exodus of Soviet Jews and large numbers of other East bloc refugees. A stable white population of 40 percent, and a rapidly growing Asian cohort that may reach 15 to 20 percent, might actually reduce New York's black and Hispanic shares below their current levels.

New York's new wellsprings of ethnic diversity are not only shatter- 6 ing stereotypes about the city's population. They are also propelling its economy. Consider the familiar paradigm of deteriorating neighborhoods. In the 1970s New York was losing more than 40,000 apartments a year to abandonment and destruction. Today many of the worst neighborhoods are reviving, and housing abandonment has been reduced to a trickle. Some of this is the product of "gentrification," but mostly it is the result of immigrants colonizing precincts that other New Yorkers have given up on.

Queens in particular has been transformed. The No. 7 IRT subway 7 line cuts an impressive international swath through the western half of the borough. It emerges from its East River tunnel to graze the edge of the vibrant Greek community in Astoria, proceeds to bisect a vast zone of Latin American settlement in Jackson Heights and Corona, and reaches its terminus in Flushing amid New York's most heterogeneous Asian complex, which is dominated by large concentrations of Koreans and Chinese with a strong admixture from the Indian subcontinent.

In Brooklyn Asians and Caribbean Hispanics have revived the badly 8 deteriorated neighborhood of Sunset Park, and Haitians, notwithstanding their status as among the poorest of immigrants, have brought new vigor to East Flatbush and Crown Heights. Jews from diverse national and theological backgrounds have imparted social stability and rising real estate values to a number of formerly troubled areas: Hasidim in Williamsburg, Syrians and other Middle Easterners in Gravesend and Sheepshead Bay, and Russians in Brighton Beach. New York's least loved neighborhoods in the Bronx and upper Manhattan are being reclaimed by Dominicans, and the expansion of Manhattan's Chinatown is reversing the severe blight of much of the Lower East Side.

The housing and settlement patterns of New York's immigrants are 9 only a reflection of their integration into the city's economic life. In addition to the well-known commercial niches that particular ethnics have carved out—Korean produce markets, Indian newsstands, Greek luncheonettes, etc.—the less skilled immigrants such as Dominicans and Haitians have proved indispensable to the success of low-wage manufacturing and service industries.

New York's ethnic profile also contradicts the popular perception of 10 the city's racial politics. Politics here do not revolve around race, or even ethnicity, because no single ethnic group commands a voting majority, and none cares to enter even transitory ethnic coalitions. The black-Hispanic coalition that New York's liberal and black political leaders have long yearned for seems an ever more distant prospect as the Hispanic bloc is increasingly fragmented by nationality and class differences. David Dinkins was elected mayor because New Yorkers had tired of Ed Koch after twelve years, not because he was black. Race may explain his appeal to the majority of black voters, but the Hispanic, Jewish, and other white voters who provided his margin of victory were attracted precisely because Dinkins promised to rise above racial politics.

There are, of course, tensions involved in this ethnic chaos: clashes 11 between old and new ethnics; resentment at rising real estate prices in booming neighborhoods; increasing crime rates owing to the youth of many new immigrant populations. But on balance, the ethnic caldron that characterizes New York's demographics is a good thing. The city's immigrant-driven culture has given it a ragged energy reminiscent of American cities at the turn of the century. How much better a fate than that of so many other American metropolises, their newly rehabilitated but half-empty downtowns surrounded by a sea of physical, social, and population decline.

## Post-Reading Questions

1.  Why do you think Salins chose "In Living Colors" as the title of his article?
2.  In the first paragraph, Salins states the main point of his article and two reasons to support his viewpoint. Identify the main point and his two reasons. How do his language choices in the first paragraph establish his *tone*? In particular, what do phrases such as "subtext of a lot of grousing" and "surface of polite discourse" suggest about Salins' attitude toward people who describe New York as a city in decline?
3.  Salins uses language to reveal his feelings about racial diversity. Review the verbs and nouns he chooses. Then write a paragraph explaining how his language choices reveal his feelings about racial diversity.
4.  How might Salins' profession as a professor of urban planning have influenced his viewpoint about New York? How might it have affected his writing strategies? Would he have written this article differently for an academic journal?
5.  This article first appeared in *The New Republic* magazine. If you are unfamiliar with this magazine, go to the library and skim through a few issues. What kinds of articles are regular features in the magazine? What can you infer about the readers just by examining the magazine? Ask some of your teachers or the reference librarian about

the magazine. What can they add to your understanding of the magazine's readers?

6. Salins teaches at Hunter College in New York City. How might his status as a New Yorker influence his viewpoint? How might non-New Yorkers interpret differently what Salins "sees" happening in New York? What reasons lie behind the different conclusions reached by New Yorkers and non-New Yorkers?

7. In paragraph ten, his concluding paragraph, Salins refers to New York as an "ethnic caldron." How does the concept of an ethnic caldron differ from that of the melting pot? Which view do you believe more closely describes American society today? Why?

8. In what ways does Salins say New York is different from other large, older cities in the East and Midwest? In what ways is it similar? What positive contributions to New York have immigrants made, according to Salins? Be specific.

9. Why does Salins begin his concluding paragraph with a concession statement? What is he willing to concede? How does the phrase "of course" affect the nature of his concession? How do his word choices temper his concession?

# 6
· · · · · · · · · · · · · ·
# OPTIONAL WRITING ASSIGNMENTS FOCUSED ON COMMUNITY

The following list of assignments provides contexts within which you can develop essays on this chapter's theme. If you choose one of these options, you will need to analyze your writing context and decide how to achieve your writing purpose for the particular readers you target (see "The Rhetorical Approach to Academic Writing" in Chapter 2).

*1. Write an essay describing one specific personal experience you had as a member of a particular community.* The experience should concern competition or cooperation among group members or between two groups. Use whatever descriptive strategies you can to help your readers (your fellow students) "see" the experience as it occurred. Your purpose in narrating this experience, however, is not only to recreate it, but to help you make your point (thesis) about competition or cooperation. You may, if your teacher agrees, compare or contrast your experience with the experiences described by Chang or Hooks.

*2. Analyze a community (social, cultural, racial, religious) to which you belong or one you wish to learn more about.* Use your own as well as others' experiences to describe the community's values, rituals, rules about behavior, and symbols. Before you write your essay, decide whether your purpose will be to explain in a very neutral and uninvolved way a main point you want to make about this community, or to persuade your readers (your fellow students) that your personal judgment or evaluation of this community should be accepted. Consider interviewing other members of this group as "experts" or insiders to obtain information about the community. Be sure to weave your personal opinions and experiences together with those of others into a balanced, complete analysis.

*3. Imagine you are a college freshman returning to your high school to address a group of students who have been accepted to your college for next fall.* The college you are attending is a large, public institution; its student and faculty population is culturally diverse. However, your high school is in a very small town. The students there have had little exposure to many of the ethnic groups they will meet as freshmen. You have been asked to offer some suggestions for adapting to college culture to those who will attend your college in the fall.

Drawing from your reading on community and from your own and others' past experiences with similar adjustments, make an argument for a particular approach to respecting cultural diversity on a college campus. Tell the students what they will find, what strategies you recommend, and why you favor this approach.

*4. Choose one of the issues raised in one or more of the readings in this chapter, perhaps immigration quotas, the biodiversity crisis, or racial and ethnic conflicts.* Take a position for or against a particular approach to the issue. Then, drawing upon your reading of the articles and essays in this chapter, your own and others' experiences, and information from some outside-of-the-classroom sources (an interview, a library article, a newspaper article or news program), state and explain the reasons for your position. Remember to consider what information your readers (your fellow students) will have, how they currently feel about this issue, and what kinds of questions they will ask about the reasons and evidence you present. You will also be expected to provide documentation for any outside-of-the-class sources to which you refer.

*5. Write an argument defending or attacking Peter D. Salins' view about New York's (or any other large city's) future.* Consider both pro and con arguments, and address what you have to say to an audience of college students. Whatever position you take, include a brief summary of Salins' main points. Then for each reason you use to defend or attack his view, provide detailed explanation in the form of information from other readings in this chapter and from your own and others' experiences and ideas.

*6. Conduct a field research experiment in which you observe some kind of animal behavior.* (Before planning your experiment, consult the section in the Research Appendix that describes field research strategies.) Plan your observations carefully for time and place. Keep the experiment simple, and make sure you have a research question before you begin. Take careful notes of your observations. Then write a report of your experiment, using the four-part format most scientists use: introduction, method and materials, results, and conclusion. Your readers are the members of the classroom community formed around the theme of animal and human communities.

*7. Conduct a field research experiment in which you observe members of a human community interacting, perhaps in a pre-school class, a college organization, or a charitable group.* Your purpose is to observe this group on a regular basis to determine the kinds of cooperative and competitive behavior members exhibit. Remember, your purpose is to observe and take notes, then analyze those notes to identify patterns of cooperative or competitive behavior. Write a report of your field research using the four-part format most scientists use: introduction, materials and methods, results, and conclusion. Your readers are the members of the classroom community developed during your reading of this chapter.

# 7

# The Power and Limits of Language

Do we control language or does it control us? How does
language work? Is language a barrier or a blessing to
cross-cultural communication? What role does language play
in communication between genders? How does language
affect the distribution of power in American society?

## 1
## DEVELOPING A RHETORICAL APPROACH

The above questions define the issues around which this chapter
revolves. Once again, you will first consider your own and your peers'
experience on these issues. Then, you will consider those experiences
and the readings included in this chapter from a rhetorical perspective:
you will ask questions concerning the authors' purposes, their audiences, their strategies for accomplishing those purposes and reaching
those audiences. In the end, you will ask the same questions of your
own writing as you develop your own purposes, senses of audience, and
strategies for accomplishing those purposes.

Why focus a chapter on language, which to most people seems an
innocuous topic best studied by English teachers, linguists, and communications experts? The answer to that question is that language is

not as simple as it seems. Scientists have long recognized the difficulties language presents even when they attempt to describe the simplest of phenomena in objective terms. Advertisers have long recognized the power of language to sell and persuade; consumers, on the other hand, have long recognized just how difficult it can be to analyze advertising language in order to make informed and rational purchases. You, as a student, might have learned the problems of dealing with the ambiguities of language when you misunderstood the requirements implied in a school assignment.

Recently, men and women have been looking closely at language to understand some of the hidden gender prejudices contained in the ways we talk about each other. Some of these gender critics argue that the perspectives we take concerning ourselves as men and women are often most influenced by the ways gender is treated in the language we use with each other.

Recently, too, many educators and language experts have been studying the whole notion of literacy. For years, literacy was defined as the ability to use language well enough to get along in society—to hold a military or civil service job, for example; to read purchasing or rental contracts; to get information from newspapers, all the basic reading and writing skills required to carry out everyday activities in an industrialized, print-oriented culture. Currently, however, many language experts have begun to question this limited definition of literacy. Rather than define literacy as society's means of using language and language education as a way of training people to fit into pre-established societal roles, these experts are suggesting that literacy should become part of the whole process of empowering individuals. This new way of considering literacy does not ask what the individual needs to do with language in order to fit into a job or social role, but what the society needs to do with its language to better fit the needs of people. Does the language of governments and public agencies need to be revised to be more accessible to a wider range of people? Does literacy education need to be changed to recognize the diverse linguistic backgrounds of a pluralistic society? These types of questions alter the whole notion of *functional* literacy from an emphasis on the individual "fitting in" to a system to one of the system coming to recognize and adapt itself to the individual.

What does it mean to take a *rhetorical* approach to the discussions of language that you find in this chapter? First, it means that you need to define the issue you want to address in your writing. Once you have defined an issue, you need to define your purpose in writing and the audience you address. You probably will not come to know your purpose and audience until you have participated in several group discussions, written and heard responses to several of your own drafts, and read at least several of the readings in this chapter. Finally, as you write drafts and hear responses to them, you will develop strategies for approaching your audience and achieving your purpose. These strategies will include making choices in organization, types of evidence, and style that you think will prove persuasive to your audience.

## 2
. . . . . . . . . . . . . .
## GENERATING IDEAS ABOUT THE POWER AND LIMITS OF LANGUAGE BEFORE READING

Language takes part in almost everything we do. To put yourself into the frame of mind to think about this chapter's contents, look closely at the role language plays and has played in your life. Think, too, about the way language functions in the public media—particularly newspapers, television, and radio. Also remember that every aspect of public life, including politics, education, professional athletics, and religion, is influenced by and influences language. Consider the following questions and activities as useful ways of generating ideas on the power and limits of language. Some you may work on in discussion groups; others you may respond to on your own in your journal or in freewriting; still others you may simply want to consider carefully before you read the essays in this chapter. Your teacher may also give you directions on how to use these questions and activities.

### Probing Personal Experience

1. *Take twenty minutes to listen in on the conversation of a group of people with whom you have everyday contact, either at work, at school, or at home.* Do not take notes while listening. Immediately after listening, however, take detailed notes; then, write a journal entry or focused writing in which you summarize and comment on the content of the conversation. What does the conversation tell you about the people involved in it? What does each person's language and way of speaking tell you about his or her character and personality?

2. *Look back at a novel or short story that you have read and liked.* Choose a character that you found interesting or important. Write a short paragraph in which you describe that character; describe the kind of person he or she was, how he or she responded to important situations, and how he or she treated other characters. Then, find a passage of dialogue in which the character you have chosen reveals him- or herself through the use of language. Show how that dialogue passage either confirms or refutes your original analysis of this character.

3. *Focus on a movie character who uses language in an original and self-defining way.* Describe some of the characterizing phrases and

features of this character's way of speaking, and explain why these features have appealed to popular audiences. For example, Marlon Brando in the 1950s, James Cagney in the 1930s and 40s, and Humphrey Bogart in the late 1930s and 40s were well-known for their styles of speaking. (You can rent their films at video stores.) Arnold Schwartzenegger has also recently become well-known for his movie dialogue, particularly in the *Terminator* films.

4. *Adolescents in every generation have developed their own distinctive speaking styles.* How has this generation of adolescents attempted to develop a style of its own? Or, if you wish to look back at the language of a previous generation—the 1950s, the Beatniks, or gangsters in the 1930s, for example—you may find information by viewing old movies, reading fiction of the period, or by interviewing those who lived in the period. Your job is to describe and summarize the style, to explain why it came into existence, and why it seemed to appeal to large groups of people.

5. *Look back at your own experience as a speaker and writer.* Have you ever had trouble moving from spoken to written discourse? Have there been times when your writing sounded too much like speech, or when your speech sounded too much like writing? Or have you simply had trouble with your writing because you mix speech patterns with formal written discourse? If any of these questions apply to your experience, describe and analyze your responses.

6. *Listen to the speech of men and women in your school, work, or home environment.* Do you hear differences in the way men and women are addressed, described, or characterized in language? If you do, describe these differences and explain why they exist. Are they in some cases motivated by gender stereotypes? Are these stereotypes caused by prejudices in the speakers, in the language itself, or by a combination of the two?

7. *Have you ever known someone who missed a job opportunity, scholarship, or prestigious position because of his or her language?* Describe that person and the situation. Then, explain what you think were the causes of this lost opportunity. Did the person involved lack some kind of skill (grammar, usage, handwriting, spelling, for example)? Was he or she penalized for using a particular dialect? Did he or she misread the requirements of the situation (use slang or informal speech when some formality was required, for example)?

## Freewriting to Capture Personal Experience

A list of topics related to language that you can freewrite about in short, ten-minute sessions follows. (For a discussion of freewriting, see pages 103 to 104.)

1. *Write a description of a situation in which your language was the primary influence on what others thought of you.* In your description,

focus on the way language defined the responses of those around you.

*2. Immediately after watching a television situation comedy, write a non-stop description and analysis of one of the characters on the show.* Focus on how that character was defined by her or his language. Also, explain why this character is humorous or interesting to a popular audience.

*3. Irony occurs when language is used in ways that suggest meanings that are not what they seem on a literal level.* Watch a network or cable news broadcast to see whether the broadcasters betray any ironic intentions. If they do, describe the situation in which the ironic message is communicated. How was the irony relayed—by tone of voice, by facial expression, or by visual–verbal contrast in the message itself?

*4. Television is, supposedly, a medium in which* put-on *is common.* Put-ons occur when, for example, a commercial advertiser makes fun of its own product, or when a television comic ridicules his own dress or habits. The effect of a put-on is complex, because viewers both laugh at and identify with the person doing the put-on. Viewers may laugh at the advertisers who ridicule their products, but they also tend to identify with them as honest folks with good senses of humor. Find a good example of put-on. Describe it and evaluate its effectiveness as communication. Does it get the desired effect? How?

*5. Interview a member of your family, a work companion, or a friend whom you think has a complex language background.* You may, for example, choose someone who has had to learn a second language in order to get along in a new country, or someone who has entered a very technical field (say medicine, science, or law) and has had to learn the jargon of that field. Write your questions beforehand. Then, listen carefully as your subject responds to your questions. As soon as you finish the interview, write (as quickly as you can and preferably without stopping) a description of your subject's responses.


# 3
· · · · · · · · · · · · ·
## DEVELOPING A RHETORICAL CONTEXT
## THROUGH GROUP ACTIVITIES

The following activities are intended for use by workshop groups of three to five people. (If you are collaborating for the first time, you should read the description of strategies for effective collaboration on pages 104 to 105.)

*1. Define a group language project in which each group member assumes a different responsibility.* First, define the purpose of your group. Do you want to find more information on a current campus or community language issue? Begin by defining the problem; then, list the kinds of information that your group thinks would help solve the problem. Assign each group member the job of getting a particular kind of information. Some may interview a person; others may use library research; still others may construct and distribute a brief survey. Finally, meet as a group, discuss findings, and write a brief group report to be distributed to the entire class.

2. *The group doing this project selects a particular public figure—a politician, a local teacher or professor who is involved in significant research, an accomplished athlete, or a well-known artist.* The purpose of the project is to report on this public figure's attitude toward language. Does this public figure think language plays an important role in his or her life? What examples of significant language-oriented experiences does this person use to explain or illustrate his or her position on language? Does the athlete or politician, for example, feel abused or fairly treated by the media? Does the artist think that the critic's words do justice to his or her work? Does the teacher think language plays an important part in teaching? Does he build an appreciation of language into his teaching? Does the researcher think that language accurately or inaccurately describes her research? Again, each group member takes on the responsibility of finding and presenting a particular kind of information. One group member may interview the public figure; a second may find and review printed material on the subject; a third may review video or photographic material on the subject.

3. *This chapter contains three clusters of professional essays on language: the first focuses on language and the issue of multiculturalism, the second on the issue of language and gender, and the third on the issue of language and power.* Looking ahead, one workshop group may want to choose one cluster, say the one on language and power, and produce a preliminary report on the issue for the entire class. Their job is to think of ways in which the language and power issue applies to the local scene (campus life, local community, or local business, industrial, and commercial interests). The group's report should show how the issue applies to a particular aspect of local culture, and it should provide several different ways of looking at the problems the issue defines. The group members should again be assigned different research and writing tasks.

# 4
## USING READINGS TO DEVELOP
## A RHETORICAL COMMUNITY

The readings in this chapter are organized into four sections. The opening essay by Lewis Thomas sets a general context for the readings that follow by focusing on the capability language has for changing and adapting to different environments and conditions. The subsequent three sections are devoted to the following issues: **language and multiculturalism, language and gender,** and **language and power.** Each issue cluster takes up in more specific terms the principle of change and adaptability introduced early in Thomas' essay.

## The Readings in This Chapter

Lewis Thomas' essay establishes several language principles that relate to one overriding quality in language: its dynamic ability to accommodate change. In fact, for Thomas, linguistic change, rather than threatening social stability, is what enables language to meet the changing social, scientific, and efficiency needs of human culture. Language's essential flexibility enables human beings to adapt to changing information, new value systems, and a dynamic natural world. This sense of the potential for change built into language is the informing principle behind all the readings in this chapter. Even when an author of one of these essays argues that a current linguistic practice is wrong or unjust, there is the underlying assumption that language itself would allow for, even encourage, the change of that practice, without in any way decreasing the expressive and communicative power of language itself.

The cluster of three essays that focus on multiculturalism provides both a general perspective on the issue of linguistic diversity and a specific focus on the language of two American minority groups (African American and Native American). Ralph E. Hamil, in "One World, One Language," summarizes many of the arguments for linguistic universalism. Underlying this position is the belief that many international economic and social problems would be resolved if people from all over the world shared a common or official language. Hamil reviews the possibility of existing languages, such as French or English, assuming that international role; he also describes the efforts of supporters of artificial languages, such as Esperanto, to establish them as an official international tongue.

The other side of this issue of linguistic universalism and diversity is represented in the essays of Dorothy Z. Seymour and Sydney J. Ortiz. In "Black Children, Black Speech," Seymour argues that English teachers, indeed all teachers of American students, must come to accept black dialects and, by implication, the dialects of *all* students as autonomous, rule-governed systems of language that warrant respect. She says that the students who speak these dialects will not feel respected by the larger society until this kind of linguistic understanding is a fact. In "The Language We Know," Ortiz makes a similar argument on behalf of Native American oral traditions, which he feels are at the center of the culture of his own people (Acoma Pueblo). Ortiz says that his people must be careful to preserve their oral tradition, its stories and poems and records, because their cultural past will be lost without them. He also believes that this particular style of speaking and living gives his people a distinct and original identity; to destroy that tradition would be to destroy that identity.

Two essays on gender and language form the second cluster in this chapter. Alleen Pace Nilsen, in "Sexism in English," argues that the English we use every day contains many kinds of gender stereotyping. Sexism will remain a part of our culture as long as we fail to eradicate this linguistic stereotyping. In "You Are What You Say," Robin Lakoff carries Nilsen's discussion a step further. She shows how conversational tone, the "way" something is said, suggests gender stereotyping; she also suggests that women in our culture often are given passive roles through customary use of language.

The third cluster of essays in this chapter focuses on the issue of language and power. In "The Disenfranchised: Silent and Unseen," Kozol describes in personal and statistical terms the frustration and lack of power experienced in our society by those who are illiterate. He attempts to persuade us to act to help those disenfranchised by their inability to read and write in our print-oriented and technological society. Kozol also argues that our government often attempts to hide the extent of the illiteracy problem from the public because, in many cases, the government does not want to spend the money needed to empower those who are illiterate. In "Adult Literacy: The Ingenuous and the Critical Visions," Freire discusses in specific terms what needs to be done to educate people for active participation in democratic government. Freire distinguishes between "functional" and "critical" literacy; he also argues that the urge to use literacy to become actively involved, critically thinking citizens of the larger society must be instilled from very early on in an individual's literacy training. For Freire, who has spent many years working on the education of Brazilian and Chilean peasants, literacy is not simply a matter of mechanically sounding out and spelling words. It is a complex process in which words and meanings grow out of each other as they are learned together; this interaction of meaning and word then becomes the individual's primary tool for expressing his or her consciousness of what needs to be done in the political and social areas of life.

William Lutz, in "Doublespeak," describes several ways in which politicians, government officials, advertisers, and other public figures use language in dishonest and duplicitous ways. Implied in Lutz's description of public doublespeak is the idea that all informed citizens should have the ability to analyze and criticize what they hear, read, and see. Lutz's argument, like those of Kozol and Freire, encourages a more active and participatory literacy than that implied by the words "functional literacy." For these writers, words can be instruments of self-expression and power.

## Developing Community

Your class and writing groups become the communities through which you develop ideas on language and power. An effective strategy for putting your small group experience to good use is to find a language issue that interests all the members of your group. Members of a writing group usually want to make it easier on themselves by focusing on one of the issues addressed in a primary way in the readings. A list of the major language issues addressed in this chapter follows:

> Language as a Tool for Describing the Natural World (Thomas)
> Language and Cultural Diversity (Seymour, Ortiz)
> The Possibilities for an International Language (Hamil)
> Language and Gender; Language and Sexual Stereotyping (Nilsen, Lakoff)
> Language as an Instrument of Power (Kozol, Freire)
> Using Language in Confusing and Dishonest Ways (Lutz)
> Using Language in Demeaning Ways (Nilsen, Lakoff, Kozol)
> Language, Culture, and Ethnic Identity (Seymour, Ortiz)

Once your group has chosen an issue, divide responsibilities among group members. Some may want to find more information than that presented in the chapter readings; others may want to coordinate and deliver in-process presentations to the whole class; still others may want to work on writing group reports. When responsibilities have been assigned, groups can work together through entire chapters. Each member of the group must understand his or her responsibilities, be able to carry out those responsibilities in a timely way, and learn something from group activity that can be effectively transferred to his or her own writing. What the group collectively discovers and passes on to its members in the process of interaction is far more significant than what the individuals in the group do along the way. The group strategies described here provide effective ways of developing content for essay assignments.

The second and most important strategy for developing useful writing communities is rhetorical. Each writing group, in other words, must ensure that it functions as a unit capable of analyzing readings and the drafts of its members from a rhetorical perspective. Groups must help their members define their purposes and audiences, develop and revise organizational and stylistic strategies, and polish and edit their written work. These rhetorical strategies help place ideas within effective essay forms that suit content as well as purpose and intended audience.

# 5

. . . . . . . . . . . . . .

## READINGS ON THE POWER
## AND LIMITS OF LANGUAGE

# LEWIS THOMAS ON SPEAKING

### Pre-Reading Questions and Activities

1. Provide examples of particular new word coinages that have come into English over the past two years.

2. Observe small children using language during play. Find a place to observe where you will not be intrusive and where you will not be interrupted. Take notes as you observe and answer the following questions. How does children's language differ from adults' language? What do children try to accomplish through language? Are they effective in controlling or manipulating their environments through language? What are they learning about language?

3. Do you think language change is a good or a bad thing? Illustrate your answer with examples drawn from your own experience.

## ON SPEAKING OF SPEAKING
### Lewis Thomas

There is nothing at all wrong with the English language, so far as I can  1
see, but that may only be because I cannot see ahead. If I were placed in charge of it, as chairman, say, of a National Academy for the Improvement of Language, I would not lay a finger on English. It suits every need that I can think of: flexibility, clarity, subtlety of metaphor, ambiguity wherever ambiguity is needed (which is more often than is generally acknowledged), and most of all changeability. I like the notion of a changing language. As a meliorist, I am convinced that all past changes were for the better; I have no doubt that today's English is a considerable improvement over Elizabethan or Chaucerian talk, and miles ahead of Old English. By now the language has reached its stage of ultimate perfection, and I'll be satisfied to have it this way forever.

But I know I'm wrong about this. English is shifting and changing  2
before our eyes and ears, beyond the control of all individuals, committees, academies, and governments. The speakers of earlier versions undoubtedly felt the same satisfaction with their speech in their time.

Chaucer's generation, and all the generations before, could not have been aware of any need to change or improve. Montaigne was entirely content with sixteenth-century French and obviously delighted by what he could do with it. Long, long ago, the furthermost ancestors of English speech must have got along nicely in Proto-Indo-European without a notion that their language would one day vanish.

"Vanish" is the wrong word anyway for what happened. The roots of     3
several thousand Indo-European words are still alive and active, tucked up neatly like symbionts inside other words in Greek, Latin, and all the Germanic tongues, including English. Much of what we say to each other today, in English, could be interpreted as Greek with an Indo-European accent. Three or four centuries from now, it is probable that today's English will be largely incomprehensible to everyone except the linguistic scholars and historians.

The ancient meanings of the Indo-European roots are sometimes     4
twisted around, even distorted beyond recognition, but they are still there, resonating inside, reminding. The old root *gheue*, meaning simply to call, became *gudam* in Germanic and then "God" in English. *Meug* was a root signifying something damp and slippery, and thousands of years later it turned into "meek" in proper English and "mooch" in slang, also "schmuck." *Bha* was the Indo-European word for speaking, becoming *phanai* in Greek with the same meaning, then used much later for our most fundamental word indicating the inability to speak: "infancy." *Ster* was a root meaning to stiffen; it became *sterban* in Germanic and *steorfan* in Old English, meaning to die, and then turned into "starve" in our speech.

The changes in language will continue forever, but no one knows for     5
sure who does the changing. One possibility is that children are responsible. Derek Bickerton, professor of linguistics at the University of Hawaii, explores this in his book *Roots of Language*. Sometime around 1880, a language catastrophe occurred in Hawaii when thousands of immigrant workers were brought to the islands to work for the new sugar industry. These people, speaking Chinese, Japanese, Korean, Portuguese, and various Spanish dialects, were unable to communicate with one another or with the native Hawaiians or the dominant English-speaking owners of the plantations, and they first did what such mixed-language populations have always done; they spoke Pidgin English (a corruption of "business English"). A pidgin is not really a language at all, more like a set of verbal signals used to name objects but lacking the grammatical rules needed for expressing thought and ideas. And then, within a single generation, the whole mass of mixed peoples began speaking a totally new tongue: Hawaiian Creole. The new speech contained ready-made words borrowed from all the original tongues, but bore little or no resemblance to the predecessors in the rules used for stringing the words together. Although generally regarded as a "primitive" language, Hawai-

ian Creole was constructed with a highly sophisticated grammar. Professor Bickerton's great discovery is that this brand-new speech could have been made only by the children. There wasn't time enough to allow for any other explanation. Soon after the influx of workers in 1880 the speech was Hawaiian Pidgin, and within the next twenty-five or thirty years the accepted language was Creole. The first immigrants, the parents who spoke Pidgin, could not have made the new language and then taught it to the children. They could not themselves understand Creole when it appeared. Nor could the adult English speakers in charge of the place either speak or comprehend Creole. According to Bickerton's research, it simply had to have been the work of children, crowded together, jabbering away at each other, playing.

Bickerton cites this historic phenomenon as evidence, incontrovert-  6
ible in his view, for the theory that language is a biological, innate, genetically determined property of human beings, driven by a center or centers in the brain that code out grammar and syntax. His term for the gift of speech is "bioprogram." The idea confirms and extends the proposal put forward by Noam Chomsky, almost three decades ago, that human beings are unique in their possession of brains equipped for generating grammar. But the most fascinating aspect of the new work is its evidence that children—and probably very young children at that— are able to construct a whole language, working at it together, or more likely *playing* at it together.

It should make you take a different view of children, eliciting  7
something like awe. We have always known that childhood is the period in which new languages as well as one's own can be picked up quickly and easily. The facility disappears in most people around the time of adolescence, and from then on the acquisition of a new language is hard, slogging labor. Children are gifted at it, of course. But it requires a different order of respect to take in the possibility that children make up languages, change languages, perhaps have been carrying the responsibility for evolving language from the first human communication to twentieth-century speech. If it were not for the children and their special gift we might all be speaking Indo-European or Hittite, but here we all are, speaking several thousand different languages and dialects, most of which would be incomprehensible to the human beings on earth just a few centuries back.

Perhaps we should be paying serious attention to the possible role  8
played by children in the origin of speech itself. It is of course not known when language first appeared in our species, and it is pure guesswork as to how it happened. One popular guess is that at a certain stage in the evolution of the human skull, and of the brain therein, speech became a possibility in a few mutant individuals. Thereafter, these intellectual people and their genes outcompeted all their speechless cousins, and natural selection resulted in *Homo sapiens*. This notion would require the

recurrence of the same mutation in many different, isolated communities all around the globe, or else one would have to assume that a lucky few speakers managed to travel with remarkable agility everywhere on earth, leaving their novel genes behind.

Another possibility, raised by the new view of children and speech, is that human language did not pop up as a special mutation, but came into existence as a latent property of all human brains at some point in the evolution of the whole species. The environment required for expression of the brain centers involved in the process was simply children, enough children crowded together in circumstances where they could spend a lot of time playing together. A critical mass of children in a sufficiently stable society could have been achieved whenever large enough numbers of families settled down to live in close quarters, as may have happened long ago in the tribal life of hunters and gatherers or in the earliest agricultural communities.

It makes an interesting scenario. The adults and wise elders of the tribe, sitting around a fire speaking a small-talk pidgin, pointing at one thing or another and muttering isolated words. No syntax, no strings of words, no real ideas, no metaphors. Somewhere nearby, that critical mass of noisy young children, gabbling and shouting at each other, their voices rising in the exultation of discovery, talking, talking, and forever thereafter never stopping.

## Post-Reading Questions

1.  Why does Thomas devote such a long paragraph (paragraph 5) to his Hawaiian Creole story? How does it fit in with the points about language that he makes in later paragraphs?
2.  Why does Thomas make so much of the possibility that children might actually have caused many of the language changes that we know today? How and why do children have more luck producing useful changes in language than adults? Why have conservative language experts experienced less success in halting language change than children have had in fomenting that change?
3.  What does play have to do with the development of language? Might early human beings have had more success experimenting in a playful way with language than they did when being serious with it? Why? Why not?
4.  Describe the two theories of the evolution of language that Thomas presents in paragraphs 8 and 9. Which one do you find more convincing? Why?
5.  Thomas seems to support the view that language is a powerful tool for developing and communicating human action and thought because it both resists and encourages change. How do you think those who wish to use language as a way of altering social conven-

tions would feel about Thomas's particular way of celebrating the dynamic qualities of language? Why might social reformers find hope in the fact that language itself will resist change only to a certain point?

6. How does Thomas achieve *coherence* (the reader's sense that the text hangs together, its parts flowing together to create a unified whole)? Where are words repeated from paragraph to paragraph to create clear connections among main ideas? Where in the text does Thomas inject analysis of his own earlier statements as a means of keeping the flow of ideas going?

7. What kind of understanding of language does Thomas wish his readers to have once they have finished this essay?

8. Who is the intended audience of this essay? Is it a well educated audience? Is Thomas addressing specialists of one kind or another? To what language features would you point in supporting your answer to this audience question?

# RALPH E. HAMIL ON ONE LANGUAGE

## Pre-Reading Questions

1. What would be gained or lost by having the whole world use one language? List advantages and disadvantages.

2. Describe a situation in which you did not speak the same language as the person with whom you had to communicate. Did you manage to communicate? How? If you did not, what did you do to solve the problem?

3. Describe a person you have known who was memorable because of the language he or she spoke. Be sure to work some of your subject's most memorable language into your description.

## ONE WORLD, ONE LANGUAGE
### Ralph E. Hamil

Language differences have often made existing economic and political conflicts worse and, in some cases, have led to bloodshed. In the twentieth century alone, language-inspired riots and terrorist attacks have occurred in Québec (English/French); Belgium (French/Flemish); Indonesia (Indonesian/Malay); India (Hindi/Urdu); and Sri Lanka (Sinhala/Tamil).

Sharing the same language does not guarantee harmony among people, but a common language does reduce the likelihood of violent strife by making diplomatic, commercial, scientific, and cultural exchanges easier and less liable to misunderstandings. If the 18 nations of Latin America each spoke a different language, wars among them would, no doubt, be far more frequent.

In the seventeenth century, improved transportation, together with    3 the decline in the use of Latin as an international language, made Europeans desire new ways to ease communication between speakers of different languages. Comenius, a Bohemian bishop and educator, recommended that the leading languages of Europe be adopted internationally, with French and English serving the West and Russian the East. Some years earlier, the French mathematician and philosopher René Descartes had suggested constructing an artificial language. Both these concepts—hegemony of one or more existing languages or the universal adoption of an artificial "second language"—have spawned many proposals and variations over the years; both ideas are still being actively pursued today.

## ELEVATING AN EXISTING LANGUAGE

At first glance, it appears easier to elevate an existing language to the    4 status of official regional or world tongue and promote its use by having it taught in the schools of every country. Suggestions for languages to be so honored have been numerous—even including Basque, a tongue spoken by only 700,000 people who live in the Pyrenees Mountains (along the border between Spain and France), but "neutral" since it is apparently unrelated to any other language on earth. Setting up French and English as co-equal world tongues has had its advocates, too. And in the 1960s, Malcom X urged American blacks to study Chinese, which he predicted was likely to become the most powerful political language of the future.

Considering the enormous difficulty of introducing an "unknown"    5 neutral language into global use, and the political and emotional resistance certain to be encountered in elevating one "major" language at the expense of others, a more practical approach, at least for the short run, is to agree upon the adoption of certain widely used tongues as the paramount or "official" language for specific regions or uses. In this spirit, English was adopted as the language to be used on manufactured goods to indicate their country of origin. Thus we read *Made in Germany,* not *Fabriziert in Deutschland,* on the souvenir we bring back from a visit to Munich. Unless, of course, it says *Made in Japan.* In the same way, English has been used for many years as the language for radio communications between aircraft and control towers at all international airports.

Examples of language dominance over a geographic region can be    6 found in former colonies of France, England, and Spain where these "imported" languages came to dominate pre-existing languages and cultures for many years. Even in India, whose cultural and linguistic traditions stretch back unbroken for thousands of years, two centuries of British rule established English as the most frequently used medium of communication between people from different parts of the country—which is the most linguistically fragmented on earth. More than 150 different languages are spoken in India, and of these no single tongue, not even the "official" language, Hindi, is spoken by more than 30% of the people.

Both H. G. Wells and Joseph Stalin expected their respective native 7 languages to gradually predominate over regions once embracing many different languages and cultural traditions. Wells thought only French and German would survive with English into the twenty-first century. Stalin believed that Russian, together with English, Spanish, and Chinese, would steamroll all rivals, and that Russian was in the best position to eventually become the world's premier language. In the early 1960s, Peking's ambassador to Jakarta predicted that Indonesian and Chinese would become the dominant languages of Asia.

The Indian philosopher Rajni Kothari has proposed a structure for 8 achieving world peace, based partly on the use of five world languages (English, French, Russian, Arabic, and Chinese) and four regional languages (Spanish, German, Arabic, and Swahili). Every child would be taught at least three languages: one world language, one regional language, and a traditional or minority language of the country in which he was born.

Precedents for such a regional arrangement of hegemonous lan- 9 guages do exist. French, which supplanted Latin as the language of European diplomacy and cultural exchange in the seventeenth century, retained its paramount position virtually unchallenged for over two centuries—despite periodic declines in France's political and military power. The first real blow to French linguistic supremacy occurred in 1878 when Britain's Prime Minister Benjamin Disraeli, who spoke French very badly, shocked his fellow statesmen at the Berlin Congress by addressing them in English. Today, English has the upper hand. Worldwide, English-speakers outnumber French-speakers four to one.

During the twentieth century, both French and English have enjoyed 10 special status as "working languages" of the League of Nations, the World Court at The Hague, and the United Nations. Although Spanish, Russian, and Chinese were included as "official" languages when the U.N. was founded in 1945, it has only been since the 1960s that they have been used as true "working languages" for U.N. meetings and publications. Following the Arab oil boycott of 1973–74, Arabic was added as the U.N.'s sixth official language. German and Japanese also enjoy important (if still unofficial) status at the U.N. thanks to the commercial and scientific activity of Japan and the German-speaking nations of Europe.

Some have suggested modifying an existing language to meet the  11 need for a universal language without seeming to enshrine the current practice of any one nation or culture as the global ideal. English, for instance, could be reformed to eliminate its unpredictable spelling; or, it might be written with Cyrillic characters to achieve a compromise between the cultural norms of Russia and the United States.

## CREATING AN ARTIFICIAL LANGUAGE

A totally different task is to create and make official an artificial language.  12 Numerous such languages have been proposed for universal use, including several based on Latin (minus its tiresome conjugations and declensions). The first of these appeared around 1880 and was called Volapük. Though not very successful, Volapük did at least inspire others to develop a better system. In fact, Esperanto, the most widely used and understood of all artificial languages (over one million speakers and readers worldwide), was developed only seven years later, and has remained virtually unchanged to this day.

Despite some slippage in popularity in recent years, Esperanto  13 cannot be ruled out as a possible world language of the future. Although based on European language roots, the language has proven easier to learn than any "natural" tongue because its grammar rules are completely consistent, and words are always pronounced exactly as they are spelled. Support for Esperanto, including newspapers, journals, and original works of fiction and poetry, is found in the socialist countries and is also strong in some of the smaller capitalist countries. Chinese, Polish, and Italian radio stations regularly schedule programs broadcast in Esperanto.

## A GLOBAL LANGUAGE: HOW DESIRABLE?

The question remains though: How useful or indeed desirable is it to  14 have one global language? Despite an enormous increase in international travel by Americans since World War II, interest in learning foreign languages has actually declined. Might it not be better to adopt a laissez-faire attitude toward language, and neither impose laws to "protect" a tongue from outside influences nor discriminate against a minority language by banning its use?

One can argue that it is pointless to make language use a subject for  15 laws and regulations even within a country, much less attempt to create a world language by decree. Instead, let all 2,796 languages compete openly with one another. The weakest—those that are least expressive, hardest to pronounce, or most cumbersome to read and write—will gradually fall out of use. Such tongues are being extinguished each year in the remote backwaters of South America, Equatorial Africa, and New Guinea. But those that are most adaptive and convenient will survive by the process of voluntary choice.

Rather than the complete domination by one language of all others, 16 the eventual result of such linguistic laissez-faire might be a merging of languages. English itself was formed in this way from the blending of Anglo-Saxon, French, Greek, Latin, and Germanic words and grammar over centuries. Afrikaans, Swahili, and Indonesian are hybrids that eventually developed a literature and received official recognition. Today, with the rapid spread of new words and ideas made possible by electronic communications, the process of language merger could occur much more rapidly.

In the twentieth century, English words have infiltrated other 17 languages in great numbers, creating hybrids such as:

- **Amideutsch**—mixture with German (also called "Deutschlisch").
- **Franglais**—mixture with French (the bane of the Académie Française).
- **Franglish**—mixture with French (for joint Anglo-French projects such as Concorde).
- **Hinglish**—mixture with Hindi.
- **Pidgin**—mixture with Chinese (English with Chinese syntax).
- **Sovangliski**—mixture with Russian.
- **Spanglish**—mixture with Spanish.

Mention should also be made of "Finnglish" (Finnish-accented 18 English), "Yidgin-English" (Yiddish-accented English), and "mid-Atlantic," which is a hybrid of British and American used by the jet set.

Despite the unifying tendencies that better transportation and mass 19 communications media bring to language, there appear to be few prospects for a quick end to global language diversity. At the present time, there are three disparate phenomena taking place:

1. Virtually every language with a significant body of speakers is increasing in number due to the population explosion centered in the Third World.
2. The spread of literacy and the saturation of the print and voice media continue to reinforce the sway of official national tongues over local languages and dialects.
3. Not only English, but also French and Russian are gaining strength within their areas of cultural influence. The result is

continued growth of bilingualism and multilingualism throughout much of the world. The eventual outcome of this competition remains uncertain.

For the immediate future, the clash of languages will continue as an 20
aspect of the larger competition between nations. But we can hope for
and encourage efforts to achieve world uniformity in such areas as traffic and
travellers' aid signs, computer "languages," and units of measurement.

The enhancement and spread of computer logic may greatly influence 21
the ways in which written and spoken languages develop in the future.
Conceivably, it could lead to the creation of an artificial, culturally
unbiased, totally logical universal tongue, adaptable both to pen and
computer console.

Even if one language should achieve global dominance, either by over- 22
whelming its competition or as an ecumenical *lingua franca*, it would not
remain unchallenged indefinitely. While saturation exposure through the
mass media might keep its position secure on a single planet, the spread of
humanity into space and eventually to other solar systems would create new
situations. Isolated colonies, light years away from Earth, would develop
their own dialects—or perhaps whole new languages—enriched by words
invented to describe physical phenomena unimagined on Earth. If contact
with alien civilizations should occur, this would surely introduce still more
new words and concepts. In time, the languages evolved in space, though
descended from Earth-based originals, might become dominant throughout the galaxy, just as French, Spanish, Portuguese, and Italian have come
to overshadow their now feeble mother language—Latin.

About the only safe prediction that can be made about the future of 23
language is that change will occur—and that the words we speak and
read today will seem odd or even incomprehensible to people living a
thousand years from now.


## Post-Reading Questions

1.  What values underlie Hamil's argument for a universal language? What
    values do you think underlie the arguments of those who oppose
    substituting official languages for native or indigenous languages?
2.  What three possible solutions to the problems created by language
    diversity does Hamil propose? Which of those solutions seems most
    reasonable to you? Why?
3.  What existing language would best serve as an "official" worldwide
    language? Support your answer with specific reasons. Who do you think
    would oppose the elevation of this language to worldwide official status?
4.  Some would describe Hamil's style as "neutral." What features of his
    style would support that description? What features call that descrip-
    tion into question?

5. What is your response to the proposal of Rajni Kothari described in paragraph 8? What would be the advantages of such an approach to the problems created by language diversity? What disadvantages would his system have?

6. Summarize in one paragraph why Hamil argues so assertively for some kind of solution to language diversity. Do his arguments seem to you to overcome the potential arguments of those who feel that too much is lost when the languages of particular peoples and cultures are replaced? Why?

7. Why does Hamil use the list at the end of paragraph 17? What function does it have in helping him make the argument for linguistic universality?

8. Analyze Hamil's use of headings in this essay. How do these headings help make the structure of the essay easy for readers to follow?

9. What is the purpose of Hamil's final paragraph? What effect is it intended to have on readers? Does it contribute to the persuasiveness of Hamil's argument? Why?

# DOROTHY Z. SEYMOUR ON BLACK SPEECH

## Pre-Reading Questions

1. Have you ever been in a situation (a job interview, a conference with a teacher or professor, a formal address on a ceremonial occasion) in which your home language had to be adapted or replaced by a more formal manner of speaking? If you have, explain how you felt and what you did in that situation.

2. Have you ever experienced or seen another person experience ridicule or criticism for using nonstandard English? If you have, describe the situation and explain the effects of this ridicule or criticism on the speaker.

3. Many people must learn to shift from the language of home and community to the language of the workplace. Why is this shift more difficult, even traumatic, for some people than it is for others?

## BLACK CHILDREN, BLACK SPEECH
### Dorothy Z. Seymour

"Cmon, man, les git goin'!" called the boy to his companion. "Dat bell 1 ringin'. It say, 'Git in rat now!' " He dashed into the school yard.

"Aw, f'get you," replied the other. "Whe' Richuh? Whe' da' 2 muvvuh? He be goin' to schoo'."

*example*

"He in de' now, man!" was the answer as they went through the 3 door.

In the classroom they made for their desks and opened their books. 4 The name of the story they tried to read was "Come." It went:

Come, Bill, come.
Come with me.
Come and see this.
See what is here.

*juxtaposition Antheny*

The first boy poked the second. "Wha' da' wor'?"

"Da' wor' *is*, you dope."

"*Is*? Ain't no wor' *is*. You jivin' me? Wha' da' wor' mean?"

"Ah dunno. Jus' *is*."

To a speaker of Standard English, this exchange is only vaguely 5 comprehensible. But it's normal speech for thousands of American children. In addition it demonstrates one of our biggest educational problems: children whose speech style is so different from the writing style of their books that they have difficulty learning to read. These children speak Black English, a dialect characteristic of many inner-city Negroes. Their books are, of course, written in Standard English. To complicate matters, the speech they use is also socially stigmatized. Middle-class whites and Negroes alike scorn it as low-class poor people's talk.

Teachers sometimes make the situation worse with their attitudes 6 toward Black English. Typically, they view the children's speech as "bad English" characterized by "lazy pronunciation," "poor grammar," and "short, jagged words." One result of this attitude is poor mental health on the part of the pupils. A child is quick to grasp the feeling that while school speech is "good," his own speech is "bad," and that by extension he himself is somehow inadequate and without value. Some children react to this feeling by withdrawing; they stop talking entirely. Others develop the attitude of "F'get you, honky." In either case, the psychological results are devastating and lead straight to the dropout route.

It is hard for most teachers and middle-class Negro parents to accept 7 the idea that Black English is not just "sloppy talk" but a dialect with a form and structure of its own. Even some eminent black educators think of it as "bad English grammar" with "slurred consonants" (Professor Nick Aaron Ford of Morgan State College in Baltimore) and "ghettoese" (Dr. Kenneth B. Clark, the prominent educational psychologist).

Parents of Negro school children generally agree. Two researchers at 8 Columbia University report that the adults they worked with in Harlem almost unanimously preferred that their children be taught Standard English in school.

But there is another point of view, one held in common by black  9
militants and some white liberals. They urge that middle-class Negroes
stop thinking of the inner-city dialect as something to be ashamed of and
repudiated. Black author Claude Brown, for example, pushes this view.

Some modern linguists take a similar stance. They begin with the  10
premise that no dialect is intrinsically "bad" or "good," and that a
non-standard speech style is not defective speech but different speech.
More important, they have been able to show that Black English is far
from being a careless way of speaking the Standard; instead, it is a rather
rigidly-constructed set of speech patterns, with the same sort of special-
ization in sounds, structure, and vocabulary as any other dialect.

## THE SOUNDS OF BLACK ENGLISH

Middle class listeners who hear black inner-city speakers say "dis" and  11
"tin" for "this" and "thin" assume that the black speakers are just being
careless. Not at all; these differences are characteristic aspects of the
dialect. The original cause of such substitutions is generally a carryover
from one's original language or that of his immigrant parents. The
interference from that carryover probably caused the substitution of /d/
for the voiced *th* sound in *this*, and /t/ for the unvoiced *th* sound in *thin*.
(Linguists represent language sounds by putting letters within slashes or
brackets.) Most speakers of English don't realize that the two *th* sounds
of English are lacking in many other languages and are difficult for most
foreigners trying to learn English. Germans who study English, for
example, are surprised and confused about these sounds because the only
Germans who use them are the ones who lisp. These two sounds are
almost nonexistent in the West African languages which most black
immigrants brought with them to America.

Similar substitutions used in Black English are /f/, a sound similar to  12
the unvoiced *th*, in medial word-position, as in *birfday* for *birthday,* and
in final word-position, as in *roof* for *Ruth* as well as /v/ for the voiced *th*
in medial position, as in *bruvver* for *brother.* These sound substitutions
are also typical of Gullah, the language of black speakers in the Carolina
Sea Islands. Some of them are also heard in Caribbean Creole.

Another characteristic of the sounds of Black English is the lack of  13
/l/ at the end of words, sometimes replaced by the sound /w/. This
makes a word like *tool* sound like *too.* If /l/ occurs in the middle of a
Standard English word, in Black English it may be omitted entirely: "I
can hep you." This difference is probably caused by the instability and
sometimes interchangeability of /l/ and /r/ in West African languages.

One difference that is startling to middle-class speakers is the fact  14
that Black English words appear to leave off some consonant sounds at

the end of words. Like Italian, Japanese and West African words, they are more likely to end in vowel sounds. Standard English *boot* is pronounced *boo* in Black English. *What* is *wha*. *Sure* is *sho*. *Your* is *yo*. This kind of difference can make for confusion in the classroom. Dr. Kenneth Goodman, a psycholinguist, tells of a black child whose white teacher asked him to use *so* in a sentence—not "sew a dress" but "the other *so*." The sentence the child used was "I got a *so* on my leg."

A related feature of Black English is the tendency in many cases not 15 to use sequences of more than one final consonant sound. For example, *just* is pronounced *jus'*, *past* is *pass*, *mend* sounds like *men* and *hold* like *hole*. *Six* and *box* are pronounced *sick* and *bock*. Why should this be? Perhaps because West African languages, like Japanese, have almost no clusters of consonants in their speech. The Japanese, when importing a foreign word, handle a similar problem by inserting vowel sounds between every consonant, making *baseball* sound like *besuboru*. West Africans probably made a simpler change, merely cutting a series of two consonant sounds down to one. Speakers of Gullah, one linguist found, have made the same kind of adaptation of Standard English.

Teachers of black children seldom understand the reason for these 16 differences in final sounds. They are apt to think that careless speech is the cause. Actually, black speakers aren't "leaving off" any sounds; how can you leave off something you never had in the first place?

Differences in vowel sounds are also characteristic of the non- 17 standard language. Dr. Goodman reports that a black child asked his teacher how to spell rat. "R-a-t," she replied. But the boy responded "No ma'am, I don't mean rat mouse, I mean rat now." In Black English, *right* sounds like *rat*. A likely reason is that in West African languages, there are very few vowel sounds of the type heard in the word *right*. This type is common in English. It is called a glided or dipthongized vowel sound. A glided vowel sound is actually a close combination of two vowels; in the word *right* the two parts of the sound "eye" are actually "ah-ee." West African languages have no such long, two-part, changing vowel sounds; their vowels are generally shorter and more stable. This may be why in Black English, *time* sounds like *Tom*, *oil* like *all*, and *my* like *ma*.

## LANGUAGE STRUCTURE

Black English differs from Standard English not only in its sounds but 18 also in its structure. The way the words are put together does not always fit the description in English grammar books. The method of expressing time, or tense, for example, differs in significant ways.

The verb *to be* is an important one in Standard English. It's used as 19 an auxiliary verb to indicate different tenses. But Black English speakers

use it quite differently. Sometimes an inner-city Negro says "He coming"; other times he says "He be coming." These two sentences mean
different things. To understand why, let's look at the tenses of West
African languages; they correspond with those of Black English.

Many West African languages have a tense which is called the 20
habitual. This tense is used to express action which is always occurring
and it is formed with a verb that is translated as *be*. "He be coming"
means something like "He's always coming," "He usually comes," or
"He's been coming."

In Standard English there is no regular grammatical construction for 21
such a tense. Black English speakers, in order to form the habitual tense
in English, use the word *be* as an auxiliary: *He be doing it. My Momma be
working. He be running.* The habitual tense is not the same as the present
tense, which is constructed in Black English without any form of the verb
*to be: He do it. My Momma working. He running.* (This means the action
is occurring right now.)

There are other tense differences between Black English and Stan- 22
dard English. For example, the non-standard speech does not use
changes in grammar to indicate the past tense. A white person will ask,
"What did your brother say?" and the black person will answer, "He say
he coming." (The verb *say* is not changed to *said*.) "How did you get
here?" "I walk." This style of talking about the past is paralleled in the
Yoruba, Fante, Hausa, and Ewe languages of West Africa.

Expression of plurality is another difference. The way a black child 23
will talk of "them boy" or "two dog" makes some white listeners think
Negroes don't know how to turn a singular word into a plural word. As
a matter of fact, it isn't necessary to use an *s* to express plurality. In
Chinese and Japanese, singular and plural are not generally distinguished
by such inflections; plurality is conveyed in other ways. For example, in
Chinese it's correct to say "There are three book on the table." This
sentence already has two signals of the plural, *three* and *are*; why require
a third? This same logic is the basis of plurals in most West African
languages, where nouns are often identical in the plural and the singular.
For example, in Ibo, one correctly says *those man*, and in both Ewe and
Yoruba one says *they house*. American speakers of Gullah retain this style;
it is correct in Gullah to say *five dog*.

Gender is another aspect of language structure where differences can 24
be found. Speakers of Standard English are often confused to find that
the nonstandard vernacular often uses just one gender of pronoun, the
masculine, and refers to women as well as men as *he* or *him*. "He a nice
girl," even "Him a nice girl" are common. This usage probably stems
from West African origins, too, as does the use of multiple negatives,
such as "Nobody don't know it."

Vocabulary is the third aspect of a person's native speech that could 25
affect his learning of a new language. The strikingly different vocabulary

often used in Negro Nonstandard English is probably the most obvious aspect of it to a casual white observer. But its vocabulary differences don't obscure its meaning the way different sounds and different structure often do.

Recently there has been much interest in the African origins of words 26 like *goober* (peanut), *cooter* (turtle), and *tote* (carry), as well as others that are less certainly African, such as *to dig* (possibly from the Wolof *degan,* "to understand"). Such expressions seem colorful rather than low-class to many whites; they become assimilated faster than their black originators do. English professors now use *dig* in their scholarly articles, and current advertising has enthusiastically adopted *rap.*

Is it really possible for old differences in sound, structure, and 27 vocabulary to persist from the West African languages of slave days into present-day inner city Black English? Easily. Nothing else really explains such regularity of language habits, most of which persist among black people in various parts of the Western Hemisphere. For a long time scholars believed that certain speech forms used by Negroes were merely leftovers from archaic English preserved in the speech of early English settlers in America and copied by their slaves. But this theory has been greatly weakened, largely as the result of the work of a black linguist, Dr. Lorenzo Dow Turner of the University of Chicago. Dr. Turner studied the speech of Gullah Negroes in the Sea Islands off the Carolina coast and found so many traces of West African languages that he thoroughly discredited the archaic-English theory.

When anyone learns a new language, it's usual to try speaking the 28 new language with the sounds and structure of the old. If a person's first language does not happen to have a particular sound needed in the language he is learning, he will tend to substitute a similar or related sound from his native language and use it to speak the new one. When Frenchman Charles Boyer said "Zees ees my heart," and when Latin American Carmen Miranda sang "Souse American way," they were simply using sounds of their native languages in trying to pronounce sounds of English. West Africans must have done the same thing when they first attempted English words. The tendency to retain the structure of the native language is a strong one, too. That's why a German learning English is likely to put his verb at the end: "May I a glass beer have?" The vocabulary of one's original language may also furnish some holdovers. Jewish immigrants did not stop using the word *bagel* when they came to America; nor did Germans stop saying *sauerkraut.*

Social and geographical isolation reinforces the tendencies to retain 29 old language habits. When one group is considered inferior, the other group avoids it. For many years it was illegal to give any sort of instruction to Negroes, and for slaves to try to speak like their masters would have been unthinkable. Conflict of value systems doubtless retards changes, too. As Frantz Fanon observed in *Black Skin, White Masks,* those who take on white speech habits are suspect in the ghetto, because others believe they are trying to "act white." Dr. Kenneth Johnson, a black linguist, put it this way: "As long as disadvantaged black children live in segregated communities and most of their relationships are confined to those within their own subculture, they will not replace their functional nonstandard dialect with the nonfunctional standard dialect."

Linguists have made it clear that language systems that are different 30 are not necessarily deficient. A judgment of deficiency can be made only in comparison with another language system. Let's turn the tables on Standard English for a moment and look at it from the West African point of view. From this angle, Standard English: (1) is lacking in certain language sounds, (2) has a couple of unnecessary language sounds for which others may serve as good substitutes, (3) doubles and drawls some of its vowel sounds in sequences that are unusual and difficult to imitate, (4) lacks a method of forming an important tense, (5) requires an unnecessary number of ways to indicate tense, plurality and gender, and (6) doesn't mark negatives sufficiently for the result to be a good strong negative statement.

Now whose language is deficient? 31

How would the adoption of this point of view help us? Say we accepted the evidence that Black English is not just a sloppy Standard but an organized language style which probably has developed many of its features on the basis of its West African heritage. What would we gain?

The psychological climate of the classroom might improve if teachers 32 understood why many black students speak as they do. But we still have not reached a solution of the main problem. Does the discovery that Black English has pattern and structure mean that it should not be tampered with? Should children who speak Black English be excused from learning the Standard in school? Should they perhaps be given books in Black English to learn from?

Any such accommodation would surely result in a hardening of the 33 new separatism being urged by some black militants. It would probably be applauded by such people as Roy Innis, Director of C.O.R.E., who is currently recommending dual autonomous education systems for white and black. And it might facilitate learning to read, since some experiments have indicated that materials written in Black English syntax aid problem readers from the inner city.

But determined resistance to the introduction of such printed 34 materials into schools can be expected. To those who view inner-city speech as bad English, the appearance in print of sentences like "My mama, he work" can be as shocking and repellent as a four-letter word. Middle-class Negro parents would probably mobilize against the move. Any strategem that does not take into account such practicalities of the matter is probably doomed to failure. And besides, where would such a permissive policy on language get these children in the larger society, and in the long run? If they want to enter an integrated America they must be able to deal with it on its own terms. Even Professor Toni Cade of Rutgers, who doesn't want "ghetto accents" tampered with, advocates mastery of Standard English because, as she puts it, "if you want to get ahead in this country, you must master the language of the ruling class." This has always been true, wherever there has been a minority group.

The problem then appears to be one of giving these children the 35 ability to speak (and read) Standard English without denigrating the vernacular and those who use it, or even affecting the ability to use it. The only way to do this is to officially espouse bi-dialectism. The result would be the ability to use either dialect equally well—as Dr. Martin Luther King did—depending on the time, place, and circumstances. Pupils would have to learn enough about Standard English to use it when necessary, and teachers would have to learn enough about the inner-city dialect to understand and accept it for what it is—not just a "careless" version of Standard English but a different form of English that's appropriate in certain times and places.

Can we accomplish this? If we can't, the result will be continued 36 alienation of a large section of the population, continued dropout trouble with consequent loss of earning power and economic contribution to the nation, but most of all, loss of faith in America as a place where a minority people can at times continue to use those habits that remind them of their link with each other and with their past.

## Post-Reading Questions

1.  What is the purpose of the first four paragraphs of this essay? What type of language contrast is the author setting up? What is the point of that contrast as far as attitudes toward dialects are concerned?

2.  Does the author agree or disagree with the view of dialects that she describes in paragraph 8? How do you know?

3.  What is the point of the reference to German in paragraph 11? What does this allusion to the difficulty German speakers have in learning English have to do with Seymour's argument regarding black dialect?

4.  Does this essay convince you that black English has a logic of its own? Do you think that is one of Seymour's main purposes? How convincing is her evidence? Do you find her organization of that evidence convincing?

5.  What do you think Seymour recommends regarding schooling? Is she recommending that teachers simply give more respect to black speech, to *all* dialect speech? Or is she arguing that black speech and other dialects should be taught? Does Seymour think that standard English should be taught along with dialects?

6. What group is the primary audience for this essay? How do you know?
7. Many experts argue that language is power. Do you think that official recognition of the value of dialects is a good way of empowering the people who speak those dialects? Why? Why not?

# SIMON J. ORTIZ
# ON NATIVE LANGUAGES

## Pre-Reading Questions

1. Consider the way Native American languages have been represented in films and on television, particularly over twenty years ago. Did these representations attempt to accurately reflect the diversity and complexity of the many Native American languages, or did they usually reduce the Native American languages to a kind of simple or "pidgin" English? If this issue has special interest to you or to your writing group, rent a video of an old Western movie (those in which Gary Cooper or John Wayne are featured make good choices) in which Native Americans play a part, and analyze its representation of native language.
2. Can you think of examples of subcultures in which the language is primarily oral? If you can, describe one of those groups and analyze what could be gained or lost by the members of this subculture because of the oral nature of their language.
3. Look at the title of this essay. What is the significance of the word *we,* given that the essay has been written by a Native American?

## THE LANGUAGE WE KNOW
### Simon J. Ortiz

I don't remember a world without language. From the time of my earliest    1
childhood, there was language. Always language, and imagination, spec-
ulation, utters of sound. Words, beginnings of words. What would I be
without language? My existence has been determined by language, not
only the spoken but the unspoken, the language of speech and the language of motion. I can't remember a world without memory. Memory,
immediate and far away in the past, something in the sinew, blood, ageless
cell. Although I don't recall the exact moment I spoke or tried to speak,
I know the feeling of something tugging at the core of the mind, something unutterable uttered into existence. It is language that brings us into
existence. It is language that brings us into being in order to know life.

My childhood was the oral tradition of the Acoma Pueblo people— Aaquumeh hano—which included my immediate family of three older sisters, two younger sisters, two younger brothers, and my mother and father. My world was our world of the Aaquumeh in McCartys, one of the two villages descended from the ageless mother pueblo of Acoma. My world was our Eagle clan-people among other clans. I grew up in Deetziyamah, which is the Aaquumeh name for McCartys, which is posted at the exit off the present interstate highway in western New Mexico. I grew up within a people who farmed small garden plots and fields, who were mostly poor and not well schooled in the American system's education. The language I spoke was that of a struggling people who held ferociously to a heritage, culture, language, and land despite the odds posed them by the forces surrounding them since A.D. 1540, the advent of Euro-American colonization. When I began school in 1948 at the BIA (Bureau of Indian Affairs) day school in our village, I was armed with the basic ABC's and the phrases "Good morning, Miss Oleman" and "May I please be excused to go to the bathroom," but it was an older language that was my fundamental strength.

In my childhood, the language we all spoke was Acoma, and it was a struggle to maintain it against the outright threats of corporal punishment, ostracism, and the invocation that it would impede our progress towards Americanization. Children in school were punished and looked upon with disdain if they did not speak and learn English quickly and smoothly, and so I learned it. It has occurred to me that I learned English simply because I was forced to, as so many other Indian children were. But I know, also, there was another reason, and this was that I loved language, the sound, meaning, and magic of language. Language opened up vistas of the world around me, and it allowed me to discover knowledge that would not be possible for me to know without the use of language. Later, when I began to experiment with and explore language in poetry and fiction, I allowed that a portion of that impetus was because I had come to know English through forceful acculturation. Nevertheless, the underlying force was the beauty and poetic power of language in its many forms that instilled in me the desire to become a user of language as a writer, singer, and storyteller. Significantly, it was the Acoma language, which I don't use enough of today, that inspired me to become a writer. The concepts, values, and philosophy contained in my original language and the struggle it has faced have determined my life and vision as a writer.

In Deetziyamah, I discovered the world of the Acoma land and people firsthand through my parents, sisters, and brothers, and my own perceptions, voiced through all that encompasses the oral tradition, which is ageless for any culture. It is a small village, even smaller years ago, and like other Indian communities it is wealthy with its knowledge of daily event, history, and social system, all that make up a people who

have a many-dimensioned heritage. Our family lived in a two-room
home (built by my grandfather some years after he and my grandmother
moved with their daughters from Old Acoma), which my father added
rooms to later. I remember my father's work at enlarging our home for
our growing family. He was a skilled stoneworker, like many other men
of an older Pueblo generation who worked with sandstone and mud
mortar to build their homes and pueblos. It takes time, persistence,
patience, and the belief that the walls that come to stand will do so for a
long, long time, perhaps even forever. I like to think that by helping to — *explain*
mix mud and carry stone for my father and other elders I managed to
bring that influence into my consciousness as a writer.

Both my mother and my father were good storytellers and singers (as   5
my mother is to this day—my father died in 1978), and for their   5 —
generation, which was born soon after the turn of the century, they were   *oral*
relatively educated in the American system. Catholic missionaries had   *tradition* —
taken both of them as children to a parochial boarding school far from   *parents* —
Acoma, and they imparted their discipline for study and quest for   *parents* —
education to us children when we started school. But it was their   *history* —
indigenous sense of gaining knowledge that was most meaningful to me.   *life - knowledge*
Acquiring knowledge about life was above all the most important item; it
was a value that one had to have in order to be fulfilled personally and on
behalf of his community. And this they insisted upon imparting through
the oral tradition as they told their children about our native history and
our community and culture and our "stories." These stories were
common knowledge of act, event, and behavior in a close-knit pueblo. It
was knowledge about how one was to make a living through work that   ✓ *work*
benefited his family and everyone else.

Because we were a subsistence farming people, or at least tried to be,   6
I learned to plant, hoe weeds, irrigate and cultivate corn, chili, pumpkins,
beans. Through counsel and advice I came to know that the rain which   *work →*
provided water was a blessing, gift, and symbol and that it was the land   *land →*
which provided for our lives. It was the stories and songs which provided   *stories →*
the knowledge that I was woven into the intricate web that was my   *rel trad →*
Acoma life. In our garden and our cornfields I learned about the seasons,   *long to*
growth cycles of cultivated plants, what one had to think and feel about   *explain it*
the land; and at home I became aware of how we must care for each
other: All of this was encompassed in an intricate relationship which had
to be maintained in order that life continue. After supper on many
occasions my father would bring out his drum and sing as we, the
children, danced to themes about the rain, hunting, land, and people. It
was all that is contained within the language of oral tradition that made
me explicitly aware of a yet unarticulated urge to write, to tell what I had
learned and was learning and what it all meant to me.

My grandfather was old already when I came to know him. I was   7
only one of his many grandchildren, but I would go with him to get

wood for our households, to the garden to chop weeds, and to his sheep camp to help care for his sheep. I don't remember his exact words, but I know they were about how we must sacredly concern ourselves with the people and the holy earth. I know his words were about how we must regard ourselves and others with compassion and love; I know that his knowledge was vast, as a medicine man and an elder of his kiva, and I listened as a boy should. My grandfather represented for me a link to the past that is important for me to hold in my memory because it is not only memory but knowledge that substantiates my present existence. He and the grandmothers and grandfathers before him thought about us as they lived, confirmed in their belief of a continuing life, and they brought our present beings into existence by the beliefs they held. The consciousness of that belief is what informs my present concerns with language, poetry, and fiction.

My first poem was for Mother's Day when I was in the fifth grade,  8 and it was the first poem that was ever published, too, in the Skull Valley School newsletter. Of course I don't remember how the juvenile poem went, but it must have been certain in its expression of love and reverence for the woman who was the most important person in my young life. The poem didn't signal any prophecy of my future as a poet, but it must have come from the forming idea that there were things one could do with language and writing. My mother, years later, remembers how I was a child who always told stories—that is, tall tales—who always had explanations for things probably better left unspoken, and she says that I also liked to perform in school plays. In remembering, I do know that I was coming to that age when the emotions and thoughts in me began to moil to the surface. There was much to experience and express in that age when youth has a precociousness that is broken easily or made to flourish. We were a poor family, always on the verge of financial disaster, though our parents always managed to feed us and keep us in clothing. We had the problems, unfortunately ordinary, of many Indian families who face poverty on a daily basis, never enough of anything, the feeling of a denigrating self-consciousness, alcoholism in the family and community, the feeling that something was falling apart though we tried desperately to hold it all together.

My father worked for the railroad for many years as a laborer and  9 later as a welder. We moved to Skull Valley, Arizona, for one year in the early 1950s, and it was then that I first came in touch with a non-Indian, non-Acoma world. Skull Valley was a farming and ranching community, and my younger brothers and sisters and I went to a one-room school. I had never really had much contact with white people except from a careful and suspicious distance, but now here I was, totally surrounded by them, and there was nothing to do but bear the experience and learn from it. Although I perceived there was not much difference between *them* and *us* in certain respects, there was a distinct feeling that we were not the same either. This thought had been inculcated in me, especially by an Acoma expression—*Gaimuu Mericano*—that spoke of the "fortune" of being an American. In later years as a social activist and committed writer, I would try to offer a strong positive view of our collective Indianness through my writing. Nevertheless, my father was an inadequately paid laborer, and we were far from our home land for economic-social reasons, and my feelings and thoughts about that experience during that time would become a part of how I became a writer.

Soon after, I went away from my home and family to go to boarding school, first in Santa Fe and then in Albuquerque. This was in the 1950s, and this had been the case for the past half-century for Indians: We had to leave home in order to become truly American by joining the mainstream, which was deemed to be the proper course of our lives. On top of this was termination, a U.S. government policy which dictated that Indians sever their relationship to the federal government and remove themselves from their lands and go to American cities for jobs and education. It was an era which bespoke the intent of U.S. public policy that Indians were no longer to be Indians. Naturally, I did not perceive this in any analytical or purposeful sense; rather, I felt an unspoken anxiety and resentment against unseen forces that determined our destiny to be un-Indian, embarrassed and uncomfortable with our grandparents' customs and strictly held values. We were to set our goals as American working men and women, singlemindedly industrious, patriotic, and unquestioning, building for a future which ensured that the United States was the greatest nation in the world. I felt fearfully uneasy with this, for by then I felt the loneliness, alienation, and isolation imposed upon me by the separation from my family, home, and community.

Something was happening; I could see that in my years at Catholic school and the U.S. Indian school. I remembered my grandparents' and parents' words: Educate yourself in order to help your people. In that era and the generation who had the same experience I had, there was an unspoken vow: We were caught in a system inexorably, and we had to learn that system well in order to fight back. Without the motive of a fight-back we would not be able to survive as the people our heritage had lovingly bequeathed us. My diaries and notebooks began then, and though none have survived to the present, I know they contained the varied moods of a youth filled with loneliness, anger, and discomfort that seemed to have unknown causes. Yet at the same time, I realize now, I was coming to know myself clearly in a way that I would later articulate in writing. My love of language, which allowed me to deal with the world, to delve into it, to experiment and discover, held for me a vision of awe and wonder, and by then grammar teachers had noticed I was a good speller, used verbs and tenses correctly, and wrote complete sentences. Although I imagine that they might have surmised this as unusual for an Indian student whose original language was not English, I am grateful for their perception and attention.

During the latter part of that era in the 1950s of Indian termination 12 and the Cold War, a portion of which still exists today, there were the beginnings of a bolder and more vocalized resistance against the current U.S. public policies of repression, racism, and cultural ethnocide. It seemed to be inspired by the civil rights movement led by black people in the United States and by decolonization and liberation struggles world-wide. Indian people were being relocated from their rural homelands at an astonishingly devastating rate, yet at the same time they resisted the U.S. effort by maintaining determined ties with their heritage, returning often to their native communities, and establishing Indian centers in the cities they were removed to. Indian rural communities, such as Acoma Pueblo, insisted on their land claims and began to initiate legal battles in the areas of natural and social, political and economic human rights. By the retention and the inspiration of our native heritage, values, philosophies, and language, we would know ourselves as a strong and enduring people. Having a modest and latent consciousness of this as a teenager, I began to write about the experience of being Indian in America. Although I had only a romanticized image of what a writer was, which came from the pulp rendered by American popular literature, and I really didn't know anything about writing, I sincerely felt a need to say things, to speak, to release the energy of the impulse to help my people.

My writing in my late teens and early adulthood was fashioned after 13 the American short stories and poetry taught in the high schools of the 1940s and 1950s, but by the 1960s, after I had gone to college and dropped out and served in the military, I began to develop topics and themes from my Indian background. The experience in my village of Deetziyamah and Acoma Pueblo was readily accessible. I had grown up within the oral tradition of speech, social and religious ritual, elders' counsel and advice, countless and endless stories, everyday event, and the visual art that was symbolically representative of life all around. My mother was a potter of the well-known Acoma clayware, a traditional art form that had been passed to her from her mother and the generations of mothers before. My father carved figures from wood and did beadwork. This was not unusual, as Indian people know; there was always some kind of artistic endeavor that people set themselves to, although they did not necessarily articulate it as "Art" in the sense of Western civilization. One lived and expressed an artful life, whether it was in ceremonial singing and dancing, architecture, painting, speaking, or in the way one's social-cultural life was structured. When I turned my attention to my own heritage, I did so because this was my identity, the substance of who I was, and I wanted to write about what that meant. My desire was to write about the integrity and dignity of an Indian identity, and at the same time I wanted to look at what this was within the context of an America that had too often denied its Indian heritage.

To a great extent my writing has a natural political-cultural bent 14 simply because I was nurtured intellectually and emotionally within an atmosphere of Indian resistance. Aacquu did not die in 1598 when it was burned and razed by European conquerors, nor did the people become hopeless when their children were taken away to U.S. schools far from home and new ways were imposed upon them. The *Aaquumeh hano*, despite losing much of their land and surrounded by a foreign civilization, have not lost sight of their native heritage. This is the factual case with most other Indian peoples, and the clear explanation for this has been the fight-back we have found it necessary to wage. At times, in the past, it was outright armed struggle, like that of present-day Indians in Central and South America with whom we must identify; currently, it is often in the legal arena, and it is in the field of literature. In 1981, when I was invited to the White House for an event celebrating American poets and poetry, I did not immediately accept the invitation. I questioned myself about the possibility that I was merely being exploited as an Indian, and I hedged against accepting. But then I recalled the elders going among our people in the poor days of the 1950s, asking for donations—a dollar here and there, a sheep, perhaps a piece of pottery—in order to finance a trip to the nation's capital. They were to make another countless appeal on behalf of our people, to demand justice, to reclaim lost land even though there was only spare hope they would be successful. I went to the White House realizing that I was to do no less than they and those who had fought in the Pueblo Revolt of 1680, and I read my poems and sang songs that were later described as "guttural" by a Washington, D.C., newspaper. I suppose it was more or less understandable why such a view of Indian literature is held by many, and it is also clear why there should be a political stand taken in my writing and those of my sister and brother Indian writers.

The 1960s and afterward have been an invigorating and liberating 15 period for Indian people. It has been only a little more than twenty years since Indian writers began to write and publish extensively, but we are writing and publishing more and more; we can only go forward. We come from an ageless, continuing oral tradition that informs us of our values, concepts, and notions as native people, and it is amazing how much of this tradition is ingrained so deeply in our contemporary writing, considering the brutal efforts of cultural repression that was not long ago outright U.S. policy. We were not to speak our languages, practice our spiritual beliefs, or accept the values of our past generations; and we were discouraged from pressing for our natural rights as Indian human beings. In spite of the fact that there is to some extent the same repression today, we persist and insist in living, believing, hoping, loving, speaking, and writing as Indians. This is embodied in the language we know and share in our writing. We have always had this language, and it is the language, spoken and unspoken, that determines our existence, that brought our grandmothers and grandfathers and ourselves into being in order that there be a continuing life.                    1987

### Post-Reading Questions

1. Ortiz, at several points, establishes the fact that he is a professional writer (paragraphs 3, 6, 7, 8, 9, 12, 13, and 14). What effect is this supposed to have? Explain the effect and give some reasons for thinking that the author had this effect in mind when he wrote the essay.

2. How did the oral tradition of his ancestors become a part of Ortiz's life despite the fact that he went to schools that discouraged his use of Native American customs and language?

3. Do you think that Ortiz has incorporated the content of his people's oral tradition in his written fiction, poetry, and essays? What makes you think that he has or has not?

4. Why do you think American mainstream culture often attempted to keep Native Americans away from their own language and customs? What advantages would there be, for the culture and the indigenous people, in encouraging this disconnection from indigenous roots?

5. Contrast Ortiz's description of his own experience with two cultures and languages to Hamil's argument for a universal, "official" language. How do you think Ortiz would respond to Hamil's argument? What does Ortiz think would be lost if indigenous languages were replaced by official, national, or universal languages?

6. Describe Ortiz's voice in this essay. How does he try to sound— stuffy, insinuating, honest, sincere? What other adjectives would you use to describe Ortiz's voice? What features of language does Ortiz use to create his writing voice? Is the voice appropriate to the purpose and subject matter? Why?

7. What is the significance of the first poem written by Ortiz on Mother's Day, when he was in the fifth grade (paragraph 8)?

8. In what ways does this essay have what Ortiz describes as a "political-cultural bent" (paragraph 14)?

9. Compare what Ortiz has to say about Acoma Pueblo and mainstream American culture. What are the strengths and weaknesses of each as he describes them?

10. What are the implications for education in the final paragraph (paragraph 15) of this essay? If you were a language teacher of a Native American child, how would you heed Ortiz's advice? What would you do in your everyday teaching to bring together Native

American and mainstream American literature and culture? How would you ensure that, while learning standard English, your Native American students would also learn to love their own literature and language?

# ALLEEN PACE NILSEN
# ON SEXISM IN ENGLISH

## Pre-Reading Questions

1. Describe your attitudes toward the idea that English is a sexist language. What does the idea mean to you? Have you ever felt any effects of sexist language? If you have, describe a situation in which you did.
2. For a group project, record, or watch and take notes on, a television program to which you think questions concerning gender and language can be applied. Talk shows, news programs, prime-time dramas and sit-coms, game shows, reruns, and commercials make good subjects. Each member of the group should be assigned to a different observational task: to record particularly relevant pieces of language, to describe visual situations in which gendered language was used, and to develop on-the-spot interpretations of particular pieces of dialogue.
3. Are males and females addressed, described, and talked about in different language in your family? If they are, describe those differences. If they are not, describe the ways in which matters of gender are handled in your family's language.
4. Examine several advertisements in popular magazines; focus on how women are portrayed. Do these advertisements use what you call "sexist language"? In what ways is the language of the advertisements sexist? If they are not sexist, how is the problem of gender-bias in language avoided by the advertisers?

## SEXISM IN ENGLISH: A 1990s UPDATE
### Alleen Pace Nilsen

Twenty years ago I embarked on a study of the sexism inherent in American English. I had just returned to Ann Arbor, Michigan after living for two years (1967–69) in Kabul, Afghanistan where I had begun to look critically at the role society assigned to women. The Afghan version of the chaderi prescribed for Moslem women was particularly confining. Few women attended the American-built Kabul University where my husband was teaching linguistics because there were no women's dormitories, which meant that the only females who could attend were those whose families happened to live in the capital city. Afghan jokes and folklore were blatantly sexist, for example this proverb, "If you see an old man, sit down and take a lesson; if you see an old woman, throw a stone."

But it wasn't only the native culture that made me question women's  2 roles; it was also the American community. Nearly six hundred Americans lived in Kabul, mostly supported by U.S. taxpayers. The single women were career secretaries, school teachers, or nurses. The three women who had jobs comparable to the American men's jobs were textbook editors with the assignment of developing reading books in Dari (Afghan Persian) for young children. They worked at the Ministry of Education, a large building in the center of the city. There were no women's restrooms so during their two-year assignment whenever they needed to go to the bathroom they had to walk across the street and down the block to the Kabul Hotel.

The rest of the American women were like myself—wives and  3 mothers whose husbands were either career diplomats, employees of USAID, or college professors teaching at Kabul University. These were the women who were most influential in changing my way of thinking because we were suddenly bereft of our traditional roles. Servants worked for $1.00 a day and our lives revolved around supervising these men (women were not allowed to work for foreigners). One woman's husband grew so tired of hearing her stories that he scheduled an hour a week for listening to complaints. The rest of the time he wanted to keep his mind clear to focus on working with his Afghan counterparts and with the president of the University and the Minister of Education. He was going to make a difference in this country, while in the great eternal scheme of things it mattered little that the servant stole the batteries out of the flashlight or put chili powder instead of paprika on the eggs.

I continued to ponder this dramatic contrast between men's and  4 women's work, and when we finished our contract and returned in the fall of 1969 to the University of Michigan in Ann Arbor I was surprised to find that many other women were also questioning the expectations that they had grown up with. I attended a campus women's conference, but I returned home more troubled than ever. Now that I knew housework was worth only a dollar a day, I couldn't take it seriously, but I wasn't angry in the same way these women were. Their militancy frightened me. I wasn't ready for a revolution, so I decided I would have my own feminist movement. I would study the English language and see what it could tell me about sexism. I started reading a desk dictionary and making notecards on every entry that seemed to tell something about male and female. I soon had a dog-eared dictionary, along with a collection of note cards filling two shoe boxes.

Ironically, I started reading the dictionary because I wanted to avoid 5
getting involved in social issues, but what happened was that my notecards
brought me right back to looking at society. Language and society are as
intertwined as a chicken and an egg. The language that a culture uses is
tell-tale evidence of the values and beliefs of that culture. And because there
is a lag in how fast a language changes—new words can easily be introduced,
but it takes a long time for old words and usages to disappear—a careful look
at English will reveal the attitudes that our ancestors held and that we as a
culture are therefore predisposed to hold. My notecards revealed three main
points. Friends have offered the opinion that I didn't need to read the
dictionary to learn such obvious facts. Nevertheless, it was interesting to
have linguistic evidence of sociological observations.

## WOMEN ARE SEXY; MEN ARE SUCCESSFUL

First, in American culture a woman is valued for the attractiveness and 6
sexiness of her body, while a man is valued for his physical strength and
accomplishments. A woman is sexy. A man is successful.

A persuasive piece of evidence supporting this view are the 7
eponyms—words that have come from someone's name—found in
English. I had a two-and-a-half inch stack of cards taken from men's
names, but less than a half-inch stack from women's names, and most of
those came from Greek mythology. In the words that came into
American English since we separated from Britain, there are many
eponyms based on the names of famous American men: bartlett pear,
boysenberry, diesel engine, franklin stove, ferris wheel, gatling gun,
mason jar, sideburns, sousaphone, schick test, and winchester rifle. The
only common eponyms taken from American women's names are *Alice
blue* (after Alice Roosevelt Longworth), bloomers (after Amelia Jenks
Bloomer) and *Mae West jacket* (after the buxom actress). Two out of the
three feminine eponyms relate closely to a woman's physical anatomy,
while the masculine eponyms (except for *sideburns* after General Burn-
sides) have nothing to do with the namesake's body, but instead honor
the man for an accomplishment of some kind.

Although in Greek mythology women played a bigger role than they 8
did in the biblical stories of the Judeo-Christian cultures and so the
names of goddesses are accepted parts of the language in such place
names as Pomona from the goddess of fruit and Athens from Athena and
in such common words as *cereal* from Ceres, *psychology* from Psyche, and
*arachnoid* from Arachne, the same tendency to think of women in
relation to sexuality is seen in the eponyms *aphrodisiac* from Aphrodite,
the Greek name for the goddess of love and beauty, and *venereal disease,*
from Venus, the Roman name for Aphrodite.

Another interesting word from Greek mythology is *Amazon*. According to Greek folk etymology, the *a* means "without" as in *atypical* or *amoral* while *mazon* comes from *mazos* meaning *breast* as still seen in *mastectomy*. In the Greek legend, Amazon women cut off their right breasts so that they could better shoot their bows. Apparently, the storytellers had a feeling that for women to play the active, "masculine" role that the Amazons adopted for themselves, they had to trade in part of their femininity.

This preoccupation with women's breasts is not limited to ancient stories. As a volunteer for the University of Wisconsin's *Dictionary of American Regional English (DARE)*, I read a western trapper's diary from the 1830's. I was to make notes of any unusual usages or language patterns. My most interesting finding was that he referred to a range of mountains as *The Teats*, a metaphor based on the similarity between the shapes of the mountains and women's breasts. Because today we use the French wording, *The Grand Tetons*, the metaphor isn't as obvious, but I wrote to mapmakers and found the following listings: *Nippletop* and *Little Nipple Top* near Mt. Marcy in the Adirondacks, *Nipple Mountain* in Archuleta County, Colorado, *Nipple Peak* in Coke County, Texas, *Nipple Butte* in Pennington, South Dakota, *Squaw Peak* in Placer County, California (and many other locations), *Maiden's Peak* and *Squaw Tit* (they're the same mountain) in the Cascade Range in Oregon, *Mary's Nipple* near Salt Lake City, Utah, and *Jane Russell Peaks* near Stark, New Hampshire.

Except for the movie star Jane Russell, the women being referred to are anonymous—it's only a sexual part of their body that is mentioned. When topographical features are named after men, it's probably not going to be to draw attention to a sexual part of their bodies but instead to honor individuals for an accomplishment. For example, no one thinks of a part of the male body when hearing a reference to Pike's Peak, Colorado or Jackson Hole, Wyoming.

Going back to what I learned from my dictionary cards, I was surprised to realize how many pairs of words we have in which the feminine word has acquired sexual connotations while the masculine word retains a serious businesslike aura. For example, a *callboy* is the person who calls actors when it is time for them to go on stage, but a *callgirl* is a prostitute. Compare *sir* and *madam*. *Sir* is a term of respect while *madam* has acquired the specialized meaning of a brothel manager. Something similar has happened to *master* and *mistress*. Would you rather have a painting by *an old master* or *an old mistress*?

It's because the word *woman* had sexual connotations as in "She's his woman," that people began avoiding its use, hence such terminology as *ladies room, lady of the house,* and *girls' school* or *school for young ladies*. Feminists, who ask that people use the term *woman* rather than *girl* or *lady,* are rejecting the idea that *woman* is primarily a sexual term. They have been at least partially successful in that today *woman* is commonly used to communicate gender without intending implications about sexuality.

I found two hundred pairs of words with masculine and feminine 14 forms, e.g., *heir–heiress, hero–heroine, steward–stewardess, usher–usherette, etc.* In nearly all such pairs, the masculine word is considered the base with some kind of a feminine suffix being added. The masculine form is the one from which compounds are made, e.g., from *king–queen* comes *kingdom* but not *queendom,* from *sportsman–sportslady* comes *sportsmanship* but not *sportsladyship.* There is one—and only one—semantic area in which the masculine word is not the base or more powerful word. This is in the area dealing with sex and marriage. When someone refers to a *virgin,* a listener will probably think of a female unless the speaker specifies *male* or uses a masculine pronoun. The same is true for *prostitute.*

In relation to marriage, there is much linguistic evidence showing 15 that weddings are more important to women than to men. A woman cherishes the wedding and is considered a bride for a whole year, but a man is referred to as a groom only on the day of the wedding. The word *bride* appears in *bridal attendant, bridal gown, bridesmaid, bridal shower,* and even *bridegroom. Groom* comes from the Middle English *grom,* meaning "man" and in this sense is seldom used outside of a wedding. With most pairs of male/female words, people habitually put the masculine word first, *Mr. and Mrs., his and hers, boys and girls, men and women, kings and queens, brothers and sisters, guys and dolls,* and *host and hostess,* but it is the *bride and groom* who are talked about, not the *groom and bride.*

The importance of marriage to a woman is also shown by the fact 16 that when a marriage ends in death, the woman gets the title of *widow.* A man gets the derived title of *widower.* This term is not used in other phrases or contexts, but *widow* is seen in *widowhood, widow's peak,* and *widow's walk.* A *widow* in a card game is an extra hand of cards, while in typesetting it is an extra line of type.

How changing cultural ideas bring changes to language is clearly 17 visible in this semantic area. The feminist movement has caused the differences between the sexes to be downplayed and since I did my dictionary study two decades ago, the word *singles* has largely replaced such sex specific and value-laden terms as *bachelor, old maid, spinster, divorcee, widow,* and *widower.* And in 1970 I wrote that when a man is called *a professional* he is thought to be a doctor or a lawyer, but when people hear a woman referred to as *a professional* they are likely to think of a prostitute. That's not as true today because so many women have become doctors and lawyers that it's no longer incongruous to think of women in those professional roles.

Another change that has taken place is in wedding announcements. 18 They used to be sent out from the bride's parents and did not even give the name of the groom's parents. Today, most couples choose to list either all or none of the parents' names. Also it is now much more likely that both the bride and groom's picture will be in the newspaper, while a decade ago only the bride's picture was published on the "Women's" or the "Society" page. Even the traditional wording of the wedding ceremony is being changed. Many officials now pronounce the couple "husband and wife" instead of the old "man and wife," and they ask the bride if she promises "to love, honor and cherish," instead of "to love, honor, and obey."

## WOMEN ARE PASSIVE; MEN ARE ACTIVE

The wording of the wedding ceremony also relates to the second point 19 that my cards showed, which is that women are expected to play a passive or weak role while men play an active or strong role. In the traditional ceremony, the official asks "Who gives the bride away?" and the father answers "I do." Some fathers answer "Her mother and I do," but that doesn't solve the problem inherent in the question. The idea that a bride is something to be handed over from one man to another bothers people because it goes back to the days when a man's servants, his children, and his wife were all considered to be his property. They were known by his name because they belonged to him and he was responsible for their actions and their debts.

The grammar used in talking or writing about weddings as well as 20 other sexual relationships shows the expectation of men playing the active role. Men *wed* women while women *become* brides of men. A man *possesses* a woman; he *deflowers* her, he *performs*, he *scores*; he *takes away*, her virginity. Although a woman can *seduce* a man, she cannot offer him her virginity. When talking about virginity, the only way to make the woman the actor in the sentence is to say that "She lost her virginity," but people lose things by accident rather than by purposeful actions and so she's only the grammatical, not the real-life, actor.

The reason that women tried to bring the term *Ms.* into the language 21 to replace *Miss* or *Mrs.* relates to this point. Married women resented being identified only under their husband's names. For example, when Susan Glascoe did something newsworthy she would be identified in the newspaper only as Mrs. John Glascoe. The dictionary cards showed what appeared to be an attitude on the part of editors that it was almost indecent to let a respectable woman's name march unaccompanied across the pages of a dictionary. Women were listed with male names whether or not the male contributed to the woman's reason for being in the dictionary or in his own right was as famous as the woman. For example, Charlotte Bronte was identified as Mrs. Arthur B. Nicholls, Amelia Earhart as Mrs. George Palmer Putnam, Helen Hayes as Mrs. Charles

MacArthur, Jenny Lind as Mme. Otto Goldschmit, Cornelia Otis Skinner as the daughter of Otis, Harriet Beecher Stowe as the sister of Henry Ward Beecher, and Edith Sitwell as the sister of Osbert and Sacheverell. A very small number of women got into the dictionary without the benefit of a masculine escort. They were rebels and crusaders: temperance leaders Frances Elizabeth Caroline Willard and Carry Nation, women's rights leaders Carrie Chapman Catt and Elizabeth Cady Stanton, birth control educator Margaret Sanger, religious leader Mary Baker Eddy, and slaves Harriet Tubman and Phillis Wheatley.

Etiquette books used to teach that if a woman had *Mrs.* in front of her 22 name then the husband's name should follow because *Mrs.* is an abbreviated form of *Mistress* and a woman couldn't be a mistress of herself. As with many arguments about "correct" language usage, this isn't very logical because *Miss* is also an abbreviation of *Mistress*. Feminists hoped to simplify matters by introducing *Ms.* as an alternative to both *Mrs.* and *Miss,* but what happened is that *Ms.* largely replaced *Miss* to become a catch-all business title for women. Many married women still prefer the title *Mrs.*, and some resent being addressed with the term *Ms.* As one frustrated newspaper reporter complained, "Before I can write about a woman, I have to know not only her marital status but also her political philosophy." The result of such complications may contribute to the demise of titles which are already being ignored by many computer programmers who find it more efficient to simply use names, for example in a business letter: "Dear Joan Garcia," instead of "Dear Mrs. Joan Garcia," "Dear Ms. Garcia," or "Dear Mrs. Louis Garcia."

The titles given to royalty provide an example of how males can be 23 disadvantaged by the assumption that they are always to play the more powerful role. In British royalty, when a male holds a title, his wife is automatically given the feminine equivalent. But the reverse is not true. For example, a *count* is a high political officer with a *countess* being his wife. The same is true for a *duke* and a *duchess* and a *king* and a *queen*. But when a female holds the royal title, the man she marries does not automatically acquire the matching title. For example, Queen Elizabeth's husband has the title of *prince* rather than *king*, but if Prince Charles should become king while he is still married to Lady or Princess Diana, she will be known as the queen. The reasoning appears to be that since masculine words are stronger, they are reserved for true heirs and withheld from males coming into the royal family by marriage. If Prince Philip were called *King Philip*, it would be much easier for British subjects to forget where the true power lies.

The names that people give their children show the hopes and 24 dreams they have for them, and when we look at the differences between male and female names in a culture we can see the cumulative expectations of that culture. In our culture girls often have names taken from small, aesthetically pleasing items, e.g., *Ruby, Jewel,* and *Pearl. Esther* and

*Stella* mean "star," *Ada* means "ornament," and *Vanessa* means "butterfly." Boys are more likely to be given names with meanings of power and strength, e.g., *Neil* means "champion," *Martin* is from Mars, the God of War, *Raymond* means "wise protection," *Harold* means "chief of the army," *Ira* means "vigilant," *Rex* means "king," and *Richard* means "strong king."

We see similar differences in food metaphors. Food is a passive 25 substance just sitting there waiting to be eaten. Many people have recognized this and so no longer feel comfortable describing women as "delectable morsels." However, when I was a teenager, it was considered a compliment to refer to a girl (we didn't call anyone a *woman* until she was middle-aged) as *a cute tomato, a peach, a dish, a cookie, honey, sugar,* or *sweetie-pie*. When being affectionate, women will occasionally call a man *honey* or *sweetie*, but in general, food metaphors are used much less often with men than with women. If a man is called *a fruit*, his masculinity is being questioned. But it's perfectly acceptable to use a food metaphor if the food is heavier and more substantive than that used for women. For example pin-up pictures of women have long been known as *cheesecake,* but when Burt Reynolds posed for a nude centerfold the picture was immediately dubbed *beefcake,* c.f. *a hunk of meat*. That such sexual references to men have come into the general language is another reflection of how society is beginning to lessen the differences between their attitudes toward men and women.

Something similar to the *fruit* metaphor happens with references to 26 plants. We insult a man by calling him *a pansy,* but it wasn't considered particularly insulting to talk about a girl being a *wallflower,* a *clinging vine,* or a *shrinking violet,* or to give girls such names as *Ivy, Rose, Lily, Iris, Daisy, Camellia, Heather,* and *Flora*. A plant metaphor can be used with a man if the plant is big and strong, for example Andrew Jackson's nickname of *Old Hickory*. Also, the phrases *blooming idiots* and *budding geniuses* can be used with either sex, but notice how they are based on the most active thing a plant can do which is to bloom or bud.

Animal metaphors also illustrate the different expectations for males 27 and females. Men are referred to as *studs, bucks,* and *wolves* while women are referred to with such metaphors as *kitten, bunny, beaver, bird, chick,* and *lamb*. In the 1950s we said that boys went *tomcatting,* but today it's just *catting around* and both boys and girls do it. When the term *foxy,* meaning that someone was sexy, first became popular it was used only for girls, but now someone of either sex can be described as *a fox*. Some animal metaphors that are used predominantly with men have negative connotations based on the size and/or strength of the animals, e.g., *beast, bullheaded, jackass, rat, loanshark,* and *vulture*. Negative metaphors used with women are based on smaller animals, e.g., *social butterfly, mousy, catty,* and *vixen*. The feminine terms connote action, but not the same kind of large scale action as with the masculine terms.

# WOMEN ARE CONNECTED
## WITH NEGATIVE CONNOTATIONS,
## MEN WITH POSITIVE CONNOTATIONS

The final point that my notecards illustrated was how many positive 28
connotations are associated with the concept of masculine, while there
are either trivial or negative connotations connected with the corresponding feminine concept. An example from the animal metaphors
makes a good illustration. The word *shrew* taken from the name of a
small but especially vicious animal was defined in my dictionary as "an ill
tempered scolding woman," but the word *shrewd* taken from the same
root was defined as "marked by clever, discerning awareness" and was
illustrated with the phrase "a shrewd businessman."

Early in life, children are conditioned to the superiority of the 29
masculine role. As child psychologists point out, little girls have much
more freedom to experiment with sex roles than do little boys. If a little
girl acts like a *tomboy,* most parents have mixed feelings, being at least
partially proud. But if their little boy acts like a *sissy* (derived from *sister*),
they call a psychologist. It's perfectly acceptable for a little girl to sleep in
the crib that was purchased for her brother, to wear his hand-me-down
jeans and shirts, and to ride the bicycle that he has outgrown. But few
parents would put a boy baby in a white and gold crib decorated with
frills and lace, and virtually no parents would have their little boy wear his
sister's hand-me-down dresses, nor would they have their son ride a girl's
pink bicycle with a flower-bedecked basket. The proper names given to
girls and boys show this same attitude. Girls can have "boy" names—
*Cris, Craig, Jo, Kelly, Shawn, Teri, Toni,* and *Sam*—but it doesn't work
the other way around. A couple of generations ago, *Beverley, Frances,
Hazel, Marion,* and *Shirley* were common boys' names. As parents gave
these names to more and more girls, they fell into disuse for males and
some older men who have these names prefer to go by their initials or by
such abbreviated forms as *Haze* or *Shirl*.

When a little girl is told to *be a lady,* she is being told to sit with her 30
knees together and to be quiet and dainty. But when a little boy is told to
*be a man* he is being told to be noble, strong, and virtuous—to have all
the qualities that the speaker looks on as desirable. The concept of
manliness has such positive connotations that it used to be a compliment
to call someone a *he-man,* to say that he was doubly a man. Today many
people are more ambivalent about this term and respond to it much as
they do to the word *macho*. But calling someone a *manly man* or a *virile
man* is nearly always meant as a compliment. *Virile* comes from the
Indo-European *vir* meaning "man," which is also the basis of *virtuous*.
Contrast the positive connotations of both *virile* and *virtuous* with the
negative connotations of *hysterical*. The Greeks took this latter word
from their name for *uterus* (as still seen in *hysterectomy*). They thought

that women were the only ones who experienced uncontrolled emotional outbursts and so the condition must have something to do with a part of the body that only women have.

Differences in the connotations between positive male and negative 31 female connotations can be seen in several pairs of words which differ denotatively only in the matter of sex. *Bachelor* as compared to *spinster* or *old maid* has such positive connotations that women try to adopt them by using the term *bachelor-girl* or *bachelorette*. *Old maid* is so negative that it's the basis for metaphors: pretentious and fussy old men are called *old maids* as are the leftover kernels of unpopped popcorn, and the last card in a popular children's game.

*Patron* and *matron* (Middle English for *father* and *mother*) have such 32 different levels of prestige that women try to borrow the more positive masculine connotations with the word *patroness,* literally "female father." Such a peculiar term came about because of the high prestige attached to *patron* in such phrases as *a patron of the arts* or *a patron saint. Matron* is more apt to be used in talking about a woman in charge of a jail or a public restroom.

When men are doing jobs that women often do, we apparently try to 33 pay the men extra by giving them fancy titles, for example, a male cook is more likely to be called a *chef* while a male seamstress will get the title of *tailor.* The Armed Forces have a special problem in that they recruit under such slogans as "The Marine Corps builds men!" and "Join the Army! Become a Man." Once the recruits are enlisted, they find themselves doing much of the work that has been traditionally thought of as "women's work." The solution to getting the work done and not insulting anyone's masculinity was to change the titles as shown below:

| | |
|---|---|
| waitress | orderly |
| nurse | medic or corpsman |
| secretary | clerk-typist |
| assistant | adjutant |
| dishwasher or kitchen helper | KP (kitchen police) |

Compare *brave* and *squaw.* Early settlers in America truly admired 34 Indian men and hence named them with a word that carried connotations of youth, vigor, and courage. But they used the Algonquin's name for "woman" and over the years it developed almost opposite connotations to those of *brave. Wizard* and *witch* contrast almost as much. The masculine *wizard* implies skill and wisdom combined with magic, while the feminine *witch* implies evil intentions combined with magic. Part of the unattractiveness of both *witch* and *squaw* is that they have been used so often to refer to old women, something with which our culture is particularly uncomfortable, just as the Afghans were. Imagine my surprise when I ran across the phrases *grandfatherly advice* and *old wives' tales* and realized that the underlying implication is the same as the Afghan proverb about old men being worth listening to while old women talk only foolishness.

Other terms which show how negatively we view old women as 35 compared to young women are *old nag* as compared to *filly, old crow* or *old bat* as compared to *bird*, and of being *catty* as compared to being *kittenish*. There is no matching set of metaphors for men. The chicken metaphor tells the whole story of a woman's life. In her youth she is a *chick*. Then she marries and begins *feathering her nest*. Soon she begins feeling *cooped up*, so she goes to *hen parties* where she *cackles* with her friends. Then she has her *brood*, begins to *henpeck* her husband, and finally turns into *an old biddy*.

I embarked on my study of the dictionary not with the intention of 36 prescribing language change but simply to see what the language would tell me about sexism. Nevertheless I have been both surprised and pleased as I've watched the changes that have occurred over the past two decades. I'm one of those linguists who believes that new language customs will cause a new generation of speakers to grow up with different expectations. This is why I'm happy about people's efforts to use inclusive language, to say *he or she* or *they* when speaking about individuals whose names they do not know. I'm glad that leading publishers have developed guidelines to help writers use language that is fair to both sexes and I'm glad that most newspapers and magazines list women by their own names instead of only by their husbands' names and that educated and thoughtful people no longer begin their business letters with "Dear Sir" or "Gentlemen," but instead use a memo form or begin with such salutations as "Dear Colleagues," "Dear Reader," or "Dear Committee Members." I'm also glad that such words as *poetess, authoress, conductress,* and *aviatrix* now sound quaint and old fashioned and that *chairman* is giving way to *chair* or *head, mailman* to *mail carrier, clergyman* to *clergy,* and *stewardess* to *flight attendant*. I was also pleased when the National Oceanic and Atmospheric Administration bowed to feminist complaints and in the late 1970s began to alternate men's and women's names for hurricanes. However, I wasn't so pleased to discover that the change did not immediately erase sexist thoughts from everyone's mind as shown by a headline about Hurricane David in a 1979 New York tabloid, "David Rapes Virgin Islands." More recently a similar metaphor appeared in a headline in the *Arizona Republic* about Hurricane Charlie, "Charlie Quits Carolinas, Flirts with Virginia."

What these incidents show is that sexism is not something existing 37 independently in American English or in the particular dictionary that I happened to read. Rather, it exists in people's minds. Language is like an x-ray in providing visible evidence of invisible thoughts. The best thing about people being interested in and discussing sexist language is that as they make conscious decisions about what pronouns they will use, what jokes they will tell or laugh at, how they will write their names, or how they will begin their letters, they are forced to think about the underlying issue of sexism. This is good because as a problem that begins in people's assumptions and expectations, it's a problem that will be solved only when a great many people have given it a great deal of thought.

## Post-Reading Questions

1. Why does Nilsen open this essay with a description of her return, twenty years before, from Afghanistan to America? What function does this opening fulfill in relation to Nilsen's purpose in writing this essay?
2. Characterize the style of this essay. Is it familiar, pushy, argumentative, informative, objective, or biased? Choose an adjective and support your choice with references to Nilsen's language. How does she create the stylistic effect you describe?
3. Do you find Nilsen's style appropriate to her audience and purpose? Explain your answer by describing how her style either suits or does not suit her context (the implied audience and purpose; the general social situation surrounding this issue).
4. What does simply scanning the headings and subheadings in the essay tell you about Nilsen's attitude toward sexist language? Are you in agreement with her attitude? Do you think her headings are objective? Why?
5. How does Nilsen deal with language change? Does she view linguistic change in a positive or negative light? How do you know?
6. Why is it important to know how, when, and why Nilsen began her research into sexist language in English (paragraph 4)? In what way does this set of facts add to your positive impression of Nilsen or diminish her status in your eyes? Why?
7. Is the evidence Nilsen uses scientific? Is it taken from scientific journals? In what ways is this essay unlike the standard scientific article in an academic or research journal?
8. Near the end of this essay Nilsen says, "The best thing about people being interested in and discussing sexist language is that as they make conscious decisions about what pronouns they will use, what jokes they will tell or laugh at, how they will write their names, or how they begin their letters, they are forced to think about the underlying issue of sexism." What begins as sensitivity to language, in other words, often ends in greater sensitivity to social and political issues of all kinds. How does this statement relate to language and power? Do members of subjugated groups, in this case women, gain more power when the societies in which they live become more sensitive to language issues? Why?

# ROBIN LAKOFF ON THE CONVERSATIONAL STYLES OF WOMEN AND MEN

## Pre-Reading Questions

1. In your experience, what differences have you noticed between women's and men's conversational patterns? What caused those differences?
2. Write a page or two of dialogue in which you contrast the conversational voices of men and women. You can do a straightforward rendition of a conversation, or a parody of women's and men's voices. (This exercise makes a good journal entry or group project.)
3. Look at the final sentence in Lakoff's essay, which appears as a one-sentence paragraph. To whom do you think this sentence is addressed? What do you think Lakoff wants this group of readers to"speak up" about? Given your responses to these questions, what do you think is argued in the essay itself?

## YOU ARE WHAT YOU SAY
### Robin Lakoff

"Women's language" is that pleasant (dainty?), euphemistic, never- 1
aggressive way of talking we learned as little girls. Cultural bias was built into the language we were allowed to speak, the subjects we were allowed to speak about, and the ways we were spoken of. Having learned our linguistic lesson well, we go out in the world, only to discover that we are communicative cripples—damned if we do, and damned if we don't.

If we refuse to talk "like a lady," we are ridiculed and criticized for 2
being unfeminine. ("She thinks like a man" is, at best, a left-handed compliment.) If we do learn all the fuzzy-headed, unassertive language of our sex, we are ridiculed for being unable to think clearly, unable to take part in a serious discussion, and therefore unfit to hold a position of power.

It doesn't take much of this for a woman to begin feeling she 3
deserves such treatment because of inadequacies in her own intelligence and education.

"Women's language" shows up in all levels of English. For example, 4
women are encouraged and allowed to make far more precise discriminations in naming colors than men do. Words like *mauve, beige, ecru, aquamarine, lavender,* and so on, are unremarkable in a woman's active

vocabulary, but largely absent from that of most men. I know of no evidence suggesting that women actually *see* a wider range of colors than men do. It is simply that fine discriminations of this sort are relevant to women's vocabularies, but not to men's; to men, who control most of the interesting affairs of the world, such distinctions are trivial—irrelevant.

In the area of syntax, we find similar gender-related peculiarities of 5 speech. There is one construction, in particular, that women use conversationally far more than men: the tag question. A tag is midway between an outright statement and a yes-no question; it is less assertive than the former, but more confident than the latter.

A *flat statement* indicates confidence in the speaker's knowledge and 6 is fairly certain to be believed; a *question* indicates a lack of knowledge on some point and implies that the gap in the speaker's knowledge can and will be remedied by an answer. For example, if, at a Little League game, I have had my glasses off, I can legitimately ask someone else: "Was the player out at third?" A *tag question*, being intermediate between statement and question, is used when the speaker is stating a claim, but lacks full confidence in the truth of that claim. So if I say, "Is Joan here?" I will probably not be surprised if my respondent answers "no"; but if I say, "Joan is here, isn't she?" instead, chances are I am already biased in favor of a positive answer, wanting only confirmation. I still want a response, but I have enough knowledge (or think I have) to predict that response. A tag question, then, might be thought of as a statement that doesn't demand to be believed by anyone but the speaker, a way of giving leeway, of not forcing the addressee to go along with the views of the speaker.

Another common use of the tag question is in small talk when the 7 speaker is trying to elicit conversation: "Sure is hot here, isn't it?"

But in discussing personal feelings or opinions, only the speaker 8 normally has any way of knowing the correct answer. Sentences such as "I have a headache, don't I?" are clearly ridiculous. But there are other examples where it is the speaker's opinions, rather than perceptions, for which corroboration is sought, as in "The situation in Southeast Asia is terrible, isn't it?"

While there are, of course, other possible interpretations of a 9 sentence like this, one possibility is that the speaker has a particular answer in mind—"yes" or "no"—but is reluctant to state it baldly. This sort of tag question is much more apt to be used by women than by men in conversation. Why is this the case?

The tag question allows a speaker to avoid commitment, and thereby 10 avoid conflict with the addressee. The problem is that, by so doing, speakers may also give the impression of not really being sure of themselves, or looking to the addressee for confirmation of their views. This uncertainty is reinforced in more subliminal ways, too. There is a peculiar sentence intonation-pattern, used almost exclusively by women, as far as I know, which changes a declarative answer into a question. The effect of using the rising inflection typical of a yes-no question is to imply that the speaker is seeking confirmation, even though the speaker is clearly the only one who has the requisite information, which is why the question was put to her in the first place:

(q)  When will dinner be ready?
(a)  Oh . . . around six o'clock. . . ?

It is as though the second speaker were saying, "Six o'clock—if that's 11 okay with you, if you agree." The person being addressed is put in the position of having to provide confirmation. One likely consequence of this sort of speech-pattern in a woman is that, often unbeknownst to herself, the speaker builds a reputation of tentativeness, and others will refrain from taking her seriously or trusting her with any real responsibilities, since she "can't make up her mind," and "isn't sure of herself."

Such idiosyncrasies may explain why women's language sounds 12 much more "polite" than men's. It is polite to leave a decision open, not impose your mind, or views, or claims, on anyone else. So a tag question is a kind of polite statement, in that it does not force agreement or belief on the addressee. In the same way a request is a polite command, in that it does not force obedience on the addressee, but rather suggests something be done as a favor to the speaker. A clearly stated order implies a threat of certain consequences if it is not followed, and—even more impolite—implies that the speaker is in a superior position and able to enforce the order. By couching wishes in the form of a request, on the other hand, a speaker implies that if the request is not carried out, only the speaker will suffer; noncompliance cannot harm the addressee. So the decision is really left up to the addressee. The distinction becomes clear in these examples:

Close the door.
Please close the door.
Will you close the door?
Will you please close the door?
Won't you close the door?

In the same ways as words and speech patterns used *by* women 13 undermine her image, those used *to describe* women make matters even worse. Often a word may be used of both men and women (and perhaps of things as well); but when it is applied to women, it assumes a special meaning that, by implication rather than outright assertion, is derogatory to women as a group.

The use of euphemisms has this effect. A euphemism is a substitute 14 for a word that has acquired a bad connotation by association with something unpleasant or embarrassing. But almost as soon as the new word comes into common usage, it takes on the same old bad connotations, since feelings about the things or people referred to are not altered by a change of name; thus new euphemisms must be constantly found.

There is one euphemism for *woman* still very much alive. The word, 15 of course, is *lady. Lady* has a masculine counterpart, namely *gentleman,* occasionally shortened to gent. But for some reason *lady* is very much commoner than *gent(leman).*

The decision to use *lady* rather than *woman,* or vice versa, may 16 considerably alter the sense of a sentence, as the following examples show:

(a)   A woman (lady) I know is a dean at Berkeley.
(b)   A woman (lady) I know makes amazing things out of shoelaces and old boxes.

The use of *lady* in (a) imparts a frivolous, or nonserious, tone to the 17 sentence: the matter under discussion is not one of great moment. Similarly, in (b), using *lady* here would suggest that the speaker considered the "amazing things" not to be serious art, but merely a hobby or an aberration. If *woman* is used, she might be a serious sculptor. To say *lady doctor* is very condescending, since no one ever says *gentleman doctor* or even *man doctor.* For example, mention in the San Francisco *Chronicle* of January 31, 1972, of Madalyn Murray O'Hair as the *lady atheist* reduces her position to that of scatterbrained eccentric. Even *woman atheist* is scarcely defensible: sex is irrelevant to her philosophical position.

Many women argue that, on the other hand, *lady* carries with it 18 overtones recalling the age of chivalry: conferring exalted stature on the person so referred to. This makes the term seem polite at first, but we must also remember that these implications are perilous: they suggest that a "lady" is helpless, and cannot do things by herself.

*Lady* can also be used to infer frivolousness, as in titles of organiza- 19 tions. Those that have a serious purpose (not merely that of enabling "the ladies" to spend time with one another) cannot use the word *lady* in their titles, but less serious ones may. Compare the *Ladies' Auxiliary* of a men's group, or the *Thursday Evening Ladies' Browning and Garden Society* with *Ladies' Liberation* or *Ladies' Strike for Peace.*

What is curious about this split is that *lady* is in origin a 20 euphemism—a substitute that puts a better face on something people find uncomfortable—for *woman.* What kind of euphemism is it that subtly denigrates the people to whom it refers? Perhaps *lady* functions as a euphemism for *woman* because it does not contain the sexual implications present in *woman:* it is not "embarrassing" in that way. If this is so, we may expect that, in the future, *lady* will replace woman as the primary word for the human female, since *woman* will have become too blatantly sexual. That this distinction is already made in some contexts at least is shown in the following examples, where you can try replacing *woman* with *lady:*

   (a)   She's only twelve, but she's already a woman.
   (b)   After ten years in jail, Harry wanted to find a woman.
   (c)   She's my woman, see, so don't mess around with her.

Another common substitute for *woman* is *girl.* One seldom hears a 21 man past the age of adolescence referred to as a boy, save in expressions like "going out with the boys," which are meant to suggest an air of adolescent frivolity and irresponsibility. But women of all ages are "girls": one can have a man—not a boy—Friday, but only a girl—never a woman or even a lady—Friday; women have girlfriends, but men do not—in a nonsexual sense—have boyfriends. It may be that this use of *girl* is euphemistic in the same way the use of *lady* is: in stressing the idea of immaturity, it removes the sexual connotations lurking in *woman.* *Girl* brings to mind irresponsibility: you don't send a girl to do a woman's errand (or even, for that matter, a boy's errand). She is a person who is both too immature and too far from real life to be entrusted with responsibilities or with decisions of any serious or important nature.

Now let's take a pair of words which, in terms of the possible 22 relationships in an earlier society, were simple male-female equivalents, analogous to *bull : cow.* Suppose we find that, for independent reasons, society has changed in such a way that the original meanings now are irrelevant. Yet the words have not been discarded, but have acquired new meanings, metaphorically related to their original senses. But suppose these new metaphorical uses are no longer parallel to each other. By seeing where the parallelism breaks down, we discover something about the different roles played by men and women in this culture. One good example of such a divergence through time is found in the pair, *master : mistress.* Once used with reference to one's power over servants, these words have become unusable today in their original master-servant sense as the relationship has become less prevalent in our society. But the words are still common.

Unless used with reference to animals, *master* now generally refers to 23 a man who has acquired consummate ability in some field, normally nonsexual. But its feminine counterpart cannot be used this way. It is practically restricted to its sexual sense of "paramour." We start out with two terms, both roughly paraphrasable as "one who has power over another." But the masculine form, once one person is no longer able to have absolute power over another, becomes usable metaphorically in the sense of "having power over *something.*" *Master* requires as its object only the name of some activity, something inanimate and abstract. But *mistress* requires a masculine noun in the possessive to precede it. One cannot say: "Rhonda is a mistress." One must be *someone's* mistress. A man is defined by what he does, a woman by her sexuality, that is, in terms of one particular aspect of her relationship to men. It is one thing to be an *old master* like Hans Holbein, and another to be an *old mistress*.

The same is true of the words *spinster* and *bachelor*—gender words 24 for "one who is not married." The resemblance ends with the definition. While *bachelor* is a neutral term, often used as a compliment, *spinster* normally is used pejoratively, with connotations of prissiness, fussiness, and so on. To be a bachelor implies that one has the choice of marrying or not, and this is what makes the idea of a bachelor existence attractive, in the popular literature. He has been pursued and has successfully eluded his pursuers. But a spinster is one who has not been pursued, or at least not seriously. She is old, unwanted goods. The metaphorical connotations of *bachelor* generally suggest sexual freedom; of *spinster*, puritanism or celibacy.

These examples could be multiplied. It is generally considered a *faux* 25 *pas*, in society, to congratulate a woman on her engagement, while it is correct to congratulate her fiancé. Why is this? The reason seems to be that it is impolite to remind people of things that may be uncomfortable to them. To congratulate a woman on her engagement is really to say, "Thank goodness! You had a close call!" For the man, on the other hand, there was no such danger. His choosing to marry is viewed as a good thing, but not something essential.

The linguistic double standard holds throughout the life of the 26 relationship. After marriage, bachelor and spinster become man and wife, not man and woman. The woman whose husband dies remains "John's widow"; John, however, is never "Mary's widower."

Finally, why is it that salesclerks and others are so quick to call 27 women customers "dear," "honey," and other terms of endearment they really have no business using? A male customer would never put up with it. But women, like children, are supposed to enjoy these endearments, rather than being offended by them.

In more ways than one, it's time to speak up.                    28

## Post-Reading Questions

1. What is the point behind Lakoff's title? Do you recognize the origin of the title? (It derives from the 1960s slogan, "You are what you eat.") How does considering the origin of the title affect your reading of the essay?

2. Describe the "double-bind" in which, according to Lakoff, women find themselves (paragraphs 2 and 3). Do you know women who have experienced this double-bind, or have you experienced it yourself?

3. What reasons lie behind the fact that women use more "tag questions" than men (paragraphs 5 through 10)? What psychological characteristics of women explain their over-reliance on tag questions?

4. How are euphemisms used differently when they refer to men than they are when they refer to women (paragraphs 14 through 22)? Summarize the purpose behind Lakoff's extended analysis of gender euphemisms. Show how this analysis fits into her overall thesis regarding gender bias in everyday conversation.

5. Lakoff uses quite a few relatively short paragraphs in this essay. Many language experts claim that short paragraphs serve either a *transitional* (connecting one set of paragraphs with another) or *emphatic* function. Analyze Lakoff's use of the short paragraph. Do her short paragraphs serve one or both of these functions? Do you find that they fulfill other functions?

6. Describe Lakoff's tone. Is she direct and determined or formal and scientific? Is she somewhere in between? What gives her style the effect you describe?

7. Taken together, the essays by Nilsen and Lakoff provide thorough discussions of ways in which a group of people, in this case women, can be kept in a subjugated role by the conventions of language. In these cases, language limits people rather than empowering them. Can you think of, or have you experienced, other situations in which an already disadvantaged group of people are kept in that state by the language used to refer to them? If you can, describe that group and list some of the language features used to keep them in a disadvantaged state.

# JONATHAN KOZOL ON ILLITERACY

## Pre-Reading Questions

1. Have you ever felt helpless because you could not understand language that you needed to understand in order to get something important done? Think back over occasions when you could not understand, for example, test questions or instructions, assembly instruction manuals, the conditions of a contract, or a difficult passage in a science or literature text. If you have had this kind of experience, describe it and explain how you felt. (This makes a good journal entry.)

2. Interview a family member or friend who does not have enough schooling to do much reading or writing, or who is new to the English language, about his or her experiences with print. Write down particularly significant statements by your subject. Then write a report in which you summarize your subject's responses.

**3.** What is your general impression of illiteracy in America? Is it a significant problem? Do you think large numbers of people have trouble reading and writing? Do you think being illiterate is a significant handicap in American society? Why? Why not? From what sources have your impressions been developed?

## THE DISENFRANCHISED:
## SILENT AND UNSEEN
### Jonathan Kozol

Im 33 now and finly made a go. But the walls are up agent. and this time I don't think I can go around them. What Im I to do. I still have some engeny left. But running out. Im afraide to run out. I don't know if I can settle for noting.

*—letter to the author, 1983*

It is difficult for most Americans to place full credence in the facts described above.    1

If we did, we would be forced to choose between enormous guilt    2 and efficacious action. The willingness of decent people to withhold belief or to anaesthetize their capability for credence represents the hardest problem that we need to overcome in dealing with the dangers that we know in abstract ways but somehow cannot concretize in ways that force us to take action.

One reason for the nation's incredulity, of course, is the deceptive    3 impact of the U.S. census figures. Until recent years, these figures have been taken as authoritative indices of national reality. While it has been recognized for decades that the nonwhite population has been underrepresented in the census, it may be that it is not black people but illiterate adults who represent, in categorical terms, the largest sector of invisible Americans. Many blacks and other minorities decline, for fear of government intrusion, to respond to written forms. Illiterates do not "decline"; they cannot read the forms at all.

This, however, is not the only explanation. Illiterates find it painful to    4 identify themselves. In a print society, enormous stigma is attached to the adult nonreader. Early in the game we see the evolution of a whole line of defensive strategies against discovery by others. "Lying low" and watching out for "traps" become a pattern of existence.

An illiterate young man, nineteen years of age, sits beside me in a    5 restaurant and quietly surveys the menu. After a time he looks at the waitress, hesitates as if uncertain of his preference, then tells her: "Well, I guess I'll have a hamburger—with french fries." When she asks what he would like to drink, he pauses again, then states with some conviction: "Well, I guess I'd like a Coke."

It took me several months, although I was this young man's  6
neighbor, to discover that he could not read a word. He had learned to
order those three items which he felt assured of finding in all restaurants.
He had had a lot of hamburg and french fries in nineteen years.

Peter had been victimized initially by some incredibly incompetent  7
officials in the Boston schools. He could not look for backup to his
family. His father could not read. His mother had died when he was very
young. This was a one-parent family which, unlike the stereotype that is
accepted as the norm, was headed not by an unmarried woman but by an
undereducated and religious man. But Peter had been victimized a final
time by some of those (myself included) who were living in his
neighborhood and who ought to have perceived that he was literally
frozen in the presence of the written word.

Being ingenious and sophisticated far beyond his years, he was able  8
to disguise his fear of words to a degree that totally deceived me. I might
never have identified his inability to read if it had not been for an entirely
social happenstance. One day, driving by the ocean north of Boston, I
stopped to take him to a seafood restaurant in Gloucester. He broke into
a sweat, began to tremble, and then asked if we could leave. He asked
me, suddenly, if we could go to Howard Johnson's.

This, I discovered, was the one escape hatch he had managed to  9
contrive. Howard Johnson's, unattractive as it may appear in contrast to
a lobster restaurant beside the sea, provided Peter with his only opportunity for culinary options. Here, because of the array of color photographs attached in celluloid containers to each item on the menu, he was
able to branch out a bit and treat himself to ice cream sodas and fried
clams. Howard Johnson's, knowingly or not, has held for many years a
captive clientele of many millions of illiterate adults.

Today, the other fast-food chains provide the pictures too. Certain  10
corporations, going even further in the wish to give employment to
illiterate teenagers, now are speaking of a plan to make use of cash
registers whose keys are marked with product symbols in the place of
numbers. The illiterate employee merely needs to punch the key that
shows "two burgers" or one "Whopper." It is a good device for giving
jobs to print (and numerate) nonreaders. Obviating errors and perhaps
some personal embarrassment, it pacifies the anguish of illiterates but it
does not give them motivation to escape the trap which leaves them
powerless to find more interesting employment. Illiterates, in this way,
come to be both captive customers and captive counter workers for such
corporations.

An illiterate cattle farmer in Vermont describes the strategies that he  11
employs to hide his inability to read. "You have to be careful," he
explains, "not to get into situations where it would leak out . . . You
always try to act intelligent . . . If somebody gives you something to read,
you make believe you read it."

Sooner or later, the strategies run out. A man who has been able to 12
obtain a good job in a laboratory testing dairy products for impurities
survives by memorizing crystals and their various reactions. Offered
promotion, he is told that he will be obliged to take a brief exam. He
brings home the books that have been given to him by his boss for
preparation. Knowing the examination is a written one, he loses heart.
He never shows up at his job again. His boss perhaps will spend some
hours wondering why.

Husbands and wives can sometimes cover for each other. Illiterates 13
may bring home applications, written forms of various kinds, and ask
their spouse or children to fill in the answers. When this stratagem no
longer works (when they are asked, for instance, to check out a voucher
or a bill of lading on the job) the game is up, the worker disappears.

Once we get to know someone like Peter, we can understand the 14
courage that it takes for an illiterate adult to break down the defenses and
to ask for help. Our government's refusal to provide an answer for the
millions who have found the nerve to ask seems all the more heartbreaking for this reason. One hundred forty thousand men and women in the
State of Illinois alone have asked for literacy help from local agencies
which have been forced to turn them down for lack of federal funds.
They have been consigned to waiting lists. How many of these people,
having asked and been refused, will find the courage to apply for help
again?

On the streets of New York City or Chicago, one out of every three 15
or four adults we pass is a nonreader. Unlike the stranger who does not
speak English, or whose skin is brown or black, the person who is
illiterate can "pass." By virtue of those strategies that guard them from
humiliation, illiterates have also managed to remain unseen.

Political impotence may represent an even larger obstacle to recog- 16
nition than the fear of personal humiliation.

Others who have been victimized at least are able to form lobbies, 17
organize agendas, issue press releases, write to politicians, and, if they do
not receive responsive answers, form a voting bloc to drive those
politicians out of office. Illiterates have no access to such methods of
political redress.

We are told in school that, when we have a problem or complaint, we 18
should write a letter "to our representative at City Hall" or to an elected
politician in the nation's capital. Politicians do not answer letters that
illiterates can't write. The leverage of political negotiation that we take
for granted and assign such hopeful designations as "the Jeffersonian
ideal" is denied the man or woman who cannot participate in print
society. Neither the press release nor the handwritten flier that can draw
a crowd into a protest meeting at a local church lies within the reach of
the nonreader. Victims exist, but not constituencies. Democracy is
posited on efficacious actions that require print initiative. Even the most

highly motivated persons, if they do not read and write, cannot lobby for their own essential needs. They can speak (and now and then a journalist may hear) but genuine autonomy is far beyond them.

Illiterates may carry picket signs but cannot write them and, in any 19 case, can seldom read them. Even the rock-bottom levels of political communication—the spray paint and graffiti that adorn the walls of subways and deserted buildings in impoverished neighborhoods—are instruments of discourse which are far beyond the range of the illiterate American. Walking in a ghetto neighborhood or in a poor white area of Boston, we see the sprawl of giant letters that decry the plight of black, Hispanic, women, gay, or other persecuted groups. We read no cogent outcries from illiterates.

The forfeiture of self-created lobbies is perhaps the major reason for 20 political inaction. Those who might speak, however, on behalf of the illiterate—neighborhood organizers, for example, or the multitude of private literacy groups—tend to default on an apparent obligation. For this, there seems to be at least one obvious explanation.

Community leaders—black leaders in particular—have been reluc- 21 tant to direct the focus of attention to the crisis of adult illiteracy within the lowest economic levels of the population. Their reticence is based upon misguided fear. In pointing to the 44 percent of black adults who cannot read or write at levels needed for participation in American society, they are afraid that they may offer ammunition to those racist and reactionary persons who are often eager to attribute failure to innate inadequacy or who, while they may refrain from stating this, will nonetheless believe it. Naming the victim should not be equated with the age-old inclination to place blame upon the victim. Indeed, it tends to work the other way around. Refusal to name a victim and, still more, to offer details as to how that victimization is perpetuated and passed on is a fairly certain guarantee that people in pain will not be seen and that their victimization will not be addressed. Well-intentioned white allies of black political groups are even more susceptible to this mistake than most black leaders. (For an important exception, see description of the black-run organization "Assault on Illiteracy," cited in Notes.)

Sensible organizers understand that silence on this subject is a 22 no-win strategy. If people are injured, injury must be described. If they have not been injured—as the silence of some partisans dogmatically implies—then they have no claim upon compassion and no right to seek corrective measures. Blaming the victim is vindictive. Naming the victim is the first step in a struggle to remove the chains.

If understandable, this hesitation on the part of many leaders is 23 politically unsound. They lose the massive voting bloc which otherwise might double and, in certain urban areas, quadruple their constituencies. Black citizens, illiterate or not, may vote in overwhelming numbers for black candidates. When, as in some recent mayoral elections and in the campaign of Jesse Jackson in the presidential primaries of 1984, the options are a single black and one or more white candidates, the voting power of black people is self-evident. But when, in the more common situation, the choices are among a number of white candidates of widely differing positions (or, for that matter, a number of black candidates of widely differing degrees of merit), a black electorate which is substantially excluded from print access cannot make discerning or autonomous decisions. A physically attractive demagogue who knows the way to key his language to immediate and short-term interests of poor people may win himself a large part of the vote from those for whom his long-term bias and his past performance ought to constitute a solemn admonition.

Illiterate voters, cut off from the most effective means of repossession  24 of the past, denied the right to learn from recent history because they are denied all access to the written record of the candidate (or to the editorial reminders of that record which most newspapers supply), are locked into the present and enslaved by the encapsulated moment which is symbolized by the sixty-second newsclip on TV or the thirty-second paid advertisement that candidates employ in order to exploit the well-organized amnesia of Americans.

Illiterate Americans, denied almost all contact with the print-  25 recorded past, cannot effectively address the present nor anticipate the future. They cannot learn from Santayana's warning. They have never heard of Santayana.

Exclusion from the printed word renders one third of America the  26 ideal supine population for the "total state" that Auden feared and Orwell prophesied: undefended against doublespeak, unarmed against the orchestrated domination of their minds. Choice demands reflection and decision. Readers of the press at least can stand back and react; they can also find dissenting sources of opinion. The speed and power of electric media allow no time for qualified reflection. The TV viewer, whether literate or not, is temporarily a passive object: a receptacle for someone else's views. While all of us have proven vulnerable to this effect, it is the illiterate who has been rendered most susceptible to that entire domination which depends upon denial of the full continuum of time and its causations.

There is some danger of implicit overstatement here. Illiterate people  27 do not represent a single body of undifferentiated human beings. Most illiterates do not remain all day in front of the TV, silent and entranced, to "drink it in." Many, moreover, draw upon their own experience to discount or refute nine tenths of what they see before them on TV. Others can draw on oral history, the stories they hear, the anecdotes they have been told by parents or by older friends. Injustice itself is a profound instructor. Intuitive recognition of a fraud—a politician or a product—can empower many people to resist the absoluteness of control which television otherwise might exercise upon their wishes or convictions.

Nonetheless it is the truth that many illiterates, deeply depressed and 28 socially withdrawn, do not venture far from home and, out of the sheer longing for escape and for the simulation of "communication," do become for hours and weeks the passive addicts of the worst of what is offered on TV. Their lives and even eating schedules have been parcelled out to match the thirty-minute packages of cultural domestication and the sixty-second units of purported information which present the news in isolation from the history that shaped it or the future that it threatens to extinguish.

Many of these people would not choose to undermine or to refute a 29 form of entertainment which has come to take a permanent place within their home—their one fast-talking friend. Many more have been so long indoctrinated to indict themselves, and not society, for their impoverished and illiterate condition that there is no chance of taking lessons from injustice. They cannot denounce what seems to them to be the normal world of those who have the "know-how" to enjoy it. Nor can they profit from the learnings of an older family member who is frequently too weary and depressed to speak at length about a lifetime (or a recent history) which he or she may not desire to remember and may have been led to view not as a blessing to pass on but as a curse to be denied or wished away.

For people like these (and there are many millions, I believe) the 30 following is true: They live in a truncated present tense. The future seems hopeless. The past remains unknown. The amputated present tense, encapsulated by the TV moment, seems to constitute the end and the beginning of cognition.

Many black children, when they speak about their lives, do not seem 31 to differentiate between the present, past, and future. "I be doing good today." "Last year I be with my family in Alabama." "Someday I be somebody important." In the year that I began to teach, knowing little about sociology and less about linguistics, I perceived this first as inability, then as unwillingness, to conjugate. I summarized my explanation of the matter in somewhat these terms: People who are robbed of history, whether by slavery or by the inability to read, do not have much reason to distinguish between past and present. Those who have been robbed of opportunity to shape a future different from the ones their parents and grandparents knew do not have much reason to distinguish between now and never.

I was equally perplexed by something else about the patterns of my 32 students' speech. Even the continuous present tense that seemed to me to be the common usage of these kids was not expressed in present indicative but in a form that seemed to hold conjunctive implications. The children did not say: "I am." They said: "I be." This too appeared to me to carry metaphoric meaning. Existence itself, I felt, had been grammatically reduced to a subjunctive possibility.

Now it turns out that all of this is true except the starting point, 33 which is entirely incorrect and which derives from my lack of awareness of some basic points of history and speech. Many scholars I have studied since have made it clear that nonwhite children "conjugate" as well as anybody else, that what I heard was not exactly what the children really said, that I was missing out on words as well as intonations that conveyed a sense of tense and mode to anyone (all of their friends, for instance) who shared in a knowledge of the language which they chose to use and one that had a logic and consistency that I could not perceive. It is not "a failure to differentiate" which was at stake. The differentiation was effected, rather, by a different body of linguistic rules.

Metaphors have a curious way of living beyond the point at which 34 the evidence from which they grew has been discarded. It is now quite obvious to me that nonwhite children, whatever the thefts they have incurred, distinguish very well between the past and present. No matter how grim the future may appear, they also distinguish clearly between "now" and "never." The fact that they can do so, and persist in doing so, may be regarded as a tribute to their courage and indomitable refusal to accede before appalling odds. The metaphor, born of my first encounter with their pain and with a world I did not understand, remains to haunt me.

Whatever the language children use, the fact that matters here may 35 be established in few words: Illiterate adults have been substantially excluded from political effectiveness by lack of access to the written word. Political impotence, in turn, diminishes the visibility of those in greatest verbal subjugation and makes it all the harder for the rest of us to recognize the full dimensions of their need.

It is argued by some cynical observers that elected leaders are 36 politically astute to follow policies which keep out of the voting booth those who, reinforced by substantive decision-making data, could not quite so easily be led to vote for those who do not serve their needs. I suspect that such observers have attributed a little too much shrewdness and a great deal too much keen farsightedness to those whose actions seem more often motivated by a nineteenth century myopia than by a sinister anticipation of the future.

Enlightened politicians, if they wish to win at once political success 37 and moral credibility, soon may demonstrate the acumen of picking up an issue which can hardly fail to better their position. Few of the votes of those who have been viewed for so long as expendable are likely to be cast for politicians who have done their best to cut off aid to programs that have given even fleeting glints of hope to those who cannot read and write.

This is the point at which to take a second look at the miscalculations 38 of the census.

For one hundred years, starting in 1840, the census posed the 39
question of the population's literacy level in its ten-year compilations.
The government removed this question from its survey in the 1940
census. The reason, according to a U.S. Census Bureau publication, was
a general conviction that "most people [by this time] could read and
write . . ."

In 1970, pressured by the military, the Bureau of the Census agreed 40
to reinstate the literacy question. Even then, instead of posing questions
about actual skills, the census simply asked adults how many years of
school they had attended. More than 5 percent of those the census
reached replied that they had had less than a fifth grade education. For no
known reason, the government assumed that four fifths of these people
probably could read and, on this dangerous assumption, it was publicly
announced that 99 percent of all American adults could read and write.
These are the figures which the U.S. government passed on to the United
Nations for the purposes of worldwide compilations and comparisons.

The numbers in the 1980 census improved a bit on those of 1970. 41
This time it was found that 99.5 percent of all American adults could
read and write.

It will help us to assess the value of the U.S. census figures if we 42
understand the methods used in 1980. First, as we have seen, the census
mailed out printed forms and based most of its calculations upon written
answers in response to questions about grade-completion levels. A
second source of information was provided by a subdivision of the
Bureau of the Census known as "Current Population Surveys." This
information, based on only a small sample, was obtained by telephone
interviews or home visits. In all cases the person was asked how many
years of school he (she) had completed. If the answer was less than five,
the person was asked if he or she could read. This was the full extent of
the investigation.

It is self-evident that this is a process guaranteed to give a worthless 43
data base. First, it is apparent that illiterates will not have much success in
giving written answers to a printed questionnaire. The census believed
that someone in the home or neighborhood—a child or a relative
perhaps—could read enough to interview those who could not and that
that person would complete the forms. This belief runs counter both to
demographics and to the demands of human dignity. Illiterate people
tend to live in neighborhoods of high illiteracy. In the home itself, it is
repeatedly the case that mother, father, grandparent, and child are
illiterate. Parents, moreover, try very hard to hide their lack of competence from their children and indeed, as we have seen, develop complicated masking skills precisely to defend themselves against humiliation.
The first assumption of the Census Bureau, therefore, must be viewed as
fatuous at worst, naive at best.

Illiterates, being the poorest of our citizens, are far less likely to have 44
telephones than others in the population. Those who do are likely to
experience repeated cutoffs for nonpayment. Anyone who organizes in a
poverty community takes it as a rule of thumb that mail and telephone
contacts are the worst of ways to find out anything about the population.
Experienced organizers also understand quite well that doorway interviews are almost certain to be unsuccessful if the occupant does not know
or trust the person who is knocking at the door. Decades of well-justified
distrust have led poor men and women to regard the stranger with his
questionnaire and clipboard as the agent of a system which appears
infrequently and almost never for a purpose which does not portend
substantial danger. Bill collector, welfare worker, court investigator,
census taker, or encyclopedia salesman—all will be received with the
same reticence and stealth. If the census taker should elicit any facts at all,
there is a good chance they will be facts contrived to fence him out, not
to enlighten him as to the actualities of anyone's existence.

In the case of illiterates, moreover, living already with the stigma of a 45
disability that is regarded as an indication of inherent deficit, there is an
even stronger inclination to refuse collaboration with the government's
investigator. Many will profess a competence which they do not possess.

Finally, there is a problem with the question that the census seeks to 46
pose. The fact that someone has attended school through fifth grade
cannot be accepted as an indication that that person reads at fifth grade
level. People who are doing well in school are likely to continue. Those
who drop out are almost always people who already find themselves two
years or more behind the class and see no realistic hope of catching up.
With the sole exception of those children who (as in the migrant streams)
drop out of school because their families need another pair of hands to
add a tiny increment of income, those who leave the schools in
elementary years are those who have already failed—or who have *been*
failed by the system. The census, therefore, in asking people how long
they have sat it out in public school, is engaging in a bit of foolishness
which cannot easily be justified by ignorance or generosity. At best, by
asking questions keyed not to attainment but to acquisition of grade
numbers, the Bureau of the Census might be learning something vague
about the numbers of adults who read at any point from first to third
grade level. As we have seen, however, even this much information is
unlikely to be gleaned by methods flawed so badly and so stubbornly
maintained.

A census, of course, may have more than one purpose in a modern 47
nation. Certain information is desired for enlightened national self-
interest. Other forms of information are required for the purposes of
international prestige. Literacy statistics are one of the universal indices
of national well-being. The first statistics listed in the "nation profiles"
that are used for international comparisons include illiteracy, infant

mortality, per capita income, life expectancy. It can be argued, from the point of view of chauvinistic pride, that it is in the short-term interest of an unwise nation to report the lowest possible statistics for illiterates. In a curious respect, therefore, the motives of the Census Bureau coincide with those of the distrustful or humiliated adult who is frightened to concede a problem that is viewed as evidence of human failing. A calamitous collusion is the obvious result: The nation wants to guard its pride. The illiterate needs to salvage self-respect. The former want to hide its secret from the world; the latter wants to hide it from the nation. It is easy to understand, in light of all of the above, why a nation within which 60 million people cannot even read the 1980 census should offer census figures to UNESCO that announce our status as a land of universal literacy.

In the preface to a 1969 edition of *The Other America*, Michael 48 Harrington pointed to "the famous census undercount" of 1960. "Almost six million Americans, mainly black adults living in Northern cities, were not enumerated. Their lives were so marginal—no permanent address, no mail, no phone number, no regular job—that they did not even achieve the dignity of being a statistic."

The same may be said in 1985 for the much larger number—not 6 49 million this time, but some tens of millions—who do not exist within the inventories of the Bureau of the Census. The census tabulations would be less alarming if at least the nation's scholars would agree to disavow them. Instead, too many scholars take these figures with a certain skepticism but proceed to rescue them from condemnation by allowing that they hold at least one particle of truth. Their resolution of the conflict works somewhat like this: They interpret the census as an accurate indication that there are "no absolute nonreaders" in the nation. They then go on to indicate that—on a higher level, and by using definitions more appropriate to a developed nation—we are doing much less than we can. The second of these two points is correct. The first one is not.

The census itself, though unintentionally, suggests that 5 percent 50 (over 8 million adults) read at third grade level or below. If we make some rough adjustments for the recent immigrants and the undocumented residents, but especially for all those the census doesn't reach and those who claim that they can read to get the census taker off their back, we can bet that well above 10 million adult residents of the United States are absolute or nearly absolute illiterates. The government, as we have seen, has now conceded an enormous crisis constituted by the "functionally illiterate" in our society; but it has attempted to convey the somewhat reassuring thought that none of these people are "nonreaders" in the sense that word would hold for Third World nations. In all likelihood, almost one third of those defined as "functional" nonreaders would be judged illiterate by any standard and in any social system.

It was Michael Harrington who spoke of "an underdeveloped 51
nation" living within the borders of America. This is an accurate
description. There is a Third World hidden in the First World, because its
occupants must live surrounded by the constant, visible, and unavoidable
reminders of the comforts and the opportunities of which they are
denied, their suffering may very well be greater than that which is
undergone by those who live with none of those reminders in a nation
where illiterate existence is accepted as the norm.

Even for those who read at fifth or sixth grade levels in this nation, 52
the suffering, by reason of the visible rewards identified with verbal and
with arithmetic competence around them, must be very, very great. "The
American poor," wrote Michael Harrington, "are not poor in Hong
Kong or in the sixteenth century; they are poor here and now in the
United States. They are dispossessed in terms of what the rest of the
nation enjoys, in terms of what the society could provide if it had the will.
They live on the fringe, the margin . . . They are internal exiles."

We know enough by now to treat the census figures with the 53
skepticism and the indignation they deserve. History will not be gener-
ous with those who have compounded suffering by arrogant conceal-
ment. Sooner or later, the world will find us out. Neither our reputation
nor our capability for self-correction can fail to suffer deeply from the
propagation of these lies.

NOTES

¶ 4. Stigma attached to the nonreader: "Not being able to read is 20th century
leprosy, is what it is . . . Maybe you won't understand that. Let me explain
it to you. Before you know it, you're being treated as a kid, as half what
you used to be treated. That's the major reason why I'm staying as Mr. X."
(Interview with an anonymous man, in *The Adult Illiterate Speaks Out,*
cited above.)

¶11. "You have to be careful . . ." *The Adult Illiterate Speaks Out,* cited above.

¶12. "Sooner or later, the strategies run out . . ." *The Adult Illiterate Speaks
Out.*

¶14. 140,000 illiterates turned away for lack of funds: *The Ladder,* September/
October 1982. *The Ladder* is the newsletter of a community-based literacy
group, "PLAN," directed by Michael Fox. The newsletter is edited by Pat
Gatlin. Fox has recently begun a project, "Operation Wordwatch," to
assess the readability of public documents and other printed items, and to
insist that all materials essential to American consumers be rewritten at a
level they can understand. For information on this project or for a
subscription to *The Ladder,* write: Push Literacy Action Now, 2311
Eighteenth Street N.W., Washington, D.C. 20009.

¶18. "Victims exist, but not constituencies . . ." Ernest Boyer, president of the
Carnegie Foundation for the Advancement of Teaching, makes this
comment: "When I testified on [Capitol] Hill for all the programs, the
ABE one brought a big yawn. Most of the programs launched are backed

by articulate, strong, organized public-interest groups . . . These people don't have a voice." (Washington *Post,* November 25, 1982)

¶21. The National Assault on Illiteracy is a network of over 80 black-run groups throughout the nation. Its national chairman Ozell Sutton and administrative coordinator Meille Smith report that 90 percent of their support comes from black-owned publications associated with Black Media, Incorporated. The organization publishes *The Advancer,* a community-oriented newspaper written at a fourth or fifth grade level. For copies of the paper, and for reprints of a powerful article by its national vice-chairperson, Carrie Haynes, write: Assault on Literacy, 507 Fifth Avenue (Suite 1101), New York, New York 10017.

This organization has been so totally ignored by the white press that virtually no literacy groups run by white people have been aware of its existence. Information provided here was obtained only with great difficulty and received only as this manuscript went to press. For this, I offer my sincere apologies.

¶32. For discussion of the linguistic and historical issues raised by the speech patterns of my pupils, see *Black English,* by J. L. Dillard, Vintage Books, New York, 1973; *Minority Education and Caste,* by John U. Ogbu, Academic Press, New York, 1978; and "Literacy and Schooling in Subordinate Cultures," by John U. Ogbu, in *Literacy in Historical Perspective,* cited above.

¶38. Miscalculations of the U.S. census: See "Education of the American Population," by John K. Folger and Charles B. Nam, U.S. Department of Commerce, Bureau of the Census, Washington, D.C., 1960; "American Education: The ABCs of Failure," special supplement to the Dallas *Times Herald,* December 11–21, 1983; "Plain Talk on the Non-census," by Michael Fox, in *The Ladder,* May/June 1982.

Detailed information on methods used in 1970 and 1980 census tabulations: interviews with Dr. Paul M. Siegel, Chief of Education and Social Stratification Branch, Population Division, U.S. Bureau of the Census, January 19, 1984, and with Roslyn Bruno, assistant to Dr. Siegel, March 19, 1984. Additional data provided by Greg Weyland, Current Population Surveys/Demographic Survey Division, U.S. Bureau of the Census, and by Richard Ning, Information Services Department, Boston Regional Office, U.S. Bureau of the Census, August 1984. See also: "Statistical Abstract of the United States, 1984 (104th edition)," U.S. Bureau of the Census, U.S. Department of Commerce, Washington, D.C., 1983. Any effort to extract clear and consistent information from the Bureau of the Census is doomed to be an arduous and frustrating task. Despite the full cooperation of all persons I have named, every explanation of the methods used in order to arrive at final figures has in some respect conflicted with all others. In twenty years of research, I have never found a comparable morass of tangled and, at times, incomprehensible statistics. If it is this difficult to get at three or four essential facts, how can those who handle and assemble such material feel any confidence at all that they are in possession of an accurate impression of the nation they describe? I have said that any nation that cannot perceive itself is subject to the dangers that we see in classic tragedy. In this instance, comedy and tragedy are mercilessly intertwined. I am convinced of the good will of those I have consulted, but I do not envy them their thankless task.

In its *1983 Book of the Year,* the Encyclopedia Britannica reports that the United States has a near 100 percent literacy rate. The source for this figure is UNESCO. UNESCO's source: the 1970 U.S. census.

¶46. Years of school attendance and real skills: According to Hunter and Harman, 30 states insist on only eighth grade competence for the receipt of a twelfth grade diploma (Hunter and Harman, cited above). Jeanne Chall (cited above) reports that studies of eight states, in the latter 1970s, indicate that "minimum competency" tests for grade eleven revealed an average of seventh/eighth grade competence as adequate to pass. A gap of three to four years between grade-completion numbers and achieved proficiency seems standard.

¶48. Michael Harrington is quoted from *The Other America,* cited above.

## Post-Reading Questions

1. Why does Kozol use a letter from a semi-literate person to open his essay? What effect is this letter intended to have on Kozol's readers? Does this opening tell you right away where Kozol's sympathies lie? Why?

2. Why does Kozol say that most citizens' choices would be between "enormous guilt and efficacious action" (paragraph 2) when and if they accept that large-scale illiteracy exists in America? What reasons explain the guilt? What kind of action is in order?

3. What is the point of the restaurant menu story in paragraphs 5 through 9? How does that point tie in with Kozol's thesis?

4. Why is Kozol negative about television and the effect it has on illiterate people (paragraphs 24 through 28)? Describe that effect and explain why it has such a negative impact on the life of an illiterate person.

5. What are Kozol's criticisms of the Census Bureau's data on illiteracy (paragraphs 40 through 53)? Why are the census counts on illiteracy misleading? Why is it important for Kozol to establish the inaccuracy of the census figures on illiteracy?

6. What does Kozol want his readers to do about the illiteracy problem? What programs can college students get involved in? What political action can they take to help alleviate the problem?

7. Why are illiterates by definition politically disadvantaged (paragraphs 16 through 20)? Describe some of the political activities from which they are excluded. Why are politicians and political activists often unwilling to support the cause of eradicating illiteracy?

8. Why are illiterates "silent and unseen," as Kozol claims in his title? What factors contribute to their invisibility?

9. Evaluate Kozol's evidence. How effective is the combination of statistics and personal stories? Does he do a thorough job of

analyzing his evidence? Does he create an effective combination of emotional and rational appeals? Are you convinced that there *is* an illiteracy problem in America by the time you have finished this essay? Why?

# PAULO FREIRE ON CRITICAL LITERACY

## Pre-Reading Questions

1. What does the term "critical literacy" mean to you? What is the difference between someone who is "critically literate" and someone who is "functionally literate" or uses reading and writing only in very mechanical ways to carry out basic everyday tasks? What can the critically literate person do that the functionally literate person cannot? Which person would be able to fill out a form or read simple directions on how to run a machine? Which person would be able to find a contradiction in a political candidate's speech? Could one person do both? Why or why not?
2. Choose an article from a newspaper that you read on a fairly regular basis. Explain how that article can be read from a functional and a critical perspective. What would a critical reading produce that might be missed by a functional reading?
3. What kind of literacy did the English and reading courses you have taken in school try to teach? Do you think those courses could have striven to teach you more than they did? If you do, explain what they did not teach that you now wish they had. If you were satisfied with these courses, explain what they taught you that you now find useful.

## ADULT LITERACY: THE INGENUOUS
## AND THE CRITICAL VISIONS
### Paulo Freire

Our concept of illiteracy is naive, at best, when we compare it, on the one          1
hand, to a "poison herb" (as is implied in the current expression "eradication of illiteracy") and, on the other, to a "disease" that's contagious and transmitted to others.[1] Again, sometimes we see it as a depressing "ulcer" that should be "cured". Its indices, statistically compiled by international organizations, distort the level of "civilization" of certain societies. Moreover, from this ingenuous or astute perspective, illiteracy can also appear as a manifestation of people's "incapacity," their "lack of intelligence," or their proverbial "laziness."

When educators limit their understanding of this complex issue,          2
which they may not appreciate (or not wish to appreciate), their solutions

are always of a mechanical character. Literacy, as such, is reduced to the mechanical act of "depositing" words, syllables, and letters *into* illiterates. This "deposit" is sufficient as soon as the illiterate student attaches a magical meaning to the word and thus "affirms" himself or herself.

Written or read, words are, as it were, amulets placed on a person 3 who doesn't say them, but merely repeats them, almost always without any relation to the world and the things they name.

Literacy becomes the result of an act by a so-called educator who 4 "fills" the illiterate learner with words. This magical sense given to words extends to another ingenuity: that of the Messiah. The illiterate is a "lost man." Therefore, one must "save" him, and his "salvation" consists of "being filled" with these words, mere miraculous sounds offered or imposed on him by the teacher who is often an unconscious agent of the political policies inherent in the literacy campaign.

## THE TEXTS

From a methodological or sociological point of view, primers developed 5 mechanistically, like any other texts, cannot escape a type of original sin however good they may be, since they are instruments for "depositing" the educator's words into the learners. And since they limit the power of expression and creativity, they are domesticating instruments.

Generally speaking, these texts and primers are developed according 6 to mechanical and magical-Messianic concepts of "word-deposit" and "word-sound." Their ultimate objective is to achieve a "transfusion" in which the educator is the "blood of salvation" for the "diseased illiterate." Moreover, even when the words from which a text is developed coincide with the existential reality of illiterate learners (and this rarely occurs), they are presented as clichés; the words are never created by the ones who should have written them.

Most often these words and texts have nothing to do with the actual 7 experience of illiterate learners. When there is some relationship between the words and the learners' experience, its expression is so contrived and paternalistic that we don't even dare call it infantile.

This way of handling illiterates implies a distorted opinion—it is as if 8 illiterates were totally different from everyone else. This distortion fails to acknowledge their real-life experience and all the past and ongoing knowledge acquired through their experience.

As passive and docile beings (since this is how they are viewed and 9 treated), illiterate learners must continue to receive "transfusions." This is, of course, an alienating experience, incapable of contributing to the process of transformation of reality.

What meaning is there to a text that asks absurd questions and gives 10 equally absurd answers? Consider this example. *Ada deu o dedo ao urubu?* "Did Ada give her finger to urubu?" The author of the question answers, "I doubt that Ada gave her finger to the bird!"

First, we don't know of any place in the world where one invites the urubu to land on one's finger. Second, in supplying an answer to his own strange question, the author implicitly doubts that the *urubu* is a bird, since he expects the student to answer that Ada gave her finger to "the bird," rather than "to *urubu*."[2]

What real meaning could texts such as these have for men and women, peasants or urbanites, who spend their day working hard or, even worse, without working. Let us consider these texts, which must be memorized: *A asa é da ave*—"The wing is of the bird"; *Eva viu a uva*—"Eva saw the grape"; *João já sabe ler. Vejam a alegria em sua face. João agora vai conseguir um emprego*—"John already knows how to read. Look at the happiness in his face. Now John will be able to find a job."

These texts are usually illustrated with cute little houses, heartwarming and well decorated, with smiling couples fair of face (usually white and blond), well-nourished children sporting shoulder bags, waving goodbye to their parents on their way to school after a succulent breakfast.

What positive view can peasants or urban workers gain for their role in the world? How can they critically understand their concrete oppressive situation through literacy work in which they are instructed with sweetness to learn phrases like "the wing of the bird" or "Eva saw the grape"?

By relying on words that transmit an ideology of accommodation, such literacy work reinforces the "culture of silence" that dominates most people. This kind of literacy can never be an instrument for transforming the real world.


## THE LEARNERS

If this literacy approach does not have the necessary force in itself to fulfill at least *some* of the illusions it transmits to the students (such as the implicit promise in one example that the illiterate who learns to read will now "find a job"), sooner or later this approach will end up working against the soothing objectives of the very system whose ideology it reproduces.

Consider ex-illiterates who were "trained" by reading texts (without, of course, their analyzing what is involved in the social context) and who can read, even though they do so mechanically. When looking for work or better jobs, they can't find them. They, at least, understand the fallacy and impossibility of such a promise.

Critically speaking, illiteracy is neither an "ulcer," nor a "poison herb" to be eradicated, nor a "disease." Illiteracy is one of the concrete expressions of an unjust social reality. Illiteracy is not a strictly linguistic or exclusively pedagogical or methodological problem. It is political, as is the very literacy through which we try to overcome illiteracy. Dwelling naively or astutely on intelligence does not affect in the least the intrinsic politics.

Accordingly, the critical view of literacy does not include the mere 19 mechanical repetition of *pa, pe, pi, po, pu* and *la, le, li, lo, lu* to produce *pula, pélo, láli, pulo, lapa, lapela, pílula,* and so on. Rather, it develops students' consciousness of their rights, along with their critical presence in the real world. Literacy in this perspective, and not that of the dominant classes, establishes itself as a process of search and creation by which illiterate learners are challenged to perceive the deeper meaning of language and the word, the word that, in essence, they are being denied.

To deny the word implies something more: It implies the denial of 20 the right to "proclaim the world."[3] Thus, to "say a word" does not mean merely repeating any word. Indeed, such repetition constitutes one of the sophisms of reactionary literacy practice.

Learning to read and write cannot be done as something parallel or 21 nearly parallel to the illiterates' reality. Hence, as we have said, the learning process demands an understanding of the deeper meaning of the word.

More than writing and reading "the wing is of the bird," illiterate 22 learners must see the need for another learning process: that of "writing" about one's life, "reading" about one's reality. This is not feasible if learners fail to take history in hand and make it themselves—given that history can be made and remade.

Both the learner and the educator need to develop accurate ways of 23 thinking about reality. And this is achieved, not through repeating phrases that seem to be nonsensical, but by respecting the unity between practice and theory. It is most essential to liberate the equivocal theory by which learners usually become victims linked to verbalism, to nonsensical syllables that are just a waste of time.

This explains such oft-repeated expressions as "You'd have much 24 better results if education were less theoretical and more practical," or "We need to eliminate these theoretical courses."

This also explains the distinction made between theoretical and 25 practical men and women, the former considered to be at the periphery of action while the latter realize it. A distinction should be made, however, between theoreticians and verbalists. Theoreticians then would also be practitioners.

What should be contrasted with practice is not theory, which is 26 inseparable from it, but the nonsense sounds of imitative thinking.

Since we can't link theory with verbalism, we can't link practice with 27 activism. Verbalism lacks action; activism lacks a critical reflection on action.

It's not that strange, then, for verbalists to retreat to their ivory 28
tower and see little merit in those who are committed to action, while
activists consider those who conceptualize an act as "noxious intellectu-
als," "theoreticians," or "philosophers" who do nothing but undercut
their work.

For me, I see myself between both groups, among those who won't 29
accept the impossible division between practice and theory, since all
educational practice implies an educational theory.


## THEORY AND PRACTICE

The theoretical foundations of my practice are explained in the actual 30
process, not as a *fait accompli*, but as a dynamic movement in which both
theory and practice make and remake themselves. Many things that today
still appear to me as valid (not only in actual or future practice but also in
any theoretical interpretation that I might derive from it) could be
outgrown tomorrow, not just by me, but by others as well.

The crux here, I believe, is that I must be constantly open to 31
criticism and sustain my curiosity, always ready for revision based on the
results of my future experience and that of others. And in turn, those
who put my experience into practice must strive to recreate it and also
rethink my thinking. In so doing, they should bear in mind that no
educational practice takes place in a vacuum, only in a real context—
historical, economic, political, and not necessarily identical to any other
context.

A critical view of my experience in Brazil requires an understanding 32
of its context. My practice, while social, did not belong to me. Hence my
difficulty in understanding my experience, not to mention in my applying
it elsewhere without comprehending the historical climate where it
originally took place.

This effort toward understanding, required of me and others, again 33
highlights the unity between practice and theory. But understanding the
relationship between practice and theory in education also requires seeing
the connection between social theory and practice in a given society. A
theory that is supposed to inform the general experience of the dominant
classes, of which educational practice is a dimension, can't be the same as
one that lends support to the rejustification of the dominant classes in their
practice. Thus, educational practice and its theory cannot be neutral. The
relationship between practice and theory in an education oriented toward
liberation is one thing, but quite another in education for the purpose of
"domestication." For example, dominant classes don't need to worry
about the unity between practice and theory when they defer (to mention
only one example) to so-called skilled labor because here the theory
referred to is a "neutral theory" of a "neutral technique."

Adult literacy is now heading toward another alternative.     34

The first practical requirement that a critical view of literacy imposes 35 is that of generative words. These are the words with which illiterate learners gain their first literacy as subjects of the process, expanding their original "restrictive vocabulary universe." These words incorporate a meaningful thematic of the learners' lives.

The educator can organize a program only through investigating this 36 vocabulary universe; the world defined by the given words. The program in this form comes from the learners and is later returned to them, not as a dissertation, but as a problem or the posing of a problem.

Conversely, through the other kind of practice we discussed earlier, 37 when the educator develops his primer, at least from a sociocultural point of view he arbitrarily selects his generative words from books in his library, a process generally considered valid throughout the world.

In a critical approach, it's most important to select generative words 38 in relation to language levels, including the pragmatic. Further, these words cannot be selected according to purely phonetic criteria. A word can have a special force in one area, for instance, and not in others: This variation in meaning can occur even within the same city.

Let's consider another point. In a mechanical practice of literacy, the 39 primer's author selects words, decomposes these words for the purpose of analysis, and composes them in conjunction with other words with identical syllables; then, using these fabricated words, he writes his texts. In the practice that we defend, generative words—people's words—are used in realistic problem situations ("codifications") as challenges that call for answers from the illiterate learners. "To problematize" the word that comes from people means to problematize the thematic element to which it refers. This necessarily involves an analysis of reality. And reality reveals itself when we go beyond purely sensible knowledge to the reasons behind the factors. Illiterate learners gradually begin to appreciate that, as human beings, to speak is not the same as to "utter a word."

## ILLITERACY AND LITERACY

It is essential to see that illiteracy is not in itself the original obstacle. It's 40 the result of an earlier hindrance and later becomes an obstacle. No one elects to be illiterate. One is illiterate because of objective conditions. In certain circumstances "the illiterate man is the man who does not need to read."[4] In other circumstances, he is the one to whom the right to read was denied. In either case, there is no choice.

In the first case, the person lives in a culture whose communication 41 and history are, if not always, at least mostly oral. Writing does not bear any meaning here. In a reality like this, to succeed in introducing the written word and with it literacy, one needs to change the situation qualitatively. Many cases of regressive literacy can be explained by the introduction of such changes, the consequence of a Messianic literacy naively conceived for areas whose tradition is preponderantly or totally oral.

From various opportunities I have had to converse with Third World 42 peasants, especially in areas where conflicts arose in their experiments with agrarian reform, I've heard expressions like these: "Before agrarian reform we didn't need letters. First, because we didn't used to think. Our thinking belonged to master. Second, because we didn't have anything to do with letters. Now, things are different." In this case, the person recognizes his or her illiteracy to be the result of objective conditions.

In the second case, by participating in a literate culture, the person 43 who cannot read comes to be considered illiterate. The illiterate in this instance is one who hasn't had the opportunity to become literate.

I'll never forget the description given by a peasant from the Brazilian 44 northeast during a discussion of two codifications that we presented. The first presented an Indian hunting with his bow and arrow; the second, a peasant like himself, also hunting, with a rifle. "Between these two hunters," he asserted, "only the second can be illiterate. The first is not."

"Why?" I asked him. Smiling as if surprised by my question, he 45 answered, "One cannot say that the Indian is illiterate because he lives in a culture that does not recognize letters. To be illiterate you need to live where there are letters and you don't know them."

Truthfully, the illiterate learner can understand this in its deeper 46 sense only when he or she recognizes that his or her own illiteracy is problematical. And this awareness won't come through phrases like "Eva saw the grape" or "the wing of the bird" or "Ada gave her finger to the *urubu*."

Again we emphasize that in the practice we propose, learners begin 47 to perceive reality as a totality; whereas in a reactionary practice learners will not develop themselves, nor can they develop a lucid vision of their reality. They will overuse what we call a focalist vision of reality, by which components are seen without integration in the total composition.

## TRANSFORMATIVE LITERACY

As illiterate learners go on to organize a more precise form of thinking 48 through a problematical vision of their world and a critical analysis of their experience, they will be able increasingly to act with more security in the world.

Literacy then becomes a global task involving illiterate learners in 49 their relationships with the world and with others. But in understanding this global task and based on their social experience, learners contribute to their own ability to take charge as the actors of the task—the praxis. And significantly, as actors they transform the world with their work and create their own world. This world, created by the transformation of another world they did not create and that now restrains them, is the cultured world that stretches out into the world of history.

Similarly, they understand the creative and regenerative meaning of 50 their transformative work. They discover a new meaning as well. For instance, chopping down a tree, cutting it into pieces, and processing the logs according to a plan will create something that is no longer a tree. Thus they come to appreciate that this new thing, a product of their efforts, is a cultural object.

From discovery to discovery, they reach these fundamental truths:    51

(a)  Obstacles to their right to "utter the word" are in direct relationship to the establishment's lack of appreciating them and the product of their work.

(b)  Given that their work provides them a certain knowledge, it's not highly significant that they are illiterates.

(c)  Finally, human ignorance and knowledge are not absolute. No one knows everything. No one is ignorant of everything.

From my experience in Brazil and from my past practice in Chile, these truths have been continually confirmed.

In discussing the meaning of work, an old Chilean peasant once said, 52 "Now I know that I'm a cultured man." When asked why he felt cultured, he replied, "Because through work and by working I change the world."

This type of affirmation reveals people seeing at a truly practical level 53 that their presence in the world (through a critical response to this presence) is implied by the knowledge that they are not only in the world but *with* the world.

It's an important new awareness when we realize we are cultured 54 because through work and by working we change the world (even though there's a lot to be done between the recognition of this and the real transformation of society). This understanding cannot be compared with the monotonous repetition of *ba, be, bi, bo, bu.*

"I like talking about this," a woman said, also a Chilean, pointing to 55 the codification of her own living situation, "because that's the way I live. But while I am living this way, I don't see it. Now, yes, I can see the way I am living."

Challenged by her own way of living as depicted in the codification, 56 this woman could understand her life in a way she couldn't see before. She did this by an "immersion" in her own existence, by "admiring" it. Making the way she lives obvious in her consciousness, describing it and analyzing it, amount to an unveiling of her reality, if not a political engagement for her transformation.

Recently we had a chance to hear similar statements during a 57 discussion of a neighborhood street scene from a man who lives in New York.

After quietly studying the scene in some detail—trash cans, garbage, 58 other typical aspects of a slum—he suddenly said, "I live here. I walk on these streets every day. I can't say that I ever noticed all this. But now I understand what I didn't used to see."[5] Basically, this New Yorker understood on that night his previous perception. He could correct his distorted view by distancing himself from his reality through its codification.

Correcting one's earlier perception isn't always easy. The relation 59 between subject and object means that revealing an objective reality equally affects its subjective qualities, and sometimes in an intensely dramatic and painful manner.

Under certain circumstances, in a kind of consciousness awakening, 60 instead of accepting reality, one avoids this through wishful thinking, which becomes real. During another discussion group in New York, we were looking over an impressive photomontage of city streets with various kinds of buildings that were representative of different social levels. Though the members of this group were doubtlessly from the lowest rung on the economic ladder, they chose a middle rung when asked to examine the montage and to find their own level.

I have also found this same resistance to accepting reality—a kind of 61 defensiveness—among peasants and urban workers in Latin America. In Chile, during a debate on their new experience in the *asentamiento* ("settlements"), there were those who expressed a certain lingering nostalgia for their old masters as well as others who went on deciphering their reality in critical terms. Conditioned by dominant ideology, those who remain nostalgic not only wipe out their capacity to see their reality, but sometimes they sheepishly submit themselves to the myths of that ideology as well.

Adult literacy, as we understand it, like postliteracy, comprises some 62 crucial elements that must be confronted.

At a time when his relationship to man and world was made 63 problematical, another Chilean peasant claimed, "I see now there isn't any man without the world." The educator asked him one more problematical question. Suppose all human beings were dead, but there were still trees, birds, animals, rivers, the sea, the mountains—would this be a world? "No," he answered emphatically, "someone who could say 'This is the world' would be missing."

Through his response, our philosopher-peasant (an "absolute igno- 64 rant" by elitist standards) raised the dialectical question of subjectivity-objectivity.

After two months of participation in cultural discussion group 65
activities, another peasant explained, "When we were tenants and the
master would call us naive, we would say, 'Thank you, Master.' To us,
that was a compliment. Now that we're becoming critical, we know what
he meant by *naive*. He was calling us fools." We asked him, "What do
you mean by becoming critical?" "To think correctly," he answered, "to
see reality as it is."

There is one last point to consider. All these oral reactions from 66
cultural discussion groups should be transcribed into texts that are then
given back to illiterate learners so that they can begin to discuss them.

This hardly relates to the criticized practice of having learners repeat
twice, three times, and memorize "the wing is of the bird."

On the basis of the social experience of illiterates, we can conclude 67
that only a literacy that associates the learning of reading and writing
with a creative act will exercise the critical comprehension of that
experience, and without any illusion of triggering liberation, it will
nevertheless contribute to its process.

And, of course, this is no task for the dominant classes.                  68

## NOTES

1. When I say "concept of illiteracy is naive at best," it is because many people
   who could be considered as "naive", when they express the above concept,
   they are, in fact, astute. They know very well what they are doing and where
   they want to go, when, in literacy campaigns, they "feed" the illiterates with
   alienating slogans under the cover of neutrality of education. Objectively,
   they identify themselves as both naive and astute.
2. *Urubu* means "vulture" in Portuguese.
3. On this subject, see Ernani Maria Fiori, Preface to *Pedagogy of the Oppressed*.
4. Alvaro Vieira Pinto, *Consciência e realidade* (Rio: ISEB, 1960).
5. This work was part of the institute called Full Circle, directed by Robert Fox,
   a Catholic priest. It was a post-literacy program. There is something similar
   between the work of these educators and the work we did in Brazil and tried
   to do in Chile. However, we did not have any influence on their concept of
   education. I met them when I visited their program at the suggestion of Ivan
   Illich.

## Post-Reading Questions

1.  For Freire, literacy must "transform" the consciousness of the
    literate person. What are the common characteristics of a previously
    illiterate adult once he or she has gained literacy? Use the peasants
    that Freire cites in this essay to illustrate your answer.
2.  Explain why "distance" from the world becomes one of the qualities
    that literacy brings to the critically literate person. Why does learning
    to read and write provide a person with the ability to stand back and

view reality from a distance? What is the benefit accrued from this ability to stand back?

3. What is wrong with the literacy texts that Freire describes in paragraphs 5 through 15? How would he rewrite those texts (paragraphs 34 through 38)?

4. Review the overall structure of this essay. Notice how the headings of the essay follow a problem–solution format. Early headings emphasize the disadvantages and problems associated with what Freire calls "mechanical" literacy in which people use reading and writing simply to repeat or reproduce the thinking of those who hold power over them. What happens to the headings as the essay draws to a close? How do they reflect the new emphases of more critical literacy as a solution to the problems posed by mechanical approaches to literacy?

5. Why is this essay addressed to an audience of teachers? What does Freire hope his readers will do with his ideas?

6. What does Freire mean when he says that newly literate people develop a "problematical" view of the world (paragraph 48)?

7. Freire opens this essay by developing an analogy between teachers of literacy and Christian missionaries (see the references to the "Messiah," to "amulets," to the "lost man," and to "miraculous sounds" in paragraphs 3 and 4). Why is this analogy particularly effective in distinguishing between the mechanical and critical teachers of literacy and their respective students?

8. How does Freire's system of teaching literacy empower students? Why are critically literate students better able to participate in public life?

# WILLIAM LUTZ ON DOUBLESPEAK

## Pre-Reading Questions

1. Working with other writing group members, choose an example of public speech (a political address, a public service announcement, or a television news commentator's remarks on a current issue). Assign group member responsibilities as follows: one to tape the address, another to develop a set of questions that would enable its users to analyze the truth level of the address, and a third to actually use the set of questions to analyze the address' content. Turn the analysis results into a brief oral report to the whole class. The presentation of the report should also be a shared endeavor by the entire group.

2. Ask several college students about the credibility of the information they receive from the media. Do they believe what they hear on television network or cable channel news? Do they expect the truth when a politician addresses an issue? Do they believe what they read

in college textbooks? What about the accuracy of newspaper articles? What about the descriptions they read in college catalogs and bulletins? What level of credibility do your respondents give to media advertising? Write a brief summary of the results of your informal interviews, supporting them with references to several responses from your subjects.

3. What does the term "friendly fire" mean to you? In what way does the combined meaning suggested in those two words seem illogical? What other examples of phrases that contain such inconsistencies can you identify?

# DOUBLESPEAK
## William Lutz

There are no potholes in the streets of Tucson, Arizona, just "pavement deficiencies." The Reagan Administration didn't propose any new taxes, just "revenue enhancement" through new "user's fees." Those aren't bums on the street, just "non-goal oriented members of society." There are no more poor people, just "fiscal underachievers." There was no robbery of an automatic teller machine, just an "unauthorized withdrawal." The patient didn't die because of medical malpractice, it was just a "diagnostic misadventure of a high magnitude." The U.S. Army doesn't kill the enemy anymore, it just "services the target." And the doublespeak goes on.

Doublespeak is language that pretends to communicate but really doesn't. It is language that makes the bad seem good, the negative appear positive, the unpleasant appear attractive or at least tolerable. Doublespeak is language that avoids or shifts responsibility, language that is at variance with its real or purported meaning. It is language that conceals or prevents thought; rather than extending thought, doublespeak limits it.

Doublespeak is not a matter of subjects and verbs agreeing; it is a matter of words and facts agreeing. Basic to doublespeak is incongruity, the incongruity between what is said or left unsaid, and what really is. It is the incongruity between the word and the referent, between seem and be, between the essential function of language—communication—and what doublespeak does—mislead, distort, deceive, inflate, circumvent, obfuscate.

## HOW TO SPOT DOUBLESPEAK

How can you spot doublespeak? Most of the time you will recognize doublespeak when you see or hear it. But, if you have any doubts, you can identify doublespeak just by answering these questions: Who is saying what to whom, under what conditions and circumstances, with what intent, and with what results? Answering these questions will usually help you identify as doublespeak language that appears to be legitimate or that at first glance doesn't even appear to be doublespeak.

### First Kind of Doublespeak

There are at least four kinds of doublespeak. The first is the euphemism, an inoffensive or positive word or phrase used to avoid a harsh, unpleasant, or distasteful reality. But a euphemism can also be a tactful word or phrase which avoids directly mentioning a painful reality, or it can be an expression used out of concern for the feelings of someone else, or to avoid directly discussing a topic subject to a social or cultural taboo.

When you use a euphemism because of your sensitivity for someone's feelings or out of concern for a recognized social or cultural taboo, it is not doublespeak. For example, you express your condolences that someone has "passed away" because you do not want to say to a grieving person, "I'm sorry your father is dead." When you use the euphemism "passed away," no one is misled. Moreover, the euphemism functions here not just to protect the feelings of another person, but to communicate also your concern for that person's feelings during a period of mourning. When you excuse yourself to go to the "rest room," or you mention that someone is "sleeping with" or "involved with" someone else, you do not mislead anyone about your meaning, but you do respect the social taboos about discussing bodily functions and sex in direct terms. You also indicate your sensitivity to the feelings of your audience, which is usually considered a mark of courtesy and good manners.

However, when a euphemism is used to mislead or deceive, it becomes doublespeak. For example, in 1984 the U.S. State Department announced that it would no longer use the word "killing" in its annual report on the status of human rights in countries around the world. Instead, it would use the phrase "unlawful or arbitrary deprivation of life," which the department claimed was more accurate. Its real purpose for using this phrase was simply to avoid discussing the embarrassing situation of government-sanctioned killings in countries that are supported by the United States and have been certified by the United States as respecting the human rights of their citizens. This use of a euphemism constitutes doublespeak, since it is designed to mislead, to cover up the unpleasant. Its real intent is at variance with its apparent intent. It is language designed to alter our perception of reality.

The Pentagon, too, avoids discussing unpleasant realities when it refers to bombs and artillery shells that fall on civilian targets as "incontinent ordnance." And in 1977 the Pentagon tried to slip funding for the neutron bomb unnoticed into an appropriations bill by calling it a "radiation enhancement device."

## Second Kind of Doublespeak

A second kind of doublespeak is jargon, the specialized language of a  9
trade, profession, or similar group, such as that used by doctors, lawyers,
engineers, educators, or car mechanics. Jargon can serve an important
and useful function. Within a group, jargon functions as a kind of verbal
shorthand that allows members of the group to communicate with each
other clearly, efficiently, and quickly. Indeed, it is a mark of membership
in the group to be able to use and understand the group's jargon.

But jargon, like the euphemism, can also be doublespeak. It can  10
be—and often is—pretentious, obscure, and esoteric terminology used
to give an air of profundity, authority, and prestige to speakers and their
subject matter. Jargon as doublespeak often makes the simple appear
complex, the ordinary profound, the obvious insightful. In this sense it is
used not to express but impress. With such doublespeak, the act of
smelling something becomes "organoleptic analysis," glass becomes
"fused silicate," a crack in a metal support beam becomes a "discontinuity," conservative economic policies become "distributionally conservative notions."

Lawyers, for example, speak of an "involuntary conversion" of  11
property when discussing the loss or destruction of property through
theft, accident, or condemnation. If your house burns down or if your
car is stolen, you have suffered an involuntary conversion of your
property. When used by lawyers in a legal situation, such jargon is a
legitimate use of language, since lawyers can be expected to understand
the term.

However, when a member of a specialized group uses its jargon to  12
communicate with a person outside the group, and uses it knowing that
the nonmember does not understand such language, then there is
doublespeak. For example, on May 9, 1978, a National Airlines 727
airplane crashed while attempting to land at the Pensacola, Florida
airport. Three of the fifty-two passengers aboard the airplane were killed.
As a result of the crash, National made an after-tax insurance benefit of
$1.7 million, or an extra 18¢ a share dividend for its stockholders. Now
National Airlines had two problems: It did not want to talk about one of
its airplanes crashing, and it had to account for the $1.7 million when it
issued its annual report to its stockholders. National solved the problem
by inserting a footnote in its annual report which explained that the $1.7
million income was due to "the involuntary conversion of a 727."
National thus acknowledged the crash of its airplane and the subsequent
profit it made from the crash, without once mentioning the accident or
the deaths. However, because airline officials knew that most stockholders in the company, and indeed most of the general public, were not
familiar with legal jargon, the use of such jargon constituted doublespeak.

## Third Kind of Doublespeak

A third kind of doublespeak is gobbledygook or bureaucratese. Basically, 13
such doublespeak is simply a matter of piling on words, of overwhelming
the audience with words, the bigger the words and the longer the
sentences the better. Alan Greenspan, then chair of President Nixon's
Council of Economic Advisors, was quoted in *The Philadelphia Inquirer*
in 1974 as having testified before a Senate committee that "It is a tricky
problem to find the particular calibration in timing that would be
appropriate to stem the acceleration in risk premiums created by falling
incomes without prematurely aborting the decline in the inflation-
generated risk premiums."

Nor has Mr. Greenspan's language changed since then. Speaking to 14
the meeting of the Economic Club of New York in 1988, Mr. Greenspan,
now Federal Reserve chair, said, "I guess I should warn you, if I turn out
to be particularly clear, you've probably misunderstood what I've said."
Mr. Greenspan's doublespeak doesn't seem to have held back his career.

Sometimes gobbledygook may sound impressive, but when the 15
quote is later examined in print it doesn't even make sense. During the
1988 presidential campaign, vice-presidential candidate Senator Dan
Quayle explained the need for a strategic-defense initiative by saying,
"Why wouldn't an enhanced deterrent, a more stable peace, a better
prospect to denying the ones who enter conflict in the first place to have
a reduction of offensive systems and an introduction to defensive
capability? I believe this is the route the country will eventually go."

The investigation into the Challenger disaster in 1986 revealed the 16
doublespeak of gobbledygook and bureaucratese used by too many
involved in the shuttle program. When Jesse Moore, NASA's associate
administrator, was asked if the performance of the shuttle program had
improved with each launch or if it had remained the same, he answered,
"I think our performance in terms of the liftoff performance and in terms
of the orbital performance, we knew more about the envelope we were
operating under, and we have been pretty accurately staying in that. And
so I would say the performance has not by design drastically improved. I
think we have been able to characterize the performance more as a
function of our launch experience as opposed to it improving as a
function of time." While this language may appear to be jargon, a close
look will reveal that it is really just gobbledygook laced with jargon. But
you really have to wonder if Mr. Moore had any idea what he was saying.

## Fourth Kind of Doublespeak

The fourth kind of doublespeak is inflated language that is designed to 17
make the ordinary seem extraordinary; to make everyday things seem
impressive; to give an air of importance to people, situations, or things

that would not normally be considered important; to make the simple seem complex. Often this kind of doublespeak isn't hard to spot, and it is usually pretty funny. While car mechanics may be called "automotive internists," elevator operators members of the "vertical transportation corps," used cars "preowned" or "experienced cars," and black-and-white television sets described as having "non-multicolor capability," you really aren't misled all that much by such language.

However, you may have trouble figuring out that, when Chrysler 18 "initiates a career alternative enhancement program," it is really laying off five thousand workers; or that "negative patient care outcome" means the patient died; or that "rapid oxidation" means a fire in a nuclear power plant.

The doublespeak of inflated language can have serious consequences. 19 In Pentagon doublespeak, "pre-emptive counterattack" means that American forces attacked first; "engaged the enemy on all sides" means American troops were ambushed; "backloading of augmentation personnel" means a retreat by American troops. In the doublespeak of the military, the 1983 invasion of Grenada was conducted not by the U.S. Army, Navy, Air Force, and Marines, but by the "Caribbean Peace Keeping Forces." But then, according to the Pentagon, it wasn't an invasion, it was a "predawn vertical insertion."

## DOUBLESPEAK THROUGHOUT HISTORY

Doublespeak is not a new use of language peculiar to the politics or 20 economics of the twentieth century. In the fifth century B.C., the Greek historian Thucydides wrote in *The Peloponnesian War* that

> revolution thus ran its course from city to city. . . . Words had to change their ordinary meanings and to take those which were now given them. Reckless audacity came to be considered the courage of a loyal ally; prudent hesitation, specious cowardice; moderation was held to be a cloak for unmanliness; ability to see all sides of a question, inaptness to act on any. Frantic violence became the attribute of manliness; cautious plotting, a justifiable means of self-defense. The advocate of extreme measures was always trustworthy; his opponent, a man to be suspected.

Julius Caesar, in his account of the Gallic Wars, described his brutal 21 and bloody conquest and subjugation of Gaul as "pacifying" Gaul. "Where they make a desert, they call it peace," said an English nobleman quoted by the Roman historian Tacitus. When traitors were put to death in Rome, the announcement of their execution was made in the form of saying "they have lived." "Taking notice of a man in the ancestral manner" meant capital punishment; "the prisoner was then led away" meant he was executed.

In his memoirs, *V-2*, Walter Dornberger, commanding officer of the 22 Peenemünde Rocket Research Institute in Germany during World War II, describes how he and his staff used language to get what they needed from the Bureau of Budget for their rocket experiments. A pencil sharpener was an "Appliance for milling wooden dowels up to 10 millimeters in diameter," and a typewriter was an "Instrument for recording test data with rotating roller." But it was the Nazis who were the masters of doublespeak, and they used it not just to achieve and maintain power but to perpetrate some of the most heinous crimes in the history of the human race.

In the world of Nazi Germany, nonprofessional prostitutes were 23 called "persons with varied sexual relationships"; "protective custody" was the very opposite of protective; "Winter Relief" was a compulsory tax presented as a voluntary charity; and a "straightening of the front" was a retreat, while serious difficulties became "bottlenecks." Minister of Information (the very title is doublespeak) Josef Goebbels spoke in all seriousness of "simple pomp" and "the liberalization of the freedom of the press."

Nazi doublespeak reached its peak when dealing with the "Final 24 Solution," a phrase that is itself the ultimate in doublespeak. The notice, "The Jew X.Y. lived here," posted on a door, meant the occupant had been "deported," that is, killed. When mail was returned stamped "Addressee has moved away," it meant the person had been "deported." "Resettlement" also meant deportation, while "work camp" meant concentration camp or incinerator, "action" meant massacre, "Special Action Groups" were army units that conducted mass murder, "selection" meant gassing, and "shot while trying to escape" meant deliberately killed in a concentration camp.

## Post-Reading Questions

1. Lutz begins his essay by defining doublespeak. Why is that a good opening strategy for this essay? How effective are his definitions? Are they precise and clear enough?

2. How convincing do you find the evidence of doublespeak that Lutz scatters throughout his essay? Does he provide sufficient analysis of these examples to persuade you that you should pay more attention to doublespeak in your own life?

3. Describe Lutz's style in a sentence or two. Do you find it *direct, clear, complicated,* or *elegant*? Or would you describe Lutz's style in some other way? What language features would you point out to support your description?

4.  What effect do Lutz's short, declarative sentences have on readers? Why is this sentence technique especially appropriate for the purposes of this essay?

5.  How would you describe Lutz's purpose in writing this essay? Does he want to inform or persuade his readers? (*Persuasion* is usually meant to cause a change in attitude or to instigate an action on the part of readers. *Informative* writing usually simply intends to enable readers to understand an issue or subject more fully than they did before reading.)

6.  What effect is the final section on the history of doublespeak meant to have on readers? Do the historical examples given effectively add significance to the whole issue of doublespeak? Why?

7.  Does Lutz's strategy of describing both the positive and negative uses of the first two types of doublespeak, euphemisms and jargon, serve as an effective way of convincing readers that he is an unbiased and objective commentator on this issue? If the strategy does accomplish this end, why is it effective? If it does not, then what contributes to its failure?

8.  In what ways does becoming aware of doublespeak, how it works and why it is used, contribute to your abilities as a critical reader?

9.  Why do consumers who understand how doublespeak works have an edge on consumers who are unaware of or give little credence to doublespeak? How would this advantage, if it exists, work?

# 6
· · · · · · · · · · · · ·
# OPTIONAL WRITING ASSIGNMENTS FOCUSED ON THE POWER AND LIMITS OF LANGUAGE

Each of the following assignments addresses issues raised by one of the clusters of essays in this chapter. Some are creative assignments with emphases on narrative; others are critical assignments with emphases on arguing different perspectives on the issues raised. A few are informative essay assignments in which you should do some additional research and use that research to add to your readers' knowledge of these language issues.

With each assignment that is suggested here, it is important to consider the rhetorical context within which you present the resulting essay. Some of these assignments assume that you address your essay to an audience of peers, those who have shared in the discussions and reading experiences associated with this chapter. Other assignment options include some basic information on audience and purpose that you should use to define the rhetorical context of your essay (review "The Rhetorical Approach to Academic Writing" in Chapter 2 as part of your planning process).

*1. Focus on a language and power issue that your class found interesting but did not know enough about to consider in a knowledgeable way.* Define what new information would help complete your class's knowledge of this language issue; decide where you can find that information; then, plan an essay in which you present this new information to your class peers. You also need to define the relevance of the new information by relating it to the issue being considered.

*2. Define an issue that was discussed, but without full resolution, in your class or writing group.* Then, plan and write an argument in which you take a side or develop an alternative resolution to this issue. An effective argument usually must appeal to both the emotions and the intellect of readers; it must make an honest attempt to deal with all sides of an issue; and it must appeal to readers' good sense and character by having a reasonable tone and style.

*3. Write a short story in which one of the language issues covered in this chapter is a major theme.* Consider using conversations that define characters; address the issue indirectly (customary in fiction), rather than directly (customary in essays). Plan the situation around which your story will revolve before you begin writing.

*4. Choose an advertisement that you find either particularly offensive because of its deceptive or questionable rhetoric, or particularly praiseworthy because of its positive ethical appeal.* Write a letter to the firm or sponsor of the advertisement in which you explain your reaction; support that reaction with specific references to the text of the advertisement. Consider your purpose in writing this letter. Do you simply want to encourage your audience to do more of the same by pointing out the positive qualities of their advertisement? Or do you want to move your audience to change their advertising by pointing out the damaging results of their approach? Your style needs to be appropriate for your purpose and audience.

*5. Find an example of public doublespeak.* Write a critical essay in which you analyze the example, using Lutz's definitions to guide your analysis. Before you begin writing, decide on the purpose and audience of your essay. Will your purpose be to inform, so that your readers will know how to find and respond to doublespeak when they confront it? Or will you expect your audience to do something about the particular example of doublespeak that you have analyzed—they may write a letter of complaint to a congressman, for example, or decide to vote against a particular political candidate, or boycott a particular product. These different purposes call for different writing styles.

*6. Use the essays by Jonathan Kozol and Paulo Freire as a basis for an address to elementary or secondary teachers on the most effective ways of teaching literacy.* Kozol is most useful in pointing out the importance of literacy and the extent of the problem of illiteracy in America. Freire discusses specifically what he feels are the most effective theory and practice for teaching literacy. Find ways to appeal directly to an audience of teachers. Write this address as if you intended to deliver it as a speech at a teachers' meeting. Provide examples likely to appeal to teachers.

7. *Write a two- or three-page dialogue that addresses the theme of gender bias and language.* Define the purpose of your dialogue before you begin writing. Will you satirize a particular kind of sexist language by having a man and woman address a particularly sensitive matter? Or will you deal more straightforwardly with a complex aspect of language by having two individuals talk the aspect through in a particular situation? You will need to define the context within which your dialogue will take place before you begin writing. Define your dialogue characters by the kind of language they use. Most important, however, is your success or failure in providing your readers with a clear but indirect focus on a particular language and gender issue.

8. *Write an essay in which you discuss the advantages and disadvantages of official languages.* What disadvantages are there for particular speech communities (minority and ethnic groups, for example); what advantages are there for commerce, trade, and international business and political transactions? Create an audience for your essay by considering the particular groups who are addressed or implied in the essays by Seymour, Hamil, and Ortiz in this chapter. Would you, for example, address your essay to teachers of minority children, to businessmen, or to concerned citizens? Once you have defined a target audience, you need to develop strategies for presenting your arguments. You need to decide why you want to address that audience. Are you trying to change the audience's attitudes toward the idea of official languages? Are you simply trying to inform your audience regarding this complex issue?

9. *Write an essay in which you explain why a particular ethnic or minority group (perhaps your own) is against the sacrifice of its own language to some kind of official or standard language.* What would the group lose by making this sacrifice? Your audience for this essay is concerned citizens who simply do not understand why a particular group of people wants to hold on to their language.

# 8

# Perspectives on Healthcare
# Ethics and Society

What healthcare issues face society?
What role do ethics play in medicine?
What factors affect medical decisions involving ethics?

## 1
## DEVELOPING A RHETORICAL APPROACH

This chapter deals with healthcare issues facing physicians, patients, and society. Biomedical and technological advances in the last twenty years have caused dramatic changes in healthcare delivery. In addition, societal attitudes and governmental policies have affected the nature of healthcare in America. Some of the readings illustrate ethical dilemmas healthcare providers and medical researchers wrestle with daily. Others focus on these medical ethics issues in terms of their effects on patients and their families.

Although these readings do not cover all of the ethical issues related to healthcare as it is practiced and will be practiced in the future, they serve as a basis for examining your own experiences with illness and with healthcare providers. Your responses to these readings, the connections you establish between what the authors say and your own experiences and views, along with your classmates' responses, provide a foundation for the rhetorical community you will develop together. As you consider the ethical issues facing physicians and patients, you will find they raise some difficult questions. Who should bear the costs of healthcare? How should healthcare be administered? Do physicians have a right to terminate treatment? Do the families of patients have that right? Where should research dollars be spent? Should physicians be held accountable for their mistakes?

At some point in this chapter, one of these questions, or one you or your classmates generate, may become the focus of your essay. Perhaps you will decide to enter the debate concerning national healthcare insurance, or you may choose to explore the history of a particular disease and its effect on society. As you narrow your topic for your essay, the rhetorical community you have developed with your classmates will provide you with a clear sense of *purpose* (what you want to say in this essay) and *audience* (whom you want to read this essay), which will guide your decisions about your essay's contents, organization, and style.

## 2
. . . . . . . . . . . . . .
## GENERATING IDEAS ABOUT HEALTHCARE ETHICS AND SOCIETY BEFORE READING

Your own experiences and knowledge of health and illness will provide valuable background information, serve as a baseline for your responses to what the different writers are saying, and contribute to the meaning you construct about some of the dilemmas physicians, patients, and researchers face. The activities that follow provide a framework for your reading and writing, and help you develop ways to respond in meaningful ways to the readings.

### Probing Personal Experience

Write short, informal answers to the following questions. If you are keeping a course journal, write your answers there. Be sure your answers are written in a form that can be used in class.

*1. How do you feel about the physicians who have treated you?* Describe some of your experiences as a patient. Do you believe your doctors gave you (or your parents) enough information about your condition and your treatment options? Did they make you feel comfortable about asking questions? Has a member of your family ever had to make a difficult decision about treatment? Did the physician guide the family member through the decision-making process?

*2. Describe the way you choose a physician.* What factors affect that choice? Which of those factors do you control and which factors are beyond your control?

*3. Do you believe we should have national health insurance in America?* If you do, how do you think it should operate? If you don't, explain why you are against national health insurance.

*4. Do you believe that a doctor's gender affects his or her ability to practice medicine?* Does gender affect your response to a physician? Are you more comfortable with either male or female physicians? Explain your answer by referring to your own experiences with male and female physicians.

*5. If you worked for a government agency responsible for allocating funds for medical research, what criteria would be most important for determining which research projects should be funded?* For example, would you distribute more dollars to those researchers seeking cures for illnesses that affected the greatest number of victims, or would more dollars go to researchers seeking cures for the most devastating illnesses, regardless of their impact on the population? How would these criteria for allocating funds be determined and by whom?

*6. Would you have a living will drawn up for yourself?* If you would, explain why and what it might say. If you wouldn't, explain your reasons.

*7. What does the term "quality of life" mean to you?* What would be your criteria for evaluating someone's quality of life? For example, would an individual need to be mobile? Would an individual need to be self-sufficient? What would a person need to be able to do? Do you think that one individual's criteria for evaluating quality of life could differ from another's? How might that create a medical dilemma for a physician or a family member of a critically ill patient? Give an example to explain your answer.

*8. How has the AIDS epidemic touched your life?* Do you know someone who has tested HIV positive or someone who has died from this disease? Has the AIDS epidemic caused you to change your sexual behaviors? Has it affected your attitudes towards medical research or medical treatment?

*9. How did you react to the news that public figures such as Arthur Ashe and Magic Johnson are HIV positive?* Did it change the way you feel about them? Did it change the way you feel about AIDS? How does knowing that celebrities are HIV positive impact society's response to this disease?

## Freewriting to Capture Personal Experience

Here is a list of topics related to healthcare ethics and society that you can freewrite about in short, ten-minute sessions. Each of these topics relates in some way to the readings in this chapter. Your teacher may assign a topic or ask you to choose one yourself. If you are keeping a journal, do your freewriting there. As you freewrite, consider narrating an experience you have had that relates to your topic. Telling a personal story is an effective initial strategy for generating ideas about a particular topic. You may find that writing about this personal experience and the details surrounding it stimulates other ideas about the topic and leads you to new insights. (For a discussion of freewriting, see pages 103 to 104.)

AIDS
Malpractice suits
Medical research
Women in medicine
Medical ethics
Physicians' responsibilities
The media and healthcare coverage
Epidemics

Your freewriting will be most effective if you follow this sequence: **Reread, Focus, Rewrite (RFR).** (For a discussion of RFR, **see** page 104.)

## 3
. . . . . . . . . . . . .
## DEVELOPING RHETORICAL CONTEXT
## THROUGH GROUP ACTIVITIES

Each of the following collaborative activities asks you to work with other students in revising a freewriting. The purpose of these revision activities is to experience other readers' responses to your writing and to develop a better sense of what writers consider as they compose for particular readers. These collaborative experiences help evaluate and refine your own ideas about this chapter's theme before you further develop them, and prepare you for the reading you will do on this topic. (If you are collaborating for the first time, you should read the earlier discussion of conventions guiding group work on pages 104 to 105.)

- Exchange your freewriting with a partner. Read your partner's freewriting without a pen or pencil in your hand. When you have finished reading, *summarize* what your partner has written. Then *list* any questions you have about what your partner wrote. Is there a word that you didn't understand? Does a personal experience your partner described remind you of something that happened to you? Were you confused by a section of the freewriting because you needed more information? Finally, *re-spond* to your partner by adding any information about your own experiences related to the contents of the freewriting. Do you know something that would be helpful to your partner? Can you recommend a source that could provide additional information? After you have completed your work with your partner's freewriting, exchange your responses, take a few minutes to read them, and discuss them with one another. If you have both done freewriting on the same topic, you may discuss how the contents of the two freewritings compare and contrast. In what ways are they alike? In what ways are they different? What kind of essay could the two of you develop if you were working as a collaborative writing team?

• Work with a group of three or four students to compose a mission statement and a set of guidelines for a hospital medical ethics committee. Use each member's freewriting as a source for the collaboratively composed draft. Have group members read their freewritings aloud while the rest of the group comments and responds. Ask one member to take notes as the entire group brainstorms common threads found in members' freewritings. As you generate ideas for the mission statement, consider what the goals of a medical ethics committee might be. Why would a hospital begin such a committee? What would be its responsibilities? Then consider what guidelines physicians would find helpful in making ethical decisions on a daily basis. What steps or processes could the committee institute that doctors could turn to? After brainstorming, the temporary secretary can read the notes aloud and the group can develop the mission statement and guidelines for the medical ethics committee. Return to the freewritings for examples that explain the guidelines being composed.

## 4
• • • • • • • • • • • • •
# USING READINGS TO DEVELOP
# A RHETORICAL COMMUNITY

The readings in this chapter discuss several aspects of the healthcare ethics and society topic, among them ethical decisions faced by doctors and patients, relationships between gender and medical research, disease and its effect on society, and healthcare information and the media. The information in these readings will produce different reactions from you and your classmates, and your responses and discussions about these readings will provide opportunities for the members of the developing rhetorical community to work toward a deeper understanding of these aspects of the chapter's theme.

Your reading will also create opportunities for you to analyze how writers make decisions about their texts with their readers and writing purposes in mind. For example, you may find that a writer trying to persuade skeptical readers to change their viewpoint on a controversial issue has included lots of quotations from "experts" that readers would respect. A writer trying to introduce a new topic to a large, nonspecialized group of readers may include several examples to help the readers follow the new information being presented. Your discussions about these readings with your classmates will give you a chance to exchange ideas about how to apply these strategies to defining your own audiences. And as you read, write about, and discuss these readings, you will be able to decide what ideas you would like to explore in more detail in your essay.

## The Readings in This Chapter

The first article provides a foundation for the other articles in this chapter. In it, Katherine Bouton, a journalist, introduces readers to the new profession of bioethics, explaining what bioethicists do and why the profession is becoming more important to physicians.

The rest of the readings focus on particular ethical issues related to healthcare. William DeVries, the cardiologist who earned a national reputation for his work with the artificial heart, discusses the "spectacular" case and the ethical decisions physicians involved in such cases must make. His personal essay, published in the *Journal of the American Medical Association* (*JAMA*), seeks to convince his readers, physicians, that such cases require a particular approach by physicians and representatives of the media alike. A second *JAMA* article discusses healthcare practices as they relate to gender. Three other readings have been written by physicians for readers without the specialized knowledge physicians bring to their reading. Richard Selzer, a retired surgeon, relates a personal experience with a malpractice suit and, in narrating that story, raises critical ethical issues related to all malpractice suits. William A. Nolen, also a surgeon, discusses the public's "thirst for medical knowledge" and its positive and negative consequences. Perri Klass, a pediatrician, speaks from her own experiences of the ethical dilemmas physicians face when delivering premature babies.

Two readings deal with AIDS. Robert M. Swenson, a medical school professor and immunologist, traces the history of AIDS and compares it with other epidemics. Kim Folz, a reporter for *The New York Times* who has tested positive for the HIV virus, shares his personal experiences with the disease.

As you read and react to the articles and essays in this chapter, consider what these writers say, how they say it, and for whom. Remember that, like these writers, you are using reading as a learning tool. Your reading will lead to a better understanding of the various rhetorical contexts these writers faced and the kinds of decisions they made in response to those contexts; it will also provide opportunities for you to consider how you feel about their ideas and what their information adds to your own understanding of some of the ethical issues they discuss. Finally, your reading and reacting will help you develop your own rhetorical context for writing. As you write in response to what you read and discuss those responses with your classmates, you will begin to narrow your own area of interest and to generate a reason for writing for a particular set of readers, just as the writers whose work you have read must do. Your reading is thus an important part of your composing process.

# 5
# READINGS ON HEALTHCARE ETHICS AND SOCIETY

# KATHERINE BOUTON ON THE ROLE OF THE MEDICAL ETHICIST

## Pre-Reading Questions

1. What does the word "ethical" mean to you? Describe the most difficult ethical decision you have made in your life. Why was it a difficult decision to make? How did you make the decision? What kinds of questions did you ask yourself as you considered your decision? Why did you make the decision you did?

2. How do you feel about prolonging life using extraordinary means? Who should decide whether life support is terminated or continued? How should this decision be made? By whom? What experiences have people you know had in which difficult medical decisions had to be made? How were these decisions made? How do you feel about the decisions these people made?

## PAINFUL DECISIONS
### Katherine Bouton

"The most difficult case I ever had?" Ruth Macklin pauses, momentarily—   1
and most uncharacteristically—at a loss for words as she thinks back over the hundreds she has considered in her years as ethicist in residence at

Albert Einstein College of Medicine and its affiliated hospitals in New York City.

"There was a woman in active labor in the ninth month, a full-term 2 pregnancy," she says. As the delivery proceeded it became apparent that the baby was in a breech position, a complication that these days virtually insures a Caesarean section. "The baby's foot was actually hanging out," Macklin says. But the mother refused to consent to the surgery.

"First she said she was a Jehovah's Witness and couldn't have 3 transfusions, and then that she didn't believe in medical procedures. I've recently been lecturing about the rights of pregnant women, the right not to be incarcerated if you're a drug addict, the right not to be forced to have a Caesarean. But this case was a very tough one, because once the baby is a newborn it has a different status altogether. Two minutes later and the mother would not have the right to deny treatment. But she could now." The right of autonomy—to accept or refuse treatment—is generally thought to extend to the pregnant woman. In principle.

In fact, however, there was that foot. The baby was all too visibly a 4 person. The obstetricians called a judge, then told the woman he was on his way over. The psychological pressure paid off. The woman agreed to the Caesarean.

"The tragic but ethically right decision would have been to allow her 5 to refuse," Macklin insists. She shrugs, acknowledging the emotional weight of the argument against her: "I told you this was the most difficult case I've encountered."

This case was brought to Macklin's attention a week or so later by 6 doctors who were troubled by their decision. Macklin and Dr. Alan R. Fleischman, a pediatrician and director of the Einstein division of neonatology, meet on a regular basis with obstetricians and pediatricians to consider issues of maternal-fetal conflict—variants of the breech-baby case—where the rights of a pregnant woman conflict with the rights of the unborn child. This session brings together a medical team working in a highly sensitive area and two senior faculty members—one proficient in ethics, the other in medicine. Together, they work out—case by case— some of the toughest problems facing doctors today.

Macklin oversees more than a dozen such conferences, teaching 7 rounds and committee meetings, often attending as many as three a day. Some deal with the big issues of bioethics: the right to die; when to withdraw or withhold treatment for an adult; the treatment of a severely handicapped newborn. But many involve the crucial small ones: in- formed consent; the right to confidentiality; the right to choose treat- ment; the right to know who is treating you.

Ruth Macklin does not sit in Solomonic judgment on these cases. 8 Rather, she and the medical personnel tease out the issues in a time- honored Socratic dialogue, with Macklin playing Socrates. Sometimes the decisions have already been made, and the discussion is primarily educational. Other times, life and death hang in the balance. Often the discussions go astray, and—unfailingly energetic, in the rat-a-tat-tat staccato of her native New Jersey—she leads her medical colleagues back on course.

Macklin doesn't give answers. She doesn't tell physicians what to do. 9 What she brings to a problem, she says, is clarity: "The ability to structure a set of moral principles that gives us a way to discuss the issues." There isn't always a right and wrong. Principles may clash. Reality may loom too large. And it doesn't mean that mistakes won't continue to be made—but, as one of her physician colleagues says, "maybe less serious ones."

Bioethics is a new profession. The term entered the language only in 10 1971, according to Webster's Ninth New Collegiate Dictionary. Macklin joined the staff of Einstein just six years later, in the department of epidemiology and social medicine. Her presence there is indicative of the revolution in medicine over the last quarter century.

Macklin entered this field, she says, by accident. In 1970, with a 11 doctorate in philosophy from Case Western Reserve, she was teaching at the university when a colleague, Samuel Gorovitz, asked if she would be interested in working with him on a project in medical ethics.

"Medical what?" was her response. 12

There was then no such thing as medical ethics as a formal field of intellectual pursuit. Although unscrupulous or vindictive or impaired doctors have always existed, the profession was considered to be ethical by its very nature. The doctor's code of ethics concerned itself as much with etiquette as ethics: doctors should not advertise, they should not profit excessively from their work, they should extend professional courtesy to colleagues, they should not allow a patient to see that they disagreed with a colleague's diagnosis or choice of treatment. Not much for a philosopher to grapple with.

But medicine was changing. In the mid-1960's, amniocentesis was 13 first used to test for fetal abnormality, meaning that prenatal diagnosis was available but abortion often was not, until Roe v. Wade in 1973. Kidney failure could finally be treated, with hemodialysis, but there weren't enough dialysis machines for all the people who needed them. When a committee in Seattle choosing candidates for dialysis was found to be relying on criteria of putative social worth (married people over single, pillars of the community over prostitutes, men over women), it started a debate over the allocation of scarce resources that continues today. And in neonatology, medical advances allowed very premature and badly damaged babies to survive—sometimes to face painful and severely compromised lives.

Gorovitz wanted to study how traditional philosophical tenets might 14 be applied to the emerging issues. At first the students in their course were from the Case Western department of philosophy; increasingly, however, the course attracted students from the medical school. And sometime during the third year, Macklin was asked to come to the university hospital to consult on a case.

"I was quaking in my boots," she recalled recently. "They were 15 looking for answers." But gradually it became clear that what the doctors wanted was to ask questions. "Much to my great surprise, even though I never gave any answers, time after time people came up afterward and thanked me, and said how much they'd learned."

Today Macklin, who is 52 years old, lives on the 10th floor of a 16 Riverdale cooperative overlooking the Hudson. Her two daughters, the products of an 11 ½-year marriage that began in college, are grown and pursuing their own lives, and her work schedule is luxuriously intense. Mornings and evenings, she writes on the computer in her bedroom. (Her many books include "Mortal Choices: Bioethics in Today's World," published by Pantheon in 1987.) The rest of the day is spent talking—fast and in great profusion. "I've been talking long enough," I once heard her say to a group at a state psychiatric hospital. "Not long enough for me, because I can go on endlessly, but long enough."

The Einstein-affiliated Bronx Municipal Hospital Center and its 17 acute-care center, Jacobi Hospital, where Macklin does much of her consulting work, are on Pelham Parkway, a leafy boulevard of handsome semidetached houses in the northeast Bronx. But the hospitals serve a larger and troubled neighborhood. Some 135,000 patients a year crowd the emergency rooms, many suffering from gunshot wounds, drug abuse and AIDS. Other Einstein hospitals, among them the private and not-for-profit Montefiore Medical Center (with its public affiliate, North Central Bronx Hospital) and Bronx-Lebanon Hospital Center, also carry a heavy urban load.

It is, then, paradoxically surprising and logical that these overbur- 18 dened hospitals have made such a commitment to a program of bioethics.

Each of these Einstein hospitals has a formal ethics committee, and 19 they share an Infant Bioethical Review Committee. This degree of commitment is not unusual. Sixty percent of the medium- and large-sized hospitals in the country have what they call an ethics committee. Their functions vary: some make policy, some hear cases, some do a little of each and some don't really do anything. In addition, some 300 people identify themselves as "clinical bioethics consultants"—people who are actively involved in ethics consultation in a medical setting. They may be philosophers, doctors, nurses, lawyers or clergy.

But the Einstein hospitals go well beyond the usual, with regularly 20 scheduled conferences in pediatrics, neonatology, perinatology, new reproductive technology and forensic psychiatry—as well as countless ad hoc sessions. Joining Macklin in these activities, and participating in many others separately, are Nancy Neveloff Dubler, a lawyer, and

John D. Arras, a philosopher, who work together as a bioethics consulting team at Montefiore.

Nurses and social workers attend these meetings, as do the hospital's 21 lawyers, when the situation seems to warrant it. But it is the attitude of the physicians that determines the degree of seriousness with which an institution takes the formal discussion of ethics. With the enthusiastic participation of many prominent doctors, Einstein has become, in fact if not in name, a leading center of bioethics in the country.

To the lay person, it seems that doctors face life-and-death decisions 22 daily, and that dealing with them must have become routine. In fact, they remain rare and as difficult as ever. An attending physician brought such a case to the ethics committee of an Einstein hospital. (To protect the patient's privacy, the hospital requested it not be identified.) "I've never been involved with something like this before in 10 years as an attending," the doctor explained. "I want to do what's best for the patient." But he wasn't at all sure what that was.

As always, the discussion began with a description of the patient's 23 condition and medical history. An elderly woman with a degenerative disease had been admitted to the hospital a little over a year before with flulike symptoms and general malaise. "She had a debilitating disease that has followed its natural course," the doctor explained, adding that since then she had had several invasive procedures—the insertion of a feeding tube and resuscitation after several respiratory arrests. With each resuscitation, he added, "her mental state has deteriorated." She had been on a respirator for a year. Unless she was sedated she was very agitated, and she seemed not to recognize anyone, including her husband, who visited her every day.

The doctor who related the story had met the patient twice in the 24 years before this admission, and even then she had led a severely limited life. She was wheelchair-bound and wore a diaper.

On admission to the hospital, for what she thought would be a brief 25 time, she had indicated—in writing, because she wasn't able to talk—that she wanted everything done in the event something went wrong.

Then things *had* gone wrong, and "everything"—respirator, feeding 26 tube—had been done. She hadn't had an opportunity to consent to any of them. She once pulled the feeding tube out of herself. Her doctor said she seemed very depressed. She was no longer able to communicate at all.

The week before this meeting, her husband had come to the doctor 27 and asked that she be removed from the respirator.

"We have to distinguish between what her husband wants and what 28 she would want," Macklin began. "There is a distinction from an ethical point of view."

The husband felt strongly that his wife would not wish to be kept 29 alive in this condition. Everyone agreed that the husband was devoted.

"He's taken care of her so many years," one nurse said. "I can't believe he would not have some feeling of what she would want."

It quickly became clear that almost everyone felt it would be in the 30 patient's best interest—a good standard for determining what is "ethically correct"—to remove her from the respirator. The air was tense with the knowledge that this group might hold her life in its hands, that as this hour came to an end a decision might be made to allow her to die.

This is a terribly difficult decision for a physician. Doctors are trained 31 to save lives, to do everything in their power to keep people alive. Andrew Mezey, a pediatrician who is medical director at the Bronx Municipal Hospital Center, told me a story that poignantly illustrated this. A few years ago, a 4-month-old grandchild of his died of viral pneumonia. As the baby's condition deteriorated, in spite of aggressive treatment, the family and the baby's doctor sat down together and talked about the baby's condition. They agreed that nothing more could be done, that the baby should not be resuscitated, that the time had come to allow her to die in peace.

Dr. Mezey recalled, as we talked in his office, a photograph of the 32 infant girl on the window sill behind him, how he sat by the baby that morning, "watching the blips on the monitor. It was clear the baby had only a few hours to live. I found myself thinking, 'I have to do something.' " The doctor in him was unable to let go. "The doctor's education is to ride roughshod," he said. He finally had to leave the baby's room.

Still, it seemed that this afternoon, in the case of the elderly woman, 33 the difficult decision was to be made. Then Macklin shifted the course of the argument.

A 1981 judgment by New York's highest court, the Court of 34 Appeals, allows the withdrawal of treatment from patients who cannot speak for themselves, provided there is "clear and convincing evidence" that this would be their wish. The standard of proof is among the most stringent in the country. Casual remarks are not good enough. Explaining this, Macklin returned to the case at hand. "It doesn't fit the clear-and-convincing evidence standard," she said. But she urged the group to consider the case purely on ethical principles.

"Does she get any pleasure out of life?" Macklin asked. Ordinarily, in 35 a benefit-burden analysis, continued life is considered to be a benefit, though the burden of treatment might outweigh it. This woman had always led a very constricted life; who was to say it was now measurably worse?

What exactly does it mean for a patient to be removed from a 36 respirator, Macklin asked. Is it painful? Perhaps the pain could be eased—with morphine, say, she added mischievously. The doctors reacted as if she'd suggested they shoot the woman. Morphine depresses respiration.

"Doesn't removing the respirator depress respiration?" she said.          37

The husband had merely asked them to remove the respirator, one 38 doctor disingenuously maintained, "not to kill his wife."

"So you're acting as an equipment mover?" Macklin remarked.          39

"No, we're removing a therapy," he insisted.

In the end, Macklin suggested to the doctor that the decision—from an ethical standpoint—could be made on the basis of whether the patient was suffering more than she was benefiting from life. "I don't like the term 'quality of life,' " she said, "but if you try to ascertain whether living in that state—conscious but uncomfortable—is better than not living at all. . . ." "And," she added, "if you are comfortable that her husband is acting as she would want, not as he wants."

"He's doing it because he believes she is suffering," the doctor said. 40 "I agree with his thoughts: I think she *is* suffering." Then, he paused. "On the other hand, if he asked me to do anything I could to save her, I would do it."

Macklin smiled. "But that's consistent with your view that he should 41 be the decision maker," she said.

Ethically, the course was clear. But legally was another matter. "It's a 42 case with inherent ambiguity," Macklin said at last. "My feeling is that ethically it is permissible to go either way."

But some on the committee, and the doctor himself, were reluctant 43 to act without the approval of the hospital's lawyers.

A few days later, a hospital administrator said there was no way the 44 hospital would honor the husband's request. The husband, meanwhile, had changed his mind, having been swayed by a conversation with a doctor opposed to the withdrawal of the treatment.

Every two weeks Macklin joins Dr. Harold N. Adel, co-director of 45 medical services at the Bronx Municipal Hospital Center, and Dr. Saul Moroff, associate director of medicine at Jacobi Hospital, in a seminar for a small group of third-year medical students. Although she regards all her work as a kind of teaching, these discussions take a more didactic form. By now—nine years after they started this course at Jacobi—Dr. Adel, Dr. Moroff and Macklin have seen just about everything, and they often take deliberately provocative positions. Saul Moroff, a genial gray-haired man, is what Macklin calls a facilitator; he moves the discussions right along, often by acting as devil's advocate.

Late in June, Macklin and Dr. Moroff met with a group of students 46 just beginning the third year, the so-called clinical clerkship, when they put on stethoscopes and white coats and treat patients for the first time. They had been on the wards for exactly a week and a half and were still starry-eyed. But it doesn't take long to get cynical in these hospitals, and we could see it developing even in the course of this hour-long discussion.

Moise Danielpour, a 25-year-old U.C.L.A. graduate, had been part 47 of a team treating a 41-year-old intravenous drug user who had checked into Jacobi with blood in his urine and a rash. He was put on methadone, treated for the rash, and given Narcan, a drug that depresses the effect of narcotics. At several points, Danielpour said earnestly, he and the patient had a "heart-to-heart discussion about the need to give up drugs."

He noted without comment that the patient had several times 48 become lethargic and developed pinpoint pupils and that he'd asked to be taken off the methadone, because "he was afraid of becoming addicted." Dr. Moroff gently pointed out that methadone dulls the effect of heroin.

It soon became inescapably clear to everyone that the patient was 49 taking heroin while he was being treated, and that he was somehow getting it there in the hospital. ("It's not difficult to buy drugs in city hospitals," Dr. Moroff commented blandly.)

What is the doctor's obligation to treat such a patient? The students 50 were reluctant to admit that they could be pushed to the point of feeling a patient was no longer qualified for care. Dr. Moroff pointed out that though a doctor on Park Avenue might "fire" a noncompliant or disruptive patient, the patient in the public hospital doesn't have the option of going to another doctor. Macklin suggested, however, that there could come a time when a patient becomes so combative, so violent "that you can no longer provide medical care."

What about the patient's right to fire the doctor or simply to refuse 51 treatment? What if a patient has a horror of needles and refuses an intravenous antibiotic? One student thought it would be immoral to allow him to take an oral antibiotic—a second-best choice that might not work. Dr. Moroff demurred: it's the patient's right to choose.

The discussion went around and around, touching on many everyday 52 ethical issues doctors face. What about the kind of language doctors use, and the patient's right to informed consent? "You never give up until you're sure they understand what you're saying," Dr. Moroff said. Then he smiled, acknowledging that the doctor's moral authority sometimes makes truly informed consent almost impossible: "With a lot of patients, if you say, 'Hello there. I'd like to remove your carotid artery and the right lobe of your brain,' they'll say, 'O.K.' "

In the world of ethics, as in the world outside, children have a special 53 status. The issues are not so different—revolving around death and dying, the right to refuse treatment, the right to informed consent—but they take on not only a special poignancy, but additional complications as well.

Most cases that come to the four-hospital committee on infant 54 bioethics involve conflicts between doctors and families: most often between doctors who want to treat an infant and a family that wants to do nothing. Sometimes, however, an infant is hopelessly ill and death is inevitable; the physician feels further treatment will only painfully pro-long life but the family still wants everything done. These cases may go to the infant ethics committee to resolve.

Some subjects that come up in Alan Fleischman's meetings on 55
neonatal ethics reflect the particular patient population in the Bronx. In
these days of crack babies, Dr. Fleischman says, infants may be born
weighing a pound or less, only 20 to 22 weeks gestational age, but
having a heartbeat. Does a doctor resuscitate such a baby? A 22-week
fetus is not viable, but what if the date of conception has been
miscalculated and the baby is actually 25 weeks old? "A young physician
faced with that in the delivery room. . . ." Dr. Fleischman shrugs. "We
never send the really young ones in alone, though other hospitals do."

In the field of neonatology, the Federal Government has sought to 56
impose standards of treatment for newborns that many physicians feel
compromise ethical behavior. Federal regulations mandate full treatment
for all handicapped newborns, with a few exceptions, often despite the
pain and suffering that the infant might be experiencing. "I believe
strongly that American hospitals are overtreating babies," Fleischman
says of the effect of these regulations. "Babies who would die anyway are
being kept alive by physicians who feel it's their obligation to do that."

A 1988 article in *The New England Journal of Medicine* found that 57
500 of the 1,000 neonatologists polled felt they were overtreating
handicapped infants out of fear of prosecution. "We are not doing that,"
Dr. Fleischman says of his staff. "We are not hurting babies for no
benefit." But no hospital is immune from fear of repercussion; ethics
meetings on infants at Einstein are attended by hospital lawyers.

AIDS plays a major role in the neonatal units. As many as 4 percent 58
of the children born in municipal hospitals in New York City test positive
for the HIV virus; of these, 30 percent will develop the disease. Up to 10
percent of the infants in intensive care are HIV positive. The issues in the
units mostly concern how aggressively to treat them, but concerns also
arise about the protection of medical workers; obstetrics and neonatal
procedures both involve a lot of blood and fluids.

Among older children the issues are more complex, and more 59
wrenching. Once a week Macklin attends a meeting held at the Children's Evaluation and Rehabilitation Center, affiliated with the medical
school. (Though the session is not primarily for the discussion of ethical
matters, Macklin attends every week anyway.) The meeting is held by the
center's AIDS team—a group of doctors, nurses, physical therapists,
social workers and educational specialists—that goes by a deliberately
obscure set of initials intended to disguise the fact that the children they
treat have AIDS. New York State law insures complete confidentiality for
children with AIDS. Even within the hospital they are not to be
identified, although warnings about the need for caution in handling the
blood and bodily fluids of these patients, posted in their rooms, are a
clear tip-off.

Many children treated by this group, though desperately ill, leave the 60
hospital womb at age 5 or 6 and go to schools for the handicapped. A

teacher and her aides from one of these schools came one afternoon to discuss a younger girl in their care. It took a few minutes of confused exchanges to realize that the visiting group had no idea it was meeting an AIDS team, that only two of the four visitors knew the child they worked with daily had AIDS, and that the two who knew she had the disease didn't know the Einstein team knew she had AIDS.

Once all that was settled—to the immense relief of everybody—they got on with the issue of how to best take care of this very ill child, who seemed to be deteriorating quickly. Simply to feed her took her teacher more than an hour, and even then, because she couldn't swallow properly, they weren't sure she was getting any nutrition. One school aide worried that more food was going into her lungs than her stomach. [61]

It was a deeply depressing case and the discussion of it became more of a therapy session than anything else. The group's leader, a young pediatrician named Karen Hopkins, who also treats non-AIDS patients, handled the discussion with skill and almost saintly serenity. Outside the door we could occasionally hear children in the corridor howling the unnatural cry of the very debilitated. Most issues raised were purely medical ones, about the course of treatment. The matter of the breach of confidentiality was easily resolved, when the school aides said they wouldn't treat the child any differently now that they knew she had AIDS. [62]

The very idea of a philosopher in the hospital has been slow to meet with the approval of some doctors. Dr. Mark Siegler, director of the Center for Clinical Medical Ethics at the University of Chicago, used to be adamant in his position that only physicians should be party to these medical discussions. Recently, his positive experiences working with what he refers to as "professional ethicists" have persuaded him to soften his views. [63]

Even some of Macklin's own physician colleagues still seem to resent discussion of these issues. At a session attended only by medical staff, Macklin cited a case where coercion had been used on a woman for the sake of a fetus. After the meeting, she said, "a physician came up yelling and screaming, furious at me for identifying the hospital" where this had happened. "The case had been written up in two law journals!" she says. "They had both named the hospital." [64]

Some doctors simply don't have the time or inclination for these discussions. Nancy Dubler says that doctors in primary care (internists, pediatricians, obstetricians and the like) most readily recognize the need for this kind of analysis but that doctors "in some subspecialties, who don't deal with the whole person, who don't see the dilemmas, the life, the hopes and fears of the person," are less responsive. Once, Macklin recalls, when one ethics committee suggested to a surgeon that he bring a case for discussion, he declined, saying, "We don't really have any ethical problems." [65]

Clinical researchers, too, often come up against ethics in a less than collegial way: the medical school's institutional review board, of which [66]

Macklin is a member, reviews all research proposals involving human subjects. Ethics sometimes comes into conflict with scientific curiosity.

In view of recent developments it must take an effort of will to deny the 67 necessity for consideration of problems in medical ethics. In the weeks this article was being researched, bioethical issues made the news with dizzying frequency:

- The Supreme Court, venturing for the first time into the "right to die" area, decided in the Nancy Beth Cruzan case that a person has the right to have life supports removed. But it affirmed the state's right to set a high standard of proof of the patient's wishes—the "clear and convincing evidence" standard that is the law in New York as well as in Cruzan's home state of Missouri.
- On the same day, the Court ruled that a state may require a teen-age girl to notify her parents or get a judge's permission before she has an abortion, raising important ethical questions about autonomy.
- Oregon dealt with the high cost of medical care and allocation of resources by making a list of illnesses and conditions, in order of the efficacy and cost of treatment, that would determine coverage under the state's Medicaid program.
- The Food and Drug Administration waived its usual requirements on drug testing and approved the use of AZT for children, reasoning that because the drug is relatively safe and effective in mitigating the symptoms of AIDS in adults it will also work for children.
- A Pennsylvania employer is challenging the estimated $1.25 million bill for a heart, liver and kidney operation on a patient who later died, even though she was covered by the corporation's health insurance policy, citing the excessively high cost of the care and the apparently low return.
- New York State passed a long-debated health-care proxy bill, which allows the designation of a surrogate to make decisions for an incapacitated patient.
- A California couple announced that they had conceived a child in the hope the baby might be a bone-marrow donor for their 17-year-old daughter, who was dying of leukemia. Against great odds, the resulting baby proved to be a suitable donor.
- An estranged father sued to force his 3-year-old twins to be tested to see if they were suitable bone-marrow donors for their critically ill 12-year-old half-brother. A judge in Chicago dismissed the suit.
- Two Christian Scientists, David and Ginger Twitchell, were convicted of manslaughter in the death of their 2½-year-old son. The couple had failed to seek medical treatment for the boy, who died of a bowel obstruction.

- Dr. Jack Kevorkian assisted Janet Adkins, a Portland, Ore., woman whose condition was diagnosed as Alzheimer's disease, in committing suicide. Macklin, who does not necessarily oppose physician-assisted suicide, argued that the case had procedural flaws, because Adkins was not terminally ill or in great pain, and because the physician who evaluated her condition also helped in the suicide. And it was all done too fast. "There should be evidence of repeated, enduring requests on the part of the patient," she says.

A physician's options in treating patients have changed so dramati- 68 cally in the last 25 years, thanks primarily to technology, that many doctors are confronted almost daily with ethical questions that would not have been asked two decades ago. Medicine can now keep a patient alive almost indefinitely, substituting respirators for breathing, artificially de- livered food and fluids for the ability to eat and drink, catheters for urination, highly sophisticated antibiotics to fight infection, artificial and transplanted organs and tissue for the ones a person is born with. Doctors often face the question of whether they should keep the patient alive. It has sometimes become hard to tell what being "alive" means.

And, paradoxically, in an age when the patient is more an object than 69 ever—when the person is divided up into parts and dealt with as a series of unrelated subspecialties—the patient is also seen as having the right to make decisions about his treatment. Nothing could be more different from the way it was in the days of the family doctor, who decided what you wanted whether you thought you wanted it or not.

Ruth Macklin meets weekly, biweekly or monthly with a dozen 70 different groups who want her help on dealing with issues on a consultative basis, or developing policy for the Einstein hospitals. She makes it a point never to turn down an invitation from a colleague to lecture to students or consult with staff. On a typical day she may spend six or eight hours talking. It is an exhaustive and exhausting process.

Andrew Mezey formed a monthly pediatric ethics group with Mack- 71 lin and Dr. Fleischman back in 1982, and recently has been involved in a lengthy series of meetings to develop a role for a hospital "ward advocate," who would act as proxy in decision making for abandoned children with AIDS in the Einstein hospitals. When I sat in on the ward advocate meeting, it was the third time this group had met on this matter. Mezey (who happens to be the designated ward advocate), Dr. Fleischman, and several representatives of the Einstein administration circled around the issues and sticking points for an hour and a half— making some progress but nowhere near enough. Another meeting was scheduled for another week.

Do you ever feel as if there's just too much talk? I asked Dr. Mezey a 72 few days later. His answer was a decided no. "The more you hang out with people like Ruth," he says, "the more you see the value of turning some-thing over and over. You'll still make errors, but maybe less serious ones."

## Post-Reading Questions

1. Who is Ruth Macklin? Why is her job a difficult one?
2. What strategy has Bouton used to introduce her article? Where does the introduction end? How effective is her introduction? Why? What writing goals does this introduction accomplish for Bouton? How does her choice of strategy reflect her sense of her readers?
3. What is the field of "bioethics"? Identify two or three examples of bioethical issues in Bouton's article.
4. Write a paragraph summarizing the development of the field of bio-ethics. How did it develop? What forces influenced its development?
5. Why would physicians resist organizing a Medical Ethics committee at a particular hospital? What reasons does Bouton offer? What other reasons would doctors have for resisting?
6. Do you think the field of bioethics will grow more or less important to the daily work physicians perform in the future? Explain your answer by using some of the information in Bouton's article and your own experiences.
7. What problems arise when "the patient's best interest" is the standard used to determine an ethical course of medical action or treatment? How should such problems be resolved?
8. In addition to describing what medical ethicists do, what other pur-pose or purposes does Bouton have for this article? How do you know?
9. What strategies does Bouton use to help her readers understand what she is writing about? For each strategy you identify, give an example from the article.
10. Why do children have a special place in the world of medical ethics? Give an example of a medical decision involving a real or hypothet-ical child.
11. Why does Bouton end her article by emphasizing "talk?"
12. In paragraph 67, Bouton identifies several specific bioethical cases. Choose one, and explain how you would go about finding out how that case was resolved. What sources would you turn to? Why?

# RICHARD SELZER
# ON MALPRACTICE CASES

## Pre-Reading Questions

1. Under what circumstances would you sue a physician for malprac-tice? Why would you consider such a suit justified? Describe a situation where you or someone you know or have read about has

sued a physician. Why did the person sue? How did the suit turn out?

2.  What reasons can you think of to explain why the number of malpractice suits is rising? In light of your reasons, do you think this number will continue to rise in the next ten to twenty years, or will it fall?

3.  What kinds of social problems does the rise in the number of malpractice suits cause? How does this rise affect healthcare delivery systems? Which prospective patients would be most affected? Why? How would healthcare costs be affected?

# TRIAL AND TRIBULATION
## Richard Selzer

**November 1986.** I learn this morning that a colleague has died. Suicide, the newspaper reported. Although I never met him, my sadness at his passing is no less acute than had we been good friends, for George Laszlo and I endured the same misfortune, and nothing binds men together like shared pain. George F. Laszlo was a general practitioner in the town of Woodbury, L.I. He was 72 years old at the time his wife, Maritza, discovered his lifeless body in their house. It had been 48 years since he graduated from medical school in Budapest. Then came the war and the Hungarian Revolution. From 1960 until the day he killed himself, he practiced medicine on Long Island.

It seems that a man experiencing chest pain went to see Dr. Laszlo, who advised him to go to the hospital for tests. Instead, the man went home. The next day, the clinical picture crystallized, and the man suffered a heart attack. In due course, the patient brought suit against Dr. Laszlo for malpractice, claiming that he had not "taken care of the condition or warned him of the severity of the situation." George Laszlo was not protected by malpractice insurance. In Hungary, as in most parts of the world, it would seem, there persists that unspoken understanding that the doctor is doing his best and that the patient is accepting his advice. The trial had been set for January 1987. Now it would have to be conducted without George Laszlo. After months of depression, sleeplessness and anguish, the accused killed himself. I leave it to a jury of his peers to decide upon guilt or innocence.

In February of that year, two years after my retirement from surgery, I too was ordered to stand trial for malpractice. But while George Laszlo had stood naked in the gale, I was well padded against any damage. (Though I had never been sued before, I had several million dollars worth of medical malpractice insurance.) Nor did I kill myself, although the thought crossed my mind.

Now I wish to make an offering of this, the record of my anguish—as 4
I recall it—to whatever of George Laszlo is still reachable. It was an
ordeal that—out of wisdom or folly, who can say?—he spared himself.
This record is not the presentation of a court trial with verbatim
testimony and all the flash and clamor of legal argument. Nor is it a
statement upon the fairness of the tort laws. (It happens sometimes that
a doctor will make an egregious error by which the patient will be
injured. In such a case, litigation is justified.) Far from it. My spirits do
not soar at the prospect of a battle. I am Ferdinand the Bull; I much
prefer to lie down and smell the flowers.

**St. Valentine's Day 1986.** For weeks I have been living with the vain 5
hope that the trial would never take place. After a lifetime of placating
Fate, She would call it off; She wouldn't have the nerve. But She did.

Here is what happened: Eight years ago I performed a cryohemor- 6
rhoidectomy upon a woman. It was what some might term minor
surgery, but I am well aware that a minor operation is one that is done on
someone else. Cryohemorrhoidectomy involves no cutting or suturing,
but rather the application of an extremely cold metal probe to excessive
internal hemorrhoidal tissue in order to destroy it, much as one uses
extreme heat to cauterize, or to burn away unwanted growths. Heat and
cold and, increasingly, light and sound are displacing the scalpel as the
preferred technique in surgery. Often quicker and safer than the making
of incisions and the stitching up, these new methods have fewer
complications, and are less painful. Still, they share with the knife an
undiminished vulnerability to malpractice litigation. Ever afterward, my
patient claimed that she was ill and incapacitated, requiring 8 to 10
enemas each day. A year ago, she died of causes unrelated to this
operation. The lawsuit is being continued by her widower.

She is dead; I am retired. We are two ghosts brought into a 7
courtroom to battle over "money damages." Would it not be more
sensible, I wonder, to delay the trial a while? The way things are going, it
ought not to be too long before she and I can sit down together and
discuss it in heaven. Or wherever. Still, I have to hand it to her. She had
taken her grievance to seven malpractice lawyers, each of whom turned it
down. Undaunted, she became her own lawyer, wrote up the documents, met the court deadlines. In legal parlance it is called *pro se*. Then,
at last, she found a lawyer who agreed, with enthusiasm, to take her case.
Together, they would spend the rest of her life in this pursuit. Such
persistence, such stamina surely ought to be rewarded, you say? Let us
see.

Yesterday a headline appeared across four columns of the front page 8
in the New Haven Register: "City Surgeon May Face 'King of Torts.'"
It seems that their lawyer has put it abroad that Melvin Belli will be his
co-counsel. The rest of the article reports the allegation that I have

"badly botched" the operation, that since, and because of, my ministra-
tions the patient suffered greatly, that I have written "several books of
fiction," that the amount of money sought is $2.6 million.

"Melvin Belli isn't going to come," I told the reporter the next day      9
at the courthouse.

"I know," he said, "I phoned him."                                       10

"Then why? . . ."

"We were told he might."

"I have never written a novel," I told him.

"Then what were they?" he asked.

"Where did you get 'badly botched?' "

"From the plaintiff's lawyer."

"Listen," I said, "we are both writers. I have never knowingly
injured anyone with a single sentence of mine. Why are you doing this to
me?"

He explained it is because I am "high profile."

"Because I wrote those books?"

"Fame," he told me, "is a two-way street."

Thus was I educated in the ways of the American press. Each day of the   11
trial, the proceedings would be reported prominently in the newspaper.

**Day One.** For some weeks I have experienced anorexia, insomnia and a   12
sense of bereavement as though, 50 years later, I am once again grieving for
my father. The nights are full of tobacco smoke and black coffee. Whatever
sleep is punctuated by dreams of courtroom humiliation. Enough. It is time
to go. I shall attend the trial by myself. The sympathy of others would
further unman me.

Do I have everything? My notebook, a pencil and, oh yes, a green         13
stone of polished malachite from Vermont, about the size and shape of a
robin's egg. It was given to me long ago by someone who loved me. This
will keep you safe, she had whispered. In the absence of faith, supersti-
tion will do. For the six days of the trial I am never to be without the
little green stone.

The courthouse has a white marble face, as pitiless as it is neutral. Up  14
wide stone steps and through a revolving door; the municipal odor of
tobacco and urine; spittoons. A uniformed guard is stationed at the door
with a metal detector, which suspects the rings of my notebook. I
surrender it to the guard and pass through. Before giving the notebook
back to me, he riffles the pages.

The courtroom is without windows, like an operating room or a           15
mausoleum. Straight ahead is the raised platform, the banc, where the
judge will be enthroned. Already, the benches are filling with lawyers,
newspaper reporters and townspeople who have come to watch Melvin
Belli perform. Their disappointment is palpable when it is learned that he

will not be coming. Their attention is lowered to me. I do not know any of them. I think of the observers who attended anatomical dissections at the medical schools of Italy and the Netherlands, at the time of the Renaissance, each carrying at the nose a vinegar-soaked handkerchief. The two lawyers, theirs and mine, are both big and handsome, each with a full complement of good white teeth. They wear large oxblood, wing-tip shoes and dark pin-striped suits. They exude confidence. The widower and I are at the height of our beshrivelment—round-shouldered, gray-faced members of a stunted, avitaminotic race. So, then, we are evenly matched.

"Banc!" It is a loud sharp command from the bailiff. The entire 16 court rises and the judge appears from the wings. He is splendid. His face is the color of mulligatawny soup. He has full white hair that is cast in motionless waves, with a part that appears to have been made with a scalpel. His nose is fleshy and ridged. There is a pearl stickpin in his pearl-gray silk tie.

It begins. One by one my peers are brought in, sworn and ques- 17 tioned. The lawyers size them up, then either accept them or challenge. If it were up to me, I should have picked the first eight. But the lawyers are finicky. The endless churning of their minds!

Here is the widower's lawyer leaning toward a prospective juror, one 18 foot braced on a step, an elbow resting on his knee. His voice is soft, utterly reassuring:

"Do you believe it is possible for a doctor to lie?"                    19

"Yes."

"Do you believe that a doctor could injure someone, then try to cover it up?"

"Yes."                    20

"If, after it were proved to you that a doctor did do such a thing, would you have any trouble awarding money damages to his victim?"

"No."                    21

"Do you believe doctors are special privileged people who should be treated differently from you and me?"

Then it is my lawyer's turn.

Two hours later, a recess is called. The corridor of a courthouse is a 22 casbah seething with plots and counterplots. Plaintiffs and defendants eye each other with cold curiosity. Lawyers whisper in the ears of clients, covering their mouths to foil the errant lip reader. The faces of the people are indignant, tense, afraid. But here, at least, I am among my colleagues—the other defendants whose trials have been recessed. We loiter in the halls, smoking and drinking coffee—no throng more forlorn than we, leaning against the walls—we, the alleged child molesters, we who are said not to have paid our alimony, we who may or may not have robbed a gas station. Here, too, those of us who insist that we have been battered by our husbands and those of us who absolutely deny having done it. Now and then someone speaks:

"What are you up for?"                                                        23

"Up?"

"He's a doctor. A case of malpractice."

"Yeah?" A gaze of profound interest. "I had an uncle once. . . ." But I have already moved away. My glance happens to meet that of the widower. Unaccountably, he smiles. Of what, I wonder, could he be thinking? Surely it is not the smile of acquaintanceship? Nor is it a gloat. No, I think he means to tell me there is nothing personal, that none of this has to do with us, not really. I am utterly dashed by this smile.

**Day Two.** Being on trial is infinitely boring, infinitely interesting. At the   24
moment, it is infinitely boring. The plaintiff's lawyer has brought a large satchel from which he is holding up, one at a time, rubber syringes, enema bags, tubes of lubricant.

"This is an enema bag," he says. "Here is the nozzle, the tubing."   25
The jurors eye with controlled distaste all of the anguished paraphernalia of spastic colitis. Each article must be labeled and entered as an exhibit.

A nurse in a white uniform is called to testify that she has seen the   26
woman give herself from 6 to 10 enemas each day. The courtroom is crowded and as hot as Nebuchadnezzar's oven. I long for a punkah wallah in a loin cloth so as to provide both breeze and entertainment.

We recess for lunch. Outside the courthouse, New Haven goes on   27
being New Haven, the way a watch keeps running in the pocket of a dead man. People saunter or hurry past on matters of importance. The grace of the unaccused, their serene faces—I cannot take my gaze from such beauty. Why should I feel hurt at their cool indifference to my plight, when I have walked past so many and did not consider theirs?

Afternoon. It is the widower's turn on the stand. He is terribly ill at   28
ease. Now and then, having been caught in a contradiction, he taps his forehead, gives a self-deprecating little smile, as if to say: There I go again. Time and again my lawyer throws him in the air and catches him in his jaws. In spite of myself, I have no rancor toward the man. There is just no sense in elevating him to the satanic. Once, even, I think he glanced in my direction as if to ask for help. It is clear that he is in over his head. Never mind. I am next and will do no better. But why is he doing this to himself? Perhaps it is his way of memorializing her? Or is it an attempt to keep her alive, by continuing her suit? No, I think, it is the money.

**Day Three.** Strange, how at the bailiff's sharp cry of "Banc!" the entire   29
court rises to its feet until His Honor has sat and settled his robes. Strange, how every gaze is fixed upon his halo of bright hair. This unanimous rising to greet the judge is more deferential than courteous.

Courtesy is composed of half respect and half generosity of spirit. This is deference, an acceptance of one's inferior position, a salaam at court.

Now it is I called to the witness stand. How I must look sitting in 30 this box—like a sad-faced monkey in a cage. I, who have never stuttered, am stuttering! I must try to look more innocent, less like a culprit who is waiting to be found out. Their lawyer, questioning me on the stand, spends the entire day in a state of outraged disbelief:

"Are you asking us to believe"—he makes a gesture to include the 31 jurors and himself in a single fraternity—"that you do not remember at what hour you received that phone call on Aug. 12, 1978?"

"I am asking the jury to believe it."                       32

"To believe what?"

"That I do not remember and so forth. It was eight years ago."

"That, I submit, is a lie."

This raises the whole question of memory. Is memory involuntary or not? Ought one to be punished for his forgetfulness? Does torture succeed in getting people to remember things?

**Day Four.** I am preyed upon by dread. And full of smoke, coffee and 33 that gray-faced thing—fatigue. As for sleep, it is a doorway barred to me until the early hours of morning. I begin to wonder whether I have a future with this body of mine. A friend has suggested that I read the "Terrible" sonnets of Gerard Manley Hopkins. It is a mistake. This kind of misery is not eased by reading:

> Here! creep,
> Wretch, under a comfort serves in a whirlwind: all
> Life death does end and each day dies with sleep.

Among today's crowd, two jovial men eating doughnuts, snuffing up 34 the crumbs; a woman with an eager foraging look wielding a notebook and pencil. Another reporter, I assume.

"No," she tells me, "a legal secretary. I'm thrilled to be here." 35 Another, a big woman who climbs over the laps of the doughnut-eaters into the middle of the pew, using her bosom and knees for leverage. And the court reporter from the newspaper. All day I shall listen to the hissing of his pencil.

The expert witness for the plaintiff has arrived, a visiting potentate 36 from lands afar. Like me, he is a retired surgeon. But unlike me, he is tall, straight, hawk-nosed and white-haired. His voice is deep and meaty. Immediately having left his mouth, it sinks to the floor and spreads out across the room, drifting among the benches. I can feel its timbre in the soles of my feet. Now *there* is an instrument of authority.

Now we hear that the expert witness has never performed a cryohe- 37 morrhoidectomy. (Nor would he! he says disapprovingly.) Has he ever seen one performed? No. It is a procedure developed since his retirement. But, he insists, he has read extensively in the literature. He has personally discussed the technique with leaders in the field. He has spoken with Melvin Belli. (That one again.) His fee for testifying is $5,000 per day. In all his years of surgery, he rumbles *andante pomposa*, he has never seen a more blatant case of malpractice. Is he aware that cryohemorrhoidectomy is an operation that is now performed many times a day, in this city as elsewhere? If so, it must not be allowed to go on, he says. If the expert witness cannot be profound, he will be emphatic.

Yet another recess. Justice, I see, is as much a matter of coffee and 38 cigarettes as it is of evidence and debate. My body has an entire repertory of aches and pains. I take it off into a corner, give it a hug of commiseration. The reporter discovers me cringing:

He: "I admire you a lot. Your writings and all. I've been reading 39 them."

Me: "What?"                                                               40

He: "As a matter of fact, I've been doing some writing too. Science fiction. I'd like to show it to you sometime. See what you think. After this is all over."

He follows me to the drinking fountain, then to the toilet.              41

News! My lawyer informs me that they have come down from $2.6 million to $250,000.

"We have got them on the run," he says.                                   42

**Day Five.** I am still on the witness stand. The lawyers have grown testy. 43 The judge, too. His principal concern is that no two of us speak at the same time lest the court stenographer be unable to reproduce the proceedings accurately. Each time such a vocal overlap occurs, he barks and shows hackles. It does away with any of the stirring antiphonal choral music that might arise from spontaneity of argument. I much prefer the rough and tumble of men shouting at each other out of the windows of their cars in hard traffic. All morning I watch the two lawyers flirting their capes, brandishing their rapiers.

Now and then, I take out my pocket watch. Not so much to see what 44 time it is as to look at a familiar face. For the third time in 10 minutes, I have been accused of lying, for the third time my lawyer has leaped to object. I am having trouble understanding the questions. I have to ask that a question be repeated. While it is asked again, I look down at my hands. All my life, my hands have been my most reliable parts. And they are stronger than my slightness of build would suggest. I can crush two walnuts in my fist, and have done so often to win the admiration of my children. But what is this! In the middle of each palm, I see a bunched yellowish nodule of hard tissue rising between the transverse creases and extending in a cord to the base of my fourth finger. For heaven's sake!

Dupuytren's Contracture. How is that I never noticed it before? Or is it. . . ? I shouldn't be a bit surprised, if all it takes is suffering. During recess, I show it to my lawyer.

"What's that?" he asks.                                                                              45

"The stigmata," I tell him, "I'm getting them. By tomorrow I'll have holes in my forehead." He is skeptical, but worried.

"Whatever you do, don't show it to the jury."                                                      46

**Day Six.** Time to leave for the courthouse. Do I have everything? 47
Notebook, pencil. My stone.

For two hours, their lawyer labors to undermine my honesty and my  48
competence. Each question is sprayed upon my cheek from a distance of 12 inches.

"What exactly is a hemorrhoid? Do you know? Do you know the  49
difference between an external and an internal hemorrhoid?" From where I sit in the witness box, it appears that something other than his necktie has him by the throat. His face is red; his forehead blistered with sweat. Each time he speaks, he throws every one of his fingers at my face.

"Answer yes or no," he wets me down.                                                               50

"Yes *and* no," I tell him.

"That is no answer," he yells. "Yes *or* no."

"Yes and no," I say again. I see him pause as if to skim off his seething thoughts. Then he wheels at me.

"Did you or did you not, answer yes or no, write a book called  51
"Confessions of a Knife?" The word "confessions" is held in his mouth, then rolled out with relishment. I am to be tarred by the word. If I have made other confessions in the past, then why not one more? I think for a moment of that small volume of personal reflections and stories having to do with the pain and joy of being a surgeon. All at once I hear a singing from my pocket. Pick me up, chants the little green stone.

"Yes," I answer. "I did write that book."                                                          52

"And what," he asks, "is the name of that book?"

"Confessions of a Knife."

"No further questions," he says.

Out into the rank and sour corridor for yet another recess. You could float up and down on the wave of indignation today. Overheard a snatch of conversation between two lawyers:

"Rape."                                                                                            53

"Rape?"

"Nothing kinky. Just your basic rape."

"Oh well, then."

I stand near the widower. There is no longer any point in trying to avoid him. I see that he looks half-dead, ashen, with black smudges beneath his eyes. It is a race to see which one of us will die of this first.

But if the case were to be decided by single combat, today I could probably take him.

Now I am back on the witness stand. It is my lawyer's turn:      54
"Tell us, please, why you became a doctor?"

"I object!" interposes his opposite number.

"Overruled," from His Honor. For half an hour the two lawyers joust, each lance splintering on my breast. At the end of which, mine is still horsed.

"Why did you become a doctor?" he repeats, sending all sorts of 55 messages to the jury by means of body English and inflection.

"Go ahead," he urges me. And so I tell him about my father, who 56 was a general practitioner in Troy, N.Y., during the Depression and who died when I was 13. Since I could no longer find him in the flesh, I would become a doctor and find him through his work.

"And then what?" my lawyer prompts. Each time I fall still, he is 57 there, nudging. At 11:45, a recess is called. The lawyers repair to the judge's chambers. The rest of us scurry out to the casbah. A strange man winks at me. Could that be the alleged child molester?

At 1:30, the lawyers emerge.      58
"They have come down to $50,000. How about it?" my lawyer says.
"How about what?"

"They have spent four years on this case. Their lawyer feels it is worth something. He wants to get a little something out of it."

"No," I say, "It is too late."

At 2 o'clock, the court is reconvened. "Banc!" is hollered. We all 59 rise, then sit. The judge speaks to the jurors.

"Ladies and gentlemen, this case has been withdrawn." He thanks 60 them for their time and patience.

"Smile," my lawyer says. "You won." But I cannot smile. I feel no 61 elation.

It took the same amount of time for the whole world to be created as it 62 did to establish my innocence.

On the steps of the courthouse, my lawyer and I shake hands and say 63 goodbye. Can the gates of hell swing open so lightly?

Waiting nearby, the reporter from the newspaper. On his face, the 64 tiniest snake of a smile. "Congratulations," he says. "Do you wish to make a statement?" I search all over my mouth for a word or two, but there are none there.

From the courthouse, I walk up Church Street to where it flows 65 seamlessly into Whitney Avenue. At this point, there is a small triangular park islanded by thoroughfares on its three sides. Even in the spring, when the ornamental quince trees are in bloom, no one seems to sit there. This abandoned park constitutes a place outside the precincts of law and medicine, outside of time itself. I cross the street, push open the iron gate to the park and sit on one of the benches. It is cold, cold. The exhaust fumes are gathered and caught by the low evergreen shrubs. I cannot stop shivering. All at once, it occurs to me that it is over. I do not have to go back to that courtroom. I am free. Why do I not rejoice? What I feel is not relieved, only bruised.

I have learned that civilization, like this park, is a tiny island in a wild 66 sea. There is always the danger of being engulfed. And I now know for certain that I am no longer a doctor. The search I began for my father 50 years ago is ended. May he rest in peace.

In the newspaper that night, a small piece—"Malpractice Suit 67 Withdrawn"—with the insinuation that money must have been paid. The last rattle of the snake's tail.

## Post-Reading Questions

1. How is Selzer's essay organized? Why do you think he chose this organizational pattern?
2. How does knowing Selzer is a retired surgeon affect your reading of his essay? How does it make you feel about him and what he is saying? How did it affect his writing style and content? Does his writing remind you more of literature or journalism? Why?
3. Why do you think Selzer begins his essay by describing what happened to George Laszlo? Why do you think he did not begin by discussing his own case?
4. Write a brief summary of the malpractice case Selzer was involved in. Why was he being sued? By whom? How was the suit resolved?
5. Where in this essay does Selzer reveal his medical background? Give at least two examples. Where does Selzer indicate that he recognizes his readers may not share his medical knowledge? Give at least two examples.
6. How does Selzer feel about his experience? Where in the essay does Selzer reveal his feelings? Do you believe his feelings are justified? Why?
7. How would the widower of the patient Selzer treated have written this essay differently? What information would he have included that Selzer does not include? What information would he leave out that Selzer includes? How might his writing style have differed?
8. What insight into medical malpractice suits does Selzer's essay provide that you found helpful to you as a non-physician? Does the essay make you feel less or more sympathetic to physicians who are sued? Does it change your mind about how you feel about suing physicians? Why?
9. Do you believe laws should regulate how much doctors can be sued for in malpractice suits? What would be the positive and negative effects of legislating such limits?

# WILLIAM C. DEVRIES
# ON THE PHYSICIAN
# AND THE 'SPECTACULAR' CASE

## Pre-Reading Questions

1. What do you remember hearing or reading about the artificial hearts used to prolong the lives of victims of heart disease? How would you feel about being the recipient of such a life-sustaining device? Why?

2. How do you feel about the public's right to information about the progress of individuals being treated with innovative or "miracle" medical procedures? What information about the patient's condition, treatment, emotional state, and family should we be entitled to know? What information should be considered private or confidential? Why?

3. Do you think the media sensationalize medical news? Explain your answer by referring to the media's handling of at least one particular medical case or issue.

## THE PHYSICIAN, THE MEDIA,
## AND THE 'SPECTACULAR' CASE
### William C. DeVries, MD

The press came into the operating theatre 20 years ago when Christiaan  1
Barnard, MD, electrified the world by performing the first human heart transplant. Since then, physicians with a "spectacular" medical case have found themselves, their patients, and their projects in the unwavering spotlight of the press. In our media-intrusive society, the spectacular case confronts physician-researchers with dilemmas unknown to their professional forebears.

If the research happens to be conducted in the United States, the  2
problems—or opportunities—tend to be intensified. American press organizations are unique in that their freedom to report news is guaranteed by the national constitution, and freedom and protection from previous restraint cannot be limited by government. Legislation and judicial decisions during the past quarter century have tended to make reporters' access to information easier, and citizens' recourse in libel actions more difficult.

Consider these factors in relation to a spectacular, newsworthy  3
medical case, especially one where the medical research is funded by a publicly supported government agency, and the question, I submit, is no longer *whether* physicians will cooperate with the press, but *when, how,* and *to what degree* they will cooperate.

On balance, cooperating with the press is more advantageous to   4
everyone concerned than taking the opposite tack. Although cooperation
may entail some bother and risk, noncooperation may well be more
troublesome—if the flow of information is shut off, reporters may
infiltrate the hospital and publish all manner of unofficial comments from
uninformed sources. Incorrect information may be published just to get
the physician back on record—to deny the inaccuracies, if for no other
reason. This tactic was used effectively in the aftermath of the first
artificial heart implant in Utah. I had decided to release less information
to the media, and when I called a reporter to complain about an
error-filled article, he acknowledged the inaccuracies, but said he used
the only information he could get. He added that I would get accurate
coverage when I again released information to the press.

The American public's appetite for medical information is at an   5
all-time high. Recent surveys indicate that 40% of all stories in daily
newspapers are health related.[1] Clinical investigations that once took
place in relative obscurity (with release of details pending publication of
the outcome in the medical literature), are now monitored day by day,
sometimes hour by hour via the mass media.

Medicine is undergoing intense upheaval in its structure, as well as its   6
technologies. This is not happening quietly, and members of the medical
profession have become very public "public servants," although not
always by choice. Sometimes, this means serving the media, as Nelkin[2]
has pointed out:

> Those working on the costly frontiers of modern medicine must maintain
> their legitimacy and their sources of public support. Many researchers
> believe that scholarly communication is no longer sufficient to maintain
> their enterprise, that national visibility through the mass media is strategi-
> cally necessary to assure a favorable public image and adequate research
> support ... they employ sophisticated public relations techniques and
> communication controls to manage the news ... promising therapeutic
> advances and dramatic medical interventions are front-page news. The
> difficult ethical choices brought about by the increasingly sophisticated
> technological possibilities are of broad public interest.

Amid the pressures, physician-researchers must attempt to reconcile   7
conflicting obligations to their patient, the medical profession, and the
public. What is best for the principal investigator, the manufacturer, the
sponsoring hospitals, the press, the regulatory agencies, and society as a
whole? It is only realistic to expect that at least some of these considerations will make themselves felt; still, the single most important question
for physicians must remain: What is best for my patients?

While physicians grapple with such difficulties, the journalists have   8
troubling problems of their own: Where does the public's right to know

end and the rights of a suffering patient begin? Should those directly involved in the case be paid for their stories?

Issues, such as these, are examined in this essay. Recognize that the   9 perspective is a biased one, of a physician meeting the press and confronted with the novel challenge of dealing with a medically naive institution that nonetheless has a significant impact on the conduct of medical research.


## THE PHYSICIAN

> It is easier for eight or nine elderly men to feel their way towards unanimity if they are not compelled to conduct their converging maneuvers under the microscopes and telescopes of the press, but are permitted to shuffle about a little in slippers.
>                                    Herbert Albert Laurens Fisher[3]

Fisher was referring to the founders of the League of Nations, but he   10 could as easily have been talking about any group of professionals conducting an experiment. Certainly, his remarks apply to physicians. Not only is the medical profession more comfortable operating under its own governance, but it is relatively unaccustomed to being questioned by anyone, let alone the press.

This unwillingness to deal with the press could be rooted in the   11 traditional reticence of the medical profession when it comes to publicity; as recently as the late 1970s, by some accounts, medical students were *taught* that a physician's name should appear in the newspaper only at birth, marriage, and death. This training and its effects are brought forcibly home to physicians involved in a spectacular case. By cooperating with the media, physicians endanger their professional reputation, and their livelihood, by losing the respect of peers who accuse them of hyping whatever project has attracted the media's attention.

Tradition, however, is not the only reason physicians are reluctant to   12 cooperate with the press. Physicians may be in charge in the operating room, but the press is in charge during an interview. Someone else decides how much of an interview will be used, how it will be edited, who else will be asked to comment on the "physician's" story, and what weight their comments will be given.

Although physicians may prefer to withhold comment until comple-   13 tion of the investigation and publication of the results in a professional journal, physicians with a spectacular case are unlikely to have that option as a first choice. The press will come to physicians, who owe it to the patient, the project, and the medical profession to be prepared. Media involvement in a spectacular medical case will immediately raise five major concerns for physician-researchers: (1) the patient's privacy,

(2) the effects of the media on the treatment of the patient, (3) the integrity of the experiment, (4) hospital disruptions, and (5) the negative reactions of peers who will perceive physician-researchers as advertising or self-aggrandizing.

## Patient Privacy

Historically, the physician's protection of patient privacy was assumed, 14 even demanded as part of the physician-patient relationship. Today, the ancient principle of complete medical confidentiality no longer exists, and "efforts to preserve it appear doomed to failure and often give rise to more problems than solutions."[4] The publicity surrounding the total artificial heart implants—although well anticipated with a waiver of confidentiality included in each lengthy consent form[5]—has created as much controversy as the surgery itself. The patient may be offered substantial amounts of money by the media for exclusive rights to his or her story. This practice, becoming known as "checkbook journalism," could lead to a troubling scenario, ie, even if physicians choose not to cooperate with the press, the *patient* might well choose differently.

Patients do in fact have varying degrees of interest in cooperating 15 with the media. My first artificial heart patient, Dr. Barney Clark, endured the press because he believed his story could educate the public. William Schroeder, my second patient, enjoyed the press attention; Murray Haydon, the third recipient, chose to avoid it as best he was able. Physicians need to be sensitive to the patients' desires in this area, as well as realistic with them about potential media demands.

## Media Effects on Patient Care

Media interest may actually affect the treatment of a patient. Many 16 medical decisions are difficult in themselves, and the involvement of the press adds another complication—how will a decision be perceived by the reporter and presented to the public (including the physician's peers and the patient's family). Reflecting on the time when cardiac transplantation was "news," Dr. Christiaan Barnard described being able to obtain permission to recover the kidneys or corneas, but not the heart, from a teenage suicide victim. The reason, the father believed that if his daughter's heart was donated, media interest in this organ donation would also reveal the nature of her death and bring further disgrace on the family.[6]

This is not to imply that the effect of the media has been entirely 17 negative: wide publicity of the need for donor organs has benefited hundreds of patients. New regulations that require specific requests for organ donation at the time of death can be attributed to the concern of an informed public.

A more serious problem is the effect of media coverage on those 18
persons intimately involved in the experiment itself, especially the patient. The necessary strong tincture of positive thinking about a disease
process or complication may be diluted rapidly by a patient's chance
reading of the morning newspaper. Physicians are very careful about how
they present the facts to the patient and family. However, with a
newsworthy case, this communication is complicated by press reports
that may vary from those of the physicians, if not in content, then in
emphasis. I will never forget going into Bill Schroeder's room to explain
the news reports announcing his depression. He asked incredulously,
"Am I depressed? Is my life in danger from depression?"

## *Integrity of the Experiment*

While the effects of media coverage are difficult to quantify, discussing 19
results as they are generated rather than retrospectively at the conclusion
of the investigation can introduce an unpredictable factor into what
should be a controlled environment. If the commentary generated by
these disclosures is influential—if, for instance, physician-researchers are
tempted to modify procedures because of critique evolving from news
reports, the scientific data may become worthless, regardless of any
apparent therapeutic value for the patient. Thus, Joseph F. Boyle, MD,
former president of the American Medical Association (AMA) was not
entirely wrong when he said that experimental data should be saved for
publication in scientific journals when the experiment is over.[7] To release
this information beforehand may threaten the validity of the investigation. Talking publicly about the results as they are being generated
destroys objectivity.

Conversely, a valid point is made by Lawrence K. Altman, MD, 20
medical reporter for *The New York Times* (Dec 31, 1985, p 13):

> Suppressing publicity while waiting to publish the results in scientific lan-
> guage can be compared to publishing a scientific box score long after the
> event spectators were not allowed to witness is over. Human experimentation
> is serious public business, not entertainment. Unless daily accounts of im-
> portant ones (i.e., experimental procedures) are available, people not directly
> involved might not know significant details that could affect public policy.

Altman[8] also made the following point: "Mutual responsibility of 21
physicians and the press in reporting the news of medicine is vital to both
the progress of medicine and to the public's welfare."

Questions inevitably arise in every investigator's mind regarding the 22
release of data to the press. How is science best served? The medical
community is best prepared to analyze data that are presented in an

organized manner from hypothesis through methodology, results, and conclusions. After years of research, however, the resulting scientific publications tend to describe tersely the experiments and results but neglect to consider developmental problems encountered. In this process, generations of physicians come to believe that research is a clear-cut process, much more simple and direct than it really is. Does it then become "the business of the press to report the developments and steps, controversial or not, in the process of reporting such an historic case?"[8] Perhaps the lengthy diaries of old, which have so enriched medical history, should return to vogue.

It is one of the ironies of being involved in a spectacular medical case that physician-researchers are simultaneously criticized by some members of the profession for cooperating with the press and by others for not publishing project data "even though this data is incomplete information from on-going studies."[9] This public demand for publication of findings has been peculiar to the artificial heart project; while premature publication may have had some immediate advantages, certain research priorities would have been jeopardized.

*Hospital Disruptions*

Running a hospital in a highly competitive market forces administrators to seek avenues to distinguish themselves from other institutions.[10] In this respect, the University of Utah Medical Center, Salt Lake City, and Humana Heart Institute International, Louisville, are involved in the same business practices. Each would like to be recognized as outstanding in the health care industry, with commitments to science and teaching, as well as to high-quality care. The artificial heart project is exciting and attractive; it has the potential to make an institution stand out as "the" hospital in town and to attract more students to the university or more patients to the hospital and, thus, greater profit and positive recognition (*The Washington Post*, Nov 27, 1984, p 1).

Despite the potential benefits that might accrue, a large-scale press onslaught is not without problems. The snowbound cadre of almost 300 reporters who camped in the main cafeteria at the University of Utah Hospital to cover the first permanent total artificial heart implant was, not surprisingly, far more disruptive than either the required physical plant alterations or the changes in patient monitoring and care. Patients, their families and visitors, and hospital staff had a difficult time with a simple lunch; many (unrelated to the case) were accosted by reporters seeking information. Police were stationed outside the intensive care unit to discourage the curious. One reason Humana established a downtown media center away from the hospital was to lessen the confusion at their institution until press interest diminished.

*Peer Reactions*

> In the life of every successful physician there comes the temptation to toy with the Delilah of the press—daily and otherwise. There are times when she may be courted with satisfaction, but beware! Sooner or later she is sure to play the harlot, and has left many a man shorn of his strength, viz, the confidence of his professional brethren.
>
> Sir William Osler[11]

Osler's statement rang true for me. In the wake of Dr. Clark's 26 surgery, some physicians in Salt Lake City stopped referring patients to me for cardiac surgery. At the height of media interest in Mr. Schroeder's implant, Joseph Boyle, MD, then president of the AMA, was quoted in newspapers around the world as saying that news coverage of the artificial heart surgery had created a "circus" atmosphere, and he called for AMA-sanctioned guidelines to govern "the apparent commercialization of this whole process by widespread publicity."[7] Others in the profession joined in taking the position that cooperating with the media, to the extent of responding to reporters' questions in news conferences, was tantamount to seeking publicity. Similar—and similarly unfair—charges were leveled against Leonard Bailey, MD, during the "Baby Fae" case and against Jack Copeland, MD, after his first use of an artificial heart as a bridge to transplant.

Although at times hard to take, review by one's peers is indispensable 27 to researchers. Our project has benefited from the professional review and critique to which it has been subjected.[12] What may be dispensable, however, are media-generated requests to one physician to critique another's work. While physicians have an ethical obligation to the public, as well as to the profession, to be well informed, to render an "expert" opinion, public "professional vulturism" violates ethical principles within the medical profession.

## THE MEDIA

> It is impossible to keep the media on a leash of predetermined length.
> Ted Koppel, *Viewpoint*, Louisville,
> Feb 7, 1985

Medical professionals have largely ignored the popular press as a 28 means of disseminating research findings; thus, physicians can be at a disadvantage in dealing with reporters covering a spectacular case. Physicians are not trained to relate to the media. As highly skilled professionals who have been allowed to practice only after years of arduous study, physicians may think of reporters in the same terms—as members of a monolithic profession dedicated to upholding a narrow set of standards, inculcated in them during their years of training. In fact, however, the standards and interests of news organizations vary incredibly, and reporters' approaches to a story reflect that diversity.

A local newspaper needs a local angle: "Does the patient have any 29 relatives here in East Overshoe?" The radio reporter needs a sound-bite: "Doctor, I know you just answered this question, but the guy next to me was talking and I didn't get it clearly. Would you repeat your answer?" The reporter from the supermarket tabloid wants drama and conflict, the more macabre, the better: "What did Dr. Clark look like when you turned off his artificial heart?" The feature writer wants the "soft" side of the story, the human detail: "Did Mrs. Schroeder cry when you told her Bill came through the operation all right?"

When the stories eventually appear, the diversity reflected by ques- 30 tions posed at a press conference comes astoundingly to life. It is sometimes hard to believe the reports all have to do with the same case. The press, one discovers, is like the Cheshire cat in *Alice's Adventures in Wonderland:* you can see the smile, and the teeth, but you never know where the body is.

The many media teams covering a spectacular case compete intensely 31 for innovative ways of *reporting, telling,* and *selling* the story.[10] At times, they highlight seemingly unimportant events for unknown reasons. The medical team experiencing the story as it unfolds remains bewildered, wondering if the reporters really want to get at the heart of the story or would rather tiptoe around the edges looking for a dramatic detail that nobody else has.[10, 13]

Physicians involved in a spectacular case are often criticized for 32 underestimating the media—minimizing its persistence and ferocity when aroused,[14] and most importantly, its capacity to help decide the fate of an experiment by influencing public opinion. Care must also be taken not to overestimate the media. Stories in the press are no substitute for the physician-researcher's eventual reports in the medical literature. Ultimately, however, the researcher's and the reporter's interests in an experiment—especially an experiment drawn out over time, with many patients and many ups and downs—are at odds.

First, the reporter must satisfy the demands of an episodic medium, 33 ie, the hourly radio news report, the nightly television show, or the daily newspaper. The experiment is described in a series of pieces, sometimes connected, sometimes not.

Second, every report must have an attention-getting "lead," even if 34 the experiment does not supply one. The media acts on extremes, running the catchy headline, the exciting first line, spectacularizing however slightly to sell newspapers, up the ratings, improve their professional standing, or simply "one-up" each other (*The Wall Street Journal,* March 1, 1985).[10] This is why a headline about a rise in Mr. Schroeder's temperature might have been followed the next day by a headline about the delivery of a case of beer from a well-wisher. It is not that Mr. Schroeder's temperature had necessarily gone back to normal—it might, indeed, have gone up—but rather that, having reported the rise already, it would not do to report it again so prominently so soon. The news is, above all, new.

The greatest impact of media coverage, however, has been the effect on public and professional perception of the investigation. Since media reports must be simplified for the audience, the conclusions drawn are often simplistic. What is intended to be a long experimental series is assessed on a case-by-case, quality-of-life basis. If a patient does well, the experimental device must be good. If the patient dies in a week, it must be bad. 35

If many other experiments in the recent history of medicine had been subjected to the kind of scrutiny the artificial heart has received, we might today be without the following: dialysis, which did not succeed until the 17th patient; mitral commissurotomy, which did not succeed until the fifth patient and numbered only five successes among the first 15 patients; and cardiopulmonary bypass, which succeeded on the first patient but failed on four subsequent patients.[15] This list could go on and would include cardiac valve replacement, pacemakers, intra-aortic balloon pumps, arterial grafts, and organ transplantation—in the field of cardiothoracic surgery alone. 36

These procedures now save thousands of lives each year, but it took time and the courage of countless patients to perfect them. These medical advances took years to come to fruition, and might not have occurred at all, if their initial success rate had been the deciding factor in their development.[16] "Spin-off advances," which sometimes came about as a direct result of perceived failures, would have been lost permanently to science and to mankind. Temporary use of the artificial heart as a bridge to transplantation, an application predicated on the permanent experience, has currently allowed over 30 patients to survive until a donor heart was available. 37

Despite the problems it may have caused us, we fully recognize that we can neither ignore nor disdain the impact of the media. There is no better way to inform the public about medical progress. Physician-researchers benefit directly in terms of public acceptance, foundation grants, and government support when reports of their work are published and broadcast. The public benefits indirectly when it becomes more educated about health matters. Reports about the artificial heart informed vast numbers of scientifically unsophisticated persons about the workings of the heart and the threats posed by poor dietary habits, cigarette smoking, insufficient exercise, and certain inherited factors. Even the adverse consequences had a positive impact on the general populace. When Mr. Schroeder suffered a stroke, for example, a Louisville television station put together an excellent segment on what a stroke is, what it means for the patient and the family, and how to get help. The 38 dignity of the professions of medicine and journalism—their compassion and utility—is enhanced by reporting of this kind.

## THE SPECTACULAR CASE

What was it about the human heart that so excited people?
Dr. Christiaan Barnard[17]

It is no surprise that the idea of a man-made replacement for the 39 human heart caught the imagination of the storytellers of today—the press. Because of the mythical and societal values associated with the heart, heart research occupies a unique position in the scientific community. It has been said that, "At a symbolic level, the [artificial] heart is a sign of the expectations of the American public and of medical and scientific researchers."[18] The artificial heart story touches on such diverse topics as government influence in medical research, medical education, the role of private enterprise in medical research, the right to life, and the right to die.[7] It illuminates the fight for existence that begins at birth and ends at death, and the extremes to which we will go to win this losing battle. It is the stuff of which unlikely, but all the more compelling, heroes are made. Most of the recipients publicly acknowledged that if they must die, they would do so in an effort that would generate knowledge that might benefit mankind.

Every human is threatened by another's suffering, fascinated by the 40 struggle with death, and—with the story of the artificial heart— simultaneously repelled and attracted by the idea that humans could have the audacity to replace the human heart with a device made of metal and plastic.

In our experience, everyone wanted to see the artificial heart 41 patients, meet them, touch them, photograph them, and wish them well. Nurses were proud to be the first to deal with such unusual patients, medical students clamored to join physicians on rounds to see the patients, and housekeepers lingered in their rooms.

It was, in the parlance of journalists, "a good story," and it is a story 42 that may belong as much to the media as to medicine.

## CONCLUSION

If we are to assume that there is a necessary symbiosis in present-day 43 relations between physicians and the media, there are three principles that appear to be in the interests of both parties:

1.  Concern for the patient and family is paramount. It takes precedence over the public's right to know, because a human

being is not public property. In interactions with the media, physician-researchers should distinguish between the project-oriented aspects of the story, which may be disclosed, and the patient-oriented ones, which should be discretionary.

2.   Accuracy is nonnegotiable. Neither the press nor the medical staff can be excused for the release of inaccurate information. All suffer when this occurs, and all must bear the consequences.

3.   Advance preparation is essential. Before the spectacular medical event occurs, the hospital and researchers should develop a team to handle the logistics of reporting the news quickly and accurately. A medical spokesperson, preferably a physician not directly involved in the experiment, should be appointed and trained. He or she should act as a liaison among the hospital, the researchers, and the media. Similarly, the media representatives need to be prepared as well. A tremendous effort was made at the University of Utah and at Humana to educate the press in advance. In our opinion, those who participated in these advance briefings benefited themselves and their audiences.

Constant adherence to the above principles is not easy, but it is, I believe, good for medicine and good for journalism. There remain many problems to be resolved between physicians with newsworthy accomplishments and the media representatives clamoring to report on these. Above all, we need to demand responsible behavior from each other and to respect the goals that each seeks to achieve. I believe Keith Reemtsma, MD,[19] was speaking for many of us when he said: [44]

> I can say that we certainly want greater public understanding of our work, of the success we've been able to achieve in this field. . . . However, we must balance this with respect for the privacy of our patients and their families, and the need to treat what seem to be major advances with caution, restraining our excitement until they are proven and available.

## REFERENCES

1. Hicks N: 1986 newspaper survey by Hill and Knowlton Hospital Marketing and Communications Services. *Hospitals* 1986;60:6.
2. Nelkin D: Managing biomedical news. *Soc Res* 1985;52:625-646.
3. Fisher Hal: *The International Experiment.* Oxford, England, Clarendon Press, 1921, pp 1-40.
4. Siegler M: Confidentiality in medicine: A decrepit concept. *N Engl J Med* 1982;307:1518-1521.
5. *Special Consent for the Implantation of the Total Artificial Heart and Related Procedures.* Salt Lake City, University of Utah, 1983, section 13.0.
6. Barnard C: Distinguished Lecture Series, Dallas, Southern Methodist University, Sept 30, 1986.

7. Boyle JF: Address before the 38th Interim Meeting of the American Medical Association's House of Delegates, Honolulu, Dec 2, 1984.
8. Altman LK: Communicating with the public: A physician's responsibility. *Bull Am Coll Physicians* 1976;8:6-10.
9. Pennington G: Statement of Dr Glenn Pennington, chairman of Society of Thoracic Surgery Ad Hoc Committee on Circulatory Assist Devices and Artificial Hearts. US Food and Drug Administration: Open Public Hearing and Open Committee Discussion, FDA Circulatory System and Cardiovascular Devices Advisory Panel, Hearing on Artificial Heart Implants, Dec 20, 1985.
10. Winsten JA: Sciences and the media: The boundaries of truth. *Health Aff,* spring 1985, p 14.
11. Osler W: *Aequanimitas With Other Addresses: Internal Medicine as a Vocation.* Philadelphia, P Blakistone Son & Co, 1905.
12. DeVries WC: The technological, economic, social and ethical questions raised by the artificial heart program: 'Status of the artificial heart program,' in *Hearings Before the Subcommittee on Investigations and Oversight of the Committee on Science and Technology,* US House of Representatives, 99th Congress, Second Session, 1986, p 212.
13. Goodell R: What's a nice scientist doing in a place like the press? in *The Visible Scientist.* Boston, Little Brown & Co, Inc., 1977, pp 120-162.
14. Metherell M: Doctor bashing: Tall poppies or tall stories? *Med J Aust* 1984; 141:846-847.
15. Comroe JH Jr: Courage to fail, in: *Retrospectroscope: Insights Into Medical Discovery.* Menlo Park, Calif, Von Gehr Press, 1977, p 131.
16. Swazey JP, Watkins JC, Fox RC: Assessing the artificial heart: The clinical moratorium revisited. *Int J Technol Assessment Health Care* 1982; 2:387-410.
17. Barnard C: *One Life.* New York, Macmillan Publishing Co, Inc, 1970, p 435.
18. Simmons PD: Ethical considerations of artificial heart implantations. *Ann Clin Lab Sci* 1986;16:1-12.
19. Reemtsma K: Introductory remarks to Arden House Conference on Organ Recovery and Organ Transplantation, Harrison, NY, Dec 8, 1985.

## Post-Reading Questions

1. What does DeVries mean by a "spectacular" medical case? In addition to the artificial heart, what other medical cases might DeVries categorize as spectacular? Why?

2. Summarize DeVries' reasons for and against releasing medical information to the media. How do you feel about those reasons? Which make more sense to you? Why? Which make less sense? Why?

3. Why did DeVries write this essay? What position is he trying to persuade his readers to accept? How do you know?

4. How would DeVries' work with artificial heart patients have influenced his position on releasing medical information to the media? What personal insights into his experiences does he share with his readers? Why does he share those particular insights?

5. This essay appeared in *JAMA,* a journal published by the American Medical Association. What does this fact tell you about DeVries' readers? What kind of readers could he have imagined? In what ways would your reading of this essay be different than theirs? Why?

6. In your own words, summarize DeVries' views on physicians' responsibilities to their patients, the press, and the medical profession. What factors influenced the development of his views? Why?

7. What ethical issues raised in this essay also apply to medical cases not considered spectacular? Give an example for each issue you identify.

8. How could you find out the treatment the artificial heart cases received in print media (newspapers, periodicals, journals)? Write a paragraph describing the research process you would use to answer this question. How would conducting such a research project help you evaluate the arguments DeVries makes in this essay?

9. Examine the references listed at the end of the essay. What do they tell you about DeVries, the journal, and his readers? Do the articles mentioned in the list of references seem to have "sensationalized" the cases involved? Explain your answer.

10. Identify a current medical case or disease that receives a great deal of media attention. What kind of attention does it receive? In what ways is that treatment similar to and different from the treatment DeVries describes? What accounts for these similarities and differences?

# WILLIAM A. NOLEN ON MEDICAL ZEALOTS

## Pre-Reading Questions

1. Do you think people have a tendency to place doctors on pedestals? Drawing from your own experiences, describe the way you and other members of your family feel about doctors in general. Why do you and the other members of your family feel as you do?

2. What does the word "zealot" mean to you? If you are unfamiliar with it, check a dictionary for the meaning. Describe the qualities you would find in a zealot. How could a doctor be a zealot? Would a doctor-zealot have a positive or negative connotation for you? Why?

## MEDICAL ZEALOTS
### William A. Nolen

Over the last few years the general public has been deluged with medical    1
information. One has only to turn on one's television set to the evening
news to hear the newscaster say something like, "Rebellion in South

Africa; Congress to vote on farm bill; stocks hit new high; doctor in Oregon claims thousands of unnecessary operations for low-back pain are being done every year—all this, and the weather, too, in the next half hour."

When, twenty minutes later, we get to the doctor in Oregon, he is given ninety seconds to explain why he thinks too many back operations are being performed. He tries to discuss the subject intelligently, but the problem of low-back pain and its proper treatment is controversial and complex, and in ninety seconds he can barely mention physiotherapy, enzyme injection, manipulation, disk surgery, acupuncture, and the half-dozen or so other methods of available treatment. What's more, it is often left unclear whether the doctor is a rheumatologist, an osteopath, an orthopedist, a chiropractor, or perhaps even a quack with a Ph.D. from some completely unaccredited institution in California (a state that seems to be waist deep in unaccredited institutions). We are certainly likely to emerge with no idea whether his contention that back surgery is being overdone is based on comprehensive statistical studies or is simply his opinion based on personal prejudice or experience. This bit of medical "information" is likely to leave the viewer more confused than enlightened. The viewer still does not know what, if anything, he ought to do about his backache. And if he is scheduled to have an operation for low-back pain in the next few days, this television snippet may raise his anxiety level to astounding heights.

That there is among the general public a thirst for medical news is undeniable. Television stations, magazines, and newspapers regularly run surveys to see what their viewers and readers want; if no one wanted medical news, one can be sure it would disappear. Every woman's magazine runs at least one medical column a month (for twelve years, 1970–1982, I myself wrote "A Doctor's World," a sort of "disease of the month" column for *McCall's*). I did not realize quite how far this thirst for medical information had gone until, one afternoon in October of 1985, I happened to step into the Kroch's & Brentano's bookstore near the Palmer House in Chicago and found a hefty stack of the current issue of the *New England Journal of Medicine* on the newsstand. Suffice it to say that at least half of the physicians I know find the scientific articles in the *New England Journal* too esoteric (and complicated) for their tastes. I find it difficult to believe that anyone without a formal medical education could read or understand these articles, yet there they were. I don't imagine that Kroch's & Brentano's would grant them shelf space if they didn't sell.

This thirst for medical knowledge would, of course, be harmless— might even be good—if we could be sure that the medical information the public was receiving was accurate; but we can't be sure. In fact, I know that the taste for the sensational leads to the distribution of a great deal of medical misinformation to the public—not only in papers like the

*National Enquirer,* where no one in his right mind expects scientific accuracy—but on respectable or semi-respectable television shows, regional and national. I could, for example, cite a segment of "Sixty Minutes"—the producers of "Sixty Minutes" are particularly adept at implying things without specifically saying them—that more or less promoted a kooky cancer treatment center in the Bahamas as a possible salvation for desperate cancer victims. But it would take too long and might seem self-serving (I made a personal investigation of the center and found the treatment it dispensed was worthless). Rather, I shall try to make my point by using examples of medical misinformation that have emanated from highly respected medical centers. If these centers can produce nonsense, one would be foolish to pay much attention to medical data that comes from sources with a significantly lesser degree of medical credibility.

"The most difficult thing in the world to prove is something that is    5 untrue." I don't know who first said that, but whoever it was didn't take physicians into account. We have little difficulty proving that the untrue is true. Consider, for example, the October 24, 1985, issue of the *New England Journal of Medicine,* easily the most prestigious and highly respected of all American medical journals. In that issue are two articles, one of which proves beyond a reasonable doubt that by giving female hormones to postmenopausal women you can "substantially" protect them against heart attacks. The second article, equally well substantiated, proves that if you give female hormones to postmenopausal women you "substantially" increase their chances of having a heart attack.

It is obvious that one of these articles is flawed—or, to put it more    6 bluntly, wrong. The editors of the *Journal* ("the *Journal*" in medical circles always refers to the *New England Journal of Medicine*), being very intelligent physicians, realized, of course, that one of these articles was wrong; but neither they nor their "referees" (experts in the subject written about who scrutinize articles before they are accepted for publication) could find a significant flaw in either article. Therefore, they published them both. In addition, they published an editorial by one of their consulting experts who wrote, among other things, "I simply cannot tell from the present evidence whether these hormones add to the risk of cardiovascular disease, diminish the risk, or leave it unchanged, and must resort to the investigator's great cop out: More research is needed." From the practical point of view, this negated the proposed effect of both articles. A doctor in clinical practice, having labored through both articles, still wouldn't know whether he ought to tell his women patients if it was safe to take "the pill." But, whatever advice the physician gave her, he could back it up with an appropriate scientific article.

It seems to me likely that this is an illustration of one of the problems    7 that afflict medical research; researchers have often decided what they are convinced is true before they embark on the research. One noted professor of surgery (who shall remain nameless because he is deceased) was widely known as a man who would often assign a surgical resident or two to the dog laboratory for six months with instructions to prove some thesis or other true, usually that a clever new operative procedure would cure one or another disease. And woe unto the resident who emerged six months later to report that the operation the professor had devised did not achieve what it was supposed to achieve. That resident would, in all probability, spend his remaining years of surgical training in some small community hospital. If you couldn't prove what the Chief wanted you to prove, what good were you?

One flagrant example of this sort of thinking is the relationship 8 between cigarette smoking and lung cancer. There is little doubt in my mind or in the minds of thousands of doctors who have studied lung cancer that cigarette smoking is linked with lung cancer. There are probably very few lay people who do not assume that it has been proven that cigarette smoking causes lung cancer. When the cigarette companies run advertisements implying that the link has not been as solidly established as the medical profession claims, one wants to go after the executives of the cigarette companies with machetes. How can these people be so callous as to put their economic self-interest ahead of the misery and suffering of those afflicted by that dread cancer?

The fact is, however, that no one has yet proven—in the strict scientific 9 sense of the word—that cigarette smoking causes lung cancer. A few years ago, in their zeal to establish this claim as fact, doctors from the American Cancer Society called a well-publicized press conference at which they announced that they had, in fact, proven that cigarette smoking caused lung cancer in dogs. If they could prove cigarettes caused lung cancer in dogs, we were supposed to accept the fact that, by extrapolation, it caused lung cancer in humans. This is not something one automatically does in science—species differences mean that what happens in one species does not necessarily happen in another—but we can hardly demand that an attempt be made to use cigarettes to produce lung cancer in humans. What the Cancer Society doctors had done was perform tracheotomies on a breed of beagles and force the beagles to smoke several packages of cigarettes a day for several months. The doctors then sacrificed the beagles and found changes in their lungs that the researchers called "pre-cancerous." This was their "proof" that cigarette smoking caused lung cancer.

Once the hullabaloo of the press conference was over, experts who 10 were not associated with the American Cancer Society reviewed the beagle research and found it so flawed as to be worthless. Among other things, the Cancer Society people had chosen a species of beagle that was genetically prone to the development of lung tumors, and the tumors found in their dogs were no different either in type or in number from the tumors that non-smoking beagles of the same species developed. The presentation by the American Cancer Society had been so widely publicized that, apparently, the doctors who found the evidence flawed were reluctant to embarrass their colleagues by criticizing them too loudly. In any event, I think it's safe to say that most of the general public—and many if not most physicians—were left with the impression that the American Cancer Society had proven that cigarette smoking causes cancer. That wasn't true then (about 1965), and it isn't true now.

In fact, if one looks at some of the evidence collected by the cigarette 11 companies, one can hardly fail to find it interesting. For example, between 1930 and 1960 the incidence of lung cancer in human residents of Philadelphia, Pennsylvania, went up significantly. Since cigarette smoking was increasing in popularity at that time, the anti-cigarette people were tempted to attribute the lung cancer to the cigarettes. Unfortunately, for their purposes, between 1901 and 1964 every animal that died in the Philadelphia Zoo was autopsied, and guess what? The incidence of lung cancer in the zoo animals increased at almost exactly the same rate as in humans. In fact, in fourteen types of animals (those that spent almost all their time in the open air), the incidence of lung cancer between 1934 and 1962 was six times greater than in the previous twenty-eight years. Need I say that the zoo animals did not smoke? It is also true that, although the British smoke far more cigarettes per capita than we do in the United States, the incidence of lung cancer in England is lower than it is in the United States. If cigarettes cause lung cancer, how do we explain this discrepancy?

I am not an advocate of cigarette smoking. I am convinced that 12 cigarette smoking makes one more likely to get bronchitis, emphysema, heart disease, and, yes, lung cancer. But for the medical profession to insist that cigarette smoking, in and of itself, causes lung cancer is simply dishonest. It hasn't been proven, and no one should claim that it has. . . .

In 1984 the results of an extensive long-term study by many 13 cooperating hospitals was published in the *Journal of the American Medical Association*. It delighted the anti-cholesterol doctors because it showed that after five years the incidence of coronary artery disease in a group of patients who took medications designed to lower blood cholesterol was lower than in those patients who did not take these drugs. Unfortunately, what was also mentioned—though certainly not emphasized—was that the death rates in the two groups were the same. Since the deaths of the drug takers were, in the main, attributed to accidents, the researchers chose to ignore them. However, in a letter to the *J.A.M.A.* (February 1985) a physician on the staff of the Helsinki University Psychiatric Clinic pointed out:

> There have recently been findings that impulsive homicidal and suicidal aspects can be connected with low cholesterol levels, although the exact reason for these findings is unclear. Also, low serum cholesterol levels have

been found to be related to poorly internalized social norms, irresponsibility, and poor self-control. And one earlier coronary heart project, which used prisoners as a control group, found that the prisoners had very low cholesterol levels and small variance in cholesterol level. So "there is the possibility that the high figure of violent and accidental deaths was not a matter of chance but the result of cholesterol lowering or some metabolic aspects connected with this, making some males more prone to impulsive violent death."

The benefits gained from taking anti-cholesterol drugs (which are, 14 incidentally, not only expensive but terribly distasteful) are perhaps more apparent than real. Instead of dying of a heart attack, you may die in a car accident; or, if you live, you might spend the rest of your life in prison. In fact, for those of us over age forty-five, a recently published study (*J.A.M.A.*, October 18, 1985) seems to make it not only useless but dangerous to try to avoid heart attacks. In this study 1,604 men between the ages of thirty-nine and fifty-four, all of whom were free of cardiovascular disease but who had at least one risk factor (i.e., elevated blood pressure, high blood cholesterol, obesity, cigarette smoking, etc.) were divided into two roughly equal groups. One group was given counseling and appropriate medication, including cholesterol-lowering drugs; the second group was left to go its merry way. Five years later the two groups were compared. The incidence of heart attacks in the treated group was twice as high as in the nontreated group (3.1% vs. 1.5%). Why? The investigators could only guess: "The possibility cannot be excluded that harmful side effects of the drugs used in the program outweighed the benefits of the improved risk factor profile."

I have no desire to belittle the researchers who are working so 15 diligently to make our lives longer and more comfortable. I am simply advising readers that they should take medical news, particularly that which seems on the surface to be a bit farfetched, "cum grano salis," as Stephen Potter was wont to say. For example, recently we have been notified, on the basis of one study, that we may increase the chance of developing heart disease if we drink more than two cups of coffee a day. If you like coffee, and it doesn't bother you (give you heartburn, make you jumpy, or cause insomnia) then you should ignore this warning. The evidence that it will lead to heart disease is thin and equivocal at best. I would guess that within a year or two someone else will prove there is no correlation between coffee drinking and heart disease. Someone may even "prove" that coffee helps prevent heart attacks. (You may recall that about five years ago we were warned that coffee drinking might lead to cancer of the pancreas. That theory has long since been discarded.)

I would also ignore the dangers supposedly inherent in secondhand 16 cigarette smoking. In fact, I do ignore it. I have heart disease—I have twice had coronary artery bypass operations, equipping me with six bypasses—and my wife smokes two packages of cigarettes a day, but I certainly have no intention of deserting our home to avoid the smoke that, I suppose, swirls in the air of our domicile. I simply don't believe it hurts me at all, and I have read nothing in the medical literature that persuades me to the contrary.

There are in the medical profession a good number of zealots. These 17 doctors are absolutely convinced that they know the best rules for the human race to live by, from the physical point of view. (They are comparable to religious zealots who are certain they know how we should live morally and spiritually.) They don't lie—they don't even intentionally exaggerate—but their enthusiasm sometimes carries them away so that they claim more for their research than the results actually warrant. Because many of them are researchers in the academic world, they are eager to publish their results and, if possible, to be the first to do so. Sometimes, despite relatively close scrutiny by the editors of the medical journals, "breakthrough" material is published prematurely that later has to be recanted. One of the major monthly surgical journals used to run a regular "reappraisal" section in which some expert would take a second look at a "breakthrough" that had been published a year or two earlier. Often this reappraisal would amount to a negation of the previous article.

What may be most germane to readers of this article is this: At the 18 moment there is no persuasive evidence that those of us leading lives of relative moderation can increase our well-being or prolong our lives by radically changing our style of living. Most of us know that it is not only unsightly but unhealthy to be grossly overweight; we all realize that at least a minimal amount of exercise is probably good for us; smoking three packages of cigarettes a day is certainly not going to do our health any good. But the evidence that moderate amounts of cholesterol will hurt us, that vigorous regular exercise will add to our longevity, or that two or three cigarettes a day will cause lung cancer simply does not exist.

Most of us pay little or no serious attention to the messages of the 19 religious evangelists who flood the radio and television airwaves every Sunday morning. We should be equally wary of the medical evangelists. A white coat and a stethoscope don't necessarily endow the owner with common sense.

## Post-Reading Questions

1.  In your own words, explain Nolen's main point (thesis). Where in his essay does he state the thesis for the first time? How convincing is Nolen? Explain why you were or were not convinced.
2.  Describe the strategy Nolen uses to introduce his essay. Why do you think he chose to begin the essay this way?

3. What kind of evidence does Nolen use to develop his ideas? Where does his evidence come from? What do his choices tell you about his background?

4. Where does Nolen demonstrate that he is writing for readers who may not be familiar with specialized medical vocabulary? Be specific. How could he revise this essay for a journal such as *The New England Journal of Medicine*?

5. Do you believe that the public gets enough, too much, or too little medical information from the media? Explain your answer using your own experiences and some information Nolen presents in his essay.

6. How does Nolen define a medical zealot? Do you agree with his definition? Does he convince you that some physicians are zealots? Why or why not?

7. How might medical information the public obtains from the media be harmful? Describe a real or imagined situation in which medical information obtained from the media was actually harmful. Who was harmed? How? Why?

8. What issues related to medical research and how it is conducted are raised directly or indirectly in this essay? Make a list of two or three of these issues. Write them as questions that could be answered in at least two different ways.

9. In what ways would a physician and a non-physician respond differently to Nolen's essay? What would explain the differences in their reading experiences?

10. Look at the last paragraph of Nolen's essay. Why do you think Nolen ended the essay this way? What is he trying to accomplish? How successful, in your opinion, is he? Why?

# ROBERT M. SWENSON ON EPIDEMICS

## Pre-Reading Questions

1. Would knowing someone had tested positive for HIV affect how you relate to that person? Why? How has the AIDS epidemic changed your attitudes or behaviors?

2. Evaluate America's response to AIDS. Do you believe the government (federal, state, local) has responded ethically and effectively? How do you feel about the way the media portray AIDS? How has the administration of your college responded to AIDS? What could or should be done that is not done, in your opinion?

3. If you have attended a presentation on AIDS in school or at work, describe what you were told and what you think the underlying message of the presentation was.

# EPIDEMICS AND HISTORY
## Robert M. Swenson

Infectious diseases have had a major influence on Western history. [1] Although epidemics have been frequent and devastating, one can categorize easily the small number of different ways in which epidemics have produced these effects. The first of these is through a widespread epidemic affecting the entire population relatively uniformly, resulting in the disruption of social structures and in long-term historical change. The most obvious, and perhaps only, example of this is the epidemic of bubonic plague that occurred in Europe in the fourteenth century. Epidemics may also have markedly different effects on different populations, resulting in significant shifts in the previous balance of power. The importation of smallpox into the Central American Indian population by the Spanish is a dramatic example of this effect. Many military battles, in which one military force is more severely affected than the other, can be viewed as a more common example of this phenomenon. In the last 150 years, many smaller epidemics have produced change through laws enacted in response to the epidemic. Many of our present-day public health laws were enacted during the recurrent cholera epidemics in the United States and England in the mid-nineteenth century.

The most recent worldwide epidemic was the outbreak of influenza [2] A that swept the world in 1918–19. The first cases of influenza were recognized at Camp Funston, Kansas. Two months later massive epidemics began in Spain, France, and England. The attack rates (number of cases per one hundred people) were extremely high, particularly among young adults. Despite massive public health measures, influenza spread rapidly throughout the world. By the time the pandemic ended in 1919, there had been one million deaths in the United States, ten million in India, and an estimated thirty million deaths throughout the world. Despite being the largest epidemic in history, it had little long-term effect, because, unlike the plague epidemic, the influenza epidemic was relatively short-lived and the population losses were rapidly replaced. (It seems callous, but it is true to say that the population itself is our most easily replaced resource.)

Throughout history, infectious diseases have had a major effect on [3] military battles. Frequently, one army has suffered from disease more severely than the opposing force, drastically altering the outcome of the battle. In general, since the defending forces tend to be more resistant to their own endemic diseases, this differential effect is most marked on the invading force. A dramatic example occurred during Napoleon's invasion of Russia.

In June 1812, Napoleon assembled an army of almost five hundred [4] thousand men to invade Russia. While traveling through Poland and western Russia, almost half of his troops died or were immobilized by typhus. By the time Napoleon began his retreat from Moscow, only eighty thousand able-bodied men remained. These catastrophic losses continued, and by June 1813 only three thousand soldiers remained alive to complete the retreat. The vast majority of deaths were the result of typhus and dysentery rather than battle injuries or exposure to the severe Russian winter. Thus, the power of Napoleon in Europe was broken more by diseases, especially typhus, than by military opposition.

From the mid-nineteenth century to the present, as government 5 bureaucracies became larger and took control of more of society's functions, much smaller epidemics produced change through the legislation enacted in response to the epidemics. The cholera epidemics in the United States in 1832, 1849, and 1866 provide excellent examples of these changes.

The largest cholera epidemic began in 1832. The city of New 6 Orleans was hardest hit with five thousand cases. By historical standards, this was a very small epidemic, but it engendered the clear beginnings of public health policy. In early 1832, the New York state legislature passed laws enabling communities to establish local boards of health, and in the summer of 1832 the New York City Board of Health was created. Quarantine regulations were passed and enforced. Cholera hospitals were established. Housing and care for the destitute were set up. Slum clearance was begun, and early efforts of food and drug control were undertaken. As the epidemic subsided, however, the government felt that these measures were no longer necessary, and the New York City Board was disbanded.

In 1854 John Snow demonstrated that cholera was spread through 7 the contaminated water supply. By 1866 few physicians doubted that cholera was portable and transmissible. With the threat of a third cholera epidemic, New York State then passed a law creating the Metropolitan Sanitary District and Board of Health in New York City. This first strong, permanent board of health in the United States exists to this day. The sanitary and public health measures were similar to those employed in 1832 but were more extensive and rigidly enforced. They were also much more effective, as only 591 cases of cholera occurred in New York City during this epidemic. Many of these regulations remain in effect and form the basis of present-day public health policy.

One can also examine what I have referred to as the internal anatomy 8 of an epidemic, by which I mean the behavioral response of both individuals and society to a given epidemic. It soon becomes apparent that there are certain attitudes and behaviors that recur during all epidemics.

First is the denial that the disease in question is even occurring. On 9 June 26, 1832, the first cases of cholera developed in New York City. When the New York Medical Society stated publicly that these nine cases had been diagnosed, the announcement was immediately attacked by New Yorkers who felt it was premature or unwarranted. Business leaders were particularly upset, realizing that even the fear of cholera and a possible quarantine would be disastrous for the city's business. Not until six weeks later, when the evidence of the epidemic could no longer be suppressed, was it officially recognized by the New York Board of Health. Denial also occurs at a national level. Following the initial outbreak of influenza in 1918 at Camp Funston, Kansas, major epidemics occurred two months later in England, France, and Spain. Initially each country attempted to deny the occurrence of influenza within its borders (noting, of course, that influenza was already present somewhere else).

Once an epidemic is recognized, it follows quickly that someone (or 10 something) else is blamed for it. As bubonic plague swept through Europe in 1348, it was claimed that it was caused by Jews who had poisoned wells. As a result, thousands of Jews were burned at the stake. The cholera epidemics in the United States fell disproportionately on the poor. At that time, poverty was viewed as a consequence of idleness and intemperance. The latter was also clearly felt to make one more suscep- tible to cholera. Since new immigrants were often the most poor, they were blamed for their own susceptibility to cholera, as well as for bringing the disease into the country. Prostitutes were also blamed for the epidemic, even though cholera was not thought to be a venereal disease. Many felt that their "moral corruption" caused them, as well as their clients, to develop cholera. Blame could also be placed at a national level. After the initial outbreak of influenza in the United States, epidemics occurred in Spain, England, and France. In addition to attempting to deny their own epidemics, the countries blamed one another. The French referred to the epidemic as the Plague of the Spanish Lady, and the English called it the French Disease. (Even today we refer to the Asian Flu.)

Epidemics occur in part because old diseases are not yet understood 11 or new diseases have arisen. In either case, physicians do not have the knowledge either to prevent the epidemic or to treat its victims effec- tively. As a result, society views the physicians and medicine of the time as having failed. A corollary of the failure of the existing methods of medicine is the rise of alternative therapies during an epidemic. During the plague epidemic, innumerable remedies and preventatives arose. This is hardly surprising since existing texts provided no effective treatment. During the first cholera epidemic in the United States, physicians routinely employed a limited array of unpleasant, even dangerous, therapies. The most common were calomel (a mercury compound that frequently resulted in mercury poisoning), laudanum (an opium com- pound), and bleeding. These measures failed to treat cholera and also had numerous untoward side effects. Given the failure and hazards of traditional medicine, it is no surprise that it was surpassed in popularity by botanical medicine during these early cholera epidemics.

A final effect that is common to all epidemics is that they stimulate a 12 variety of new laws. Initially, these laws are viewed as immediately necessary to prevent or control an epidemic, but often they remain in effect long after the epidemic has subsided. For example, many laws were enacted prior to and during the cholera epidemics. Many of these laws continue in virtually their same form one hundred years later.

## Post-Reading Questions

1. What bearing does the history of epidemics have on the current AIDS epidemic? What can be learned from such a comparison?
2. How does Swenson organize his discussion of epidemics? In what order does he present the information? What kinds of information about epidemics does he include? What does he achieve by organizing this section of his essay this way? What does his approach to organization suggest about his consideration of readers?
3. Identify the epidemics that Swenson describes in his essay. What do those epidemics have in common? What do those epidemics have in common with AIDS?
4. What does Swenson mean by the "internal anatomy" of an epidemic? Using his definition, explain the internal anatomy of America's response to AIDS.
5. What societal issues are raised because of AIDS' status as an epidemic? Would society's response to AIDS differ if it had not reached epidemic proportions? Would the government's response have been different? Why?
6. How have healthcare professionals responded to epidemics in the past? How has the medical community responded to the AIDS epidemic? What differences in response exist among healthcare professionals? What accounts for these differences in response?
7. Swenson teaches in a medical school. How would his professional background have influenced what he says, how he says it, and why he says it?

# KIM FOLTZ ON AIDS

## Pre-Reading Questions

1. From what you have heard and read, describe the life of a person suffering from AIDS. In what ways is the person's daily routine affected? How are the person's professional and personal relationships affected? How is the person's body affected? Explain the source

of your description. Does most of what you know about the AIDS patient come from your own experiences, your reading, or the media?

2.   How much discrimination do you believe exists against AIDS patients? What form or forms does this discrimination take? How does this discriminatory behavior affect the AIDS patient? What reasons do individuals offer to defend these forms of discrimination? In your opinion, how legitimate are their reasons?

# TESTING POSITIVE
## Kim Foltz

A few months after I found out I had the virus that causes AIDS, I   1
learned exactly what this disease was going to mean to me. It happened while I was riding a bus up Eighth Avenue. A young man sat next to me, and then a few stops later he suddenly moved to a seat across the aisle. I was busy scribbling in a journal I'd been keeping since I learned last year that I am H.I.V. positive and didn't pay much attention to him. Then, in quick succession, an elderly woman and a teen-age girl sat down next to me, and switched to other seats. I was overcome with paranoia. Although I hadn't developed any of the telltale signs of AIDS, and there was no way for them to know, had they somehow figured out that I was H.I.V. positive?

In the following weeks, the virus seemed to tighten its psychological   2
grip on me. If I coughed too much in a crowd, I felt guilty, even though I knew I hadn't put anyone at risk. I shied away from kissing friends.

The paranoia eventually passed. But it taught me that who I am is   3
irrevocably tied to being H.I.V. positive. When the basketball player Earvin (Magic) Johnson recently announced that he had H.I.V., I—like almost everyone else—applauded his candor. But I suspect he has probably not begun to realize the extent to which H.I.V. will shape his future.

Having the AIDS virus isn't the death sentence I thought it would   4
be. Unlike the early victims of AIDS, who were quickly overwhelmed by rapidly deteriorating health and radical medical treatments, I have discovered that my biggest task is learning to live with H.I.V. I waited until April 1990, when AZT was well established as a treatment, before being tested for the virus. I didn't want to know, if there was nothing that could be done. Now that drugs like AZT and DDI can slow the progress of the disease, I could be relatively healthy for years.

Still, every step is a new one for me, as it is for anyone affected by   5
H.I.V. Every medical advance creates a rush of excitement and anxiety. In the year and a half since I tested positive, the antiviral drug DDI has

been approved by the F.D.A., and other antiviral drugs, like DDC, have been tested. Several AIDS vaccines that may help those already infected with the virus are also being tested. There are new drugs to treat AIDS-related infections, including the drug foscarnet for an eye disorder caused by a cytomegalovirus, and fluconazole to treat fungal infections.

Knowledge about the disease changes so rapidly that you feel as if you have to become an instant medical expert. Every time I insist against my physician's advice that I should try some new treatment, I know I could be making a dangerous mistake. Lately, I've wondered whether my doctor is too conservative. Some people I know who have had similar doubts have switched to more aggressive doctors and are happy with the results. My doctor swears by AZT, and I decided to take it even though the drug's detractors argue that the highly toxic compound can do more harm than good. But several times during the past year, I have panicked after discussions with friends about the dangers of AZT and have stopped taking it, only to begin again after a week.    6

I began to get more involved in planning my treatment after I developed anemia as a result of AZT, which had suppressed my bone marrow's ability to produce red blood cells. I discussed with my doctor whether I should try DDI, an antiviral treatment that has been effective for people who cannot tolerate AZT. He feels DDI is too dangerous, since it can cause seizures and damage the pancreas. Instead, he put me on Epogen, a new drug that stimulates the production of red blood cells. I inject the medicine into my leg every other day. So far, it is working.    7

Since so little is known about H.I.V., I don't want to rule out any possibilities. I've read several books on AIDS that seemed helpful but, just a year or two after their publication, were already outdated. More useful have been publications from organizations like Project Inform, which discuss the pros and cons of the latest treatments. I'm better informed now, but that doesn't make me a doctor.    8

The confusion and anxiety associated with H.I.V. become overwhelming at times. I talk often with my longtime companion, James Baker, who is also a journalist and has written many stories about AIDS; he's been a reassuring source of facts about the disease. But there have been some issues I thought it would be too upsetting to bring up with him. I needed to talk to other people. Last year, I turned to a nonprofit organization called Body Positive, set up by people who are H.I.V. positive to offer support to others in that situation. There were 12 men in my group, all of us gay. We gathered every Monday night in the rundown recreation room of a church near Times Square. We met for three months, and talked about our fears and hopes.    9

During several meetings, we discussed how H.I.V. has created a kind of sexual limbo for many of us. Finding the right person has never been an easy proposition, even in the best of times. H.I.V. creates nerve-racking complications. When do you tell a prospective partner that you    10 are H.I.V. positive? Safe sex is nothing more than protected sex. There still are risks.

One group member said the first time he made the confession, to a  11 young man he'd just met in a bar, the man turned his back on him and walked away without a word of explanation. Waiting until a relationship develops during a series of platonic dates isn't the solution either. When you finally come clean, the response is often: "I don't want to waste my time with someone who's going to die."

One evening, we talked about our biggest fears. Mine is the indignity  12 of ending up destitute. I make a good salary, but once I have AIDS and am too disabled to work, I will not be able to make ends meet. Now that I have H.I.V., it's too late to sign up for private disability insurance. My two years at the newspaper entitle me to only a few months' disability pay. After that, I would have to manage on $600 a month from a Federal disability program. That wouldn't begin to cover my share of the rent, food and utilities.

It wasn't until one of the last sessions that we finally tackled the topic  13 that had been on everyone's mind: suicide. Most said they would probably kill themselves if the suffering became too much to bear. I had always thought I would do the same. The alternative for many people with AIDS is to waste away slowly, ending their days in intense pain. But when I was asked what I would do, I surprised myself by replying that suicide was not the answer for me.

I never thought I would be on such intimate terms with death. I am  14 only 43 years old and, like many gay men, have watched a string of friends die. But one of the things I've learned in dealing with H.I.V. is never to give up hope. Each day, the first thing I do is get on the scale to make sure I haven't lost weight. Next, I take my AZT. Then I tell myself I'm ready for the next round.

## Post-Reading Questions

1. Explain how Foltz introduces his personal essay on AIDS. How would you categorize his strategy for introducing his topic and main point? How effective is his introduction? Why?

2. Summarize in your own words how being HIV positive has affected Foltz's life. How has it affected his daily routine? How has it affected his long-term goals? How has it affected his philosophy of life?

3. Identify two or three ethical issues Foltz alludes to in his essay. How could each issue be described as a problem with several possible solutions?

4. All of the information in this essay comes from Foltz's own experiences. What kinds of experiences does Foltz share with his readers? Be specific. How do you think he decided which experiences he would include? What kinds of experiences do you believe

he could have decided *not* to include? Why would he have left those experiences out of the essay?

5. Describe how Foltz ends his essay. What is he trying to accomplish in the conclusion? How effective is he? Why?

6. What information can Foltz present, as an HIV-positive individual, that a journalist might not be able to convey as effectively? Why?

7. What kinds of readers do you believe Foltz considers his audience? Describe these readers. How might Foltz's analysis of his readers' attitudes and knowledge about AIDS have influenced what he says in the essay?

8. Analyze the organization of this essay. What are the sub-topics Foltz covers? In what order are the sub-topics presented to the reader? What reasons would Foltz have had for organizing his essay this way?

9. What effect did reading this personal account of AIDS have on you in terms of your knowledge, opinions, and feelings about AIDS? Which individuals would benefit most from reading this essay? Why?

10. What is Foltz's purpose in writing? What attitudes and experiences did he want to clarify or change?

# THE AMA'S COUNCIL ON ETHICAL AND JUDICIAL AFFAIRS ON MEDICAL DECISION MAKING

## Pre-Reading Questions

1. Would you be more comfortable being examined and treated by a physician of your own gender? Have you ever been treated by a physician of the opposite gender? Explain your answer by referring to your own experiences with physicians.

2. What are your expectations when you visit a doctor? What do you expect in terms of advice, medical treatment, and "bedside manner"? Do you expect your gender to influence the doctor's handling of your care? Explain your answer by referring to your own experiences with doctors.

## GENDER DISPARITIES IN CLINICAL DECISION MAKING

### Council on Ethical and Judicial Affairs, American Medical Association

*Members of the Council on Ethical and Judicial Affairs of the American Medical Association include the following: Richard J. McMurray, MD, Flint, Mich, Chair; Oscar W. Clarke, MD,*

*Gallipolis, Ohio, Vice Chair; John A. Barrasso, MD, Casper, Wyo; Dexanne B. Clohan, Arlington, Va, Medical Student; Charles H. Epps, Jr, MD, Washington, DC; John Glasson, MD, Durham, NC; Robert McQuillan, MD, Kansas City, Mo, Resident Physician; Charles W. Plows, MD, Anaheim, Calif; Michael A. Puzak, MD, Arlington, Va; David Orentlicher, MD, JD, Chicago, Ill, Secretary; Kristen A. Halkola, Chicago, Ill, Associate Secretary. Dr Orentlicher and Ms Halkola were staff authors of this article.*

Recent evidence has raised concerns that women are disadvantaged because of inadequate attention to the research, diagnosis, and treatment of women's health care problems. In 1985, the US Public Health Service's Task Force on Women's Health Issues reported that the lack of research data on women limited understanding of women's health needs.[1]

One concern is that medical treatments for women are based on a male model, regardless of the fact that women may react differently to treatments than men or that some diseases manifest themselves differently in women than in men. The results of medical research on men are generalized to women without sufficient evidence of applicability to women.[2-4] For example, the original research on the prophylactic value of aspirin for coronary artery disease was derived almost exclusively from research on men, yet recommendations based on this research have been directed to the general populace.[4]

Some researchers attribute the lack of research on women to women's reproductive cycles. Women's menstrual cycles may constitute a separate variable affecting test results.[5] Also, researchers are reluctant to perform studies on women of childbearing age, because experimental treatments or procedures may affect their reproductive capabilities. However, the task force pointed out that it is precisely because medications and other therapeutic interventions have a differential effect on women according to their menstrual cycle that women should not be excluded from research.[6] Research on the use of antidepressant agents was initially conducted entirely on men, despite apparently higher rates of clinical depression in women.[6,7] Evidence is emerging that the effects of some antidepressants vary over the course of a woman's cycle, and as a result, a constant dosage of an antidepressant may be too high at some points in a woman's cycle, yet too low at others.[2,3]

In response to the task force, the National Institutes of Health promised to implement a policy ensuring that women would be included in study populations unless it would be scientifically inappropriate to do so.[4] However, in June 1990, the General Accounting Office reported that the National Institutes of Health had made little progress in implementing the policy and that many problems remained.[4]

In addition to these general concerns raised by the task force about    4
women's health, recent studies have examined whether a patient's gender
inappropriately affects the access to and use of medical care. Three
important areas in which evidence of gender disparities exists are
(1) access to kidney transplantation, (2) diagnosis and treatment of
cardiac disease, and (3) diagnosis of lung cancer. Other studies have also
revealed gender-based differences in patterns of health care use. Although biological factors account for some differences between the sexes
in the provision of medical care, these studies indicate that nonbiological
or nonclinical factors may affect clinical decision making. There are not
enough data to identify the exact nature of nonbiological or nonclinical
factors. Nevertheless, the existence of these factors is a cause for concern
that the medical community needs to address.

## EVIDENCE OF DISPARITIES

### Gender Differences in Health Care Use

Some evidence indicates that, compared with men, women receive more    5
health care services overall. In general, women have more physician visits
per year and receive more services per visit.[8] Several studies have examined
the issue of differences in health care use between men and women.[8-14]
The results of these studies vary and some are contradictory. One of the
most extensive studies on gender differences in the use of health care
services found that when medical care differs for men and women (in
approximately 30% to 40% of cases), the usual result is more care for
women than for men. Women seem to receive more care even when both
men and women report the same type of illness or complaint about their
health.[8] Women undergo more examinations, laboratory tests, and blood
pressure checks and receive more drug prescriptions and return appoint-
ments than men. However, the reasons for this are not clear.

Studies that have examined gender as a factor for receiving several    6
major diagnostic or therapeutic interventions, however, suggest that
women have less access than men to these interventions.

### Disparities in Providing Major Diagnostic
### and Therapeutic Interventions

Kidney dialysis and transplantation.    Gender has been found to correlate    7
with the likelihood that a patient with kidney disease will receive dialysis
or a kidney transplant. In one study researchers analyzed the percentage
of patients in the United States with endstage renal disease who received
dialysis.[15] Of men who needed dialysis, 37.3% were given dialysis,

compared with 31.1% of women. Ninety percent of the difference resulted from the fact that younger people have a greater likelihood of receiving dialysis than older people.

Disparities based on gender are more pronounced for the likelihood   8 of receiving a kidney transplant. An analysis of patient dialysis data from 1981 through 1985 indicated that women undergoing renal dialysis were approximately 30% less likely to receive a cadaver kidney transplant than men.[16] Another study, done during the period 1979 through 1985, showed that a female dialysis patient had only three-quarters the chance of a male patient to receive a renal transplant.[17] Controlling for age did not significantly reduce gender as a factor in the likelihood of receiving a transplant. Men were more likely to receive a transplant in every age category. The discrepancy between sexes was most pronounced in the group 46 to 60 years old, with women having only half the chance of receiving a transplant as men the same age.[18]

*Diagnosis of lung cancer.* Recent autopsy studies have revealed that in as   9 many as a quarter of patients with lung cancer, a diagnosis is not made while they are alive.[18-20] A comparison between the population in which lung cancer is diagnosed and the population in which it is not diagnosed shows that a detection bias favors the ordering of diagnostic testing for lung cancer in patients who are smokers, have a recent or chronic cough, or are male.[20]

One study compared the rates of lung cancer detected at autopsy 10 with the way cytologic studies of sputum were ordered in a hospital setting to detect lung cancer. Men and women have relatively equal rates of previously undiagnosed lung cancer detected during autopsy. In addition, other studies have shown that women and men with similar smoking practices are at essentially equivalent risk for lung cancer.[21] However, men were twice as likely to have cytologic studies of sputum ordered as women. Once smoking status and other medical considerations were taken into account, men still had 1.6 times the chance of having a cytologic test done.[20]

*Catheterization for coronary bypass surgery.* Men seem to have cardiac 11 catheterizations ordered at a rate disproportionately higher than women, regardless of each gender's likelihood of having coronary artery disease. A study done in 1987 showed that in a group of 390 patients, of those with abnormal exercise radionuclide scans, 40% of the male patients were referred for cardiac catheterization, while only 4% of the female patients were referred for further testing.[22] The study showed that once researchers controlled for the variables of abnormal test results, age, types of angina, presence of symptoms, and confirmed previous myocardial infarction, men were still 6.5 times more likely to be referred for catheterization than women, although men have only three times the likelihood of having coronary heart disease than women.

Of those patients whose nuclear scan test results ultimately were 12 abnormal, women were more than twice as likely to have their symptoms attributed to somatic, psychiatric, or other noncardiac causes as men. For patients whose test scans were normal, men and women had a relatively equal chance of having their symptoms attributed to cardiac causes.

The authors concluded that the wide difference in referral rates 13 between men and women could not be explained by gender-based differences in the accuracy of nuclear scans. Even after abnormal test results had been established, men were referred significantly more often than women. It is unlikely that the discrepancy results from a higher likelihood of referral in some types of nuclear scan abnormalities, since men had higher referral rates in every category of abnormality. Men were also more likely to be referred regardless of the probability of their having coronary artery disease before the nuclear scan.

## POSSIBLE EXPLANATIONS

### Biological Differences Between the Sexes

Differences in biological need between male and female patients proba- 14 bly account for a large part of the differences in the use of health care services. The kind and number[23] of illnesses that are reported differ somewhat for women and men. Possibly, women get more care because they have more illnesses or because the types of illnesses they have require more overall care. Some figures show that the generally lower socioeconomic status of women may be associated with poorer health. Also, women tend to live longer than men and individuals of older ages may have more morbidities.[8] However, real differences in morbidity and mortality between the sexes would not explain the fact that women seem to receive more care than men for the same type of complaint or illness.[8]

Real biological differences also cannot account for the gender 15 disparities in rates of cardiac catheterization, kidney transplantation, or lung cancer diagnoses. For instance, the discrepancy in dialysis rates might be explained by the existence of coexisting diseases in women that lessen the potential effectiveness of dialysis. However, the Health Care Financing Administration reports that female patients receiving dialysis have a slightly better survival pattern than male patients.[24]

Also, biological differences between the sexes, such as the level of 16 cytotoxic antibodies, number of complications after transplantation, or differences in the type of renal disease between men and women did not explain the disparity in the likelihood of receiving a kidney transplant.[17] It is unlikely that the difference reflects either patient or physician preference; successful transplantation is generally considered superior to lifetime dialysis by both patients and physicians.[16,17]

The difference in sputum cytologic findings between male and female [17] patients may reflect the historical association between male sex and cigarette smoking. Traditionally, more men than women have been smokers.[21] In fact, past demographic data showed that men were more likely to have lung cancer than women. Physicians, in turn, may view smoking and being male as independent risk factors for lung cancer and therefore tend to suspect cancer more readily in patients who either smoked or were men even though gender is not an independent risk factor.[21]

Differences in disease prevalence between men and women have [18] been cited to explain the disparity in cardiac catheterization rates.[25] However, the difference in disease prevalence between men and women is 3:1, whereas the difference in catheterization rates was almost 7:1.[22,26] Additionally, the similarities in use of antianginal drug treatment indicates that the patients were clinically comparable.[22]

Other evidence also suggests that women may be disadvantaged by [19] inadequate attention to the manifestations of cardiovascular disease in women. There is some evidence that cardiovascular disease is not diagnosed or treated early enough in women. Studies show that women have a higher operative mortality rate for coronary bypass surgery[27,28] and a higher mortality rate at the time of an initial myocardial infarction.[29–31] The higher mortality rates reflect the fact that cardiovascular disease is further advanced in women than men at both the time of surgery and the time of an initial heart attack.[29]

The lack of research done specifically on women may have resulted in [20] a failure to develop diagnostic criteria and treatments that are appropriate for cardiovascular disease in women. Cardiovascular disease in women differs from the disease in men in several significant ways. One study showed that diabetes is a greater risk factor in women for morbidity and mortality from coronary heart disease than in men.[32] The same study also showed that the level of high-density lipoprotein cholesterol is a stronger predictor of heart disease in women than in men.[32] These differences between the sexes in the manifestation of cardiovascular disease may affect diagnostic and treatment indications for women. Yet, research on cardiovascular disease has concentrated almost entirely on men[3] despite the fact that cardiovascular disease is the leading cause of death in women in the United States.[2,29] Also, tests traditionally used to detect cardiovascular disease in men, such as treadmill testing, are not as sensitive or specific for detecting cardiovascular disease in women as for men.[28]

### Societal Attitudes May Affect Decision Making in the Health Care Context

Data that suggest that a patient's gender plays an inappropriate role in [21] medical decision making raise the question of possible gender bias in clinical decision making. Gender bias may not necessarily manifest itself as overt discrimination based on sex. Rather, social attitudes, including stereotypes, prejudices and other evaluations based on gender roles may play themselves out in a variety of subtle ways.

For instance, some evidence suggests that physicians are more likely 22 to attribute women's health complaints to emotional rather than physical causes.[33-35] Women's concerns about their health and their greater use of health care services have been perceived to be due to "overanxiousness" about their health.[35] However, characterizing women's use patterns as a result of emotional excess or overuse risks providing inadequate care for women. For example, in the study of catheterization rates, attributing a disproportionate percentage of women's abnormal nuclear scan results to psychiatric or noncardiac causes for their symptoms may have compromised their care.[22]

Perceiving men's use practices as normal and attributing *over*anxious- 23 ness to women's concerns about their health may be doing a disservice to both sexes. One study concluded that "women's greater interest in and concern with health matters and their greater attentiveness to bodily changes may be part of a set of behaviors that do contribute to women's lower mortality rates."[12] Men may tend to be "*under*anxious" about their health or to ignore symptoms or illnesses and, consequently, underuse health care. Statistics that show that men tend to have a lesser number but more severe types of health problems may reflect men's resistance to seeking care until a health problem has become acute.

Societal value judgments placed on gender or gender roles may also 24 put women at a disadvantage in the context of receiving certain major diagnostic and therapeutic interventions, such as kidney transplantation and cardiac catheterization. A general perception that men's social role obligations or of their contributions to society are greater than women's may fuel these disparities.[9] For instance, altering one's work schedule to accommodate health concerns may be viewed as more difficult for men than women. Overall, men's financial contribution to the family may be considered more critical than women's. A kidney transplant is much less cumbersome than dialysis. Coronary bypass surgery, for which catheterization is a prerequisite, is a more efficient and immediate solution to the problem of coronary artery disease than continuous antianginal drug therapy. However, judgments based on evaluations of social worth or preconceptions about the probable roles of men and women are clearly inexcusable in the context of medical decision making.

### Role of the Medical Profession in Examining Gender Disparities and Eliminating Biases

Available data do not conclusively demonstrate a connection between 25 gender bias and gender disparities in the provision of health care. Designing a study that can control for the myriad social, economic, and cultural factors that might influence decision making in a clinical context has proved extraordinarily difficult.

Historically, societal perceptions regarding women's health status 26 have often disadvantaged women. Throughout the mid-19th and well into the 20th century, women's perceived disposition toward both physical and mental illness was used as a rationale for keeping them from worldly spheres such as politics, science, medicine, and law. For women, behavior that violated expected gender-role norms was frequently attributed to various physical or mental illnesses[36,37] and in turn often was treated in a variety of ways, including gynecological surgeries, such as hysterectomies and, occasionally, clitoridectomies.[38] Society and medicine have addressed and are working to remedy sex stereotypes and biases. Yet, many social and cultural attitudes that endorse sex-stereotyped roles for men and women remain in our society.

The medical community cannot tolerate any discrepancy in the 27 provision of care that is not based on appropriate biological or medical indications. The US Public Health Service's Task Force on Women's Health Issues concluded that "[b]ecause health care is a legitimate concern of all people, the health professions are obligated to seek ways of ensuring that clinical decisions are based on science that adequately pertains to all people."[6] Insufficient research on women is not only discriminatory but may be dangerous; medical care or drug treatments that prove effective in men may not always be safely generalizable to women.[4] The influence that social attitudes and perceptions have had on health care in the past suggests that some biases could remain and affect modern medical care. Such attitudes and perceptions may disadvantage both women and men by reinforcing gender-based stereotypes or inhibiting access to care. Current evidence of possible discrepancies indicates a need for further scrutiny.

## SUMMARY OF RECOMMENDATIONS

Physicians should examine their practices and attitudes for the influence 28 of social or cultural biases that could affect medical care. Physicians must ensure that gender is not used inappropriately as a consideration in clinical decision making. Assessments of need based on presumptions about the relative worth of certain social roles must be avoided. Procedures and techniques that preclude or minimize the possibility of gender bias should be developed and implemented. A gender-neutral determination for kidney transplant eligibility should be used.

More medical research on women's health and women's health problems should be pursued. Results of medical testing done solely on 29 men should not be generalized to women without evidence that results can be applied safely and effectively to both sexes. Research on health problems that affect both sexes should include male and female subjects. Sound medical and scientific reasons should be required for excluding women from medical tests and studies, such as that the proposed research does not or would not affect the health of women. An obvious example would be research on prostatic cancer. Also, further research into the possible causes of gender disparities should be conducted. The extent to which physician-patient interactions may be influenced by cultural and social conceptions of gender should be ascertained.

Finally, awareness of and responsiveness to sociocultural factors that [30] could lead to gender disparities may be enhanced by increasing the number of female physicians in leadership roles and other positions of authority in teaching, research, and the practice of medicine.

## REFERENCES

1. US Public Health Service. *Women's Health: Report of the Public Health Service Task Force on Women's Health Issues.* Washington, DC: US Dept of Health and Human Services; 1985;2.
2. Cotton P. Is there still too much extrapolation from data on middle-aged white men? *JAMA.* 1990;263:1049-1050.
3. Cotton P. Examples abound of gaps in medical knowledge because of groups excluded from scientific study. *JAMA.* 1990;263:1051-1052.
4. *Hearings Before the House Energy and Commerce Subcommittee on Health and the Environment,* 101st Congr, 1st Sess (1990) (testimony of Mark V. Nadel, associate director, US General Accounting Office).
5. Hamilton J, Parry B. Sex-related differences in clinical drug response: implications for women's health. *J Am Med Wom Assoc.* 1983;38:126-132.
6. Hamilton JA. Guidelines for avoiding methodological and policy-making biases in gender-related health research in Public Health Service. *Women's Health: Report of the Public Health Service Task Force on Women's Health Issues.* Washington, DC: US Department of Health and Human Services; 1985;2.
7. Raskin A. Age-sex differences in response to antidepressant drugs. *J Nerv Ment Dis.* 1974;159:120-130.
8. Verbrugge LM, Steiner RP. Physician treatment of men and women patients: sex bias or appropriate care? *Med Care.* 1981;19:609-632.
9. Marcus AC, Suman TE. Sex differences in reports of illness and disability: A preliminary test of the 'fixed role' hypothesis. *J Health Soc Behav.* 1981;22:174-182.
10. Gove WR, Hughes M. Possible causes of the apparent sex differences in physical health: an empirical investigation. *Am Sociol Rev.* 1979;44:126-146.
11. Cleary PD, Mechanic D, Greenley, JR. Sex differences in medical care utilization: an empirical investigation. *J Health Soc Behav.* 1982;23:106-119.

12. Hibbard JH, Pope CR. Another look at sex differences in the use of medical care: illness orientation and the types of morbidities for which services are used. *Women Health.* 1986;11:21-36.

13. Armitage KJ, Schneiderman LF, Bass RA. Response of physicians to medical complaints in men and women. *JAMA.* 1979;241:2186.

14. Natanson CA. Illness and the feminine role: a theoretical review. *Soc Sci Med.* 1975;9:57-63.

15. Kjellstrand CM, Logan GM. Racial, sexual and age inequalities in chronic dialysis. *Nephron.* 1987;45:257-263.

16. Held PJ, Pauly MV, Bovbjerg RR, et al. Access to kidney transplantation. *Arch Intern Med.* 1988;148:2594-2600.

17. Kjellstrand CM. Age, sex, and race inequality in renal transplantation. *Arch Intern Med.* 1988;148:1305-1309.

18. McFarlane MJ, Feinstein AR, Wells CK. The 'epidemiologic necropsy': unexpected detections, demographic selections, and the changing rates of lung cancer. *JAMA.* 1987;258:331-338.

19. McFarlane MJ, Feinstein AR, Wells CK. Necropsy evidence of detection bias in the diagnosis of lung cancer. *Arch Intern Med.* 1986;146:1695-1698.

20. Wells CK, Feinstein AR. Detection bias in the diagnostic pursuit of lung cancer. *Am J Epidemiol.* 1988;128:1016-1026.

21. Schoenberg JB, Wilcox HB, Mason TJ, et al. Variation in smoking-related lung cancer risk among New Jersey women. *Am J Epidemiol.* 1989;130:688-695.

22. Tobin JN, Wassertheil-Smoller S, Wexler JP, et al. Sex bias in considering coronary bypass surgery. *Ann Intern Med.* 1987;107:19-25.

23. Verbrugge LM. Sex differentials in health. *Prevention.* 1982;97:417-437.

24. Eggers PW, Connerton R, McMullan M. The Medicare experience with end-stage renal disease: trends in incidence, prevalence, and survival. *Health Care Fin Rev.* 1984;5:69-88.

25. Karlin BG. Sex bias and coronary bypass surgery. *Ann Intern Med.* 1988;108:149.

26. Tobin JN, Wassertheil-Smoller S, Wexler J, et al. Sex bias and coronary bypass surgery. *Ann Intern Med.* 1988;108:149.

27. Khan SS, Nessim S, Gray R, Czer LS, Chans A, Matloff J. Increased mortality of women in coronary artery bypass surgery: evidence for referral bias. *Ann Intern Med.* 1990;112:561-567.

28. Wenger NK. Gender, coronary artery disease and coronary bypass surgery. *Ann Intern Med.* 1990;112:557-558.

29. Wenger NK. Coronary disease in women. *Ann Rev Med.* 1985;36:285-294.

30. Fiebach NH, Viscoli CM, Horwitz RI. Differences between women and men in survival after myocardial infarction. *JAMA.* 1990;263:1092-1096.

31. Dittrich H, Gilpin E, Nicod P, Cali G, Henning H, Ross J. Acute myocardial infarction in women: influence of gender on mortality and prognosis variables. *Am J Cardiol.* 1988;62:1-7.

32. Lerner DJ, Kannel WB. Patterns of coronary heart disease morbidity and mortality in the sexes: a 26-year follow-up of the Framingham population. *Am Heart J.* 1986;III:383-390.

33. Bernstein B, Kane R. Physicians' attitudes toward female patients. *Med Care.* 1981;19:600-608.
34. Colameco S, Becker L, Simpson M. Sex bias in the assessment of patient complaints. *J Fam Pract.* 1983;16:1117-1121.
35. Savage WD, Tate P. Medical students' attitudes towards women: a sex-linked variable? *Med Educ.* 1983;17:159-164.
36. Waisberg J, Page P. Gender role nonconformity and perception of mental illness. *Women Health.* 1988;14:3-16.
37. Broverman IK, Broverman DM, Clarkson FE, et al. Sex-role stereotypes and clinical judgments of mental health. *J Consult Clin Psychol.* 1970;34:1-7.
38. Barker-Benfield B. 'The spermatic economy.' In: Gordon M, ed. *The American Family in Sociohistorical Perspective.* New York, NY: St Martin's Press; 1973.

## Post-Reading Questions

1. This article was written by the American Medical Association's Council on Ethical and Judicial Affairs. What are the responsibilities of the group? Why is it interested in gender and its relationship to healthcare practices?
2. Explain the different kinds of gender disparities the Council outlines in this article. In your opinion, which area has the potential to have the most serious negative effects on the American healthcare delivery system? Why?
3. What evidence can you identify in the article that it is intended for readers of a medical journal? What would these readers be like in terms of their interests, questions, and reactions to the article's contents?
4. Describe your personal reaction to the claims in the article. How would your reaction to the information about disparities in decision making differ from those of doctors reading the same information?
5. What does the term "male model" (paragraph 2) mean to doctors? Explain the connection between a male model in medicine and gender disparities in clinical decision making.
6. How would you describe the Council's approach to developing the article's claims? What kind of support seems most critical to supporting their claims? Why is this kind of support appropriate for their article?
7. How is the article organized? In what order is the information presented? Why is the organization effective? How does it help the Council achieve its writing purposes?
8. Summarize the Council's suggestions for eliminating the disparities it outlines. What is your reaction to their suggestions? Are they appropriate? Are some more likely to be tried than others?

# PERRI KLASS ON THE GENETIC TESTING OF UNBORN BABIES

## Pre-Reading Questions

1.  How do you feel about genetic testing? Do you feel all prospective parents should undergo such testing? What kinds of information about their baby should parents have? How should they use that information?
2.  The original title of the Klass essay was "The Perfect Baby?" What kinds of expectations does that title create? How do the "Before They're Born" and "The Perfect Baby?" titles differ? What could have prompted Klass or her editor to change titles?
3.  When Perri Klass wrote this essay, she was a pediatric resident at a Boston hospital. What kinds of experiences motivated her to write this essay? Why would she choose to write a personal essay rather than a straightforward journalistic piece? What is she able to accomplish in an essay that she couldn't accomplish in a magazine article?

## BEFORE THEY'RE BORN
### Perri Klass

Shakespeare, allowing Richard III to explain the origins of his villainy,    1
had him announce that he had been "Deformed, unfinished, sent before my time/Into this breathing world scarce half made up" (Act I, Scene 1). What could be worse than a birth defect, what tragedy greater than a baby born abnormal?

So you want to have a baby. Naturally, a healthy baby, a perfect baby.    2
You'll give up alcohol, drink your eight glasses of milk a day. You won't even take Tylenol. Maybe you'll finally go ahead and test your house for radon.

As medicine marches forward, one of the benefits we seek is    3
certainty: give me the diet that will keep me healthy, the special bran muffin to lower my cholesterol. Do as many tests as you need, doctor, just make sure there's nothing wrong with me. And above all, promise me a healthy child. The astronomical rate at which obstetricians are sued by their patients reflects this; a good obstetrician is expected to deliver a perfect baby, and to foresee and circumvent any of the possible problems in pregnancy, labor and delivery.

In medicine in general, and in obstetrics in particular, this search for    4
certainty leads to many invasive procedures. Now the search for a perfect baby is leading us further and further back into pregnancy, as the possibilities for prenatal diagnosis multiply.

Prenatal diagnosis starts before there is a fetus to diagnose. If two    5
people are thinking of having a child together, they should give some

thought to whether any genetic diseases run in their families, from the relatively common well-known disorders, such as hemophilia and muscular dystrophy, to such rare disorders as ceramidase deficiency and glycogen-storage disease. Any prospective parent whose family tree includes a number of childhood deaths, or a succession of congenital anomalies, should get genetic counseling promptly.

Even if there isn't any such family history, those who come from 6 high-risk populations may want to be tested to see if they carry defective genes. Those with African ancestry can be tested for the sickle cell anemia gene; those with Eastern European Jewish forebears, for Tay-Sachs.

O.K., so now you're pregnant. And the obstetrician does the usual 7 checkup on the fetus, listens to the heartbeat, measures the uterus—but what about the new, high-tech ways of making sure the baby is going to be all right?

The only prenatal screen routinely recommended for *every* pregnancy 8 is an alpha-fetoprotein, or AFP, level. This is done on a small sample of the mother's blood, measuring a protein produced by the fetus. A protein level too low or too high for the stage of pregnancy prompts the doctor to do an ultrasound, using sound waves to create a picture of the fetus. Usually, it turns out that the estimated gestational age was wrong; ultrasound allows accurate dating of the pregnancy, and a high AFP level turns out to mean a baby due sooner than expected.

However, if the AFP is really too high, it raises the specter of 9 congenital anomaly. AFP is elevated in spinal-cord defects, where the spinal column never fuses properly, causing spina bifida, for example. Other malformations that leave the internal organs exposed can also raise the AFP; such as gastroschesis, in which the intestines are outside the abdomen. Ultrasound detects most such major defects. But others— Turner syndrome, for example, a chromosomal abnormality in which a fetus has only one sex chromosome (a single X, instead of XX or XY)—cannot be diagnosed on ultrasound.

An AFP level that is too low is associated with Down's syndrome, as 10 well as with another, more serious syndrome: trisomy 18. In trisomy 18, instead of the extra 21st chromosome seen in Down's, the fetus has an extra 18th chromosome; these babies will have multiple birth defects, and will not survive. These chromosomal syndromes really require amniocentesis for detection.

Although the American College of Obstetricians and Gynecologists 11 does not actually recommend ultrasound as a routine test in a normal untroubled pregnancy, more and more doctors seem to be doing routine ultrasounds on more and more women. Some of this probably grows out of the parents' desire to be assured that all is well with the fetus; some grows out of the doctor's desire to guard against lawsuits by doing every test.

Ultrasound may or may not be accompanied by amniocentesis, in 12 which a sample of amniotic fluid is withdrawn by needle, and the fetal cells are cultured and their chromosomes analyzed. This test is now recommended for women over the age of 35, a somewhat arbitrary number. As women age, the frequency of Down's syndrome in their offspring increases, and 35 marks the age at which this risk was thought to surpass the risk to the fetus from the procedure itself—there is a small incidence of miscarriage following amniocentesis. Now, women over 35 tend to have amniocentesis done, and the vast majority of babies with Down's syndrome are born to younger mothers; the younger group has a lower frequency of the defect, but a much higher birth rate, so the rare events add up.

Let me point out that morally we are already in deep weeds. Prenatal  13 diagnosis, after all, carries with it the implication that, if an abnormality is found, the parents intend to consider the possibility of doing something about it, i.e., terminating the pregnancy. But the various abnormalities I have just listed constitute a wide spectrum. On one end, a trisomy 18, or a trisomy 13, is a fetus that many parents would choose to abort. If carried to term, these babies are profoundly abnormal, severely retarded, and tend to die soon. On the other hand, girls with Turner syndrome have only mildly unusual facial features, and grow up mentally normal. They suffer from certain medical problems—short stature and infertility, to name two—but they are by no means devastated.

Or take Down's syndrome, the reason for most over-35 amnios.  14 Many women choose to abort fetuses with Down's—but I know parents who have raised children with the syndrome and are indignant at the idea of not allowing the birth of such babies, proud of their children's achievements. Such parents are quick to point out that their children are happy and loving.

Amniocentesis cannot be done until the second trimester, but the  15 relatively new technique of chorionic villus sampling, or C.V.S., can sample fetal chromosomes as early as the ninth week.

Although geneticists can now ask a multitude of questions, the vast  16 majority are not routinely broached with the average pregnancy. A 37-year-old woman has an amnio, and the fetal cells are checked for major chromosomal abnormalities, such as trisomys. However, without specific indications, no one looks at this DNA to find any other subtle genetic diseases. If there is a family history of cystic fibrosis, say, or of some enzyme deficiency, then that test is done, but most genetic diseases are so rare that it would make no sense to screen the general population.

The availability of these specific tests is a tremendous boon to  17 families cursed with a deadly genetic disease. Consider Duchenne's muscular dystrophy, which is an X-linked disorder, a condition, like hemophilia, in which the mother is a carrier, with one normal X chromosome, and one that carries the muscular dystrophy. If her son inherits that one, he develops the disease and slowly loses his strength, ending up wheelchair-bound by 12 or 13, then losing the power of his respiratory muscles, and dying, usually of lung disease, often before the age of 20. Once, doctors told parents who were watching one well-loved son undergo this agony: next time have an amniocentesis, and if the fetus is male, consider abortion. There was no specific prenatal screen to tell whether a male had inherited the defective X. Now, the difficult decision of whether or not to carry a pregnancy to term can be fully informed. We can screen for muscular dystrophy.

But certainty cannot be bought. Geneticists caution that even if all 18 the currently available genetic tests were done, they would not guarantee a perfect baby. Although we can test for a number of syndromes, which include mental retardation, these syndromes account for far fewer than half of the children diagnosed with mental retardation. Most have causes we cannot possibly pick up prenatally. And congenital anomalies occur more often than many people realize; by one recent estimate, one in every 50 babies has a defect, which vary in medical, cosmetic, or surgical significance. Most of these defects are not life-threatening, and even if we could detect them all prenatally, would we want to start terminating pregnancies for comparatively minor cardiac defects? Or for extra fingers and toes?

I believe that prospective parents are entitled to as much information 19 as they feel they need, entitled to good genetic counseling, accurate testing and medical support for their decisions. I also believe they are entitled to do whatever they want with this information. I just think that before we reach out eagerly for all the new knowledge our expanding technology can offer, we need to stop and think about how we are going to use this information, how much of it we need, how much of it we want.

And as the technology for prenatal testing gets better and better, 20 prospective parents will need to ask themselves some major questions: how, exactly, do they feel about abortion? How great is their need for a perfect child? And, if not a perfect child, how much imperfection can they tolerate—or love? How great a handicap would they want a child of theirs to bear? And we have to acknowledge that, for all the technology, the growth of a fetus and the birth of a baby remain processes that are not completely under our control; perfect babies, in the end, are born, not made.

## Post-Reading Questions

1. What strategy does Klass use to introduce her essay's topic? How does her choice of this strategy reflect her sense of audience? What expectations does she have about her readers, based on this introductory strategy?

2. What do the terms "prenatal diagnosis" and "invasive procedures" (paragraph 2) mean to you? How are the two terms related?

3. According to Klass, who should consider genetic counseling? Why?

4. Where in the essay does Klass acknowledge her readers' lack of medical knowledge? How does she accommodate this difference between herself and many of her readers?

5. Why do you think Klass wrote this essay? What was her writing purpose? How do you know?

6. Summarize the kinds of genetic testing Klass describes. Why does she include those descriptions in the first part of her essay? What organization is she setting up for the body of her essay?

7. What does Klass mean when she says that "morally we are already in deep weeds" (paragraph 13)? In your own words, explain some of the ethical issues facing people who are in deep weeds.

8. Where in this essay does Klass answer the question she poses in the title? What is her answer? How appropriate is her placement of the answer? Why? Do you agree with her answer? Why?

# 6
. . . . . . . . . . . . .
## OPTIONAL WRITING ASSIGNMENTS FOCUSED ON HEALTHCARE ETHICS AND SOCIETY

Several possible topics have been introduced and discussed throughout this chapter. The following list of essay suggestions provides contexts within which you can compose essays on this chapter's theme of healthcare ethics and society. Whether you choose one of these options or develop another focus for your essay, you need to analyze your writing context and decide how to achieve your writing purpose for the particular readers you target (to review "The Rhetorical Approach to Academic Writing," see Chapter 2).

*1. Write a personal essay describing one particular experience you or someone close to you had related to healthcare in America.* The experience you choose should involve some kind of ethical dilemma or healthcare issue raised by one or more of the readings or by classroom discussions. Use whatever descriptive strategies you can to help your readers (your classmates) "see" the experience as it occurred. Your purpose in narrating this experience, however, is not only to recreate it—the experience you choose must help you make a point (thesis) about healthcare ethics and society. You may, if your teacher agrees, compare or contrast your experiences with those described in one or more of the readings in this chapter.

*2. Imagine you are a college student preparing a talk for a group of medical school professors.* They are considering whether or not medical students should be required to take a course in medical ethics. Such a course does not currently exist. Before making a decision, they are seeking input from experienced physicians, individuals currently working in healthcare settings, and lay persons whose lives will be affected by the future physicians being trained at the medical school. What recommendation would you make?

Drawing from your reading on healthcare ethics and society, and from your own and others' past experiences with the healthcare system, make an argument for or against creating a required medical ethics course. Identify and fully explain the reasons for your viewpoint. You should also convince your readers that you have considered opposing viewpoints and identified their weaknesses.

3. *Choose one of the medical dilemmas raised in one or more of the readings in this chapter, perhaps allocating more research dollars to find a cure for AIDs, ceilings for malpractice suits, or controlled public access to medical information.* Take a position for or against a particular approach to solving the dilemma. Then, drawing on your reading of the articles and essays in this chapter, your own and others' experiences, and information from some outside-of-the-classroom sources (an interview, a library article, a newspaper article, or news program), state and explain the reasons for your solution. Remember to consider what information your readers (your fellow students) have, how they currently feel about this dilemma, and what kinds of questions they will ask about the reasons and evidence you present. You will also be expected to document any outside-of-the-classroom sources you refer to in your essay.

4. *Write an argument defending or attacking Nolen's view that public access to medical knowledge does not always produce positive results.* Consider both pro and con arguments, and address what you have to say to an audience of local journalists. Whatever position you take, include a brief summary of Nolen's position. Then, for each reason you use to defend or attack his position, provide detailed explanation in the form of information from other readings in this chapter and from your own and others' experiences and ideas.

5. *Investigate some medical research currently being conducted at a local medical school.* Your goal is to analyze the kinds of research being done and to evaluate the potential effects of their results on society. You may also choose to analyze these research projects in terms of their possible benefits to particular groups in society, for example, a particular gender or individuals suffering from a particular illness. To conduct this investigation, identify individuals who may consent to being interviewed. Once you have obtained their consent, generate a short but specific list of questions to ask each researcher or administrator. Take careful notes during the interview (or request permission to record it). Analyze the results and prepare a report of your findings. If your teacher requires it, use an organization pattern (review pages 84 to 85) that reflects a scientist's format for reporting

the results of an investigation (refer to the Research Appendix for information on how to document interviews). If you do not live in a community with a medical school nearby, you may conduct this investigation by examining several issues of a variety of periodicals that cover health- care topics.

6. *Conduct a survey of attitudes towards some healthcare issue raised by the readings or in classroom discussions.* If your teacher agrees, you may conduct this investigation with a group of two or three students who are also interested in learning more about public attitudes. Conduct some library research, perhaps reading about some of the issues raised in Bouton's article, and develop a questionnaire that will produce information about your survey respondents' (your subjects) beliefs about this issue. You need to decide which attitudes you are interested in learning more about and which individuals you are interested in surveying. You also need to consider the ethics of conducting a survey. How will you obtain permission from the subjects? From your college, if necessary? How will you guarantee your subjects' anonymity? Administer the survey, trying to create a representative sample of subjects. Analyze your results and report them to your classmates using this format: introduction (in which you review your reading on the particular healthcare issue and explain what you were trying to learn more about and what you expected to find), method (in which you describe what you did), results (in which you present the subjects' responses), and discussion (in which you analyze and explain the results and suggest future research on the topic).

7. *Using library sources, investigate one or more court cases involving medical ethics issues, perhaps a case identified in one of this chapter's readings or one that has piqued the local community's interest.* Generate a list of questions your readers (classmates) need answers to; identify possible library sources that would give you those answers. Once you have read and taken notes from those sources, develop a thesis for a report on the case or cases you have been researching. Do you want to explain, for example, how this case has set a precedent for a particular aspect of healthcare practice, or do you want to persuade your class- mates that this case demonstrates that your position on a particular healthcare issue is justified? Once you have decided what point you will make about this case (your thesis), you can reconsider your notes and your own experiences and begin to plan a strategy for presenting your ideas to your readers. To plan this strategy, you need to make some decisions about how to introduce the focus of your report to your readers and pique their interest as well. You also need to decide how to organize support for the thesis most effectively. Finally, you need to plan a way to conclude your report in a way that reviews its main points and suggests its implications to your readers.

*8. Investigate current viewpoints concerning mandated HIV testing.* Find out whether any local, state, or federal legislation requires such tests for particular groups. Learn as much as you can about how people feel about such legislation and what reasons they offer to support their viewpoints. Then write a persuasive personal essay, explaining your opinion about mandated HIV testing. Be sure you state and explain your reasons clearly and thoroughly. You must also convince your readers that you have considered opposing viewpoints, but have reasons to reject those viewpoints. Finally, consider the kinds of emotional and logical appeals that would convince your readers to respect your position.

*9. Imagine you have been asked to speak to a group of high-school students at a science fair assembly.* The focus of this assembly is "Frontiers of Healthcare: Issues in the Twenty-First Century." Your particular presentation focuses on genetic testing and its possibilities in the future. Prepare the speech you would present at this fair. First, choose a particular type of genetic testing to investigate. Then, using the Klass essay as a starting point, generate a list of questions that your listeners (high-school juniors and seniors) may have about this kind of testing. Next, locate library sources that can furnish the answers to your questions. Finally, draft your speech. Consider how to introduce your topic to your readers and how you can interest them in what you are about to say. You need to organize your presentation carefully so your listeners are able to follow what you are saying. What strategies, for example, would you use to remind your readers of what you have just covered and what your next point will be? What adjustments do you have to make because your rhetorical context is a listening one, not a reading one? Finally, how will you conclude? What will you say to these high-school readers that will focus on your main points and help them understand the long-term issues associated with genetic testing?

# 9

## Women and the Corporate Workplace

What problems do women experience in corporate environments? What causes these problems? How can these problems be solved?

### 1
### DEVELOPING A RHETORICAL APPROACH

The readings in this chapter focus on the recent changes that have occurred for women and, as a result, for men in the workplace, particularly the corporate workplace. Some of the readings describe women who seek executive positions in large corporations and those who choose to become entrepreneurs, running their own businesses. Other readings provide background information on the changes that have occurred and will continue to occur as more women enter the workforce and remain there for longer periods of time. Finally, some readings discuss issues related to these changes from both personal and professional perspectives.

Although these readings focus on women as leaders in corporate environments, the pre- and post-reading questions and activities ask you to consider what they say both in terms of women *and* men in corporate environments. As you read and respond to some of these

402

articles, review your own experiences in the workplace, your career goals, and your perceptions about gender as it relates to employment. You will have opportunities to consider some of the questions these readings raise. How does gender affect a woman's career path? What cultural forces influence how men and women interact in workplace settings? What changes are taking place in the workplace? Can women succeed in traditional male careers? What societal values must be shared before women can succeed in careers traditionally pursued by men? Have affirmative action laws accelerated or diminished female progress in the workplace? What role has the women's rights movement played in the careers of women employed in corporate settings?

As you and your classmates discuss some of these questions and generate questions of your own, you will be able to narrow your focus on one aspect that interests you. This narrowed focus will help you to develop a clear sense of *purpose* (what you want to do in this essay) and *audience* (whom you want to read this essay) for your chapter essay.

## 2
## · · · · · · · · · · · · ·
## GENERATING IDEAS ABOUT WOMEN AND THE CORPORATE WORKPLACE BEFORE READING

Your own job experiences and knowledge about other work experiences provide a useful foundation for the reading, writing, and discussing you will do for this chapter. You can compare what you know to what the writers are saying. The information you bring to your reading contributes to the meaning you construct as you learn more about women and the corporate workplace; after reading, it affects your responses and contributes to the rhetorical community you and your classmates develop around this subject. It also helps develop a sense of audience for the essay you write as part of this unit.

The activities that follow provide a framework for your reading and writing by helping you develop ideas with which to respond in more meaningful ways.

### Probing Personal Experience

Write short, informal answers to the following questions. If you are keeping a course journal, write your answers there. Write your answers in a form that can be used in class.

*1. Have the genders of the people with whom you have worked affected the way they were treated?* Were the men you worked with treated differently from the women? Was the treatment men or women received from fellow employees the same as treatment they received from supervisors?

*2. How did you learn appropriate behavior for workplace settings?* What experiences at home provided lessons for how to act at work? How did the actual workplace provide models for behavior? What specific job-related experiences can you describe that modeled behaviors for you?

*3. Describe some of the working women you have seen on television.* What kinds of jobs did they have? How did they manage the responsibilities of work and family? In what ways are these television portrayals realistic? Unrealistic? Be specific.

*4. Describe a job that you feel you did well.* How did your gender affect your ability to fulfill your job responsibilities? If gender was not related to job responsibilities, explain why it was not a factor.

*5. What kinds of jobs have the men in your family traditionally held?* How did they choose their jobs? What role did their gender play in these job choices? What other factors influenced their job choices?

*6. Compare two jobs that you have had.* How did your gender affect your choosing or getting these jobs? How did your gender affect your experiences in those jobs?

*7. Describe the career choices of three male and three female friends.* In what ways are they alike and different? What accounts for the similarities or differences? How might gender have affected these friends' career choices? What other factors might have influenced their choices?

*8. Describe the job histories of three women in your family whom you identify as belonging to "the older generation."* How do their work histories compare with yours? What accounts for the differences and similarities?

*9. Describe a case of sexual harassment that you have heard about, read about, or experienced yourself.* Could it have been avoided? Why or why not? In your opinion, how serious a problem is sexual harassment on the job? Explain your answer.

### Freewriting to Capture Personal Experience

Here is a list of topics related to women and the corporate workplace that you can freewrite about in short, ten-minute sessions. Your teacher may assign a topic or ask you to choose one yourself. If you are keeping a journal, do your freewriting there. You may begin freewriting by narrating an experience you had that relates in some way to the topic. Recall as many details about the experience as you can to give your writing a personal, interesting flavor. Writing about this personal experience may lead to connections between what has happened to you and some other ideas you have. (For a discussion of freewriting, see pages 103 to 104.)

Affirmative action
Comparable worth
Sexual harassment
Performance evaluation
Entrepreneurship
The glass ceiling
Leadership in the workplace

Freewriting is most effective if you follow this sequence: **R**eread, **F**ocus, **R**ewrite (**RFR**). (For a discussion of RFR, see page 104.)

## 3
## • • • • • • • • • • • • • •
## DEVELOPING RHETORICAL CONTEXT
## THROUGH GROUP ACTIVITIES

Each of the following collaborative activities involves working with your and your classmates' freewriting. The purpose of these collaborative activities is to subject these freely expressed observations and opinions to the questions and responses of others who are working with you. Their responses should help you develop and refine your own ideas before you develop them any further and vice versa. (If you are collaborating for the first time, you should read the description of conventions guiding group work on pages 104 to 105.)

- Exchange your freewriting with a partner. Read your partner's freewriting without a pen or pencil in your hand. When you have finished reading, write a few sentences to your partner saying what you think is expressed in the freewriting. In other words, *summarize* what your partner has written. Then *list* any questions you have about what your partner wrote. Did a particular sentence pique your curiosity? Was some idea difficult to follow because there is not enough information? Are you interested in knowing why your partner wrote a particular statement? Finally, *respond* to your partner by adding any information about your own experiences. Is there something in the freewriting that reminds you of a personal experience? Have you seen or heard something that could be helpful to your partner? After you have completed your work with your partner's freewriting, exchange your responses, take a few minutes to read them, and discuss them with one another.
- Work with a group of three or four students to compose a definition of sexual harassment. Use each member's freewriting

as a source for the collaboratively composed draft. Have group members read their freewritings aloud while the rest of the group comments and responds. Then ask one member to take notes as the entire group brainstorms common threads found in members' freewritings. The temporary secretary can then record the definition of sexual harassment as the group develops it. Return to the freewritings for examples that explain the definition the group has composed.

# 4
## . . . . . . . . . . . . . .
## USING READINGS TO DEVELOP
## A RHETORICAL COMMUNITY

The readings on women in the corporate workplace in this chapter will help your class create a body of shared knowledge and become a rhetorical community. The readings contain information about several aspects of this topic: trends of female representation in the workplace, kinds of leadership roles women have and seek in the workplace, factors that affect the choices women make and are offered, how women combine personal and career goals, and inequities in pay and treatment women experience.

Your reading creates opportunities for you to analyze how different kinds of writers respond to different rhetorical contexts of the same topic. Some writers, for example, rely only on statistics to support their claims, while others combine statistics with their personal experiences and the experience of others to present their ideas. Your understanding of how these differences reflect writers' responses to writing purposes and audiences—important aspects of any writing context—will enhance your ability to analyze any writing context.

## The Readings in This Chapter

The first reading provides some background information about changes in female employment patterns. Susan E. Shank, an economist in the Division of Labor Force Statistics, Bureau of Labor Statistics, provides a statistical analysis of these changes. Focusing on women aged 25 to 54, she explains how and why this age group in particular has experienced great changes in recent decades. Barbara F. Reskin and Heidi Hartmann, sociologists, also provide background information. Reporting the results of an extensive investigation, they describe cultural beliefs about gender and work, and explain how these beliefs affect female workers.

Four articles focus on women managers and entrepreneurs. Barbara Ehrenreich offers a feminist's perspective on the experiences of women in corporate environments. Ann M. Morrison, Randall P. White, and Ellen Van Velsor detail the results of an investigation of female executives. They define what they call "the glass ceiling" and suggest strategies that contribute to a woman's ability to break through it. Susan Fraker, a business writer for *Fortune* magazine, analyzes why so few women become chief executive officers (CEO's) of Fortune 500 corporations. Her analysis suggests that the reasons for this situation are difficult to identify and even harder to deal with. Finally, Lisa I. Fried, a managing editor of *Management Review,* explains why women leave corporate management positions and become entrepreneurs.

Teresa Amott and Julie Matthaei outline a feminist perspective on the issue of comparable worth. They argue that comparable worth can eliminate sexual inequalities not only in the workplace but throughout society. They suggest a comprehensive approach to salary and worth factors in the workplace.

# 5
. . . . . . . . . . . . .
## READINGS ON WOMEN AND THE
## CORPORATE WORKPLACE

# SUSAN E. SHANK ON WOMEN AND THE
# LABOR MARKET

### Pre-Reading Questions

1. Describe the employment history of the women in your family. How are the jobs held by women of your generation similar to those of female relatives of other generations? How are they different?
2. How do you feel about families in which both parents work? What are the advantages and disadvantages? Why are such families becoming more common? Use examples from your own experience to answer these questions.

## WOMEN AND THE LABOR MARKET: THE LINK
## GROWS STRONGER
### Susan E. Shank

Women's attachment to the labor market has increased dramatically since    1
the end of World War II—especially for those between age 25 and 54. More than 7 of 10 women in this age group are now in the labor force, up from about 3 of 10 four decades earlier. The rise in women's

attachment to market work is clearly both a product and a cause of many profound social and economic changes that have occurred in the United States over the last 40 years.

One result of this surge has been a narrowing of the gap between  2 male and female participation rates. Also, women today display a pattern of labor force participation by age group that is very different from that evident 15 years ago. Until the mid-1970's, female participation rates by age formed an "M" shape, dipping between the early twenties and the main child-bearing years of 25 to 34. That pattern has now shifted to an inverted "U" and thus is very similar to that for men.

Another result is that labor market activity has become the norm for  3 most women today. This is true for women in each 10-year group in the 25 to 54 age bracket, for whites, for blacks, and for all marital status groups. Moreover, the majority of mothers are in the labor force today—even mothers of infants and toddlers. As recently as 1975, a Bureau of Labor Statistics study found sharp differences in participation rates of women by marital status and presence and age of children.[1] Such differences have been reduced very substantially over the ensuing decade.

Finally, women today work more hours per week and more weeks per  4 year than they did 10 or 20 years ago. The majority of 25- to 54-year-old women who worked in 1986 did so full time, year round.

This article focuses on women 25 to 54, the age group where job  5 market links are especially strong. Most people in these "prime working ages" have completed school and not yet started to withdraw (permanently) from the labor force. Women in these ages increased their labor market participation throughout the post-World War II period, and the rate of increase accelerated in the mid-1960's. Labor force participation rates of women are projected to continue rising to the year 2000, although at a slower pace than during the past two decades.

## HISTORICAL TRENDS

Women in the United States have been entering the labor market in in-  6 creasing numbers over the past century, but, until the advent of the Second World War, the changes were small and gradual. However, between 1940 and 1944, the number of women in the labor force jumped by 5 million—or more than one-third.[2] Over the same period, about 10 million men entered the Armed Forces and, as their number in the civilian work force plummeted, women moved in and took their places. This pattern was reversed in the following two years. As the GI's returned home, the number of men in the civilian labor force rebounded, while millions of women withdrew from the work force. However, fewer women left at the end of World War II than had entered during the war years, and many of those who exited in the 1944–46 period returned a few years later.

*Age.* The flood of 25- to 34-year-olds into the labor market during the 7
last 20 years changed the long-standing pattern of female participation
rates by age (Figure 1). The historical "M" shape was replaced by an
inverted "U," as the dip in female participation that had been evident
between the 20 to 24 and 25 to 34 age groups almost disappeared. Also,
after the mid 1970's, women 45 to 54 no longer had the highest rates
among the three groups within the prime working-age bracket. In 1987,
the rate for the 45 to 54 age group averaged 67 percent, compared to 74
percent for 35- to 44-year-olds, and 72 percent for 25- to 34-year olds.

The unprecedented changes discussed above can be seen clearly in 8
the participation rates of women in the same birth cohort as they move
from their early to late twenties. As the following tabulation shows,
almost half of the women who were 20 to 24 in 1960 were in the labor
force, but the proportion dropped substantially when these women
entered the peak childbearing ages of 25 to 29:

|  | *Age 20–24* | *Age 25–29* |
|---|---|---|
| Year born: |  |  |
| 1936–40 | *in 1960* | *in 1965* |
|  | 46.1 | 38.9 |
| 1946–50 | *in 1970* | *in 1975* |
|  | 57.7 | 57.3 |
| 1956–60 | *in 1980* | *in 1985* |
|  | 68.9 | 71.4 |

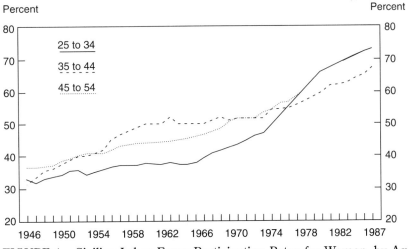

FIGURE 1   Civilian Labor Force Participation Rates for Women, by Age,
1946–87

The first of the baby-boom generation, born only 10 years later,   9
displayed markedly different patterns. Their participation rates were
much higher than those of women born 10 years earlier, and participation rates did not drop between their early and late twenties. Women
born in the latter part of the 1950's showed further remarkable changes.
Not only were their participation rates higher again, but the rates actually
rose as these women moved from their early to late twenties—a reversal
of the pattern just 20 years earlier.

*Marital status.*   Most married women did not work outside the home in   10
the postwar years. In 1957, for example, only about 33 percent of
married women 25 to 54 were in the labor force, compared with
approximately 80 percent of single women and 65 percent of widowed,
divorced, and separated women combined. These differences shrank
dramatically in the following three decades. Between 1957 and 1987,
married women entered the labor market in record numbers and their
participation rate more than doubled—to 68 percent, while the rate for
single women remained around 80 percent, and that for widowed,
divorced, or separated women rose to 79 percent.

At the same time that differences in labor force activity rates   11
narrowed across marital status groups, the number of single and divorced
women rose substantially. The following tabulation shows that the
proportion of divorced women in the prime working-age population
increased fourfold, and the proportion of single women also jumped:

|  | *1957* | *1987* |
|---|---|---|
| Never married | 7.5 | 12.9 |
| Married, spouse present | 80.5 | 68.2 |
| Married, spouse absent | 4.3 | 4.9 |
| Widowed | 4.6 | 2.2 |
| Divorced | 3.0 | 11.8 |

In 1987, divorced and never-married women together accounted for 1 of
4 prime working-age women—up from about 1 of 10 in 1957. The
marked expansion in these groups, which have high labor force activity
rates, was matched by contraction in the married and widowed groups,
where rates are somewhat lower.

## WORK ATTACHMENT

The phenomenal rise in female labor force activity has been accompanied   12
by major changes in the nature and extent of women's connections to
market work. Not only are most women currently in the labor market,

but the vast majority are full-time, career-oriented workers. This applies across virtually all age, race, and marital status groups. It applies whether or not women have children at home and even for those with very young children.

Only in the last few years have women decided to remain in the labor 13 force for a large part of their adult years and to work even when they have young children at home. As recently as 20 years ago, it was more typical for women to work for a few years after they finished school and then leave the labor force when their first child was born. In many cases, these women did not return to market work at all or did so only after an absence of several years.

*Marital status and children.* Labor market activity is now the norm for 14 women, and high participation rates are evident in nearly all demo-graphic groups. For example, in March 1987, rates ranged from 85 percent among divorced women to 66 percent for widows (Table 1). Women 35 to 44 generally had the highest activity rates of the three 10-year groups of the prime working ages. However, this was not the case among the single women group, where 25- to 34-year-olds regis-tered the highest participation rate. Moreover, the rate was nearly 90 percent for women in this younger age group who did not have children.

TABLE 1   Civilian Labor Force Participation Rates of Women, by Age, Marital Status, and Presence and Age of Children, March 1987

| Characteristic | Age 25–54 | Age 25–34 | Age 35–44 | Age 45–54 |
|---|---|---|---|---|
| **Marital status** | | | | |
| Never married | 81.5 | 82.9 | 81.8 | 68.5 |
| Married, husband present | 68.1 | 67.5 | 71.7 | 64.0 |
| Married, husband absent | 70.9 | 68.2 | 76.0 | 67.6 |
| Widowed | 65.7 | 52.7 | 68.7 | 66.5 |
| Divorced | 84.7 | 83.3 | 87.3 | 82.7 |
| **Presence and age of own children** | | | | |
| No own children under age 18 | 79.0 | 89.0 | 82.1 | 68.1 |
| Own children under age 18 | 66.7 | 63.1 | 71.7 | 63.8 |
| Age of youngest child: | | | | |
| 14 to 17 | 74.8 | 82.4 | 78.7 | 67.8 |
| 6 to 13 | 72.0 | 72.9 | 73.8 | 58.7 |
| 3 to 5 | 62.4 | 63.1 | 61.1 | 52.7 |
| Under age 3 | 55.2 | 55.2 | 55.9 | (1) |

[1]Participation rate not shown where population is less than 75,000.

The presence of children, especially very young children, tends to 15 moderate the labor force participation of women, but this effect is much less marked today than it was 20 years ago. In 1987, 79 percent of women with no children under age 18 were in the labor force, compared to 67 percent for women with children. Activity rates for mothers fell steadily in line with the age of their youngest child—from about 75 percent for mothers of high school age children (none younger) to 55 percent for mothers with children under the age of 3. The fact that more than half of all mothers with toddlers were in the labor market in 1987 indicates the magnitude of social and economic change in recent years. As recently as 1967, less than one-fourth of mothers with children under age 3 were in the labor force.

*Hours per week.* The number of hours worked per week or per year is a 16 measure of the intensity of a person's connection to the labor market. Despite a common impression to the contrary, most employed women work full time, that is, 35 hours or more per week. In 1986, for example, 78 percent of all employed women ages 25 to 54 worked full time; an additional 5 percent worked fewer than 35 hours but wanted full-time jobs; and only 17 percent worked part time voluntarily. The proportion of women who work full time has been essentially stable for the past two decades. However, among those working part time, the proportion doing so voluntarily has declined, while the fraction wanting full-time jobs has increased.

Even though most women work full time, they tend to work fewer 17 hours per week than do men. In 1986, prime working-age women employed in nonagricultural industries averaged about 37 hours per week, compared with 44 hours for men in the same age group. Employed women are heavily concentrated in the retail trade and service industries in which part-time work is common. Approximately 6 of 10 prime working-age women were in these two industries in 1987, in contrast to only 3 of 10 prime working-age men.

*Weeks per year.* In addition to hours per week, labor force attachment 18 can also be viewed in terms of weeks worked per year. During 1986, 68 percent of women 25 to 54 who worked did so for a full year, and an additional 10 percent worked 40 to 49 weeks.[3] At the other extreme, only about 15 percent of these women worked for less than half the year. Women's year-round employment rose substantially between 1966 and 1986, especially in the 25 to 34 age group. Over these two decades, the fraction of these younger women who worked for the full year jumped from 45 to 65 percent, while the proportion who worked only 1 to 13 weeks dropped from 18 to 7½ percent.

Combining weeks worked per year with usual hours per week offers  19
additional insights into the degree of workers' job attachment. Persons
who work full time 50 to 52 weeks per year clearly have a strong work
commitment. In 1986, 57 percent of all employed women 25 to 54 were
in this year-round, full-time category; the comparable proportion for
men was 78 percent. As was true of hours per week, work patterns over
the calendar year have been converging for men and women of prime
working age. Two decades earlier, 46 percent of the employed women
and about 84 percent of employed men were year-round, full-time
workers.

Younger women have followed the lead of their older counterparts in  20
moving toward year-round, full-time employment, as they did in entering the labor force. By 1986, fully 55 percent of employed women 25 to
34 were year-round, full-time workers, up from 39 percent in 1966. The
proportion of women in this age group working full year but part time
also rose considerably. This latter pattern—full-year work on a part-time
basis—was the second most common schedule (after year round, full
time) for women in the prime working-age group in 1986.


## FUTURE OUTLOOK

Will women continue to enter the labor force in greater numbers? How  21
high will their participation rates go? How large will the proportion of
women who work year round, full time become? While there are no
definite answers to these and some other questions about women's labor
market behavior in the future, BLS recently introduced projections to
the year 2000 which describe some probable scenarios.[4] The projections
presume a continued increase in female labor force participation, but at a
much slower rate than during the preceding two decades.

*Slower increases.*  Between 1986 and 2000, the labor force participation  22
rate for women in the prime working-age group is projected to increase
10 percentage points, from about 71 percent to 81 percent (assuming
the "middle growth" scenario). While very large by most standards, this
would be only half the size of the increase that took place in the previous
14 years, when the rate jumped from 51 percent to 71 percent.

The primary reason for the projected slower rate of increase is that  23
the huge gains of the past have brought female participation rates to
relatively high levels. There is simply much less room to grow from a
70-percent participation rate than there was from a 40- or 50-percent
rate. A second reason is that the projections assume that participation
rates for prime working-age women will not exceed those for men. This
constraining assumption is built into the projection methodology. A

third reason for the projected slowing is that most of the population growth will take place in the oldest 10-year group in this study (45- to 54-year-olds), where participation is lower. During the 1990's, this group will account for virtually all of the population growth in the prime working-age group—as the first of the baby-boom generation moves into their mid-forties and early fifties.

*Gender differences shrink.* While participation rates for women are 24 expected to continue rising through the end of the century, those for men are projected to edge further down. As a result, the longstanding gap between male and female rates will shrink even more. The following tabulation shows that the difference in the prime working-age group, which was about 60 percentage points in 1950 (and 23 points in 1986), will narrow to 12 points by the year 2000. For 25- to 34-year-olds, the gender difference is expected to shrink to only 10 points.

|  | *Actual, 1950* | | *Projected, 2000* | |
|---|---|---|---|---|
|  | *Women* | *Men* | *Women* | *Men* |
| 25 to 54 years | 36.8 | 96.5 | 80.8 | 92.6 |
| 24–34 years | 34.0 | 96.0 | 82.3 | 93.6 |
| 35–44 years | 39.1 | 97.8 | 84.2 | 93.9 |
| 45–54 years | 37.9 | 95.8 | 75.4 | 90.1 |

Moreover, as the gap between male and female rates continues to 25 narrow, the outline traced by these rates over the life cycle is expected to become increasingly unisex. In the year 2000, activity rates of women are projected to rise steadily from the teen years to a peak in the 35 to 44 age group, then to decline in the 45 to 54 age group before dropping off sharply for those 55 and over.

The shift in the outline of women's participation rates from the "M" 26 shape to an inverted "U," which started in the 1970's, will be even more prominent by 2000. In fact, women's participation rates (in terms of both level and pattern by age) are projected to be more similar to those for men than to women's rates in 1960 or 1970. Moreover, as male rates decline over time—especially in the older age groups—the right side of their inverted "U" shifts to the left and thus becomes more like that for women.

Differences between labor market behavior of men and women shrank 27 dramatically in the four decades following World War II. This was due largely to a tremendous increase in labor market activity by women. Over the past 40 years, the proportion of 25- to 54-year-old women in the labor force jumped from one-third to more than 70 percent. Furthermore, among employed women, 3 of 4 worked full time in 1986, and well over half of them worked year round and full time. BLS projections to the year 2000 call for continued increases in market activity of women, and as a result, further convergence in male and female labor force patterns over the life cycle.

## NOTES

1. See Deborah Pisetzner Klein, "Women in the labor force: the middle years," *Monthly Labor Review*, November 1975, pp. 10–16.
2. These are Current Population Survey (CPS) data for persons 14 years and over. When the lower age boundary for labor force statistics was raised to 16 years, historical data were revised, but only back to 1948. The CPS is a monthly household survey, conducted for the BLS by the Census Bureau.
3. These data are from the March 1987 work experience supplement to the Current Population Survey. This supplement (conducted in March of each year) obtains labor force information for each week of the previous calendar year.
4. Howard N. Fullerton, Jr., "Labor force projections: 1986 to 2000," *Monthly Labor Review*, September 1987, pp. 19–29.

## Post-Reading Questions

1. How is the increase in the number of women in the workplace both a "product and a cause" of social and economic change in the United States, according to Shank?
2. What does Shank mean when she says that the rates of female participation in the workplace resemble an "M" or a "U"?
3. Shank is an economist for the Bureau of Labor Statistics, Division of Labor Force Statistics. How are the natures of her work and audience reflected in the article? How would a sociologist investigate and write about the same subject? How would a psychologist investigate this subject?
4. Describe the way Shank organizes the article. In what order does she present her information? How does this organization reflect her writing purposes and her audience?
5. Summarize the patterns Shank describes for working women aged 25 to 54. Why does she focus on this age group?
6. Describe Shank's tone. How does she sound as she presents her information? If you have read another article in this chapter, compare Shank's tone with the tone of another article. What language choices contribute to that tone?
7. What are Shank's predictions for labor in the future? Where are they found in the article? Why has she placed them there?

8. How would you use information in this article to speak to high-school students about the role their jobs will play in their future? What other kinds of information could you draw on that Shank has not used? Why would you use them?

9. Read the footnotes at the end of the article. Describe the information they contain. Why has Shank included this information in notes rather than in the body of her article?

# BARBARA F. RESKIN AND HEIDI I. HARTMANN ON CULTURAL BELIEFS ABOUT GENDER AND WORK

## Pre-Reading Questions

1. What expectations for the kind of work you intend to do as an adult did you learn as a child? Where and from whom did you learn these expectations? Why do you believe you received the advice you did? In what way were these expectations taught? Were they taught indirectly or directly?

2. Describe your extended family's work history. What kinds of jobs do your family's females have? The males? Why do you think these family members chose the jobs they did? What factors (social, cultural, economic, cultural, historical) might have affected their decisions? In what ways are the factors influencing your career choice similar to and different from those influencing other family members' choices?

## CULTURAL BELIEFS ABOUT GENDER AND WORK

### Barbara F. Reskin and Heidi I. Hartmann

Beliefs about differences between the sexes, many of them taken as axiomatic, play an important role in the organization of social life. These assumptions are often so much a part of our world view that we do not consciously think about them. As one anthropologist put it, they are "referentially transparent" to us (Hutchins, 1980). It is their transparency that gives them their force: because they are invisible, the underlying assumptions go unquestioned, and the beliefs they entail seem natural to us. Even when we do question and revise certain of these beliefs—for instance, when we realize that they are prejudicial to women—the implicit assumptions that engendered them remain intact and can serve as the foundation for future, perhaps somewhat altered, sex stereotypes. The cultural axioms that have been used to exclude women from the workplace, to restrict them to certain occupations, or to condition their wage labor fall into three broad categories: those related to women's role in the home, those related to male-female relationships, and those related to innate differences between the sexes.[1]

## WOMEN'S ROLE IN THE HOME

The first category consists of those assumptions that hold that women's "natural" place is in the home. This group of assumptions underlies many specific attitudes about women and work held by employers, male workers, lawmakers, parents, husbands, and women themselves. It seeks to legitimate women's exclusion from the public sphere and hence the workplace and implies that a woman who is committed to her job is unwomanly. This axiom is neither universal nor timeless. It is an expression of cultural beliefs elaborated especially over the last two centuries and perhaps most fully developed and widely disseminated, through the popular media, in the contemporary United States. The assumption that women's place is in the home follows from the premise that men support women, so women do not need to do wage work to earn a living. By implication, if women are employed, it must be for extras or diversion from domestic life, so their concentration in low-paying, dead-end jobs is of little importance. The corollary to this set of assumptions, that men do not belong in the home during working hours, also accounts for the almost totally segregated occupation of housewife and may help to explain the resilience of the traditional sexual division of domestic work among couples in which both partners are employed full time.

Historically as well as today, the notion that women's place is in the home has not reflected the actual behavior of large sectors of the population; hence it has been in fundamental conflict with the reality of many women's lives. Women have worked to support themselves and their families; they have worked because their labor was needed. Women have replaced men gone to war. They have done heavy labor on family farms when necessary. They have sought wage work when there was no means of support for them on the farm. They have taken in boarders and devised other ways to earn money at home. Women who are urban and minority, recent immigrants, and poor in general have done menial work for low wages, without the primacy of women's domestic role being invoked. And highly educated women, earning better salaries, have also worked as nurses, teachers, social workers, office workers, and businesswomen since late in the last century. As women from all parts of the

[1]This section on cultural beliefs relies heavily on di Leonardo (1982).

social and economic spectrum have increased their labor force participation, the contradiction between the underlying belief about women's place and reality has become more visible.

We can now see ways in which the belief system has been modified    4
with changing circumstances and ways in which reality has been reconciled to the belief system (di Leonardo, 1982). For example, those who insist that women should not work claim the incompatibility of paid employment with women's domestic roles, in that paid work interferes with proper child care. Those who wish to justify women's employment outside the home, by contrast, try to show that it is compatible with, even complements, their home roles. The latter justification permits or even promotes jobs for women that minimize interference with child care through flexible scheduling (e.g., school teaching or part-time work), low demands on incumbents (e.g., retail sales), or work that can be done at home (e.g., data processing, typing, sewing). Certain occupations (e.g., teaching home economics) that are believed to enhance women's ability to carry out domestic duties later in their lives may be considered more acceptable than others. Other occupations (e.g., nursing, social work) have been acceptable because they have been defined as an extension of women's domestic roles, a rationale that has been used to justify paying workers in these jobs low wages (Kessler-Harris, 1982).

Thus, despite the strong contradiction between the notion of wom-    5
en's place and reality, the former continues to provide the foundation for beliefs about the conditions under which women should and should not do wage work. Most important for the present endeavor are beliefs as to which occupations are appropriate for them.


## MALE-FEMALE RELATIONSHIPS

A second category of beliefs includes those about gender differences that    6
are relevant in male-female relationships. For example, an ancient and pervasive belief in Western thought is that women lack reason and are governed by emotion (N. Davis, 1975; Jordanova, 1980). This line of thought offers a logical basis for assuming "natural" male dominance and underlies social values that men should not be subordinate to women. Whenever the two sexes interact outside the family, women are viewed as subordinate, and when they enter the workplace, they are expected to fill subordinate occupational roles. Caplow (1954) elaborates this point, arguing that attitudes governing interpersonal relationships in our culture sanction only a few working relationships between men and women and prohibit all others. He contends that according to these values, "intimate groups, except those based on family or sexual ties, should be composed of either sex but not both" (p. 238). Intimate work groups in which men and women have unequal roles are sometimes

allowed. These norms of sexual segregation and male dominance have frequently guided employers' hiring decisions. Women are rarely hired in positions of authority (Wolf and Fligstein, 1979a, 1979b). Some employers explain that they defer to workers' preferences. Male managers surveyed one and two decades ago indicated that they felt both women and men would be uncomfortable working under a woman supervisor (Grinder, 1961; Bass et al., 1971). They also thought that women in supervisory roles have difficulty dealing with men in subordinate positions.

In several recent studies, it is clear that attitudes about female supervisors have changed. Two-thirds of the respondents in a 1980 Roper survey said it made no difference to them whether they worked for a man or a woman, and only 28 percent preferred a male supervisor (Barron and Yankelovich, 1980: Table 5). A survey of 1,402 university employees revealed a preference for male bosses and professionals providing personal services (accountants, dentists, lawyers, physicians, realtors, and veterinarians), but it was weaker among women, the more educated, and those who had had positive experiences with female bosses or professionals (Ferber et al., 1979). A study of women in several traditionally male jobs in public utilities found that most subordinates of both sexes held positive attitudes toward women managers (U.S. Department of Labor, Employment and Training Administration, 1978). Of particular interest is the admission by several men that they had been initially concerned but that their apprehensions disappeared when they found that their supervisors performed effectively. More generally, this study revealed that attitudes changed quite rapidly with experience with female bosses, even when those bosses held jobs that traditional values label "very masculine" (p. 10). The effects of education and experience suggest that we may expect continued change in employee attitudes toward women supervisors. For women's occupational opportunities to increase, however, the behavior of those making employment decisions must also change.

Sexual relations, as well as power relations, are also relevant in the workplace, and fears of sexual relations particularly may contribute to occupational segregation. The folk theory that women unwittingly tempt men and that men, vulnerable to their provocation, may be prompted to seduction has been used to justify excluding women from certain occupations or work settings that are thought to heighten men's vulnerability to female sexuality. Examples include shipboard duty or jobs that involve travel with coworkers. Women have been denied certain jobs because their presence may suggest the appearance of impropriety. MacKinnon (1979) cites the example of the South Carolina Senate, which refused to hire women as pages in order to foster public confidence in the Senate by protecting its members from appearing in a possibly damaging way. Not only men but women themselves may be depicted as the victims of their unwitting sexual provocation. Reformers around the turn of the century argued that permitting the sexes to work side by side would lead women to stray, either because their presence tempts men or because corrupt men will exploit innocent and vulnerable women who have left the protection of their homes. This concern reflects the belief in women's sexuality as an autonomous force over which neither they nor the men with whom they work have control. And it also reveals, once again, the assumption that women's primary place is in the home: for the consequence of women's employment alongside men feared by reformers was that these women, once having strayed sexually, would be forever disqualified from their domestic roles as wife and mother. Kessler-Harris quotes Robert McClelland, Secretary of the Interior, in the middle of the last century: "There is such an obvious impropriety in the mixing of the sexes within the walls of a public office that I am determined to arrest the practice" (1982:100–101). Such reasoning ultimately led several states to pass laws making it illegal for women to hold a variety of occupations, including bartender, messenger, meter reader, and elevator operator, but it did not prevent women from entering offices in large numbers (J. Smith, 1974; Kessler-Harris, 1982).

More recently, the stereotype of woman as sexual temptress has been invoked to account for women's sexual harassment: simply by entering the workplace, women subject men to their sexuality and invite harassment. Sexual harassment is pervasive in male-dominated occupations that women have recently entered (Enarson, 1980; Martin, 1980; Walshok, 1981a; Westley, 1982). Gruber and Bjorn (1982) suggest that men may use it to gain the upper hand in situations in which men and women have similar jobs and earn equal wages, especially in unskilled jobs in which male coworkers cannot punish entering women by denying them work-related information. The important point here is that the unquestioned assumptions about the sexuality of both men and women underlie the limiting of women's occupational choices.

## INNATE DIFFERENCES BETWEEN THE SEXES

A third category of beliefs that shape women's occupational outcomes are those that assume innate differences between the sexes. We have already seen that women are regarded as innately less rational and more emotional, a view that has been used to justify excluding them from positions of authority. In addition, women have variously been thought to lack aggressiveness, strength, endurance, and a capacity for abstract thought and to possess greater dexterity, tolerance for tedium, and natural morality than men. A body of research reviewed in Lueptow (1980) indicates that the public continues to hold many of these stereotypes about female and male "personalities." Some of these differences further justify women's greater responsibility for family care.

For example, women's supposed natural sense of morality suits them for raising children and bringing a civilizing influence to family life.

Other stereotypes contribute directly to occupational segregation by 11 asserting sex differences in what are alleged to be occupationally relevant traits. Women's dexterity is offered to explain their employment as clericals and sometimes as operatives; their supposed passivity and compliance have been seen as uniquely fitting them for clerical work (Grinder, 1961; Davies, 1975; Kessler-Harris, 1982) as well as other jobs involving boring, repetitive tasks. One employer's explanation, offered in the 1960s, for preferring women illustrates both points: "We feel that jobs requiring manual dexterity call for women. Also this work is particularly tedious and painstaking—definitely a woman's job" (G. Smith, 1964:24). Construction firms cite women's alleged weakness and intolerance of harsh working conditions as reasons for denying them jobs (U.S. Department of Labor, Employment Standards Administration, 1981; Westley, 1982). The social expectations that women should uphold moral standards and care about the needy, perhaps because of their innate nurturance, limit their occupational opportunities. As Epstein (1981) noted, women have been encouraged to perform good works in service-oriented occupations such as social work and nursing, which, coincidentally, have often had poor career potential. And women have been believed to be "too good" for politics. They are also thought to be too sentimental and timid to enforce the law or serve in combat (Epstein, 1981). Women's alleged emotionality may disqualify them in many employers' minds for higher-level positions, especially those in law, medicine, or science that require rationality and tough-mindedness (for a brief review, see Miller and Garrison, 1982).

## SEX STEREOTYPES AND OCCUPATIONAL SEGREGATION

Many of these beliefs about women's innate traits and their natural social 12 roles persist, despite women's increasing participation in a large number of formerly male occupations, even among students training for professions (Quadagno, 1976; Beattie and Diehl, 1979). A single woman worker who violates the stereotype can be explained as exceptional; when the behavior of many women clearly belies a particular stereotype, a different one may emerge to maintain the gender homogeneity with which members of an occupation have become comfortable. For example, women lawyers were dismissed in the 1960s as "too soft" for the courtroom. When they showed themselves to be competent in court, they were restereotyped by male lawyers as tough and unfeminine—and hence implicitly unsuited to their proper role as wife and mother (Epstein, 1981).

Stereotypes about appropriate and inappropriate occupations for 13 women and men encourage sex-typical occupational choices by affecting workers' aspirations, self-image, identity, and commitment. The stereo-typed views that masculine men would not pursue certain occupations, nor feminine women others, for instance, is deterrent enough for most people. Their misgivings are realistic: the femininity or masculinity of individuals who are not so deterred is questioned (Bourne and Wikler, 1978), and they may experience disapproval, especially from males (Nilson, 1976; Jacobs and Powell, 1983). The prospects of sexual harassment or of being prejudged as incompetent at one's work may also discourage those who might otherwise opt for sex-atypical occupations.

Another way that assumed sex differences affect the jobs women and men fill is that employers' beliefs that members of one sex do not want to do certain kinds of work influence their personnel decisions. For ex-ample, individuals who made hiring decisions for entry-level semiskilled jobs in several firms in one city commented to the researcher, "Women wouldn't like this," and "Men wouldn't like to see women (coworkers) this way." Another employer who hired primarily women said, "The work is clean and women like that" (Harkess, 1980).

### Statistical Discrimination

Economists (Arrow, 1972; Phelps, 1972) have termed one form of employers' reluctance to hire certain persons "statistical discrimination," a concept that refers to decision making about an individual on the basis of characteristics believed to be typical of the group to which he or she belongs. The wide acceptance of assumptions of sex differences in characteristics related to productivity provides the basis for statistical discrimination by employers (e.g., Bass et al., 1971). According to this model, employers do not hire anyone who is a member of a group thought to have lower productivity; statistical discrimination serves for them as a cheap screening device. Statistical discrimination often rests on unquestioned assumptions about women's domestic roles. For example, employers may refuse to hire a woman in the childbearing years for certain jobs—especially those that require on-the-job training—because they assume that many young women will leave the labor force to have children, irrespective of any individual applicant's childbearing or labor market intentions. In a study of book publishing, Caplette (1981) discovered that women were automatically excluded from the primary route to upward mobility, the college traveler job, on the assumption that extensive traveling would conflict with their domestic responsibili-ties. According to this explanation of discrimination, employers practice statistical discrimination against women solely on economic grounds and presumably would ignore gender if they came to recognize that their cheap screening device was too costly in terms of misapplied human resources. Employers might, for example, become convinced that young men were equally likely to quit their jobs or take time off to share childbearing responsibilities or that many qualified women will not quit because of family responsibilities.

Statistical discrimination contributes to sex segregation in two ways. 16 First, employers' beliefs that the sexes differ on work-related traits may bias them to favor one or the other sex for particular occupations. Second, if they expect that women are more likely than men to drop out of the labor force, they will hire women only for jobs that require little or no on-the-job training (e.g., retail sales) or involve skills whose training costs workers themselves assume (e.g., typing, hairdressing). Using data for 290 California establishments, Bielby and Baron (1986) examined whether employers seemed to reserve some jobs for men and others for women in a manner consistent with their perceptions of sex differences in skills, turnover, costs, and work orientations. They found that employers assigned jobs involving nonrepetitive tasks, spatial skills, eye-hand-foot coordination, and physical strength to men and those requiring finger dexterity to women. The concept of statistical discrimination also encompasses employers' favoring members of a group whose performance they believe they can predict more reliably. Even if the sexes were equally productive and performed equally well on some valid employment test, if the test predicted women's performance less reliably, employers would make fewer errors by hiring men (Aigner and Cain, 1977; Osterman, 1978). For this type of statistical discrimination to help explain sex segregation, employers must believe that women's performance is less reliably predicted than that of men, and so exclude them from some occupations.[2]

### Sex Labeling and Sex Typing

In an influential 1968 study, Oppenheimer argued that the individual 17 decisions of workers and employers are reinforced by a historical process through which most occupations have come to be labeled as women's work or men's work, and hence reserved for members of the appropriate sex. Oppenheimer contended that sex labeling reflected employers' beliefs that certain occupations required attributes that were characteristic of one sex or the other or, for women, represented an extension of domestic nonwage work. To job seekers, occupations take on the characteristics of current incumbents; custom then tends to make the sex labels stick.

The related concept of sex typing implies both that an occupation 18 employs a disproportionate number of workers of one sex and the normative expectation that this is as it should be (Merton, in Epstein, 1970a:152). Manifest in language and the mass media, sex labels and the

---

[2]One study offers evidence that this is the case. Although Osterman (1979) rejected less reliable predictions of women's absenteeism as a basis for wage differentials, Kahn (1981) showed that he used the wrong indicator of predictability. Using the appropriate one, Kahn found that female absenteeism was predicted less reliably, a finding that could support statistical discrimination in wages.

associated norms are learned through childhood and adult socialization by current and future workers and employers. An obvious example of sex typing in the mass media is classified advertisements stipulating a particular sex or segregated by sex, now not permissible under Title VII of the Civil Rights Act of 1964. Some sex-specific occupational titles (e.g., "lineman," "stewardess") are still common, although most were eliminated in the newest revision of the *Dictionary of Occupational Titles* (U.S. Department of Labor, 1977) and other government publications. Job descriptions often use sex-specific pronouns. Television, movies, magazines, and billboards consistently depict occupational incumbents in stereotyped ways (Marini and Brinton, 1984). These labels influence the occupations to which people aspire, for which they prepare, and ultimately in which they seek employment. Influenced also are gatekeepers—parents, educators, employers, friends, and neighbors—who guide or control decisions regarding training and hiring. . . .

REFERENCES

Aigner, Dennis and Glen Cain. 1977. "Statistical theories of discrimination in labor markets." Industrial and Labor Relations Review 30:175–187.
Arrow, Kenneth. 1972. "Models of job discrimination." Pp. 83–102 in Anthony H. Pascal (ed.), Racial Discrimination in Economic Life, Lexington, Mass.: D.C. Heath.
Barron, Deborah Durfee and Daniel Yankelovich. 1980. Today's American Woman: How the Public Sees Her. Prepared for the President's Advisory Committee for Women by the Public Agenda Foundation (December).
Bass, Bernard M., Judith Krussell, and Ralph A. Alexander. 1971. "Male managers' attitudes toward working women." American Behavioral Scientist 15:221–36.
Beattie, Muriel Yoshida and Leslie A. Diehl. 1979. "Effects of social conditions on the expression of sex-role stereotypes." Psychology of Women Quarterly 4:241–55.
Bielby, William T. and James N. Baron. 1984. "A woman's place is with other women: sex segregation within organizations." Pp. 27–55 in Barbara F. Reskin (ed.), Sex Segregation in the Workplace: Trends, Explanations, Remedies. Washington, D.C.: National Academy Press.
Bourne, Patricia and Norma Wikler. 1978. Employment Among Mothers of Young Children: Changing Behavior and Attitudes. Center for Demography and Ecology working paper no. 82–25. University of Wisconsin, Madison.
Bumpass, Larry 1982. Employment Among Mothers of Young Children: Changing Behavior and Attitudes. Center for Demography and Ecology working patper no. 82–25. University of Wisconsin, Madison.
Caplette, Michele K. 1981. Women in Book Publishing: A Study of Careers and Organizations. Ph.D. dissertation, State University of New York, Stony Brook.
Caplow, Theodore. 1954. The Sociology of Work. Minneapolis: University of Minnesota Press.
Cherlin, Andrew, and Pamela B. Walters. 1981. "Trends in United States men's and women's sex-role attitudes: 1972 to 1978." American Sociological Review 46 (August):453–60.

Davis, Natalie Zemon. 1975. "Women on top." Pp. 124–51 in Natalie Zemon Davis (ed.), Society and Culture in Early Modern France, Stanford, Calif.: Stanford University Press.

di Leonardo, Micaela. 1982. Occupational Segregation and Cultural Analysis. Paper presented at the Workshop on Job Segregation by Sex, Committee on Women's Employment and Related Social Issues, National Research Council, Washington, D.C. (May).

Enarson, Elaine. 1980. Sexual Relations of Production: Women in the U.S. Forest Service. Paper presented at the annual meetings of the Pacific Sociological Association.

Epstein, Cynthia Fuchs. 1970a. Woman's Place: Options and Limits in Professional Careers. Berkeley: University of California Press.

———. 1981. Women in Law. New York: Basic Books.

Ferber, Marianne, Joan Huber, and Glenna Spitze. 1979. "Preference for men as bosses and professionals." Social Forces 58 (December):466–76.

Grinder, Charles E. 1961. "Factor of sex in office employment." Office Executive 36:10–13.

Gruber, James E. and Lars Bjorn. 1982. "Blue-collar blues: the sexual harassment of women autoworkers." Work and Occupations 9 (August):271–98.

Harkess, Shirley. 1980. Hiring Women and Blacks in Entry-Level Manufacturing Jobs in a Southern City: Particularism and Affirmative Action. Paper presented at the annual meetings of the Society for the Study of Social Problems, New York.

Hutchins, Edwin. 1980. Culture and Inference: A Trobriand Case Study. Cambridge, Mass.: Harvard University Press.

Jacobs, Jerry and Brian Powell. 1983. Occupational Prestige and Sex Segregation: Further Evidence. Paper presented at the Southern Sociological Society meetings, Atlanta.

Jordanova, L.J. 1980. "Natural facts: a historical perspective on science and sexuality." Pp. 42–69 in C. MacCormack and M. Strathern (eds.), Nature, Culture and Gender. Cambridge: Cambridge University Press.

Kahn, Lawrence M. 1981. "Sex discrimination in professional employment: a case study." Industrial and Labor Relations Review 43 (January):273–76.

Kessler-Harris, Alice. 1975. "Where are all the organized women workers?" Feminist Studies 3(1–2 Fall):92–110.

———. 1982. Out to Work. New York: Oxford University Press.

Lueptow, Lloyd B. 1980. "Social change and sex-role change in adolescent orientations toward life, work, and achievement: 1964–1975." Social Psychology Quarterly 43 (1):48–59.

MacKinnon, Catherine A. 1979. Sexual Harassment of Working Women. New Haven: Yale University Press.

Marini, Margaret Mooney and Mary Brinton. 1984. "Sex typing in occupational socialization." Pp. 192–232 in Barbara F. Reskin (ed.), Sex Segregation in the Workplace: Trends, Explanations, Remedies. Washington, D.C.: National Academy Press.

Martin, Susan E. 1980. Breaking and Entering: Policewomen on Patrol. Berkeley: University of California Press.

Mason, Karen Oppenheim, John L. Czajka, and Sara Arber. 1976. "Change in U.S. women's sex role attitudes, 1964–1974." American Sociological Review 41:573–96.

Miller, Joanne and Howard H. Garrison. 1982. "Sex roles: the division of labor at home and in the workplace." Annual Review of Sociology 8:237–262.

Nilson, Linda Burzotta. 1976. "The occupational and sex-related components of social standing." Sociology and Social Research 60:328–36.

Osterman, Paul. 1978. Sex, Marriage, Children, and Statistical Discrimination. Unpublished paper, Department of Economics, Boston University.

———. 1979. "Sex discrimination in professional employment: a case study." Industrial and Labor Relations Review 32 (July):451–64.

Phelps, Edmund S. 1972. "The statistical theory of racism and sexism." American Economic Review 62 (September):659–66.

Quadagno, Jill. 1976 "Occupational sex-typing and internal labor market distributions: an assesssment of medical specialties." Social Problems 23:442–53.

Smith, Georgina M. 1964. Help Wanted—Female. A Study of Demand and Supply in a Local Job Market for Women. New Brunswick, N.J.: Institute of Management and Labor Relations, Rutgers University.

Smith, Judith. 1974. The "New Woman" Knows How to Type: Some Connections Between Sexual Ideology and Clerical Work, 1900–1930. Paper presented at the Berkshire Conference on Women's History.

Thornton, Arland, Duane F. Alwin, and Donald Camburn. 1983. "Causes and consequences of sex-role attitude change." American Sociological Review 48 (April):211–27.

U.S. Department of Labor. 1977. Dictionary of Occupational Titles, Fourth edition. Washington, D.C.: U.S. Department of Labor.

U.S. Department of Labor, Employment Standards Administration. 1981. Participation of Females in the Construction Trades. Report prepared by Office of Federal Contract Compliance Programs (September 4).

U.S. Department of Labor, Employment and Training Administration. 1978. Women in Traditionally Male Jobs: The Experiences of Ten Public Utility Companies. R&D Monograph 65. Washington, D.C.: U.S. Department of Labor.

Walshok, Mary Lindenstein. 1981a. Blue-Collar Women. Garden City, N.Y.: Anchor Books.

Westley, Laurie A. 1982. A Territorial Issue: A Study of Women in the Construction Trades. Washington, D.C.: Wider Opportunities for Women.

Wolf, Wendy C. and Neil D. Fligstein. 1979a. "Sex and authority in the workplace." American Sociological Review 44 (April):235–52.

———. 1979b. "Sexual stratification: differences in power in the work setting." Social Forces 58:94–107.

## Post-Reading Questions

1.  This reading is from a book-length report published by the National Academy of Science. What kinds of researchers belong to this academy? What kind of research do these members conduct?

2.  What is meant by the statement that some beliefs of differences between males and females are "taken as axiomatic" (paragraph 1)?

3.  How is information provided about the sources of information? Why is this particular kind of documentation provided?

4.  What is an "invisible" assumption (paragraph 1)? Why is an invisible one more dangerous than a visible one?
5.  Into what three categories are cultural axioms that work against women in work environments divided?
6.  Summarize the assumptions of a woman's role in the home. How do these assumptions affect womens' job choices and options?
7.  What is the authors' purpose? In what way do their language choices reflect their purpose?

# ANN M. MORRISON, RANDALL P. WHITE, AND ELLEN VAN VELSOR ON "THE GLASS CEILING" IN CORPORATIONS

## Pre-Reading Questions

1.  Describe a woman you know who holds a high management position. What obstacles do women seeking high-level management positions face professionally and personally?
2.  How are women in the workplace portrayed on television? How do these portrayals affect viewers' feelings or attitudes about working women?

## BREAKING THE GLASS CEILING

### Ann M. Morrison, Randall P. White, and Ellen Van Velsor

Women in management have carried an enormous load. Many women 1 have paid their dues, even a premium, for a chance at a top job, only to find a glass ceiling between them and their goal. The glass ceiling is not simply a barrier for an individual, based on the person's inability to handle a higher-level job; it applies to women as a group who are kept from advancing higher *because they are women*.

The glass ceiling may exist at a different level in different companies 2 or industries, but just short of the general manager job often marks the glass ceiling for women in large companies. Even in the more progressive companies, it is rare to find women at the general management level.

The general management level also varies from company to company, 3 but as a rule, it means taking responsibility for more than one type of business/function or more than one division's functions. Attaining this level represents a major transition in responsibility according to both the female and the male executives we interviewed, a transition so difficult that failure is a distinct possibility. Executives at the general management level may have an idea of what goes on in each area, but they are not expert in more than one or two, at most, of those areas. These positions are what some of our 76 executives called "real management" because accountability is broad and visible.

Women are often kept from general management. Perhaps this is 4 because of the quantum leap in responsibility general management represents—many senior managers are unwilling to risk putting a woman where she might fail. They may doubt the ability of a woman to cope with such expansive or far-flung responsibilities, and they may fear the visibility a woman would have at such a level.

General management is also the point at which managers are 5 admitted into the "club" at many companies, not unlike a community country club. Prospective members are reviewed carefully by a committee of current members and assessed on criteria that aren't always concrete, even though applicants must pay their dues. As in a country club, people lacking the proper background, image, sex, or whatever, can be blackballed.

Because of general attitudes toward women and the lack of familiar- 6 ity many men have with executive women, the club is often closed to women. Despite the dues they have paid, women typically are not seen as appropriate members. They may be blackballed because the criteria go beyond professional abilities into the broader, but murky, area of compatibility. Men may not be comfortable around executive women. In her 1985 *Working Woman* article "The Breakthrough Generation: 73 Women Ready to Run Corporate America," Basia Hellwig reported that "studies have shown that top executives tend to promote people into leadership positions who are as much like them as possible," because "men are simply more comfortable with and seem to gravitate toward people like themselves. . . . Because of this, gender will be a barrier to women," according to 44 percent of the recruiters *Working Woman* interviewed.[1]

There are risk and discomfort associated with admitting women to 7 the general management team. Another factor that may be involved in barring women from the club is the benefit package that often goes with the rank. Bonuses and special perks often accompany the general manager title and, to the extent that male executives may be reluctant to let women share in these symbolic rewards, they may foster even greater reluctance to bring women into the ranks. There are still some people who believe that women should be paid and otherwise rewarded less than men, which makes women a business bargain and, consequently, tolerable at least to a point.

Many talented female executives, then, are closed out before their 8 time. The fact that *any* women make it into general management may be a minor miracle. Only a small number of women have broken the glass ceiling to enter general management. In our study of 76 executive women, we classified only 52 of them as general managers—the other 24 were one level below general manager. The most we interviewed from any one company was 7, and these are companies that may each have as many as three hundred or more general managers. There were some companies with more female general managers than we interviewed, but most of the companies in our study had only one or two women at that level.

The 52 general managers we interviewed had done what very few  9 other women have been able to do—break through the glass ceiling. They were smart, worked hard, and achieved a great deal, but the same can be said of many other women who lose out on general management jobs even though they may be at least as motivated and capable. The women who entered general management seem to have some "extras" on their side that may have enabled them to break through.

From our research, we have identified three types of extras that the  10 vast majority of general managers mentioned as they told us about their careers and their lives. These extras include credibility and presence, either outside the company or inside, often with a prestige connotation; the unusually strong advocacy of at least one influential person higher in the company; or pure luck that facilitated their career movement in some way. Fifty of the 52 general managers mentioned at least one of these extras, and 36 of the 52 mentioned having two or all three.

We know the savvy insiders believe that getting help from above can  11 make the difference between success and derailment. Yet winning support and sponsorship from higher executives is terribly difficult because of the risks to executives if their female protégée bombs. Most executives want to get as close to a performance guarantee as possible before advocating a woman for general management. Credibility and prestige may be the extras that lead to other extras—getting active support from others or coming out ahead in a reorganization. The combination, then, of establishing credibility in special ways and having the support of influential people seems to give high-potential women enough ammunition to break through the ceiling. If that's not enough, the timing of opportunities may add the extra bit needed.

## EXTRA 1: CREDIBILITY

Women in management still must prove their suitability for executive  12 positions before they can be promoted into these jobs. Yet often the only acceptable evidence of suitability is to do the job successfully. This problem is a critical one for many women—a plight similar to that of the young graduate who cannot get job experience because all potential employers want someone with experience.

We have already noted that women need to be consistently outstand-  13 ing to move ahead in their careers. The general managers in our group were able to build a case for their own competence so compelling that senior executives were convinced they would succeed. The risk to them as advocates of a woman was reduced to a tolerable level. These women built their case by demonstrating their professional abilities for the executives in person, or if they relied on the testimony of others, it was from other executives they respected.

Within the company, it was clear from the interviews, more than half 14 of the general managers had worked directly with senior executives on a project or as an adviser on sensitive or confidential matters. Those who were in staff roles at the time advised top management on compensation practices, tax policy, speaking and public relations, and various other sticky issues. They were the experts from whom the executive committee sought counsel on everything from whom to hire or fire to what business to buy or sell.

The general managers had sometimes served on a task force that also 15 involved senior executives as another way of having direct contact. These included women who were in line jobs at the time, as well as in staff jobs, since those in line jobs could be experts in such areas as cost-cutting or the ins and outs of a new region where they were in charge.

Formal education is one area in which the general managers excelled. 16 Forty percent had academic credentials from well-known, top-notch schools, including the most prestigious institutions. They had earned undergraduate and higher degrees from Barnard, Bryn Mawr, Columbia, Cornell, Harvard, Hunter, MIT, Smith, Stanford, Wellesley, Wharton, and Yale, among others. Some had placed very high in their class, and some had been honored with scholarships and awards.

This is not to say that students at other institutions less well known 17 are not similarly challenging or noteworthy. For top management, the issue is one of reducing uncertainty about the level at which women can perform. To win academically at a big-league school is proof of one's ability. It also implies a level of sophistication and a network of useful contacts that will contribute to overall corporate performance. At other schools, particularly less well known and respected, the standards and the overall value of the educational experience are open to doubt.

Other arenas also can command corporate respect. A few of the 18 general managers had become recognized figures on the political scene nationally, internationally, or at the statewide level. Through very high appointed positions, they achieved prominence in the government sector. Their visible savvy and other talents made them attractive candidates for corporate jobs.

Community leadership is another domain that intersects corporate 19 life and can enhance one's credibility. Several general managers were active on local boards of directors and played key roles in the United Way campaign. In taking on these responsibilities, they worked with business leaders several levels above them, from their own company as well as from others. They interacted with senior executives as peers in some cases because of the comparable roles they held in outside governance and fund-raising activities. And more senior executives got to know them personally and see them in action. One executive remarked: "My vice president was very hard to please. Strangely enough, it was the way I ran our United Way campaign that won him over."

Being prominent in the social life of the community may also have 20 helped some general managers get the attention of senior executives and, subsequently, a chance to take on a corporate job. Some were clearly in the right social circles and, in that realm, were peers of the top executives who create career opportunities for them. Again, the direct contact these women had with senior executives at social functions may have played a part in convincing the executives that they had marketable skills.

Perhaps the most compelling of the outside activities that the general 21 managers took on were those related to the trade or profession. One woman was elected president of the national association in which the senior executives of her company were active, which gave her added credibility:

> The company supported my being president. . . . It gave me great visibility. In that speaking role, people saw me, and I got job offers.


## EXTRA 2: ADVOCACY

Women need help from above to get the kind of experience they need to 22 be promoted, as we noted earlier. The extra credibility makes them more fail-safe for the general management ranks; still, women probably won't break the glass ceiling without the unusually strong advocacy of a senior manager. A senior manager might spot a woman who is doing something unusual for a woman or in general. Investigation into her background might reveal some undisputable abilities. With this reasonable assurance that she is talented and able to command respect, the senior manager might give her a visible assignment in the corporation. When she performs up to par, her credibility grows and she gets another visible assignment.

Those who were willing to advocate for any of our general managers 23 to get a visible assignment were usually those who had worked directly with them—presumably those most certain of their capabilities. Women spoke of their gratitude to a helpful boss who was special for several reasons, one often being a willingness to push them into the direct vision of senior executives. Once they were in the limelight, a higher-level executive who saw them in action sometimes picked up the ball and invited them to work directly for him or her, or placed them in yet another visible, perhaps prestigious, role in the company.

The reasons for sponsoring a woman are not entirely clear from our 24 study. Some executives may have backed a competent woman in a move toward social justice, unhappy that women equal to men in ability were denied the chance to contribute as fully. Other sponsors may have had different motivations for supporting a woman, but the Equal Employment Opportunity pressure probably made it easier for all of them to make a case for promoting high-potential women. Nearly 40 percent of the general managers made reference to the EEO requirements during their career that represented for them an extra in reaching their high level.

## EXTRA 3: OUTRIGHT LUCK

One savvy insider commented that executive women, more than men, 25 need "a break or two." Sometimes serendipity makes all the difference in a career—meeting someone who is hiring people in your field, getting into a business that is on the upswing, and playing a role in a project that attracts national attention are all examples of how luck and timing can help your career. Naturally, luck and ability are often related. Getting a boss who is willing to promote a woman, being a young professional when the Equal Employment Opportunity Commission pushed strongly for women in management, or being the only one around at the time who knows something about a problem are all examples of how luck can join with ability to help someone succeed.

One break that 13 of our 52 general managers mentioned was a 26 reorganization of the company that opened some career opportunities to them. Some got to play an active role in the merger or divestiture itself—the process of reorganization was the forum for them to take on new responsibilities, work with top executives, or represent the company. For others, an acquisition created new testing grounds that they entered and in which they proved themselves.

Luck and timing work to the good of aspiring executives, but they 27 also work to their detriment. Some women were said to have derailed once a reorganization took place, and some of our general managers recounted the career setbacks they had as a result of a reorganization. Women succumb to the whims of fate just as men do. If there is a difference between women and men, it may be that women need more luck (along with more ability) to get ahead because of the barriers they confront. Even good luck can be hazardous to a woman's career, however, because many people are more than willing to attribute her progress or achievements to luck and not to her capabilities.

Two researchers from the University of Texas at Arlington, Howard 28
Garland and Kenneth Price, in examining a number of studies on
perceptions of why people succeed, found that people attribute the
above-average performance of a man more to his skill than to luck.
However, the same level of performance by a woman is attributed more
to luck than to her abilities. These authors conclude:

> An individual could maintain a strong bias against women in management in
> the face of information about a successful female manager by attributing her
> success to some external cause . . . the female manager is not given personal
> credit for her success.[2]

Another example of luck being used to explain the success of women 29
is the story of Katharine Graham. Many people know that, for more than
twenty years, since 1963, she was the only female CEO of a Fortune 500
company. Many people also know that she took control of the *Washington Post* after her husband's death, as *Forbes* and other publications are
quick to reveal in their reports.[3] In other words, she inherited the reins
of power from her husband, which casts some doubt on her ability. We
are left with the question, Without that marriage and her husband's
untimely death, could she have reached that level? Was she just lucky?

What most people *don't* know about the *Washington Post* situation is 30
that Katharine's father bought that business in 1933, and he chose her
husband, Philip Graham, to run the family affairs. Philip had as much of
an advantage via family connections as did Katharine. He was just as
"lucky," but few people mention it or are particularly bothered by it.
Probably a fair number of male CEOs of large companies had family
connections or other forms of luck, but perhaps we hear less about them
because people tend to attribute men's success to their own skills.

Executive women do need some luck to break the glass ceiling, but 31
luck alone does not work. Luck in combination with competence and
support makes this milestone possible. These three extras are not always
within one's control, but they may make the difference between women
who have succeeded to general management and those who still see the
glass ceiling above them.

NOTES

1. Basia Hellwig, "The Breakthrough Generation: 73 Women Ready to Run
   Corporate America," *Working Woman* (April 1985): 148.
2. Howard Garland and Kenneth H. Price, "Attitudes toward Women in
   Management and Attributions for Their Success and Failure in a Managerial
   Position," *Journal of Applied Psychology* 62 (1977): 30.
3. Pamela Sherrid, "Embarrassment of Riches," *Forbes*, 9 April 1984, pp. 45–46.

## Post-Reading Questions

1.  How do the authors explain "the glass ceiling" in corporations? At what level is it found in an organization's management structure? Why is this ceiling there? Why do the authors describe it as made of glass?
2.  How do jobs above the glass ceiling differ from those below it? How do these differences explain the existence of this glass ceiling, according to the authors?
3.  What "extras" do the authors believe may help women who are trying to break through the glass ceiling?
4.  Do you think the glass ceiling will disappear in time? If so, when and why? What factors would contribute to its disappearance? If you do not think it will disappear, explain why it will remain in place.
5.  What are the authors' writing purposes? How do they achieve these purposes? How would they change their approach if they were writing about their research for a magazine such as *Good Housekeeping* or *Ms.*?
6.  Describe the tone of this article. How do the authors sound as they present their information? How does their tone help them accomplish their writing purposes?
7.  The authors use the phrase "our research" in this chapter. Although they do not describe their research methods, how does the kind of information they present suggest particular research methods? Are there any other clues in the reading that help you understand how they obtained their information?
8.  Read the first paragraph in Barbara Ehrenreich's article on corporate women (page 435). How is her first paragraph different from this reading's? How is it similar? How are these differences or similarities related to the authors' purposes and audiences?

# BARBARA EHRENREICH ON CORPORATE WOMEN

## Pre-Reading Questions

1.  How has the women's movement affected your life? What impact may it have on your future? Describe the women you know who have been active in the movement. What are they like? What beliefs do they share? How do they differ?
2.  What does the expression "liberated woman" mean to you? Do you consider it a positive or negative term (or both)? Why? In what ways has the liberated woman been stereotyped? How do such stereotypes compare to your own experiences with "liberated" women? Is this

expression used to describe a woman as often now as it might have been used during the 1960s and 1970s? Why or why not?

## STRATEGIES OF CORPORATE WOMEN
### Barbara Ehrenreich

Some of us are old enough to recall when the stereotype of a "liberated woman" was a disheveled radical, notoriously braless, and usually hoarse from denouncing the twin evils of capitalism and patriarchy. Today the stereotype is more likely to be a tidy executive who carries an attaché case and is skilled in discussing market shares and leveraged buy-outs. In fact, thanks in no small part to the anger of the earlier, radical feminists, women have gained a real toehold in the corporate world: about 30 percent of managerial employees are women, as are 40 percent of the current MBA graduates. We have come a long way, as the expression goes, though clearly not in the same direction we set out on. [1]

The influx of women into the corporate world has generated its own small industry of advice and inspiration. Magazines like *Savvy* and *Working Woman* offer tips on everything from sex to software, plus the occasional instructive tale about a woman who rises effortlessly from managing a boutique to being the CEO of a multinational corporation. Scores of books published since the mid-1970s have told the aspiring managerial woman what to wear, how to flatter superiors, and when necessary, fire subordinates. Even old-fashioned radicals like myself, for whom "CD" still means civil disobedience rather than an eight percent interest rate, can expect to receive a volume of second-class mail inviting them to join their corporate sisters at a "networking brunch" or to share the privileges available to the female frequent flier. [2]

But for all the attention lavished on them, all the six-figure promotion possibilities and tiny perks once known only to the men in gray flannel, there is a malaise in the world of the corporate woman. The continuing boom in the advice industry is in itself an indication of some kind of trouble. To take an example from a related field, there would not be a book published almost weekly on how to run a corporation along newly discovered oriental principles if American business knew how to hold its own against the international competition. Similarly, if women were confident about their role in the corporate world, I do not think they would pay to be told how to comport themselves in such minute detail. ("Enter the bar with a briefcase or some files. . . . Hold your head high, with a pleasant expression on your face. . . . After you have ordered your drink, shuffle through a paper or two, to further establish yourself [as a businesswoman]," advises *Letitia Baldridge's Complete Guide.*) [3]

Nor, if women were not still nervous newcomers, would there be a  4
market for so much overtly conflicting advice: how to be more impersonal and masculine (*The Right Moves*) or more nurturing and intuitive
(*Feminine Leadership*); how to assemble the standard skirted suited
uniform (de rigueur until approximately 1982) or move beyond it for the
softness and individuality of a dress; how to conquer stress or how to
transform it into drive; how to repress the least hint of sexuality, or
alternatively, how to "focus the increase in energy that derives from
sexual excitement so that you are more productive on the job" (*Corporate Romance*). When we find so much contradictory advice, we must
assume that much of it is not working.

There is a more direct sign of trouble. A small but significant number  5
of women are deciding not to have it all after all, and are dropping out of
the corporate world to apply their management skills to kitchen decor and
baby care. Not surprisingly, these retro women have been providing a feast
for a certain "I told you so" style of journalism; hardly a month goes by
without a story about another couple that decided to make do on his
$75,000 a year while she joins the other mommies in the playground. But
the trend is real. The editors of the big business-oriented women's magazines are worried about it. So is Liz Roman Gallese, the former *Wall St.
Journal* reporter who interviewed the alumnae of Harvard Business
School, class of '75, to write *Women Like Us*.

The women Gallese interviewed are not, for the most part, actual  6
dropouts, but they are not doing as well as might have been expected for
the first cohort of women to wield the talismanic Harvard MBA.
Certainly they are not doing as well as their male contemporaries, and
the gap widens with every year since graduation. Nor do they seem to be
a very happy or likable group. Suzanne, the most successful of them, is
contemptuous of women who have family obligations. Phoebe, who is
perhaps the brightest, has an almost pathological impulse to dominate
others. Maureen does not seem to like her infant daughter. Of the 82
women surveyed, 35 had been in therapy since graduation; four had
been married to violently abusive men; three had suffered from anorexia
or bulimia; and two had become Christian fundamentalists. Perhaps not
surprisingly, given the high incidence of personal misery, two-fifths of the
group were "ambivalent or frankly not ambitious for their careers."

What is happening to our corporate women? The obvious antifeminist  7
answer, that biology is incompatible with business success, is not borne
out by Gallese's study. Women with children were no less likely to be
ambitious and do well than more mobile, single women (although in
1982, when the interviews were carried out, very few of the women had
husbands or children). But the obvious feminist answer—that women are
being discouraged or driven out by sexism—does gain considerable
support from *Women Like Us*. Many of the women from the class of '75

report having been snubbed, insulted, or passed over for promotions by their male co-workers. Under these circumstances, even the most determined feminist would begin to suffer from what Dr. Herbert J. Freudenberger and Gail North call "business burnout." For non-feminists—or, more precisely, post-feminists—like Gallese and her informants, sexism must be all the more wounding for being so invisible and nameless. What you cannot name, except as apparently random incidents of "discrimination," you cannot hope to do much about.

Gallese suggests another problem, potentially far harder to eradicate 8 than any form of discrimination. There may be a poor fit between the impersonal, bureaucratic culture of the corporation and what is, whether as a result of hormones or history, the female personality. The exception that seems to prove the rule is Suzanne, who is the most successful of the alumnae and who is also a monster of detachment from her fellow human beings. In contrast, Gallese observes that men who rise to the top are often thoroughly dull and "ordinary"—as men go—but perhaps ideally suited to a work world in which interpersonal attachments are shallow and all attention must focus on the famed bottom line.

To judge from the advice books, however, the corporate culture is 9 not as impersonal, in a stern Weberian sense, as we have been led to believe. For example, *The Right Moves,* which is a good representative of the "how to be more like the boys" genre of books for corporate women, tells us to "eliminate the notion that the people with whom you work are your friends"—sound advice for anyone who aspires to the bureaucratic personality. But it also insists that it is necessary to cultivate the "illusion of friendship," lest co-workers find you "aloof and arrogant." You must, in other words, dissemble in order to effect the kind of personality—artificially warm but never actually friendly—that suits the corporate culture.

Now, in a task-oriented, meritocratic organization—or, let us just 10 say, a thoroughly capitalist organization dedicated to the maximization of profit—it should not be necessary to cultivate "illusions" of any kind. It should be enough just to get the job done. But as *The Right Moves* explains, and the stories in *Women Like Us* illustrate, it is never enough just to get the job done; if it were, far more women would no doubt be at the top. You have to impress people, win them over, and in general project an aura of success far more potent than any actual accomplishment. The problem may not be that women lack the capacity for businesslike detachment, but that, as women, they can never entirely fit into the boyish, glad-handed corporate culture so well described three decades ago in *The Lonely Crowd.*

There may also be a deeper, more existential, reason for the corporate 11 woman's malaise. It is impossible to sample the advice literature without beginning to wonder what, after all, is the point of all this striving. Why not be content to stop at $40,000 or $50,000 a year, some stock options, and an IRA? Perhaps the most striking thing about the literature for and about the corporate woman is how little it has to say about the purposes, other than personal advancement, of the corporate "game." Not one among the Harvard graduates or the anonymous women quoted in the advice books ever voices a transcendent commitment to, say, producing a better widget. And if that is too much to expect from postindustrial corporate America, we might at least hope for some lofty organizational goals—to make X Corp. the biggest damn conglomerate in the Western world, or some such. But no one seems to have a vast and guiding vision of the corporate life, much less a Gilderesque belief in the moral purposefulness of capitalism itself. Instead, we find successful corporate women asking, "Why am I doing what I'm doing? What's the point here?" or confiding bleakly that "something's missing."

In fact, from the occasional glimpses we get, the actual content of an 12 executive's daily labors can be shockingly trivial. Consider Phoebe's moment of glory at Harvard Business School. The class had been confronted with a real-life corporate problem to solve. Recognizing the difficulty of getting catsup out of a bottle, should Smucker and Co. start selling catsup out of a wide-mouthed container suitable for inserting a spoon into? No, said Phoebe, taking the floor for a lengthy disquisition, because people like the challenge of pounding catsup out of the bottle; a more accessible catsup would never sell. Now, I am not surprised that this was the right answer, but I am surprised that it was greeted with such apparent awe and amazement by a professor and a roomful of smart young students. Maybe for a corporate man the catsup problem is a daunting intellectual challenge. But a woman must ask herself: Is *this* what we left the kitchen for?

Many years ago, when America was more innocent but everything 13 else was pretty much the same, Paul Goodman wrote, "There is nearly 'full employment' . . . but there get to be fewer jobs that are necessary or unquestionably useful; that require energy and draw on some of one's best capacities; and that can be done keeping one's honor and dignity." Goodman, a utopian socialist, had unusually strict criteria for what counted as useful enough to be a "man's work," but he spoke for a generation of men who were beginning to question, in less radical ways, the corporate work world described by William H. Whyte, David Riesman, Alan Harrington, and others. Most of the alienated white-collar men of the 1950s withdrew into drink or early coronaries but a few turned to Zen or jazz, and thousands of their sons and daughters eventually joined with Goodman to help create the anticorporate and, indeed, anti-careerist counterculture of the 1960s. It was the counterculture, as much as anything else, that nourished the feminist movement of the late 1960s and early 1970s, which is where our story began.

In the early years, feminism was torn between radical and assimila- 14
tionist tendencies. In fact, our first sense of division was between the
"bourgeois" feminists who wanted to scale the occupational hierarchy
created by men, and the radical feminists who wanted to level it.
Assimilation won out, as it probably must among any economically
disadvantaged group. Networks replaced consciousness-raising groups;
Michael Korda became a more valuable guide to action than Shulamith
Firestone. The old radical, anarchistic vision was replaced by the vague
hope (well articulated in *Feminine Leadership*) that, in the process of
assimilating, women would somehow "humanize" the cold and ruthless
world of men. Today, of course, there are still radical feminists, but the
only capitalist institution they seem bent on destroying is the local adult
bookstore.

As feminism loses its critical edge, it becomes, ironically, less capable of 15
interpreting the experience of its pioneer assimilationists, the new
corporate women. Contemporary mainstream feminism can understand
their malaise insofar as it is caused by sexist obstacles, but has no way of
addressing the sad emptiness of "success" itself. Even the well-worn
term "alienation," as applied to human labor, rings no bells among the
corporate feminists I have talked to recently, although most thought it an
arresting notion. So we are in more or less the same epistemological
situation Betty Friedan found herself in describing the misery—and, yes,
alienation—of middle-class housewives in the early 1960s; better words
would be forthcoming, but she had to refer to "the problem without a
name."

Men are just as likely as women to grasp the ultimate pointlessness of 16
the corporate game and the foolishness of many of the players, but only
women have a socially acceptable way out. They can go back to the
split-level homes and well-appointed nurseries where Friedan first found
them. (That is assuming, of course, they can find a well-heeled husband,
and they haven't used up all their child-bearing years in the pursuit of a
more masculine model of success.) In fact, this may well be a more
personally satisfying option than a work life spent contemplating, say, the
fluid dynamics of catsup. As Paul Goodman explained, with as much
insight as insensitivity, girls didn't have to worry about "growing up
absurd" because they had intrinsically meaningful work cut out for
them—motherhood and homemaking.

There is no doubt, from the interviews in *Women Like Us* as well as 17
my own anecdotal sources, that some successful women are indeed using
babies as a polite excuse for abandoning the rat race. This is too bad from
many perspectives, and certainly for the children who will become the
sole focus of their mothers' displaced ambitions. The dropouts themselves would do well to take a look at *The Corporate Couple,* which

advises executive wives on the classic problems: how to adjust to the annual relocation, how to overcome one's jealousy of a husband's svelte and single female co-workers, and how to help a husband survive his own inevitable existential crisis.

Someday, I believe, a brilliantly successful corporate woman will suddenly look down at her desk littered with spread sheets and interoffice memos and exclaim, "Is this really worth my time?" At the very same moment a housewife, casting her eyes around a kitchen befouled by toddlers, will ask herself the identical question. As the corporate woman flees out through the corporate atrium, she will run headlong into a housewife, fleeing into it. The two will talk. And in no time at all they will reunite those two distinctly American strands of radicalism—the utopianism of Goodman and the feminism of Friedan. They may also, if they talk long enough, invent some sweet new notion like equal pay for . . . meaningful work.

## Post-Reading Questions

1. Ehrenreich refers to several "advice" books in her article. Name a few. What do they have in common? What do they try to accomplish? How does Ehrenreich feel about these books? Why?

2. What is Ehrenreich trying to accomplish in this article? What is her main point? How effective is she in achieving her writing goals? Why?

3. Analyze paragraph 4. How many sentences does it contain? How do they differ? What is the point the author wants to make? How does the structure of the first sentence in the paragraph help her achieve this goal?

4. What does Ehrenreich mean by "retro women" (paragraph 5)? Why does the number of retro women concern Ehrenreich?

5. What is the intended audience for this article?

6. Analyze the sources Ehrenreich draws on in this article. What effects do these different kinds of sources have on you as a reader? How do the sources help her achieve her writing purposes and reach her intended audience?

7. Where in the article does Ehrenreich reveal her personal intentions and political goals? How does this kind of insight into Ehrenreich's political and personal intentions affect readers' reactions to her ideas? How would readers' personal and political values affect their reactions to Ehrenreich's ideas?

8. Read Ehrenreich's conclusion again. How does she restate her main point? How effective is her conclusion? Why?

9. What specific groups of women may not be able to relate to Ehrenreich's discussion of "meaningful" work? Why would they find it difficult?

10. Write a brief summary of Ehrenreich's explanation of why women are not making it in the corporate world. What other reasons could be added to the list that she does not mention? Why might she have not included these reasons in her article?

# LISA I. FRIED
# ON FEMALE ENTREPRENEURS

## Pre-Reading Questions

1. What does the term "entrepreneur" mean to you? Describe an entrepreneur you know personally or from reading or watching films or television. What was this person like? How did he or she treat employees? How did he or she become successful? How does American society in general feel about entrepreneurs?
2. Why would it be difficult for a woman to become an entrepreneur? What obstacles would she face professionally and personally?

## A NEW BREED OF ENTREPRENEUR—WOMEN
### Lisa I. Fried

After 21 years of service at a leading photography and graphic arts firm, 1 Judie Eakins, the president of the company's Dallas subsidiary, found herself out of a job. Five months earlier, a stockholders' dispute over management philosophies prompted the termination of Sidney Gayle, the chairman of the board and president. Eakins' pink slip came when the new management team at The Alderman Co. converted the Dallas operation from a wholly owned subsidiary to a division, eliminating her position.

At that point in April 1987, Eakins had two choices: go work for 2 someone else or work for herself. Eakins had worked for Gayle in a number of capacities at The Alderman Co. So three months after losing her job, she teamed up with him to start two design and photography studios. Eakins, who had managed the turnaround of Alderman-Dallas from a loser into a $6 million company in three years, now heads up Omega Studios Inc. Southwest in Irving, Texas. Gayle heads up a twin studio in North Carolina, Omega Studios Inc. Southeast, and is chairman of the board of the Texas studio. (Postscript: Alderman-Dallas closed its doors one year after Eakins' position was eliminated.)

In an era marked by widespread mergers, acquisitions and downsiz- 3 ing, the circumstances leading to Eakins' departure from Alderman are not that surprising. However, it may surprise some that she jumped into her own business less than three months after losing her job. But Eakins' decision probably wouldn't shock analysts at the Small Business Administration (SBA), who have been watching the escalation of female entrepreneurs for some time now. From 1980 to 1986, the number of women owning small-business sole proprietorships—those with 500 employees or less—increased by almost 63 percent to more than 4 million. During the same period, the growth rate for male owners was 35 percent. And with women owning 30 percent of all small-business sole proprietorships by 1986, women have clearly become a driving force in the economy.

With that in mind, *Management Review* set out to get a closer look   4 at this new breed of entrepreneurs. We interviewed women who head up businesses in the broadcasting, wine making, advertising, computer consulting and photography industries. Their visions for their companies, career motivations and management styles may surprise you.


## A LOOK AT PAST JOBS

When executives leave the corporate life to start their own ventures, their   5 past employment experiences weigh heavily on their management and leadership styles. For these women, the lessons of how *not* to manage have sometimes been the strongest. "I knew that I wanted to do things differently than Alderman had done," explains Eakins, referring to her former employer. "We had four stockholders all involved in the company, all in upper management . . . who wanted to run things their way. Decisions were typically made by committee, and in many cases, the necessary sense of urgency was not there."

While Eakins recognizes the value in having a lot of people partici-   6 pate in management, ultimately one person needs to make the final decision, she says. "You need one person willing to take responsibility and make the decision—right or wrong."

As a result, Eakins has set up her studio with thin layers of   7 management. In addition, her organizational chart is an inverted one; she is on the bottom, responsible to everyone above her. The next positions up the organizational chart are filled by the operations manager (her husband), the controller and leaders. Leaders "are supervisors but not in the traditional sense," explains Eakins, who is a member of AMA's General Management Council for Growing Organizations. "We are not stressing the supervisory aspect as much as leadership. We want them to lead other people and to get them to buy into what they want them to do—not create a dictatorial situation."

Elaine Lyerly, who started her own marketing/advertising/public   8 relations firm in Charlotte, N.C., in 1977, was familiar with many management styles before her startup. Her six years at Group C, another Charlotte public relations agency, exposed her to many types of clients and, as a result, many different management styles. "When you're servicing an account, you learn the inner workings of a company," she says. "There were a number of different companies and management styles that I liked, that motivated employees and that produced the greatest results. I guess I'm sort of a smorgasbord of management styles."

Lyerly refers to Group C, which went out of business in the late '70s, as a creative-driven agency with lots of room for expression. This philosophy seems to have carried over into her firm, Lyerly Agency, as well. Elaine and her sister, Melia, the firm's executive vice president, hold meetings regularly for employees to complain, acknowledge accomplishments, discuss problems and, in general, air their views. "Employees are going to complain," Elaine contends. "And if these complaints are not dealt with, managers are really out of touch with a big pull on the company's effectiveness. Our approach is that we welcome complaints. We view them as an opportunity to interact with employees." 9

For example, if an employee complains about the copy machine, in many companies that person is labeled as a complainer, she says. But if, instead, managers realize that employees don't complain about things unless they are committed to them, they will deal with the incidents differently. One approach is to recognize that the employee may be interested in having an operation run in a more efficient way. "Look at how employees can impact the growth, direction and results of the company," Lyerly advises. 10

Barbara Lamont, president and CEO of WCCL-TV and the New Orleans Teleport, a satellite facility, has certainly heeded that advice. "In broadcasting, there are the 'them's' and the 'us's.' The them's are the unskilled who panic at the slightest thing, and there's always one of them in charge. I try to avoid those types in my business, explains Lamont, whose broadcast career included stints at ABC, CBS, Metromedia in New York and several stations outside of the United States before she started her own television station. "If something happens here, no one looks for whom to blame. Everyone just jumps in to help. 11

"We have a very high ratio of women and blacks and, in general, very highly skilled people. . . . It's most important to me that this be a healthy place for people to work—a place where freedom and creativity is encouraged, where people don't lay blame or [play] politics, one of racial and sexual equality—and, eventually, healthy financially. It shows up on the screen . . . and in our relationships with the community, our viewers and advertisers." Lamont believes that the work environments at WCCL-TV and the teleport are the "most supportive" ones she and her staff have ever worked in. 12

## FOSTERING A POSITIVE ENVIRONMENT

Several female presidents cite the importance of fostering a positive 13 environment for employees. Some measure their success by it, while others consider their emphasis on it a typically "female" management response. "If you're having fun, the people that work for you are having fun, and if you are satisfying your customer base, that spells success," explains Eakins, whose firm employs 67. "The people working with me are the whole company. It's not the building or the equipment that makes our company. It's our people's talent, and that is what makes us what we are and better than our competitor down the street. Seeing these people develop . . . into superior talent, good managers and good leaders is exciting to me.

"I would probably never make it in a *Fortune* 500 company," she 14 admits. "They're probably more bottom-line oriented. You have to be bottom-line oriented, but you also have to have all those people working toward the same goal, and you have to pay attention to them. I consider it a challenge to take someone who's been a problem for others to deal with and figure out how to make that person a star," she says.

Eakins' outlook is common among women business owners. In fact, 15 the need for self-fulfillment, the desire to achieve and an interest in helping others motivate women owners *more* than the quest for profits, according to the 1989 Avon Report, a national survey of successful women entrepreneurs. Only 12 percent of 319 women entrepreneurs surveyed regard profits as the primary hallmark of success. More than one-third say it is self-fulfillment; 30 percent equate success with achievement, and almost 20 percent say success is in helping others.

Nevertheless, women entrepreneurs who focus on these nonmon- 16 etary factors can make just as much money as those who concentrate on sales growth and profit, according to the study. "Women entrepreneurs may choose different paths to success, yet each path can lead to a profitable enterprise," explains Marilyn Frasier Pollack, Ph.D., an expert on women entrepreneurship and co-owner of New World Decisions, the research firm that conducted the Avon Report. "In fact, successful women entrepreneurs who pursue goals other than sales or profit are found slightly more often at the highest level of annual gross sales [indicated by respondents]—$500,000 and above," she adds.

All the female entrepreneurs *MR* interviewed have staffs of fewer 17 than 100 people. Thus, it's not surprising that many thrive on their personal involvement with employees. Deborah Aguiar-Velez, president and owner of Sistemas Corp., a Princeton, N.J.-based computer consulting and training firm, exemplifies this approach. This past year she took a leave of absence from her firm to run New Jersey's Office for the Development of Small Businesses and Women and Minority Businesses, which assists entrepreneurs throughout the Garden State.

Of the 33 employees in the division, she replies, "I love these people 18 dearly. . . . They're like my children. I try to nurture them." At the same time, Aguiar-Velez has surprised some staff members by saying "I love you and respect you and that's why I'm being very tough with you." For example, consider a conversation she had with the secretaries. "I told [them] that they should dress for the future. One asked if that meant a dress code was being established. I said, 'No, if you want to acquire power you have to dress in a different way. You dress for the position you want in the future.' Everyone changed their dress," she reports.

Other female entrepreneurs point out that their management style is 19 a people-oriented one, which requires skills that may come more naturally to women than to men.

For example, Carolyn Martini, who became president of her family's 20 winery after a more than 50-year patriarchy, comments on the impact of gender in international business deals: "American males are pretty straightforward in how they do business," explains Martini, who is also a member of AMA's General Management Council for Growing Organizations. "If they want something or want to sell something, they find someone who wants to buy it. They work out a deal and it's done. They're considerably less concerned with getting to know someone or feeling they trust someone.

"There has been the suggestion that the Japanese think more like 21 women. They, of course, don't feel that way. But they definitely take a different approach than an American male manager would normally take. Women go into business trusting their intuition and men can't understand what that is. The person feels good, you get to know them a bit. For women, it's the way they operate."

## EMPLOYEE RELATIONSHIPS ARE CRUCIAL

Lyerly, who started her agency with a sister, runs her firm with what she 22 terms a "transformational" or "New Age" management style. Dictatorial management is becoming extinct, she explains, noting that some may label it a "male" style because companies have been traditionally run by men. "What my agency is about—and I think women bring this to the table—is a transformational type of management. It's not motivation by fear. It's empowerment and team building. It eliminates some things from the old style, such as jockeying for position, power and authority," and encourages employee input.

She credits women for taking this approach since "they're the ones 23 who are really good at listening and interacting and [don't tend to say] 'this is the way it is.'" Lyerly says her agency's employee discussion meetings signify this approach. Departments meet weekly and the entire staff—12 employees—meets monthly. "There's an opportunity to discuss the agency, complain and acknowledge. The acknowledgement is really important. When someone in the art department acknowledges the media buyer for the great job that was done for a particular client on a tight deadline, it's great."

She is quick to point out, however, that employees are free to 24 comment both positively and negatively. "Melia and I know we're accountable for the results we produce and accountable for our employees. We have to create the right environment for that, so we can't judge them by what they say. And, we stress that it is safe [for them] to say anything." Lyerly says that employees feel free to have frank discussions. "It's usually what's *not* said in companies that is devastating," she continues. "Sometimes Melia and I are there to moderate and keep things going in a positive direction; other times we're not. People usually leave feeling great about themselves. . . ."

If one gets the impression that these women take their relationships 25 with employees seriously, it's because they do. At the same time, these managers have learned that, despite their efforts, some skills just can't be taught and some employees just don't work out. And, in small companies like these, the responsibility for firing someone often falls on their shoulders. "This has always been a real difficult thing for me to do," explains Eakins, who had to fire a large number of employees during the turnaround of Alderman-Dallas. "I go over things again and again to be sure that when I do fire someone, I'm doing the right thing.

"You don't just walk in and fire people. You work with them and 26 give them time to make changes. . . . To some degree you feel as if you've failed if you can't bring those people around. But if they don't work out, you do fire them."

These decisions can be particularly difficult when another manager 27 disagrees with the president's decision. It can be especially troublesome when that other manager is a spouse. Sistemas' Deborah Aguiar-Velez experienced that recently. A programmer who made client presentations was not bringing in new business. Debbie's husband, German Velez, who joined the firm as vice president and senior consultant two years after its startup, thought the employee needed more time to develop. Both German and Deborah agreed to wait it out for three months.

"After three months, he still wasn't getting contracts," Deborah 28 says, "and my husband didn't want to let him go. He thought that long term he was the best programmer we'd ever find. I kept thinking, 'he's not costing us any money but he's not making us any either.' " Hoping he would improve, she allowed him to stay for two more months to finish his computer science training, which would help his career outside of Sistemas. At the end of that time, she and her husband agreed he had to go.

## Post-Reading Questions

1. Where does Fried define the term *entrepreneur* formally? Paraphrase her definition.
2. Where does Fried announce her purpose? What is that purpose? What strategy does she rely on, for the most part, to achieve her goal?
3. What is the intended audience for this article? How does Fried's sense of her readers affect the information she presents?
4. Describe the process Fried might have used to obtain the information she presents in this article. How do the kind of sources and information presented reflect her sense of audience? What do they suggest about her sense of herself as a writer?
5. Identify three women Fried describes. What two qualities do these women seem to share? Provide evidence from the article to support your answer.
6. Why did Fried begin her article with a description of Judie Eakins' decision to start her own business? What effect does this description have on her readers? Describe another way Fried might have begun this article. How would your strategy for introducing the article create a different response in a reader?
7. Why does Fried use headings in this article? How do they help her achieve her writing goals? How do they help the reader?
8. How realistic is Fried's description of female entrepreneurs? What details about female entrepreneurs receive less attention than those qualities Fried emphasizes? What accounts for Fried not discussing these other details?
9. Do you believe the number of female entrepreneurs will increase or decrease in the future? Explain your answer.
10. In what ways might Fried's gender have influenced her treatment of female entrepreneurs? How might a male author have handled the subject differently? How might a sociologist have approached the study of female entrepreneurship? A psychologist? A short story writer? An economist? Why would these writers' perspectives differ?

# SUSAN FRAKER ON WOMEN IN MANAGEMENT POSITIONS

## Pre-Reading Questions

1. How would you describe a woman who has "made it" in the corporate world? Is your description of such a woman different from your description of male success? If so, how? If not, why not?

2. How would you define sexual harassment on the job? Describe some experiences with sexual harassment, either personal ones or those you have heard or read about. Why do women find it difficult to cope with sexual harassment?

3. What does the title "Why Women Aren't Getting to the Top" suggest to you about the article's contents? What does it suggest about the intended readers?

# WHY WOMEN AREN'T GETTING TO THE TOP
## Susan Fraker

Ten years have passed since U.S. corporations began hiring more than   1
token numbers of women for jobs at the bottom rung of the management ladder. A decade into their careers, how far up have these women climbed? The answer: not as far as their male counterparts. Despite impressive progress at the entry level and in middle management, women are having trouble breaking into senior management. "There is an invisible ceiling for women at that level," says Janet Jones-Parker, executive director of the Association of Executive Search Consultants Inc. "After eight or ten years, they hit a barrier."

The trouble begins at about the $75,000 to $100,000 salary level,   2
and seems to get worse the higher one looks. Only one company on *Fortune*'s list of the 500 largest U.S. industrial corporations has a woman chief executive. That woman, Katharine Graham of the Washington Post Co. (No. 342), readily admits she got the job because her family owns a controlling share of the corporation.

More surprising, given that women have been on the ladder for ten   3
years, is that none currently seems to have a shot at the top rung. Executive recruiters, asked to identify women who might become presidents or chief executives of *Fortune* 500 companies, draw a blank. Even companies that have women in senior management privately concede that these women aren't going to occupy the chairman's office.

Women have only four of the 154 spots this year at the Harvard   4
Business School's Advanced Management Program—a prestigious 13-week conclave to which companies send executives they are grooming for the corridors of power. The numbers aren't much better at comparable programs at Stanford and at Dartmouth's Tuck School. But perhaps the most telling admission of trouble comes from men at the top. "The women aren't making it," confessed the chief executive of a *Fortune* 500 company to a consultant. "Can you help us find out why?"

All explanations are controversial to one faction or another in this   5
highly charged debate. At one extreme, many women—and some men—maintain that women are the victims of blatant sexism. At the

other extreme, many men—and a few women—believe women are unsuitable for the highest managerial jobs: they lack the necessary assertiveness, they don't know how to get along in this rarefied world, or they have children and lose interest in—or time for—their careers. Somewhere in between is a surprisingly large group of men and women who see "discrimination" as the major problem, but who often can't define precisely what they mean by the term.

The discrimination they talk about is not the simple-minded sexism    6
of dirty jokes and references to "girls." It is not born of hatred, or indeed of any ill will that the bearer may be conscious of. What they call discrimination consists simply of treating women differently from men. The notion dumbfounds some male managers. You mean to say, they ask, that managerial women don't want to be treated differently from men in any respect, and that by acting otherwise—as I was raised to think only decent and gentlemanly—I'm somehow prejudicing their chance for success? Yes, the women respond.

"Men I talk to would like to see more women in senior manage-    7
ment," says Ann Carol Brown, a consultant to several *Fortune* 500 companies. "But they don't recognize the subtle barriers that stand in the way." Brown thinks the biggest hurdle is a matter of comfort, not competence. "At senior management levels, competence is assumed," she says. "What you're looking for is someone who fits, someone who gets along, someone you trust. Now that's subtle stuff. How does a group of men feel that a woman is going to fit? I think it's very hard."

The experience of an executive at a large Northeastern bank illus-    8
trates how many managerial women see the problem. Promoted to senior vice president several years ago, she was the first woman named to that position. But she now believes it will be many years before the bank appoints a woman executive vice president. "The men just don't feel comfortable," she says. "They make all sorts of excuses—that I'm not a banker [she worked as a consultant originally], that I don't know the culture. There's a smoke screen four miles thick. I attribute it to being a woman." Similarly, 117 of 300 women executives polled recently by UCLA's Graduate School of Management and Korn/Ferry International, an executive search firm, felt that being a woman was the greatest obstacle to their success.

A common concern among women, particularly in law and invest-    9
ment banking, is that the best assignments go to men. "Some departments—like sales and trading or mergers and acquisitions—are considered more macho, hence more prestigious," says a woman at a New York investment bank. "It's nothing explicit. But if women can't get the assignments that allow them to shine, how can they advance?"

Women also worry that they don't receive the same kind of construc-    10
tive criticism that men do. While these women probably overestimate the amount of feedback their male colleagues receive, even some men

acknowledge widespread male reluctance to criticize a woman. "There are vast numbers of men who can't do it," says Eugene Jennings, professor of business administration at Michigan State University and a consultant to a dozen large companies. A male banking executive agrees: "A male boss will haul a guy aside and just kick ass if the subordinate performs badly in front of a client. But I heard about a woman here who gets nervous and tends to giggle in front of customers. She's unaware of it and her boss hasn't told her. But behind her back he downgrades her for not being smooth with customers."

Sometimes the message that has to be conveyed to a woman manager 11 is much more sensitive. An executive at a large company says he once had to tell a woman that she should either cross her legs or keep her knees together when she sat. The encounter was obviously painful to him. "She listened to me and thanked me and expressed shock at what she was doing," he recalls, with a touch of agony in his voice. "My God, this is something only your mother tells you. I'm a fairly direct person and a great believer in equal opportunity. But it was damn difficult for me to say this to a woman whom I view to be very proper in all other respects."

Research by Anne Harlan, a human resource manager at the Federal 12 Aviation Administration, and Carol Weiss, a managing associate of Charles Hamilton Associates, a Boston consulting firm, suggests that the situation doesn't necessarily improve as the number of women in an organization increases. Their study, conducted at the Wellesley College Center for Research on Women and completed in 1982, challenges the theory advanced by some experts that when a corporation attained a "critical mass" of executive women—defined as somewhere between 30% and 35%—job discrimination would vanish naturally as men and women began to take each other for granted.

Harlan and Weiss observed the effects of different numbers of 13 women in an organization during a three-year study of 100 men and women managers at two Northeastern retailing corporations. While their sample of companies was not large, after their results were published, other companies said they had similar experiences. Harlan and Weiss found that while overt resistance drops quickly after the first few women become managers, it seems to pick up again as the number of women reaches 15%. In one company they studied, only 6% of the managers were women, compared with 19% in the second company. But more women in the second company complained of discrimination, ranging from sexual harassment to inadequate feedback. Could something other than discrimination—very different corporate cultures, say—have accounted for the result? Harlan and Weiss say no, that the two companies were eminently comparable.

Consultants and executives who think discrimination is the problem 14 tend to believe it persists in part because the government has relaxed its commitment to affirmative action, which they define more narrowly than some advocates do. "We're not talking about quotas or preferential treatment," says Margaret Hennig who, along with Anne Jardim, heads the Simmons College Graduate School of Management. "That's stupid management. We just mean the chance to compete equally." Again, a semantic chasm separates women and men. Women like Hennig and Jardim think of affirmative action as a vigorous effort on the part of companies to ensure that women are treated equally and that sexist prejudices aren't permitted to operate. Men think the term means reverse discrimination, giving women preferential treatment.

Legislation such as the Equal Employment Opportunity Act of 1972 15 prohibits companies from discriminating against women in hiring. The laws worked well—indeed, almost too well. After seven or eight years, says Jennings of Michigan State, the pressure was gone and no one pushed hard to see that discrimination was eliminated in selecting people for senior management. Jennings thinks the problem began in the latter days of the Carter Administration, when the economy was lagging and companies worried more about making money than about how their woman managers were doing. The Reagan Administration hasn't made equal opportunity a priority either.

What about the belief that women fall behind not because of 16 discrimination, but because they are cautious, unaggressive, and differently motivated than men—or less motivated? Even some female executives believe that women derail their careers by choosing staff jobs over high-risk, high-reward line positions. One woman, formerly with a large consumer goods company and now president of a market research firm, urges women to worry less about sexism and more about whether the jobs they take are the right route to the top. "I spent five years thinking the only reason I didn't become a corporate officer at my former company was because of my sex," she says. "I finally had to come to grips with the fact that I overemphasized being a woman and underemphasized what I did for a living. I was in a staff function—the company didn't live and die by what I did."

Men and women alike tend to believe that because women are raised 17 differently they must manage differently. Research to support this belief is hard to come by, though. The women retail managers studied by Harlan and Weiss, while never quarterbacks or catchers, had no trouble playing on management teams. Nor did they perform less well on standardized tests measuring qualities like assertiveness and leadership. "Women don't manage differently," Harlan says flatly.

In a much larger study specifically addressing management styles, 18 psychologists Jay Hall and Susan Donnell of Teleometrics International Inc., a management training company, reached the same conclusion. They matched nearly 2,000 men and women managers according to age, rank in their organization, kind of organization, and the number of people they supervised. The psychologists ran tests to assess everything from managerial philosophies to the ability to get along with people, even quizzing subordinates on their views of the boss. Donnell and Hall concluded, "Male and female managers do not differ in the way they manage the organization's technical and human resources."

Data on how women's expectations—and therefore, arguably, their [19] performance—may differ from men's are more confusing. Stanford Professor Myra Strober studied 150 men and 26 women who graduated from the Stanford Business School in 1974. When she and a colleague, Francine Gordon, polled the MBA's shortly before graduation, they discovered that the women had much lower expectations for their peak earnings. The top salary the women expected during their careers was only 60% of the men's. Four years later the ratio had fallen to 40%.

Did this mean that women were less ambitious or were willing to [20] take lower salaries to get management jobs? Strober doesn't think so. She says a major reason for the women's lower salary expectations was that they took jobs in industries that traditionally pay less, but which, the women thought, offered opportunities for advancement. Almost 20% of the women in her sample went into government, compared with 3% of the men. On the other hand, no women went into investment banking or real estate development, which each employed about 6% of the men. Strober points out, however, that investment banking and big-time real estate were all but closed to women in the early 1970s. "One way people decide what their aspirations are," she says, "is to look around and see what seems realistic. If you look at a field and see no women advancing, you may modify your goals."

Some of what Mary Anne Devanna found in her examination of [21] MBA's contradicts Strober's conclusions. Devanna, research coordinator of the Columbia Business School's Center for Research in Career Development, matched 45 men and 45 women who graduated from the Columbia Business School from 1969 to 1972. Each paired man and woman had similar backgrounds, credentials, and marital status. The starting salaries of the women were 98% of the men's. Using data collected in 1980, Devanna found a big difference in the salaries men and women ultimately achieved, though. In manufacturing, the highest paying sector, women earned $41,818 after ten years vs. $59,733 for the men. Women in finance had salaries of $42,867 vs. $46,786 for the men. The gap in the service industries was smallest: $36,666 vs. $38,600. She then tested four hypotheses in seeking to explain the salary differences: (1) that women are less successful because they are motivated differently than men, (2) that motherhood causes women to divert attention from their careers, (3) that women seek jobs in low-paying industries, and (4) that women seek types of jobs—in human resources, say—that pay less.

Devanna found no major differences between the sexes in the [22] importance they attached to the psychic or monetary rewards of work.

"The women did not expect to earn less than the men," she says. Nor did she find that motherhood led women to abandon their careers. Although several women took maternity leaves, all returned to work full time within six months. Finally, Devanna found no big differences in the MBAs' choice of industry or function, either when they took their first jobs or ten years later.

Devanna concluded that discrimination, not level of motivation or choice of job, accounted for the pay differences. Could the problem simply have been performance—that the women didn't manage as well as men? Devanna claims that while she couldn't take this variable into account specifically, she controlled for all the variables that should have made for a difference in performance—from family background to grades in business school. 23

In their discussions with male executives, researchers like Devanna hear a recurrent theme—a conviction that women don't take their careers seriously. Even though most female managers were regarded as extremely competent, the men thought they would eventually leave—either to have children or because the tensions of work became too much. Both are legitimate concerns. A woman on the fast track is under intense pressure. Many corporate types believe that she gets much more scrutiny than a man and must work harder to succeed. The pressures increase geometrically if she has small children at home. 24

Perhaps as a result, thousands of women have careers rather than husbands and children. In the UCLA-Korn/Ferry study of executive women, 52% had never married, were divorced, or were widowed, and 61% had no children. A similar study of male executives done in 1979 found that only 5% of the men had never married or were divorced and even fewer—3%—had no children. 25

Statistics on how many women bear children and then leave the corporation are not complete. Catalyst, a nonprofit organization that encourages the participation of women in business, studied 815 two-career families in 1980. It found that 37% of the new managers in the study returned to work within three months; 68% were back after 4½ months; 87% in eight months. To a company, of course, an eight-month absence is a long time. Moreover, the 10% or so who never come back—most males are convinced the figure is higher—represent a substantial capital investment lost. It would be naive to think that companies don't crank this into their calculation of how much the women who remain are worth. 26

Motherhood clearly slows the progress of women who decide to take long maternal leaves or who choose to work part time. And even those committed to working full time on their return believe they are sometimes held back—purposely or inadvertently. "Men make too many assumptions that women with children aren't free to take on time-consuming tasks," says Gene Kofke, director of human resources at 27

AT&T. Karen Gonçalves, 34, quit her job as a consultant when she was denied challenging assignments after the birth of her daughter. "I was told clearly that I couldn't expect to move ahead as fast as I had been," she says. Later, when Gonçalves began working at the consulting firm of Arthur D. Little Inc. in Cambridge, Massachusetts, she intentionally avoided discussions of family and children: "I did not keep a picture of my daughter in the office and I would travel anywhere, no matter how hard it was for me."

Sometimes pregnancy is more of an issue for the men who witness it 28 than for the women who go through it. Karol Emmerich, 35, now treasurer of Dayton Hudson Corp., was the first high-level woman at the department store company to become pregnant. "The men didn't really know what to do," she recalls. "They were worried when I wanted to take three months off. But they wanted to encourage me to come back. So they promoted me to treasurer when I was seven months pregnant. Management got a lot of good feedback." Emmerich's experience would please Simmons Dean Anne Jardim, who worries that most organizations aren't doing enough to keep women who want to have children. "It's mind-boggling," she argues. "Either some of the brightest women in the country aren't going to reproduce or the companies are going to write off women in whom they have a tremendous investment." To the corporation it may seem wasteful to train a woman and then be unable to promote her because she won't move to take the new job. The Catalyst study found that 40% of the men surveyed had moved for their jobs, vs. only 21% of the women. An argument can be made that an immobile executive is worth less to the corporation—and hence may be paid less.

Where women frequently do go is out of the company and into 29 business for themselves. "When the achievements you want aren't forthcoming, it makes going out on your own easier," says a woman who has set up her own consultancy. "I was told I wouldn't make it into senior management at my bank. Maybe I just didn't have it. But the bank never found any woman who did. They were operating under a consent decree and they brought in a lot of women at the vice president level. Every single one of them left." Karen Gonçalves left Arthur D. Little to do part-time teaching and consulting when she was pregnant with her second child. "I didn't think I would get the professional satisfaction I wanted at ADL," she says.

From 1977 to 1980, according to the Small Business Administra- 30 tion, the number of businesses owned by women increased 33%, compared with an 11% increase for men—though admittedly the women's increase started from a much smaller base. While it's not clear from the numbers that women are entering the entrepreneurial ranks in greater numbers than they are joining corporations, some experts think so. "It's ironic," says Strober of Stanford. "The problem of the 1970s was bringing women into the corporation. The problem of the 1980s is keeping them there."

A few companies, convinced that women face special problems and that it's in the corporation's interest to help overcome them, are working hard at solutions. At Penn Mutual Life Insurance Co. in Philadelphia, where nearly half the managers are women, executives conducted a series of off-site seminars on gender issues and sex-role stereotypes. Dayton Hudson provides support (moral and financial) for a program whereby women in the company trade information on issues like personal financial planning and child care. 31

What women need most, the experts say, are loud, clear, continuing statements of support from senior management. Women have come a long way at Merck, says B. Lawrence Branch, the company's director of equal employment affairs, because Chairman John J. Horan insisted that their progress be watched. Merck has a program that identifies 10% of its women and 10% of minorities as "most promising." The company prepares a written agenda of what it will take for them to move to the next level. Progress upward may mean changing jobs or switching functions, so Merck circulates their credentials throughout the company. "We have a timetable and we track these women carefully," says Branch. Since 1979 almost 40% of the net growth in Merck's managerial staff has been women. 32

Sensitive to charges of reverse discrimination, Branch explains that Merck has for years singled out the best employees to make sure they get opportunities to advance. Women, he notes, were consistently underrepresented in that group. In his view the tracking program simply allows women to get into the competition with fast-track men. Others might not be so charitable. Any company that undertakes to do something on behalf of its managerial women leaves itself open to the charge that it too is discriminating—treating women and men differently. 33

What everyone may be able to agree on is that opening corporations to competition in the executive ranks is clearly good for performance and profits. But how can a company do this? It can try to find productive part-time work for all employees who want to work part time—even managers. It can structure promotions so that fewer careers are derailed by an absence of a few months or the unwillingness to relocate. It can make sure that the right information, particularly on job openings, reaches everyone. Perhaps most importantly, it can reward its managers for developing talent of all sorts and sexes, penalize them if they don't, and vigilantly supervise the process. 34

## Post-Reading Questions

1. What topic does Fraker announce in the first paragraph of this article? What strategy does she use to interest her readers? How effective is this strategy? Why?

2. What kind of reader does Fraker have in mind? How do you know? What kind of reader may not be interested in reading Fraker's article? Why?

3. What kinds of information does Fraker present in paragraphs 1 to 4 to support the claim she makes about women in high-level management positions? How persuasive is this information? Why?

4. What are the possible explanations, according to Fraker, for the reality that "women aren't making it" (paragraph 4)? Does her explanation make sense to you? Why or why not?

5. What does Fraker mean when she says that the greatest hurdle women face is "comfort, not competence" (paragraph 7)? From your own experience, why does this hurdle exist? What would have to change for the hurdle to disappear? How likely are such changes?

6. What methods would you use to learn about the Bush administration's policy on affirmative action and on discrimination in the workplace?

7. Describe the organization of this article. What major topics does Fraker present and in what order? Why did she choose this organization?

8. Summarize the research findings Fraker describes in her article. How do they help her achieve her writing purpose?

9. What strategy does Fraker use to conclude her article? Explain your answer with reference to the last paragraph. What effect may this conclusion have on her implied audience?

10. How does Fraker feel about the situation she describes for women in management positions? Where in the article does she reveal her personal feelings about this situation? Do those expressions help or hinder her appeal to this article's audience? Why?

# TERESA AMOTT AND JULIE MATTHAEI ON COMPARABLE WORTH

## Pre-Reading Questions

1. Explain "affirmative action" as you understand it. Why were affirmative action laws enacted originally? How would affirmative action work at a college and in a corporation?

2. Do you believe that men and women doing the same job generally receive the same pay? Explain your answer using your own experiences or those of someone you know or have read about.

# COMPARABLE WORTH, INCOMPARABLE PAY
Teresa Amott and Julie Matthaei

## THE EMERGENCE OF THE
## COMPARABLE-WORTH STRATEGY

When the Equal Pay Act of 1963 prohibited unequal pay for equal work   1
and the broader Civil Rights Act of 1964 set affirmative action into
motion, many assumed that the gap between men and women's wages
would close. Instead, the average salary for a woman working full-time
year-round remained roughly 60 percent of the salary earned by a man.
The constancy of the wage gap in the face of anti-discrimination
legislation drew attention to the fact that women and men rarely hold the
same jobs. Traditional sex roles and outright sex discrimination by
employers and workers have had the result of excluding women from
most occupations other than homemaking and its labor market extensions. Those paid occupations open to women shared low pay, few
opportunities for advancement, and often centered around nurturing
and serving others. Throughout the decade of the 1970s, over 40
percent of all women workers were concentrated in 10 occupations, most
of which were over 70 percent female—for example, nursing, secretarial
and clerical work, teaching, and food service. In contrast, men, especially
white men, had more job options and more opportunity for high pay and
promotion. For instance, stock clerks, predominantly male, earn more
than bank tellers, who are predominantly female, and registered nurses
earn less than mail carriers. As a result of this occupational segregation,
legislation prohibiting unequal pay for equal jobs failed to address the
heart of pay inequity between the sexes: men and women earning
unequal pay for different jobs.

The idea of comparable worth was devised to raise women's wages in   2
female-dominated occupations up to the level paid in male occupations of
"comparable worth." Also known as pay equity, comparable worth means
that jobs deemed to be of "equal value to the employer" should pay the
same, regardless of their sex or race-typing. The first wage comparability
case before the courts was based on race.[1] However, subsequent attempts
to apply the Civil Rights Act to non-identical jobs have focused on wage
differences origins from gender-based job segregation.

Some of the first attempts to broaden the concept of equal pay   3
emerged during World War II, when unions such as the UAW and the
IUE fought differential pay for men and women workers in order to
prevent an overall reduction in pay scales and to generate greater unity
between men and women workers.[2] Since then, the ranks of pay equity
advocates have grown and a more feminist construction has been placed
on the concept. Women's rights groups, working women's organizations

and unions representing women workers are currently pursuing three strategies for achieving comparable worth corrections to pay inequities based on sex or color: litigation, collective bargaining, and legislation. Often a combination of these strategies is utilized by pay equity advocates.

## Litigation

Prior to a 1981 Supreme Court decision, the courts were uniformly 4 unfriendly to charges of sex discrimination in pay across different jobs. In Denver, where nurses charged discrimination because the city paid them less than tree trimmers and sign painters, the judge ruled against the nurses, arguing that the doctrine of comparable worth was "pregnant with the possibility of disrupting the entire economic system."[3] In 1981, however, the Supreme Court ruled that Title VII of the 1964 Civil Rights Act could be applied to prohibit wage differences in similar, but not identical, jobs.[4] Since then, there have been lower court decisions, such as one in the state of Washington, which have awarded back pay to women whose jobs have been systematically undervalued.

## Collective Bargaining

A variety of unions, including AFSCME, CWA, IUE, SEIU, UAW, UE 5 and others, have adopted pay equity as a goal in bargaining, as well as in membership education and lobbying. Most efforts have focused on public employees, largely because information on pay scales is more accessible, and state agencies may be more vulnerable to public pressure brought through community-labor alliances. Local 101 of AFSCME in San Jose, California is one of the public sector success stories. These city employees struck to win a substantial pay increase and "special adjustments" to upgrade jobs held predominantly by women.[5] Unions often combine litigation with bargaining, as in the case of an IUE local which won pay equity raises for women workers employed at a Massachusetts General Electric plant.

## Legislation

Many states have adopted legislation calling for a pay equity study of 6 state employment, and others, including California, Minnesota and Washington, have passed statutes which require public sector wages to be set on the basis of comparable worth.[6] In Idaho, a law which assigns pay in state positions on the basis of skill and responsibility has produced a 16 percent increase in pay for female clerical workers. Other states have begun to raise wages in predominantly women's jobs without explicit recourse to comparable worth. In New Mexico, for instance, over

$3 million was appropriated in 1983 to raise the wages of the lowest paid state employees, over 80 percent of them women, even though a job evaluation study has not yet been completed.

## IMPLEMENTING COMPARABLE WORTH

The primary mechanism for implementing comparable worth in wage    7
structures is the job-analysis/job-evaluation study, and efforts for pay equity usually involve ridding an existing study of inherent sex bias and/or demanding a formal job evaluation study where one does not exist.

Job evaluation studies were in use long before pay equity advocates    8
recognized their potential in comparable-worth struggles. Generally speaking, most large, bureaucratic firms and state agencies do not negotiate a wage directly with each employee, but rather assign an employee to a particular rung of a job ladder. The worker's position on the job ladder determines his or her wages. Workers in the same job would thus receive the same salary, while workers in different jobs would be paid differently. To determine pay scales, large firms use fairly systematic job analysis/evaluation schemes, often prepared by outside consultants. The first step of the study analyzes jobs through examination of job descriptions and, sometimes, discussions with workers. In the most common type of evaluation, known as a point-factor system, points are assigned to each job on the basis of criteria (factors) such as skills, effort, responsibility, and working conditions. In the final stage of the process, dollar values are assigned to the points in each category. The same procedures, and often the same consultants, are used for job evaluations in pay equity cases. In smaller firms, the process is much more informal, but rankings of jobs are still undertaken.

Despite the aura of objectivity surrounding these studies, there is no    9
objective way to determine the relative productivity of jobs. Due to the division of labor, a myriad of different workers contribute to the output of any product, and it is impossible to distinguish their different contributions. How can one technically measure the relative importance of dieticians, nurses, or pharmacological staff to a hospital? Normally, hospital administrators pay market wages—the amount needed to attract workers—and infer the relative worth of these different workers from their wage rates. Job evaluation studies, on the other hand, attempt to determine relative productivity of jobs apart from the market. To do this, they must subjectively choose a set of factors and weights. There are many ways in which sex, race, and class bias can enter into the calculations.

One critical area is the selection and definition of factors to be    10
evaluated. For example, it is common to define responsibility as supervisory responsibility over other workers, machines, or money. In this case,

child care workers would receive low points for "responsibility" even though their jobs entail enormous responsibility for children under their care. Similarly, skilled activities such as nurturing and guidance are rarely counted, causing traditional women's jobs to receive lower points than men's jobs. Boredom from routinized work is not commonly considered worthy of points as an adverse working condition, although outdoor work and heavy lifting are.

Another critical area is the weighting of different factors, accom- 11 plished either through the number of points allocated to each factor or by the method which assigns dollars to points. This has the effect of determining the relative worth of different factors, and generally involves sophisticated statistical techniques such as multiple regression analysis. In effect, consulting firms specializing in job evaluations rely on previous correlations between existing pay scales and measured factor points to predict for new clients what a job's salary should be. From the perspective of the employer, the best point rankings are those which duplicate the existing pay hierarchy as closely as possible, since this seemingly "objective" technique can then be used to legitimize pay differentials. This means that job evaluation schemes usually embody existing pay practices, complete with sex, race, or gender bias. For example, the maximum number of points assigned for responsibility may be 2000, while adverse working conditions are awarded only a maximum of 200 points; this would ensure that managerial jobs pay more than service or operative jobs.

Despite these biased methods, current methods of evaluating jobs 12 can still be used to win pay raises for those in "undervalued" work. For example, most studies have found that male and female jobs with equal point evaluations are paid differently because of the weighting of different factors mentioned above or because firms use different ranking schemes for different types of jobs. In these cases, legislation or bargaining agreements mandating equal pay for jobs of equal point value (under the same ranking scheme) can achieve somewhere between 5 and 25 percent pay increases.[7]

Much more can be won by eliminating bias from the technique. This 13 requires wide access to information about existing or contemplated job evaluation studies. We need to disseminate information on how consulting firms such as Hay Associates, which serves approximately 40 per cent of the Fortune 500 companies,[8] conduct their studies, and we need to bargain for input at all stages of the evaluation process. The more we involve ourselves in the technique, taking power from the technocrats, the more success we will have. Progress has already been achieved in this area. Most unions have staff members who are experts on the technique; feminist proponents of comparable worth are currently at work expanding the definitions of factors so as to recognize the value of women's traditional work skills. (One of the most important redefinitions has been the inclusion of responsibility for children as a compensable factor.) More work needs to be done to rid the method of race and class bias.


## HOW RADICAL IS COMPARABLE WORTH?

While comparable worth directly challenges sexual inequality in the labor 14 market, it may also have the potential for other radical change.

Comparable worth promises to undermine male supremacy outside 15 the labor market as well. Feminists have long noted the way in which the lower wages of women have reinforced the traditional nuclear family and women's responsibility for unpaid work in the home.

As long as women are denied access to men's jobs, and few women's 16 jobs pay a living wage, women are under strong economic pressure to marry. Married women's financial dependence upon their husbands contributes to sexual inequality within marriage. The economic costs of leaving or being left by one's husband are illustrated by the high percentage of women heading families on their own who live in poverty. The risk of poverty is highest for women of color; in 1982, 56.2 percent of black and 55.4 percent of Latino families headed by women were poor.

In addition, comparable worth subjects the pay structure to scrutiny 17 it rarely receives. Conventional economic wisdom argues that in the "perfectly competitive market economy," workers are paid according to their "marginal product," that is, according to their contributions to the production process. (In graduate school, one of our teachers built models which assumed that women were 60 percent as productive as men, justifying this with the fact that full-time women workers earned on average, 60 percent as much as men!) Comparable worth debunks such convenient rationalizations of the pay structure, and the sexist assumptions they both reflect and create, by showing that the force behind pay differences has not been productivity differences but rather power and discrimination. Thus, it presents a radical critique of our system of income distribution through the "free market," and presents an alternative way of achieving what the market had promised: the distribution of income to workers according to their contributions in a manner which is fair and incentive-creating at the same time.

Finally, while comparable worth does not directly attack occupational 18 segregation by sex, it may do so indirectly. On the one hand, by making traditionally feminine jobs palatable to women, comparable worth may reduce the incentives for women to seek entrance into male-dominated, more privileged jobs. On the other hand, as traditionally feminine jobs begin to offer wages comparable to those of masculine jobs, more men will find them attractive. Also, as women begin to fight for and expect working conditions comparable to those of men, they may find men's jobs more desirable, and be more willing to fight to get them.


## BROADENING THE COMPARABLE-WORTH AGENDA

Comparable worth gains effectiveness and constituency when combined with other progressive demands. [19]

Conservative economists have warned that raising wages for women's work would create uncontrollable inflation. While firms will try to increase their prices (and state agencies, their tax revenues), the inflationary impact would depend upon the magnitude and speed of the pay equity adjustment, as well as the ability of firms and governments to pass on the costs. (This, in turn, depends upon the degree of monopoly power and citizen resistance to tax increases.) Finally, inflation is not the worst of all evils, and can be limited by the use of wage-price controls, long a demand of progressives. [20]

What is more worrisome are the other possible reactions of firms and state agencies to an increase in the price of women's labor: automation, elimination of state programs, and runaway shops to countries in which women still provide a super-exploitable labor force. Already, computerization is threatening clerical workers and job flight has created massive structural unemployment in the U.S. In order for comparable worth struggles not to exacerbate these problems, they must be pursued in conjunction with demands for job security, retraining, and plant-closing legislation. [21]

So as to aid all undervalued workers, pay equity must also be extended to include comparisons between comparable but racially segregated jobs. Even this extension will not solve all workers' problems. Workers without jobs will not benefit, nor will workers in those jobs calculated to have the least worth. Since these are the main job problems faced by men of color, comparable worth offers little to them. Raising pay for women in certain jobs reduces inequality between women and men on the same level of the job hierarchy, but increases the relative poverty of those at the bottom of the hierarchy. Their problems can only be solved by a more comprehensive restructuring of work and by a deeper and more radical discussion of the worth of work. [22]

As currently practiced, the doctrine of comparable worth accepts the idea of a hierarchy of workers, more or less "worthy" on the basis of some objective criteria. However, as radicals become involved in decisions about what factors should merit higher pay, we may well begin to question the rationale for the hierarchy itself. If the discussion of what makes work worthy is extended to the grass roots, we may well determine that all jobs are equally worthy. We may decide that workers in [23] unskilled, routinized jobs may be doing the hardest work of all, for such work saps and denies their very humanity. Why should those whose jobs give them the most opportunity to develop and use their abilities also be paid the most? The traditional argument—that higher pay must be offered as an incentive for workers to gain skills and training—is contradicted by the fact that our highly paid jobs attract many more workers than employers demand. And given unequal access to education and training, a hierarchical pay scheme becomes a mechanism for the intergenerational transmission of wealth privilege, with its historically linked racism, sexism, and classism.

We see comparable worth as one of the most innovative and promising approaches to redressing sexual inequality. In fact, given the present reactionary climate, it is one of the few struggles in which tangible progress against injustice is being achieved. Furthermore, as we have pointed out, it raises larger questions about the fairness of the "free market" system, questions which may even undermine the rationale for income inequality.

NOTES

1. The case was *Quarles* v. *Phillip Morris*. For more information, see Judy Scales-Trent, "Comparable Worth: Is This a Theory for Black Workers?" Unpublished paper, State University of New York at Buffalo Law School, 1984.
2. Ruth Milkman, "The Reproduction of Job Segregation by Sex: A Study of the Sexual Division in the Auto and Electrical Manufacturing Industries in the 1960s." Ph.D. Dissertation, University of California at Berkeley, 1981.
3. League of Women Voters Education Fund, "Women and Work: Pay Equity," Publication No. 110, 1982.
4. Ibid. The decision was *County of Washington, Oregon* v. *Gunther*, and involved female jail matrons who were paid 70 per cent of the salary for male guards.
5. Ibid.
6. A good source of information on state and local government pay equity initiatives is "Who's Working for Working Women," published by the Comparable Worth Project, the National Committee on Pay Equity and the National Women's Political Caucus in 1984. The pamphlet contains an excellent bibliography and a list of resource groups in each state. To order, write the National Committee on Pay Equity, 1201 16th Street, N.W., Suite 422, Washington, D.C., 20036.
7. For more information on the uses and limitations of job evaluation schemes, see Helen Remick, ed., *Comparable Worth and Wage Discrimination: Technical Possibilities and Political Realities*, Temple University Press, 1981, and Donald Breiman and Heidi Hartmann, *Women Work and Wages: Equal Pay for Jobs of Equal Value*, National Academy of Sciences, 1981.
8. Ronnie Steinberg, "A Want of Harmony: Perspectives on Wage Discrimination," in Remick, op. cit.

**Post-Reading Questions**

1. According to Amott and Matthaei, why do we still have a wage gap, even though the Equal Pay Act has been law since 1963? How is occupational segregation related to this wage gap?
2. Explain the concept of "comparable worth." Summarize how feminists are attempting to achieve comparable worth for female workers.
3. How would a college develop a job analysis or job evaluation study? How would a consultant analyze jobs at the college and determine pay scales? How would bias affect the consultant's analysis?
4. Why do Amott and Matthaei devote so much space in their article to discussing possible bias in job evaluation studies? What in their political, professional, or personal backgrounds accounts for this strategy? Where in the article are the clues to these influences?
5. Provide some examples of "undervalued" work.
6. In your own words, summarize the authors' purpose. What main point are they trying to make? What is the "reasoning" that helps them make that point? What kind of evidence do they offer to support their claims?
7. How does the authors' feminist perspective affect readers' reactions to their article? How would readers' commitment (or lack of it) to feminist perspectives affect their reaction to the argument the authors make?
8. Explain what the authors mean when they say, "Comparable worth promises to undermine male supremacy outside the labor market as well" (paragraph 15). How do you feel about their claim? Why?
9. Both Amott and Matthaei are economists. Where in the article do they reveal their professional background?
10. Examine the notes at the end of the article. What kinds of information do they contain? Why is this information not included in the body of the essay?

# LAURA MANSNERUS
# ON SEXUAL HARASSMENT

**Pre-Reading Questions**

1. How would you define sexual harassment on the job? Give some examples from your own experience and knowledge to explain your definition. Why is proving sexual harassment difficult? Why do women refrain from pressing charges of sexual harassment? Do you believe the number of sexual harassment complaints in America will increase, decrease, or remain about the same? Why?

2. What is the difference between "job discrimination" and "sexual harassment"? In what ways are the two terms alike? How do they differ? Is one type of behavior more common than the other? Why?
3. Have you ever observed or been the victim of sexual harassment? Describe the incident as you recall it, focusing on both the evidence of harassment and the response of the victim.


## DON'T TELL
### Laura Mansnerus

Sometimes discrimination announces itself like pie in the face to the most 1
wide-eyed young worker. I know this from a talk I had 18 years ago with the executive editor of the first newspaper I worked for. I made an appointment with the busy man and asked if he thought I could ever move from copy editing into a reporting job. He called for the results of the battery of tests I'd taken as a job applicant, he frowned over them and then he said no. A machine-scored personality profile, which he helpfully posed in front of me to let me see that science compelled his answer, showed that I was much too female a type to work as a reporter for him.

So much for my career plans. The news was a surprise (Nurturing 2
and compliant? Me?), a non sequitur and an insult, and it looked like a violation of the employment-discrimination laws. So what did I do? I chatted up the editor at the press club. At parties, I pasted on a smile of rapt interest in his anecdotes. With my boyfriend of the moment, a protégé of the editor—bad coincidence—I went to dinner at the editor's apartment and surely said, "Wonderful to see you." The man was widely loathed, but no one, except the poor boyfriend, heard a word of grievance from me; I was as sweet as the test said I was. A year later, after I'd quit to take a job that then evaporated, I wrote the editor a warm, ingratiating letter asking him to take me back. His response left the door open, but fortunately another job materialized.

I demonstrated a complete failure of moral resolve. Nearly two 3
decades later, having held many other jobs, having become a lawyer, having seen the sex-discrimination laws evolve and having watched the United States Senate recently consider an account of sexual harassment from the most impeccable witness that a plaintiff's lawyer could invent, I know I did the right thing.

Now, I haven't suffered degradation; the sexual advances I've 4
received from superiors have consisted mostly of peculiar remarks from guys who were stranded in the era of pledge formals and hope chests. But I had plenty of answers for the senators and witnesses who demanded to know about Anita Hill: Why didn't she report these incidents? Why

didn't she take notes? Why did she continue to speak highly of Clarence Thomas? Why did she follow him into another job?

One answer is that in trying to patch up the humiliations of daily life, you probably do not consult the rules of evidence, even if you're a lawyer, expecting that someday you'll have to explain any lapses in strategy to Senator Specter. Another is that your tormentor can also be your friend, which might or might not stop you from telling the truth if the F.B.I. comes around 10 years later to ask what it was like to work for him.

But the easiest answer is that a young woman who brings enthusiasm and hope to a job is going to try, sometimes with heartbreaking docility, to get along. And nobody likes a tattletale. We know now that the uglier the tale, the more savage the raking that the victim gets. But we knew all along that to squeal on one's mentor, or even one's boss, is an idiotic thing to do. (You'd think a senator wouldn't have any trouble understanding that proposition.)

A tattletale is by definition a weakling who asks for intervention, which is exactly what the grievance procedures available to workers are all about. The laws and company policies and sensitivity-training seminars are supposed to aid victims and whiners, and that's why the authorities are just as happy that they don't work.

Begin with the Equal Employment Opportunity Commission: last year it received about 33,000 sex-discrimination complaints and filed suit in 197 cases. For a woman who is somehow able to retain her own lawyer—and the plaintiff, incidentally, has typically already been fired—the odds are better, but not by much.

Legislated remedies are fine. They're absolutely necessary. And Congress is stunningly proud of itself for this year's Civil Rights Act, which liberalizes the rules in job-discrimination cases, in ways that a worker can understand if she is also a civil rights lawyer. But most people, civil rights lawyers included, can understand that sworn accusations, discovery motions and depositions are going to have a horrifying effect around the office. Even a discreet inquiry by the company's Human Resources Department will mark the complainer as, well, a complainer—and probably, eventually, as a loser too.

What of the view that the woman who speaks up is a fighter rather than a whiner? Well, it's something you might believe if you're very young or extraordinarily aggressive. But fights take place between adversaries, not between the boss man and a pesky underling. That Anita Hill emerged from the hearings without looking like a perpetually kayoed cartoon character is testament to a dignity that most people don't have.

It's clear that the senators didn't view Professor Hill, who found none among them inclined to be combative on her behalf, as an actual challenge to Clarence Thomas. After all, they were themselves cowed by

Clarence Thomas. Would anybody be cowed by Anita Hill? At best the senators were oily and patronizing.

At worst, of course, they blithely slandered her, which is usually the 12 case when the charge is the kind that would upset the accused's wife. Delusion and vindictiveness are handy explanations, easier and at the same time more cruel to the aggrieved woman than the traditional defense of calling her a slut.

So I look at my own little potential sex-discrimination case from 13 1973. Suppose I had lodged a complaint. I would not have been cross-examined by Orrin Hatch. I would not have had to watch some preening egomaniac I'd spoken to at a party appear on national television to accuse me of romantic fantasizing. No one would have suggested that I'd asked for whatever was said to me. Not at all. As a union member, I probably wouldn't have lost my boring job. But I wouldn't have got another one, at that newspaper or any other, and that seems like enough of a deterrent to me.

Anita Hill, law professor, said hesitantly to her questioners that in 14 declining to invoke the legal process she might have used poor judgment. No, no, no. The 25-year-old who shut up proceeded with a recommendation and no muss or fuss to a university teaching job. Now she has tenure. Her judgment was dead on.

## Post-Reading Questions

1. Describe the experience Mansnerus recounts in her introductory paragraph. Why does she begin her essay with it? What effect did reading it have on you? Why? The experience she describes happened about 20 years ago. How likely do you think the repetition of such an experience is today? Why?

2. What does Mansnerus mean by "I demonstrated a complete failure of moral resolve" (paragraph 2)? Does Mansnerus blame herself for her lack of moral resolve? Do you? Why? How typical do you believe her response is?

3. How does the title of this personal essay forecast its contents to readers? What connection does it have to her thesis? What would a sociologist's title for an article on the same topic sound like? Why would it be different?

4. What is Mansnerus' main point or thesis? Where does she first state it?

5. In your own words, summarize the information Mansnerus presents to support her thesis. How convincing is her support? Why?

6. In what ways does Mansnerus see herself as like Anita Hill? In what ways does she see herself as different? Do you agree with her assessment? Why?

7. Reread the last paragraph of this essay. What does Mansnerus accomplish in this paragraph? In what ways is this paragraph like the

introductory paragraph? What is their connection? In what ways do the introductory and concluding paragraphs differ?

8.   This is a personal essay. What writing strategies does Mansnerus use to convey to readers the personal nature of this essay? In what ways would a journalist's article on the same topic differ? Why?

# 6

. . . . . . . . . . . . . . .

# OPTIONAL WRITING ASSIGNMENTS FOCUSED ON WOMEN AND THE CORPORATE WORKPLACE

Several possible topics have been introduced and discussed throughout this chapter. The following list of essay suggestions provides contexts within which you can compose essays on this chapter's theme. Whether you select one of these options or develop a focus on your own, you need to analyze the rhetorical context within which you are composing and decide how that context will affect your decisions about how you will achieve your writing purposes for the particular readers you target. (To review "The Rhetorical Approach to Academic Writing," see Chapter 2.)

*1. Write a personal essay describing one specific experience you had as an employee.* The experience you choose should involve some kind of problem created while you were employed. Use whatever descriptive strategies you can to help your readers (your classmates) "see" the experience as it occurred. Your purpose in narrating this experience, however, is not only to recreate it. The experience you choose must help you make a point (your thesis) about gender in the workplace. You may, if your teacher agrees, compare or contrast your experience with those described in one or more of the readings in this chapter.

*2. You are a college student preparing a talk for a group of local businesspersons.* You have been asked to focus on the issues that you believe young men or women (or both) seeking business careers identify as gender-related. Many of these businesspersons have been working for twenty or more years and have few opportunities to interact with the current crop of college graduates. Many grew up in an era when men and women had distinctly different career goals. What issues will you present to them and what suggestions will you make for resolving these issues? Draw from your reading on women and the corporate workplace, and from your own and others' past experiences with jobs.

*3. Choose one of the issues raised in one or more of the readings in this chapter, perhaps affirmative action, comparable worth, or women in nontraditional jobs.* Take a position for or against a particular approach to the issue. Then, drawing on your reading of the articles and essays in this chapter, your own and others' experiences, and information from some outside-of-the-classroom sources (an interview, a library article, a newspaper article or news program), state and explain the reasons for your position. Remember to consider what information your readers have, how they currently feel about this issue, and what kinds of questions they will ask about the reasons and evidence you present. Make sure to document any outside-of-the-classroom sources you refer to in your essay.

4. *Write an argument defending or attacking Amott and Matthaei's view that comparable worth is "one of the most innovative and promising approaches to redressing sexual inequality."* Consider both pro and con arguments, and address what you have to say to an audience of local business leaders, perhaps members of the Chamber of Commerce's Executive Board. Whatever position you take, include a brief summary of Amott and Matthaei's position. For each reason you use to defend or attack their position, provide detailed explanation in the form of information from other readings in this chapter and from your own and others' experiences and ideas.

5. *Conduct an investigation of women (or men and women) in management positions.* Identify individuals who may consent to being interviewed. Once you have obtained their consent, generate a short but specific list of questions to ask each businessperson. Take careful notes during the interview (or request permission to tape record). Analyze the results and prepare a report of your findings about these managers, comparing your results to the findings presented in one or two of the readings in this chapter. If your teacher requires it, use an organization pattern that reflects a social scientist's format for reporting on an investigation (see the Research Appendix for information on how to document interviews and organize this kind of report).

6. *Conduct a survey of beliefs about gender and work.* If your teacher agrees, you may conduct this investigation with a group of two or three other interested students. Conduct some library research, perhaps locating and reading sources mentioned in Reskin and Hartmann's article. Then develop a questionnaire that will produce information about your subjects' beliefs about gender and work. Decide which beliefs you are interested in learning more about and which individuals you are interested in surveying. Then administer the survey, trying to create a representative sample of subjects. Analyze your results and report them to your classmates using this format: introduction (in which you review your reading and explain what you were trying to learn and what you expected to find), method (in which you describe what you did), results (in which you present the subjects' responses), and discussion (in which you analyze and explain the results and suggest future research on the topic). Consider the ethical issues involved with survey work. How, for example, will you guarantee

confidentiality for your subjects? How will you maximize the sincerity in their responses? Consider these issues and any others you and your classmates raise with your teacher before administering your survey.

7. *Write a proposal for conducting an evaluation of the jobs at a particular organization.* Conduct some library research about job analysis studies; then obtain permission from a local business to observe or interview employees, perhaps the personnel manager and the affirmative action officer, if the company employs one. Write your proposal as a consultant would, identifying a problem within the organization, suggesting a solution (the job evaluation), providing reasons for hiring you to do it, and describing the cost.

8. *Using library sources, investigate two or three affirmative action or comparable worth cases.* Who were the people involved in these cases? What were their concerns? How were their complaints resolved? What do the results of these cases suggest about the future of affirmative action? Using the information you have gathered from sources, write a report detailing the events surrounding these cases and the short and long-term effects the cases have had on corporate practices in the United States. Your report's thesis should state clearly your personal interpretation of the impact of affirmative action or comparable worth cases on American business practices.

# 10

# Consumerism

How do consumers differ? What factors influence purchasing decisions? How are products marketed?

## 1
## DEVELOPING A RHETORICAL APPROACH

In this chapter, you will be reading about American consumers. During this century, consumer behavior has undergone great change. Researchers who study consumers and their buying practices have found that consumers behave differently at different stages of their lives because their attitudes towards buying and their needs change from one life stage to another. Some readings in this chapter describe consumers at different stages of life. Others focus on research that contrasts different groups of consumers. Finally, some readings analyze marketing strategies and the forces that affect consumers' purchasing decisions. You are encouraged to respond critically to American consumerism by questioning the moral, ethical and commercial motivations that lie behind the phenomenon.

These readings provide a solid information base with which you can develop a rhetorical community focused on consumer behavior. The pre- and post-reading questions and activities ask you to consider your own experiences as a consumer and to respond to the information in this chapter. As you discuss your experiences and responses to the readings with classmates, this rhetorical community will solidify.

Class discussion may modify your views on some of the consumer issues raised in the readings or trigger an idea for your chapter essay on consumerism; similarly, your input in these discussions will contribute to your classmates' considerations of these consumer issues. How do consumers differ from one stage of life to another? What forces shape their purchasing decisions? Why is ownership so important to American consumers? How powerful are the brand-name marketers? What role should government play in regulating advertising? Or, if you decide to take a critical perspective, you may inquire into moral and ethical questions related to these buying and selling behaviors.

The rhetorical community you develop around consumerism will influence your decision about what aspect to focus on in your essay. It will guide your decisions about *purpose* (what you want to do in this essay) and *audience* (whom you want to read this essay). In this sense, your work as a writer is interconnected with your work as a member of the classroom community; your contributions to classroom discussions affect the context within which you compose your essay.

## 2
· · · · · · · · · · · · ·
## GENERATING IDEAS ABOUT CONSUMERISM

The activities that follow provide a framework for your reading and writing by asking you to focus on your own experiences as a consumer. Those experiences and your knowledge about how other people make purchases provide a useful starting point for the reading, writing, and discussing you will do on this subject. They will allow you to contrast what you know about consumerism with what the writers are saying and contribute to the meaning you construct as you learn more about consumers and their behavior. After reading, they will affect your responses to the ideas in the readings and contribute to the shared knowledge base developing in your class around this subject. Finally, understanding your own point of view on consumerism will also help you develop a clearer sense of your audience.

### Probing Personal Experience

Write short, informal answers to the following questions. If you are keeping a course journal, write your answers there. Be sure your answers are written in a form that can be used in class.

*1. Describe what you were like as a child consumer.* Did you have your own money to spend? How much? Who gave it to you? What kinds of things did you buy? Where did you spend your money? Who or what influenced your purchasing decisions? Can you remember a particular item you wanted to buy? How did you get it?

*2. As a child, did you have any influence on the purchases your family made?* Were there items you wanted to have or items you wanted the family to have? What efforts did you make to have those items bought? How successful were you? Describe one particular family purchase and your role in the decision-making process.

*3. When you were growing up, how did your family spend the income generated by family members?* Was there a family budget? What items were considered priorities or necessities? What items were considered luxuries? Who made decisions about how money was spent?

*4. Compare the consumer you are now with the consumer you were as an adolescent.* Have your purchasing behaviors changed or remained the same? Were your reasons for making purchases the same then as they are now? Are the things you spend your money on different now? Is your source of money the same? Are the forces influencing your purchasing decisions the same?

*5. How loyal are you to brand names?* What brand name products do you insist on buying? Do you have a particular brand of shampoo or deodorant, for example? What features of these brand-name products attract you? What is responsible for your loyalty? Do other people you know prefer the same brands or do they use different ones? If you have no loyalty to brand-name products, explain why.

*6. How do you feel about store-brand or generic products?* Do you buy them? Which ones do you buy? If you don't do any grocery shopping yourself, which ones do you think you would buy? What would you find attractive about store brand products? What would cause you to choose a national brand over a store brand?

*7. Compare your behavior as a consumer with your parents' and grandparents'.* In what ways are your purchases like theirs? How do your purchases differ? What explains these similarities and differences?

*8. What role do advertisements and commercials play in your purchasing decisions?* Do you believe consumers are controlled by the media? How powerful are commercials and advertisements? What products or services can you think of that became popular because of a media campaign?

*9. What influence do your friends have on your consumer behavior?* Do you buy things because your friends have them? What kinds of things would you buy because friends had them? How do the individuals responsible for marketing campaigns take advantage of the influence friends have on one another?

*10. What role should government play in regulating the production and marketing of goods and services?*  Do we need stricter laws about package labeling, for example? Do we need stricter laws about what advertisements and commercials can say about particular products? Explain your answer using your own experiences with particular products.

*11. Are you aware of connections among television shows and commercials and other types of media advertising?*  Are actors in popular series shown on visual displays in the stores at your local mall, for example? Do you support or oppose this kind of media "saturation" as a selling technique? Why?

## Freewriting to Capture Personal Experience

Here is a list of topics related to consumerism that you can freewrite about in short, ten-minute sessions. These topics are discussed in the articles in this chapter. Your teacher may assign a topic or ask you to choose one yourself. Begin your freewriting with personal experiences triggered by a topic. These personal experiences give your responses an interesting, personal flavor. If you are keeping a journal, do your freewriting there. (For a discussion of freewriting, see pages 103 to 104.)

Marketing
Consumer behavior
Brand-name and store-name products
Consumer loyalty
Advertising campaigns
Children as consumers
Compulsive buying
The ethics of advertising

Freewriting is most effective if you follow this sequence: **R**eread, **F**ocus, **R**ewrite (**RFR**). (For a discussion of RFR, see page 104.)

# 3
· · · · · · · · · · · · ·
# DEVELOPING RHETORICAL CONTEXT
# THROUGH GROUP ACTIVITIES

Each of the following collaborative activities involves sharing your freewriting with other group members, either to revise it for use later or to incorporate parts of it into a group-composed text. The purpose of these activities is to subject your freely expressed personal observations and feelings to the questions and responses of others who are working with you on the consumerism topic. Their responses to what you have written, as well as your responses to their freewritings, should help you develop and refine your own ideas. (If you are collaborating for the first time, you should read the description of strategies for effective collaboration on pages 104 to 105.)

- Make two copies of your freewriting. Form groups of three and have group members distribute copies of their freewriting to the other two members. Then take about 15 to 20 minutes to read your groupmates' freewritings. For each freewriting, do the following on a separate response sheet: 1) Read the freewriting without stopping and write a few sentences summarizing what the writer says; 2) Read the freewriting again and write 2 or 3 questions about what the writer says or why he says it; 3) Read the freewriting again and write a personal response to what the writer says, indicating how you feel and what you know or have experienced that has some connection to the content of the freewriting. Once the three group members have completed this part of the collaborative task, have the leader conduct a sharing session. The two readers of each freewriting should report to the group their summaries, questions, and responses. The group should then discuss the similarities and differences between the two responses and what accounts for them. Finally, brainstorm ways in which the writer of the freewriting could use it as a starting point for an essay on consumerism.
- In groups of three or four students, use each student's freewriting on consumer behavior to develop a classification system that could be used to analyze or criticize consumer behavior. Begin by having the group's leader direct a sharing session where group members take turns reading their freewriting aloud, while the rest of the group comments and responds. Then ask one member to serve as a recorder while the entire group brainstorms the categories that can be derived from the contents of the freewritings. The recorder should take notes on the possible classification systems that the group considers. The categories the group finally agrees to use should be mutually exclusive. For example, if the group decides to analyze consumer behavior using age categories, any particular age should fit into only one category. Similarly, the categories should be parallel. For example, if categories are based on age, each category should be mutually exclusive and of the same size (20–29 years old; 30–39 years old). Or, if media are the basis for classification, each category should represent a single medium. Once the group has determined the categories it will use to analyze consumer behavior, the group leader should lead a second brainstorming session to identify ideas and examples in the freewritings that explain the individual categories. Once all of the groups have

completed these activities, each group should choose a reporter, who shares the group's work with the entire class.

## 4
. . . . . . . . . . . . .
## USING READINGS TO DEVELOP
## A RHETORICAL COMMUNITY

The readings on consumerism in this chapter are meant to help you and your classmates write, create a body of shared knowledge, and become a rhetorical community. The readings contain information about several aspects of this topic: stages in consumer behavior, the development of consumerism in America, various aspects of marketing, and trends in consumer behaviors. The information in these readings will elicit different reactions from you and your classmates. Those reactions will shape and reshape your own views on this topic and some of the issues related to it. It will be your and your classmates' job to work toward a deeper understanding of these aspects of consumerism through discussion.

Reading creates opportunities for you to analyze how different writers respond to different rhetorical contexts or situations. Because the writers in this chapter represent different professional backgrounds, you will be able to note differences and similarities in the kinds of information they present and the ways they present it, even though they are all writing about the same topic. Some of these differences and similarities will stem from the writers' writing contexts: their readers, their writing purposes, and their own knowledge of the material in the article, for example. As you discuss with your classmates the rhetorical contexts these readings reflect, your ability to define and create your own rhetorical approach in your chapter essay will develop.

### The Readings in This Chapter

Several articles discuss consumers themselves. Robert B. Settle and Pamela L. Alreck's piece on adult stages of consumerism, part of a chapter from their book *Why They Buy,* provides a foundation for understanding how and why various adult consumers act differently. Their information is complemented by two articles on children as consumers. James U. McNeal's article on "The Littlest Consumers" was originally published in *American Demographics.* A professor of marketing, McNeal's article reports the results of his recent research on the influence children have on family purchasing behaviors. In contrast, the excerpt from Vance Packard's influential book *The Hidden Persuaders,* originally published in 1957, provides an opportunity to contrast young consumers of today with their predecessors. It also provides a critical perspective on advertising in the 1950s. John M. Rogers' article on how urban and rural consumers spend their money also affords readers an opportunity to learn more about different groups of consumers.

Other articles deal more with the products consumers buy and why they buy them. Richard S. Tedlow, a professor at the Harvard Business School, discusses the history of consumerism in America during the past century. He reviews three stages in the development of American marketing and their impact on consumer behavior. The closing paragraphs of this reading, originally part of a chapter in Tedlow's book *New and Improved: The Story of Mass Marketing in America,* raise some interesting questions about criticism of America's consumer society. "Brands in Trouble," by journalist Julie Liesse, analyzes changes in consumer loyalty to brand-name products and makes some interesting predictions about how future consumers will behave. Finally, Gail Tom's article presents an academic perspective on marketing. Tom, a professor of marketing, reports the results of her study of the effects of music on consumer behavior. Her article, originally published in *The Journal of Consumer Marketing,* not only explains one aspect of marketing affecting consumers' purchasing but provides an example of how researchers write about their studies of consumer behavior for other specialists studying the same behavior.

Finally, this chapter closes with two articles that take a more critical look at aspects of consumerism in the last decade. Bernice Kanner, in "The Secret Life of the Female Consumer," describes the marketing strategies behind the advertising of an upscale product at General Foods. The article provides the kind of factual description that can link directly with more critical questions concerning the media's manipulation of consumers. Laurence Shames, in "What a Long, Strange (Shopping) Trip It's Been: Looking Back at the 1980s," argues that in the 1980s America returned to the "conspicuous consumption" of the 1890s. He implies that such a return could have very negative effects on social, moral, and ethical values in America. Shames provides the overt criticism that Kanner implies.

# 5
· · · · · · · · · · · · ·
## READINGS ON CONSUMERISM

## RICHARD S. TEDLOW ON CONSUMERISM IN THE TWENTIETH CENTURY

### Pre-Reading Questions

1. What does the term "consumer advocate" mean to you? Do you identify any particular individuals with this term? Can you identify any consumer issues that are important to you?

**2.** From what you have read and heard, explain how being a consumer in America is different at the end of the twentieth century than at the beginning. How does being a consumer in another country (Russia, for example) differ from being a consumer in America? Why?

**3.** Do you like being labeled a "consumer"? Why? Why not?

## THE ALL-CONSUMING CENTURY
### Richard Tedlow

#### THE AMERICAN AS CONSUMER

Americans are choosers. They cherish the right to choose what they   1
will do and what they will be. One of the enduring attractions of Benjamin Franklin's *Autobiography* lies in how it epitomizes the American notion of choosing one's very self. Thomas Mellon, founder of a great American fortune, wrote that reading Franklin's *Autobiography* was "the turning point in my life."[1] It inspired him to leave the family farm and take up finance. Another farm boy inspired by Franklin was Jared Sparks, who became the president of Harvard in 1849. The *Autobiography* "first roused my mental energies . . . prompted me to resolutions, and gave me strength to adhere to them." Astutely capturing the book's essence, Sparks explained that it "taught me that circumstances have not a sovereign control over the mind."[2]

America has been peopled by a great mass migration in which   2
millions of individuals chose to join the nation of choosers.[3] Here they found not only freedom of religion, but also the right not to support any church established by law.[4] They found the right to choose their potential leaders in periodic elections. And they found the right to choose what to buy.

More than any other nation in the history of the world, the United States during the course of the past century has been a nation of consumers. A higher percentage of the population has been able to purchase a greater variety of goods and services than even the most visionary dreamer in the mid-nineteenth century would have imagined possible. In transportation and communication, in food and clothing, in entertainment, in household appliances, and in all the other devices that make life easier and more enjoyable, Americans have indeed been a "people of plenty."[5]

Americans fully appreciate, perhaps even overestimate, the appeal of   3
our ideas of civil and political liberty to people in other countries. They underestimate the attractiveness of simply having things. Yet the opportunity to come to this New World and to be granted full membership in society after satisfying minimal residence requirements has so often been

seized because along with it comes the chance to better one's station in life and by so doing to own more things.[6]

Not only is consumption possible in America, it is also good. This is an attitude that should not be taken for granted. An English Socialist once complained of the "damned wantlessness of the poor," but that has not been a problem in the United States. Here, wanting is approved. What one wants and what one purchases have become an important part of self-definition. Moreover, being in the business of catering to the wants of the people is also good.

The emphasis on mass consumption in American society—our habit of identifying how well-off people are with how many things they have—is so pervasive that we tend to take it for granted. Yet mass consumption is a rare phenomenon in the history of the world. Even in the present day, a nation's focus on the welfare of the mass of its citizens as consumers is not universally accepted. Japan, for example, is a rich nation. However, since World War II it has been far more geared toward an ethos of production and the penetration of international markets than it has been toward delivering consumer products to its own citizens at the lowest possible prices.[7]

There is nothing "natural" about mass consumption. It is a cultural and social construction. One of the keystones of the edifice is the marketing function in the modern, large American corporation.

In broad outline, it is possible to discern a progression in American marketing through three phases that correspond to the broader evolution of the American economy and society. During the first phase, the domestic market was fragmented among hundreds of localities. The major factor dictating this fragmentation was the absence of a transportation and communication infrastructure spanning the continent. National brands were few in number, and national advertising was almost unknown. This was an era of vertical and horizontal nonintegration. Firms were small and exercised limited control over the market. The principal business strategy was to make profits by charging high prices and thus making high margins but at the expense of low volume. This, then, was the era of market fragmentation.

Toward the end of the nineteenth century, the completion of the railroad and telegraph network set the stage for the second phase of American marketing. This was the era of the national mass market, in which a small number of firms realized scale economies to an unprecedented degree by expanding their distribution from coast to coast and border to border. The profit strategy during this phase was to charge low prices, which permitted only small margins per unit but made possible greatly increased total profits because of high volume.

In Phase II, the national market was united by manufacturers in some product lines and by retailers in others. Where once there had been no national brands, now there were many. In Phase II—the unification phase—the national product market was dominated by an aggressive leading company or a small number of such companies. Through advertising and publicity, through forward integration into company-owned wholesaling, through franchise agreements with retailers, through the creation of sales programs and their implementation, and through the systematic analysis of carefully collected data, the large firm came to exercise an impact on the consumer market far greater than anything contemplated in Adam Smith's day. In the commodity world of Phase I, the market had dictated the terms of business. In the new Phase II world of brands, the market still played a key role in the sense that consumer acceptance was essential, but the firm's power to shape and mold the market was vastly increased.

Many consumer products such as automobiles and household me- 10 chanical refrigerators, did not exist prior to the twentieth century. For these products especially, the firm had to organize and educate a mass market. This is what Ford did in automobiles and what Frigidaire, General Electric, and Sears did in refrigerators.

The third phase of American marketing has been characterized by 11 market segmentation.[8] This era bears certain similarities to the nineteenth-century phase of market fragmentation, in that divisions in the market have become the primary focus of the consumer marketing effort rather than the unification of the market by a dominant brand or product form. But market segmentation today is far more complex than were the market divisions of a hundred years ago. Transportation costs still matter, so geography is still important. However, marketers (a term unknown in the previous century) use such additional considerations as demographics (age, income, and education) and psychographics (life-style) to create divisions in markets that they can exploit with competitive advantages. These segments have to be sufficiently large so that scale economies are obtained. The goal, however, has been not only to achieve scale economies, but also to gain the freedom to "value price"—to price in accord with the special value that a particular market segment places on the product, independent of the costs of production.

Phase II products and marketing strategies had a changeless quality 12 about them. For instance, Coca-Cola and the Model T Ford were conceived of as the best possible answers to market needs in their respective product categories. Coca-Cola's proprietor, Asa G. Candler, was devoted to his product because of its medicinal (he believed it cured headaches) and refreshing qualities. He wanted to share it with the nation and also with the world. Candler did not bring out a new version of his soft drink each year, nor did he experiment with diet beverages or other line extensions. Indeed, until 1955, Coca-Cola was available in only two forms—at the soda fountain and in the traditional 6½-ounce, hobble-skirted bottle. Coke was, the company believed, perfect for everyone. There was no need to devote special attention to one group or another.

The story at Ford in the early years was similar. After the Ford Motor 13 Company settled on the Model T as its sole market entry in 1908, it stuck with the product doggedly. Indeed, an important reason for Ford's early success was that the company seized on the idea of reducing the price of the automobile by producing large numbers of high-quality vehicles in a progressively more efficient factory. Henry Ford explicitly conceived of the Model T as the "universal" car. Market segmentation played no part in his thinking. There was no reason, in Ford's view, for anyone to buy another model.

Phase III products have attacked the Phase II strategy through 14 change and segmentation. General Motors introduced the price pyramid with the "car for every purse and purpose" in the 1920s. Each make was supposed to appeal to a different set of customers. Each make also changed every year. There was no sense that a 1923 Chevrolet or a 1927 Buick was supposed to be a "universal" car.

Likewise, Pepsi-Cola answered Coca-Cola's Phase II strategy with a 15 vigorous Phase III approach. Pepsi's advertisements in the 1950s did not tout the product as much as they did the context in which the product was consumed.[9] "Be sociable, look smart. Be up to date with Pepsi."

This strategy was brilliantly refined with the inauguration of the 16 "Pepsi Generation" in the 1960s. Margaret Mead once remarked that the world was divided into two groups—those who lived through World War II and those who experienced it only as a memory. By the early 1960s, the postwar baby boomers had reached their teenage years. Perhaps never before in the history of the nation had the generation gap been so fundamental. The baby boomers' parents grew up amid depression and war. But during the 1960s, the spread of wealth in the United States put cash in the pockets of many teens who had never earned a penny. These young people sought badges of belonging in language, in hairstyle, in clothing, and in music.[10] Pepsi zeroed in on them, combining an appeal to peer approval with life-style. Unlike Coke, Pepsi was always about variety and change. When Coca-Cola tried to change its formula in 1985, there was an uproar among loyal customers. Pepsi changed its formula in the early 1930s and again in the early 1950s, and nobody cared. People expected Pepsi to change.

### Some Historical Examples of Marketing Phases

The three phases of American marketing—from fragmentation to unifi- 17 cation to segmentation—will help organize the complex historical narrative that follows. This basic progression recurs in the industries under study here.

*Soft drinks.* The soft drink industry was in Phase I through most of the 18
nineteenth century. There were dozens of local brands, compounded by
druggists who tried to brighten the day of their customers by concocting
new flavors at the soda fountain. In the early 1890s, Asa G. Candler of
Atlanta gained control of one such beverage, Coca-Cola.

Candler quickly established a market presence all over the country 19
and abroad through exceptionally heavy national advertising and, after
the turn of the century, through a bottler network that relied in large
part on independent franchises. Coca-Cola's advertising in the early
1900s did not attempt to segment the market. Coca-Cola was for
everyone—young or old, rich or poor. It was the universal cola—a classic
example of a Phase II product.

Pepsi-Cola was developed in the 1890s, but it had a checkered career 20
until the 1930s. At that time the company attempted to segment the
market but not through psychographics or demographics. Rather, Pepsi
underpriced Coke in the famous "Twice as Much for a Nickel, Too"
campaign. Pepsi made some headway among people watching their
pennies, of whom there were many during the Depression. However, this
modified Phase II strategy became impossible to maintain as the industry's costs rose in the postwar inflation. By the late 1940s, Pepsi was
looking for a new *raison d'être*. This it found first with psychographic
segmentation ("Be sociable") and then with the combination of psychographic and demographic segmentation (Pepsi Generation). Coca-Cola
responded; and by the 1980s, with line extensions, the proliferation of
packaging, and narrow market targeting, the soft drink industry had
clearly entered Phase III.

*Automobiles.* The automobile moved through its first phase with speed. 21
Inventors, mechanics, and hobbyists were tinkering with contraptions
that can be considered ancestors of the automobile in the 1880s. As
numerous companies organized themselves at the turn of the century,
the usual strategy was to produce a number of different models in
relatively small runs. In those early years of fragmented competition, no
product design was yet dominant. Gasoline, steam, and electricity were
all vying for acceptance.

Henry Ford devised a strategy that called for total concentration on 22
a single, "universal" car aimed at everyone. With economies of scale and
learning-curve advantages, Ford successfully reduced the price of the car
and in the process greatly widened the market. This was Phase II—the
profit-through-volume stage of the automobile industry.

In the 1920s, the automobile market grew large enough and the 23
problems posed by the used car proved vexing enough that there was an
opportunity for a new strategy of segmentation. This opportunity was
seized by Alfred P. Sloan, Jr., at General Motors; and, as a result, industry
leadership was seized as well.

Since the 1920s, there have been many attempts to re-create Ford's 24
success. Most noteworthy was the Volkswagen Beetle, another changeless "universal" car that eventually outsold even the Model T. At this
writing, however, the automobile industry seems to be moving, thanks to
flexible manufacturing and computerization, even more firmly into Phase
III with mass customization.

## BUSINESS BATTLES AND BATTLERS

The strategy of profit through volume is a distinctively American 25
contribution to marketing, facilitated by both our culture and our
economy. Although cultural and economic preconditions were necessary,
they could not alone move an industry from Phase I to Phase II. An
added element was required: entrepreneurial drive and vision.

American entrepreneurs discovered in their attempts to implement 26
the profit-through-volume strategy that reliance solely on market relationships was impossible. They had to build an organization through
which they could coordinate manufacturing and marketing. Once created, this organization could, under certain circumstances, generate large
profits. It also stood as a barrier to the entry of new competition desiring
to share in those profits. Potential new entrants were faced with the
choice of either replicating the successful strategy of the first-mover or of
finding some fundamentally new way to compete. The firms that
succeeded in the long term were those that managed their organizational
capabilities against the backdrop of changes in the economy and society.
In other words, the strategy of profit through volume—selling many
units at low margins rather than few units at high margins—historically
has been the distinctive signature of the American approach to marketing. By making products available to the masses all over the nation—by
democratizing consumption—the mass marketer did something profoundly American.

Examples are numerous. Personal transportation was once a signa- 27
ture of social privilege, until Henry Ford made it available to everyone.
More recently, acetaminophen was a high-priced pharmaceutical specialty drug, marketed primarily with the help of recommendations from
physicians. James E. Burke at Johnson & Johnson cut the price of the
drug, advertised heavily, and distributed intensively; he thus created in
Tylenol one of the biggest brands in American history. Acetaminophen
started in the province of the experts. Burke democratized it.[11]

Mass marketing did not spontaneously develop because of the 28
existence of necessary technological, economic, and social preconditions.
Entrepreneurs had to have the creativity to see new business opportunities and the willingness to take the risks involved in transforming their
visions into realities. The business firms that such people made the

instruments of their will had to create mass markets by shaping and molding the unorganized, inchoate demand for their products.

Tylenol, for example, did not create itself. To be sure, there has always 29 been a market for safe pain relief. Yet the market for acetaminophen was, to an important degree, created by James Burke. He saw the product's potential when others did not. He created a new company within Johnson & Johnson—McNeil Consumer Products—to pursue a vigorous con- sumer marketing strategy to develop the market.[12] Had he not done so, there might never have been a mass-marketed acetaminophen; and there certainly would not have been a Tylenol. This is precisely what I mean by "creating mass markets." Of course, if Tylenol had not been efficacious, no amount of marketing expenditure or strategizing could have turned it into a successful brand. The product had to work. But merely working would not have turned it into a successful brand either. The world would not have beaten a pathway to it. Burke's entrepreneurial insight, drive, and investment were essential to its success.

To implement the strategy of profit through volume, the entrepre- 30 neur had to create a vertical system through which raw materials were sourced, production operations were managed, and products were delivered to the ultimate consumer. Scale at one level was useless without scale at the others. Mass production demanded mass marketing. The vertical system usually involved integration within the firm of some of the steps involved and contractual relations for the others.

The early years of the Singer Sewing Machine Company illustrate 31 the need for the marriage of mass distribution to mass production. In the 1870s and 1880s, Singer built the largest sewing machine factories in the world. If this large fixed investment were to pay off, these plants had to operate near rated capacity. Unfortunately, the independent distributors through which Singer sold made the smooth scheduling of production very difficult. These distributors failed to maintain inven- tories properly. They always seemed to be either overstocked or out of stock. Just as problematic, they were late in remitting payments and deficient in supplying the various services that the market for a new, complex, and expensive consumer durable required.

## SOME THOUGHTS ON CONSUMPTION
## AND COMMUNITY IN THE UNITED STATES

In a remarkable passage, Alexis de Tocqueville wrote:                    32

> [N]ot only does democracy make every man forget his ancestors, but it hides his descendants and separates his contemporaries from him; it throws him back forever upon himself alone and threatens in the end to confine him entirely within the solitude of his own heart.[13]

Tocqueville was so accustomed to a more hierarchically organized society that when he came to the United States he was surprised—more than that, in fact, he was deeply shocked—that the country could stick together absent the glue of aristocracy that he and so many Europeans took for granted. Other observers also have looked on the United States as a nation in which the sense of community was relatively weak. Especially as the twentieth century got under way, Americans came to share less and less the same ethnicity or religion. Language, too, was a barrier to the integration of the millions of immigrants who migrated here.

But an interest in purchasing consumer goods came to be an 33 important attribute shared by these diverse peoples. Indeed, the purchase of a branded, standardized item established a bond, in a sense at least, among the purchasers. Men who saw that eyepatch advertisement and bought a Hathaway shirt as a result of it probably did share some attitudes. For many years, though less so today, driving a Cadillac constituted a public declaration that the driver had "made it." Or that he thought he had made it. Or at least that he wanted other people to think he had made it.

Daniel J. Boorstin brought the existence of these "consumption 34 communities" to our attention in *The Americans: The Democratic Experience*. "Invisible new communities were created and preserved by how and what men consumed," he explained.

> Nearly all objects from the hats and suits and shoes men wore to the food they ate became symbols and instruments of novel communities. Now men were affiliated less by what they believed than by what they consumed.[14]

This is doubtless an overstatement, yet there is an element of truth in it. And it is here that so much of the criticism of America's consumer society is located. For a century, commentators have objected to the substitution of material things for matters of the spirit. It is interesting to note that many early advertising agents were the sons of ministers.[15] Advertising almost literally seemed to be the equivalent of preaching in our secular age. Preaching what? Not God. Not Goodness. Toothpaste.

Much of what critics have written about mass consumption is 35 valuable and thought-provoking. The net effect of all the advertisements to which the average American is exposed over a lifetime must be to increase his or her concern with material possessions. It takes an act of will to keep in mind that who one is counts for more than how much one has. The appeal of much advertising does have a debasing aspect to it. The depersonalization associated with mass marketing is as disturbing as the other types of massification in modern mass society. Advertising is often misleading, at least implicitly. The economist Robert Heilbroner has observed that one of its most important effects is to teach children that adults are willing to lie for money.[16]

To the extent that these observations are true, they are genuinely 36
disturbing. There has been a price, a high price, for the explosion of
consumption in the past hundred years. But it is a price which, by and
large, most Americans have believed to be worth paying. There are
refrigerators in American homes because Americans want them there.
Cars are in their garages for the same reason. Coca-Cola exists because
many people think it tastes good. For all the commercial persuasion in
our society, consumer goods exist because consumers—we, that is—have
chosen them. In the words of Richard Wightman Fox and T. J. Jackson
Lears:

> It will not do to view [the consumer culture] as an elite conspiracy in which
> advertisers defraud the "people" by drowning them in a sea of glittering
> goods. The people are not that passive; they have been active consumers,
> preferring some commodities to others.[17]

Choice, then, is at the center of the modern American consumer 37
economy. Some of the choices consumers have made have been wrong.
Some choices have carried costs of which the consumers were unaware.
On the whole, however, most of their choices have been reasonable. And
the corporations that have provided American consumers with the
alternatives from which to choose have done something worth doing.

## NOTES

1. Quoted in Leonard W. Labaree et al., eds., "Introduction," *The Autobiog-raphy of Benjamin Franklin* (New Haven: Yale University Press, 1964), 10.
2. Labaree et al., *Autobiography,* 10–11.
3. Of course, many people, especially large numbers of enslaved Africans, did not choose to come here but were, rather, brought against their will.
4. Alexander Hamilton made a point of this in the "Report on Manufactures." See Henry Cabot Lodge, ed., *Works of Alexander Hamilton* (New York: Houghton Mifflin, 1885), 92–93. There were established churches on the state, as opposed to the federal, level until as late as 1833. See Lawrence H. Fuchs, *The American Kaleidoscope* (Middletown, Conn.: Wesleyan University Press, forthcoming).
5. David M. Potter, *People of Plenty: Economic Abundance and the American Character* (Chicago: University of Chicago Press, 1954).
6. Fuchs, *Kaleidoscope.*
7. Thomas K. McCraw and Patricia A. O'Brien, "Production and Distribution: Competition Policy and Industry Structure," in *America Versus Japan,* ed. Thomas K. McCraw (Boston: Harvard Business School Press, 1986), 77–116.
8. See the concluding chapter of Daniel Pope, "Advertising Today: The Era of Market Segmentation," in his *The Making of Modern Advertising* (New York: Basic Books, 1983), 252–98. This chapter is full of illuminating observations, many of which I elaborate upon in this book. Another

important source for my characterizing Phase III as an era of market segmentation is my colleague at the Harvard Business School, Professor John A. Quelch of the Marketing Area. In two lengthy critiques of my work, which he delivered at the school's Business History Seminar, Professor Quelch emphasized the importance of market segmentation and product proliferation during the recent past.

9. See Pope's shrewd comments in *Modern Advertising,* 280.
10. For most of the material in this paragraph, I am indebted to conversations with Professor Lawrence H. Fuchs of the Brandeis University American Studies Department. The source for Margaret Mead's observation is Donald R. Katz, *The Big Store: Inside the Crisis and Revolution at Sears* (New York: Viking, 1987), 209.
11. Wendy K. Smith with Richard S. Tedlow, "James Burke: A Career in American Business (A)," in *Managerial Decision Making and Ethical Values,* ed. Thomas R. Piper (Boston: Harvard Business School Press, forthcoming).
12. Ibid.
13. Alexis de Tocqueville, *Democracy in America,* vol. 2, ed. Phillips Bradley (New York: Vintage, 1945), 105–106.
14. Daniel J. Boorstin, *The Americans: The Democratic Experience* (New York: Vintage, 1973), 89–90. For a brief critique of Boorstin's idea of consumption communities, see Michael Schudson, *Advertising: The Uneasy Persuasion* (New York: Basic Books, 1984), 159–60.
15. Pope, *Modern Advertising,* 178–79.
16. Robert L. Heilbroner, *Business Civilization in Decline* (New York: W. W. Norton, 1976), 114.
17. Richard Wightman Fox and T. J. Jackson Lears, eds., "Introduction," in *The Culture of Consumption: Critical Essays in American History, 1880– 1980* (New York: Pantheon, 1983), x.

## Post-Reading Questions

1. This reading is part of a chapter in Tedlow's book, *New and Improved: The Story of Mass Marketing in America.* How would you describe the way Tedlow introduces this chapter on consumerism? What strategy does he use? How effective is it? What does it suggest about the readers Tedlow has in mind?
2. What does Tedlow mean when he says, "Here, wanting is approved. What one wants and what one purchases have become an important part of self-definition"? Do you agree? Why?
3. Where in this reading does Tedlow describe three historical phases in American marketing? Summarize those three phases in your own words.
4. How do the products and marketing strategies of Phase II differ from those of Phase III? What accounts for those differences?
5. Although Tedlow does not describe his research process, the information in this reading provides clues to how he obtained his information. In your own words, describe Tedlow's research process. Refer to the reading in your description.

6.  Identify four or five individuals whose words Tedlow incorporates in this reading. What can you say about these individuals? Why did Tedlow find their statements helpful to his writing purposes?
7.  Although Tedlow seems primarily interested in presenting information to his readers, he does at some points in the essay inject his personal views. Find a place in the reading where you have a sense of how Tedlow feels. What does he reveal to the readers about his own feelings? How do you know?
8.  Make a list of the headings in this reading. What do the headings suggest about Tedlow's organization? Why do you think this organization works for him?
9.  Summarize the criticism of America's consumer society as Tedlow explains it. How does Tedlow feel about this criticism? How do you know? Do you think Tedlow's feelings are reasonable? Do you share them? Explain your answer by referring to your own experiences as a consumer or a consumer-observer.
10. How would you analyze the ways in which a particular consumer product is marketed? Using one product, cars or shampoo or beer, for example, describe your research process. What kinds of information would you need to locate to conduct this analysis? How would you decide what kinds of information would be most helpful? Where would you find this information? Whom could you turn to for advice?

# ROBERT P. SETTLE AND PAMELA L. ALRECK ON CONSUMER LIFE STAGES

## Pre-Reading Questions

1.  From your own experiences, describe how purchasing behaviors differ among the young and mature adults you know. What differences exist in what, when, how, where, and why they buy?
2.  How are decisions made in your home about what brand of cereal will be purchased? Who makes the decision? Why? What influences that decision? Has the preferred brand or brands of cereal remained constant over the years? What, if anything, has influenced the change in preference?

## THE STAGES OF ADULT LIFE
### Robert P. Settle and Pamela L. Alreck

There was a time when developmental psychology was synonymous with "child" psychology—not so today. We know now that adult consumers go through a process of growth and change as they mature. The phases of adult life don't necessarily correspond to age decades, but there's enough commonality to make that breakdown meaningful. So we'll identify the typical patterns for consumers in their twenties, thirties, forties, and so forth, mostly because these periods are easy to understand and recall.


## CONSUMERS IN THEIR TWENTIES

This is a time of search and conformity for young people, who are fully aware of the fact that they're setting the course for later life. For the first time, many of the decisions they make will have an impact on their life beyond the next few days, weeks, or months. They have a strong concern for what's "right" and "wrong," what they "should" and "shouldn't" do, according to social norms. Sensitivity to group and societal norms is the earmark of people at this stage. Marketing to this segment often relies heavily on appeals to conformity, citing group or social norms, without reference to experts who are authority figures. The norms are based on relevant reference groups, rather than on individual authority.

| Factor | Typical Condition in Their Twenties |
| --- | --- |
| Family status | Young single, early married, or young child. |
| Occupational status | Ending formal education, starting a career. |
| Social conditions | Many casual friends, many changes with marriage. |
| Principal concerns | Popularity with peers, getting a good start. |
| Major decisions | What career to pursue, with whom to mate? |
| Dominant needs | Independence, sexuality, exhibition, diversion. |
| Value emphasis | Social, intellectual, then economic, political. |
| Appeal sensitivity | To their own peers, as a reference group. |

General Motors promotes their Celebrity Eurosport, "Today's Chevrolet," with print ads strongly appealing to young adults beginning their careers. Listen to the copy verse, under the headline, *Corporate Blue:*

> Imagine a color
> in all its hues
> what some call success
> is just chasing the blues.
>
> Well, the day has dawned
> and the sun's getting hot
> your heart says go
> don't ever stop.

It's how you move
it's what you see
you know where you're going
where you want to be.

If you start right now
you can light the fuse
pull out all the stops
we're gonna chase the blues.

Sun on the left
sea on the right
got the good life ahead
and the car in flight.

Point it down the road
there's no time to lose
in your heart you know
how to chase the blues.

The copy of this *Cosmopolitan* magazine ad (jointly sponsored by designer Anne Klein II, whose clothes the model wears) is rife with double meanings relevant to consumers in their twenties, concerned with conflicts between independence and responsibility, peer pressure and personal values.

## CONSUMERS IN THEIR THIRTIES

This is a time of solidification and commitment. Even those highly ₃ committed to experimentation and change often feel a strong pull toward greater stability, mostly in the spheres of family and vocation. Those who married early have either survived the "seven year itch" or uncoupled from their original partner. Those who postponed the process of pairing and family creation are likely to feel that "this is the time" and maybe that it's "now or never." This stage may contain a strong sense of frustration for many. It's a time of great aspirations and few resources. New parents often approach that role very seriously. Minor mishaps at home or at work can be fanned into major catastrophes with terrible consequences.

There's often a pull toward traditional values and conventional ₄ lifestyles, defined by societal norms rather than peer groups. This is a time to "put down roots" and solidify tastes and preferences—to start "the long pull" toward complete maturity and eventual seniority and authority. Personal anxiety can be a problem, but they may feel that agitation and discontent are signs of instability or failure. But this stage is also filled with energy, enthusiasm, a high level of idealism, and often fruitful dedication to both personal and social principles and causes.

| Factor | Typical Condition in Their Thirties |
|---|---|
| Family status | Married couple only or with young children. |
| Occupational status | Career path identified, now settling in. |
| Social conditions | Attention to family and job limits contacts. |
| Principal concerns | To become sure and stable at home and at work. |
| Major decisions | Whether or not to have any (more) children. |
| Dominant needs | Achievement, nurturance, security, recognition. |
| Value emphasis | Economic, social, then intellectual, aesthetic. |
| Appeal sensitivity | Acceptance and approval from society at large. |

By contrast to the auto promotion just mentioned for those in their twenties, Chrysler Corp. promotes the Dodge Lancer in magazine ads with the headline "We hid a sports car inside." One of several of a new breed of cars, the Lancer combines the practical aspects of a family sedan with the performance of a sports car. The copy deals with "First, the fun." Then, "As for practicality . . . ." Both the conception of such cars and their promotion are geared to drivers in their thirties, meeting their compulsion to conform without relinquishing some youthful abandon.

## CONSUMERS IN THEIR FORTIES

This is often a period of uncertainty and discontent, when people 5 turn inward toward their own desires. Caught in the bind between durable commitments and strong desires for personal satisfaction, many experience a midlife crisis. The route divides into two paths at that fork in the road: Those choosing conformity and conventionality find a smooth, straight, well-paved, clearly marked, and often exceedingly boring path. Those who choose personal gratification over convention are on an unmapped, narrow, twisting, rocky road that's also exciting, exhilarating, and novel.

Positive marketing appeals to youth and vigor are effective, but 6 negative (fear) appeals to prevention of aging may backfire. One way or the other, most of these consumers resolve their contentions with society: Conventionalists reluctantly conform and self-satisfiers reject social norms, so appeals to conformity are ill-advised. People of this age are more comfortable with self-indulgence—they feel they've earned it—and more hospitable to luxury as opposed to utility. Appeals based on personal values and self-determination work well compared to those based on family or job necessity.

| Factor | Typical Condition in Their Forties |
|---|---|
| Family status | Full nest of children, often separation, divorce. |
| Occupational status | In the long pull or mid-life career change. |
| Social conditions | Well-established affiliations and routines. |
| Principal concerns | Coping with boredom and maintaining momentum. |
| Major decisions | Whether or not to change marriage or career? |
| Dominant needs | Diversion, consistency, nurturance, sexuality. |
| Value emphasis | Economic, aesthetic, then social, intellectual. |
| Appeal sensitivity | To respected, well-recognized authority figures. |

> With two-page ads in such magazines as *Ladies' Home Journal* and *Good Housekeeping*, famous TV actress Linda Evans introduces Clairol's New Ultress gel hair colorant to middle-aged homemakers with the slogan, "You could be the best you've ever been. . . ." Whether in a stable state or in transition, women of this age group are responsive to *credible* (but not exaggerated) glamour appeals, especially those portraying an authority figure as well-recognized, glamourous, and admired as this one.

## CONSUMERS IN THEIR FIFTIES

This time is of fruition and attainment of authority, when consumers really come into their own. Accepting the impossibility of their impossible dreams, they abandon them, but they're compensated by the realization of maturity and recognition while health and energy are yet barely on the wane. Cynicism is held at bay as they take command of their social and material world. Long experience in many roles has demonstrated both their capabilities and their limitations. Declining health may be acknowledged as inevitable, but it's not imminent, it's still well beyond the horizon. Recognition of competence and authority arrive simultaneously at home and at work. In family life, elders pass the mantle of authority to the next generation. On the job, their seniority and experience gain the respect of peers, subordinates, and superiors. Consumers' attitudes are in part a function of the external social situation, so these interactions have a significant effect on their attitudes and values, and they learn to see themselves as "having arrived." Even though they may realize they haven't reached the lofty position they once aspired to and probably never will, the daily satisfactions and rewards of seniority are an effective balm for the disappointment.

| Factor | Typical Condition in Their Fifties |
|--------|-----------------------------------|
| Family status | Children departed or departing, few demands. |
| Occupational status | Well-established, assuming command posture. |
| Social conditions | More time for and devotion to outside interests. |
| Principal concerns | Solidification of position, preparing to retire. |
| Major decisions | Which commitments to maintain or to terminate? |
| Dominant needs | Achievement, dominance, recognition, stimulation. |
| Value emphasis | Political, aesthetic, then economic, religious. |
| Appeal sensitivity | To the self as the most competent judge. |

Rather than basing marketing appeals on authority or conformity, it's 8 more effective to present the facts and tell these consumers, "You be the judge." They feel they're competent to evaluate and choose for themselves. They would rather set the standards themselves than bow to social norms. Nor are they likely to take the word of what they see as *another* authority. They respond well to consumer goods that assist them in the process of personalization and individuation. With fewer fears and uncertainties than others, they're relatively unresponsive to marketing appeals based on fear or those offering reassurance.

Magazine ads for German-made Merkur XR4Ti, imported by Ford's Lincoln-Mercury division, illustrate very well how facts are presented to mature consumers who prefer to judge for themselves. Superimposed on the low-angle photo of the car, a 6 column, 20 row table has a detailed comparison of the Merkur with the BMW 318i, Saab 9000 Turbo, Audi 4000S Quattro, and Volvo Turbo. The headline for the car notes that "Its objective is not to compete with the (others), but frankly, to surpass them."

## CONSUMERS SIXTY AND BEYOND

Because many consumers, and especially males, tend to retire during their 9 sixties, there are some significant differences at this stage between the time before and after retirement. Generally this is an era of gratification and fulfillment. Despite the prevalent (and erroneous) assumption that "old" people are largely tired, poor, and sick, these consumers are mostly occupied with the harvest of their life's work. Only a small minority are destitute, in ill health, and experiencing hard times. In the main, consumers in this age bracket are well-off from most points of view.

Often people this age relinquish much of their authority and 10 responsibility but retain positions of influence, becoming the "power behind the scenes." They may provide advice and counsel to their juniors at work and at home. While their dependence on others may increase, they rarely become submissive, and many become more assertive or even openly aggressive. With the feeling that they've been there and back already, they sense that they have little to gain by conformity and observance of the social niceties and little to lose by their protagonism, expression of judgment, or exceptional candor. Often practical, down-to-earth, and unpretentious, they are their own people and they know it.

This market for consumer goods seeks products and services that are  11 safe, reliable, practical, and perhaps traditional. Marketers shouldn't rely on fear appeals. They contain too much threat for those very aware of danger and limitation. Nor do appeals to conformity or to authority have great potential for this market. Instead, they find clean, simple, straight-forward presentations of product or service value most appealing. They also have fewer psychological prohibitions against self-indulgent luxury.

| Factor | Typical Condition in Their Sixties |
|---|---|
| Family status | Empty nest, maybe sole survivor, grandparenting. |
| Occupational status | Preparing to retire, retired, part-time work. |
| Social conditions | Strong affiliations with their age cohort group. |
| Principal concerns | Economic security and finding social purpose. |
| Major decisions | What to down-grade and how much to change? |
| Dominant needs | Security, independence, affiliation, succorance. |
| Value emphasis | Religious, social, then aesthetic, political. |
| Appeal sensitivity | To functional utility and economy of the goods. |

> Print ads for Lindsay's Know It All brand water conditioning appliance sport the headline "Smart Buy." With this brand, says the copy, "What you need is what you get. No more, no less." The tag line is "Quality water at a price you can afford." Both the product itself and the promotion are appropriate to consumers of any age, but especially for the more mature, who neither shy away from a little luxury such as soft water, nor willingly spend more than they must to get it.

Remember that these descriptions are only tendencies and there's no ironclad boundary between consumers of adjacent age cohort groups. There's some overlap and some who are exceptions to the modal patterns identified here.

## Post-Reading Questions

1.  This is an excerpt from a chapter in the book *Why They Buy*. Reread the first paragraph of the excerpt. How does it differ from the kind of introduction a journalist would write for an article on adult consumers in *Time* or *Newsweek*? How would a personal essay on adult consumers begin?

2.  What purpose do Settle and Alreck announce in their first paragraph? How well, in your opinion, do they succeed? Why?

3.  What kinds of readers did Settle and Alreck have in mind for this book? How do you know?

4.  Make a list of the adult stages Settle and Alreck explain. Next to each stage, write a key word or phrase describing the adult consumer during that stage. Then examine your list. Write a paragraph analyzing the pattern(s) suggested by your key phrases. What general statements can you make about adult consumers from your list?

5.  For each adult stage described by Settle and Alreck write the name of someone you know. Then examine your list of names. Write a paragraph analyzing how closely these people match the descriptions in the reading. What are the similarities and differences between the textbook descriptions and the people you know?

6.  Use Settle and Alreck's descriptions to explain how different members of your family would purchase a new car. What factors would influence their decision-making process? How do these factors differ among family members? Why?

# JAMES U. MCNEAL
# ON CHILDREN AS CONSUMERS

## Pre-Reading Questions

1.  What things did you most want to buy as a teenager? Why did you want to have those things? How successful were you in getting them? What factors affected your success as a teenaged consumer? Compare your consumer habits in high school to your consumer habits now. How similar and different are they? What, in your opinion, explains these similarities and differences?

2.  In what ways are children exploited by marketing experts and advertisers? How would these experts and advertisers defend their marketing strategies?

## THE LITTLEST SHOPPERS
### James U. McNeal

Children are not shy about shopping. During a store visit, children aged 1 12 or under may take 15 purchase requests to their parents. Children also make purchase requests while they are at home, in cars, at the movies, during television viewing, on vacation, at mealtimes, and even in church, according to our research. One mother reported that during church services, her 5-year-old always suggests a place to eat afterwards.

The total income of young children was estimated at almost $9 2 billion in 1989. But children have an even more extensive influence on how their parents buy products and services. They often influence purchase decisions in three areas: items for children, such as snacks, toys, electronic gadgets, clothes, and hobby supplies; items for the home, such as furniture, television sets, stereos, and yard equipment; and items for the family, such as vacations, automobiles, food, and recreation. We estimate that their influence on consumer spending in 62 product categories adds up to more than $132 billion. That is a vast sum, more than the Gross National Product of Taiwan.

## LEARNING TO BE CONSUMERS

The influence of children on family purchases has been a research topic 3 among marketers since the 1950s. But in recent years, the influence of children has grown rapidly. There are four main reasons. First, parents are having fewer children, thereby increasing the influence of each child. Second, rapid increases in the number of one-parent families also increase the number of children who do some of their own shopping. Third, an increasing number of women now delay childbearing, and these women usually have more to spend on their children. Finally, almost 70 percent of households with children are dual-earner households. Working couples foster household participation and self-reliance among their children, out of necessity.

Parents have always perceived their children as influences, or even as 4 nagging influences, on household purchase decisions. But today, purchase decisions are increasingly being viewed by parents as part of the children's responsibility. A child's request for certain play items, snack foods, clothes, and even medicines is often the main influence on what a parent buys, simply because the requests give direction to a hassled working mother or father.

On the most fundamental level, children learn to get things by asking 5 their parents. Asking a parent for something is essentially the first stage in the development of consumer behavior.

Parents completely determine how their child's needs are satisfied 6 only until the age of 2 or 3. After age 3, children are permitted some choices: for example, in flavors of ice cream and beverages, and in types of toys. As they develop their choices, most children become the targets of an ever-increasing number of advertisements. The information in these messages, combined with the information children receive during store visits with parents, fuels consumer development.

By the age of 5 or 6, a child's wants and needs may have grown 7 beyond the parent's ability to pay. This is the beginning of the second stage of consumer development, when youngsters start developing their persuasive techniques. Often learned from peers, these are tricks children play on parents to satisfy a few of their many wants. Parents are soon treated to pleas like "I gotta have one," "I'll die if I don't get one," and "Everyone's got one except me."

## $132 BILLION IN INFLUENCE

What do children try to get from their parents? The total amount has 8 never been estimated before, although estimates have been made for several product categories where children's influence is extensive.

This study examined children's influence on parental purchases, 9 using a variety of sources. The first were any estimates that have appeared in business publications since 1988. When two or more figures for a category existed, we used the more conservative one. If no estimate existed, we contacted company officials in various consumer-goods industries to get their assessments of children's influence.

We next examined published estimates of children's influence on 10 household spending as provided by parents and children. These results were usually obtained by researchers who asked both parents and children in a household about the degree of the child's influence. We averaged the parental and child estimates when they differed.

Finally, we combined the estimates of industry officials with those of 11 families to produce an influence index for children ages 2 through 12. We matched this index with annual U.S. sales figures for 62 product categories among households containing children aged 12 and under.

We estimate that children influence about $132 billion in parental pur- 12 chase decisions every year. Their influence totals $82.4 billion in food and beverage purchases, $13.2 billion in clothing, $16.9 billion for play items, and $3.1 billion for health and beauty aids. This figure does not include major categories for which figures were not available, such as family vacations.

This study is not precise. Its estimates assume that a child's degree of 13 influence is the same for each category, that the extent of a child's influence is the same in all households, and that parity exists among researchers who measure this influence. It also derives estimates from estimates. But its point still comes through loud and clear. The goal of any business is to find and influence the primary decision-makers for purchases. That is why businesses, in increasing numbers, are targeting children.

# Little Pleas & Big Bucks

On average, children influence 17 percent of family spending in 62 product categories.

*(total sales, percent of sales influenced by children, and volume of child-influenced sales, in billions of 1990 dollars)*

|  | Total Industry Sales ($ billions) | Percent of Sales Influenced by Children | Volume of Child-Influenced Sales ($ billions) |
|---|---|---|---|
| Athletic shoes | $ 5.60 | 20% | $ 1.12 |
| Automobiles | 221.70 | 4 | 8.87 |
| Bakery goods | 26.10 | 10 | 2.61 |
| Bar soap | 1.50 | 20 | 0.30 |
| Batteries | 3.00 | 25 | 0.75 |
| Beauty aids (kids') | 1.20 | 70 | 0.84 |
| Bicycles | 1.00 | 40 | 0.40 |
| Blank audio cassettes | 0.39 | 15 | 0.06 |
| Bottled water | 2.00 | 10 | 0.20 |
| Bread | 13.00 | 20 | 2.60 |
| Cameras (still) and film | 4.55 | 12 | 0.55 |
| Candy and gum | 10.43 | 33 | 3.44 |
| Canned pasta | 0.57 | 60 | 0.34 |
| Casual dining | 21.00 | 30 | 6.30 |
| Cereals (cold) | 6.90 | 20 | 1.38 |
| Cereals (hot) | 0.74 | 50 | 0.37 |
| Clothing (kids') | 18.40 | 60 | 11.04 |
| Consumer electronics | 32.60 | 10 | 3.26 |
| Cookies (packaged) | 4.30 | 40 | 1.72 |
| Dairy goods | 40.20 | 10 | 4.02 |
| Deli goods | 11.10 | 8 | 0.89 |
| Fast foods | 65.00 | 35 | 22.75 |
| Fragrances (kids') | 0.30 | 70 | 0.21 |
| Frozen breakfasts | 0.55 | 10 | 0.06 |
| Frozen novelties | 1.40 | 75 | 1.05 |
| Frozen sandwiches | 0.27 | 30 | 0.08 |
| Fruit snacks | 0.30 | 80 | 0.24 |
| Fruits and vegetables, canned | 3.00 | 20 | 0.60 |
| Fruits and vegetables, fresh | 43.40 | 6 | 2.60 |
| Furniture, furnishings (kids') | 5.00 | 35 | 1.75 |
| Hair care | 3.80 | 5 | 0.19 |
| Hobby items | 1.00 | 40 | 0.40 |
| Home computers | 3.10 | 10 | 0.31 |
| Hotels (mid-price) | 5.50 | 10 | 0.55 |
| Ice cream | 7.60 | 23 | 1.75 |

## Little Pleas & Big Bucks—*continued*

| | Total Industry Sales ($ billions) | Percent of Sales Influenced by Children | Volume of Child-Influenced Sales ($ billions) |
|---|---|---|---|
| Isotonic drinks | $ 0.70 | 15% | $ 0.11 |
| Jellies and jams | 2.60 | 20 | 0.52 |
| Juices and juice drinks | 10.00 | 33 | 3.30 |
| Meats (packaged) | 17.10 | 13 | 2.20 |
| Meats (fresh) | 43.10 | 10 | 4.30 |
| Microwave meals | 2.30 | 30 | 0.69 |
| Movies | 4.20 | 30 | 1.26 |
| OTC drugs | 11.00 | 12 | 1.32 |
| Peanut butter | 1.40 | 40 | 0.56 |
| Pet foods | 7.20 | 12 | 0.86 |
| Pizza (frozen) | 0.92 | 40 | 0.37 |
| Pudding and gelatin | 0.93 | 25 | 0.23 |
| Recorded music | 3.40 | 20 | 0.68 |
| Refrigerated puddings | 0.20 | 20 | 0.04 |
| Salty snacks | 8.30 | 25 | 2.08 |
| School supplies | 1.80 | 35 | 0.63 |
| Seafood | 7.30 | 10 | 0.73 |
| Shoes (kids') | 2.00 | 50 | 1.00 |
| Soda | 46.60 | 30 | 13.98 |
| Sporting goods | 5.50 | 10 | 0.55 |
| Spreadable cheese | 0.25 | 20 | 0.05 |
| Toaster products | 0.25 | 45 | 0.11 |
| Toothpaste | 1.00 | 20 | 0.20 |
| Toys | 13.40 | 70 | 9.38 |
| Video games | 3.50 | 60 | 2.10 |
| Video rentals | 6.50 | 25 | 1.63 |
| Yogurt | 1.20 | 10 | 0.12 |
| Total | $769.15 | — | $132.87 |

Source: Author's research

## Post-Reading Questions

1. According to McNeal, what influence do children have on consumer spending? What evidence does he use in paragraphs 1 and 2 to support his claim about that influence? How effective is his evidence? Why? Why do you think he uses that kind of evidence in the first paragraphs of his article?

2. Why are researchers interested in the influence of children on family purchasing behaviors? Give an example from your own experience to explain your answer.

3. In your own words, summarize the reasons for the increased influence of children on family purchasing behaviors. From your own experiences, how convincing are these reasons?

4. Describe the different stages children go through as consumers. How do these stages differ? Do you believe children have always gone through these stages, or do the stages change from one historical period to another? Explain your answer.

5. McNeal is a professor of marketing. Much of the information he presents in this article is based on his own research. In your own words, summarize the research process used to obtain this information. Who are the "we" he alludes to in paragraphs 9 to 12? What does the use of the word "we" suggest about the research process?

6. Analyze the table McNeal presents ("Little Pleas & Big Bucks"). What purchases are most influenced by children? What influence patterns are suggested in the table? Where in the article is the information in the table mentioned? How do the table and the discussion of the information in the table differ?

7. After reading this article, what kind of readers do you believe McNeal had in mind? How do you know? What changes might McNeal have made in this article if he had wanted to submit it to an academic journal read primarily by other marketing professors? Why would he have made those changes?

8. Reread the last paragraph of the article. What is McNeal trying to do in this paragraph? Why? How do the beginning and end of this last paragraph differ? What reasoning connects them?

9. Reread the first and last paragraphs of McNeal's article. In what ways are they different? How are they alike? Why?

10. Examine two or three children's magazines or television programs. What kinds of advertisements or commercials are children exposed to in those media? How do your observations compare and contrast to what McNeal says in this article?

11. How do your own parents or other parents that you know feel about advertising appeals to children?

# VANCE PACKARD ON MARKETING TO CHILDREN

## Pre-Reading Questions

1. What can you remember about the television commercials you watched as a child? Do you believe they influenced what you wanted to have? Can you remember any particular toys that you wanted because you saw them advertised on television? Do you believe children today are influenced by television commercials in the same way you were? Do you believe television exerts too much control over children, particularly in terms of how it influences their decisions about what they want to own?

2. This is an excerpt from Vance Packard's famous book *The Hidden Persuaders*. Published over thirty years ago (1957), it deals with television and its impact on children at a time when television itself was in its infancy. What do you think Packard had in mind when he selected this title? What did he want to suggest about television? Why were his ideas considered ground breaking at the time?

3. Do you feel that children's television shows are too commercial in their appeals? What about cartoon shows that promote products that can then be purchased at department stores—Ninja Turtles, and others?

## MARKETING TO MOPPETS
### Vance Packard

"Today the future occupation of all moppets is to be skilled consumers."
—David Riesman, *The Lonely Crowd*

Dr. Riesman in his study of the basic changes taking place in the American character during the twentieth century (i.e., from inner-directed to other-directed) found that our growing preoccupation with acts of consumption reflected the change. This preoccupation, he noted, was particularly intense (and intensively encouraged by product makers) at the moppet level. He characterized the children of America as "consumer trainees." 1

In earlier more innocent days, when the pressure was not on to build future consumers, the boys' magazines and their counterparts concentrated on training the young for the frontiers of production, including warfare. As a part of that training, Dr. Riesman pointed out in *The Lonely Crowd*, the budding athlete might eschew smoke and drink. "The comparable media today train the young for the frontiers of 2 consumption–to tell the difference between Pepsi-Cola and Coca-Cola, as later between Old Golds and Chesterfields," he explained. He cited the old nursery rhyme about one little pig going to market while one stayed home and commented dourly: "The rhyme may be taken as a paradigm of individuation and unsocialized behavior among children of an earlier era. Today, however, all little pigs go to market; none stay home; all have roast beef, if any do; and all say 'wee-wee-wee.' "

The problem of building eager consumers for the future was consid- 3 ered at a mid-fifties session of the American Marketing Association. The head of Gilbert Youth Research told the marketers there was no longer any problem of getting funds "to target the youth market"; there were plenty. The problem was targeting the market with maximum effectiveness. Charles Sievert, advertising columnist for the *New York World Telegram and Sun,* explained what this targeting was all about by saying, "Of course the dividend from investment in the youth market is to develop product and brand loyalty and thus have an upcoming devoted adult market."

A more blunt statement of the opportunity moppets present appeared 4 in an ad in *Printer's Ink* several years ago. A firm specializing in supplying "education" material to school-teachers in the form of wall charts, board cutouts, teachers' manuals made this appeal to merchants and advertisers: "Eager minds can be molded to want your products! In the grade schools throughout America are nearly 23,000,000 young girls and boys. These children eat food, wear out clothes, use soap. They are consumers today and will be the buyers of tomorrow. Here is a vast market for your products. Sell these children on your brand name and they will insist that their parents buy no other. Many farsighted advertisers are cashing in today . . . and building for tomorrow . . . by molding eager minds" through Project Education Material supplied to teachers. It added reassuringly: "all carrying sugar-coated messages designed to create acceptance and demand for the products. . . ." In commenting on this appeal Clyde Miller, in his *The Process of Persuasion,* explained the problem of conditioning the reflexes of children by saying, "It takes time, yes, but if you expect to be in business for any length of time, think of what it can mean to your firm in profits if you can condition a million or ten million children who will grow up into adults trained to buy your product as soldiers are trained to advance when they hear the trigger words 'forward march.' "

One small phase of the seduction of young people into becoming 5 loyal followers of a brand is seen in the fact that on many college campuses students can earn a part of their college expenses by passing among fellow students handing out free sample packages of cigarettes.

The potency of television in conditioning youngsters to be loyal 6 enthusiasts of a product, whether they are old enough to consume it or not, became indisputable early in the fifties. A young New York ad man taking a marketing class at a local university made the casual statement that, thanks to TV, most children were learning to sing beer and other commercials before learning to sing "The Star-Spangled Banner." Youth Research Institute, according to *The Nation,* boasted that even five-year-olds sing beer commercials "over and over again with gusto." It pointed out that moppets not only sing the merits of advertised products but do it with the vigor displayed by the most raptly enthusiastic announcers, and do it all day long "at no extra cost to the advertiser." They cannot be turned off as a set can. When at the beginning of the decade television was in its infancy, an ad appeared in a trade journal alerting manufacturers to the extraordinary ability of TV to etch messages on young brains. "Where else on earth," the ad exclaimed, "is brand consciousness fixed so firmly in the minds of four-year-old tots? . . . What is it worth to a manufacturer who can close in on this juvenile audience and continue to sell it under controlled conditions year after year, right up to its attainment of adulthood and full-fledged buyer status? It CAN be done. Interested?" (While the author was preparing this chapter he heard his own eight-year-old daughter happily singing the cigarette jingle: "Don't miss the fun of smoking!")

The relentlessness with which one TV sponsor tried to close in on preschool tots brought protests in late 1955. Jack Gould, TV columnist of *The New York Times,* expressed dismay at a commercial for vitamin pills that Dr. Francis Horwich, "principal" of TV's *Ding Dong School* for preschool children, delivered. It seems she used the same studied tempo she used in chatting to children about toys and helping mother while she demonstrated how pretty the red pills were and how easy to swallow they were. She said she hoped they were taking the pills every morning "like I do," and urged them to make sure the next time they visited a drugstore that their mother picked out the right bottle. Gould commented: 7

"To put it as mildly as possible, Dr. Horwich has gone a step too far in letting a commercial consideration jeopardize her responsibility to the young children whose faith and trust she solicits." First, he pointed out, was the simple factor of safety. Small children should be kept away from pills of all kinds and certainly not be encouraged to treat them as playthings. A lot of different pills (including mama's sleeping pills) can be pretty and red and easy to swallow, and after all prekindergarten children can't read labels. Gould doubted whether TV had any business deciding whether tots do or do not need vitamin pills. He felt that a vitamin deficiency is better determined "by a parent after consultation with a physician" rather than a TV network. Finally, he observed, "Using a child's credibility to club a parent into buying something is reprehensible under the best of circumstances. But in the case of a product bearing on a child's health it is inexcusable." Doctors wrote in commending Gould for his stand; and a mother wrote that she found herself "appalled at the amount of commercialism our children are being subjected to." 8

Mr. Gould's complaints notwithstanding, the merchandisers sought to groom children not only as future consumers but as shills who would lead or "club" their parents into the salesroom. Dr. Dichter advised a 9 major car maker to train dealer salesmen to regard children as allies rather than nuisances while demonstrating a car. The salesmen, instead of shoving them away, should be especially attentive to the kiddies and discuss all the mechanisms that draw the child's attention. This, he said, is an excellent strategy for drawing the understanding permissive father into the discussion.

In late 1955 a writer for *The Nation* offered the opinion that the 10 shrewd use of premiums as bait for kiddies could "mangle the parent's usual marketing consideration of need, price, quality and budget." He cited as one example General Electric's offer of a sixty-piece circus, a magic-ray gun, and a space helmet to children who brought their parents into dealers' stores to witness new GE refrigerators being demonstrated.

Sylvania reportedly offered a complete Space Ranger kit with not 11 only helmet but disintegrator, flying saucer, and space telephone to children who managed to deliver parents into salesrooms. And Nash cars offered a toy service station. This writer, Joseph Seldin, concluded: "Manipulation of children's minds in the fields of religion or politics would touch off a parental storm of protest and a rash of Congressional investigations. But in the world of commerce children are fair game and legitimate prey."

Herb Sheldon, TV star with a large following of children, offered this 12 comment in 1956: "I don't say that children should be forced to harass their parents into buying products they've seen advertised on television, but at the same time I cannot close my eyes to the fact that it's being done every day." Then he added, and this was in *Advertising Agency* magazine, "Children are living, talking records of what we tell them every day."

Motivational analysts were called in to provide insights on the most 13 effective ways to achieve an assured strong impact with children. Social Research got into this problem with a television study entitled "Now, for the Kiddies . . ." It found that two basic factors to be considered in children's TV programs are filling the moppet's "inner needs" and making sure the program has "acceptability" (i.e., appease Mom, for one thing, so that she won't forbid the child to listen to it, which is an ever-present hazard). Social Research offered some psychological guideposts.

A show can "appeal" to a child, it found, without necessarily offering 14 the child amusement or pleasure. It appeals if it helps him express his inner tensions and fantasies in a manageable way. It appeals if it gets him a little scared or mad or befuddled and then offers him a way to get rid of his fear, anger, or befuddlement. Gauging the scariness of a show is a difficult business because a show may be just right in scariness for an eight-year-old but too scary for a six-year-old and not scary enough for a ten-year-old.

Social Research diagnosed the appeal of the highly successful Howdy 15 Doody and found some elements present that offered the children listening far more than childish amusement. Clarabelle, the naughty clown, was found consistently to exhibit traits of rebellious children. Clarabelle, it noted, "represents children's resistance to adult authority and goes generally unpunished." The report stated: "In general the show utilizes repressed hostilities to make fun of adults or depict adults in an unattractive light. The 'bad' characters (Chief Thunderthud, Mr. Bluster, Mr. X) are all adults. They are depicted either as frighteningly powerful or silly." When the adult characters are shown in ridiculous situations, such as being all tangled up in their coats or outwitted by the puppets, the child characters in the show are shown as definitely superior. "In other words," it explained, "there is a reversal process with the adults acting 'childish' and incompetent, and children being 'adult' and clever." It added that the master of ceremonies, Buffalo Bob, was more of a friendly safe uncle than a parent.

All this sly sniping at parent symbols takes place while Mother, unaware 16 of the evident symbology, chats on the telephone, content in the knowledge that her children are being pleasantly amused by the childish antics being shown electronically on the family's wondrous pacifier.

In turning next to the space shows the Social Research psychologists 17 found here that the over-all format, whether the show was set in the twenty-first century or the twenty-fourth, was: "Basic pattern of 'good guys' versus 'bad men' with up-to-date scientific and mechanical trapping." Note that it said bad men, not bad guys.

The good guys interestingly were found to be all young men in their 18 twenties organized as a group with very strong team loyalty. The leader was pictured as a sort of older brother (not a father symbol). And the villains or cowards were all older men who might be "symbolic or father figures." They were either bad or weak.

Much of this fare might be construed as being antiparent sniping, 19 offering children an exhilarating, and safe, way to work off their grudges against their parents. "To children," the report explained, "adults are a 'ruling class' against which they cannot successfully revolt."

The report confided some pointers to TV producers for keeping 20 parents pacified. One way suggested was to take the parent's side in such easy, thoughtful ways as having a character admonish junior to clean his plate. Another good way was to "add an educational sugar coating. Calling a cowboy movie 'American history' and a space show 'scientific' seems to be an effective way to avoid parental complaints." A final hint dropped was: "Cater a little more to parents. . . . The implication that children can be talked into buying anything . . . irritates parents. Slight changes along these lines can avoid giving offense without losing appeal for the children."

Some of the United States product makers evidently solicit the favor 21 of moppets by building aggressive outlets right into their products. Public-relations counsel and motivational enthusiast E. L. Bernays was reported asserting in 1954 that the most successful breakfast cereals were building crunch into their appeal to appease hostility by giving outlet to aggressive and other feelings. (He has served as a counsel to food groups.) The cereal that promises "pop-snap-crackle" when you eat it evidently has something of value to kiddies besides calories.

One aspect of juvenile merchandising that intrigued the depth 22 manipulators was the craze or fad. To a casual observer the juvenile craze for cowboys or knights or Davy Crockett may seem like a cute bit of froth on the surface of American life. To fad-wise merchandisers such manifestations are largely the result of careful manipulation. They can be enormously profitable or disastrously unprofitable, depending on the merchandiser's cunning.

An evidence of how big the business can be is that the Davy Crockett 23 craze of 1955, which gave birth to 300 Davy Crockett products, lured $300,000,000 from American pockets. Big persuasion indeed!

American merchandisers felt a need for a deeper understanding of 24 these craze phenomena so that they could not only share in the profits, but know when to unload. Research was needed to help the manufacturers avoid overestimating the length of the craze. Many were caught with warehouses full of "raccoon" tails and buckskin fringe when, almost without warning, the Crockett craze lost its lure. One manufacturer said: "When they die, they die a horrible death."

This problem of comprehending the craze drew the attention of such 25 motivation experts as Dr. Dichter and Alfred Politz. And *Tide* magazine, journal of merchandisers, devoted a major analysis to the craze.

The experts studied the Crockett extravaganza as a case in point and 26 concluded that its success was due to the fact that it had in good measure all of the three essential ingredients of a profitable fad: symbols, carrying device, and fulfillment of a subconscious need. The carrying device, and the experts agreed it was a superb one, was the song "Ballad of Davy Crockett," which was repeated in some form in every Disney show. Also it was richer in symbols than many of the fads: coonskin cap, fringed buckskin, flintlock rifle. *Tide* explained: "All popular movements from Christianity's cross to the Nazis' swastika have their distinctive symbols."

As for filling a subconscious need, Dr. Dichter had this to say of 27 Crockett: "Children are reaching for an opportunity to explain themselves in terms of the traditions of the country. Crockett gave them that opportunity. On a very imaginative level the kids really felt they were Davy Crockett. . . ."

What causes the quick downfall of crazes? The experts said overex- 28 ploitation was one cause. Another cause was sociological. Mr. Politz pointed out that crazes take a course from upper to lower. In the case of adult fads this means upper-income education groups to lower. In the case of children, Politz explained: "Those children who are leaders because of their age adopt the fad first and then see it picked up by the younger children, an age class they no longer wish to be identified with. This causes the older children deliberately to drop the fad."

Both Politz and Dichter felt not only that with careful planning the 29
course of fads could be charted to ensure more profits to everybody, but
also that profitable fads could actually be created. *Tide* called this
possibility "fascinating." Dr. Dichter felt that with appropriate motivation research techniques a fad even of the Crockett magnitude could be
started, once the promoters had found, and geared their fad to, an
unsatisfied need of youngsters.

Politz felt that the research experts could certainly set up the general 30
rules for creating a successful fad. In a bow to the professional persuaders
of advertising he added that once the general rules are laid down, the
"creative" touch is needed. Both he and Dr. Dichter agreed that this
challenging task for the future—creating fads of the first magnitude for
our children—is the combined job of the researcher and the creative man.

## Post-Reading Questions

1. This excerpt from Packard's book begins with a quotation and
   additional references to sociologist David Riesman's book *The
   Lonely Crowd*. What does Packard tell his readers about Riesman's
   book? Why? What does Riesman say that Packard obviously agrees
   with? Why would he begin a section of the book about children
   with these references to Riesman?

2. What is Packard's main point (thesis)? Describe his strategy for
   developing that thesis. How does he organize this section of his
   book? What kinds of support does he use to develop his thesis?
   How convincing do you believe his support was to his 1957
   readers? Why? Would a 1990s reader react the same way? Explain.

3. Where in this excerpt are the clues that this was written in 1957? If
   you were writing an essay about the same topic today, what
   examples would you substitute? Identify two or three of Packard's
   examples and compare them with ones you would use.

4. Can you identify two or three statements in Packard's excerpt that
   would no longer be true today? Why are they no longer true? What
   has changed?

5. In your opinion, is Packard's thesis still correct? Explain your
   answer by referring to specific aspects of how products are marketed
   to children today.

6. How would you complete this sentence: Because children are subject to the powerful influence of television, . . . . After you complete
   this sentence, write a paragraph explaining the point you make. Refer
   to something Packard says in the excerpt as you develop your idea.

7. Where in this excerpt can you identify references to psychology and
   sociology? Be specific. What do these references suggest about the
   impact psychological and sociological research had on Packard's
   ideas?

8.  Explain what Packard means by "the seduction of young people" in paragraph 5. Why is the word "seduction" used?
9.  Using information in Packard's excerpt, explain how television commercials have changed since 1957. Is the industry subject to stricter or more lenient controls? Use current commercials to support your claim.
10. Packard says that children learn to sing beer commercials before they learn "The Star-Spangled Banner." Do you believe that is still true? Explain your answer by referring to specific commercials.
11. What kinds of readers did Packard envision for his book? How might the reader in 1957 have differed from the readers of the 1990s? Why?
12. In your opinion, what is the relationship between sociological and psychological research and marketing today? Do you think the relationship today is the same or different than the relationship that existed in 1957? Why?
13. What do you think Packard's reaction would be to children's programs such as *Sesame Street* and *Mr. Rogers' Neighborhood* (developed during the late 1960s and early 1970s)? Use information in this excerpt to support your answer.

# JOHN M. ROGERS ON URBAN AND RURAL CONSUMERS

## Pre-Reading Questions

1.  Describe the neighborhood you grew up in. Was it urban or rural? How did your neighborhood affect your family's purchasing behavior: what, where, why, and how you bought?
2.  Describe yourself as a consumer. What purchases do you consider the most important? How do you decide to spend your money? Do different factors influence different purchasing decisions? Why?
3.  Using percentages, estimate how much of your household's total expenditures are put toward food, transportation, and housing. Compare your estimates to Rogers' data, taking the time difference into consideration.

## EXPENDITURES OF URBAN AND RURAL CONSUMERS, 1972–73 TO 1985

### John M. Rogers

Social and economic comparisons of urban and rural populations have   1
long been of interest to public policymakers. The migration of families

between urban and rural areas, the financial problems of the American farmer, and the incidence of poverty by type of area are but a few of the urban versus rural topics that have received much attention.[1] This report focuses on another socioeconomic aspect of the urban and rural populations, namely, how the expenditure patterns of the two populations compare.[2] Expenditures, income, and family characteristics are compared for 1985, and changes in expenditure levels and expenditure shares between 1972–73 and 1985 are discussed using data from the Bureau of Labor Statistics Consumer Expenditure (CE) Survey.

## METHOD OF THE EXPENDITURE SURVEY

The CE Survey consists of two separate components, each with its own   2 questionnaire and sample: 1) a quarterly interview survey in which expenditures and income of consumer units are obtained in five interviews conducted every 3 months and, 2) a diary or recordkeeping survey completed by consumer units for two consecutive 1-week periods. The Interview survey is designed to obtain data on the types of expenditures which respondents can recall for a period of 3 months or longer. In general, these include relatively large expenditures, such as automobile purchases, and those that occur on a regular basis, such as rent or utility payments. Including "global estimates" of spending for food, about 95 percent of expenditures are covered in the Interview survey. The diary survey obtains data on small, frequently purchased items which normally are difficult for respondents to recall, such as detailed food expenses. Data cited in this report are from the interview survey. Differences in expenditures and expenditure shares discussed here are based on population estimates rather than sample estimates.

## URBAN VERSUS RURAL, 1985

Rural consumer units[3] accounted for about 16 percent of the total in   3 1985. However, the portion of the consumer units classified as rural varied substantially by region of the country. Almost 22 percent of the units in the South were rural, compared with only 9 percent of the units in the West. About 19 percent of units in the Midwest region and 12 percent in the Northeast were in rural areas. The data also show that urban consumer units averaged higher incomes in 1985 than did their rural counterparts. Urban consumer units had slightly fewer members and were headed by persons about 2 years younger than heads of rural units. The numbers of earners, children under age 18, and persons over 65 were about the same for the two groups. Rural consumer units owned more vehicles per unit and were more likely to own their own homes.

Total expenditures accounted for a larger proportion of total income of rural units than of urban units.

Expenditure levels of the two population groups showed substantial 4 differences across expenditure components. As might be expected from their higher average incomes, urban consumer units had higher levels of total expenditures—they spent about $3,600 more on average than did rural units in 1985. Higher food, housing, and apparel expenditures accounted for much of the difference. However, despite lower average incomes, rural consumer units spent more for transportation, health care, tobacco, and life and other personal insurance than did urban units.

Results show that, in 1985, urban consumer units spent more for 5 housing than did their rural counterparts, and the amount spent accounted for a larger share of total expenditures than that of rural units. Expenditure shares, the percent of total expenditures spent on each component, are shown in Table 1. Urban consumer units spent an average of $7,005, or 31 percent of their total expenditures, on housing compared to an average of $5,064, or 26 percent of the total, spent by rural units. A higher percentage of rural consumer units were homeowners and rural homeowners were more likely to have paid off their mortgages—38 percent having done so versus 21 percent of urban units. Despite lower total housing expenditures, rural units spent almost as much on fuels and utilities as urban units, $1,579 compared to $1,661. These costs accounted for a larger share of rural consumers' housing costs than of urban consumers'—31 percent versus 24 percent. The higher share spent by rural consumer units may be partially explained by the fact that renter families frequently do not pay directly for fuels and utilities—payments are included in the rent—and a higher proportion of urban families are renter families.

Rural consumers spent a larger share of their total unit expenditures 6 on transportation, 25 percent versus 20 percent spent by urban consumers, due largely to higher expenditures for vehicles and gasoline.[4] This is as expected, because rural consumers own more vehicles than do urban consumers—2.4 per consumer unit compared to 1.8 owned by urban consumers. Also, rural consumers probably drive longer distances than do urban consumers.

Rural consumers also spent more per unit on health care than did 7 urban consumers—$1,168 versus $1,011. This accounted for about 6 percent of rural consumers' total unit expenditures versus 4 percent of urban consumers' total. Higher health care expenditures by rural consumers can be attributed to their being older, on average, than urban consumers. Also, data from the survey show that rural consumer units more frequently paid the full cost of their health insurance policies while employers more frequently paid the costs of policies for urban consumers.

## CHANGES IN EXPENDITURE SHARES

Changes in the shares of total expenditures spent on different compo-    8
nents are used to show how consumers' expenditure patterns change
over time. Increases or decreases in shares show changes in the way
consumer units allocate their expenditures on individual components
relative to the change in total expenditures. Changes in shares can take
place gradually over a period of years as consumers alter their expenditures in response to changes in tastes, preferences, or lifestyle, or in
response to sudden economic changes. For example, the share of the
food dollar spent on food at home has been declining over time and can
be attributed in part to the increase in the number of two-earner
households. Families have had to adjust their schedules to meet job
requirements, which has resulted in multiple-earner families taking more
meals outside the home. An example of a more sudden change was the
sharp increase in expenditures on gasoline in the 1970's as a result of the
1973–74 oil embargo that depleted supplies and forced up prices.

Data in Table 1 show how expenditure shares for urban and rural    9
consumer units changed between 1972–73 and 1985. Shares are also
shown for 1980 because, for some components such as food and
gasoline, the shares over the entire period from 1972–73 to 1985 were
not steadily increasing or decreasing. Food expenditure shares for urban
and rural consumer units each increased about 1 percentage point
between 1972–73 and 1980. Subsequently, food expenditure increases
slowed relative to increases in expenditures for other goods and services,
and this is reflected in the drop in food expenditure shares between 1980
and 1985:

Food Expenditure Shares (percent of total expenditures)

|  | Urban | | | Rural | | |
|---|---|---|---|---|---|---|
|  | 1972–73 | 1980 | 1985 | 1972–73 | 1980 | 1985 |
| Food, total | 17.8 | 19.0 | 15.2 | 19.5 | 20.4 | 15.6 |
| Food at home | * | 14.3 | 10.3 | * | 16.6 | 11.5 |
| Food away | * | 4.7 | 5.0 | * | 3.8 | 4.2 |

*Data not available.

Food expenditure shares dropped for both urban and rural consumer
units, but more for rural units than urban. In 1972–73, food accounted
for a larger share of rural consumers' total unit expenditures than of
urban consumers'—20 percent versus 18 percent—but, by 1985, this
difference had almost disappeared. The decline in food expenditure
shares from 1980 to 1985 was accounted for entirely by the drop in the

TABLE 1 Expenditure Shares of Urban and Rural Consumer Units, Interview Survey, 1972–73, 1980, and 1985[1] (in percent)

| Item | Urban | | | Rural | | | Significance Test[2] |
|---|---|---|---|---|---|---|---|
| | 1972–73 | 1980 | 1985 | 1972–73 | 1980 | 1985 | |
| Total expenditures: | | | | | | | |
| Average (in dollars) | $ 9,420 | $16,723 | $22,810 | $ 7,760 | $13,663 | $19,197 | — |
| Percent of total | 100.0 | 100.0 | 100.0 | 100.0 | 100.0 | 100.0 | — |
| Food | 17.8 | 19.0 | 15.2 | 19.5 | 20.4 | 15.6 | * |
| Food at home | (3) | 14.3 | 10.3 | (3) | 16.6 | 11.5 | * |
| Food away | (3) | 4.7 | 5.0 | (3) | 3.8 | 4.2 | * |
| Alcoholic beverages | .9 | 1.7 | 1.3 | .6 | 1.4 | 1.1 | — |
| Housing | 28.0 | 29.3 | 30.7 | 24.5 | 25.2 | 26.4 | * |
| Shelter | 16.0 | 16.3 | 17.9 | 11.5 | 11.8 | 13.6 | * |
| Owned dwellings | 7.9 | 9.5 | 10.3 | 7.2 | 8.4 | 9.5 | * |
| Rented dwellings | 6.9 | 5.3 | 5.7 | 3.2 | 2.1 | 2.8 | * |
| Other lodging | 1.2 | 1.5 | 1.9 | 1.1 | 1.2 | 1.2 | * |
| Fuels and utilities | 6.2 | 7.1 | 7.3 | 7.6 | 8.4 | 8.2 | * |
| Household operations | 1.5 | 1.6 | 1.6 | 1.1 | 1.2 | 1.3 | * |
| House furnishings and equipment | 4.4 | 4.3 | 3.9 | 4.4 | 3.2 | 3.3 | * |

| | | | | | | |
|---|---|---|---|---|---|---|
| Apparel and services | 7.8 | 5.4 | 6.8 | 4.5 | 4.4 | * |
| Transportation | 18.7 | 20.4 | 22.0 | 24.7 | 25.0 | * |
| Vehicles | 7.5 | 7.0 | 9.6 | 9.4 | 12.6 | * |
| Gasoline and motor oil | 4.3 | 7.1 | 5.7 | 9.4 | 6.0 | * |
| Other vehicle expenses | 5.7 | 5.1 | 6.2 | 5.7 | 5.9 | * |
| Public transportation | 1.2 | 1.3 | .4 | .5 | .5 | * |
| Health care | 4.6 | 4.4 | 5.8 | 5.2 | 6.1 | * |
| Entertainment | 4.1 | 4.3 | 3.9 | 4.1 | 4.7 | | |
| Personal care | 1.1 | .9 | 1.0 | .8 | .7 | * |
| Reading | .5 | .7 | .5 | .6 | .6 | | |
| Education | 1.3 | 1.2 | 1.0 | .7 | 1.1 | * |
| Tobacco | 1.4 | 1.0 | 1.5 | 1.3 | 1.3 | * |
| Miscellaneous | 1.1 | 1.5 | 1.0 | 1.5 | 1.1 | * |
| Cash contributions | 3.9 | 2.9 | 3.8 | 2.5 | 2.8 | * |
| Personal insurance and pensions | 8.7 | 9.1 | 8.2 | 7.0 | 9.1 | | |
| Life and other personal insurance | 3.9 | 1.2 | 3.6 | 1.8 | 1.7 | * |
| Retirement, pensions, and Social Security | 4.8 | 7.9 | 4.5 | 5.2 | 7.5 | — |

[1]Expenditure shares are the percent of total expenditures spent on each component.

[2]A chi-square test of the significance of the difference between proportions was used to test whether the difference between urban and rural shares in 1985 was significant at the 5-percent level. Those components for which the difference was significant are marked by an asterisk.

*Data not available.

food at home component, as expenditure shares for food away from home actually increased slightly over the period. As a result, food away from home accounted for an increasing portion of overall food expenditures. The drop in expenditure shares for food at home corresponds to the slower price rise of food at home items relative to the price increases of all goods and services. From 1980 to 1985, food at home prices as measured by the CPI-U rose only 18 percent compared to a 31-percent increase in the All-Items CPI-U.

Housing expenditure shares increased steadily from 1972–73 to 1985 for both urban and rural consumer units; the share that urban units spent on housing rose about 3 percentage points, from 28 percent in 1972–73 to 31 percent in 1985, while the rural units' share rose about 2 percentage points, from 25 percent to 27 percent over the period. The percentage of units that were homeowners rose about 3 percentage points for both urban and rural consumers.

Transportation expenditure shares rose over the period 1972–73 to 1985, but more for rural than for urban consumer units. Shares rose from 22 to 25 percent for rural units compared to an increase from 19 to 20 percent for their urban counterparts. The sharp increase in gasoline prices contributed to a rise in gasoline expenditure shares from 1972–73 to 1980. However, the subsequent decline in prices, coupled with conservation measures, resulted in gasoline shares dropping to about the same level as in 1972–73 by 1985. Increases in expenditures on vehicles were responsible for the larger increases in the overall transportation component for rural consumers than for urban consumers. Vehicle shares dropped slightly from 1972–73 to 1980 for both urban and rural consumer units. However, they then rose sharply from 1980 to 1985 and more rapidly for rural than for urban units. Other transportation components accounted for about the same share of total expenditures in 1985 as in 1972–73.

Expenditure shares for retirement, pensions, and Social Security also increased from 1972–73 to 1985. Shares rose about 3 percentage points for both urban and rural consumer units, with much of the increase occurring between 1980 and 1985. Over that period, the annual maximum taxable earnings for Social Security rose from $25,900 to $39,600 and the employee contribution rate rose from 6.13 percent to 7.05 percent.[5]

This report shows that there are differences in the way that urban and rural consumers allocate their expenditure budgets. Also, the differences in expenditure shares between the two groups are not static, but rather fluctuate in response to socioeconomic changes. As more data become available, analysts will have the opportunity to compare and follow changes in expenditure patterns of the two groups. The data provided by the Consumer Expenditure Survey can be of help in developing economic programs specific to each of the two different population groups.

NOTES

1. See Kathleen K. Scholl, "Income and Poverty Rates: Farm and Nonfarm Residence," *Family Economics Review,* no. 1, 1983, pp. 16-19; and Kathleen K. Scholl, "Economic Outlook for Farm Families: 1986," in U.S. Department of Agriculture, *Outlook '86: Proceedings,* Agricultural Outlook Conference, Dec. 4, 1985, pp. 279-88.
2. Urban, as defined in this survey, includes the rural population within metropolitan areas.
3. A consumer unit comprises: 1) all members of a particular household related by blood, marriage, adoption, or other legal arrangements; 2) a person living alone or sharing a household with others or living as a roomer in a private home or lodging house or in permanent living quarters in a hotel or motel but who is financially independent; or 3) two or more persons living together who pool their income to make joint expenditure decisions. For the purposes of this report, consumers and consumer units may be used interchangeably.
4. Data on fuel consumption are from *Statistical Abstract of the United States, 1987* (Bureau of the Census, 1987), p. 590, table 1032, "Domestic Motor Fuel Consumption, By Type of Vehicle: 1970 to 1984."
5. Data are from *Statistical Abstract of the United States, 1987,* p. 348, table 586, "Social Security (OASDHI)—Contribution Rates: 1970 to 1990."

**Post-Reading Questions**

1. Why are public policy makers interested in differences and similarities among rural and urban populations? What public policies are influenced by knowledge of such differences?
2. What is the purpose of Rogers' report? What evidence does he use to achieve his purpose? Where does his evidence come from?
3. Summarize the differences reported by Rogers between rural and urban consumers. Why do these differences exist?
4. What changes have occurred in urban and rural consumers? What accounts for these changes?
5. In Rogers' concluding paragraph, he states that "differences in expenditure shares between the two groups are not static, but rather fluctuate in response to socioeconomic changes." What are some of these socioeconomic changes? Why does Rogers not explain these changes?
6. What is the Consumer Expenditure Survey? What are its components? What component does Rogers rely on for his information? What does Rogers mean when he says that data from this survey can be helpful for individuals responsible for planning economic programs for urban or rural consumers?

7.  This article was published in the *Monthly Labor Review*. What kind of readers subscribe to this journal? Why? What information would they expect to find? Why do they read it regularly? How does your reading of this article differ from theirs? Why?

8.  Examine two or three issues of the *Monthly Labor Review*. Analyze the tables of contents. What can you learn about the readers of this journal and the information they seek from reading the table of contents? Scan the issues. What can you learn about readers' expectations for how information in these articles will be presented simply from the format and appearance of the articles?

9.  Examine the notes at the end of the article. What do they tell you about why writers use notes? What information do they contain? What do they tell you about the readers' needs and expectations?

# JULIE LIESSE ON BRAND NAME LOYALTY

## Pre-Reading Questions

1.  How loyal are you to brand name products? Which brand name products are important to you? Why are brand names important to you? How does a particular product become your preferred one? Has your loyalty to particular brands remained constant, or has it changed? Explain why you have remained loyal to or rejected particular brand products?

2.  Would you buy a generic or store brand? What is it about such brands that attracts or repels you? Where do you think your attitude toward such products was developed? What factors are responsible for your attitudes?

3.  Do you think the whole concept of "brand names" is created in order to keep you buying certain products, or does the concept actually have value in defining quality? Explain your answer by describing your own experiences as a consumer.

## BRANDS IN TROUBLE

### Julie Liesse

Brands are under siege—and losing the battle.                                    1

Once the foundation of the marketing world, package-goods com-   2
panies are being buffeted by internal and external forces threatening the future of their brands.

Marketers have made it easy for consumers to trade down and tune   3
out presumably venerable brand names—by siphoning ad dollars to fund

trade promotions, by producing all too similar ad messages, by losing the edge in product innovation.

While such top-flight product marketers as Kellogg Co. and Coca- 4 Cola Co. seem to stumble, retailers including Wal-Mart Stores, Target Stores and Price Club are proving they understand the consumer of the 1990s. In the process, they've become arguably the best U.S. marketers.

By playing price as a trump card, these retailers are diverting 5 consumer loyalty from brands to themselves.

Does this shift in how Americans shop indicate greater vulnerability 6 for brand name products? Will they survive the changing landscape? If so, in what form? Is the industry's concern about a return to brand-building too little and too late?


## ERODING LOYALTY

The future of brands is of critical importance not just to marketers, but 7 to retailers, ad agencies and the media.

"So much of what we take for granted comes from brands—all of 8 our media systems depend on brand marketing," says Don Schultz, professor in the integrated advertising/marketing communications program of Northwestern University's Medill School of Journalism.

Logically, as the time pressures of modern life grow, the reliance on 9 brands should be growing, too.

"A brand is a memory shortcut," says Russ Ferstandig, a practicing 10 psychiatrist and head of Competitive Advantage Consulting.

Brands are "guideposts," says Marylin Silverman, exec VP-director 11 of strategic planning and international research for Backer Spielvogel Bates, New York.

"Brand credibility brings a convenience of decisionmaking into 12 consumers' lives," says Dave Murphy, president of the Betty Crocker division of General Mills.

Is that still true today?                                                  13

The Roper Organization for a decade has measured brand loyalty to 14 a broad group of packaged goods. Three years ago, 56% of those polled by Roper said they know what brand they want to buy when they enter a store. That figure fell to 53% in April 1990 and plunged to 46% by mid-1991.

"The recession has served as a catalyst, accelerating the underlying 15 trends toward eroding brand loyalty," says Bradford Fay, project director at Roper. "But the trend preceded the recession and may well outlast it."

DDB Needham Worldwide's 15-year-old study of consumer habits 16 has shown a drop in loyalty to well-known brands. The number of consumers saying they try to stick to well-known brand names has fallen to about 61% now from 75% in the late '70s. The big drop occurred in the recession of the early '80s—and "brand loyalty has never fully recovered from that drop," says Martin Horn, VP-associate director of the Delta Group research arm of DDB Needham, Chicago.

These recessionary trends, combined with the changed role of brands, mean the '90s have become "one of the most dynamic periods ever for brand loyalty," says Sanford Bredine, president of Bishop/Bredine Associates, a marketing agency.

"The relationship of a brand with a consumer in the 1960s was usually as a problem solver," Backer's Ms. Silverman says. "Then as brands became less and less different in the '70s and '80s, they were sold as badges."

It's not unusual that perfumes or apparel are bought and sold on their emotional values. But in the continuing evolution of brand messages, everyday products like toothpaste and frozen dinners today use marketing messages based not on practical value or product differentiation but on their emotional appeal.

What makes for brand loyalty today are all the intangibles—it's finding a consumer's need and filling it, whether it be sexual aspirations, social needs or self-esteem, says Tom Pirko, principal of Bev-Mark, a food and beverage consultancy.

Consumers, particularly the MTV generation, are comfortable with that.

"It's OK to say, 'Part of the reason I drink Pepsi is that it's cooler than Coke,' " says Melody Douglas-Tate, senior VP-group research director at Leo Burnett USA, Chicago.

If a brand's advantage over its competitor is expressed as a largely emotional one, however, its success hinges more than ever on advertising. And many experts believe not only that advertising isn't working but that emotional messages aren't what consumers want to hear today.

"We have a marketplace that's overglutted with brands that are undifferentiated—brands that have not really identified themselves to the consumer as products that can't be substituted," Backer's Ms. Silverman says.

Part of the problem is the number of new products and new brands arriving on store shelves each year. The average supermarket carries more than 16,000 items, a 45.5% increase since 1985.

"Just the sheer proliferation of brand names has led to consumers viewing them as parity," says DDB Needham's Mr. Horn.

But experts also blame advertising.

"In package goods, the difference between one product and another is often a differentiated idea that comes out of the marketing," says Laurel Cutler, vice chairman-worldwide director of marketing planning for FCB/Leber Katz Partners, New York. "As brands have to deal with an ever-smarter, ever-more pinched consumer, they must keep differentiating to earn the loyalty of their franchise. Some are doing that; some aren't."

A tenet of today's market research is that consumers formerly loyal to 29 a single brand in a given category are increasingly becoming "brand switchers": They're loyal to a set of brands they view as essentially equal. Each individual purchase decision is based on shelf price, the availability of a coupon or other factors unrelated to the brand's equity.

The erosion of ad dollars has exacerbated the problem, says Richard 30 Furash, national director-consumer products for Deloitte & Touche's consultancy group.

"The problem with branding today is that consumer goods market- 31 ers aren't investing in their brands; 70% of their marketing monies are being spent to push products through the retail channel," he says.

"Then it becomes a self-fulfilling prophecy: Manufacturers decreas- 32 ing the amount of advertising behind their brands is one big reason people don't have the same brand loyalties they used to," Mr. Furash says.

An ongoing analysis of brand loyalty trends by the NPD Group arm 33 of A.C. Nielsen Co. shows consumer loyalty to a brand usually declines when the brand doesn't maintain its share of voice in its category.

The growth of couponing has even changed the habits of those 34 consumers already tagged "price-driven" by Leo Burnett USA's research department. Among those price-oriented consumers, many who were "brand experimental"—occasionally trying a new brand if they held a coupon for it—are now "brand irrelevant."

It's not just the message, though; differences between brands have 35 eroded as well.

"The problem is that the majority of R&D is set to develop parity 36 products—and then the majority of advertising is offering parity claims," says Gary Stibel, principal of the New England Consulting Group. "Knowing that both Eveready and Duracell are good is *not* OK. Advertising that communicates that products are simply 'good' is unaffordable."

Even if a brand does claim superiority, consumers may not respond. 37

"Whereas brands formerly were given the benefit of the doubt, 38 brands now have to earn your trust," Competitive Advantage's Mr. Ferstandig says. "They are deceptors until proven innocent."

With pressure on to increase sales and profits in a country with flat 39 population growth, package-goods marketers are cutting product costs— usually under the "productivity" banner. But by shaving a little here and a little there off product quality, marketers are at least partly responsible for the gap in consumer trust.

"Product quality has become a problem," says Scott Rahn, VP- 40 corporate development for ConAgra, the country's No. 2 food marketer.

"Some companies have sacrificed quality for making more money or holding to a specific price point. It's a valid criticism."

The trend in product quality alarms Tod Johnson, president of NPD    41
Group. NPD regularly uses its focus groups to test product reformulations for its marketer clients.

"When we tested products in the '60s and '70s, I'd say 75% of the    42
changes were product improvements," he says. "Today, two-thirds or even three-quarters of the testing we do is asking for consumer opinion on cost reductions. Product quality is being ignored."

National brands also lose their cachet when confronted by today's    43
generation of lower-price store brands. Unlike their generic ancestors of the '70s, these brand alternatives make quality a priority, a critical ingredient to bargain-hunting shoppers. Private-label sales in supermarkets are at $24.7 billion, up 13% since 1989, Nielsen Marketing Research says, and are making serious inroads into classic marketing categories like ready-to-eat cereal, pet food and beverages.

"If everyone takes advantage, like the cereal people do—by raising    44
prices at every opportunity—there will be a problem for brands," says retail consultant Gene Hoffman, of Corporate Strategies International. "Marketers will have created too many price voids for private-label to move in."

There's also a quality void.                                        45

"We tend to look at brand support in terms of media support, but as    46
a brand leader, you have to continue to innovate," says Paul Walsh, joint chief operating officer of Grand Metropolitan Food Sector and head of Pillsbury Co. "When times are tough, the easiest things to cut are new products and R&D. If you do that over a protracted period of time, you're inviting private-label into your category."

Conventional wisdom holds that private-label products fare well in    47
tough economic times, when shoppers feel a need to trade down.

As consumers "trade down" this time around, "They're finding the    48
quality of the private-label products is better," says Mr. Furash of Deloitte & Touche. "So when all is said and done, private-label is going to have gained more long-term share in this recession."


## A SHIFT IN POWER

Private-label products are only the tip of the iceberg. Retailers are    49
playing a broader and fast-growing role in controlling consumers' brand loyalties.

At a 1990 meeting, Ralston Purina Co. Chairman-CEO William    50
Stiritz was asked, by a Wall Street analyst eager to see better profits, when his company could raise the price of Eveready batteries. His answer was both frustrated and matter of fact.

"One of the dominant trends in our business is the tilting of power 51 to mass merchandisers and away from grocery chains and drug chains— whether they recognize it or not," Mr. Stiritz said. As a result, he said, "We may now be seeing our peak profit margins—we're getting drug-product margins on cereals, for God's sake. We're seeing the emergence of Wal-Mart—and Wal-Mart pricing—as the prototype for the retail business. It will happen, long-term."

Long-term? In just two years, Wal-Mart has added 357 stores, for a 52 total of 1,882, with 1990 sales of $32.6 billion. Its store count has doubled in five years; its sales in four years.

In those two years, deep-discount drug chains Phar-Mor, Drug 53 Emporium and F&M Distributors together have opened more than 200 new outlets, for 616 total stores nationwide. Estimates show warehouse clubs ringing up $32 billion in sales in 1992, nearly double the $17 billion total from 1989.

"The marketing world has underestimated some of the changes that 54 have taken place at the retail level," says Sid Doolittle, managing partner at McMillan/Doolittle, a retail consultancy. "The marketplace will never be the same again."

For now, brands are an important ingredient in the new discount 55 channel.

"The fundamental thrust of a Drug Emporium, or a Pace warehouse 56 club, is to make a price impression," says consultant Mr. Hoffman, a former president of Kroger Co. and Super Valu Stores. "Well, the best way to make a price impression is with a recognized brand—a national brand rather than a private brand. When these retailers can take a brand that's constantly escalating in price and discount it, the brands are serving a purpose for these retailers."

But a tour of a Phar-Mar warehouse club is evidence that brands 57 aren't necessarily treated as valuable allies.

If one strength of brands is that they allow consumers to buy on 58 habit, without making decisions, discounters' merchandising strategy seems to defeat that goal; giving consumers a consistent selection of merchandise frequently takes a back seat to "power buying": buying large quantities at discount prices.

"These discounters often buy what they can get a good deal on—and 59 if they don't have it the next week, they don't care," says consultant Mr. Bredine.

Through their inventory choices—which frequently include making 60 one brand the "exclusive" supplier in a given category—discounters have eliminated brand choice in many aisles.

"These retailers have narrowed the purchase decision for consumers, 61 while still offering the right items, or at least the right number of items," BevMark's Mr. Pirko says. "But in the transition, brands become less important and price more important to the purchase decision."

Despite the care that manufacturers expend on packaging, their 62 products are often merchandised in haphazard fashion.

"There are floor displays all over the place in many of these stores," 63 says Christie Hunt, associate at Willard Bishop Consulting. "It's a style that in general runs contrary to the careful merchandising philosophy of supermarkets."

Simply, the discount channel's focus on saving money—from "every- 64 day low price" to double couponing—relegates choosing a brand to an afterthought.

"It's what we call the commoditization of American package 65 goods," New England Consulting Group's Mr. Stibel says. "It's not just in Wal-Marts, but also in Food Lions and Krogers: Retailers are driving toward 'everyday low pricing' in a more effective fashion. In that setup, the value of the brand will deteriorate over time, right there in the stores."

Consumers are shopping at the new discount outlets because saving 66 money makes them feel good—and paying more makes them feel chumped.

"With all the options out there today, the consumer is asking, 'Am I 67 stupid to maintain my brand loyalty?' " Competitive Advantage's Mr. Ferstandig says. "On the other hand, saving money offers consumers the power of doing something smart; it's a positive stroke. You'd be surprised at the number of consumers of all income levels who are terribly proud when they save $1.50."

The recession has made saving money a more serious proposition. 68

"The need for minimal price outlay is going to grow as our society 69 polarizes based on income," says Josh McQueen, exec VP-director of research at Leo Burnett USA, Chicago. "For many consumers, what that will mean is they'll be trying to get 'good enough' quality at the lowest price."

## HIGH-INCOME BARGAIN HUNTERS

But a surprising number of discount shoppers are not those who *need* to 70 save money. The typical frequent buyer at a discount drugstore has a household income higher than $30,000, according to Nielsen Marketing Research information. Consumers with a household income greater than $50,000 are 38% more likely to be frequent buyers at warehouse clubs than the average.

The lesson: It's not only the prices that draw shoppers to discount 71 stores.

A trip to a warehouse club is "usually a bulk-up trip, for people who 72 don't like to have to buy these products all the time," says Glen Terbeek, managing partner of the food and package-goods industry program at

Andersen Consulting. "These consumers have the financial and storage capacity to stock up. And they're buying products for which the only possible shopping enjoyment is getting them cheaper."

Warehouse club shopping can be fun in its own way, though. 73 Although package-goods marketers largely are failing to captivate consumers with their new products, consumers are intrigued with what they find at warehouse clubs: odd sizes and packaging, foodservice and institutional products, things they can't find anywhere else.

Although the reality is that many discounters carry only one brand of 74 plastic wrap, light bulb or battery, Willard Bishop's Ms. Hunt maintains consumer perceptions may be different.

"Consumers may be looking at the deep-discount drugstores, for 75 instance, as providing *more* variety than supermarkets. Usually each chain has a couple of key categories, like haircare or cosmetics, in which they carry unusual products and lots of variety. And they make that big variety statement as soon as you walk in the store."

## THE FUTURE OF BRANDS

So where do brands fit into this emerging discount channel of retailing? 76 What happens when Wal-Mart, Target, Drug Emporium, Sam's Club, Pace Membership Warehouse, F&M and the rest have blanketed the country?

"At some point, most package goods will be sold in these high- 77 volume emporiums," Corporate Strategies' Mr. Hoffman says. "Then, an individual store's ability to [establish and promote a] price differential disappears, because all the retailers price low and consumers use those low prices as a benchmark.

"Right now, discount retailers are using brands as power, because 78 they can price lower than supermarkets. But at some point, when the low-price philosophy has become the norm, the retailer will have to find new ways of doing his price philosophy."

That's when the forecasts get *really* interesting.                          79

"When the retailer needs to get a price advantage, he can try to cut 80 his own costs further or work out an arrangement for a new line of products that only he can carry," Mr. Hoffman says. "And that's where private-label could come in."

It's already happening. Although Wal-Mart has built itself with 81 national brands, the retailer is experimenting with a Sam's American Choice brand of soft drinks and juices. Chairman Sam Walton's signed message on the cans reads: "Innovative products, made to our own standards, that we're proud to call Sam's American Choice. We believe these products, available only at Wal-Mart, offer better value than the leading national brands."

Northwestern's Mr. Schultz asks: "Brands won't go away, but will 82 they be manufacturer brands, retailer brands or someone else's brands?"

Perhaps manufacturers will be able to tweak products enough to give 83 each retailer something distinctive.

"There may be brands to be developed specifically for those kinds of 84 outlets," says ConAgra's Mr. Rahn.

Mr. Doolittle points to an emerging trend he calls "divisive packag- 85 ing": Manufacturers split products into different packaging to create a unique assortment for each retailer.

"We're giving different retailers different combinations of merchan- 86 dise and working out different promotions so no one has exactly the same program this Christmas season," says Donna Gibbs, Mattel's director of media relations.

Wal-Mart's wholesale Sam's Club chain this fall got a unique version 87 of Mattel's popular "Bathtime Barbie" with a bathtub, packaged together for an end-aisle display that no other retailer has.

Another point of difference for national brands could be a *higher* 88 price.

"Price is one of the last variables in marketing; companies are 89 blatantly using low price as a tool, assuming that low price is better. Maybe it's not," says Mr. Stibel of New England Consulting Group.

One of the real fears for brand marketers is that retailers will create 90 brand loyalties not just with private-label goods but with a broader store image. Consumers can shop the Wal-Mart brand—"always the low price"—trusting they will get the best deal in each product category. Does it matter if that "best deal" is on Colgate, Crest or Aqua-fresh?

"It's reached a point where the manufacturer-retail circus is getting so 91 out of control that brands don't have as much meaning as they used to. . . .People are transferring their loyalty from the brand to the retailer," Mr. Doolittle says. "It's hard to get people to give up on brands, and the fact that brands are important to consumers is part of the reason discounters have been so successful. But brand marketers are going to lose some ground as a result of all this change in the retail sector."

## PLANNING FOR THE FUTURE

Marketers and conventional retailers need to learn how to deal with the 92 new discount channel now—"rather than waiting till we're forced in the year 2000," says Mr. Hoffman of Corporate Strategies.

Almost everyone in marketing agrees: In the face of this level of 93 retailer power, manufacturers tempted to reduce marketing costs must resist.

"As a consumer-goods marketer, you have leverage to the extent that 94 the customer wants your product. . . ." says Mr. Furash of Deloitte &

Touche. "Some products regularly are sold below cost, because the manufacturer is able to command a premium in the consumer's eyes. The consumer draws that product through the channel even though retailers don't make money on it. A product like that is the closest thing to a diamond you can get in this industry."

Even those companies who've already struck long-term deals with 95 discounters need to be vigilant.

"The man who has an exclusive deal with Wal-Mart has to know that 96 he got that deal on price and that tomorrow a competitor will come in with a lower price," Mr. Stibel says. "When that happens, that manufacturer must . . . through product quality and consumer marketing, have convinced his retail customers that the product can't be dropped."

Marketers have seen the danger of cutting advertising too far.        97

"I see a trend toward companies making a serious effort to reallocate 98 money to media, thereby streamlining promotion," says Maurice Kelley, VP-marketing services at SmithKline Beecham Consumer Products. "We've overdone the price thing in stores . . . and brand loyalties have eroded a tad there."

## BRANDS' WORST ENEMY

Protecting established brand equity and mining new "diamonds" isn't 99 easy, though. Unfortunately, many experts believe the package-goods marketers themselves—their organizational setups and corporate mentalities—represent the worst threat to brand health and the greatest obstacle to developing breakthrough products.

Corporate megamergers brought brand equity into the spotlight 100 during the '80s. But Wall Street's increased input in brand decisions and the huge bureaucracies that have developed at the megamarketers have left companies unable to properly manage those equities.

A lack of integrated marketing systems is a key problem that leading 101 ad agencies and marketers are trying to address with executive training programs and new organizational setups.

"Corporations are not set up to handle brand equity," Burnett's Ms. 102 Douglas-Tate says. "Decisions aren't based on the brand's needs."

Bureaucracies don't produce the best new products, either. Despite a 103 general belief that the supermarket is saturated with undistinguished products, new items are racing into supermarkets—and failing at a faster and faster rate. The most innovative new products of the recent past, from Gatorade to Budget Gourmet to Iams dog food to Chicken by George, usually have been developed outside the expansive research & development departments of the leading package-goods marketers.

While small companies are launching breakthrough concepts, many 104 larger marketers lament their overreliance on line extensions.

"The line extension strategy is going to play itself out at some point; 105 it can't go on forever," says Mr. Pirko of Bevmark.

But the difficulty and expense of establishing a truly new brand name 106 will force marketers to continue using their existing brands as umbrellas for new products—but with better-defined extensions.

"I think megabrands with microvarieties is the future of brands," 107 says Burnett's Mr. McQueen, whose agency works on several, like Procter & Gamble Co.'s Cheer detergent.

Big marketers can score big hits, too—and not just with line 108 extensions. The food industry's hottest brand remains ConAgra's Healthy Choice, which seeks to revolutionize the rest of the supermarket in the way it's dominated the freezer case in the past three years.

"We've gone through and analyzed why Healthy Choice worked," 109 Mr. Rahn says. "Last February, at a management presentation, we agreed that one reason for its success was that there was a singular focus from the beginning on what it was. The objective was clear, the mandate from on top was there—but we were left alone to develop it. [Chairman-CEO] Mike Harper told us what he wanted, but he was not an interferer."

"We're seeing top management getting more and more actively 110 involved in new products," says consultant Mr. Bredine. "Plus, companies are trying to find ways to reward people for developing new products."

That's one positive trend for new products and brands. Tangible new 111 product and brand opportunities may also exist in consumers' interest in eating right and being environmentally correct.

Package-goods companies also have a perhaps underutilized chance 112 to build consumer loyalty to broader, more corporate identities.

With billions of dollars at stake, package-goods marketers won't give 113 up on brands despite the challenges emerging in the '90s. And they won't stop mining for gold, because of the power potential of a strong brand name.

"In the end, there are only a couple of things a company has—its 114 people and its brands, both the trademarks and the good will they carry with consumers," says John Blair, VP-marketing services and new ventures for Quaker Oats Co. "And once you have a brand that's established in the minds of consumers, it's a crown jewel."

## Post-Reading Questions

1. What is Liesse's main point or thesis? Where does she first present it to the reader? Why? What effect does this placement have?
2. Where does Liesse's introduction end? What does she do to interest her readers and introduce them to her topic?

3. What readers would be interested in learning more about the future of brand name products? Why? What strategies does Liesse use to present her information in a way that meets the needs of these readers?

4. What sources does Liesse rely on to support her claims about brand name loyalty? As a journalist, how did she obtain information from these sources? In what ways does the research process of a college student writing about brand name loyalty differ from Liesse's? Why?

5. According to Liesse, what explains the decrease in brand name loyalty?

6. How has the relationship between consumers and particular brand name products changed since the 1960s? Describe the changes from one decade to another.

7. Why does John Blair, a marketing executive for Quaker Oats, compare an established brand to a "crown jewel"? What does he mean? Why is the comparison effective? What, from your experiences, are some of the crown jewels of brand names?

8. What is a "brand switcher"? Why is the number of brand switchers increasing?

9. What are "megabrands with microvarieties" (see paragraphs 105 to 107)? Identify some examples. Is Liesse hopeful about the future of these megabrands? How does she explain her prediction?

10. After reading this article, what is your general impression of American consumers? Does Liesse want her readers to envision consumers as pawns of marketers or does she paint a picture of consumers as thoughtful shoppers? What can you point to in her article that supports your analysis of her viewpoint? How does her viewpoint compare with yours? How would you evaluate the average American consumer? Why?

11. What point lies behind Liesse's discussion of discount retailing stores such as Wal-Mart and Drug Emporium? Are they helping or hindering brand name products? How?

# GAIL TOM ON MARKETING WITH MUSIC

## Pre-Reading Questions

1. What strategies used to make goods and services more attractive to consumers appeal to you? Would a sale entice you to buy? What about a testimonial by a celebrity? A coupon? Attractive packaging? Use your own experiences as a consumer to describe how marketing affects your consumer behavior.

2. Why do you think music is used in commercials? What television commercials can you identify in which music is a major element? Write about some of the commercials you know that use music. What kinds of music do you usually hear in television commercials? How do you react to commercials containing music?
3. Do you more quickly associate original or hit music with particular products? Cite examples.

# MARKETING WITH MUSIC
## Gail Tom

The recent usage of previously popularized hit music and parodies of hit [1] music along with the traditional usage of originally scored music for products advertised in television commercials has created a natural setting to explore the role of music as a memory factor. A tape of nine television commercials with deletions of all mention of the advertised product was played to a sample of 151 students. Each participant rated the familiarity of each song on a five-point Likert scale and attempted to recall the product/ brand that came to mind for each song. The results indicate that the music created specifically for the advertised product is a more effective retrieval cue than parodies, which in turn are more effective than the use of original hits. These findings are in the direction of previous research that found that the more similar the information at the points of input and output, the more effective they are as cues for recall.

Recent research in consumer behavior investigating memory factors has [2] demonstrated the importance of encoding factors, such as the context of information presentation, and retrieval cues, such as its absence or presence on recall.[1,2,3,4] Although music is an integral part of the majority of television commercials, the role of music as a retrieval cue for the advertised products has not received focused attention.

Research investigating the role of music on other aspects of con- [3] sumer behavior has demonstrated its effectiveness. For example, research has shown that music affects the rate and quantity of consumption at restaurants[11,16] and the speed and quantity of purchases at supermarkets.[9,10] Research investigating the role of background music in television commercials on the formation of brand attitudes has indicated that such background music has a facilitating effect on the formation of brand attitudes under low involvement conditions,[7] a distracting effect under high involvement, and a mixed effect under high affect involvement.[12] In addition to the long-standing practice of using originally scored music for the advertising product, television commercials have recently incorporated songs that were previously popularized by radio broadcasts such as the use of the Beatles' "Revolution" for Nike tennis shoes, or incorporated parodies of hit songs, such as the modification of the lyrics of Stevie Wonder's "You Are the Sunshine of My Life" to include mention of the name of the advertised product, Minute Maid.[6,13,15] This situation has created a natural setting to conduct an exploratory study investigating the role of music as a memory factor.

Consistently, research on memory factors has demonstrated that recall is dependent upon the similarity of information at input and cues at output.[5,8,14] For the three types of music under consideration, the similarity of information at input and cues at output is highest for products advertised with originally scored music, intermediate for products using parodies of previously popularized music, and lowest for products using original versions of the previously popularized music. While the lyrics of the originally scored music and the parodies both purposely include the name of the advertised product, the lyrics of the original hit music usually do not mention the name of the product. Whereas originally scored music has been presented only in association with the advertised product, the consumer had most likely been exposed to the original hits and original versions of the parody music in other contexts. Thus, we would expect originally scored music to be the most effective retrieval cue and hit songs to be the least effective retrieval cue, with parody music somewhere in between.

4

## METHODOLOGY

The purpose of this study is to explore the recall effectiveness of three types of music currently being used in television commercials: (1) hit music, (2) parodies of hit music, and (3) music scored specifically for television commercials. An audiotape of commercials aired during prime time on the three major networks (ABC, CBS, and NBC) was made during the last week of the month of August, 1987. The commercials were recorded in such a way that all mention of the product's name was deleted. The tape was played to a group of 23 participants, who rated each musical selection for its familiarity on a five-point Likert scale. From this original tape, a second tape was made of nine commercials selected for their equally high level of familiarity. (See Table 1 for a listing of the nine songs and their average familiarity rating.)

5

A researcher played the tape of the nine commercials to a sample of 151 students. After listening to each commercial, the respondents rated the familiarity of each song on a five-point Likert scale and identified the brand or product that came to mind when they heard the commercial.

6

TABLE 1  Frequency of Correct Product Identifications and Median Familiarity Ratings of T.V. Commercials

| Type of Music | Advertised Product | Correct Product Identifications | | Median Familiarity Rating |
| | | Frequency | Percent | |
|---|---|---|---|---|
| Hit original | Time Magazine | 41 | 27% | 4 |
| Hit original | Nike Tennis Shoes | 34 | 22% | 5 |
| Hit original | Stridex | 34 | 22% | 4 |
| Parody | Minute Maid Orange Juice | 53 | 35% | 4 |
| Parody | Shield Soap | 45 | 30% | 4 |
| Parody | 7-Up | 100 | 66% | 4 |
| Original | Oreo Cookies | 125 | 83% | 4 |
| Original | Nestle Candy Bar | 123 | 81% | 4 |
| Original | Safeway Supermarket | 96 | 69% | 4 |

## RESULTS

As Table 1 shows, the respondents' familiarity with the music was high 7
for all nine songs. Even though the familiarity of the music was relatively
uniform, their effectiveness as a retrieval cue was not. Music scored
specifically for the advertisement had the greatest recall, followed by
parody music, with original hits being least effective. On the average,
77.6 percent of the participants correctly identified the advertised
product associated with music scored specifically for the product, compared with 43.6 percent for products paired with parody music, and 23.6
percent for products using original versions of the rock hits.

Table 2 shows the number of correctly identified products for each of 8
the five levels of familiarity. These results indicate that the familiarity of
the songs does influence the correct identification of the advertised
product, more so when the music used is a parody or original music than
when hit music is used.

## DISCUSSION

The recent usage of popularized songs and parodies of popularized 9
songs, as well as original music, in television commercials created a
natural setting to conduct this exploratory study investigating the
retrieval effect of the various types of music.

The findings are in the direction suggested by consumer behavior 10
research on memory factors. The more similar the information at the
points of input and output, the more effective they are as cues for recall.

On a practical basis, the role of music as a retrieval cue is limited 11
because the music cannot be presented at the point of purchase. Thus, an
area for future research is the incorporation of pictorial and/or verbal
cues at the point of purchase that reference the music featured with the
advertised product. The California Raisin Board's current advertising
campaign featuring the "dancing raisins" along with Marvin Gaye's hit
song "Heard It Through the Grapevine" is a current example of the
effective usage of combined verbal and pictorial cues that incorporate
the music of the advertised product. The California Raisins are shown
on the product at the point of purchase and serve as a retrieval cue that
incorporates the music of the advertised product.

Because of the exploratory nature of this study, the results should be 12
considered as only tentative. However, because music is ubiquitous in
television commercials, its role as a memory factor should receive
empirical attention. The natural setting of this study did not allow for the
control of significant factors such as the exposure rates of the television
commercials, level of involvement within the commercial, attitude toward

TABLE 2   Summary Variance Results of the Recall Effectiveness of Television Commercials

| | | Frequency and Percent of Correct Product Identifications for the Five Familiarity Groups[†] | | | | | | | | |
| | | Groups Familiarity Rating | | | | | | | | |
| | | 1 I definitely have not heard this song before | | 2 I probably have not heard this song before | | 3 I probably have heard this song before | | 4 I definitely have heard this song before | | 5 I can name the title of the song and/or the performer(s) | |
| Type of Music | Advertised Product | % | # | % | # | % | # | % | # | % | # |
|---|---|---|---|---|---|---|---|---|---|---|---|
| 1. Hit original | Time Magazine | 0 | (4) | 0 | (1) | 21 | (14) | 19 | (64) | 38 | (68) |
| 2. Hit original | Nike Tennis Shoes | 0 | (5) | 0 | (4) | 11 | (17) | 11 | (36) | 32 | (89) |
| 3. Hit original | Stridex | 0 | (8) | 0 | (3) | 11 | (9) | 25 | (72) | 25 | (59) |
| 4. Parody | Minute Maid Orange Juice | 0 | (4) | 0 | (6) | 13 | (16) | 35 | (83) | 52 | (42) |
| 5. Parody | Shield Soap | 0 | (4) | 0 | (7) | 17 | (22) | 33 | (75) | 40 | (43) |
| 6. Parody | 7-Up | 0 | (9) | 0 | (7) | 37 | (19) | 77 | (83) | 92 | (33) |
| 7. Original | Oreo Cookies | 0 | (3) | 0 | (0) | 60 | (19) | 89 | (93) | 91 | (36) |
| 8. Original | Nestle Candy Bar | 0 | (3) | 0 | (3) | 66 | (6) | 84 | (104) | 91 | (35) |
| 9. Original | Safeway Supermarket | 0 | (7) | 0 | (7) | 30 | (10) | 70 | (92) | 83 | (35) |

[†]Percent calculated by dividing total number of correct product identifications for the song by total number of respondents in the familiarity group for the song.

the commercial, evaluation of the brand, and other factors. Future research needs to control for such factors in order to measure more conclusively the role of music as a memory factor.

Research indicates that the structure of music in memory is orga- [13] nized along nonmusical characteristics such as themes and content and not upon musical characteristics such as first interval.[8] Future research could focus upon the selection of familiar songs for advertised products based upon an understanding of the salient nonmusical characteristics associated with songs.

## NOTES

1. Alba, J. W., and J. W. Hutchinson, "Dimensions of Consumer Expertise," *Journal of Consumer Research,* 13 (March 1987), 411–54.
2. Burke, R. F., and T. K. Srull, "Competitive Interference and Consumer Memory for Advertising," *Journal of Consumer Research,* 15 (June 1988), 55–68.
3. Chattopadhyay, A., and J. W. Alba, "The Situational Importance of Recall and Inference in Consumer Decision Making," *Journal of Consumer Research,* 15 (June 1988), 1–12.
4. Cox, D. S., and A. D. Cox, "What Does Familiarity Breed? Complexity as a Moderator of Repetition Effects in Advertisement Evaluation," *Journal of Consumer Research,* 15 (June 1988), 111–16.
5. Craik, F. I. M., "Encoding and Retrieval Effects in Human Memory," *Attention and Performance,* Vol. 9, ed. A. D. Baddeley and J. Long. Hillsdale, NJ: Lawrence Erlbaum, 1981.
6. Demkowych, C., "Music on the Upswing in Advertising," *Advertising Age,* 57 (March 31, 1986), S-5.
7. Gorn, G. J., "The Effects of Music in Advertising on Choice Behavior: A Classical Conditioning Approach," *Journal of Marketing,* 46 (Winter 1982), 94–101.
8. Halpren, A., "Organization in Memory for Familiar Songs," *Journal of Experimental Psychology: Learning, Memory, and Cognition,* 10 (1984), 496–512.
9. Keller, K. L., "Advertising Retrieval Cues on Brand Evaluations," *Journal of Consumer Research,* 14 (December 1984), 316–33.
10. Linsen, M. A., "Like Our Music Today, Ms. Shopper?" *Progressive Grocer,* October 1975, p. 156.
11. Millerman, R. E., "Using Background Music to Affect the Behavior of Supermarket Shoppers," *Journal of Marketing,* Summer 1982, pp. 86–91.
12. Millerman, R. E., "The Influence of Background Music on the Behavior of Restaurant Patrons," *Journal of Consumer Research,* September 1986, pp. 280–85.
13. Park, C. W., and S. M. Young, "Consumer Response to Television Commercials: The Impact of Involvement and Background Music on Brand

Attitude Formation," *Journal of Marketing Research,* 23 (February 1986), 11–24.

14. Sherrid, P., "Emotional Shorthand," *Forbes,* 136 (November 4, 1985), 214–15.

15. Tulving, E., "Relation Between Encoding Specificity and Levels of Processing," *Levels of Processing in Human Memory,* ed. L. S. Cermak and I. M. Fergus. Hillsdale, NJ: Lawrence Erlbaum Associates.

16. Vail, J., "Music as a Marketing Tool," *Advertising Age,* 56 (November 4, 1985), 24.

## Post-Reading Questions

1. Reread the abstract of this article (the short paragraph preceding the article itself). What kind of information does it contain? What is the purpose of the abstract? What words in it are unfamiliar to you? Why? Who would be more familiar with those words than you are? Why?

2. Use a psychological dictionary to find a definition of *Likert scale.* Explain it in your own words.

3. Describe how this article is organized. Into what sections is it divided? What does Tom accomplish in each section?

4. Reread the first sentence in the article. Why does Tom place the numbers "1,2,3,4" at the end of the sentence? What do they tell her specialist readers (other marketing researchers)?

5. Why does Tom call her research an "exploratory study" (paragraph 2)? What future research does she suggest? Where does she make her suggestions? Why does she include her suggestions where she does?

6. How does Tom reinforce the idea that her findings are tentative? What words does she use to suggest this?

7. Explain the relationship between music and memory described by Tom. How does Tom know that this relationship exists? How do you know? Why does she explain this relationship in the article? Where in the article does she explain this relationship? Why does she discuss it there?

8. This article was written for academic readers—other marketing researchers. In what kind of non-specialist magazine article would you find Tom's research discussed? How would a journalist use the information in Tom's article? What changes would a journalist make in order to use the information in an article meant to be read by non-specialists?

9. Examine the two tables in Tom's article. What kind of information is in the tables? Where in the article does Tom refer to the information in the tables? In what ways does her discussion of that information in the text differ from the actual tables? Why? To what kind of readers would these tables appeal?

# BERNICE KANNER
# ON FEMALE CONSUMERS

## Pre-Reading Questions

1.  What products are directly marketed to women? Can you name some
    of these products? How would you describe the commercials and
    print advertisements that feature these products? What kinds of
    women are shown using or promoting these products? What appeals
    do these commercials and advertisements make to female consum-
    ers? Why are they successful?
2.  What do feminist organizations find offensive in television commer-
    cials and advertisements promoting female products? What do they
    find offensive in commercials and advertisements marketed to both
    men and women? Can you identify at least one commercial and one
    advertisement that would be particularly offensive to feminists?
    Explain the offensive qualities in each example you offer.

## THE SECRET LIFE
## OF THE FEMALE CONSUMER
### Bernice Kanner

Women who drink General Foods International Coffees take their ads  1
light and sweet. Scenes that show best friends chatting do well. So do
images of women relaxing with their husbands and kids. And women
respond favorably when soft, relaxing music plays in the background.

How does General Foods know all this? Because the executives who  2
market the brand conduct extensive tests that tell them how far they can
push your hot buttons. They know, for instance, that high-tech images,
blue light or a close-up of an ice cube moving along a woman's neck will
turn you off. They also know that you'll react warmly to an ad showing
a man canceling a golf game to be with his wife, or one that shows a
mother having a heart-to-heart with her daughter.

Scoff if you like, but the touchy-feely approach works. Between July  3
1989 and July 1990, sales of General Foods International Coffees
(GFIC) were $115.9 million, an 11 percent rise over the same period a
year earlier. This is startling when you consider that sales in the
instant-coffee category as a whole, estimated to be worth $1.1 billion,
are off by 9.4 percent. In fact, nearly all supermarket brands are down,
the victims of rising health concerns about caffeine, the gourmet-bean
trend and morning cola consumption.

But GFIC isn't like other coffees. It's presweetened and positioned  4
as a specialty product, not a commodity. This gives it a designer image.

GFIC is also aimed at women, who have been the brand's biggest consumers since its introduction in 1974 (although there is talk now of targeting men).

"GFIC is the closest coffee comes to the fashion or perfume 5 business," says Tom Pirko, president of Bevmark Inc., a Los Angeles consultancy. "It's selling the sizzle as much as the steak."

As one of the largest consumer-products companies in the world, 6 General Foods has long depended on consumer research to market its brands. But as the roles of American women have changed, it has become more difficult to peg female consumers. Today it is important for marketers to define not only who consumers are but also who they would like to be. Increasingly, women, like men, buy products because they identify—or strive to identify—with the kind of people they think use them.

"This has confused many food companies," says Carol Brady Blades, 7 president and chief operating officer of The Softness Group, a New York–based consultancy that specialized in marketing to women. "Many shoot for a hot, contemporary feel in ads but overlook the fact that women need to identify with the actress. If your female audience doesn't empathize with her, you've lost them."

To make sure that doesn't happen, GFIC's marketers stress an 8 emotional benefit—"more the feeling than the function," says Nancy Wong, director of marketing for General Foods' Maxwell House division, located in White Plains, New York. And that feeling? When it comes to GFIC, it's self-indulgence and traditional values represented by a series of emotional moments in commercials.

## WHAT DO WOMEN WANT? ASK THEM

The team behind GFIC is headed by Wong, 48, who supervises all 9 aspects of selling the brand, including product development, packaging, advertising and promotion. To determine what women want from the brand, the team stages hundreds of focus groups each year and mails out thousands of questionnaires. Reporting to Wong is Cathy Ko, 36, the brand's senior product manager. Sarita Nayyar, 30, an associate product manager, monitors product development, consumer research and media planning, and is the team's liaison with the advertising agency. David Hirschler, 29, also an associate product manager, oversees the budget, business analysis and planning, and sales coordination; Margaret Block, 32, is in charge of GFIC's consumer promotions.

Over the years, GFIC's research techniques have become more 10 complex as its audience has grown more sophisticated. It is no longer enough to ask, "What do you like about the taste?" While the GFIC team does not hire anthropologists or sociologists to study the cultural environment of the brand's consumers, as some companies do, it does employ psychologists to run the focus groups. They draw out and interpret women's feelings about coffee and the brand.

"How do you feel before you've had a cup?" the psychologist might 11 ask. "And after?" He or she then might direct women to draw pictures illustrating the transformation. "If you were having a dream in which GFIC played a part, what would it be?" There are even questions to tease out the brand's "personality": "How old is GFIC?" "Is it male or female?" "What music does it listen to?" "What kind of car does it drive?" Women are also given stacks of photographs and asked to create a collage using pictures of ordinary people who they think would consume the brand.

During these sessions, the women might be asked to fill in balloon 12 captions of cartoon characters or "read" their feelings into a picture, a technique called a "thematic appreciation test." This reveals not just what consumers think about the brand but how they feel about everything.

From the research, the team has determined that the typical con- 13 sumer is a baby boomer or younger, earns a middle income, is warm, friendly, and drinks coffee on a regular basis. And although she works, research reports, she's not obsessed with her career.

Research also tells General Foods how to position existing 14 products—and when to launch new ones. In keeping with the times, sugar-free versions appeared in 1984 and decaffeinated ones were introduced in 1989. Last year single-serving envelopes were rolled out after women said they especially like curling up with a cup when traveling. The newest variety, Hazelnut Belgian Cafe, was added in July. The team decided on the name because hazelnut is a popular gourmet-bean flavor and in Belgium hazelnut is often used in pastry.

## TURNING RESEARCH INTO ADS

Once GFIC's marketers know what turns women on, they create a series 15 of test ads. These are shown to focus groups to learn what might work in ongoing campaigns. "Because we're dealing with image advertising," Wong says, "we have to continuously check the tone and manner to be sure it's effective."

The GFIC team won't discuss details of the findings, but advertise- 16 ments for the brand provide insight into their thinking. In the most recent television commercial, "Home Movies," a 30-something couple is shown sitting in their living room, sipping from mugs of Hazelnut Belgian Cafe. They're watching a black-and-white home movie of a backpacking trip they took to Belgium some years ago. Phoebe Snow's earthy voice is heard in the background.

"The ad works because it's comforting, not patronizing" says 17
Blades, of The Softness Group. "It acknowledges that it's late in the
feminist age. While the woman is shown with a man, she's in control, the
product works for her."

Young & Rubicam, the agency that created the advertisement, has 18
worked on the brand since it was introduced. Back in the early 1970s,
actress Carol Lawrence was GFIC's spokeswoman. Lawrence, best
known as Maria in the Broadway version of *West Side Story*, was chosen
for her European looks. At the time, the General Foods marketers
working on the brand wanted to emphasize its international personality.
College-age women, the target audience, had traveled abroad or intended to, and the coffee stirred up their wanderlust.

Bill Burgess, a former member of the original GFIC team and now a 19
principal with Weston Group, a Westport, Connecticut, consulting firm,
recalls, "With Lawrence we were tapping into the heartbeat of the prime
prospect at the time—homebodies who kaffeeklatsch, who are nurturers,
who wanted to use this as an experience to treat themselves as they would
company."

By 1980 the brand's marketers felt that Lawrence should be replaced 20
by unknown actors playing consumers in real-life situations. The ads
positioned the brand as the coffee to drink when bonding with family,
friends or co-workers. But that wasn't the only change. Men, who had
always appeared in the ads, were given more prominent roles in the late
1980s. In one ad, a woman pauses in the kitchen while drinking a cup of
GFIC to watch her husband and child snuggle in the living room. *It's a
laugh, it's a cry . . . all the moments that you want to celebrate . . . You don't
need an invitation,* croons Snow.

The team is now studying ways to attract larger numbers of men 21
without triggering a rebellion among loyal female consumers. "We're
not going to do macho stuff," says Wong. "We have to take it slow. We
need to know more about the way they feel, but we have to be careful.
Men don't always open up as easily when we ask our type of questions."

## Post-Reading Questions

1. Why does the article's title refer to "the secret life" of female buyers?
   What is its connection to the article's contents?
2. Why would the editors of *Working Woman* include an article about
   how a particular product is marketed to female consumers? What
   does including this article suggest about the magazine's editorial
   policies? What does it suggest about the women who read this
   magazine?
3. Why is the International Coffees product line a good example of the
   relationship between research and marketing? Why does Kanner
   focus the entire article on this product?

4. What is Kanner's writing purpose? What do you believe she is trying to accomplish by describing how these coffee products are marketed? What strategies does she use to achieve her writing purpose?

5. What is Kanner's thesis? In your own words, write the main point she is making in the article.

6. Using what Kanner says and what she implies, describe the research a company would do before developing a marketing approach for a particular product.

7. Why is research important to marketing products? What can marketers learn about consumers from research?

8. In what ways are the commercials Kanner describes considered manipulative and controlling? What are the negative, long-term ramifications of applying research to marketing? How may such knowledge be abused or misused? Do you consider the applications of research Kanner describes manipulative? Why?

# LAURENCE SHAMES ON CONSUMERISM IN THE 1980s

## Pre-Reading Questions

1. From what you can remember of the 1980s, describe its biggest sellers. What were the products that were most popular for consumers? What were some of the items children, teens, and adults just **had** to have? Which products were things you wanted to own? Why did you want them so badly? Which products were items other members of your family wanted? What made them so attractive to those family members?

2. Read the title of this article. What does it say directly? What does it imply? Why would such a title appeal to readers of the periodical in which it was excerpted, *The Utne Reader,* an alternative press publication?

3. Have you heard the term "conspicuous consumption" before? What does it mean to you? Give an example or two.

## WHAT A LONG, STRANGE (SHOPPING) TRIP IT'S BEEN: LOOKING BACK AT THE 1980s
### Laurence Shames

Conspicuous consumption is as old as Babylon, but it took American 1
society of the late 1800s—the Gilded Age, a time not unlike the 1980s—to give it a name. The phrase was coined in 1899 by Thorstein

Veblen, economist, social critic, author of *The Theory of the Leisure Class.*
"Conspicuous consumption of valuable goods" was a notion at the very
heart of Veblen's social theory. "To gain and hold the esteem of men,"
he observed, "it [was] not sufficient merely to possess wealth or power.
The wealth or power must be put in evidence."

Veblen arrived at this theory not by abstract thought but by shrewd  2
observation of the life going on around him—a life of gross inequality in
which, for example, Andrew Carnegie's untaxed income was more than
20,000 times as great as that of the average workingman, and William K.
Vanderbilt lived in a house with 45 bathrooms and a garage for 100 cars.
Moreover, the 1890s, like the 1980s, were a period of plutography, when
newspapers routinely published accounts of the banquets of the rich—
published the *menus*—chronicling consumption down to the last bottle
of Madeira and breast of canvasback duck. No small part of the pleasure
of being wealthy was the knowledge that one would be publicly flattered
for being so.

These practitioners of conspicuous consumption might have flattered  3
themselves as being at the pinnacle of modern refinement, yet they were,
ultimately, slaves to ancient and primitive rituals of *more*. Folks had
dressed to kill in Sumeria. There were influential show-offs in the age of
Genghis Khan. Persian harlots wore their jewels in their belly buttons;
the matrons of Newport in the Gilded Age pinned theirs to their bodices
or hung them from their ears. How much difference was there?

This is neither to deny nor knock the enjoyment that people have  4
always gotten from their possessions. What people are buying, after all,
once you get past the bare necessities, is the promise of pleasure. But an
odd thing seems to happen during periods when conspicuous consumption is in vogue. During these times people spend extraordinary amounts
of money on things beyond what they need. They also invest a lot of
caring, a lot of ego, a lot of anxious thought. And so they ask a lot—too
much—of their possessions in return.

A certain line gets crossed. People look to their goods not just for  5
pleasure but for meaning. They want their stuff to tell them who they
are. They ask that inanimate objects serve as stand-ins for deeper
qualities. Not just pretty flowers but a built-in serenity is taken to exist in
a Laura Ashley wallpaper pattern. Not just style but the character of a
person is presumed to be made manifest by a Ralph Lauren blazer.
People disappear into their clothes. Their conversation becomes merely a
part of the ambience of the restaurants they frequent.

Certainly this has been true through the 1980s, a time when we  6
pointed each other out as *the guy in the Armani jacket* or *the woman with
the rose-colored Saab*, when *New York* magazine called shopping "the
unifying principle by which . . . [some people] structure days."

Shopping, for some, had become a detour in the otherwise unstylish  7
quest to find oneself. When you bought "taste," you bought yourself a

personality, and it was that, over and above the much-blabbed-about "quality" of the goods, which justified the price.

But what justified the price of, say, an $800 pair of shoes? Nothing 8 short of a fairy-tale magic presumably contained in them. That, at least, would seem to be the conclusion to be drawn by a salesperson at the ultra-expensive Susan Bennis/Warren Edwards store: "You can almost hear [the customers] thinking, 'If I had those shoes, what wonderful things would happen to me?' "

Back in 1971, Charles Reich, in *The Greening of America*, identified 9 a dynamic he called "impoverishment by substitution." What consumer society tended to do, Reich argued, was to withhold such basic gratifications as a sense of purpose, of community, of simply being comfortable in one's skin, and to offer up in place of those things the whole glittering panoply of stuff that could be purchased. The impoverishment came from the fact that while feeding one's life on consumer goods might distract one from the more basic hungers, it could never really satisfy them—and the basic hungers didn't go away.

Given that dynamic, it was not surprising that one of the 1980s' 10 characteristic emotional maladies was "compulsive shopping"—a phrase that moved into widespread clinical use in 1984. There are people out there who literally shopped till they dropped, who spoiled their marriages, wrecked their finances, and occasionally committed felonies because they simply could not stop buying. There was the young woman, described by *Newsweek*, who resorted to the subterfuge of "slipping dry cleaners' bags over her new clothes" so her husband wouldn't know she'd been on another buying binge. Not that compulsive shopping is the sole domain of women. Men might be less likely to go haywire over clothes, but there was no shortage of males who simply could not stay out of electronics stores, upgrading the $3,000 speakers to a $5,000 pair, whipping out the wallet-warm Visa card for a high-tech television with more dots in its screen.

In America through the 1980s, you saw billions of dollars being 11 spent on advertising and promotion, encouraging just the sort of material competitiveness and display that Veblen had described almost 100 years before. You saw millions if not tens of millions of folks who had bought into the fashion of rabid consuming and who looked at spending money as perhaps the most consistently enjoyable thing they did. Yet you had a situation that seemed neither to be making most people happy nor functioning in a way that promoted the well-being of the system itself.

Economists were bewailing high levels of personal debt and low 12 levels of saving, claiming that the pattern discouraged meaningful investment in new growth—and backing the claim with comparisons to Japan, West Germany, and Korea. In 1986, around $5 were owed for every dollar that was being saved in America, and interest payments alone—not counting mortgage interest—accounted for nearly as big a chunk of average household expenditures as did health care.

It has been argued that the Reagan "recovery" was basically a 13 recovery in spending. It was a false euphoria, but in the near term it was better than no euphoria at all. Pull the plug on conspicuous consumption, and you pull the plug on the rebound.

So what was the "right" degree of acquisitiveness? What was the 14 "healthy" level of craving stuff?

That point was awfully difficult to locate. For one thing, the cravings 15 of the obsessive spenders were not foreign to the rest of us. 'Fess up—we all wanted the cashmere and the leather and the pewter and the oak; the out-of-control ones were just a notch or two more avid in their hankering.

Then there was the confusing tendency, as we have seen, to regard 16 what is "healthy" in terms of what is "normal." What were taken to be normal spending patterns in America in the 1980s, however, probably hadn't seemed normal since Germany in the days of the Weimar Republic. In most other times and places, people went into hock in the face of catastrophe, not each time they wanted a new pair of boots. A virtually universal consumer indebtedness, in most times and places, would have signaled crisis. In America it's become business as usual.

Conspicuous consumption was the hallmark of the 1980s from the 17 very beginning. As early as 1981, *U.S. News & World Report* noted that although inflation was 10.4 percent and almost 8.5 million people were unemployed, "there [was] no recession in the luxury market." The magazine reported that in New York, "Russian sables starting at $40,000" were selling briskly, and in Texas, silk sheets were "being snapped up" at $1,500 a set. Leg of lion was being sold in Washington for $19.99 a pound, and in San Francisco, gold belts were moving well at $30,000. "[What] you're seeing," commented Sandra Shaber of Chase Econometrics, is "the moderate and lower-income American going down the tubes, while other groups of households are doing well."

Under the umbrella of Reaganism, high-income households did even 18 better as the decade progressed, and they seemed ever more intent on flaunting it. Between 1983 and 1984 alone, sales of stretch limousines doubled. As of 1977, the average age of a first-time fur coat owner was 50; by 1987 it had tumbled to 26.

It should be understood that the 1980s were far more gilded, far 19 more mercenary, far more narrowly defined by bucks than even Veblen's Gilded Age. Through the decade, most people were getting functionally poorer, the middle class was splintering, and there was beginning to be a broad suspicion that the American way of life was well past its peak. Yet at the same time the *arriviste* was being hailed as a patriot.

This actually made perfect sense if you considered not the substance 20 but the symbol. It didn't matter that the new fortunes, as in the case of the corporate raiders and greenmailers, tended to come at the expense of other people's jobs, or, as in the case of certain real estate developers, that they cost some people their homes, neighborhoods, or small businesses. More important to people, apparently, was the vicarious pick-me-up the new rich provided in demonstrating what we all wanted to believe—that America is indeed the Land of Opportunity. Maybe it was no longer the land of opportunity for *most;* opportunity was becoming something of a spectator sport. Still, it was reassuring to see that not everyone in America was getting hammered by a shifting economy, that some people could still wring princely rewards from the system.

In 1962 the novelist Ralph Ellison wrote a book called *Invisible* 21 *Man.* The title came from Ellison's contention that the humiliating and enraging thing about being black in America was not so much that white folks treated you badly, but that they acted as if you weren't there at all. Well, through the 1980s, something like that was coming to be the situation for Americans of any color who were outside the top echelons of consumption.

In 1986 it was observed in *Fortune* that "in the metaphysics of the 22 market, only those who buy and sell truly exist." And as the market became ever more narrowly defined by its top end, the closer to non-existence came anyone who couldn't spring for the choice labels and the choice materials: the "quality" goods. Retailers no longer courted these customers. Service people didn't particularly care about their trade. Magazines didn't even want their subscriptions, as it watered down their demographics. To those whose business was *more,* the people who had less simply didn't matter.

## Post-Reading Questions

1.  Having read the article, what do you take its title to mean now? How does the title relate to the article's contents? How does it relate to Shames' writing purpose?
2.  What is "conspicuous consumption"? Why does Shames begin his article with a brief description of the term's origin and definition? How does this kind of introduction serve his writing purpose?
3.  What is Shames' criticism of conspicuous consumption? How does he develop his explanation of his criticism? How close does your own opinion of conspicuous consumption match Shames'? Why?
4.  What kinds of evidence does Shames present to support his criticism of consumerism? How effective is that support? Why?
5.  What does the term "impoverishment by substitution" mean (paragraph 9)? Does this condition, in your opinion, exist in the 1990s? Explain your answer using specific examples of consumer products.

6. In your own words, summarize Shames' comparison between the 1890s and the 1980s. Which decade, in his opinion, was worse? Why?

7. Explain the impact of Shames' concluding paragraph. How effective is the quotation from *Fortune* magazine? Why? What is the connection between that quotation and the rest of the sentences in the conclusion? What does his purpose seem to be in this last paragraph?

8. How closely does the description Shames paints of the 1980s match consumer behavior in the 1990s? What evidence can you point to in support of your assessment of the similarities and differences between the two decades?

9. How would an advertising executive respond to the criticism of consumerism Shames presents? What would she say in defense of conspicuous consumption? Why?

# 6
# . . . . . . . . . . . . .
# OPTIONAL WRITING ASSIGNMENTS FOCUSED ON CONSUMERISM

What follows is a list of essay suggestions; each assignment provides a context within which you can write an essay on consumerism. Whether you choose one of these options or develop one on your own, you need to analyze your writing context and decide how you are to achieve your writing purpose for the particular readers you target (to review "The Rhetorical Approach to Academic Writing" see Chapter 2).

*1. Write a personal essay describing one particular experience you have had as a consumer.* The experience you choose should be related in some way to one of the aspects of consumerism discussed in one or more of the articles in this chapter. Use whatever descriptive strategies you can to help your readers (your classmates) "see" the experience as it happened. Your purpose in narrating this experience, however, is not only to recreate it. The experience you choose as the focus of your essay must help you make a point (your thesis) about consumerism. You may, if your teacher agrees, compare or contrast your experience with those described in one or more of this chapter's readings.

*2. Imagine consumer advocate Ralph Nader's name has been suggested as a speaker for your college's commencement next year.* You have been asked to write to Mr. Nader inviting him to deliver the commencement address. Because Mr. Nader receives many invitations like yours, you have decided that he may be persuaded to accept your invitation if you convince him that you, as a representative of your college's student body, are aware of some consumer concerns facing America as it approaches the twenty-first century. Draft the invitation letter to Nader, incorporating the information you have learned from your work with the consumer topic. Invent any details you feel would be contained in a letter of this kind. If you choose this option, look Ralph Nader up in a biographical dictionary at the reference desk of your library. A reference librarian can guide you to the appropriate dictionary. Incorporate relevant facts describing Nader into your letter.

3. *Take a position for or against stricter regulation of television commercials (or some other consumer-related issue).* Drawing from this chapter's readings, your own and others' experiences, and information from some outside-of-the-classroom sources (an interview or an article from a newspaper or periodical), state and explain the reasons for your position. Remember to consider what information your readers (your classmates) have, how they currently feel about this issue, and what kinds of questions they will ask about the reasons and evidence you present. Document all sources you refer to in your essay.

4. *Analyze how a particular consumer product is marketed.* Consider the different media approaches used. Explain how these ways of marketing reflect your understanding of some of the sociological and psychological aspects of consumer behavior. Examine several commercials, advertisements, or billboards that promote the product. Analyze the similarities and differences among them. Is the product marketed differently to different groups of consumers? Take detailed notes as you conduct your analysis. Then write a report that reflects the results of your in-depth analysis. The report should develop a thesis that is suggested by the notes you took while studying the marketing of the product. Use your notes and information from some of the readings in this chapter (as well as outside-of-the-classroom sources, if your teacher requests them) to convince your reader (your teacher) that you understand some of the theories of marketing discussed as your class read and responded to the articles on consumerism.

5. *Write a report describing how psychological and sociological research affects advertising campaigns.* First, conduct some library research to obtain some additional information on the relationship between research and advertising. Then, interview one or two individuals who work for an advertising agency (if you cannot interview individuals working at advertising agencies, consider interviewing a professor of marketing at your college). Once they have consented to an interview, generate a short but specific list of questions to ask them. Take careful notes during the interview (or request permission to tape record). Analyze your notes and tapes. Drawing from your interview notes, your library research, and information in this chapter's readings, write a report explaining the impact of sociological and psychological research on advertising campaigns. Your report's thesis should state clearly what you think this relationship is. The body of your report should convince your reader (a psychology professor) that your claim

is sufficiently supported and credible. You will need to document your library sources using the American Psychological Association's (APA) documentation system (see the Research Appendix for information on how to document sources using APA guidelines).

6. *Conduct your own investigation of children as consumers.* Use what you have learned from the readings and classroom discussions to develop a research question. Then develop a research plan for answering your research question (observations of children watching television, interview questions, or a controlled laboratory experiment). Conduct your investigation, taking detailed notes of what you do with the children you study. Analyze your results and then report them to your classmates using this format: introduction (in which you review your reading and explain what you were trying to investigate and why), method (in which you describe what you did), results (in which you present the data your investigation produced), and discussion (in which you analyze and explain the results, and suggest future research on the topic). If you choose this option, review the article by Gail Tom to see how this format is applied. If your teacher agrees, conduct this investigation with two or three other interested students. Finally, with your teacher's approval, develop a research plan for an investigation into some other aspect of consumer behavior.

7. *Investigate the history of subliminal advertising.* Using the library, find out what subliminal advertising is, how it was used, and why it is no longer legal to use it. Then write an essay comparing advertisements with subliminal messages to current advertisements and commercials. Use specific examples to explain the similarities and differences in the advertisements and commercials, as well as information you obtained from the readings in this chapter and from your library research. Your thesis should indicate whether you believe these two kinds of advertisements are more alike than different or more different than alike. You will also need to consider what aspects of subliminal advertising need to be explained to your readers. Remember to document the information from library sources that you use in your essay.

8. *Write an essay in which you argue that Shames' "conspicuous consumption" idea applies or does not apply to the 1990s.* Support your thesis with references to readings in this chapter, personal experience, and interviews with classmates. Combine references to personal experience with references to readings as you write.

# 11

## Perspectives on Television Culture

Is television really "the bad guy"? How do we learn to control what we see? Is it possible to be a critical consumer of television? Can television educate?

### 1
#### DEVELOPING A RHETORICAL APPROACH

Detractors and supporters of television abound. Some experts say that we allow our lives to be controlled to too large a degree by "the tube." Large parts of our daily routines are often defined by our desire to see morning, evening, and late evening news programs; favorite shows at regular times; and special events and sports programming. Too many people, critics say, identify with television characters and figures—from soap-opera, prime-time-drama, and situation-comedy stars to talk-show hosts and guests—without considering the values these characters and figures represent.

Other critics of television argue that the medium is too closely allied with commercial interests. They assert that television commercials, even the shows that are supported by these commercials, are extensions of the corporations that make the products represented in those commercials. Viewers, these critics assert, are actually treated as consumers, not as independent individuals who have a citizen's need for information, education, and entertainment. Viewers are given what the advertisers think they want and what corporations want them to crave, not what they need to function as informed, thoughtful citizens.

Almost all the negative criticism of television stems from the critics' belief that television is a mesmerizing medium, one that encourages its audiences to absorb rather than criticize, to consume rather than act in a socially responsible way.

Positive critics of television emphasize the medium's ability to reach multitudes of people, to cross international and cultural boundaries, and to represent the views of different peoples from very different social classes. They also applaud television's commercialism because it helps the country's economy by creating markets, new businesses, and more jobs. Positive critics argue that television advertising provides viewers with greater knowledge of what's available.

These critics also focus on television's potential for educating children and adults who otherwise do not have access to further education. Working parents who did not attend school are able to take early morning and evening television courses; people who live far from urban areas are able to take community college courses from home. Television also enables high-school teachers to have students view films that supplement a course's reading list.

Almost all the positive critics of television emphasize the medium's potential for reaching larger segments of society with useful information and entertainment. Although many of them believe that television programmers have yet to exploit that potential to anywhere near its full capacity, they argue that the medium could become a major democratizing influence on American society.

Keep this broad context in mind as you read and write your way through this chapter. When you approach discussions and writing assignments, consider the general positions put forward by critics of television, positive and negative. Then probe your own experience, consider the views and experiences of your classmates, and analyze the arguments put forward by the authors of this chapter's readings as you develop ideas for your own oral and written contributions to the ongoing television debate. The final step in this process is an essay in which you develop your own thesis on one of these television issues.

## 2
## GENERATING IDEAS ABOUT TELEVISION AND CULTURE

You have probably watched thousands of hours of television as you grew up. As a member of family, school, and work groups, you have shared conversations with other viewers concerning the function, value, and content of television. Some of your own values have been either directly or indirectly shaped by television viewing experiences. Some of your buying habits have most likely been influenced by television commercials. Your role models might, to some degree, have been drawn from television programs.

The following sequence of questions will help you recall and organize your thoughts concerning past experiences with television. Record your responses to these questions in your reading journal if you are keeping one. Write your responses so that you will be able to make specific contributions to workshop groups and class discussions.

## Probing Personal Experience

*1. Recall your viewing habits when you were a child.* Did you watch television at certain times of the day? What types of programs did you watch? Do you recall being especially interested in certain characters? Who were they? What kinds of values and behaviors did they represent?

*2. Did your parents or other family members control your viewing?* What form did this control take? Has this control either positively or negatively affected your current viewing habits?

*3. Consider recent responses to television programming: choose a particular show or television character and explain your response to it.* What are the purposes behind the show? Does it intend to entertain or instruct, or both? How well does it accomplish its purpose? Does the show or character attempt to represent a current social condition? Does it do a good or poor job of representation? In what ways?

*4. Choose a show you have had a good deal of experience watching.* Define the show's intended audience and explain what parts of the show seem to you to be most obviously directed to that audience. What values and tastes would that audience have? How does the show appeal to those values and tastes?

*5. Describe a particularly effective commercial.* To whom is the commercial addressed (age group, gender, and the like)? Toward what psychological and physical needs is it directed? Why is the commercial effective?

*6. Many media experts criticize television's lack of seriousness.* Do you agree or disagree with this criticism? Describe particular viewing experiences that either reinforce or contradict this criticism.

*7. What do you think the latest viewing technologies, such as VCRs, have added to the television viewing experience?* How have VCRs given viewers more control over what they watch? How have they broadened the range of programs to which most viewers have access?

*8. In your experience, has television offered enough in the way of educational programming?* Do you think American viewers would take advantage of increased educational programming if it were offered? Why? Why not? Would you? What incentives need to accompany increased programming to ensure that viewers will take advantage of it (opportunities to pursue degrees at home, or to apply what they learn on their jobs, for example)?

9. *Many critics of news programming argue that television news is sensational and superficial, seldom precise or thorough.* Watch one half-hour news program and refer to it in developing your own response to this often-heard criticism. Are the issues covered thoroughly? Do you perceive evidence of sensationalism in the way anchor persons introduce particular news stories? Is there sufficient time to address important issues in thorough ways?

10. *Do you think television is excessively violent?* What examples can you give to support your answer? How do you define "excessive violence"?

## Freewriting to Capture Personal Experience

The following list of controversial statements contains good subjects for freewriting about television. Choose one or two and write without editing on each for ten minutes, twenty at the most. (For a discussion of freewriting, see pages 103–104.) Freewriting is most helpful if you follow the sequence **R**eread, **F**ocus, **R**ewrite (**RFR**). (For a discussion of **RFR,** see page 104.)

- Television is only good for those times when you are too tired to think. That is why it is called the "boob tube."
- Television is the most effective medium for making viewers feel a part of what they see.
- Television and delayed gratification are contradictions in terms.
- Television is focused on commercial purposes to the detriment of all others.
- Television destroys the minds and souls of the young.
- Television news programs are objective in their presentation of the news.
- Television is *the* most democratic medium of communication.
- Political campaigns are controlled by television.
- Television makes a serious effort to represent men and women in complex ways and to avoid all gender stereotypes.

## 3
. . . . . . . . . . . . . .
## DEVELOPING RHETORICAL CONTEXT THROUGH GROUP ACTIVITIES

As in previous chapters, this section provides a group of collaborative activities that help you generate ideas for essays. Some of these group activities help you as you revise freewritings. Others simply provide advice about how to go about directing group discussions. (If you are collaborating for the first time, read the earlier description of strategies for effective collaboration on pages 104 to 105.)

- Exchange your freewriting with a partner. You and your partner should then play devil's advocate. Imagine yourselves as part of an audience that is either skeptical of or opposes what your partner has said in his or her essay. Perhaps that audience does not agree with the proposition that television is controlled by commercial interests. How can your partner's argument that television *is* controlled by commercial interests be presented in a convincing way? How can it be presented to take into consideration opposing positions without weakening the force of the argument? How can your partner present his or her argument without antagonizing that audience? By exchanging roles in this way, you and your partner will be better able to imagine what an audience with different views would say and how their different positions can be acknowledged in an essay that effectively presents a different perspective.
- Write a collaborative statement explaining why your group either agrees or disagrees with one of the following opinions:

> Television caters to viewers' worst appetites.
> Television news is slanted.
> Television distorts viewers' images of women.
> Television misrepresents minority cultures.
> Television does a good job of educating the young.
> Television provides positive role models for our youth.

Members of your group need to sort out their own differences *before* they write the position paper, which should be straightforward and no longer than three pages. Then, while drafting the position paper, group members should read aloud and comment on the evolving statement, asking questions that push for more detailed explanations or clarifications and identifying possible mismatches between the intended position and the ideas in the draft.

An effective way to draft a position paper is to have each group member contribute one section, with follow-up discussion of what needs to be done to tie the sections together into a coherent statement. Once written, the position paper can become part of your overall composing process in one of two ways: Write your own response to the position stated in the paper, or collaborate with some or all of your group peers to produce a collaboratively written extended argument essay based on the original position paper. This second option needs your teacher's approval.

- Plan to participate in a television research workgroup with peers in your class. This group begins by planning a television research strategy. What do members of your group want to know more about? Why do they want this further information? Where and how can they get this information? Does the *library reference desk* have materials that establish some base information in each research area that the group decides is important? (One group member can read the Research Appendix in this book and consult a library reference desk staff person before reporting back to the group.) Would the group prefer to administer a *survey* before discussing a particular aspect of television programming? (Another member of the group can read the section on field research in the Research Appendix and talk with a social science professor or advanced student about doing surveys before reporting back to the group.) A third member can report back to the group on the possibility of using *interviews* to get a sense of how individuals have responded to particular aspects of television programming or advertising. (This person would review the material on interviewing in the field research section of the Research Appendix and discuss interviewing techniques with a local news reporter [the campus newspaper often works well as a source for reporters in this case], social science professor, or student before reporting back to the group.) A fourth person might have read a particular book on television that she wishes to summarize for the rest of the group to provide useful material for essays.

    This activity should serve as a useful source of collective information on television for all group members, no matter what particular subjects they choose for their essays. Even more important, however, will be the insight such group work can provide into the use of different kinds of research. The discussion following the individual reports in these research groups should encourage group members to consider how to use the different kinds of research results in their individual essays.

# 4
. . . . . . . . . . . . . .
## USING READINGS TO DEVELOP
## RHETORICAL COMMUNITY

You need at this point to take the results of your personal and group work and synthesize it with your reading of this chapter's professional essays and articles. In most cases, you will disagree with some but not all of every essay you read. You need, first, to give a fair and open reading to every essay you are assigned to read, but you then need to develop your own perspective out of some combination of critical reading, your own experience, and what you have heard others in your class say.

## The Readings in This Chapter

The readings in this chapter are organized into four consecutive clusters. The first focuses on how television influences viewers. Robert W. Kubey and Mihalyi Csizkszentmihalyi, in "The Structuring of Television," argue that television influences the way we organize our lives, especially our time. Programming, they tell us, influences when we decide to relax and, to some degree, when we work. It often has a great deal to do with how we arrange our living space and what furniture we decide to put into the rooms in which television is present. Neil Postman, in "Now ... This," argues that television has had a dramatic effect on how we think. He asserts that we are now accustomed to receiving disconnected information without looking for connections; we are, Postman argues, willing to live within a chaos of undefined and unrelated sequences of visual and verbal information. We have lost our critical perspective, and television must share, Postman says, much of the blame.

The second cluster includes two essays that address the issue of minority cultural representation on television. Both also raise related cultural issues. The first essay, Mark Crispin Miller's "The Cosby Show," criticizes this very successful situation comedy's implied commercialism and its emphasis on narrow middle-class values. It also raises general objections to what Miller thinks is the extreme commercialism of all television programming. Miller implies that "The Cosby Show," despite its focus on a black upper-middle-class family, actually offers blacks a distorted picture of black life in America and of social complexities in general. In contrast, Eric Copage, in "Prime-Time Heroes," presents a more positive view of network television's presentation of black culture. Drawing from his own childhood experience, Copage argues that television images of successful individuals, black or white, can provide positive role models for black and white children. Copage finds value in television's tendency to dramatize and commercialize everyday life.

The third cluster addresses the issues of television technology and viewer control over television scheduling and programming. Kiku

Adatto, in "The Incredible Shrinking Sound Bite," illustrates how television news programs have, over the past two decades, moved to increasingly briefer segments covering political campaigns. This tendency, Adatto says, makes it difficult for viewers to interpret the messages of political candidates in any kind of thorough or critical way. Adatto's analysis of the visual technology of television news ties in with Neil Postman's criticism of television's dependence on nonlogical or disjointed narratives. Both writers think that television is destroying viewers' ability to construct coherent messages out of what they see, hear, and experience every day.

Kimberly K. Massey and Stanley J. Baran, in "VCRs and People's Control of Their Leisure Time," analyze the potential effects of VCRs on viewers' structuring of their outside-of-work lives. These researchers and authors find cause for optimism in the advent of VCR technology because it has the potential to release viewers from the bondage of network programmers who previously set the time slots within which all shows would be watched. VCRs also enable people to watch programs over and over again if they choose, which encourages more critical and analytical responses to television programming. Massey and Baran take a more positive view of the potential of television than either Adatto or Postman.

The fourth and final cluster in this chapter focuses on the influence television has and could have on the emotions and intellects of viewers. Christine Hall Hansen and Ranald D. Hansen, in "The Influence of Sex and Violence on the Appeal of Rock Music Videos," bring up the long-standing question of what kinds of effects television's representation of sex and violence has on viewers. This piece is this chapter's sole example of the scientific article: it includes the conventional introduction, methods, results, and discussion sections, although at times these exact words are not used. Hansen and Hansen attempt to measure the effects of sexual and violent visual and verbal imagery on actual human subjects under controlled laboratory conditions. They come up with some definite evidence of effect on emotions. It will be up to you as a general reader to decide how far you can go in making value judgments about television based on this study.

Edward L. Palmer, in "Our Crisis in Children's Television," argues that the medium has done little to reach its full potential for educating the young. He provides the history of children's programming over the past three decades, including a good deal of attention to the history of *Sesame Street*. Working from that history, he compares what American television has done in the area of children's educational programming to what he thinks could be done. Palmer's judgment of the past is negative; his vision of the future is positive.

# 5
. . . . . . . . . . . . . .
## READINGS ON TELEVISION CULTURE

# ROBERT W. KUBEY AND MIHALYI CSIZKSZENTMIHALYI ON THE STRUCTURE OF TELEVISION

## Pre-Reading Questions

1. Grant Tinker, a television executive who is cited in this article (see paragraph 20), says, "I think what is probably the biggest sin of the medium as it exists is that so little sticks to your ribs, that so much effort and technology goes into—what? It's like human elimination. It's just waste." Do you agree or disagree? Think of some examples to support your answer.

2. What television programs have recently "stuck to your ribs"? What common qualities made them stick? Why would you like to see more programs of this kind?

3. In general, why do you watch television? Does it usually provide escape and relaxation, or does it usually provide information or understanding? Provide some examples to support your answers.

## TELEVISION AND THE STRUCTURING OF EXPERIENCE
### Robert W. Kubey
### Mihalyi Csizkszentmihalyi

A sound education consists in training people to find pleasure and pain in the right objects.

—Plato

Nothing is so damaging to good character as the habit of lounging at the games.

—Seneca

Hardly any teaching can mean more for our community than the teaching of beauty where it reaches the masses.

—Munsterberg (1916)

Much remains to be said about the role television plays in the quality of   1
everyday life, individual development, and the future and health of human societies. Does television help people live more rewarding and

meaningful lives? Is television viewing different from other forms of
leisure? Is it just as well that people continue to use television as they are
doing now or could changes in the audience make a difference in how
television is used and experienced, or in how it is created? Why is
television programming the way it is, and could it be changed?

## ORDER AND COMPLEXITY REVISITED

We earlier pointed out that human attention was limited, and that    2
attention was required to bring order to experience. Experience is not
naturally ordered, and, without a focus for attention that provides
patterns for thoughts, experience rarely remains in an ordered state for
very long.

### Television and Routine Reality Maintenance

Food and sleep are not enough to maintain psychological order. Certain    3
types of information are also necessary. To help restore assurance in the
world as we know it, "reality-maintenance" work is regularly needed
(Berger & Luckmann, 1967). *Emergency* reality maintenance is called for
when events suddenly threaten our most basic goals. A war, the loss of a
job, the inevitable death of loved ones or the approach of one's own,
will often put ordered reality into question. At such times, more than
ever, messages are needed to confirm the value of the goals by which we
live.[1]

But routine reality maintenance is just as crucial for daily mental    4
well-being. We typically engage in such maintenance unconsciously by
falling into the routines of social living. Upon awaking we tell our
spouse, "A gloomy day outside again," and when he or she absent-
mindedly agrees we get a small confirmation that the world is indeed as
we believe it to be. Then we glance at the paper,[2] listen to the radio, have
breakfast, and so on—at each step compiling further messages that
reassure us of the order in the world. Without such reassurance it would
be difficult to make plans for our personal goals, and disorder might
enter consciousness in the form of a disabling anxiety.

For Gregory Bateson (1972), as for Berger and Luckmann, much of    5
the information we seek out and produce for ourselves is aimed at
creating redundancy that will help maintain a reliable sense that things
are as they seem. So, although we often seek novelty and complexity,
reassuring redundancy is also necessary to maintain consciousness in an
organized state.[3] (Klapp, 1986, called this "good"—or functional—
redundancy and included rules, codes, customs, and traditions among
the redundant phenomena that help provide order and meaning to
experience.)

Berger and Luckmann also posited that it is ordinary conversation    6
that is the primary mechanism of routine reality maintenance. People
keep their subjective universes in recognizable shape by constantly
talking about them. When we exchange words about our work or the
weather, yesterday's football games or television shows, useful information in the sense of increasing knowledge is rarely exchanged. Yet the
information is often valuable because it helps connect and integrate us
with our fellow human beings while confirming what we already know,
but might begin to doubt unless confirmed. Redundancy reminds us of
the order in the universe—of what is "real," what is worth paying
attention to, working for, and living for.

For many of us, television now performs some of the function that    7
conversation once played in maintaining everyday order. Whether it is
because modern life is increasingly privatized, offering fewer opportunities to have friendly or meaningful chats, or because it is easier or seems
more enjoyable to watch television than to hold a conversation,[4] most
people in our culture now spend 2 to 4 hours daily in contact with
televised information, the bulk of which can be thought of as redundant,
particularly in its repetitive use of well accepted genres, "frames," and
scenarios (Gamson, 1988; Gitlin, 1980; Tuchman, 1974).

Indeed, the majority of television viewers interviewed by the Corpo-    8
ration for Public Broadcasting (1978) said that they preferred commercial television over public television because in watching commercial TV
they were more likely to see familiar actors and episodes of programs they
had viewed previously. In fact, many viewers are disappointed and even
outraged if their expectations are not met by the programs they regularly
watch. The CBS comedy "Rhoda" began to lose its audience when an
unconventional plot element was added: Rhoda's new marriage was not
working and she and her TV husband separated. CBS also received
thousands of angry letters and telephone calls after a favorite leading
character in the comedy "M*A*S*H" was killed on his way home from
the war. In both instances, the comedies in question were taken to task
for breaking with the tradition of amusement and escape, by conflicting
with viewers' expectations and thus producing psychic entropy. In this
sense, television may not only perform some of the reality-maintenance
functions of conversation, but also those of a much repeated fairy tale; it
is familiar and predictable.

As television comedy writer and producer Stu Silverman told Kubey    9
(1989d), "Television reassures us, it's 'nice,' it doesn't offend or
challenge an audience. It's designed to do the opposite of art, to reassure
rather than excite. That often is what people want." Bob Shanks, a
successful television producer and writer has drawn similar conclusions:

> Television is used mostly as a stroking distraction from the truth of an
> indifferent and silent universe and the harsh realities just out of sight and

sound of the box. Television is a massage, a "there, there," a need, an addiction, a psychic fortress—a friend. (see Fowles, 1982, pp. 46–47)

Steven Bochco (1983), creator of "Hill Street Blues" and "L.A. Law," 10 has concluded that many viewers wish to be left "in a very pleasant state of semiconsciousness" (p. 160) before going to bed, and Aaron Spelling, the creator of more fanciful programs such as "Fantasy Island" and "Charlie's Angels," has observed that workers "come home and use the TV set as a paintbrush to paint over the horrors of the day, to forget what real life is" (see Fowles, 1982, p. 43). Television critic William Henry (1983), in examining his own viewing motivations would concur: "I run to television for solace. In times of personal turmoil it provides familiarity, emotional connections, and the promise of resolution" (p. 48).

The "days of the week" and the "hours of the day," are also among 11 the most powerful social conventions that help structure experience and maintain reality.[5] Activities such as sleeping, eating, working, leisure, and religious observance take place at particular times and intervals based exclusively, or in large part, on what day of the week and what hour of the day it is, thereby providing order and regularity as well as giving direction to what we believe we should be doing and experiencing at any given time.

Regarding television, specific programs are also available at certain 12 times of the day and on particular days of the week and, especially in the United States, these programs are neatly packaged into familiar and regular "time slots" of 30 minutes, 60 minutes, and so on. Indeed, the timing of viewing depends to a great extent on the day of the week, the time of day, and the scheduling of work and meals.

Because the scheduling of different kinds of television programs is 13 dependent on these same social conventions, television viewing itself reinforces the already existing time structure that society has devised for itself and thereby helps further communicate a sense of regularity and orderliness. Indeed, it might be disorienting if one suddenly found children's cartoons on all of the major networks late one night or "The Wide World of Sports" airing on a weekday morning. In fact, since the early 1950s the TV industry has titled a good many of its entertainment and news programs by what time of day they were broadcast, in part, as a reminder to viewers and to help increase ratings ("The Noon News," "The Eleven O'Clock News," and so on). (Among NBC's longest running programs have been "Tonight" and "Today," and more recently, "Tomorrow," "Late Night," and "Later.")

Many viewers, particularly those with less structure in their lives such 14 as retired persons and the unemployed, use television to give shape to the day and to demarcate time (Davis, 1973; Kubey, 1980; Schalinske, 1968). A quote from one of Steiner's (1963) older respondents provides evidence of how television can help provide structure and psychological order, particularly for someone who has lost many of his previous social roles:

> I'm an old man and the TV brings people and music and talk into my life. Maybe without TV I would be ready to die; but this TV gives me life. It gives me what to look forward to—that tomorrow if I live, I'll watch this and that program.

Our colleague Marten deVries (personal communication, June 9, 1989) has reported that in an ESM study of drug abusers in the Netherlands, 45% of all responses from one recovering heroin addict were instances of television viewing. The subject's feelings during viewing were more relaxed and less sad and angry than normal, and he reported that his thoughts during viewing were more pleasant and less confused. The subject explained that he used television as a self-control mechanism that helped him contain his craving and get his mind "off dope."

But television may also structure experience in ways that are less 15 desirable, and that signal a dependence at variance with the viewer's long-term interests. In one example, another aging man, hospitalized for alcoholism, told Kubey, "I have my drinking under pretty good control. I don't have my first drink of the day until noon when the '$20,000 Pyramid' comes on."

Emphasis on the maintenance functions of television should not 16 imply that the medium does not also produce complex messages. Television can and does provide interesting and thought-provoking information. Some programs are sophisticated and, regardless of content, many viewers derive complex interpretations of what they view. Television can also influence viewers so that their ways of seeing, thinking, and feeling change, and the capacity to order experience is enhanced. Both drama and comedy can help deepen our understanding of ourselves and our culture, while news and educational programs frequently provide information that helps people realize their plans and enriches their store of knowledge.*

### Reality Maintenance, Television Content, and the Existing Social Order

But when we speak of the reality-maintenance functions of television, 17 what kind of *reality* does television maintain? Certainly not an absolute reality "out there," but a model of it. Although televised messages can

---

*Of course, much television news, especially at the local level, is purposely sensationalized with the primary goal of attracting and holding viewers in order to boost ratings. Critics regularly point out that news programs tend to be a hodgepodge of facts unrelated to any meaningful context; in one jaundiced view, they merely provide information that can be used effectively in a game of Trivial Pursuit (Nystrom, 1984).

contribute to keeping the individual consciousnesses of viewers in an ordered state, they simultaneously keep attention focused on common societal concerns, thereby contributing to cultural integration (Hirsch, 1977a; Loevinger, 1968). Of course, some critics argue that this integration is likely to benefit the goals of those who own and/or control the communication process more than it benefits the goals of individual viewers. Hence, there are enormous political and ethical implications of television as a medium for shaping consciousness.

But even though most of what appears on the screen exists for 18 commercial reasons, for advertisers to make money by attracting the attention of tens of millions of prospective consumers, television fare must at the same time appeal to many of the goals of the public if it is also to benefit the owners' goals. It must have high enough negentropy and complexity quotients to attract and hold viewer attention, but not so high as to turn them off. As we have shown, most television fare is experienced as mildly pleasant and requiring little mental effort, offering bits of novelty safely packaged in a familiar context. As a result, the information conveyed can be processed in a relaxed manner for several hours each day.

But, again, some critics claim that mass viewing causes a wholesale 19 imitation of TV reality and greater conformity on the part of the public.* And certainly it is the case that television often emphasizes those messages that directly or indirectly will best serve the goals of the people who own or control the medium and who pay for the production of programs.† And as is argued shortly, tens of thousands of hours spent watching television may well help foster an acceptance and attraction for the aims of the commercial world.

Furthermore, although television helps provide psychological order, 20 our research also suggests that the medium may not enrich life as much

---

*As the Paddy Chayefsky character, Howard Beale, in the movie *Network* put it when he chastised the viewing audience, "You think like the tube, you dress like the tube, you eat like the tube."

†The idea that the mass media serve the interests of the power elite has a long and distinguished history. One of the seminal statements on the topic and the one that underlies many critiques of mass culture is Marx's statement in *The German Ideology* that "the ideas of the ruling class are in every epoch the ruling ideas."

Frankfurt School theorists later held that the mass media tended to lull and assimilate the working class to the ruling elite's interests and thus subverted the revolutionary change forecast by Marx (Horkheimer & Adorno, 1972; Marcuse, 1964). Gramsci (1971) and Hall (1982) were concerned less with the base and class determinants of ideology, focusing instead on the process of hegemony itself (i.e., how dominant ideologies are represented in mass media content and how through the mass media they reproduce themselves in consciousness). Much of George Gerbner and his colleagues' research on "cultivation" effects similarly suggests that heavy viewers tend to share a more narrow, mainstream set of political and social beliefs than light viewers (see Gerbner et al., 1986, for a review). Among many others who have delineated how the mass media serve ruling interests are Gitlin (1980); Herman and Chomsky (1988); Parenti (1986); and Schiller (1973).

as one might hope. Like Tantalus, the Lydian king who in Hades was condemned to stand up to his neck in water that always flowed away when he tried to drink it, the modern television viewer is surrounded by interesting stimulation that too often flickers away without slacking his thirst. Or as the former President of MTM, NBC, and current CEO of his own GTG Entertainment Company, Grant Tinker, has said, "I think what is probably the biggest sin of the medium as it exists is that so little sticks to your ribs, that so much effort and technology goes into—what? It's like human elimination. It's just waste" (see Gitlin, 1983, p. 16).*

The irony is that television may benefit most those who least need it. 21 People who are already reasonably happy and in control of their lives will be more inclined to find useful information on television and will be less inclined to become dependent on the medium. Those who are less happy and less able or skilled in creating order in their experience are more likely to become dependent, and yet derive less enjoyment from their viewing.

That those in better emotional condition may be more inclined to 22 use television for serious ends is illustrated in an intriguing study by Zillmann et al. (1980). Subjects in whom a good mood was experimentally induced were more likely to become quickly disenchanted with viewing a game show and gravitated instead to a drama. The authors concluded that these subjects possessed the necessary patience to stick with the drama. In contrast, subjects in whom a bad mood was induced did the opposite—those who first picked the drama deserted it quickly in favor of viewing the game show. Zillmann and Bryant (1985) concluded from this study and similar research that certain programs are selected not because of "particular excitatory and hedonic reactions but primarily because they contain soothing, comforting information" (p. 182).

An examination of one's own use of television may confirm these 23 findings. If you come home anxious and depressed from a particularly frustrating and defeating day at work and you have two movies available on videotape that you very much want to eventually view, are you more likely to pick a light comedy or a very serious, complex drama?

Attraction to comforting, low-complexity easy-to-digest information 24 is one of the prime reasons that television viewing typically supports the viewer's existing set of beliefs, why use of the medium will tend to support the status quo. David Mumford, senior vice president for research at Columbia Pictures Television confirmed that viewers do not

---

*Edward R. Murrow also took a dim view of much that his industry offered:

And if there are any historians . . . a hundred years from now and there should be preserved the kinescopes for one week of all three networks, they will find recorded, in black-and-white or color, evidence of decadence, escapism and insulation from the realities of the world. . . . If we go on as we are, then history will take its revenge, and retribution will [catch] up with us. (cited in Friendly, 1968, p. 99)

want "challenging" programs; they want "leisure-time activity that is absent of discomfort" (cited in Topolnicki, 1989, p. 74).

Dissonance theory (Festinger, 1957), affect-dependent stimulus ar-  25 rangement theory (Zillmann & Bryant, 1985), cognitive balance theory (Heider, 1946), and our own model of information and experience each predict that people who are unhappy for one reason or another will tend to seek out nonthreatening, confirmatory messages, and will avoid information that challenges their belief system. Of course some people who are unhappy for long periods of time will eventually gravitate to new belief systems to make themselves feel better.

But people who are reasonably happy and who possess greater  26 cognitive complexity are more likely to seek out television programs that contain more complex and challenging information. Even watching the same program, a person more skilled in interpreting information can generally extract more complexity and order. For as Wright and Huston (1981) pointed out:

> Informativeness . . . is a meaningful property only to the viewer who is actively seeking to understand the content at a level of processing beyond superficial enjoyment. To appreciate features for their informativeness, the viewer must be able to encode content, form hypotheses, and develop a context of expectations. (p. 77)

Furthermore, a viewer's expectation about the viewing enterprise  27 plays a role in how the medium is experienced. The research of Salomon and Leigh (1984) confirms that children readily form a "context of expectations" that causes them to approach television with an attitude that precludes actively seeking to understand television content at deeper levels. Still, those children who can order their experiences more actively and who appreciate and seek complexity are more likely to retain greater control and mastery over the information provided by any medium, and therefore will derive more useful information from it.

Viewer expectations are the result of a system of complex reciprocal  28 causality. The nature of television programming is shaped by audience ratings while past viewing experiences and the programs themselves simultaneously help set certain expectations in viewers. These in turn affect how viewers will respond to what is on TV and what will be on in the future. Therefore, both the nature of television form and content, and the nature of television use and experience, are the results of repeated interactions of medium, mind, and the past experiences of both producers and audiences.

This is a good place to debunk the much repeated idea that television  29 is a medium best suited to transmitting emotions, and that it either "cannot" or is not "good" at transmitting ideas. We believe that those who make this claim often confuse what they are accustomed to seeing on television with what television can transmit.

A single example may prove instructive. Every year, for a variety of 30 reasons, many students successfully receive their introductory college lectures in chemistry, biology, and physics via television and/or on videotape. This often happens because lecture halls are overcrowded or as a means of accommodating students' schedules. Regardless of the reason, it is clearly the case that very complex ideas can be readily and inexpensively transmitted via television. We might keep this in mind when considering why television is only occasionally used in this manner. Indeed, it is ironic that the greatest expense in commercial production is involved in taking very simple things—say, a deodorant or a bathroom tissue—and, by employing very costly special effects or a celebrity spokesperson, making these products seem more interesting and more complex than they are.

The answer to why we see what we see on television lies in a 31 combination of how audiences have come to conceive of the medium, what audiences want to watch (or have grown accustomed to watching), and what the people who control and sponsor television believe needs to be created and broadcast in order to maximize profit.

But the medium and the industry can be held only partly accountable 32 if people become dependent on television for escape. Nor is television solely responsible if people have either not obtained, or have lost, the ability to find meaningful goals by which to direct their consciousness.

Rather, television content, and how people use and experience the 33 medium, are certainly as much a result of human nature and existing economic and cultural arrangements as their cause. Or as Utley (1948) wrote, "TV appeals to the inherent laziness in all of us" (p. 137). Moreover, if television always presented information requiring substantial effort to interpret and to assimilate, it would fail to provide its therapeutic function, if for no other reason than that people simply lack the inclination and the mental energy to process complex messages all of the time. Thus there is something to be said for the fact that television does not tax the mind—especially if much of life is already challenging, or if one's usual experience alternates between boredom and anxiety.

At one time or another, most of us have come home after a day of 34 dealing with complex problems and dropped in front of the television, appreciatively receiving its attractive, easy-to-receive entertainment. Certainly it can be argued that using television in this manner habitually is no worse, and may indeed be better, than habitually using alcohol or other mood-altering substances.

Although this argument has merit, it is also true that television has 35 become too important a part of daily life for us to ignore what happens during the time it is viewed. Just as a drug that masks pain but does not heal may be of limited value in the long run or may cause addiction, so can viewing encourage a false sense of well-being in some people who might be better off taking active steps to change the conditions of their "real" lives.

If one of the goals of life is to realize one's latent potentialities—the 36
ideal held, among others, by Aristotle, the Christian Tomists, as well as
by Marx and most modern psychologists—then the prolonged and
indiscriminate viewing of television is likely to present an obstacle in
achieving that purpose.

## NOTES

1. Kubey and Peluso (1990) have shown that rapid news diffusion following
   tragic events such as an assassination or the destruction of the space shuttle is
   partly driven by this same need for reality maintenance.
2. Stephenson (1967) and Glasser (1982) have claimed that much newspaper
   reading is ritualistic and serves a reality-maintenance function as much or
   more than it is driven by a need to obtain new information. Many a sports fan
   is as likely to read the account of a game he or she has witnessed the day
   before as the account of a game he or she did not witness.
3. Or as Sylvan Tomkins (1962) wrote:

   > Stimuli are extremely attractive to the human organism if they possess
   > both sufficient novelty and sufficient familiarity so that both positive
   > affects are reciprocally activated, interest-excitement by the novel aspects
   > of the stimulus and enjoyment-joy by the recognition of the familiar and
   > the reduction of interest-excitement. (pp. 127–128)

   Fiske and Maddi (1961) and Zuckerman (1979), among others, have also
   explored the alternating affinity for both novelty and familiarity.
4. It has been claimed that conversation, which is so central to the transmission
   of ideas and the creation of meaning, has begun to be outpaced by the speed
   of electronic communications. Franco Ferrarotti (1988) argues that the art of
   simple conversation is being lost because it is antithetical to the imperatives of
   mass society and mass media.

   Andre Gregory (1983) reported that he and Wallace Shawn became
   interested in making *My Dinner with Andre,* a full-length film that consists
   almost entirely of a conversation between the two men, because:

   > Wally and I were struck by the fact that we found that nobody talked
   > about anything anymore that came from the heart, that we felt. We
   > sensed that most conversation had become automatic. . . . And that there
   > was no real communication going on. As a result we were collectively
   > going into a kind of psychological ice age—becoming so blocked that
   > positive action was becoming impossible. Because in order to have
   > positive action you have to communicate: you have to think and feel.
   > When social intercourse becomes deadly and boring and unlife-
   > enhancing—as it is becoming—then what happens is that humanity starts
   > to become atrophied. (p. 20)

   It is also possible that conversation today is no more boring or meaningless than conversation at any other time. In 1732, Berkeley wrote that people
   "prefer doing anything to the ennui of their own conversation."

5. E. P. Thompson (1967) focuses on how mechanized production required a new "time sense" that would help discipline workers and separate them from natural forms of time perception.

## Post-Reading Questions

1. According to Kubey and Csizkszentmihalyi, what is "routine reality maintenance" (paragraphs 3 and 4)? How does television become part of routine reality maintenance? Why do people need it?
2. Do Kubey and Csizkszentmihalyi imply that the reality-maintenance function of television has been emphasized at the expense of other, more creative and imaginative functions? Where in this essay do Kubey and Csizkszentmihalyi most explicitly develop their position on the role television plays in the lives of most viewers?
3. Do you think that more recent technologies such as VCRs provide viewers with more control over their viewing schedules? In what ways is this the case?
4. What do Kubey and Csizkszentmihalyi mean by this sentence from paragraph 21: "The irony is that television may benefit most those who least need it"? To which people might they be referring? What negative effects does television have on these individuals?
5. What changes in television programming do Kubey and Csizkzent-mihalyi recommend? Why?
6. How are "viewer expectations" created (paragraphs 27 and 28)?
7. As one of Kubey and Csizkszentmihalyi's readers, what do you think they want you to *do* with the information and ideas you get by reading their article? Do they want you to consider changing your viewing behavior? If they do, what kinds of changes do they suggest? If not, why do they not encourage change in your individual viewing habits? Do they want to change your attitude toward television programming and to get you to demand more of the medium than you are now getting from network programmers? Where do you find evidence of this desire on their part for an attitude change on your part as reader and viewer? Or do you find other kinds of reader attitude changes recommended? Where?

# NEIL POSTMAN ON THE INCOHERENCE OF TELEVISION

## Pre-Reading Questions

1. What is your response to television news programming? Do you find it informative? What is your assessment of how the news is presented? Is it presented objectively, in sufficient depth, and with

enough explanation? Do you find some of it sensational or superficial? When is television news programming at its best and worst? Give examples.

2. In paragraph 18, Neil Postman makes the following assertion: "Americans are the best entertained and quite likely the least well-informed people in the Western world." Explain your initial reaction to that assertion. In what ways do you find it accurate, in what ways exaggerated or wrong?

3. Name and describe your favorite news anchor persons. What qualities do they have and why do you like them? Do you think the person presenting the news gets too much or too little attention on American news media? Why? Why not?

4. Compare the news on CNN or other cable news programs to network news. What are the major differences? Do you find one more "newsworthy" than the other? Why? Why not?

## "NOW . . . THIS"
### Neil Postman

The American humorist H. Allen Smith once suggested that of all the worrisome words in the English language, the scariest is "uh oh," as when a physician looks at your X-rays, and with knitted brow says, "Uh oh." I should like to suggest that the words which are the title of this chapter are as ominous as any, all the more so because they are spoken without knitted brow—indeed, with a kind of idiot's delight. The phrase, if that's what it may be called, adds to our grammar a new part of speech, a conjunction that does not connect anything to anything but does the opposite: separates everything from everything. As such, it serves as a compact metaphor for the discontinuities in so much that passes for public discourse in present-day America.

"Now . . . this" is commonly used on radio and television newscasts to indicate that what one has just heard or seen has no relevance to what one is about to hear or see, or possibly to anything one is ever likely to hear or see. The phrase is a means of acknowledging the fact that the world as mapped by the speeded-up electronic media has no order or meaning and is not to be taken seriously. There is no murder so brutal, no earthquake so devastating, no political blunder so costly—for that matter, no ball score so tantalizing or weather report so threatening—that it cannot be erased from our minds by a newscaster saying, "Now . . . this." The newscaster means that you have thought long enough on the previous matter (approximately forty-five seconds), that you must not be morbidly preoccupied with it (let us say, for ninety seconds), and that you must now give your attention to another fragment of news or a commercial.

Television did not invent the "Now . . . this" world view. As I have tried to show, it is the offspring of the intercourse between telegraphy and photography. But it is through television that it has been nurtured and brought to a perverse maturity. For on television, nearly every half hour is a discrete event, separated in content, context, and emotional texture from what precedes and follows it. In part because television sells its time in seconds and minutes, in part because television must use images rather than words, in part because its audience can move freely to and from the television set, programs are structured so that almost each eight-minute segment may stand as a complete event in itself. Viewers are rarely required to carry over any thought or feeling from one parcel of time to another. 3

Of course, in television's presentation of the "news of the day," we may see the "Now . . . this" mode of discourse in its boldest and most embarrassing form. For there, we are presented not only with fragmented news but news without context, without consequences, without value, and therefore without essential seriousness; that is to say, news as pure entertainment. 4

Consider, for example, how you would proceed if you were given the opportunity to produce a television news show for any station concerned to attract the largest possible audience. You would, first, choose a cast of players, each of whom has a face that is both "likable" and "credible." Those who apply would, in fact, submit to you their eight-by-ten glossies, from which you would eliminate those whose countenances are not suitable for nightly display. This means that you will exclude women who are not beautiful or who are over the age of fifty, men who are bald, all people who are overweight or whose noses are too long or whose eyes are too close together. You will try, in other words, to assemble a cast of talking hair-do's. At the very least, you will want those whose faces would not be unwelcome on a magazine cover. 5

Christine Craft has just such a face, and so she applied for a co-anchor position on KMBC-TV in Kansas City. According to a lawyer who represented her in a sexism suit she later brought against the station, the management of KMBC-TV "loved Christine's look." She was accordingly hired in January 1981. She was fired in August 1981 because research indicated that her appearance "hampered viewer acceptance."[1] What exactly does "hampered viewer acceptance" mean? And what does it have to do with the news? Hampered viewer acceptance means the same thing for television news as it does for any television show: Viewers do not like looking at the performer. It also means that viewers do not believe the performer, that she lacks credibility. In the case of a theatrical performance, we have a sense of what that implies: The actor does not persuade the audience that he or she is the character being portrayed. But what does lack of credibility imply in the case of a news show? What character is a co-anchor playing? And how do we decide that the 6 performance lacks verisimilitude? Does the audience believe that the newscaster is lying, that what is reported did not in fact happen, that something important is being concealed?

It is frightening to think that this may be so, that the perception of the  7 truth of a report rests heavily on the acceptability of the newscaster. In the ancient world, there was a tradition of banishing or killing the bearer of bad tidings. Does the television news show restore, in a curious form, this tradition? Do we banish those who tell us the news when we do not care for the face of the teller? Does television countermand the warnings we once received about the fallacy of the ad hominem argument?

If the answer to any of these questions is even a qualified "Yes," then  8 here is an issue worthy of the attention of epistemologists. Stated in its simplest form, it is that television provides a new (or, possibly, restores an old) definition of truth: The credibility of the teller is the ultimate test of the truth of a proposition. "Credibility" here does not refer to the past record of the teller for making statements that have survived the rigors of reality-testing. It refers only to the impression of sincerity, authenticity, vulnerability or attractiveness (choose one or more) conveyed by the actor/reporter.

This is a matter of considerable importance, for it goes beyond the  9 question of how truth is perceived on television news shows. If on television, credibility replaces reality as the decisive test of truth-telling, political leaders need not trouble themselves very much with reality provided that their performances consistently generate a sense of verisi-militude. I suspect, for example, that the dishonor that now shrouds Richard Nixon results not from the fact that he lied but that on television he looked like a liar. Which, if true, should bring no comfort to anyone, not even veteran Nixon-haters. For the alternative possibilities are that one may look like a liar but be telling the truth; or even worse, look like a truth-teller but in fact be lying.

As a producer of a television news show, you would be well aware of  10 these matters and would be careful to choose your cast on the basis of criteria used by David Merrick and other successful impresarios. Like them, you would then turn your attention to staging the show on principles that maximize entertainment value. You would, for example, select a musical theme for the show. All television news programs begin, end, and are somewhere in between punctuated with music. I have found very few Americans who regard this custom as peculiar, which fact I have taken as evidence for the dissolution of lines of demarcation between serious public discourse and entertainment. What has music to do with the news? Why is it there? It is there, I assume, for the same reason music is used in the theater and films—to create a mood and provide a leitmotif for the entertainment. If there were no music—as is the case when any television program is interrupted for a news flash—viewers would expect something truly alarming, possibly life-altering. But as long as the music is there as a frame for the program, the viewer is comforted to believe that there is nothing to be greatly alarmed about; that, in fact, the events that are reported have as much relation to reality as do scenes in a play.

This perception of a news show as a stylized dramatic performance 11 whose content has been staged largely to entertain is reinforced by several other features, including the fact that the average length of any story is forty-five seconds. While brevity does not always suggest triviality, in this case it clearly does. It is simply not possible to convey a sense of seriousness about any event if its implications are exhausted in less than one minute's time. In fact, it is quite obvious that TV news has no intention of suggesting that any story *has* any implications, for that would require viewers to continue to think about it when it is done and therefore obstruct their attending to the next story that waits panting in the wings. In any case, viewers are not provided with much opportunity to be distracted from the next story since in all likelihood it will consist of some film footage. Pictures have little difficulty in overwhelming words, and short-circuiting introspection. As a television producer, you would be certain to give both prominence and precedence to any event for which there is some sort of visual documentation. A suspected killer being brought into a police station, the angry face of a cheated consumer, a barrel going over Niagara Falls (with a person alleged to be in it), the President disembarking from a helicopter on the White House lawn—these are always fascinating or amusing, and easily satisfy the requirements of an entertaining show. It is, of course, not necessary that the visuals actually document the point of a story. Neither is it necessary to explain why such images are intruding themselves on public consciousness. Film footage justifies itself, as every television producer well knows.

It is also of considerable help in maintaining a high level of unreality 12 that the newscasters do not pause to grimace or shiver when they speak their prefaces or epilogs to the film clips. Indeed, many newscasters do not appear to grasp the meaning of what they are saying, and some hold to a fixed and ingratiating enthusiasm as they report on earthquakes, mass killings and other disasters. Viewers would be quite disconcerted by any show of concern or terror on the part of newscasters. Viewers, after all, are partners with the newscasters in the "Now . . . this" culture, and they expect the newscaster to play out his or her role as a character who is marginally serious but who stays well clear of authentic understanding. The viewers, for their part, will not be caught contaminating their responses with a sense of reality, any more than an audience at a play would go scurrying to call home because a character on stage has said that a murderer is loose in the neighborhood.

The viewers also know that no matter how grave any fragment of 13 news may appear (for example, on the day I write a Marine Corps general has declared that nuclear war between the United States and Russia is inevitable), it will shortly be followed by a series of commercials that will, in an instant, defuse the import of the news, in fact render it largely banal. This is a key element in the structure of a news program and all by itself refutes any claim that television news is designed as a serious form of public discourse. Imagine what you would think of me, and this book, if I were to pause here, tell you that I will return to my discussion in a moment, and then proceed to write a few words in behalf of United Airlines or the Chase Manhattan Bank. You would rightly think that I had no respect for you and, certainly, no respect for the subject. And if I did this not once but several times in each chapter, you would think the whole enterprise unworthy of your attention. Why, then, do we not think a news show similarly unworthy? The reason, I believe, is that whereas we expect books and even other media (such as film) to maintain a consistency of tone and a continuity of content, we have no such expectation of television, and especially television news. We have become so accustomed to its discontinuities that we are no longer struck dumb, as any sane person would be, by a newscaster who having just reported that a nuclear war is inevitable goes on to say that he will be right back after this word from Burger King; who says, in other words, "Now . . . this." One can hardly overestimate the damage that such juxtapositions do to our sense of the world as a serious place. The damage is especially massive to youthful viewers who depend so much on television for their clues as to how to respond to the world. In watching television news, they, more than any other segment of the audience, are drawn into an epistemology based on the assumption that all reports of cruelty and death are greatly exaggerated and, in any case, not to be taken seriously or responded to sanely.

I should go so far as to say that embedded in the surrealistic frame of 14 a television news show is a theory of anticommunication, featuring a type of discourse that abandons logic, reason, sequence and rules of contradiction. In aesthetics, I believe the name given to this theory is Dadaism; in philosophy, nihilism; in psychiatry, schizophrenia. In the parlance of the theater, it is known as vaudeville.

For those who think I am here guilty of hyperbole, I offer the 15 following description of television news by Robert MacNeil, executive editor and co-anchor of the "MacNeil-Lehrer Newshour." The idea, he writes, "is to keep everything brief, not to strain the attention of anyone but instead to provide constant stimulation through variety, novelty, action, and movement. You are required . . . to pay attention to no concept, no character, and no problem for more than a few seconds at a time."[2] He goes on to say that the assumptions controlling a news show are "that bite-sized is best, that complexity must be avoided, that nuances are dispensable, that qualifications impede the simple message, that visual stimulation is a substitute for thought, and that verbal precision is an anachronism."[3]

Robert MacNeil has more reason than most to give testimony about 16
the television news show as vaudeville act. The "MacNeil-Lehrer Newshour" is an unusual and gracious attempt to bring to television some of
the elements of typographic discourse. The program abjures visual
stimulation, consists largely of extended explanations of events and
in-depth interviews (which even there means only five to ten minutes),
limits the number of stories covered, and emphasizes background and
coherence. But television has exacted its price for MacNeil's rejection of
a show business format. By television's standards, the audience is
minuscule, the program is confined to public-television stations, and it is
a good guess that the combined salary of MacNeil and Lehrer is one-fifth
of Dan Rather's or Tom Brokaw's.

If you were a producer of a television news show for a commercial 17
station, you would not have the option of defying television's requirements. It would be demanded of you that you strive for the largest
possible audience, and, as a consequence and in spite of your best
intentions, you would arrive at a production very nearly resembling
MacNeil's description. Moreover, you would include some things Mac-
Neil does not mention. You would try to make celebrities of your
newscasters. You would advertise the show, both in the press and on
television itself. You would do "news briefs," to serve as an inducement
to viewers. You would have a weatherman as comic relief, and a
sportscaster whose language is a touch uncouth (as a way of his relating
to the beer-drinking common man). You would, in short, package the
whole event as any producer might who is in the entertainment business.

The result of all this is that Americans are the best entertained and 18
quite likely the least well-informed people in the Western world. I say this
in the face of the popular conceit that television, as a window to the
world, has made Americans exceedingly well informed. Much depends
here, of course, on what is meant by being informed. I will pass over the
now tiresome polls that tell us that, at any given moment, 70 percent of
our citizens do not know who is the Secretary of State or the Chief
Justice of the Supreme Court. Let us consider, instead, the case of Iran
during the drama that was called the "Iranian Hostage Crisis." I don't
suppose there has been a story in years that received more continuous
attention from television. We may assume, then, that Americans know
most of what there is to know about this unhappy event. And now, I put
these questions to you: Would it be an exaggeration to say that not one
American in a hundred knows what language the Iranians speak? Or what
the word "Ayatollah" means or implies? Or knows any details of the
tenets of Iranian religious beliefs? Or the main outlines of their political
history? Or knows who the Shah was, and where he came from?

Nonetheless, everyone had an opinion about this event, for in 19
America everyone is entitled to an opinion, and it is certainly useful to
have a few when a pollster shows up. But these are opinions of a quite

different order from eighteenth- or nineteenth-century opinions. It is probably more accurate to call them emotions rather than opinions, which would account for the fact that they change from week to week, as the pollsters tell us. What is happening here is that television is altering the meaning of "being informed" by creating a species of information that might properly be called *disinformation*. I am using this word almost in the precise sense in which it is used by spies in the CIA or KGB. Disinformation does not mean false information. It means misleading information—misplaced, irrelevant, fragmented or superficial information—information that creates the illusion of knowing something but which in fact leads one away from knowing. In saying this, I do not mean to imply that television news deliberately aims to deprive Americans of a coherent, contextual understanding of their world. I mean to say that when news is packaged as entertainment, that is the inevitable result. And in saying that the television news show entertains but does not inform, I am saying something far more serious than that we are being deprived of authentic information. I am saying we are losing our sense of what it means to be well informed. Ignorance is always correctable. But what shall we do if we take ignorance to be knowledge?

Here is a startling example of how this process bedevils us. A *New* 20 *York Times* article is headlined on February 15, 1983:

REAGAN MISSTATEMENTS GETTING LESS ATTENTION

The article begins in the following way:

> President Reagan's aides used to become visibly alarmed at suggestions that he had given mangled and perhaps misleading accounts of his policies or of current events in general. That doesn't seem to happen much anymore.
>
> Indeed, the President continues to make debatable assertions of fact but news accounts do not deal with them as extensively as they once did. In the view of White House officials, the declining news coverage mirrors a *decline in interest by the general public.* (my italics)

This report is not so much a news story as a story about the news, 21 and our recent history suggests that it is not about Ronald Reagan's charm. It is about how news is defined, and I believe the story would be quite astonishing to both civil libertarians and tyrants of an earlier time. Walter Lippmann, for example, wrote in 1920: "There can be no liberty for a community which lacks the means by which to detect lies." For all of his pessimism about the possibilities of restoring an eighteenth- and nineteenth-century level of public discourse, Lippmann assumed, as did Thomas Jefferson before him, that with a well-trained press functioning as a lie-detector, the public's interest in a President's mangling of the truth would be piqued, in both senses of that word. Given the means to detect lies, he believed, the public could not be indifferent to their consequences.

But this case refutes his assumption. The reporters who cover the 22 White House are ready and able to expose lies, and thus create the grounds for informed and indignant opinion. But apparently the public declines to take an interest. To press reports of White House dissembling, the public has replied with Queen Victoria's famous line: "We are not amused." However, here the words mean something the Queen did not have in mind. They mean that what is not amusing does not compel their attention. Perhaps if the President's lies could be demonstrated by pictures and accompanied by music the public would raise a curious eyebrow. If a movie, like *All The President's Men*, could be made from his misleading accounts of government policy, if there were a break-in of some sort or sinister characters laundering money, attention would quite likely be paid. We do well to remember that President Nixon did not begin to come undone until his lies were given a theatrical setting at the Watergate hearings. But we do not have anything like that here. Apparently, all President Reagan does is *say* things that are not entirely true. And there is nothing entertaining in that.

But there is a subtler point to be made here. Many of the President's 23 "misstatements" fall in the category of contradictions—mutually exclusive assertions that cannot possibly both, in the same context, be true. "In the same context" is the key phrase here, for it is context that defines contradiction. There is no problem in someone's remarking that he prefers oranges to apples, and also remarking that he prefers apples to oranges—not if one statement is made in the context of choosing a wallpaper design and the other in the context of selecting fruit for dessert. In such a case, we have statements that are opposites, but not contradictory. But if the statements are made in a single, continuous, and coherent context, then they are contradictions, and cannot both be true. Contradiction, in short, requires that statements and events be perceived as interrelated aspects of a continuous and coherent context. Disappear the context, or fragment it, and contradiction disappears. This point is nowhere made more clear to me than in conferences with my younger students about their writing. "Look here," I say. "In this paragraph you have said one thing. And in that you have said the opposite. Which is it to be?" They are polite, and wish to please, but they are as baffled by the question as I am by the response. "I know," they will say, "but that is *there* and this is *here*." The difference between us is that I assume "there" and "here," "now" and "then," one paragraph and the next to be connected, to be continuous, to be part of the same coherent world of thought. That is the way of typographic discourse, and typography is the universe I'm "coming from," as they say. But they are coming from a different universe of discourse altogether: the "Now . . . this" world of television. The fundamental assumption of that world is not coherence but discontinuity. And in a world of discontinuities, contradiction is useless as a test of truth or merit, because contradiction does not exist.

My point is that we are by now so thoroughly adjusted to the "Now ... this" world of news—a world of fragments, where events stand alone, stripped of any connection to the past, or to the future, or to other events—that all assumptions of coherence have vanished. And so, perforce, has contradiction. In the context of *no context,* so to speak, it simply disappears. And in its absence, what possible interest could there be in a list of what the President says *now* and what he said *then?* It is merely a rehash of old news, and there is nothing interesting or entertaining in that. The only thing to be amused about is the bafflement of reporters at the public's indifference. There is an irony in the fact that the very group that has taken the world apart should, on trying to piece it together again, be surprised that no one notices much, or cares.

For all his perspicacity, George Orwell would have been stymied by this situation; there is nothing "Orwellian" about it. The President does not have the press under his thumb. *The New York Times* and *The Washington Post* are not *Pravda;* the Associated Press is not Tass. And there is no Newspeak here. Lies have not been defined as truth nor truth as lies. All that has happened is that the public has adjusted to incoherence and been amused into indifference. Which is why Aldous Huxley would not in the least be surprised by the story. Indeed, he prophesied its coming. He believed that it is far more likely that the Western democracies will dance and dream themselves into oblivion than march into it, single file and manacled. Huxley grasped, as Orwell did not, that it is not necessary to conceal anything from a public insensible to contradiction and narcoticized by technological diversions. Although Huxley did not specify that television would be our main line to the drug, he would have no difficulty accepting Robert MacNeil's observation that "Television is the *soma* of Aldous Huxley's *Brave New World*." Big Brother turns out to be Howdy Doody.

I do not mean that the trivialization of public information is all accomplished *on* television. I mean that television is the paradigm for our conception of public information. As the printing press did in an earlier time, television has achieved the power to define the form in which news must come, and it has also defined how we shall respond to it. In presenting news to us packaged as vaudeville, television induces other media to do the same, so that the total information environment begins to mirror television.

For example, America's newest and highly successful national newspaper, *USA Today,* is modeled precisely on the format of television. It is sold on the street in receptacles that look like television sets. Its stories are uncommonly short, its design leans heavily on pictures, charts and other graphics, some of them printed in various colors. Its weather maps are a visual delight; its sports section includes enough pointless statistics to distract a computer. As a consequence, *USA Today*, which began publication in September 1982, has become the third largest daily in the United States (as of July 1984, according to the Audit Bureau of Circulations), moving quickly to overtake the *Daily News* and the *Wall Street Journal*. Journalists of a more traditional bent have criticized it for its superficiality and theatrics, but the paper's editors remain steadfast in their disregard of typographic standards. The paper's Editor-in-Chief, John Quinn, has said: "We are not up to undertaking projects of the dimensions needed to win prizes. They don't give awards for the best investigative paragraph."[4] Here is an astonishing tribute to the resonance of television's epistemology: In the age of television, the paragraph is becoming the basic unit of news in print media. Moreover, Mr. Quinn need not fret too long about being deprived of awards. As other newspapers join in the transformation, the time cannot be far off when awards will be given for the best investigative sentence.

It needs also to be noted here that new and successful magazines 28 such as *People* and *Us* are not only examples of television-oriented print media but have had an extraordinary "ricochet" effect on television itself. Whereas television taught the magazines that news is nothing but entertainment, the magazines have taught television that nothing but entertainment is news. Television programs, such as "Entertainment Tonight," turn information about entertainers and celebrities into "serious" cultural content, so that the circle begins to close: Both the form and content of news become entertainment.

Radio, of course, is the least likely medium to join in the descent into 29 a Huxleyan world of technological narcotics. It is, after all, particularly well suited to the transmission of rational, complex language. Nonetheless, and even if we disregard radio's captivation by the music industry, we appear to be left with the chilling fact that such language as radio allows us to hear is increasingly primitive, fragmented, and largely aimed at invoking visceral response; which is to say, it is the linguistic analogue to the ubiquitous rock music that is radio's principal source of income. As I write, the trend in call-in shows is for the "host" to insult callers whose language does not, in itself, go much beyond humanoid grunting. Such programs have little content, as this word used to be defined, and are merely of archeological interest in that they give us a sense of what a dialogue among Neanderthals might have been like. More to the point, the language of radio newscasts has become, under the influence of television, increasingly decontextualized and discontinuous, so that the possibility of anyone's knowing about the world, as against merely knowing *of* it, is effectively blocked. In New York City, radio station WINS entreats its listeners to "Give us twenty-two minutes and we'll give you the world." This is said without irony, and its audience, we may assume, does not regard the slogan as the conception of a disordered mind.

And so, we move rapidly into an information environment which 30 may rightly be called trivial pursuit. As the game of that names uses facts as a source of amusement, so do our sources of news. It has been demonstrated many times that a culture can survive misinformation and false opinion. It has not yet been demonstrated whether a culture can survive if it takes the measure of the world in twenty-two minutes. Or if the value of its news is determined by the number of laughs it provides.

NOTES

1. For a fairly thorough report on Ms. Craft's suit, see *The New York Times,* July 29, 1983.
2. MacNeil, p. 2.
3. MacNeil, p. 4.
4. See *Time,* July 9, 1984, p. 69.

## Post-Reading Questions

1. What is Postman's overall message? Do you think that his purpose includes convincing his readers to do something about the situation he describes? What is it that he wants you, as a television viewer and citizen, to do?
2. Do you agree with Postman that television technology and programming encourage viewers to live with and celebrate incoherence, even chaos? Why do you agree or disagree? Can you think of specific exceptions to what Postman argues is the rule of television news programming (i.e., that television programs entertain, but do *not* inform)?
3. When you watch television, do you ever find yourself doing what Postman abhors—responding more, for example, to the image, charisma, or personality of the newscaster than to the news itself? If you do, explain why. Is it the particular newscaster, the issue involved, the setting, or a combination of these elements?
4. What are the implications of Postman's emphasis on the fact that the average television news story lasts forty-five seconds? How does this fact support his overall thesis (paragraph 11)?
5. In paragraph 6, Postman describes the experience of a young news reporter, Christine Craft, who was hired and then fired for her appearance rather than her professional skills. How does this story support Postman's thesis?
6. Select an event that you recently heard reported on your local news program. Explain how the coverage of that event either supported, contradicted, or qualified Postman's thesis.

# MARK CRISPIN MILLER
# ON THE COSBY SHOW

## Pre-Reading Questions

1. How would you describe your reaction to "The Cosby Show"? Was it an accurate image of life in America? Was Cosby the perfect dad? To what qualities would you attribute its tremendous popularity? Did you find the Huxtable family to be a suitable representation of American family life in the 1980s and 1990s?

2. List several common characteristics of television situation comedies. What kinds of humor do they manifest? What situations are most typical of them? Which ones have you found most and least entertaining? What makes this type of show appealing to American audiences?

3. Consider several shows that have featured African-American stars. Were they different from "The Cosby Show" in the images they presented of African-American life in America? Or do you find similarities among these programs that feature or featured African-American stars? Define those differences and similarities.

## THE COSBY SHOW
### Mark Crispin Miller

Cosby is today's quintessential[1] TV Dad—at once the nation's best-liked   1
sitcom character and the most successful and ubiquitous of celebrity
pitchmen. Indeed, Cosby himself ascribes his huge following to his
appearances in the ads: "I think my popularity came from doing solid
30-second commercials. They can cause people to love you and see more
of you than in a full 30-minute show." Like its star, *The Cosby Show* must
owe much of its immense success to advertising, for this sitcom is
especially well attuned to the commercials, offering a full-scale confirmation of their vision. The show has its charms, which seem to set it well
apart from TV's usual crudeness; yet even these must be considered in
the context of TV's new integrity.

On the face of it, the Huxtables' milieu is as upbeat and well stocked   2
as a window display at Bloomingdale's,[2] or any of those visions of
domestic happiness that graced the billboards during the Great Depression. Everything within this spacious brownstone[3] is luminously clean

---

[1]*quintessential:* the most perfect embodiment of something; the purest form of
something.
[2]*Bloomingdale's:* an exclusive New York-based department store.
[3]*brownstone:* a multistory row house, typically built of reddish-brown stone.

and new, as if it had all been set up by the state to make a good impression on a group of visiting foreign dignitaries. Here are all the right commodities—lots of bright sportswear, plants and paintings, gorgeous bedding, plenty of copperware, portable tape players, thick carpeting, innumerable knickknacks, and, throughout the house, big, burnished dressers, tables, couches, chairs, and cabinets (Early American yet looking factory-new). Each week, the happy Huxtables nearly vanish amid the porcelain, stainless steel, mahogany, and fabric of their lives. In every scene, each character appears in some fresh designer outfit that positively glows with newness, never to be seen a second time. And, like all this pricey clutter, the plots and subplots, the dialogue and even many of the individual shots reflect in some way on consumption as a way of life: Cliff's new juicer is the subject of an entire episode; Cliff does a monologue on his son Theo's costly sweatshirt; Cliff kids daughter Rudy for wearing a dozen wooden necklaces. Each Huxtable, in fact, is hardly more than a mobile display case for his/her momentary possessions. In the show's first year, the credit sequence was a series of vivid stills presenting Cliff alongside a shiny Dodge Caravan, out of which the lesser Huxtables then emerged in shining playclothes, as if the van were their true parent, with Cliff serving as the genial midwife to this antiseptic birth. Each is routinely upstaged by what he/she eats or wears or lugs around: In a billowing blouse imprinted with gigantic blossoms, daughter Denise appears, carrying a tape player as big as a suitcase; Theo enters to get himself a can of Coke from the refrigerator, and we notice that he's wearing both a smart beige belt *and* a pair of lavender suspenders; Rudy munches cutely on a piece of pizza roughly twice the size of her own head.

As in the advertising vision, life among the Huxtables is not only well supplied, but remarkable for its surface harmony. Relations between these five pretty kids and their cute parents are rarely complicated by the slightest serious discord. Here affluence is magically undisturbed by the pressures that ordinarily enable it. Cliff and Clair, although both employed, somehow enjoy the leisure to devote themselves full-time to the trivial and comfortable concerns that loosely determine each episode: a funeral for Rudy's goldfish, a birthday surprise for Cliff, the kids' preparations for their first day of school. And daily life in this bright house is just as easy on the viewer as it is (apparently) for Cliff's dependents: *The Cosby Show* is devoid of any dramatic tension whatsoever. Nothing happens, nothing changes, there is no suspense or ambiguity or disappointment. In one episode, Cliff accepts a challenge to race once more against a runner who, years before, had beaten him at a major track meet. At the end, the race is run, and—it's a tie!

Of course, *The Cosby Show* is by no means the first sitcom to present us with a big, blissful family whose members never collide with one another, or with anything else; *Eight Is Enough, The Brady Bunch,* and *The Partridge Family* are just a few examples of earlier prime-time idylls.[4] Here are, however, some crucial differences between those older shows and this one. First of all, *The Cosby Show* is far more popular than any of its predecessors. It is (as of this writing) the top-rated show in the United States and elsewhere, attracting an audience that is not only vast, but often near fanatical in its devotion. Second, and stranger still, this show and its immense success are universally applauded as an exhilarating sign of progress. Newspaper columnists and telejournalists routinely deem *The Cosby Show* a "breakthrough" into an unprecedented *realism* because it uses none of the broad plot devices or rapid-fire gags that define the standard sitcom. Despite its fantastic ambience of calm and plenty, *The Cosby Show* is widely regarded as a rare glimpse of truth, whereas *The Brady Bunch* et al., though just as cheery, were never extolled in this way. And there is a third difference between this show and its predecessors that may help explain the new show's greater popularity and peculiar reputation for progressivism: Cliff Huxtable and his dependents are not only fabulously comfortable and mild, but also noticeably black.

Cliff's blackness serves an affirmative purpose within the ad that is 5 *The Cosby Show.* At the center of this ample tableau, Cliff is himself an ad, implicitly proclaiming the fairness of the American system: "Look!" he shows us. "Even *I* can have all this!" Cliff is clearly meant to stand for Cosby himself, whose name appears in the opening credits as "Dr. William E. Cosby, Jr., Ed.D."—a testament both to Cosby's lifelong effort at self-improvement, and to his sense of brotherhood with Cliff. And, indeed, Dr. Huxtable is merely the latest version of the same statement that Dr. Cosby has been making for years as a talk show guest and stand-up comic: "I got mine!" The comic has always been quick to raise the subject of his own success. "What do I care what some ten-thousand-dollar-a-year writer says about me?" he once asked Dick Cavett. And on *The Tonight Show* a few years ago, Cosby told of how his father, years before, had warned him that he'd never make a dime in show business, "and then he walked slowly back to the projects. . . . Well, I just lent him forty thousand dollars!"

That anecdote got a big hand, just like *The Cosby Show,* but despite 6 the many plaudits for Cosby's continuing tale of self-help, it is not quite convincing. Cliff's brownstone is too crammed, its contents too lustrous, to seem like his—or anyone's—own personal achievement. It suggests instead the corporate showcase which, in fact, it is. *The Cosby Show* attests to the power, not of Dr. Cosby/Huxtable, but of a consumer society that has produced such a tantalizing vision of reality. As Cosby himself admits,

---

[4]*idylls:* short poems or prose works depicting the pleasant simplicity of rural life; in general terms, an ideal situation.

it was not his own Algeresque[5] efforts that "caused people to love" him, but those ads put out by Coca-Cola, Ford, and General Foods—those ads in which he looks and acts precisely as he looks and acts in his own show.

Cosby's image is divided in a way that both facilitates the corporate    7 project and conceals its true character. On the face of it, the Cosby style of pure impishness. Forever mugging and cavorting, throwing mock tantrums or beaming hugely to himself or doing funny little dances with his stomach pushed out, Cosby carries on a ceaseless parody of some euphoric eight-year-old. His delivery suggests the same childish sponta-neity, for in the high, coy gabble of his harangues and monologues there is a disarming quality of baby talk. And yet all this artful goofiness barely conceals an intimidating hardness—the same uncompromising willful-ness that we learn to tolerate in actual children (however cute they may be), but which can seem a little threatening in a grown-up. And Cosby is indeed a most imposing figure, in spite of all his antics: a big man boasting of his wealth, and often handling an immense cigar.

It is a disorienting blend of affects, but it works perfectly whenever    8 he confronts us on behalf of Ford or Coca-Cola. With a massive car or Coke machine behind him, or with a calculator at his fingertips, he hunches toward us, wearing a bright sweater and an insinuating grin, and makes his playful pitch, cajoling us to buy whichever thing he's selling, his face and words, his voice and posture all suggesting this implicit and familiar come-on: "Kitchy-koo!" It is not so much that Cosby makes his mammoth bureaucratic masters seem as nice and cuddly as himself (although such a strategy is typical of corporate advertising); rather, he implicitly assures us that *we* are nice and cuddly, like little children. At once solicitous and overbearing, he personifies the corporate force that owns him. Like it, he comes across as an easygoing parent, and yet, also like it, he cannot help but betray the impulse to coerce. We see that he is bigger than we are, better known, better off, and far more powerfully sponsored. Thus, we find ourselves ambiguously courted, just like those tots who eat up lots of Jell-O pudding under his playful supervision.

Dr. Huxtable controls his family with the same enlightened devious-    9 ness. As widely lauded for its "warmth" as for its "realism," *The Cosby Show* has frequently been dubbed "the *Father Knows Best* of the eighties." Here again (the columnists agree) is a good strong Dad maintaining the old "family values." This equation, however, blurs a crucial difference between Cliff and the early fathers. Like them, Cliff always wins; but this modern Dad subverts his kids not by evincing the sort of calm power that once made Jim Anderson so daunting, but by seeming to subvert himself at the same time.[6] His is the executive style, in

---

[5] *Algeresque:* reminiscent of the writings of Horatio Alger (1834–1899), a U.S. novelist whose rags-to-riches tales of success were popular at the turn of the century.

[6] *Jim Anderson:* father's name in the early TV series *Father Knows Best.*

other words, not of the small businessman as evoked in the fifties, but of the corporate manager, skilled at keeping his subordinates in line while half concealing his authority through various disarming moves: Cliff rules the roost through teasing put-downs, clever mockery, and amiable shows of helpless bafflement. This Dad is no straightforward tyrant, then, but the playful type who strikes his children as a peach, until they realize, years later, and after lots of psychotherapy, what a subtle thug he really was.

An intrusive kidder, Cliff never fails to get his way; and yet there is 10 more to his manipulativeness than simple egomania. Obsessively, Cliff sees to it, through his takes and teasing, that his children always keep things light. As in the corporate culture and on TV generally, so on this show there is no negativity allowed. Cliff's function is therefore to police the corporate playground, always on the lookout for any downbeat tendencies.

In one episode, for instance, Denise sets herself up by reading Cliff 11 some somber verses that she's written for the school choir. The mood is despairing; the refrain, "I walk alone . . . I walk alone." It is clear that the girl does not take the effort very seriously, and yet Cliff merrily overreacts against this slight and artificial plaint as if it were a crime. First, while she recites, he wears a clownish look of deadpan bewilderment, then laughs out loud as soon as she has finished, and finally snidely moos the refrain in outright parody. The studio audience roars, and Denise takes the hint. At the end of the episode, she reappears with a new version, which she reads sweetly, blushingly, while Cliff and Clair, sitting side by side in their high-priced pajamas, beam with tenderness and pride on her act of self-correction:

> My mother and my father are my best friends.
> When I'm all alone, I don't have to be.
> It's because of me that I'm all alone, you see.
> Their love is real. . . .

> Never have they lied to me, never connived me,
> talked behind my back.
> Never have they cheated me.
> Their love is real, their love is real.

Clair, choked up, gives the girl a big warm hug, and Cliff then takes 12 her little face between his hands and kisses it, as the studio audience bursts into applause.

Thus, this episode ends with a paean[7] to the show itself (for "their 13 love" is *not* "real," but a feature of the fiction), a moment that, for all its mawkishness, attests to Cliff's managerial adeptness. Yet Cliff is hardly a

---

[7] *paean:* a poem or song of praise.

mere enforcer. He is himself also an underling, even as he seems to run things. This subservient status is manifest in his blackness. Cosby's blackness is indeed a major reason for the show's popularity, despite his frequent claims, and the journalistic consensus, that *The Cosby Show* is somehow "colorblind," simply appealing in some general "human" way. Although whitened by their status and commodities, the Huxtables are still unmistakably black. However, it would be quite inaccurate to hail their popularity as evidence of a new and rising amity between the races in America. On the contrary, *The Cosby Show* is such a hit with whites in part because whites are just as worried about blacks as they have always been—not blacks like Bill Cosby, or Lena Horne, or Eddie Murphy, but poor blacks, and the poor in general, whose existence is a well-kept secret on prime-time TV.

And yet TV betrays the very fears that it denies. In thousands of 14 high-security buildings, and in suburbs reassuringly remote from the cities' "bad neighborhoods," whites may, unconsciously, be further reassured by watching not just Cosby, but a whole set of TV shows that negate the possibility of black violence with lunatic fantasies of containment: *Diff'rent Strokes* and *Webster,* starring Gary Coleman and Emmanuel Lewis, respectively, each an overcute, miniaturized black person, each playing the adopted son of good white parents. Even the oversized and growling Mr. T, complete with Mohawk, bangles, and other primitivizing touches, is a mere comforting joke, the dangerous ex-slave turned comic and therefore innocuous by campy excess; and this behemoth too is kept in line by a casual white father, Hannibal Smith, the commander of the A-Team, who employs Mr. T exclusively for his brawn.

As a willing advertisement for the system that pays him well, Cliff 15 Huxtable also represents a threat contained. Although dark-skinned and physically imposing, he ingratiates us with his childlike mien and enviable life-style, a surrender that must offer some deep solace to a white public terrified that one day blacks might come with guns to steal the copperware, the juicer, the microwave, the VCR, even the TV itself. On *The Cosby Show,* it appears as if blacks in general can have, or do have, what many whites enjoy, and that such material equality need not entail a single break-in. And there are no hard feelings, none at all, now that the old injustice has been so easily rectified. Cosby's definitive funny face, flashed at the show's opening credits and reproduced on countless magazine covers, is a strained denial of all animosity. With its little smile, the lips pursed tight, eyes opened wide, eyebrows raised high, that dark face shines toward us like the white flag of surrender—a desperate look that no suburban TV Dad of yesteryear would ever have put on, and one that millions of Americans today find indispensable.

By and large, American whites need such reassurance because they 16 are now further removed than ever, both spatially and psychologically, from the masses of the black poor. And yet the show's appeal cannot be explained merely as a symptom of class and racial uneasiness, because there are, in our consumer culture, anxieties still more complicated and pervasive. Thus, Cliff is not just an image of the dark Other capitulating to the white establishment, but also the reflection of any constant viewer, who, whatever his/her race, must also feel like an outsider, lucky to be tolerated by the distant powers that be. There is no negativity allowed, not anywhere; and so Cliff serves both as our guide and as our double. His look of tense playfulness is more than just a sign that blacks won't hurt us; it is an expression that we too would each be wise to adopt, lest we betray some devastating sign of anger or dissatisfaction. If we stay cool and cheerful, white like him, and learn to get by with his sort of managerial acumen, we too, perhaps, can be protected from the world by a barrier of new appliances, and learn to put down others as each of us has, somehow, been put down.

Such rampant putting-down, the ridicule of all by all, is the very 17 essence of the modern sitcom. Cliff, at once the joker and a joke, infantilizing others and yet infantile himself, is exemplary of everybody's status in the sitcoms, in the ads, and in most other kinds of TV spectacle (as well as in the movies). No one, finally, is immune.

## Post-Reading Questions

1. Miller's thesis is that "The Cosby Show" is an advertisement for the products and life styles promoted by corporate America. What do you think Bill Cosby would argue in response to Miller's criticism? Is "The Cosby Show" one big advertisement for middle-class consumerism? Is it a show that successfully promotes racial understanding? Is it both?

2. Why does Crispin compare "The Cosby Show" with other family shows such as "The Brady Bunch" and "Eight is Enough" (paragraph 4)?

3. Do you agree or disagree with Miller when he argues (paragraphs 13 to 15) that Cosby's blackness actually makes this show popular with whites? Many other television critics have argued the opposite; they say that it is the show's "color blindness" that gives it its appeal to all audiences. What line of argument does Miller develop as he attempts to persuade his readers that race is at the bottom of the appeal of "The Cosby Show"?

4. Why does Miller find Cosby's career-long promotion of his own success story unconvincing (paragraph 6)? What does Miller think is really behind Cosby's success?

5. In paragraph 11, Miller discusses an episode from one show in which Cliff Huxtable's daughter Denise writes a poem. What point about the show in general and Cliff Huxtable's character in particular is Miller trying to make by discussing this episode? How does this point tie in with Miller's thesis?

6. How would you describe Mark Miller's voice in this article? What language features (vocabulary, tone, sentence structure) help create this voice? Is the voice appropriate for Miller's purpose in writing this article?

7. What is Miller's purpose in writing this article? What does he want to contribute to his readers' understanding of "The Cosby Show"? How does he want to change their understanding of the show? Why does he want to create that change?

# ERIC COPAGE ON TELEVISION HEROES

## Pre-Reading Questions

1. American movies and television have always had a "star system." Do you recall attempting to imitate the behavior of a television or film hero during your childhood? Do you think that imitation had a positive or negative effect on your character and future life? In what ways does hero worship have negative or positive effects on children?

2. Do you think successful role models from minority groups usually have positive effects on all other members of the particular minority group? Why? Why not? How do the social or economic conditions of some members of the group have a bearing on the effect of the role model?

## PRIME-TIME HEROES
### Eric Copage

No one told me that because I am black I couldn't be Superman. No one     1
told me I couldn't be Peter Gunn, the wild, wild James West or John
Drake, Secret Agent Man.

These television paladins of yesteryear came up during a recent dinner     2
conversation. A companion told me a black friend of his, roughly my age,
had felt hobbled by the lack of African-American heroes and the prevalence of negative stereotypes on television during his childhood. While I
knew that television programs could adversely affect self-esteem, I also
knew, through my own experience, that it needn't be that way. And as my
4-year-old son and 16-month-old daughter hurtle through the world, I
know I must do my best to nurture them the way I was nurtured.

When I was growing up, virtually all the main characters on TV were     3
white. But that didn't prevent me from being lost in space with Billy
Mumy or diving under the sea with Lloyd Bridges. When "I Spy"
premiered in 1965, the precedent of Bill Cosby's starring role was lost on

my 10-year-old mind. I watched because Scotty (Cosby) and Kelly (Robert Culp) were so cool that they could wisecrack in the face of death, which was the same reason I admired John Steed and Emma Peel—"The Avengers"—played by Patrick Macnee and Diana Rigg, both of whom, of course, were white.

It's not that I was oblivious to color. I remember feeling an 4 emotional dissonance between ending the pledge of allegiance at school "with liberty and justice for all," and going home to see TV news footage of blacks fire-hosed for demanding to eat and walk where ever they chose. In the integrated and white middle-class neighborhoods of Los Angeles, racial epithets had been hurled at me. Yet the racial violence seemed distant and surrealistic, and I never went home crying as a result of a racist remark.

Rather, the reality of my home was the most powerful one I had. The 5 adults in my life told me I could do anything if I was determined and resourceful. Granted, being middle-class made this easy to accept. But the people who gave me this advice had come from backgrounds that were far from middle-class. My father, for instance, grew up during the Depression in the ghettos of Chicago, yet managed to become a successful real-estate broker and never dwelt on the disadvantages dealt him. My mother, a housewife and sometime actress, grew up poor but didn't seem alienated from society.

And when, as a youngster, I'd tell my father my big plans for the 6 future—to buy the company that made Colgate toothpaste and change the name to Copage—he'd just give me a sly smile that seemed to say proudly, "That's my boy," as any middle-class father would. I was expected to be ambitious because there was an intrinsic pleasure in excelling, not because I had to prove anything to whites.

Even the Watts riots of 1965 failed to convince me that to be black 7 was to be helpless and hopeless in America. My father owned a hamburger stand in Watts as an investment, and hired local teen-agers to work at the counter. They didn't dress as I did, and they sure didn't take the music, karate and acrobatics classes children in my neighborhood routinely attended. Yet I believed that if these teenagers continued to work hard and look for opportunities, they could make better lives for themselves, as my father had for himself.

Over the next two years, however, a sense of otherness took root in 8 me. In my mostly white junior high school, I was asked whether I preferred being called Negro or black. I began hearing chants of "black is beautiful." That being black was to be somehow tragic and full of rage was played out on the TV news, where I saw black Americans talking about revolution and shooting clenched-fist salutes in the air. In the midst of this, I began to doubt myself and the values I had grown up with. I feared I might be an "Oreo."

This conflict was brought into vivid relief for me in 1968. I was 13    9
when my 6-year-old brother, Marc, was tapped to play the part of Corey
Baker in "Julia," the half-hour sitcom that starred Diahann Carroll as a
widowed nurse trying to raise her young son (my brother). Julia was
middle-class, beautiful and smart, and lived with her son in an integrated
apartment building.

Being the first series since "Beulah" in 1950 to star a black woman,   10
"Julia" received a fair amount of publicity, and more than a fair amount
of vitriol. Black activists and some white television critics said the series,
produced and written by whites, was "unrealistic" because it did not
address the black rage blazing across America's inner cities.

But for me, "Julia" was as real as television gets, no more sanitized   11
or hyperbolic than "I Love Lucy" or "The Patty Duke Show." And
besides, the show, with its black characters functioning without pathol-
ogy in a "white" world, was enough like my life to seem grounded in
reality. Were the show's critics charging that my family had forsaken our
blackness? Yes, I avidly listened to Bach and Beethoven, but to Charlie
Parker and Miles Davis as well. True, when my grandmother cooked
chitlins, I shut the kitchen door to contain the stench, but did that make
me less black?

For years after that I had a knee-jerk response to television's   12
depiction of black people and black family life: Was the "social reality"
that was not a part of "Julia" more "black"?

Still, the fact is that no black person ever complained to me about the   13
life depicted on "Julia." On the contrary, in our conversations about the
show, blacks of my acquaintance seemed proud. Certainly, I reasoned,
seeing Greg Morris as the expert technician on "Mission: Impossible" or
Denise Nicholas as a concerned and conscientious school counselor on
"Room 222" could inspire a black child to reach beyond his social
limitations.

Recognizing the power of television made me restless for further   14
change. Sidekick status was just not good enough. Why didn't James Earl
Jones play Chief Ironside and get chauffeured by some trusty white soul?
Why couldn't Captain Kirk be black? And speaking of the Enterprise,
why hadn't it ever run into black aliens?

As my friend and I walked to his bus stop after that recent dinner   15
party, we talked about how the depiction of blacks has changed over the
past 25 years. Today my children routinely see black judges, lawyers,
obstetricians and cops on "Sesame Street," "The Cosby Show" and
"Mister Rogers's Neighborhood." This is good. And with Cosby, Oprah
Winfrey and Quincy Jones, blacks are beginning to control their own
images. That is even better.

But a parent's encouragement, regardless of his or her economic or   16
social circumstance, is more powerful than any cathode-ray-tube hero.
Besides, throughout America's history, its good will toward blacks has

always come sporadically, been slow to gather force and quick to dissipate. Television has been a mirror of that. As my friend boarded the bus and waved goodbye, I thought I'd continue to teach my children what I had been taught: that they needn't see a black become President or win the Indy 500 on television before feeling they can do it in real life.

## Post-Reading Questions

1. What is the purpose behind the first paragraph of this article? To whom is it addressed? Why is the paragraph written as a series of short, declarative sentences?
2. What organizational strategy does Copage employ to give unity to his story? In answering, note the references to the party, his friend, the bus stop, and the walk from the party.
3. What is the point behind the little story that Copage tells in paragraph 6 in which he describes how his father reacted when, as a child, Copage told him that he planned to own the Colgate-Palmolive Company someday?
4. How does Copage's response to "The Cosby Show" differ from Mark Crispin Miller's (paragraph 15)? What are the reasons behind that different kind of response?
5. How do you think Eric Copage would respond to Mark Crispin Miller's assertion that "The Cosby Show" is primarily a hype for television consumerism? Would Copage argue that corporate control of television might be a good thing for the American economy and for African-American society as well?

# KIKU ADATTO ON TELEVISION AND POLITICAL CAMPAIGNS

## Pre-Reading Questions

1. Think back over the 1992 presidential campaign. From what sources did you get most of your information during that campaign? What media sources do you think offered the most useful and informative coverage?
2. What do you think it means to say that a political campaign is "managed and orchestrated to play on the evening news" (paragraph 3)? Provide some examples of such management from your own viewing experience.
3. What do you suppose Adatto's title is meant to suggest? What does it suggest to you? Since this is an article on television coverage of political campaigns, what does the emphasis on the word "shrinking"

suggest about the attitude this writer takes toward recent television coverage of political campaigns? Will the article be positive or negative?

# THE INCREDIBLE SHRINKING SOUND BITE
## Kiku Adatto

Standing before a campaign rally in Pennsylvania, the 1968 Democratic   1 vice presidential candidate, Edmund Muskie, tried to speak, but a group of antiwar protesters drowned him out. Muskie offered the hecklers a deal. He would give the platform to one of their representatives if he could then speak without interruption. Rick Brody, the students' choice, rose to the microphone where, to cheers from the crowd, he denounced the candidates that the 1968 presidential campaign had to offer. "Wallace is no answer. Nixon's no answer. And Humphrey's no answer. Sit out this election!" When Brody finished, Muskie made his case for the Democratic ticket. That night Muskie's confrontation with the demonstrators played prominently on the network news. NBC showed fifty-seven seconds of Brody's speech, and more than a minute of Muskie's.

Twenty years later, things had changed. Throughout the entire 1988   2 campaign, no network allowed either presidential candidate to speak uninterrupted on the evening news for as long as Rick Brody spoke. By 1988 television's tolerance for the languid pace of political discourse, never great, had all but vanished. An analysis of all weekday evening network newscasts (over 280) from Labor Day to Election Day in 1968 and 1988 reveals that the average "sound bite" fell from 42.3 seconds in 1968 to only 9.8 seconds in 1988. Meanwhile the time the networks devoted to visuals of the candidates, unaccompanied by their words, increased by more than 300 percent.

Since the Kennedy-Nixon debates of 1960, television has played a   3 pivotal role in presidential politics. The Nixon campaign of 1968 was the first to be managed and orchestrated to play on the evening news. With the decline of political parties and the direct appeal to voters in the primaries, presidential campaigns became more adept at conveying their messages through visual images, not only in political commercials but also in elaborately staged media events. By the time of Ronald Reagan, the actor turned president, Michael Deaver had perfected the techniques of the video presidency.

For television news, the politicians' mastery of television imagery   4 posed a temptation and a challenge. The temptation was to show the pictures. What network producer could resist the footage of Reagan at Normandy Beach, or of Bush in Boston Harbor? The challenge was to avoid being entangled in the artifice and imagery that the campaigns dispensed. In 1988 the networks tried to have it both ways—to meet the challenge even as they succumbed to the temptation. They showed the images that the campaigns produced—their commercials as well as their media events. But they also sought to retain their objectivity by exposing the artifice of the images, by calling constant attention to their self-conscious design.

The language of political reporting was filled with accounts of 5 staging and backdrops, camera angles and scripts, sound bites and spin control, photo opportunities and media gurus. So attentive was television news to the way the campaigns constructed images for television that political reporters began to sound like theater critics, reporting more on the stagecraft than the substance of politics.

When Bush kicked off his campaign with a Labor Day appearance at 6 Disneyland, the networks covered the event as a performance for television. "In the war of the Labor Day visuals," CBS's Bob Schieffer reported, "George Bush pulled out the heavy artillery. A Disneyland backdrop and lots of pictures with the Disney gang." When Bruce Morton covered Dukakis riding in a tank, the story was the image. "In the trade of politics, it's called a visual," said Morton. "The idea is pictures are symbols that tell the voter important things about the candidate. If your candidate is seen in the polls as weak on defense, put him in a tank."

And when Bush showed up at a military base to observe the 7 destruction of a missile under an arms control treaty, ABC's Brit Hume began his report by telling his viewers that they were watching a media event. "Now, here was a photo opportunity, the vice president watching a Pershing missile burn off its fuel." He went on to describe how the event was staged for television. Standing in front of an open field, Hume reported, "The Army had even gone so far as to bulldoze acres of trees to make sure the vice president and the news media had a clear view."

So familiar is the turn to theater criticism that it is difficult to recall 8 the transformation it represents. Even as they conveyed the first presidential campaign "made for television," TV reporters in 1968 continued to reflect the print journalist tradition from which they had descended. In the marriage of theater and politics, politics remained the focus of reporting. The media events of the day—mostly rallies and press conferences—were covered as political events, not as exercises in impression management.

By 1988 television displaced politics as the focus of coverage. Like a 9 gestalt shift, the images that once formed the background to political events—the setting and the stagecraft—now occupied the foreground. (Only 6 percent of reports in 1968 were devoted to theater criticism, compared with 52 percent in 1988.) And yet, for all their image-conscious coverage in 1988, reporters did not escape their entanglement. They showed the potent visuals even as they attempted to avoid the manipulation by "deconstructing" the imagery and revealing its artifice.

To be sure, theater criticism was not the only kind of political 10
reporting on network newscasts in 1988. Some notable "fact correction"
pieces offered admirable exceptions. For example, after each presidential
debate, ABC's Jim Wooten compared the candidates' claims with the
facts. Not content with the canned images of the politicians, Wooten
used television images to document discrepancies between the candidates' rhetoric and their records.

Most coverage simply exposed the contrivances of image-making. 11
But alerting the viewer to the construction of television images proved
no substitute for fact correction. A superficial "balance" replaced objectivity as the measure of fairness, a balance consisting of equal time for
media events, equal time for commercials. But this created a false
symmetry, leaving both the press and the public hostage to the play of
perceptions the campaigns dispensed.

Even the most critical versions of image-conscious coverage could 12
fail to puncture the pictures they showed. When Bush visited a flag
factory in hopes of making patriotism a campaign issue, ABC's Hume
reported that Bush was wrapping himself in the flag. "This campaign
strives to match its pictures with its points. Today and for much of the
past week, the pictures have been of George Bush with the American
flag. If the point wasn't to make an issue of patriotism, then the question
arises, what was it?" Yet only three days later, in an ABC report on
independent voters in New Jersey, the media event that Hume reported
with derision was transformed into an innocent visual of Bush. The
criticism forgotten, the image played on.

Another striking contrast between the coverage of the 1968 and 13
1988 campaigns is the increased coverage of political commercials.
Although political ads played a prominent role in the 1968 campaign,
the networks rarely showed excerpts on the news. During the entire
1968 general election campaign, the evening news programs broadcast
only two excerpts from candidates' commercials. By 1988 the number
had jumped to 125. In 1968 the only time a negative ad was mentioned
on the evening news was when CBS's Walter Cronkite and NBC's Chet
Huntley reported that a Nixon campaign ad—showing a smiling Hubert
Humphrey superimposed on scenes of war and riot—was withdrawn
after the Democrats cried foul. Neither network showed the ad itself.

The networks might argue that in 1988 political ads loomed larger in 14
the campaign, and so required more coverage. But as with their focus on
media events, reporters ran the risk of becoming conduits of the
television images the campaigns dispensed. Even with a critical narrative,
showing commercials on the news gives free time to paid media. And
most of the time the narrative was not critical. The networks rarely
bothered to correct the distortions or misstatements that the ads
contained. Of the 125 excerpts shown on the evening news in 1988, the

reporter addressed the veracity of the commercials' claims less than 8 percent of the time. The networks became, in effect, electronic billboards for the candidates, showing political commercials not only as breaking news but as stand-ins for the candidates, and file footage aired interchangeably with news footage of the candidates.

The few cases where reporters corrected the facts illustrate how the 15 networks might have covered political commercials. ABC's Richard Threlkeld ran excerpts from a Bush ad attacking Dukakis's defense stand by freezing the frame and correcting each mistaken or distorted claim. He also pointed out the exaggeration in a Dukakis ad attacking Bush's record on Social Security. CBS's Leslie Stahl corrected a deceptive statistic in Bush's revolving-door furlough ad, noting: "Part of the ad is false. . . . Two hundred sixty-eight murderers did not escape. . . . [T]he truth is only four first-degree murderers escaped while on parole."

Stahl concluded her report by observing, "Dukakis left the Bush 16 attack ads unanswered for six weeks. Today campaign aides are engaged in a round of finger-pointing at who is to blame." But the networks also let the Bush furlough commercial run without challenge or correction. Before and even after her report, CBS ran excerpts of the ad without correction. In all, network newscasts ran excerpts from the revolving-door furlough ad ten times throughout the campaign, only once correcting the deceptive statistic.

It might be argued that it is up to the candidate to reply to his 17 opponent's charges, not the press. But the networks' frequent use of political ads on the evening news created a strong disincentive for a candidate to challenge his opponent's ads. As Dukakis found, to attack a television ad as unfair or untrue is to invite the networks to run it again. In the final weeks before the election, the Dukakis campaign accused the Republicans of lying about his record on defense, and of using racist tactics in ads featuring Willie Horton, a black convict who raped and killed while on furlough from a Massachusetts prison. . . . In reporting Dukakis's complaint, all three networks ran excerpts of the ads in question, including the highly charged pictures of Horton and the revolving door of convicts. Dukakis's response thus gave Bush's potent visuals another free run on the evening news.

The networks might reply that the ads are news and thus need to be 18 shown, as long as they generate controversy in the campaign. But this rationale leaves them open to manipulation. Oddly enough, the networks were alive to this danger when confronted with the question of whether to air the videos the campaigns produced for the conventions. "I am not into tone poems," Lane Venardos, the executive producer in charge of convention coverage at CBS, told the *New York Times*. "We are not in the business of being propaganda arms of the political parties." But they seemed blind to the same danger during the campaign itself.

So successful was the Bush campaign at getting free time for its ads 19
on the evening news that, after the campaign, commercial advertisers
adopted a similar strategy. In 1989 a pharmaceutical company used
unauthorized footage of Presidents Bush and Gorbachev to advertise a
cold medication. "In the new year," the slogan ran, "may the only cold
war in the world be the one being fought by us." Although two of the
three networks refused to carry the commercial, dozens of network and
local television news programs showed excerpts of the ad, generating
millions of dollars of free airtime.

"I realized I started a trend," said Bush media consultant Roger 20
Ailes in the *New York Times.* "Now guys are out there trying to produce
commercials for the evening news." When Humphrey and Nixon hired
Madison Avenue experts to help in their campaigns, some worried that,
in the television age, presidents would be sold like products. Little did
they imagine that, twenty years later, products would be sold like
presidents.

Along with the attention to commercials and stagecraft in 1988 came 21
an unprecedented focus on the stage managers themselves, the "media
gurus," "handlers," and "spin-control artists." Only three reports
featured media advisers in 1968, compared with twenty-six in 1988. And
the numbers tell only part of the story.

The stance reporters have taken toward media advisers has changed 22
dramatically over the past twenty years. In *The Selling of the President*
(1969), Joe McGinniss exposed the growing role of media advisers with
a sense of disillusion and outrage. By 1988 television reporters covered
image-makers with deference, even admiration. In place of independent
fact correction, reporters sought out media advisers as authorities in their
own right to analyze the effectiveness and even defend the truthfulness of
campaign commercials. They became "media gurus" not only for the
candidates but for the networks as well.

For example, in an exchange with CBS anchor Dan Rather on Bush's 23
debate performance, Stahl lavished admiration on the techniques of
Bush's media advisers:

*Stahl:* "They told him not to look into the camera. [She gestures
    toward the camera as she speaks.] You know when you look directly
    into a camera you are cold, apparently they have determined."
*Rather [laughing]:* "Bad news for anchormen I'd say."
*Stahl:* "We have a lot to learn from this. Michael Dukakis kept talking
    right into the camera. [Stahl talks directly into her own camera to
    demonstrate.] And according to the Bush people that makes you
    look programmed, Dan [Stahl laughs]. And they're very adept at
    these television symbols and television imagery. And according to
    our poll it worked."

*Rather:* "Do you believe it?"
*Stahl:* "Yes, I think I do, actually."

So hypersensitive were the networks to television image-making in 1988 24
that minor mishaps—gaffes, slips of the tongue, even faulty
microphones—became big news. Politicians were hardly without mishap
in 1968, but these did not count as news. Only once in 1968 did a
network even take note of a minor incident unrelated to the content of
the campaign. In 1988 some twenty-nine reports highlighted trivial slips.

The emphasis on "failed images" reflected a kind of guerrilla warfare 25
between the networks and the campaigns. The more the campaigns
sought to control the images that appeared on the nightly news, the
more the reporters tried to beat them at their own game, magnifying a
minor mishap into a central feature of the media event.

Early in the 1988 campaign, for example, George Bush delivered a 26
speech to a sympathetic audience of the American Legion, attacking his opponent's defense policies. In a slip, he declared that September 7, rather than
December 7, was the anniversary of Pearl Harbor. Murmurs and chuckles
from the audience alerted him to his error, and he quickly corrected himself.

The audience was forgiving, but the networks were not. All three 27
network anchors highlighted the slip on the evening news. Dan Rather
introduced CBS's report on Bush by declaring solemnly, "Bush's talk to
audiences in Louisville was overshadowed by a strange happening." On
NBC Tom Brokaw reported, "He departed from his prepared script and
left his listeners mystified." Peter Jennings introduced ABC's report by
mentioning Bush's attack on Dukakis, adding, "What's more likely to be
remembered about today's speech is a slip of the tongue."

Some of the slips the networks highlighted in 1988 were not even 28
verbal gaffes or misstatements, but simply failures on the part of
candidates to cater to the cameras. In a report on the travails of the
Dukakis campaign, Sam Donaldson seized on Dukakis's failure to play to
ABC's television camera as evidence of his campaign's ineffectiveness.
Showing Dukakis playing a trumpet with a local marching band, Donaldson chided, "He played the trumpet with his back to the camera." As
Dukakis played "Happy Days Are Here Again," Donaldson's voice was
heard from off-camera calling, "We're over here, governor."

One way of understanding the turn to image-conscious coverage in 29
1988 is to see how television news came to partake of the postwar
modernist sensibility, particularly the pop art movement of the 1960s.
Characteristic of this outlook is a self-conscious attention to art as
performance, a focus on the process of image-making rather than on the
ideas the images represent.

During the 1960s, when photography and television became potent 30
forces for documentation and entertainment, they also became powerful

influences on the work of artists. Photographers began to photograph the television set as part of the social landscape. Newspapers, photographs, and commercial products became part of the collage work of painters such as Robert Rauschenberg. Artists began to explore self-consciously their role in the image-making process.

For example, Lee Friedlander published a book of photography, *Self* 31 *Portrait,* in which the artist's shadow or reflection was included in every frame. As critic Rod Slemmons notes, "By indicating the photographer is also a performer whose hand is impossible to hide, Friedlander set a precedent for disrupting the normal rules of photography." These "postmodernist" movements in art and photography foreshadowed the form television news would take by the late 1980s.

Andy Warhol once remarked, "The artificial fascinates me." In 1988 32 network reporters and producers, beguiled by the artifice of the modern presidential campaign, might well have said the same. Reporters alternated between reporting campaign images as if they were facts and exposing their contrived nature. Like Warhol, whose personality was always a presence in his work, reporters became part of the campaign theater they covered—as producers, as performers, and as critics. Like Warhol's reproductions of Campbell's soup cans, the networks' use of candidates' commercials directed our attention away from the content and toward the packaging.

The assumption that the creation of appearances is the essence of po- 33 litical reality pervaded not only the reporting but the candidates' self-understanding and conduct with the press. When Dan Quayle sought to escape his image as a highly managed candidate, he resolved publicly to become his own handler, his own "spin doctor." "The so-called handlers story, part of it's true," he confessed to network reporters. "But there will be no more handlers stories, because I'm the handler and I'll do the spinning." Surrounded by a group of reporters on his campaign plane, Quayle announced, "I'm Doctor Spin, and I want you all to report that."

It may seem a strange way for a politician to talk, but not so strange 34 in a media-conscious environment in which authenticity means being master of your own artificiality. Dukakis too sought to reverse his political fortunes by seeking to be master of his own image. This attempt was best captured in a commercial shown on network news in which Dukakis stood beside a television set and snapped off a Bush commercial attacking his stand on defense. "I'm fed up with it," Dukakis declared. "Never seen anything like it in twenty-five years of public life. George Bush's negative television ads, distorting my record, full of lies, and he knows it." The commercial itself shows an image of an image—a Bush television commercial showing (and ridiculing) the media event where Dukakis rode in a tank. In his commercial, Dukakis complains that

Bush's commercial showing the tank ride misstates Dukakis's position on defense.

As it appeared in excerpts on the evening news, Dukakis's commer- 35 cial displayed a quintessentially modernist image of artifice upon artifice upon artifice: television news covering a Dukakis commercial containing a Bush commercial containing a Dukakis media event. In a political world governed by images of images, it seemed almost natural that the authority of the candidate be depicted by his ability to turn off the television set.

In the 1950s Edward R. Murrow noted that broadcast news was "an 36 incompatible combination of show business, advertising, and news." Still, in its first decades television news continued to reflect a sharp distinction between the news and entertainment divisions of the networks. But by the 1980s network news operations came to be seen as profit centers for the large corporations that owned them, run by people drawn less from journalism than from advertising and entertainment backgrounds. Commercialization led to further emphasis on entertainment values, which heightened the need for dramatic visuals, fast pacing, quick cutting, and short sound bites. Given new technological means to achieve these effects—portable video cameras, satellite hookups, and sophisticated video-editing equipment—the networks were not only disposed but equipped to capture the staged media events of the campaigns.

The search for dramatic visuals and the premium placed on show- 37 manship in the 1980s led to a new complicity between the White House image-makers and the networks. As Susan Zirinsky, a top CBS producer, acknowledged in Martin Schram's *The Great American Video Game*, "In a funny way, the [Reagan White House] advance men and I have the same thing at heart—we want the piece to look as good as [it] possibly can." In 1968 such complicity in stagecraft was scorned. Sanford Socolow, senior producer of the *CBS Evening News with Walter Cronkite*, recently observed, "If someone caught you doing that in 1968 you would have been fired."

In a moment of reflection in 1988, CBS's political correspondents 38 expressed their frustration with image-driven campaigns. "It may seem frivolous, even silly at times," said Schieffer. "But setting up pictures that drive home a message has become the number one priority of the modern-day campaign. The problem, of course, is while it is often entertaining, it is seldom enlightening."

Rather shared his colleague's discomfort. But what troubled him 39 about modern campaigns is equally troubling about television's campaign coverage. "With all this emphasis on the image," he asked, "what happens to the issues? What happens to the substance?"

## Post-Reading Questions

1. Why does Adatto begin her article with the Edmund Muskie anecdote? What point does this anecdote drive home about the 1968 campaign? How is that point related to Adatto's thesis?
2. In paragraphs 4 and 5, Adatto points out that network news coverage of the 1988 presidential campaign included an odd mixture of media criticism of the selling of presidential candidates and commercial hype of candidates. What does Adatto suggest caused this odd combination?
3. What is "fact correction" (paragraph 10) as practiced by the network news commentators during a political campaign? Why would Adatto argue that fact correction is the only kind of attention political commercials should get on television news programs?
4. What alternatives to network coverage of political campaigns do viewers have? What other types of media can provide political campaign coverage? In what ways are those media inferior or superior to television?
5. What persona does Adatto project in this essay? Does that persona seem sufficiently sincere or honest to be effective in the context of this essay? What is Adatto's underlying purpose in writing this essay? Does she want to encourage action on the part of readers, or is she looking only for a concerned response along with the realization in readers of how a political campaign *is* conducted?
6. What about this essay convinces you that the author has done a great deal of research? Does this fact make you more receptive to the author's argument?
7. What point is Adatto trying to make when she relates contemporary philosophy to current television political commercials (paragraphs 29 to 32)? Summarize that point and provide your own example from television news programming to support your summary. What part does the idea of visual "surfaces" or "appearances" play in Adatto's post-modernist point?
8. How are earlier television news personalities such as Edward R. Murrow and Walter Cronkite different from today's news anchor persons (paragraphs 13 and 36)? Answer this question simply by analyzing Adatto's references to them in this essay.

# KIMBERLY K. MASSEY AND STANLEY J. BARAN ON VCRs AND LEISURE

## Pre-Reading Questions

1. How has the VCR changed your use of leisure time? Do you watch more movies at home because of the VCR? How much taping of television programs do you do? Have you changed your leisure

schedule because you can tape shows and watch them when you choose? Have you changed the type of shows that you watch because of the VCR?

2.  Do you think that the question of how to spend leisure time should get more or less attention now than it has in the past? What reasons do you have for your answer to this question?

# VCRs AND PEOPLE'S CONTROL OF THEIR LEISURE TIME

Kimberly K. Massey

Stanley J. Baran

Between the end of 1987 and 1988, scientists added one second to the world's clock. It wasn't enough. "I'd like to but I don't have the time" is rapidly replacing "have a good day" as the signature line of the later 80's. In addition, stress has taken the place of paranoia as the mental affliction of the generation.

—Richard (1988)

Time seems to be on everybody's mind. As work becomes less industrial 1 and more service-oriented, it tends to revolve around time—meetings and deadlines are the order of the business day. Travel arrangements must now be made at least 30 days in advance to get the best prices. FAX machines and overnight mail services have done away with lag time (the safety cushion of the tardy) between project completion and actual delivery. Time must be planned and facilities reserved for health and recreational leisure activities such as golf and racquetball. Even sleep is structured into our busy days. Today, mastery of scheduling has become necessary to keep pace in the rat race.

Adhering to the rule of supply and demand, the American people are 2 willing to pay—and pay dearly—to get and save time. Leisure time has become an almost priceless commodity. "Time could end up being to the '90s what money was to the '80s" (Gibbs, 1989, p. 58). Savvy business minds hoping to capitalize on the time drought have invented numerous ways to help the public ease the crunch. Services can be hired to do the shopping for us out of a catalogue, pick up our dry cleaning, or cater dinner for us and our friends. Greeting cards written specifically for children with slogans varying from "Wish I were there to tuck you in" to "I will miss you today" are being marketed for busy parents to compensate for those lost "precious moments." Three-minute microwave entrees have replaced what we formerly thought of as time-saving 30-minute TV dinners and our automobiles have become offices away from work complete with telephones, lap-top computers and portable FAX machines.

Americans are running out of time, or so it seems. According to     3
Nancy Gibbs (1989), a poll for *Time* and CNN conducted by Yankelovich Clancy Schulman described this sense of "not having enough time"
as being "especially acute among women in two-income families [an
estimated 57% of American households are two-income]: 73% of the
women complain of having too little leisure, as do 51% of the men"
(p. 61). Gibbs also assured us that the pressure we feel from the clock is
certainly not a figment of our imaginations. She wrote:

> According to a Louis Harris Survey, the amount of leisure time enjoyed by
> the average American has shrunk 37% since 1973 [from 16.6 hours per week
> to 9.6]. Over the same period, the average workweek, including commut-
> ing, has jumped from under 41 hours to nearly 47 hours. In some
> professions, predictably law, finance and medicine, the demands often
> stretch to 80-plus hours a week. Vacations have shortened to the point
> where they are frequently no more than long weekends. And the Sabbath is
> for—what else? shopping. (p. 59)

John Robinson, Director of the Americans' Use of Time Project,     4
disagreed, at least in part. He wrote:

> Americans have more free time today than ever before. Men have 40 hours
> of free time a week, and women have 39 hours. Free time is defined as
> what's left over after subtracting the time people spend working and
> commuting to work, taking care of their families, doing housework,
> shopping, sleeping, eating and doing other personal care activities. (1989,
> p. 34)

In his analysis, this free time includes such activities as adult schooling,
club and other organizational activities, sports, recreation and hobby
activities, reading, visiting friends and relatives, and watching television.
And although his data indicate that the "40-hour work week is balanced
by a 40-hour play week," he conceded that many of us are under a real
time crunch. Working parents are especially beleaguered and the "baby
boomers," those between the ages of 36 and 50, have proportionately
less free time than do other age categories.

Leisure time may or may not be hard to come by, but it is difficult to     5
define and even harder to measure. In fact, the discrepancies between the
Harris results on which Gibbs reported and the Robinson analysis may be
due in part to method (survey vs. diary) and, in part, due to definition.
Robinson (personal communication, July 13, 1989) himself has substituted the term "free time" for the word "leisure" in his research. In his
seminal 1969 work on "television and leisure time" (reporting on 1965
data), for example, he defined leisure as "all daily activities outside of
work, housework, child care, shopping, sleep, and other personal care"

(p. 271). In 1981, when he wrote on his 1975 replication of that work, he still used the word "leisure" and employed "the same coding procedures for activities ... in both studies" (p. 123). This older, twice-utilized definition varies very little from that employed in his 1989 work. Why, then, the shift to "free time"? Because so much of our free (nonwork, nonmaintenance) time is filled with so many options and activities, and these options and activities have become so crucial to our mental and physical health as well as to our conceptions of ourselves that free-time often hardly seems like leisure time. Quoted in Gibbs (1989, p. 59), Robinson said, "People's schedules are more ambitious. There just isn't enough time to fit in all the things one feels have to be done." Adult schooling, for example, may consume free time, but if taken seriously, it may not be very leisurely.

Rojek (1985) used the adage that what is "work for some is leisure for others" to discuss the problems social scientists have had in defining the field, yet the majority of observers choose to equate leisure and free time. Recognizing that a precise definition of leisure time is needed for operationalization in research, he ultimately adopted Vickerman's rendition of leisure (and so do we in this chapter): "take leisure time to be roughly equivalent to free time; that time left over after meeting commitments to work and such essential human capital maintenance as sleeping, eating, and personal hygiene" (p. 14).

## LEISURE AS A CONCEPT

The concept of leisure did not receive much scientific attention until soon after the Second World War. Since that time a number of factors have combined to increase the importance and the amount of leisure time available to individuals and to create new options for filling that free time:

1. Industrialization, urbanization, and automation have caused a "natural shift" from a work-centered to a leisure-centered life.
2. The public experienced a growth in disposable income. This is especially true for younger people.
3. More employers began experimenting with 4-day work weeks and computerization.
4. In 1971 a Federal law shifted 5 midweek holidays to positions adjacent to weekends, providing a set of 4-day weeks for a majority of the U.S. work force.
5. Improved pension plans have allowed for earlier retirements.
6. Advances in science have resulted in longer life spans.
7. The scale and range of leisure goods and services have expanded.

8. Women are doing less housework than they did in "pre-appliance" days and before they were successful in enlightening their male domestic partners to the merits of labor sharing at home.
9. Fewer households have children (freeing people from the time demands of child care), and couples are marrying later, therefore spending more of their lives unmarried; single people have more free time than do married folks. (See Harvey & Rothe, 1985; Nayman, Atkins, & Gillette, 1973; Robinson, 1989; Rojek, 1985; Tinsley, Barrett, & Kass, 1977 for details.)

Although the contemporary time crunch that many of us feel may  8 make it hard to believe, these events, most related to war-driven or war-accelerated alterations in our culture, technology, and demographics, produced a sudden and unprecedented burst of leisure time and, as a result, scientific interest. Social scientists began to focus on the "progressive" phenomenon of leisure, often considering it "real evidence of free choice and personal liberty in the western democracies" (Rojek, 1985, p. 2). Researchers (e.g., Tinsley et al., 1977) began to connect leisure activity choice with an individual's satisfaction predicting that, "as leisure time increases, the life satisfaction of an individual will become increasingly dependent upon the extent to which that person is able to select leisure activities which fulfill his or her needs" (p. 111).

## TELEVISION AND LEISURE

The changes in America just enumerated occurred simultaneously with a  9 significant change in the American media environment—namely, the widespread introduction and diffusion of television.

When the Television Freeze of 1948 was lifted in 1952, there were  10 fewer than 250,000 television receivers in the United States. By 1960, a mere 8 years later, 80% of all American homes had at least one set (Baran, McIntyre, & Meyer, 1984). Because the network structure, recognizable and popular stars, and means of economic support were transferred wholesale from radio to the infant medium, people almost instantly found themselves with a new and improved method of enjoying the leisure-time bonanza. Examining the steady rise in Nielsen viewing figures, which ultimately reached and have remained constant for the last several years at approximately 7 hours a day for an average household, there can be little doubt that television viewing did in fact become a common leisure pastime.

Robinson (1969) identified this phenomenon by writing,  11

Television has had a massive impact on American daily life, responsible for a greater rearrangement of time usage than the automobile. Furthermore, the time now devoted to television is of such magnitude that it has apparently not only usurped time previously devoted to other mass media, but has eaten into substantial portions of time previously spent in other forms of leisure. (p. 211)

His analysis of the 1965 diaries indicated that "over the whole population close to 28% of all leisure time appears to be spent primarily watching television" (p. 213).

In reporting on the 1975 diaries, Robinson (1981) argued that 12 several factors should have suggested no or limited increases in the amount of leisure devoted to television. In the span between his two investigations, the number of hours devoted to the average work week failed to decline; so the amount of available nonleisure time remained static. More women entered the workforce, leaving them less time for viewing. The adult population became better educated, and a higher level of education was the single best predictor of smaller amounts of television consumption at that time. Personal income and, therefore, the number of other leisure-time options grew. Increased movement of the population to the Sun Belt meant that more people had additional outside-the-home leisure options. The country's romance with "expressive personal growth activities" would have suggested less attention to the passive, unimaginative activity of television viewing. Finally, the novelty of television may well have declined in those 10 early years of the medium's life. So, of course, he found significant increases in the amount of leisure time devoted to viewing across all demographic groups in the country. In fact, television viewing now accounted for 40% of all leisure-time activity. He attributed the increase to two factors: (a) improvements in programming content due to the programmers' and advertisers' desire to reach the better educated and heavier spending people in their audiences; and (b) improvements in technology, specifically color television and cable.


## VIDEOCASSETTE RECORDERS AND LEISURE

Now, another technology, the VCR, has entered into our leisure-time 13 equations. It not only occupies and enriches individuals' free time, but it has directly affected another leisure habit—television viewing. Concentrating on the nature and capabilities of VCR technology alone, however, may be a wasted exercise when striving for an understanding of its impact on leisure. Instead, following the advice of Marvin (1988), we should leave behind the traditional notions that new technologies fashion new audiences out of "voiceless collectives and inspire them to new uses based on novel technological properties." Rather, she suggested that emerging technologies provide a new stage for existing groups to "negotiate power, authority, representation, and knowledge with whatever resources are available" (p. 7).

When applying these ideas more specifically to media technology she  14
continued,

> Media are not fixed natural objects; they have no natural edges. They are
> constructed complexes of habits, beliefs, and procedures embedded in
> elaborate cultural codes of communication. The history of media is never
> more or less than the history of their uses, which always lead us away from
> them to the social practices and conflicts they illuminate. New media,
> broadly understood to include the use of new communication technology
> for old or new purposes, new ways of using old technologies [what VCRs do
> to television] and, in principle, all other possibilities for the exchange of
> social meaning, are always introduced into a pattern of tension created by
> the coexistence of old and new, which is far richer than any single medium
> that becomes a focus of interest because it is novel. (p. 8)

In the case of the VCR, she might argue, a most valuable means of  15
understanding its impact is to examine this technology's alterations in
how we use television and how that use has affected various aspects of
our environment. Leisure is one of those aspects. Although not speaking
exclusively of the VCR, Hornik and Schlinger (1981) labeled this more
holistic view as the analysis of "the consumption of the media situation."
That is, media technologies interacting with one another and, in combination, with the consumption environment.

From its inception, broadcasting's critics predicted that the video-  16
tape recorder would one day accompany television sets in every living
room, creating Marvin's hypothetical "new audiences." DeLuca, for
example, proposed that this accomplishment "would free viewers from
their total reliance on broadcasting and in particular on the dominant
commercial networks with their monotonous mass-taste programming"
because economically "a network could not consider programming for a
prospective audience of say 100,000 people nationwide, a producer of
prerecorded video tapes could reap a bonanza from a single program that
sold 100,000 copies" (DeLuca, 1980, p. 85). In other words, the VCR
was to become a new medium with new audiences.

On the other hand, broadcasters were initially unconcerned about  17
the use of VCRs. They did not care *when* people watched their shows as
long as they *did* watch them. In other words, *when* audiences watched
might change a bit, but not *what* and *how* they watched. Marvin would
say they underestimated the "pattern of tension" created by the coexistence of the old and new; both industry insiders and critics were wrong.

Critics, broadcasters, theater owners, film producers, and commercial  18
sponsors are now all paying close attention to what people are doing with
their VCRs, because even though the VCR was initially conceived of as a

complement to the television set, the *way* in which people are using the VCR in their viewing is changing their leisure and therefore, the television industry that for so long has prospered by successfully filling that free time. In Marvin's parlance, the VCR *and* television set form a new leisure use technology "which is far richer" than the old (television) or the new (VCR) taken alone.

The "power and authority" granted to television viewers by the VCR [19] that impact free time most obviously include:

1. *Zapping,* where viewers edit out commercials while recording programs with their remote controls and *zipping,* where viewers scan through the advertisements on taped programs at high speeds. Both grant viewers more control over how they spend their leisure time and it increases the available amount of that time. Video industry data indicate that nearly half the households that have a remote engage in this "video grazing."

2. *Time-shifting,* where television programs are recorded off-channel on the VCR, permitting viewers to watch programs when it is most convenient (more control over leisure), resolving programming conflicts (more enjoyable leisure) and allowing previewing of programs for video libraries or for children's consumption (more rewarding use of leisure). Moreover, Nielsen figures indicate that 67% of all off-station taping is devoted to television network fare, suggesting audience "prioritizing" of leisure-time viewing. Their data also show that 50% of all home taping occurs while the television set is turned off, strongly indicating that the audience is doing something other than viewing at the time; that is, in many cases they are prioritizing their leisure activities (Nielsen Media Research, 1988).

3. Establishing a controlled environment for children. VCRs provide parents an opportunity to influence the viewing behavior of their children. The controversy over advertising to children, for example, is well documented. By "playing prerecorded programs or programs recorded by the parent (with commercials deleted) [parents can] shelter children from advertising messages" (Harvey & Rothe, 1985, p. 20). However, other studies of parents and children indicate that children do not perceive the same amount of control that parents claim, and that parents often use the VCR as just more TV (see Kim, Baran, & Massey, 1988).

4. Increasing the amount of noncommercial television viewing. Viewers can now accumulate tape libraries and rent prerecorded tapes, permitting them to watch more noncommercial television. This not only allows for greater personal discretion in how free time is spent, but many critics argue that the result is an

improvement of commercial television programming as the networks strain to compete with various other VCR program
options. This echoes Robinson's (1981) argument that broadcasters maintained and even expanded the amount of viewing
between the years of 1965 and 1975 through improved programming even though many factors would seem to have
encouraged lower amounts of television consumption.

5. Faster viewing of programs. The fast-forward mechanism permits
viewers to prerecord material and view it in a condensed time
frame, allowing for more leisure. This is especially true in watching sporting events where time-outs, commercials, delays, half
times and poor plays may be viewed on fast forward. This allows
the sports fan to watch an entire football game in 30 minutes or
a hockey match in 15 minutes (see Harvey & Rothe, 1985).

## TAKING CONTROL

Instead of slouching in front of the screen, passing time, viewers are now 20
participants in the creation of the television viewing experience. People
are watching exactly what they want to watch. A wide variety of
prerecorded material is available from which to choose, such as video
cookbooks; astrology; nutrition and exercise; speech excerpts from
Kennedy, Churchill, and King; "how-to" or "self-help" programs; and
so forth (see McCullaugh, 1985). In addition, as Vale writes, people are
also participating in the "screening of America" by videotaping their
own weddings, birthdays, athletic events, and so on.

Collins (1988) provided reactions to the "active viewer" from some 21
of the more prominent names in the video industry when he quoted Ted
Turner (whose cable channels helped shape the new viewing environment) as saying, "Unquestionably, viewers have more power and control,
because they have more choices." Programming innovator Fred Silverman agreed that "viewers seem to be more and more active" (p. 13).
Researchers are also involved in observation of the viewing activity
phenomenon. Mark Levy (1983) talked about VCRs "creating a new age
for mass communication, an era in which mass media audiences have
more message choices, greater involvement with the media and increased
control over the timing and general experience of exposure" (p. 265).

There are only so many hours in a week, and only so many of them 22
represent free time, and only so much free time is spent in front of a set,
so how are broadcasters reacting to the newly empowered viewer? They
are inventing new ways in which to capture and keep their attention. The
most obvious approach is in the improvement of commercial programming. But according to Collins (1988), a variety of other innovations

have also been introduced to curb what the commercial broadcasters call "destructive" viewing activities. "One requires the TV networks to present trivia questions or puzzles before the first commercial in the pod is aired and then present the answers at the end of the pod" (p. 13). "Pods" are seen as a way to curb zapping and zipping. The idea proposes that people will "stay tuned" and watch all of the commercials in between the mini-questions or presentations. A common example of a pod would be the sports-oriented, "You Make the Call." Other approaches touted by the Association of National Advertisers include the following: prize games to guarantee viewer participation during commercial breaks, such as a sweepstakes based on Social Security numbers; using a split-screen technique to run commercials while programming continues with little or no sound and action; presenting a bingo-type game using the advertised products instead of number called TV WINGO; or, grouping compatible commercials within the same pod, such as a wine commercial with a cheese commercial ("Making the call on pods," 1986).

Interactive television may be another way to recapture lost viewers, 23 and not only with home shopping shows. The commercial, over-the-air broadcasters are trying interactive children's games, and, as in the case of the February 16, 1989 episode of "Matlock" on NBC, interactive drama where viewers were invited to phone in and vote on who was the murderer. Simply put, as audience control over leisure viewing has changed, so too has the broadcast industry as it attempts to maintain its share of that free time.

The leisure-time activity of going to the movies has also been 24 affected by the VCR. Observers such as Seideman (1986) and Robbins (1985) claimed the film industry is suffering due to VCR usage. Seideman quoted Market Facts Inc., saying "home video is rapidly becoming the leading medium through which Americans watch feature films. At least 40% of feature-film viewing is done with VCRs" (p. 39). Robbins agreed, stating that "after the first two years of box office revenues climbing despite VCR sales, now box office revenue is down while VCR sales are up" (p. 23). Others disagree, saying "VCRs were originally feared as a threat to the American film industry, but movie house attendance in the U.S. has actually been stimulated by the VCR, in much the same fashion as Music Television (MTV) fuels the sale of rock records and videos" (Howell, 1986, p. 291). Some grist for this debate can be found in a survey conducted by the Motion Picture Association of America that discovered a 56% increase in movie attendance from 1986 to 1987 by people over 40 years old. Denby (1988) attributed this surge to the VCR-created "appetite for seeing movies where they belong, in their home, their temple and universe, the movie theatre" (p. 39).

## VCRs, CHOICES, AND LIFE SATISFACTION

The relationship between television and leisure time was straightforward 25 and obvious. World War II industrialized and urbanized America, so the work day and work week were no longer bound by the sun and seasons, but by the clock. Americans then had more time for leisure pursuits. In addition, as people left the farms to work in the employ of others, they had less need to put their earnings back into their livelihoods, freeing greater amounts of money for leisure. The newly emerged yet technologically, programmatically, economically, and organizationally mature medium of television could be afforded by those who had time in need of filling and its entrenchment was assured by advertisers of consumer goods seeking to entice people to send their newly available discretionary dollars their way, making possible greater amounts of attractive programming.

Television, then, logically became a perfect free time filler; but, in 26 part because of people's relative lack of control over its content and scheduling, it was seen as just that. After analyzing the 1965 leisure time data, Robinson (1969) wrote,

> Perhaps few viewers consciously plan their TV evenings ahead of time by marking off those programs in *TV Guide* which look most appealing. Rather, if the weather is unaccommodating, if one can find nothing better to do, if one is looking for an hour or two of relaxation after a hectic day at work or with the children, if one is waiting for friends to call . . . what better noninvolving activity is there than an innocuous TV program that may be tuned in at any time? (p. 218)

In his examination 10 years later he asked his respondents to rate how much they "liked or disliked participating in various obligatory and free-time activities, on a scale running from 0 (dislike a great deal) to 10 (like a great deal)." He discovered that "while the average score of 6.1 for TV viewing did fall on the positive side of the scale, it was well below the scores of almost all other free-time activities." He concluded, "These data make it hard to conclude that by increasing their viewing, the public had enhanced the subjective quality of their leisure time or their lives in general" (Robinson, 1981, p. 129).

The relationship between VCRs and leisure, however, does suggest 27 that this subjective quality of leisure has been enhanced by the introduction of that technology and its use with home television receivers. Harvey and Rothe (1985) offered, "Not since the advent of the television set has any home electronic device began to make such a profound impact on the way Americans spend their leisure-time hours than videocassette recorders" (p. 19). Howell (1986) wrote, "Home video technology decreases the transience of television broadcasts and shifts much of the control over choice of programming and viewing time from the broadcaster to the user of the TV receiver" (p. 286).

Remembering Tinsley et al.'s (1977) linking of the amount of choice 28 and selection within leisure time with individuals' life satisfaction, it is easy to argue that VCR is more than a free-time filler; it is free time, and therefore life-quality enhancer.

Where television helped fill free time, the VCR shifts the locus of 29 control over much of our free time to us. This is an important function given either perspective on the amount of leisure available to Americans. If we have less time, the VCR allows us to make more efficient and personally meaningful use of what we have. If we have more, but it is harried by too many choices or too much to do, then it allows greater control. In either case, the VCR empowers viewers, affording them greater control over and choices within their free time, and possibly enhancing their life satisfaction.

Chicago *Sun Times* columnist Judy Markey made this point in a 30 somewhat tongue-in-cheek manner. She wrote,

> When VCRs came out, we crossed over some sort of ethical edge. Because suddenly it was actually possible to be out until midnight eating sushi and still see "thirtysomething." I mean it used to be that acts (eating sushi) had consequences (missing "thirtysomething"). But suddenly what happened was that acts (eating sushi) had second acts ("thirtysomething" on tape at midnight). (1988, p. B-2)

Instead of simply filling available leisure time (as did television) or 31 providing more attractive viewing options for today's shrinking amounts of leisure time (as was predicted for it), the VCR has put us ultimately in charge of the quantity *and* quality of a good deal of our leisure time. Moreover, there is every indication that the VCR will become even more central to our control of that free time. The technology is being improved constantly, assuring even easier and more enjoyable use and, therefore, increased options and satisfaction. Super VHS tape machines (SVHS) were introduced in 1988 by Japan Victor Corporation, utilizing 420 lines of horizontal resolution rather than the traditional 330 lines. This provides a dramatically clearer picture. Two-deck machines are now available, making possible home cassette-to-cassette dubbing and off-station taping while viewing tapes. In November 1989, ABC and machine manufacturers began experimenting with bar-code program-ming, invented by Panasonic in 1987. The network inserts a bar-code in its *TV Guide* ads, and viewers need only pass a reading wand over it to automatically program their VCRs to tape the specific program they want, making time-shifting even more common (Atkinson, 1989).

Enriching viewers' leisure options even further, the broadcasters, rat- 32 ings organizations, and advertisers are all working to better understand audience needs, wants, and viewing patterns. Presumably programming will more closely follow viewer demands and expectations, providing us with even more attractive options and choices.

It seems clear that the VCR has already affected the ways in which ₃₃ Americans are spending their leisure time. But what will this mean for leisure-time patterns of the future? What will it mean if people are spending more time at home, or spending more time watching programs on the VCR with family members or friends? Will American leisure-time patterns differ from those in other countries, and to what extent might this be correlated with patterns of VCR penetration? What will become of other traditional leisure-time activities if we spend more of what little free time we have with the VCR? These and other questions need to be investigated as VCRs are found in more homes throughout the world.

REFERENCES

Atkinson, T. (1989, July 12). VCR programming: Making life easier using bar-codes. *Los Angeles Times*, VI, p. 1.

Baran, S. J., McIntyre, J. S., & Meyer, T. P. (1984). *Self, symbols and society.* Reading, MA: Addison Wesley.

Collins, G. (1988, March 20). For many, a vast wasteland has become a brave new world. *New York Times*, p. 13.

DeLuca, S. M. (1980). *Television's transformation: The next 25 years.* San Diego: A. S. Barnes.

Denby, D. (1988, June 6). Fatal attraction: The VCR and the movies. *New York*, pp. 28–39.

Gibbs, N. (1989, April). How America has run out of time. *Time*, pp. 58–67.

Harvey, M., & Rothe, J. T. (1985). Video cassette recorders: Their impact on viewers and advertisers. *Journal of Advertising Research, 25*, 19–27.

Hornik, J., & Schlinger, M. J. (1981). Allocation of time to the mass media. *Journal of Consumer Research, 7*(4), 343–355.

Howell, W. J. (1986). *World broadcasting in the age of the satellite.* Norwood, NJ: Ablex.

Kim, W. Y., Baran, S. J., & Massey, K. K. (1988). Impact of the VCR on control of television viewing. *Journal of Broadcasting and Electronic Media, 32*(3), 351–358.

Levy, M. R. (1983). The time-shifting use of home video recorders. *Journal of Broadcasting, 27*(3), 263–268.

Making the call on pods. (1986, March 24). *Advertising Age*, p. 17.

Markey, J. (1988, October 21). VCR = Very complex recreation. *San Jose Mercury News*, p. B–2.

Marvin, C. (1988). *When old technologies were new.* New York: Oxford University Press.

McCullaugh, J. (1985, December 28). A day in the life of a video family. *Billboard*, pp. T8, T40.

Nayman, O. B., Atkins, C. K., & Gillette, B. (1973). The four-day workweek and media use: A glimpse of the future. *Journal of Broadcasting, 17*(3), 301–308.

Nielsen Media Research. (1988, Fall). *Nielsen newscast.* Northbrook, IL: Author.

Richard, J. (1988, November 28). Out of time. *New York Times,* p. A25.

Robbins, J. (1985, November 27). Fear about VCR threat renews. *Variety,* pp. 3, 23.

Robinson, J. P. (1969). Television and leisure time: yesterday, today and (maybe) tomorrow. *Public Opinion Quarterly, 33*(2), 210–222.

Robinson, J. P. (1981). Television and leisure time: A new scenario. *Journal of Communication, 31*(1), 120–130.

Robinson, J. P. (1989). Time's up. *American Demographics, 11*(7), 33–35.

Rojek, C. (1985). *Capitalism and leisure theory.* New York: Tavistock.

Seideman, T. (1986, March 8). Study shows VCR film viewing grows. *Billboard,* p. 39.

Tinsley, H. E. A., Barrett, T. C., & Kass, R. A. (1977). Leisure activities and need satisfaction. *Journal of Leisure Research, 9*(2), 110–120.

## Post-Reading Questions

1. Why, according to Massey and Baran, is time on everybody's mind? Summarize their reasons for making this assertion.

2. How do professionals define leisure time (paragraph 6)? Why is arriving at an exact definition of leisure time problematic?

3. Why is the issue of what research methods to use in gathering data on television viewing habits important and problematic? Why is the question of whether or not viewer responses were recorded in diaries or on surveys significant in interpreting data? (Paragraph 12 suggests that diary responses provide more in-depth insight into viewer habits and choices than do simply surveys. Why?)

4. Once you have read this essay, skim back over it and see if you find an organizational pattern suggested in the headings. What is that pattern? Describe it in your own words. How does it help readers move from one part of the essay to another? How does it help you define the purpose of this essay?

5. What is the purpose behind this essay? Do Massey and Baran want you to change your viewing behavior? Or are they simply interested in giving you a better understanding of how new technologies such as the VCR affect viewing habits and choices? What would a better understanding of new technologies lead to? What in the language of this essay causes you to define its purpose in a certain way?

6. Are Massey and Baran addressing other researchers and specialists or general readers? Or are they addressing both? What, in the language of their essay, appeals to either expert or general readers, or both?

7. After reading this essay, considering your own experience, and hearing others' views and experiences, do you agree that viewers have more control over leisure time because of VCR technology? If you do, provide a summary of the reasons for your response. If you do not, then explain why you think the idea that viewers have more

control over leisure time because of technologies such as VCR is an illusion. Does, for example, the need to master the technology actually mean that viewers are more rather than less controlled by it? Or has our definition of leisure time itself been distorted to the degree that what we now call leisure is actually work?

# CHRISTINE HALL HANSEN AND RANALD D. HANSEN ON SEX, VIOLENCE, AND ROCK VIDEOS

## Pre-Reading Questions

1. What are your initial opinions on the influence sex and violence have on the viewers of rock videos? (Review your initial opinions when you have finished reading this article and compare them to the findings of the article. Are you surprised? Did the results of this study cause you to change your opinions? In what ways?)

2. The following article is a research report addressed to a scientific audience. Notice the introduction, methodology, results, discussion, and conclusion sections. One effective way of preparing to read a research article is to skim the headings and first sentences of paragraphs of the article before you actually read it. Another is to read carefully the abstract that appears before the article itself. Do these two things; then list in your own words what you expect to be the major issues addressed in this article. Take notes on these issues as you actually read the article.

3. Look closely at the language of the first paragraph of this article. How is that language different from what you have found in other essays and articles in this chapter? Can you relate your response to this article's language to particular language features? Describe those features and show how they work.

## THE INFLUENCE OF SEX AND VIOLENCE ON THE APPEAL OF ROCK MUSIC VIDEOS[1]

Christine Hall Hansen

Ranald D. Hansen

*Two experiments examined the effects of sex and violence in rock music videos on viewers' judgments of the appeal of the music and visuals and emotional responses to the videos. The effects of videos with high, moderate, or low visual sex content were compared in Experiment 1. Positive emotions and the appeal of both the music and visuals were found to be positively related to the level of sexual content. In Experiment 2, the effects of videos with high, moderate, and low levels of visual violence content indicated that negative emotional responses and reduced appeal of both the music and the visuals were related to the level of violence. Evidence was obtained from both experiments that the combination of sex and violence also decreased appeal. In addition, music arousal was found to have an effect on appeal. More arousing music was positively related to appeal and positive emotions in sexy videos, but its influence was found to be independent of visual sex. In violent videos, however, music arousal was associated with decreased appeal and negative emotions and appeared to result from the "transfer" of excitation from the arousing music to the violence of the visual content.*

A generation is coming of age while watching sex and violence on television (Gerbner, Gross, Morgan, & Signiorelli, 1986; Singer & Singer, 1980). Rock music videos, in particular, have been the target of public criticism (Gore, 1987; Steinem, 1988). The National Coalition on Television Violence (1984), for example, has argued that the sexual and violent content of rock music videos makes them unwholesome viewing for young people. A similar opinion has been voiced by the American Academy of Pediatrics (Strasburger, 1988). Rock music videos hold a sizable share of the young television-viewing audience (Zimmerman, 1984), and content analyses have documented the presence of significant sexual and violent content (Brown & Campbell, 1986; Hansen & Hansen, 1989; Sherman & Dominick, 1986; Waite & Paludi, 1987). Yet, if only because the popularity and prevalence of rock music videos is relatively recent, little research has been conducted to test their effects on the viewer (Greeson & Williams, 1986; Hansen, in press; Hansen, C. H. & Hansen, R. D., 1988, in press). But, the effects of this sex and violence per se are not at issue here. Rather, our research was constructed to bear on another, related, question—why is the sex and violence there in the first place? [1]

The conventional wisdom seems to be that sex and violence "sells"; [2] that, for whatever reason, violence and sex exert an attractive force on the audience that increases enjoyment and enhances positive evaluations of rock music videos. In short, it is commonly believed that sex and violence add to a video's appeal. Is this intuitive hypothesis reasonable? The only experiment conducted to test it (Zillmann & Mundorf, 1987) did not yield overwhelming support. Zillmann and Mundorf edited R-rated sex, violence, or both into a rock music video. Sex, violence, or the combination of sex and violence did not have a positive influence on viewers' appreciation of the visual content. Although sex did increase the appeal of the music, violence had equivocal effects. And, interestingly, sex and violence together actually decreased the music's appeal. In terms of the prevailing wisdom, sex may sell, violence may or may not, and sex and violence together will not. Our research was designed to test the effects of sex and violence on appeal, employing multiple rock music videos selected for different levels of sex (Experiment 1) or violence (Experiment 2). Three formal hypotheses, relating to the conventional wisdom, were tested:

> *Hypothesis 1:* As the level of sexual imagery in rock music videos increases, subjects will find both the visual and music content more appealing.
>
> *Hypothesis 2:* As the level of violent imagery increases, subjects will find the visuals and music more appealing.
>
> *Hypothesis 3:* As the level of combined sexual and violent imagery increases, subjects will find the visuals and music less appealing.

## CAPTURING THE EFFECTS OF SEX AND VIOLENCE

Rock music videos are complex stimuli that combine music with visual content, and they can be expected to produce complex effects in the viewer. In consequence, subjects in this research were asked to evaluate both the music and the visual content of a music video, as well as to report the emotional feelings that the video produced. Recent research on emotions (Hansen, R. D. & Hansen, C. H., 1988; Schwartz & Weinberger, 1980) has indicated that emotional responses to events are rarely simple or unitary; instead, emotion-evoking stimuli typically produce a complex blend of feelings. Like other emotional events, music videos are expected to produce a blend of emotions. In addition, emotional responses should become more intense as the level of sexual or violent imagery increases. Stronger sexual feelings, for instance, should be provoked by very sexy videos than by less sexy ones. Stronger feelings of fear, anger, or aggressiveness should be provoked by very violent videos than by less violent ones. Therefore, two affect-related hypotheses were formulated; the first was tested in Experiment 1, the second in Experiment 2:

> *Hypothesis 4:* As the level of sexual imagery increases, the intensity of the complex blend of emotions engendered by sexual imagery will become greater.
>
> *Hypothesis 5:* As the level of violent imagery increases, the intensity of the complex blend of emotions engendered by violent imagery will become greater.

One additional component of rock music videos—the physiological 4 arousal produced by rock music—deserves particular attention because of its theoretical status as an important variable in affective responses. The music in many rock music videos is arousing, and the importance of arousal in emotional responses has a long history (James, 1884; Schachter & Singer, 1962; Zillmann, 1978, 1983). Zillmann's theory of excitation transfer (Zillmann, 1978, 1983, 1984) best captures the way in which arousal produced by the music of a rock video might contribute to the affective effects of visual sex or violence. Within excitation-transfer theory, physiological arousal is related to both the intensity of emotional responses to an event (Zillmann, 1978, 1983, 1984) and the strength of its appeal (Cantor & Zillmann, 1973). Thus both the intensity of the viewer's emotional responses to sexual or violent videos and how appealing viewers find them should be related to the level of arousal or excitation provoked by the sexual or violent images. In stating this, excitation transfer is similar to a number of theories (e.g., Schachter & Singer, 1962). But the theory predicts effects beyond a connection between the arousal produced by an image and the intensity of the emotional responses to that image.

Excitation-transfer theory is uniquely constructed to describe the 5 effects of complex stimuli like rock music videos—stimuli that incorporate multiple sources of excitation. The theory posits that the individual either cannot or does not discriminate the excitation produced by one source from that produced by another. Therefore, if visual sex or violence in rock music videos engenders positive evaluations and emotions, the intensity of those feelings may reflect more than just the excitation provoked by the visual images of sex or violence. The total excitation available to intensify appeal and emotions will be greater than that which would be produced by the sex or violence alone because it also reflects the excitatory contribution of arousing music. Arousing music, then, has the potential to intensify the effects of sexual and violent imagery; the excitation from arousing music would transfer to the excitatory effects of visual sex and violence on evaluations and emotions. Formally stated, two transfer effects were hypothesized:

*Hypothesis 6:* Excitation produced by arousing music augments emotional responses to sexual imagery in rock music videos and renders the images and music more appealing.

*Hypothesis 7:* Excitation produced by arousing music augments emotional responses to violent imagery and renders the images and music more appealing.

The transfer of music excitation to visual sex was tested in Experiment 1, and the transfer to violence was tested in Experiment 2.

## EXPERIMENT 1: SEX

### *Method*

*Subjects, design, and procedures.*  In return for course credit, 170 male    6
and 196 female undergraduates participated in the experiment. Almost
all subjects were either freshmen or sophomores who lived on campus. At
the time the study was conducted, cable service (with 24-hr access to
music videos) was unavailable in the residence halls. Subjects reported
that, on average, they watched about 30 min of rock videos during any
given week, but they acknowledged that this viewing time increased
when they stayed at home or off campus. Experimental sessions were
conducted in mixed-sex groups averaging about 10 per session, but
groups ranged in size from 6 to 12 people. Experiments 1 and 2 were
run concurrently over the period of a month.

On the basis of content analyses made by three independent under-    7
graduate research assistants (blind to the experimental hypotheses) and
the researchers' judgments, 15 rock music videos were selected for
inclusion in the experiment. Five videos were selected for each of three
categories, based on high, moderate, and low levels of visual sex. To
reduce variance, all videos featured male artists, and none of the videos
made use of material from recently released motion pictures (e.g., videos
that were created for motion picture title songs were excluded).

Subjects in any given session were exposed to one video in one of the    8
visual-sex conditions. Assignment to visual-sex condition and to video
within condition was randomly determined. The video was presented on
a 21-in. color monitor within comfortable viewing distance of the
subjects. The audio signal was amplified and presented through two
loudspeakers located to either side of the monitor. The experimenter,
blind to experimental condition, described the research to subjects as an
"exploratory study of music videos." She placed a questionnaire face
down in front of each subject and told subjects to complete it at the
conclusion of the video. After these instructions, she left the experimental room and did not return until after playing the appropriate video and
allowing subjects time to complete the questionnaire. Subjects were
debriefed at the conclusion of the session.

*Measurement.*  The experimental booklet contained four components    9
that appeared in counterbalanced order. As a check on the manipulation
of visual content, subjects rated the level of visual sex and of visual
violence on separate scales ranging from 1 (*nonsexual/nonviolent*) to 9
(*very sexual/very violent*). They also were asked to report how the video
made them feel on seven scales—happy, angry, sad, fear, anxious, sexual,
and aggressive—anchored at 0 (*not at all [emotion]*) and at 10 (*extremely
[emotion]*). In addition, they rated the visual content on 20 (9-point)

bipolar scales. On a separate page, they rated the music and the lyrics on the same scales.

*Visual appeal, music appeal, and music arousal measures.* Data from 10 visual and music scale items were used to construct composite measures of visual appeal, music appeal, and music arousal (i.e., excitation). To keep the measures consistent across Experiments 1 and 2, data from both experiments were combined in constructing these measures. To select items for the visual appeal measure, a factor analysis was conducted on the visual content scale items. The first factor extracted represented an appeal dimension. Items loading below .550 on this factor were dropped, and all remaining visual scale items were resubmitted to factor analysis (to calculate correct eigenvalues and variance accounted for by the factor composed of only the retained items). Cronbach's alpha coefficient was computed to ensure that the remaining items formed a unified scale. Each subject's ratings for the retained items were summed and averaged to yield a composite visual appeal score, and these scores were used as data in statistical analyses.

The same method was used to construct a measure of music appeal 11 and music arousal. Music scale items were submitted to factor analysis. The first factor extracted represented an appeal dimension, and the second factor represented an arousal dimension. Again, items loading below .550 on either factor were dropped, and the remaining items were resubmitted to factor analysis. Cronbach's alpha coefficient was computed for each of the two remaining sets of items. Subjects' ratings on retained items from the appeal factor were summed and averaged to yield a composite music appeal score, and ratings on retained items from the arousal factor were summed and averaged to yield a composite music arousal score.

## Results

*Manipulation effectiveness.* A 3 (Visual Sex) × 2 (Subject Gender) 12 ANOVA, conducted on ratings of visual sexual content, indicated that the manipulation of visual sex had been successful, $F(2, 359) = 57.89$, $p < .001$, $\eta^2 = .33$. Bonferroni $t$ tests showed that high-sex videos were seen as having more sexual content than moderate-sex videos ($M = 6.96$ and $M = 5.99$) and that low-sex videos were seen as having less sexual content ($M = 3.76$) than either moderate- or high-sex videos (all $ps < .01$). But the analysis also revealed that ratings of visual violence differed somewhat across visual-sex conditions, $F(2, 359) = 3.97$, $p < .02$, $\eta^2 = .02$. Moderate- and high-sex videos were seen as equally violent ($Ms = 5.05$ and 4.86, respectively), but both were judged more violent than low-sex videos, $M = 4.16$ ($ps < .05$). Although this effect was modest and the mean tended to be close to the midpoint of the scale in all conditions, ratings of visual violence were treated as a covariate in subsequent analyses to eliminate any potential confound of sex and violence. Subject gender entered into no significant effects; women and men agreed on the sexual and violent content of the videos.[2]

*Measures of visual appeal, music appeal, and music arousal.*   Factors used 13 to construct the composite measures were extracted using the principal factors method. Visual and music scale items were analyzed separately. Both oblique and orthogonal rotations were performed, revealing highly similar solutions; therefore the orthogonal rotation (varimax technique) was retained for simplicity. Thirteen items loaded on the visual appeal factor that was extracted from visual scale items, but 3 items with factor loadings below .550 were dropped. The remaining 10 visual scale items were reanalyzed, and the results of the visual appeal factor containing only the retained items are presented in Table 1. Ten items loaded on the music appeal factor, and 7 loaded on the music arousal factor. Again, items with factor loadings below .550 were dropped, resulting in the loss of 2 appeal and 3 arousal items. The remaining music scale items were reanalyzed. Results of the music appeal and music arousal factors containing only the retained items are presented in Table 1. In addition, an oblique (oblimin) rotation of the retained music scale items revealed that only a minimal correlation was found to exist between the two music factors ($r = .07$). As shown in Table 1, Cronbach's alpha coefficients indicated that items retained in each of the three factors showed a high degree of internal consistency. Therefore, each subject's average rating on items within the visual appeal, music appeal, and music arousal factors was used as data in subsequent analyses.

*The impact of sex on appeal.*   The hypothesis that sexual imagery 14 increases the appeal of rock music videos (Hypothesis 1) was strongly supported. Subject Gender × Visual Sex ANCOVAs indicated that visual sex had substantial effects on visual and music appeal, $F(2, 358) = 16.92$, $p < .003$, $\eta^2 = .09$, and $F(2, 358) = 7.03$, $p < .001$, $\eta^2 = .04$. Gender had no effects. Bonferroni $t$s revealed that the visual content of high-sex videos was rated more appealing ($M = 6.20$) than the visual content of either moderate- or low-sex videos ($M = 5.19$ and $M = 5.35$, both $p$s $< .01$), whereas low and moderate conditions did not differ from each other. Likewise, the music of high-sex videos was judged more appealing ($M = 6.41$) than the music of either moderate- or low-sex videos ($M = 5.82$ and $M = 6.01$, both $p$s $< .01$). In short, high sex translated into increased appeal of both music and visual content.

## SEX AND VIOLENCE

These covariance analyses also revealed effects involving the covariate 15 (visual violence) that deserve some attention because they foreshadow effects obtained in Experiment 2. The regression of visual appeal on

TABLE 1   Items loading on visual appeal, music appeal, and music
arousal factors

| Visual Scale Factor Analysis | | | Music Scale Factor Analysis | | | | | |
|---|---|---|---|---|---|---|---|---|
| Appeal Factor | | | Appeal Factor | | | Arousing Factor | | |
| Item | Loading | $(h^{2}\!*)$ | Item | Loading | $(h^{2})$ | Item | Loading | $(h^{2})$ |
| Pleasant | .890 | (.81) | Positive | .869 | (.78) | Loud | .869 | (.79) |
| Attractive | .897 | (.80) | Pleasant | .842 | (.81) | Arousing | .820 | (.65) |
| Good | .886 | (.80) | Friendly | .821 | (.71) | Active | .750 | (.64) |
| Positive | .875 | (.79) | Good | .809 | (.81) | Heavy | .718 | (.67) |
| Excellent | .867 | (.78) | Excellent | .796 | (.83) | | | |
| Nice | .811 | (.77) | Warm | .765 | (.70) | | | |
| Warm | .790 | (.77) | Happy | .711 | (.73) | | | |
| Happy | .721 | (.63) | Colorful | .704 | (.61) | | | |
| Colorful | .702 | (.60) | | | | | | |
| Bright | .697 | (.60) | | | | | | |
| Eigenvalue | | | | | | | | |
| | 7.35 | | | 5.98 | | | | 2.75 |
| Total variance accounted for | | | | | | | | |
| | 45.94% | | | 37.37% | | | | 17.19% |
| Cronbach's alpha coefficient | | | | | | | | |
| | .95 | | | .82 | | | | .86 |

*Communalities
Note. Values listed above for the visual appeal factor were the result of a factor analysis
conducted on visual scale items. Values listed for music appeal and music arousal factors were
produced by a factor analysis of the music scale items.

visual violence was significant, $F(1, 358) = 85.30$, $p < .001$; but the
direction was opposite to that predicted in Hypothesis 2. Increasing
violence predicted *decreased* appeal of the visual content, $r(358) = -.31$,
$p < .01$. The regression of music appeal on visual violence also was
significant, $F(1, 358) = 102.84$, $p < .001$, but, again, opposite to the
direction predicted. Increasing violence predicted lower music appeal,
$r(358) = -.32$, $p < .01$. An analysis of these regression lines across
visual-sex conditions proved interesting. The relationship of visual violence to music appeal did not vary among visual-sex conditions,
$F(2, 356) = 1.47$, $p < .25$. Violence diminished the appeal of the music
no matter how sexual the video.

Support for Hypothesis 3, that the combination of sex and violence 16
decreases appeal, was also obtained. The relationship of visual violence to
the appeal of the visual content differed across visual-sex conditions,
$F(2, 356) = 3.33$, $p < .04$, $\eta^{2} = .02$. Contrast analyses indicated that
violence had a more detrimental effect, $F(1, 358) = 6.26$, $p < .02$, on
visual appeal in high- and moderate-sex videos, $r(273) = -.48$, $p < .001$,

than in low-sex videos, $r(85) = -.24$, $p < .02$, suggesting that the combination of sex and violence produced particularly unappealing visuals. In summary, violence appeared to diminish the appeal of both the music and visual content of videos, particularly for videos with higher sexual content. This latter finding, of course, was consistent with the results obtained by Zillmann and Mundorf (1987). But, if only because of the truncated range of violence in these videos, this must be considered a weak test of the effect of violence on appeal (Hypothesis 2). A strong test of this hypothesis awaits the results of Experiment 2.

*The impact of sex on emotions.* The Gender × Visual Sex ANCOVAs [17] conducted on emotions produced a number of gender main effects. These effects—indicating that men and women differed on reports of anger, sadness, fear, aggressiveness, and sexual feelings—were not of particular interest here. The important finding was that gender did not qualify any of the effects produced by visual sex; the effect of visual sexual content on emotional experiences was the same for women and men.

Hypothesis 4 was strongly supported. The level of sexual imagery [18] influenced ratings on several emotions. Visual sex produced significant main effects on happy, $F(2, 359) = 8.94$, $p < .001$, $\eta^2 = .05$; sad, $F(2, 359) = 17.91$, $p < .001$, $\eta^2 = .11$; fearful, $F(2, 359) = 4.17$, $p < .02$, $\eta^2 = .03$; and, not surprisingly, sexual, $F(2, 359) = 32.31$, $p < .001$, $\eta^2 = .16$. Comparisons using Bonferroni $t$s indicated that high-sex videos made subjects feel more happy, less sad, and less fearful than either low- or moderate-sex videos (see Table 2). In addition, subjects felt more sexual after high-sex videos than after moderate-sex videos and less sexual after low-sex videos than after moderate-sex videos. In short, high-sex

TABLE 2  Means for emotions in visual sex conditions

|  | Visual Sex | | |
|---|---|---|---|
|  | *Low* | *Moderate* | *High* |
| Happy | $5.13_a$ | $4.79_a$ | $6.00_b$ |
| Angry | $2.31_a$ | $2.49_a$ | $2.69_a$ |
| Sad | $3.98_a$ | $3.90_a$ | $2.16_b$ |
| Fear | $2.65_a$ | $2.87_a$ | $2.00_b$ |
| Anxious | $3.28_a$ | $3.62_a$ | $3.93_a$ |
| Sexual | $2.17_a$ | $4.13_b$ | $5.07_c$ |
| Aggressive | $3.19_a$ | $3.75_a$ | $3.74_a$ |

*Note.* Means in the same row not sharing a common subscript are significantly different ($p < .05$).

videos produced a stronger blend of positive emotions, including sexual feelings, than did moderate- or low-sex videos.

*Arousing music: excitation available for transfer.* Visual sex produced a significant main effect on music arousal, $F(2, 359) = 8.58$, $p < .001$, $\eta^2 = .05$. Comparisons using Bonferroni $ts$ indicated that high-sex videos were more arousing ($M = 7.01$) than moderate-sex videos ($M = 6.28$, $p < .01$), and that moderate-sex videos, in turn, were more arousing than low-sex videos ($M = 4.47$, $p < .01$). This finding led us to wonder whether the effects of visual sex on appeal were actually produced by visual sex or by arousal. Inspection of the first two rows in Table 3 provides an answer to this question. Ratings of visual sex were correlated with visual appeal, music appeal, and emotional responses. As shown in the first row of Table 3, these correlations reproduced the pattern of effects in the analyses of variance reported above. Visual sex was significantly correlated with visual and music appeal as well as with happy, sad, fearful, and sexual feelings. When these correlations were partialed for the effects of arousing music (second row in Table 3), the partial correlations remained significant. This clearly indicated that the effects on appeal and emotions were produced by visual sex and not by the more arousing music of high-sex videos.

Did the excitation of arousing music transfer to the effects of sex, as predicted by Hypothesis 6? The data did not support this conclusion. As shown in the third row of entries in Table 3, music arousal had a strong association with positive emotions and increased appeal of the visuals and music. However, if excitation produced by music arousal had transferred to sex, two effects should have emerged. First, the relationships of visual sex to appeal and emotions should have been weakened substantially if the contribution of arousing music was removed (row 2 of Table 3). This

TABLE 3   Appeal and emotions correlated with visual sex and arousing music

|  | Visual Appeal | Music Appeal | Happy | Angry | Sad | Fearful | Anxious | Sexual | Aggressive |
|---|---|---|---|---|---|---|---|---|---|
| Visual sex |  |  |  |  |  |  |  |  |  |
| Zero-order | .17*** | .13** | .11* | -.01 | -.12* | -.10* | -.08 | .68*** | .05 |
| Partialed for |  |  |  |  |  |  |  |  |  |
| arousing music | .18*** | .10* | .10* | -.01 | -.09* | -.08 | -.07 | .58*** | .01 |
| Arousing music |  |  |  |  |  |  |  |  |  |
| Zero-order | .25*** | .13** | .24*** | -.10* | -.28*** | -.14** | -.17** | .02 | .04 |
| Partialed for sex | .23*** | .13** | .23*** | -.10* | -.27*** | -.14** | -.09* | .08 | .04 |

*Note.* Asterisks designate the significance levels of the correlations.
*$p < .05$; **$p < .01$; ***$p < .001$.

did not occur. The differences between the zero-order and partial correlations were examined using Fisher $z_r$ transformations. None of the $t$ tests was significant, indicating that the partialed correlations were not significantly weaker than the nonpartialed correlations. Second, the relationship of music arousal to appeal and emotions (row 3 of Table 3) should have been weakened if the transfer of excitation to the effects of visual sex were controlled (row 4 of Table 3). When the zero-order and partial correlations were transformed $(z_r)$, $t$ tests revealed no significant differences. In short, there was no evidence that excitation generated by arousing music transferred to sex.

Arousing music, however, did appear to be independently related to 21 appeal and emotions. As inspection of the third row of entries in Table 3 will show, music arousal had a strong association with increased appeal of the music and visuals and with more positive emotional experiences. Further, this association was not disturbed when these correlations were partialed for the effects of sex (last row in Table 3). In other words, in the context of these videos, which tended to produce positive emotional experiences and were generally appealing, arousing music was appreciated and enjoyed. Whether the same would occur in the context of violent videos remained to be seen.

In summary, the results of Experiment 1 demonstrated that visual sex 22 enhanced the appeal of music videos and yielded positive emotional experiences. No evidence was obtained suggesting a transfer of music arousal to these effects of visual sex. Finally, there was some evidence from the analyses of covariance that visual violence may have just the opposite effects, diminishing the appeal of both the music and the visual content. Experiment 2 was conducted to test the effects of visual violence on appeal and emotions, to investigate the potential counterinfluence of sex within violent videos, and to explore excitation-transfer effects on reactions to violence.


## EXPERIMENT 2: VIOLENCE

### Method

In all, 213 female and 174 male undergraduates participated in the 23 experiment. Experiment 2 was identical to Experiment 1 except, of course, subjects were exposed to a video containing a low, moderate, or high level of visual violence. The procedure for selecting the five videos used at each level of violence was the same as that used in Experiment 1. The procedures and measures used in Experiment 2 were the same as those used in the first experiment.

## Results

A 3 (Visual Violence) × 2 (Subject Gender) ANOVA conducted on 24 violence ratings produced a significant visual-violence main effect, $F(2, 384) = 291.72$, $p < .001$, $\eta^2 = .48$. No other effects were significant. Bonferroni $t$ tests indicated that the manipulation had been successful. High-violence videos were rated more violent ($M = 7.90$) than moderate-violence videos ($M = 5.45$, $p < .01$), and moderate-violence videos were rated more violent than low-violence videos ($M = 3.27$, $p < .01$). But an ANOVA conducted on ratings of visual sex also revealed a visual-violence main effect, $F(2, 384) = 9.09$, $p < .001$, $\eta^2 = .05$. High-violence videos were rated as less sexual ($M = 5.25$) than moderate-violence videos ($M = 5.88$, $p < .01$), and these, in turn, were rated as less sexual than low-violence videos ($M = 6.53$, $p < .01$). As in the first experiment, the stimulus materials modestly confounded sex and violence, so analyses of covariance—here, using visual sexual ratings as the covariate—were used.

### The Impact of Violence on Appeal

The hypothesis that violent imagery augments the appeal of the music 25 and visual content of music videos (Hypothesis 2) was not supported. In fact, data analyses supported the opposite conclusion—violence diminishes appeal. Subject Gender × Visual Violence ANCOVAs produced no effects involving gender. Visual violence produced significant main effects on visual appeal, $F(2, 384) = 38.24$, $p < .001$, $\eta^2 = .18$, and on music appeal, $F(2, 384) = 37.20$, $p < .001$, $\eta^2 = .12$. Bonferroni $t$ comparisons produced the same pattern on both types of appeal showing that violence decreased, rather than increased, appeal. The visual content of high-violence videos was rated less appealing ($M = 3.98$) than the visual content of moderate-violence videos ($M = 5.01$, $p < .01$), and the visual content of moderate-violence videos was judged less appealing than that of low-violence videos ($M = 5.91$, $p < .01$). Similarly, the music of high-violence videos was judged less appealing ($M = 4.52$) than the music of moderate-violence videos ($M = 5.53$, $p < .01$), which, in turn, was rated less appealing than the music of low-violence videos ($M = 6.36$, $p < .01$). In short, increasing the level of violence decreased the appeal of both music and visual content.

*Violence and sex.* Although the effects were less straightforward for 26 violent than for sexual videos, Hypothesis 3 received additional support in Experiment 2; at high levels, the combination of sexual and violent imagery tended to decrease appeal. The covariance analyses yielded effects due to the covariate (rating of visual sex) on the appeal of visual and music content that were interesting and consistent with the effects obtained in Experiment 1. The regression of visual appeal on ratings of visual sex was significant, $F(1, 384) = 3.76$, $p < .05$; and, overall, the relationship was positive ($r = .14$). But analysis of the regression revealed that the association varied across visual-violence conditions, $F(2, 384) = 4.79$, $p < .009$, $\eta^2 = .02$. Contrast analyses indicated that visual sex enhanced the visual appeal of low- and moderate-violence videos, $r(254) = .16$, $p < .001$, but had just the opposite effect, $F(1, 384) = 7.97$, $p < .005$, on the visual appeal of high-violence videos, $r(130) = -.09$, $p < .08$. Although the regression of music appeal on visual sex ($r = .05$) was not significant overall, $F(1, 384) < 1$, the association between visual sex and music appeal varied significantly across levels of visual violence, $F(2, 384) = 3.51$, $p < .03$, $\eta^2 = .02$. As found for visual appeal, contrast analyses revealed that visual sex augmented the appeal of the music in low- and moderate-violence videos, $r(254) = .16$, $p < .01$, but had the opposite effect, $F(1, 384) = 8.52$, $p < .004$, on high-violence videos, $r(130) = -.10$, $p < .07$.

Thus, in high-violence videos, visual sex diminished the appeal of both the visual and music content. Recall that in the first experiment, visual violence generally reduced appeal but had a particularly detrimental effect on the rated appeal of more sexual videos. Here, visual sex (which typically increases appeal) actually had a detrimental effect on the appeal of highly violent videos. In other words, visual violence particularly decreased the appeal of highly sexual videos, and visual sex decreased the appeal of highly violent videos, indicating that a combination of sex and violence, especially at high levels, is particularly unappealing. This relationship, found in two experiments here, replicated the effects reported by Zillmann and Mundorf (1987). 27

### The Impact of Violence on Emotions

The Gender × Visual Violence ANCOVAs conducted on emotions revealed gender main effects on feelings of aggressiveness and sexuality. These effects were not of particular interest here. Rather, the important finding was that gender did not qualify any of the obtained visual-violence effects. Visual violence produced significant effects on all seven emotions: $F(2, 384) = 14.62$, $p < .001$, $\eta^2 = .07$ for happy; $F(2, 384) = 23.41$, $p < .001$, $\eta^2 = .11$ for angry; $F(2, 384) = 4.21$, $p < .02$, $\eta^2 = .02$ for sad; $F(2, 384) = 21.10$, $p < .001$, $\eta^2 = .10$ for fearful; $F(2, 384) = 7.35$, $p < .005$, $\eta^2 = .04$ for anxious; $F(2, 384) = 10.72$, $p < .001$, $\eta^2 = .04$ for sexual; and $F(2, 384) = 40.01$, $p < .001$, $\eta^2 = .21$ for aggressive. 28

The means underlying these effects are shown in Table 4. Hypothesis 5 received strong support from the data. The blends of emotions 29

TABLE 4

|          | Visual Violence | | |
|----------|------|-----------|------|
|          | Low  | Moderate  | High |
| Happy     | 5.41$_a$ | 5.15$_a$  | 3.77$_b$ |
| Angry     | 2.27$_c$ | 3.27$_b$  | 4.47$_c$ |
| Sad       | 3.77$_a$ | 2.86$_b$  | 3.62$_a$ |
| Fear      | 2.18$_b$ | 2.69$_b$  | 4.24$_a$ |
| Anxious   | 3.19$_b$ | 4.01$_a$  | 4.48$_a$ |
| Sexual    | 4.39$_a$ | 4.17$_{ab}$ | 3.65$_b$ |
| Aggressive | 2.55$_c$ | 4.10$_b$  | 5.70$_a$ |

*Note.* Means in the same row not sharing a common subscript are significantly different ($p < .05$).

produced by violent videos became more intense as the level of violent imagery increased. With the exception of sad, the effect of visual violence on emotional experience was fairly consistent; as videos became more violent, the emotional experience became more negative. Increasing the level of violence made viewers feel less happy, more angry, more fearful, more anxious, less sexual, and more aggressive than did less violent videos.

### Arousing Music: Excitation Available for Transfer

Visual violence had a substantial effect on music arousal, [30] $F(2, 384) = 139.30$, $p < .001$, $\eta^2 = .42$. Results of Bonferroni $t$ tests revealed that the music of high-violence videos was rated more arousing ($M = 7.01$) than the music of moderate-violence videos ($M = 6.28$, $p < .01$), and the music of these videos was rated as more arousing than the music of low-violence videos ($M = 4.39$, $p < .01$). As in the first experiment, this raised the question of whether the effects ascribed above to violence might actually have been produced by music arousal (with which violence covaried). To answer this question, visual-violence ratings were correlated with each of the appeal and emotion measures and then partialed for music arousal. The correlations of visual violence with appeal and emotions can be seen in the first row of Table 5. These correlations, when partialled for music arousal, remained significant, indicating that visual violence remained a potent mediator of appeal and emotional experience. Therefore, violent imagery decreased the appeal of the music and visual content and yielded negative emotional responses.

Further, statistical comparisons of the zero-order and partial corre- [31] lations yielded evidence that supported excitation transfer as proposed in

Hypothesis 7. Excitation produced by arousing music transferred to the effects of visual violence; however, because violence produced negative effects, arousing music intensified *negative* emotions and decreased, rather than increased, appeal. The zero-order correlations in the first row and the partial correlations in the second row of Table 5 were transformed into $z_r$ scores, and pairwise comparisons were conducted to test the difference between each zero-order correlation and its partial. The difference was significant in the case of five variates: music appeal, $t(384) = 4.30$, $p < .01$; angry, $t(384) = 2.20$, $p < .05$; fearful, $t(384) = 2.12$, $p < .05$; anxious, $t(384) = 2.20$, $p < .05$; and aggressive, $t(384) = 5.50$, $p < .005$. In other words, music arousal significantly enhanced the negative effect of violence on the appeal of the music and increased the feelings of anger, fear, anxiety, and aggressiveness produced by violent videos. Although this finding suggested that the excitation produced by arousing music may have transferred to the effects of visual violence, we had to establish that the effect of arousing music on music appeal and emotions was mediated by violence and not independent of violence. The correlations of music arousal with appeal and emotions, in the third row, give the appearance that the impact of music arousal parallels that of visual violence; music arousal was associated with reduced appeal of both the visuals and music and more negative emotional experiences. However, when these were partialed for visual violence (last row of Table 5), it became obvious that the independent effect of music arousal on evaluations and emotions was negligible. In short, the augmenting effects of arousing music on music appeal, anger, fear, anxiety, and aggressiveness were mediated by violence; the excitation of arousing music transferred to the effects of violence to intensify these negative reactions.

TABLE 5   Appeal and emotions correlated with visual violence and arousing music

| | Visual Appeal | Music Appeal | Happy | Angry | Sad | Fearful | Anxious | Sexual | Aggressive |
|---|---|---|---|---|---|---|---|---|---|
| **Visual violence** | | | | | | | | | |
| Zero-order | −.51*** | −.49*** | −.40*** | .47*** | .12* | .43*** | .23*** | −.13** | .55*** |
| Partialed for | | | | | | | | | |
| arousing music | −.47*** | −.31*** | −.35*** | .38*** | .14* | .34*** | .17** | −.11** | .33*** |
| **Arousing music** | | | | | | | | | |
| Zero-order | −.25*** | −.28*** | −.14** | .21*** | .01 | .18** | .18** | .14** | .22*** |
| Partialed for | | | | | | | | | |
| violence | .07 | .01 | .10* | −.06* | −.08 | −.06 | −.06 | .11* | −.08 |

*Note.* Asterisks designate the significance levels of the correlations.
*$p < .05$; **$p < .01$; *** $p < .001$.

## DISCUSSION

### *The Impact of Sex and Violence on Appeal and Emotions*

The impact of visual sex and violence on the appeal of the music and 32 visual content of rock videos clearly emerged from these two experiments. The hypothesis that sexual imagery would increase the appeal of music videos (Hypothesis 1) was strongly supported. On the other hand, Hypothesis 2, predicting that violent imagery would have a similar positive effect, was not supported; and, in fact, the data pointed to the opposite conclusion: violence diminished the appeal of both the music and the visuals. As the amount of sex in videos increased, subjects liked both the music and the visuals more; as the amount of violence increased, subjects found them less appealing. And, as indicated by calculations of $\eta^2$, the effects produced by sexual and violent imagery were substantial. Sexual imagery accounted for about 4% of the variance in music appeal ratings, and violent imagery accounted for approximately 12%. For ratings of visual appeal, sex accounted for 9% of the variance in ratings, and violence accounted for approximately 18%.

Hypothesis 3, that increasing the combined levels of both sex and 33 violence would decrease appeal, was supported by results from covariance analyses in both experiments. In the first experiment, the detrimental effect of violence on appeal was particularly potent when videos contained high levels of sex. Here violence accounted for 23% of the variance in visual appeal scores and about 10% of the variance in music appeal. In the second experiment, a tendency for sex to increase appeal was evident in less violent videos, but actually reversed in judgments of highly violent videos, accounting for about 1% of the variance in both types of appeal. In short, the combination of sex and violence appeared to be particularly unappealing.

Because there has been relatively little research conducted to test the 34 impact of sex and violence on the appeal of rock music videos, it is important to highlight both the consistencies and the discrepancies across studies. Zillmann and Mundorf (1987) reported that visual sex increased the appeal of the music, and the combination of sex and violence tended to be detrimental to appeal. These effects were replicated here. On two other counts, however, there was divergence across studies.

First, Zillmann and Mundorf (1987) reported that sex had only a 35 minimal effect on the appeal of visual content and, in the case of women, may have had a detrimental effect. Sex, in our experiment, had a strong, positive effect on the appeal of both the music and the visuals for subjects of both genders. The most obvious explanation lies in the difference between the R-rated sexual inserts used in the Zillmann and Mundorf experiment and the milder, naturally occurring visual sex found in the videos used in our research. Zillmann and Mundorf's subjects—women in particular—voiced their disapproval of incorporating this type of (graphic) sex in publicly accessible videos. It was not surprising, then, that they also depreciated visual content. Perhaps the relationship of sexual explicitness to enhancement of appreciation is curvilinear. Beyond some point, more explicit sexual material becomes intrusive and detracts from, rather than enhances, appeal.

Second, Zillmann and Mundorf (1987) found that violence pro- 36 duced equivocal effects on appeal; whereas, in our experiments, violence produced strong detrimental effects. One explanation may lie in the locus of the violence. The violence in the videos used in our research involved members of the rock groups recording the video. Recall that videos containing violent vignettes not associated with the recording artists were excluded from our sample because the vignettes were almost always from current motion picture releases. By virtue of their manipulation, the violent vignettes in the video used by Zillmann and Mundorf were necessarily dissociated from the recording artists. It may be that dissociating visual violence from the recording artists serves to insulate the artists, the music, and even the video itself from the chilling effects of violence. This, of course, would be an interesting hypothesis for future research.

Predictions that blends of emotional responses to music videos 37 would be more intense at higher levels of sexual and violent imagery (Hypotheses 4 and 5) were strongly supported. As the level of sexual imagery increased, sexy videos had the effect of making the viewer feel happier (accounting for 5% of the variance in ratings) and more sexual (accounting for 16% of the variance) and of reducing feelings of fear (3% of the variance) and sadness (11% of the variance). In contrast, violence produced negative consequences on several emotions. Increasing violent imagery intensified feelings of apprehension, including fear (accounting for 10% of the variance) and anxiety (4%). In addition, higher violence increased feelings of anger (accounting for 11% of the variance) and aggressiveness (21%) and left viewers feeling anything but happy (7%) and sexual (4%). Given these kinds of emotional reactions, it is hardly surprising that violence diminished and sex enhanced the appeal of the music and the visual content.

The rock music videos selected for our experiments were not altered 38 in any way. This is both good and bad. Although it increases the ecological validity of the results compared to experiments in which the videos are altered in some way by researchers, it also increases the possibility that unknown or uncontrolled variables potentially may be confounding the results. For example, because of the inherent complexity of rock music videos, the sexual and violent videos might have differed on some other critical dimension(s) that we have failed to consider. However, we believe this to be unlikely as our findings paralleled those of Zillmann and Mundorf (1987) in many respects, even though their experimental procedures were quite different. In addition, the possibility exists that embellishment of some videos with sexual imagery may be due, at least in part, to the excitatory quality of the music that is being put to film. Could it be that the more exciting visual embellishers find the music, the more sexual images they include?[3] Our data are moot regarding this point, but given the number of sexual videos we have encountered with very unexciting music, we think that this systematic kind of effect is unlikely. In fact, it seems to us that video producers often attempt to counteract an inherently unexciting song by including more sexual visual imagery.

### Arousing Music: Excitation Available for Transfer

Two excitation-transfer hypotheses were also tested: Experiment 1 tested the transfer of excitation produced by arousing music to affective responses to videos containing sexual visuals (Hypothesis 6); Experiment 2 tested excitation transfer to affective responses produced by violent videos (Hypothesis 7). Only the latter hypothesis was supported. The contribution of arousing music to appeal and emotions was straightforward in the first experiment. Across videos containing sex, which were judged appealing and produced positive emotions, arousing music promoted appeal and positive emotional experiences. Further, in this positive context, the contribution of arousing music to visual and music appeal and emotions was independent of visual sex. The excitation of arousing music did not transfer to the effects of sex. Subjects liked the sex, and they enjoyed the arousing music; arousing music did not alter the effect of sex, and sex did not alter the effect of arousing music. But this changed dramatically in the second experiment.

An excitation-transfer effect (Hypothesis 7) was supported, but excitation transfer did not enhance the appeal of violent videos, as predicted. Across these videos, arousing music appeared to reduce appeal and yield negative emotional feelings; however, the presence of violence in videos mediated these negative effects. Analyses indicated that the negative effects produced by arousing music resulted from the transfer of excitation from the arousing music to the violence of the visual content. Arousing music augmented the negative effects of violence. Adding arousing music to violence enhanced the negative effect of violence on the appeal of the music and visual content and produced an even more unpleasant negative emotional experience. It was evident across these two experiments that the effect of arousing music on appeal and emotional experiences was dramatically influenced by the visual content of the video. Sexual images accompanied by arousing music produced the highest ratings of appeal and the most positive emotional experience.

Violent images accompanied by arousing music produced the lowest appeal and the most negative emotional experience.

The implications of the research for excitation-transfer theory were 41 mixed. The transfer of excitement from arousing music to violence was clearly evident in Experiment 2, but the transfer of excitement from arousing music to sex failed to appear in Experiment 1. Sex and arousing music both intensified feelings, but the excitatory contribution of arousing music remained isolated from the excitation provided by sex. This suggested a possible boundary to excitation transfer. Perhaps the physiological arousal state evoked by the sexual images was sufficiently different from that evoked by the arousing music that it did not transfer efficiently. There is a growing body of literature indicating that emotion-eliciting stimuli have the capacity to provoke a variety of physiological arousal states (e.g., Schwartz & Weinberger, 1980). It may be that emotional states with more similar physiological patterns (such as similar heart rate, blood pressure, and skin conductance changes) are more likely to transfer than emotions with differing or competing physiological response patterns. This would imply that excitation transfer may not be achieved with equal ease across all physiological states. This hypothesis merits further attention.

### Conclusions

We return to the conventional wisdom—sex and violence sells. Our data 42 indeed indicated that sex is appealing in rock music videos. Rock videos containing the highest level of sex were judged most appealing[4] and left viewers in the most positive mood. But the lesson of the experiment conducted by Zillmann and Mundorf (1987) should not be lost. An escalation of explicit sexual content in rock music videos is likely to have adverse effects. The impact of sex on appeal may be curvilinear. At some point, giving the viewer more sex and making it more explicit may yield negative consequences for appeal.

Most important, the findings of our research indicated that viewers 43 *did not enjoy* violent videos. Highly violent videos were rated as extremely unappealing and produced very negative emotional experiences. In addition, the formula for producing the least enjoyable rock video was clear: Make it highly violent, add sex and, then, arousing music. Because there is substantial evidence demonstrating a link between television violence and aggression (e.g., Berkowitz & Rogers, 1986; Geen & Thomas, 1986; Greeson & Williams, 1986; Huesmann, 1986; Rosenthal, 1986; Singer & Singer, 1980), the potential adverse effects of violence give more force to the findings of our research. In particular, if media depictions of violence have the potential to produce antisocial consequences and the viewer, in fact, does not enjoy it, why is there violence in rock music videos at all?

## NOTES

1. Many thanks to Dolf Zillmann for comments on an earlier version of this manuscript. Correspondence concerning this article should be addressed to Christine H. Hansen, Department of Psychology, Oakland University, Rochester, MI 48309-4401.
2. To ensure that failure to find significant effects was not due to lack of power in the statistical tests, the following power estimates (Cohen, 1969) were computed. For Experiment 1, power estimates of the ANOVAs indicated that the power to detect a medium gender effect on sexual visual content (equivalent to a difference in means of 1.27) and violent visual content (mean difference of 1.18) was above .99. (All mean differences refer to 1-9 scales.) The power of the ANCOVAs to detect medium gender effects for visual appeal and music appeal (a difference in means of .91 and .81, respectively) was greater than .99. Power estimates of the visual-sex ANCOVAs indicated that the power to detect a medium effect on the nonsignificant emotion variates also was above .99. A medium effect translated into differences in means of 1.55 (angry), 1.77 (aggressive), and 1.84 (anxious). For Experiment 2, the power of the ANOVAs to detect medium gender effects on visual-violence and visual-sex ratings (differences in means of 1.22 and 1.75) was above .99. Finally, the power of the ANCOVAs to detect medium gender effects on visual and music appeal (differences in means of .98 and .96) was also above .99.
3. We are grateful to an anonymous reviewer for pointing this out to us.
4. In fact, the conventional wisdom may be a bit less correct with regard to sex than the results from this study would imply. Our research has indicated that nonsexual, upbeat visuals are given significantly higher evaluations than high-sex videos.

## REFERENCES

Berkowitz, L., & Rogers, K. H. (1986). A priming effect analysis of media influences. In J. Bryant & D. Zillmann (Eds.), *Perspectives on media effects*. Hillsdale, NJ: Lawrence Erlbaum.

Brown, D., & Campbell, K. (1986). Race and gender in music videos: The same beat but a different drummer. *Journal of Communication, 36,* 94–106.

Cantor, J. R., & Zillmann, D. (1973). The effect of affective state and emotional arousal on music appreciation. *Journal of General Psychology, 89,* 97–108.

Cohen, J. (1969). *Statistical power analysis for the behavioral sciences*. New York: Academic Press.

Geen, R. G., & Thomas, S. L. (1986). The immediate effects of media violence on behavior. *Journal of Social Issues, 42,* 7–27.

Gerbner, G., Gross, L., Morgan, M., & Signiorelli, N. (1986). Living with television: The dynamics of the cultivation process. In J. Bryant & D. Zillmann (Eds.), *Perspectives on media effects*. Hillsdale, NJ: Lawrence Erlbaum.

Gore, T. (1987). *Raising PG kids in an X-rated society*. Nashville, TN: Abingdon.

Greeson, L. E., & Williams, R. A. (1986). Social implications of music videos for youth. *Youth & Society, 18,* 177–189.

Hansen, C. H. (in press). Priming sex-role stereotypic event schemas with rock music videos: Effects on impression favorability, trait inferences, and recall of a subsequent male-female interaction. *Journal of Basic and Applied Social Psychology.*

Hansen, C. H., & Hansen, R. D. (1988). Priming stereotypic appraisal of social interactions: How rock music videos can change what's seen when boy meets girl. *Sex Roles, 19,* 287–316.

Hansen, C. H., & Hansen, R. D. (1989). *The content of MTV's daily countdown: "Dial MTV" for sex, violence, and antisocial behavior.* Unpublished manuscript, Oakland University.

Hansen, C. H., & Hansen, R. D. (in press). Rock music videos and antisocial behavior. *Basic and Applied Social Psychology.*

Hansen, R. D., & Hansen, C. H. (1988). Repression of emotionally tagged memories: The architecture of less complex emotions. *Journal of Personality and Social Psychology, 55,* 811–818.

Huesmann, L. R. (1986). Psychological processes promoting the relation between exposure to media violence and aggressive behavior by the viewer. *Journal of Social Issues, 42,* 125–139.

James, W. (1884). What is emotion? *Mind, 9,* 188–204.

National Coalition on Television Violence. (1984, January 14). *Rock music and MTV found increasingly violent.* Press release.

Rosenthal, R. (1986). Media violence, antisocial behavior, and the consequences of small errors. *Journal of Social Issues, 42,* 141–154.

Schachter, S., & Singer, J. E. (1962). Cognitive, social, and physiological determinants of emotional state. *Psychological Review, 69,* 379–399.

Schwartz, G. E., & Weinberger, D. A. (1980). Physiological patterning and emotion: Implications for the self-regulation of emotion. In K. R. Blankenstein & J. Polivy (Eds.), *Self-control and self-modification of emotional behavior* (pp. 13–27). New York: Plenum.

Sherman, B. L., & Dominick, J. R. (1986). Violence and sex in music: TV and rock 'n' roll. *Journal of Communication, 36,* 79–93.

Singer, J. L., & Singer, D. G. (1980). Television viewing and aggressive behavior in preschool children: A field study. *Annals of the New York Academy of Sciences, 347,* 289–303.

Steinem, G. (1988). Six great ideas that television is missing. In S. Oskamp (Ed.), *Television as a social issue: Applied social psychology annual issue* (Vol. 8, pp. 18–29). Newbury Park, CA: Sage.

Strasburger, V. C. (1988, November 17). Rock videos may harm kids' health. *USA Today,* p. D4.

Waite, B. M., & Paludi, M. A. (1987). *Sex-role stereotyping in popular music videos.* Paper presented at the meeting of the Midwestern Psychological Association, Chicago.

Zillmann, D. (1978). Attribution and misattribution of excitatory reactions. In J. H. Harvey, W. J. Ickes, & R. F. Kidd (Eds.), *New directions in attribution research* (Vol. 2, pp. 335–368). Hillsdale, NJ: Lawrence Erlbaum.

Zillmann, D. (1983). Transfer of excitation in emotional behavior. In J. T. Cacioppo & R. E. Petty (Eds.), *Social psychophysiology: A sourcebook* (pp. 215–240). New York: Guilford.

Zillmann, D. (1984). *Connections between sex and aggression.* Hillsdale, NJ: Lawrence Erlbaum.

Zillmann, D., & Mundorf, N. (1987). Image effects in the appreciation of video rock. *Communication Research, 14,* 316–334.

Zimmerman, D. (1984, March 29). Rock video's free ride may be ending. *USA Today,* pp. D1, D2.

## Post-Reading Questions

1. What surprises, if any, do you find in the results of this study? What reasons lie behind these surprise findings as far as you are concerned? Do your reasons seem in line with Hansen and Hansen's? If not, how are they different? What factors caused you to interpret the results in a different way?

2. Describe the methods used in this study. Do you see any problems in the methodology used? What important variables were not taken into consideration? Why are they important? How could the study have been altered to include these variables?

3. If you were a rock video programmer, how would you interpret and apply the results of this study? Would you alter the appeals to sexuality in your videos? How would you alter them? Would you avoid or increase violent appeals? Why?

4. Your class probably includes some students who are majoring in areas that require mathematical and statistical expertise. In a workshop group, have these students explain the general function and meaning of the statistical analyses that are mentioned in this article. Focus these explanations and demonstrations on paragraphs that are particularly reliant on statistics (paragraphs 9, 11 to 15, 21 to 25, and 28).

5. Write a short news article for your local or campus newspaper based on this research article. Be sure that you do not distort the data and results of your source in any way. You should also avoid simply repeating the technical language and statistics of your source; these would not appeal to newspaper readers. Have other non-expert readers in your class read a draft of your article and comment on its readability.

6. What does this article suggest regarding television sex and violence in general? Does it tell you something about most viewers, or about some other particular category of viewers? Does it tell you something about appeals to sex and violence in combination, or about how people respond emotionally to sexual and violent stimulation?

7. Why do research articles usually begin with abstracts? How are these abstracts useful to other researchers? How could they be used by those who produce reference materials such as indexes, bibliographies, and readers' guides?

# EDWARD L. PALMER ON CHILDREN'S TELEVISION

## Pre-Reading Questions

1. Read the title and headnotes to this essay. What do you predict will be the thesis of this essay, given these early clues? What type of essay do you think this will be—persuasive, informative, entertaining, instructive, more than one of these, or something else?

2. Before you read this essay, review your own experiences and opinions concerning children's television. Given those experiences, what do you think Palmer means when he says that there is a "crisis" in children's education? Do you think he is referring to the amount, type, or content of children's programming?

3. From your own experience with educational programs such as "Sesame Street," what do you think makes some successful and others not? Do some do a better job than others of blending entertainment and instruction? How is this blend accomplished? Does an educational program require the same level of technical support and expertise as any prime-time entertainment in order to appeal to today's children?

## OUR CRISIS IN CHILDREN'S TELEVISION, OUR DEFICIENCIES IN CHILDREN'S EDUCATION
### Edward L. Palmer

This instrument can teach, it can illuminate; yes, and it can even inspire. But it can do so only to the extent that humans are determined to use it to those ends. Otherwise, it is merely wires and lights in a box. There is a great, perhaps decisive battle to be fought, against ignorance, intolerance and indifference. This weapon of television can be useful.

—Edward R. Murrow

. . .the first people who understood television, at least in the United States, were the advertising community. They grasped its significance immediately. The second group in the United States who figured it out were the politicians, because they saw the consequence the television would have in campaigning, in reaching the electorate. The last group which is finally awakening from its slumber are the educators, the teachers. They finally are beginning to realize that television is a monumental change in the way people think, in the way people spend their time.

—Newton Minow

*assumption*

Everything we see on television for children is a reflection of somebody's  1
vision) Programs do not just "happen"; they are a product of policy—
even if that policy is one of indifference and neglect.

What is our vision? How do we, as Americans, collectively decide (or  2
fail to decide) how this vital medium affects our children? What are the
forces that shape our vision? And how do they compare with the forces
that shape other countries' visions of children's TV?  *rhet. strat*

Somebody's vision—good or bad, actively sought or passively  3
accepted—becomes our children's television reality. In speaking of "vision," I mean not only the subjective issue of program content and quality
but, equally important, the objective quantifiable considerations on which
the entire superstructure of programming rests. Are children's programs
conveniently available at suitable viewing times, and well distributed
throughout the week and year? What total amount of new programming
is available each year? What is the ratio of new to repeat programs? Are
shows geared to narrow bands of age in keeping with growing children's
rapidly changing needs, interests, and understandings?

Two different TV systems in the U.S. have the capacity to reach and  4
serve our total child population. They are commercial broadcasting and
public broadcasting, both with penetration levels that exceed 95 percent
of all households.[1] Cablecasting and videocassette recordings are a
distant but emerging third force, although within this century neither
will reach more than perhaps three-quarters of all children in the country,
at most.

For the near term, we can look only to our commercial and PTV  5
broadcast systems to serve all our children abundantly and well, with
high-quality, age-appropriate programs, rich and varied in horizon-
expanding subject matter. Yet, by any measure we may care to use, both
of these systems are woefully deficient in their children's offerings.

## OUR BEST, OUR WORST, AND OUR CRISIS
## OF NEGLECT

The extent of our deficiency will probably surprise most Americans.  6
After all, do we not export programming all over the world? And do we
not boast of a fine weekday children's offering on public TV? What of
programs like *Sesame Street* and *Mister Rogers' Neighborhood* for preschoolers, and the *3-2-1 Contact* science series for children aged 8 to 12? It is
true that these series and *The Electric Company*, the now retired reading
series for 7- to 10-year-olds, served for many years as the four traditional
cornerstones of the PTV children's out-of-school program block.

All have been well received by parents and children, and by their  7
backers in an assortment of foundations and government agencies,

corporations, and PTV organizations. In addition, so well regarded is *Sesame Street* worldwide, and its unique model of planned education presented through television's most engaging entertainment forms, that eleven different countries have solicited cooperation from CTW in creating their own *Sesame Street* adaptations, featuring their own languages, cultural symbols, educational goals, and characters. Moreover, our traditional PTV children's favorites have been joined in the early 1980s by a lively new series called *Reading Rainbow,* which promotes books and reading, and by a new weekly series of hour-long family cultural dramas presented under the umbrella title of *WonderWorks* and scheduled for play in the early evening, to encourage shared viewing by children and their parents. *Square One TV,* a major new math series for children 8 to 12 years old, by CTW, had its premiere in 1987.

So what can be so far awry? In fact, the status of children's TV is 8 bleak in both commercial and public television.

On the commercial side, the abysmal fact is that *not one of our three* 9 *major networks supports a regular weekday program schedule for children.* With the exception of occasional late afternoon specials, commercial children's programming is geared mainly to entertainment and confined to Saturday morning. Commercial TV's neglect of children on weekdays is especially regrettable when we consider that 90 percent of all child viewing takes place on weekdays.[2]

It is true, particularly in the largest U.S. commercial TV markets, 10 containing the greatest numbers of channels, that the independent (i.e., non-network) stations frequently schedule children's programs before or after school; however, with rare exceptions, these programs are reruns of already heavily exposed Saturday morning network cartoons.

The strong swing toward deregulation in the 1980s has only 11 worsened the situation and is directly responsible for a decline in children's informational and educational features on commercial television.[3] The advocacy group Action for Children's Television had appeared before the Federal Communications Commission (FCC) in 1970 asking for regulated reforms that included daily programming for children.[4] After long delays that involved an on-again, off-again series of hearings, inquiries, proposed rule-makings, reports, policy statements, petitions, complaints, and other regulatory red tape, while we waited for improvements through industry self-regulation that were never to come, an FCC decision of December 1983 finally ruled against the ACT petition.[5]

An earlier FCC of a different mood, in 1979, had issued a task force 12 report which concluded that the industry leaves children "dramatically underserved."[6] This view was soon to be set aside, however, with hardly a moment's blush, by an administration intent upon dismantling as much as possible of the federal regulatory function. One of the first casualties to result from the massive move toward deregulation of the 1980s was the long-running and well regarded *Captain Kangaroo* children's TV series, which CBS promptly dropped from its weekday schedule.

Meanwhile, repeat programming in the PTV children's schedule 13 hovers just short of 90 percent for all children, and is even higher for children above preschool age. Public television aired 1200-plus hours of children's programs in 1982–83, according to the FCC's landmark 1983 Report and Order on children's television.[7] Yet, for children 6–13 years old, public television in a typical recent year offered, on a year-round average, an ungenerous amount of less than ten minutes of new programming each weekday. In the 1984–85 PTV broadcast season, only 41 new program hours in total were produced for 6- to 13-year-olds, counting *3-2-1 Contact*, 10 hours; *Reading Rainbow*, 2.5 hours; *Voyage of the Mimi*, 6.5 hours; and *WonderWorks*, 22 hours.

So underfunded is children's public television in the U.S. that it has 14 never yet had the need or occasion to ask what form a well-conceived and managed, comprehensive children's program schedule might take. We know, however, from other countries such as Japan and Britain, and from our own more limited experience, that for the most part the program needs of 6- to 9-year-olds are distinct from those of 10- to 13-year-olds, especially when the programs are informational or educational.

To offer each of these two age groups one program hour each 15 weekday, 260 days per year, would require 520 schedule hours per year. PTV's 41-hour offering for 6- to 13-year-olds in the 1984–85 broadcast season would constitute a program renewal rate of less than 8 percent in this modest 520-hour-per-year schedule.

Television emerged scarcely more than forty years ago, rapidly to 16 become ubiquitous in the lives of America's children. Since that time, we have seen a wide variety of program forms emerge with qualities which enrich children's lives. Many parents who grew up in the first "television generation" will remember with nostalgia some of the old favorites they loved and learned from. I am thinking of titles like Leonard Bernstein's *Young People's Concerts,* the venerable *Captain Kangaroo* series, going all the way back to the mid-fifties, and *Mr. Wizard,* whose primitive production values were more than offset by its host's earnest fascination with things of science. Or who in this generation does not remember *Kukla, Fran and Ollie* or the perils of *Lassie*?

Then came television's "wasteland" years of the 1960s, as they were 17 characterized at the time by FCC Chairman Newton Minow. Violence in the children's schedule became so great a concern that the Surgeon General undertook a major study to examine the effects on children's attitudes and behaviors.[8] It was at this time, too, in the late 1960s, that Action for Children's Television was formed.

A third milestone event in children's television came at around the 18 same time, in 1966, when *Sesame Street*'s co-conceivers, Joan Cooney and Lloyd Morrisett, sat over dinner to first discuss not just a new production idea but how television for children's at-home viewing could be tied to the national education agenda. What made this event even more significant is that they shared an extraordinarily ambitious vision. In an era when PTV children's shows were all local productions, done on shoestring budgets, and commercial cartoons were being turned out like so many sausage-factory look-alikes, Cooney and Morrisett asked for—and received—the funding to transform all of the most expensive of television's artistically and technically sophisticated forms into vehicles for teaching. To do this, they started a new organization, independent of public broadcasting: Children's Television Workshop.

Their dream was to showcase the best of what this promising but 19 underdeveloped invention could achieve. They were pioneers. And they succeeded.

Their shared vision, realized, establishes beyond any reasonable 20 question that television can be taken seriously as a cost-efficient educational tool. Independent research and testing have demonstrated that programs in the style of those produced by the Workshop can garner an impressively large following of voluntary child viewers and at the same time bring about measured educational outcomes.[9] The Workshop's heavy investment in pre-broadcast planning and in child testing to help guide program design had proved its worth.[10] A few professional reports and articles and then hundreds appeared to document the Workshop's program-design strategies, to prove measurable effects, to question and probe—and, in general, to create a body of knowledge and experience which might serve as shoulders for future practitioners to stand on.[11]

A wonderful kind of yin/yang balance pervades in the Workshop's 21 productions and approach. For example, the programs both educate and entertain, and to bring this about, they are created by collaborating academics and television artists. The goals are idealistic, and they are promoted by public relations professionals. These program series focus on the special and otherwise unmet needs of children from low-income households, and they are wholly embraced by the middle-class parents as a source of valuable educational experiences for their children.[12] The Workshop itself is chartered as a nonprofit educational corporation, but it has developed tax-paying, profit-making subsidiaries to help keep vintage series in production and develop new ones.[13]

Since *Sesame Street*'s initial appearance in 1969 as a means to prepare 22 young children for school, the Workshop has produced, in addition, three other major home-and-school educational TV series. One is *The Electric Company,* an aid to children experiencing reading difficulty. Another is *3-2-1 Contact,* which encourages career preparation in science and technology by documenting and explaining the activities of the people who work in the field. And the most recent is the mathematics series, *Square One TV,* to strengthen children's skills, understandings, and interest in this important field. The latter two are intended primarily to serve the 8 to 12 age group.

On the international front, CTW recently completed an entirely original, major TV production titled *Al Manaahil* designed to help teach reading of Arabic to Arab children. The series consists of 65 half-hour programs modeled partly on *The Electric Company* and produced in Jordan. 23

The work in production design at CTW may be looked upon as a deliberate attempt to appropriate or adapt for educational use every suitable form known in television. A great deal has been made of the fact that *Sesame Street* copies the short, punchy format of the television commercial. As a result, it succeeds at encouraging preschool children to go away from the TV humming the alphabet or singing a jingle about cooperation or geometric forms. What is often overlooked is that the series' producers also incorporate many other forms by commissioning some of the best documentary filmmakers, cartoonists, music writers, puppeteers, and performing artists. As a result, television artistry, in all its manifestations, has become one of the most powerful allies of parents and educators. Building on the tradition of Sophocles and Horace, DeFoe and Twain, Aesop and the *Laugh In* TV series, CTW set out with *Sesame Street* to couch instruction in entertaining forms. 24

Somewhere along the way, the Workshop learned that "entertaining" does not always have to mean "amusing," and nowadays its staff more often speaks of using "engaging" television approaches to attract and teach the child learners. *Sesame Street* was copied around the world by producers, some of whom assumed that the aim is always to amuse the viewing children. Actually, to engage the children with a comedy skit or visual trick may work to teach some subjects some of the time. But just as useful, under the right conditions, is simply to allow television to serve as the prism through which the inherent appeal and fascination of a subject is revealed, without embellishments. 25

*example?*

Thanks to the efforts of the Workshop and other dedicated production centers in the U.S. and around the world, proof that television confers value in children's lives, when it is thoughtfully conceived and produced, is no longer at issue. Our only problem now, at least in the U.S., is to find ways to make this quality available in sufficient quantity—to go beyond demonstrations and occasional, usually short-lived, applications to develop a comprehensive children's offering. 26

In applauding the fact that the children's PTV schedule is now partly full we must not lose sight of the fact that it is still mostly empty. Why are we Americans so stingy in allocating a fair share of our invaluable daily television broadcast time to help educate our younger generation for the awesome responsibilities they will inherit? Put another way, why cannot the United States provide its number one natural resource—its children—with the electronic sustenance that television is uniquely 27

*garnering support from reader*

capable of providing every classroom and home? Television is, after school and home, the country's most important teacher. What is more, we can harness its potential for less than a penny a day per child.

Precedents abound elsewhere. A quality children's TV schedule is an 28 institution in Great Britain and Japan. Youngsters in these countries benefit from a constant stream of fresh, new images and ideas available throughout their formative childhood years. An equitable portion of the total broadcast schedule in these countries is devoted to programs made expressly for children, and these programs are scheduled at times appropriate and convenient for child viewing. Both of these countries even strive to provide their children with a "microcosm" of the program varieties available to adults, including news, drama, sports, light entertainment, discussion, and how-to programming. Moreover, sufficient numbers of new programs are created each year to sustain a high ratio of new to repeat programming.

In Great Britain, for example, the BBC airs 785 hours of at-home 29 children's television each year, representing 12.6 percent of BBC–1 program schedule. Of these, 590 hours, making up 75 percent of the total of children's shows, are newly produced each year.[14] Our own PBS, by contrast, carried just 87.5 new program hours in the 1984–85 broadcast year—a quite typical recent year—of new out-of-school children's TV fare.[15] Great Britain's population is one-quarter the size of ours, yet its yearly volume of new PTV programming for children is more than five times greater than our own. The BBC also creates educational programs for in-school use on a regular and stable basis.[16]

## THE NEED IN EDUCATION, THE OPPORTUNITY IN TELEVISION

In the meantime, education in our country is beset with a long-building 30 crisis whose costs and consequences will be enormous. The dimensions of the problem were chronicled in no fewer than five commissioned reports and several individually authored books, whose co-appearance in 1983 fomented a major wave of national concern.[17] Former U.S. Commissioner of Education, Harold Howe II, has said of this "year of the reports":

> It is doubtful that American education has ever before received such a concentrated barrage of criticism and free advice. . . . What is even more unusual is that these outpourings are not just from academics worried about standards in the schools. They come from business and political leaders, from university presidents, from parents and students, and occasionally from educators themselves. The broad message is that the schools can and should be improved, particularly with regard to their academic function. The

recommendations are legion and sometimes conflicting; no one can count their costs. Further, there is a frustrating sense among educational leaders about who should do what and how to start.[18]

Many feel that solutions must focus primarily on conditions in the 31 nation's schools—on improving teacher recruitment, professional status and pay, on updating curricula, and on upgrading facilities, equipment, and materials. Many educators say that underlying all of these is the more fundamental need to strengthen the underpinnings of financial support. But another part of the solution lies in making fuller use of broadcast television for at-home learning. Television's unique contribution to this large task may reside in such factors as:

*why "but"*

- its ubiquity;
- its nonthreatening, nonpunitive quality as a teaching medium;
- its ability to organize and present information in clear and memorable ways through animated graphics;
- its ability to depict live role models; and
- its nondependence on reading skill or ability. *b/c of their resources*

The schools are being asked to do more than they can accomplish. As 32 a result, each time this country has identified a major deficiency in children's education in recent years, television has responded as a supplement, to help provide a part of the answer—first to help meet preschool children's need for early social, emotional, and intellectual stimulation, and subsequently, in elementary school reading and in career exploration in science and technology. The most recent area was mathematics. But do we really need to wait for future reports to reveal that television also can help children understand history, geography, health, government, the arts, and simple skills for everyday living?

A measure of our crisis in children's home-and-school television is 33 that we lack the level of assured funding that would allow us even to stand still. Funds with which to expand on or revise successful program series are almost totally lacking; funds to start new productions are in only slightly greater supply. With enough funds to create only one major new series every few years, we have had to learn to chase the most urgent education crisis of the moment.

Done without the benefit of supporting national policy, this ad hoc 34 approach at least has given us a successful and highly visible era of demonstration activities. But we are moving far too slowly, and as we step from crisis to crisis, the ground gained crumbles away behind us for want of stable funding support.[19] This is regrettable, because the needs in education which these productions address remain with us and require continuous attention.

*isn't # for schools more important?*

Given the chance, television can (1) *promote* useful activities, ranging 35 from book reading to art and music to health and safety; (2) *instruct* children in skills and ideas ranging from school subjects to household economics to the harmful effects of dangerous drugs; and (3) *inform* them about everything—world political and economic events, happenings in nature, career opportunities, and lifestyle trends and scientific discoveries which will affect their lives. It can start them off pursuing strands of life-long interests.

Well-planned television programs can help prepare children to find 36 school, the workplace, the voting booth, and events in the larger world more interesting and comprehensible. Like teachers and textbooks, television can provide learning experiences that parents have neither the time nor, in most cases, the academic expertise to provide.

Looked at from every conceivable perspective, a hybrid, home-and- 37 school schedule of children's television programming deserves to be supported. The special benefits to be realized range from social equity to educational cost efficiency. Many of these benefits hinge on what television can contribute toward filling children's lives with learning as a voluntary, everyday pastime.

Children's time is valuable, and parents need help in seeing greater 38 portions of their children's time turned to productive uses. Educational television programs, regularly and conveniently available, can be an important part of the answer.

Children's weekday television viewing averages nearly 100 hours per 39 month.[20] No one wants these children to watch more television than they already do; instead, what is needed is a useful alternative to the heavily adult-oriented program diet they now consume. What I am proposing is that at least 20 hours a month of thoughtfully crafted, age-appropriate educational fare be available as a viewing option for all children.

Like money contributed regularly to savings, a little of a child's time 40 devoted each day to learning quickly adds up—and it soon begins to yield compound interest. Suppose we provide children with an hour each weekday of solidly educational or informational TV fare. An hour each weekday—260 hours per year—is equal to about a fifth of the total time a child spends in the classroom each year. It is also about one-fifth the amount of the time the typical child spends watching television each weekday.

Ten years of TV learning at the rate of just an hour each weekday is 41 equal *in time* to two full school years. This is a very considerable amount of learning time which, if well filled, could significantly enrich our children's formative years.

One measure of the need for television as children's third educational 42 institution—after school and home—is the complexity of the world today's youngsters will reside in and manage when their turn comes.

*expert*

Alan Pifer, who headed the Carnegie Corporation when it funded the Carnegie Commission on Children, points out that upon today's youngsters will fall the threefold responsibility of supporting the largest elderly population in our nation's history and providing the nation's productive work force, while rearing their own children.[21]

Readings of the future point to only a small fraction of the challenges 43 with which today's young people must be prepared to cope. They will have to learn to refresh and retrain themselves through life-long learning. To a greater extent than ever before, education will no longer be seen as an activity to be completed early as preparation for life, but as a continuing activity throughout life. The need will be felt increasingly to provide another chance for those who fail or drop out the first time through.

Former U.S. Education Commissioner Dr. Ernest Boyer had this to 44 say about the way in which television's unique strengths as educator came into play in one TV series:

> In the push toward strengthening academics, there is the danger that young people are gathering fragments of information without developing a perspective. The scope and drama of television can help remedy that. The series, *Connections,* for example, in tracing the roots of technology related how we live today to the long sweep of discovery and invention.[22]

Dr. Boyer went on to mention another very different educational application for the medium:

> Teenagers are confused about the future. Thirty percent of our high school seniors were still undecided early in 1983 about whether they were going to college, although that question pertained to a future only a few months distant. Public television, better than high school vocational counseling programs, could show teenagers what it is like to work at various occupations.[23]

Television's established role and value in helping children explore 45 career possibilities is a key point in the rationale behind the creation of the *3-2-1 Contact* science series. *3-2-1 Contact* was funded in response to our national need to see more school children develop interest in and consider careers in science and technology. It is designed to reach youngsters in their preteens, so that later, in high school, they will choose to enroll in the courses which will admit them into further study or work in science and technology. Without this high school preparation, a career in the field is closed to them forever.

*Sesame Street,* in the meantime, has become a kind of "omnibus" 46 series, each year widening its scope by the addition of one or two new subjects—careers, computers, vocabulary, disabling conditions such as

*to cultivate the workforce we need*

deafness and blindness, and promotion of book reading and library use, to mention only a few. In addition, CTW has created the outlines of a similar series for television's now forgotten early elementary (6- to 9-year-old) age group. This series concept has as its working title the *Sesame Graduates* series. The TV possibilities are at least as varied with these older children as in the case of *Sesame Street*'s preschool learners. Yet many worthy programming ideas have failed to get off the ground in recent years for want of adequate funding support, and there is no assurance that the Workshop, in spite of its excellent fundraising record to date, will succeed in forming a new consortium of funders to support this or any other new children's series.

## FINE EDUCATIONAL GEMS: THEIR ASTONISHING COST ADVANTAGE

Children's public television in the U.S. today is stalled in a proving phase 47 that began in 1969 with the first national distribution of *Sesame Street* and *Mister Rogers' Neighborhood*. When Newton Minow described television of the 1960s as a "vast wasteland," it is certain that in the children's area, a wasteland it was. Since that time, children's television has emerged as an educational resource of proven potential. Yet, still with us are all the same in-built, systemic shortcomings in America's television institutions which encouraged Joan Cooney and Lloyd Morrisett to found CTW in the first place as an independent force in the field. Under their leadership, the Workshop proved a vision of home-and-school television which seems to have everything going for it, except—so far—to have sparked the wider growth of the field which the Workshop had anticipated as the sequel to its widely acknowledged and highly visible successes.

*Sesame Street* has been a paver of the way and a model. It has been 48 copied widely, not only in terms of surface appearance but in the unique way in which it was—and is—created: through a three-way collaboration of TV producers, subject-matter planners, and specialists in research on children's educational television.

All that this great success story lacks is a happy conclusion. Not that 49 things have gone all that badly. In that erstwhile wasteland, now, at least, we can see in one small corner, standing out here and there on the landscape, a few gems and strings of gems of real value. Their presence makes us even more painfully aware of all the gaping holes where other gems might be.

As we survey this scene, we have to ask what conditions are 50 responsible for our failure up to now to achieve the next major milestone, that of creating at least a minimally adequate, comprehensive children's television schedule, to supplement young peoples' education through an activity in which children already spend thousands of all-too-often wasted hours.

It was Joan Cooney who first described her vision for *Sesame Street* as "a Tiffany jewel." She used the ambitious metaphor to express her dream of seeing the children's corner of the wasteland eventually filled with other jewels, measured by *Sesame Street*'s high standard of combined entertainment and education. The problem with gems, Joan always knew, is that they come with a price tag, and the more massive they are, and the better their quality, the greater the cost.

It is true that television is costly, especially when to garner a voluntary child audience we have to match the technical and artistic quality children are accustomed to seeing on competing channels. Yet, even so, education through broadcast television makes abundantly sound economic sense. U.S. Commissioner of Education in the early 1970s, Dr. Sidney Marland, said of *Sesame Street* and *The Electric Company* that they are probably the best educational investment the government ever made.[24] And still today, the cost for the six million target-age preschoolers who tune in regularly each week to *Sesame Street* comes to just a penny per child per program viewed.[25] Factored across a whole year, programs like *Sesame Street* become the sort of cost-efficient bargain available nowhere else in education. The cost for *The Electric Company* when it was produced in the early 1970s was also just a cent a day per elementary school-age child reached.[26]

No complex economic analysis is required to appreciate what an extraordinary educational bargain broadcast television can be. So great is television's educational cost advantage that a few calculations, which anybody could make, literally on the back of an envelope, convey the point dramatically and well. For the 1986–87 school year we laid out an estimated $22.42 per school day to educate each child in grades one through twelve.[27] Compare this with the very large amount which could go each year to support children's PTV programs if we could somehow raise *just one cent per day* for each of the nation's 42 million children who fall in the age range of two to thirteen years.[28] The amount would be a rather astonishingly large $153 million—or more than five times the small and unstable annual amount of less than $30 million spent currently, from all sources, on public children's television.[29]

As a nation, we currently spend at the rate of about 12 cents per year per capita on programming in children's public television.[30] By contrast, our nation's projected $170 billion combined elementary and secondary school bill in fiscal 1987 translates to about $713.00 per capita.[31] Seen in this light, the yearly amount needed to markedly improve our children's educational television diet is minuscule. The amount which I propose to be minimally adequate for this purpose is $62.4 million.[32] This expenditure is easily affordable: it requires less than six tenths of a cent a day on behalf of each child in the population.

One prefers to believe that the key to a great surge forward in 55
children's home-and-school television is not mainly one of achieving the
necessary policy breakthrough in principle, since few issues of national
self-interest can be so clearly argued from the standpoint of the need, the
available but underused resource, and cost-efficiency. More complex,
both from a policy standpoint and from a standpoint of practicality, is the
question of how to collect and channel the dollars needed to support a
quality offering of children's weekday out-of-school informational and
educational TV programs.

Individual parents, no matter how wealthy, cannot buy for their 56
children the best in educational programming that television has the
potential to offer. There is no store from which to purchase or lease 260
hours—a weekday supply for a year—of age-appropriate educational TV
cassettes. Nor is cable TV the answer—not if we want to be able to reach
all children with planned education, and not if we want to reach more
than but a fraction of all children within the reasonably near future. So
far, cable has not spent the extra amounts needed to incorporate a solid
educational emphasis in its children's services, and it has little competitive reason to do so. It offers a service of unique value simply by offering
"something" for children at times in the schedule when otherwise there
is nothing. Cable's limited reach is another problem, especially in its
tendency to exclude the poor by wiring first in wealthier neighborhoods.[33] Moreover, as much as a quarter of the total population will not
yet enjoy even the option to subscribe to cable by the end of this
century.[34]

The commercial broadcasters have their "collection" mechanism, in 57
the form of advertising fees. An innovative mechanism is needed by
which to better support children's informational and educational TV
programs. Applying principles of sound business economics, it may be
seen that we are able to realize dramatic, not merely marginal, cost
advantages when we make use of nationally broadcast television as a force
in children's education. Our economic folly if we fail to do so is revealed in
the following additional illustration. A small children's learning book
which costs $1.49 will give, perhaps, as much as five hours of benefit. Yet
for just $1.49 per child, we can supply every child in the country with
260 hours per year of age-appropriate, televised learning.[35] A full hour
each weekday, week in and week out, for each of three child age groups.
In this example, the ratio of television's cost-advantage is a little more
than 50 to 1, assuming that every child watches every program.[36]
Television's advantage is still 25 to 1 if only a very conservative 50
percent of the nation's 2- to 13-year-olds view each program.

There is no shortage of educational needs and certainly no lack of 58
program ideas. Moreover, the public television signal today is available in
nearly every U.S. household, and every station could and should make

*Spring break—parents*

*Change paper grade*

abundant space available in its schedule to serve children. But there is a great shortage of funding, which can only be met with substantial government participation.

The future of children's educational television depends on our [59] government leaders' awareness of our national interest in this important, too-long-neglected area, and on the care they take in shaping a policy for long-term action. The answer lies principally with Congress and the Administration.

Sixteen years ago, we did not know enough about television's [60] usefulness as a children's at-home teaching medium to be able to justify (much less help guide) the formation of national policy to set up permanent funding support for the activity. Today we do.

## NOTES

1. Source: A. C. Nielsen.
2. *Child and Teenage Television Viewing 1981* (New York: A. C. Nielsen Co.).
3. Examples: CBS's *30 Minutes,* the award-winning TV magazine show for young people that was patterned on *60 Minutes,* was canceled. NBC's *Special Treat* moved into rebroadcasts with no new shows produced. ABC dropped *Animals, Animals, Animals* on Sunday mornings, and stopped production on *Kids Are People Too,* deciding to present reruns for its major non-cartoon effort on weekends.
4. Action for Children's Television appeared before the FCC in 1970 with a proposal that required daily programming for children, and the elimination of commercials—including selling by hosts—on children's television. The FCC accepted ACT's proposal as a petition for rulemaking.
5. Source: Federal Communications Commission (1984), "Children's Television Programming and Advertising Practices: Report and Order" (*Federal Register, 49,* 1704, January 13).
6. Source: *Television Programming for Children: A Report of the Children's Television Task Force* (five volumes) (Washington, D.C.: Federal Communications Commission, 1979).
7. Source: FCC, "Report and Order."
8. Reference: Surgeon General's Scientific Advisory Committee on Television and Social Behavior (1972), *TV and Growing Up: The Impact of Televised Violence* (Report to the Surgeon General, U.S. Public Health Service) (Washington, D.C.: U.S. Government Printing Office).
9. For various evaluations of *Sesame Street,* G. Lesser, S. Ball, G. Bogatz, J. Minton, L. Paulson, T. Cook; for various evaluations of *The Electric Company,* S. Ball, P. Dirr, R. Herriott, R. Liebert, J. Riccobono, A. Sherdon.
10. For an excellent general description of pre-broadcast planning and formative research to guide program design, see G. Lesser (1974) *Children and Television: Lessons from Sesame Street* (New York: Random House).
11. Also, currently G. Lesser of the U.S. and P. Levelt of the Netherlands are collaborating in a compilation and review of published and unpublished

studies and reports on *Sesame Street* and its various international adaptations, which number well in excess of 300 entries.

12. Evidence that children from low-income circumstances learn from watching *Sesame Street* and *The Electric Company* is contained in reports of major evaluations of the two series by S. Ball and G. Bogatz, and in studies by other researchers such as J. Minton and L. Paulson. Evidence of heavy *Sesame Street* viewership in low-income black and Spanish-speaking neighborhoods is reported in the Yankelovich surveys.

13. Examples of fully or partly CTW-owned tax-paying subsidiaries, current or previous, include Distinguished Productions, Inc., and Sesame Street Records, both subsidiaries of CTW Communications, Inc.; and Children's Computer Workshop. A Ford Foundation grant in the early 1970s helped CTW develop its capacity to produce self-generated revenues.

14. Source: *BBC Annual Report and Handbook 1986*. BBC-1 carries 746 hours of children's out-of-school programs, and BBC-2 carries 39. Their combined total is 785 hours, and the children's fraction of all schedule hours on the combined two channels is 7.2 percent. Children's out-of-school programs make up 12.6 percent of the schedule on the BBC-1 channel.

15. Sources: PBS and the several individual children's program producers who supplied PBS. The newly produced children's program hours in the 1984–85 PBS children's TV schedule were: *Sesame Street*, 39; *Mr. Rogers' Neighborhood*, 7.5; *Reading Rainbow*, 2.5; *WonderWorks*, 22; *Voyage of the Mimi*, 6.5; and *3-2-1 Contact*, 10.

16. Schools television constituted 503 hours and 10.1 percent of BBC-2's total annual broadcast schedule in 1984–85. Source: *BBC Annual Report and Handbook 1986*.

17. Harold Howe II (1984) Introduction to Symposium on the Year of the Reports: Responses from the Educational Community. *Harvard Educational Review*, Volume 5, Number 1. Reports cited by the Symposium include:

Boyer, Ernest (1983), *High School: A Report on Secondary Education in America* (Princeton, N.J.: Carnegie Foundation for the Advancement of Teaching);

Goodlad, John J. (1983), *A Place Called School: Prospects for the Future* (New York: McGraw-Hill);

Lightfoot, Sara L. (1983), *The Good High School: Portraits of Culture and Character* (New York: Basic Books);

The National Commission on Excellence in Education (1983), *A Nation At Risk: The Imperative for Educational Reform* (Washington, D.C.: U.S. Department of Education);

The National Science Board Commission on Precollege Education in Mathematics, Science, and Technology (1983), *Educating Americans for the 21st Century* (2 vols.) (Washington, D.C.: National Science Foundation);

Task Force on Education for Economic Growth (1983), *Action for Excellence: A Comprehensive Plan to Improve Our Nation's Schools* (Denver: Education Commission of the States);

The Twentieth Century Fund Task Force on Federal Elementary and Secondary Education Policy (1983), *Making the Grade* (New York: Twentieth Century Fund).

18. Harold Howe II, *Harvard Educational Review, ibid.*
19. Lack of funding caused the demise of *Zoom* and *The Electric Company,* and was responsible in part for the reduction of *Mr. Rogers' Neighborhood* to as few as ten new shows (5 hours of production) a year. *3-2-1 Contact* currently is at the end of its assured funding, with no new funding source in sight. And in spite of its highly successful premier season, *Reading Rainbow* received much less than it deserved in funding to create additional programs.
20. Source: A. C. Nielsen.
21. Source: Pifer, Alan (1978), "Perception of Childhood and Youth (Report of the President)," in *1978 Annual Report Carnegie Corporation of New York.*
22. Source: *The Dial* (June 1983).
23. *Ibid.*
24. Source: Quoted in CTW newsletters and press reports. The author himself heard Marland make this observation in public on many occasions.
25. From A. C. Nielsen data, we know that each week, *Sesame Street* attracts six million preschoolers for an average of 3.1 viewings each, giving a total of 18.6 million viewings. In 52 weeks, that comes to 967 million preschooler viewings. At a series production cost in Fiscal Year 1985 of $9,719,000, the cost per child per viewing comes to just one cent.
26. Source: CTW Newsletter. Note, however, that *The Electric Company* continued to play weekdays on PBS in repeat for eight years after its last renewed season in 1976–77. As a result, the cost-per-viewer ratio continued to improve over the course of those eight years.
27. Source: The annual back-to-school forecast from the National Center for Education Statistics projects a $4,263 annual expenditure rate per pupil for the 1986–87 school year. Assuming a 190-day school year, this translates to $22.42 per pupil per school day.
28. Population source: U.S. Bureau of the Census, Current Population Reports Series, P–25, No. 952.
29. The 1984–85 expenditure for children's programs aired on public television, new plus repeat programs, was $28.7 million.
30. Based on the total national population of 239 million men, women, and children.
31. From the annual back-to-school forecast issued by the National Center for Education Statistics. The U.S. population figure used in arriving at my per capita calculation is 239 million.
32. In 1985 dollars.
33. The right of cable companies to wire into the wealthier neighborhoods of a community first has been upheld by the courts.
34. My own projection. Nobody has argued a convincing case that more than three-quarters of U.S. homes will have access to cable by the year 2000. The National Cable Television Association reported that in the ten largest television markets, 65 percent of homes were still without access to cable in

1985. And the 1985 Field Guide from *Channels* reports that high installation costs have frightened the biggest multiple-system operators away from major markets, leaving some cities looking hard for qualified bidders. Also, in the largest cities cable faces the greatest amount of broadcaster competition for TV advertising. According to *TV and Cable Factbook* (Washington: Television Digest, annual) cable had 37.5 million subscribers in 1986, not all of which are households. There are about 88 million TV households nationwide.

35. I propose a rate of funding support for children's out-of-school public TV programs of $62.4 million per year, to provide 260 days per year of weekday programming. Given that there are 42 million 2- to 13-year-olds in the U.S., the cost per year per child is $1.49.

36. The cost for the television in the example above is less than six-tenths of a cent per child per day ($0.0057). The cost for the book is $1.49 divided by five, or 30 cents a day. Television's cost-advantage is 53 to one.

## Post-Reading Questions

1. This is one of the few persuasive essays in this chapter. What is persuasive about its style? How is its style different from the more scientific essays in this or other chapters?

2. Why does the essay begin with three paragraphs that include a large number of questions? How is Palmer's audience supposed to be affected by these questions? What role do these questions play in setting up his audience? What are the implied answers to these questions?

3. Why does Palmer think that television holds the key to the locked door of education in America? What are the advantages of educational television compared to school education, for example?

4. Why does Palmer think that "Sesame Street" has been as successful as it has been? What did the show and its producers do to make it successful?

5. Why has "Sesame Street" not spawned a whole series of similar educational programs? Why have the total number of hours of children's educational programming remained as low as they have?

6. What administration does Palmer seem to hold accountable for the government's recent lack of interest in children's educational television (paragraph 11)? What role did government deregulation play in this de-emphasis on support for children's educational television?

7. In arguing for greater support for children's educational programming, Palmer balances pessimism regarding private or corporate sponsored television and optimism regarding federally sponsored programming. Why is that? Why is he skeptical of commercial interests when it comes to looking for support for educational television?

**8.** Why are Japan and the United Kingdom ahead of the United States in monetary support of educational television for children?

# 6
. . . . . . . . . . . . . .
## OPTIONAL WRITING ASSIGNMENTS FOCUSED ON TELEVISION AND CULTURE

The following optional list of assignments should prove useful if you choose not to develop your own essay topic. Whether you choose one of these options or develop your own, remember that you need to analyze your writing context to decide how to achieve your writing purpose for the particular readers you target (see "The Rhetorical Approach to Academic Writing" in Chapter 2).

*1. Write an essay based on research you conducted after identifying an issue while reading and discussing this chapter.* Begin by defining the issue in precise terms, then consider where you might find a book, article, or statistics that would enable you to address the issue in a convincing way. Why is this additional information useful to your readers? How does it clarify a complicated situation? Refer to Chapter 3 on the research process for ideas on how to go about doing research and to the Research Appendix for ideas on sources of information.

*2. Write an argument.* Begin by stating a thesis with which others in your class disagree. List your reasons and support for this thesis. Then, do the planning that a writer of a strong argument needs by addressing these questions: What will my intended readers think of my reasons and support? How can I ground my thesis in assumptions that I think my readers will accept? How can I appeal to my readers' need for information related to the thesis? How can I appeal to their emotions as I support my thesis? What appeals will give my readers a positive image of my character as I develop my thesis? What style and organization will effectively address my audience on this issue? The following list of questions could be turned into workable theses for an essay:

- What kind of an impact does television have on our daily lives?
- How does television affect our ability to think coherently?
- How does television, in its drive to entertain, oversimplify important issues?
- How does television enhance our lives?
- How fairly are minorities represented on television?
- Does television promote too much or too little hero worship?
- Does television have a positive or negative effect on individual character?

- What must television do to reach its full potential?
- Does television have a positive or negative effect on education?

*3. Write an essay in which you describe in detail an occasion in which you, a friend, or your family were influenced by a television program.* As you describe the occasion, suggest whether the effect was positive or negative—not only by what you say, but by how you say it. Consider, for example, how adjectives, adverbs, and verbs or figures of speech convey emphatically the program's impact to your readers.

*4. Some television experts say that character is the primary emphasis in most television dramatic programs.* With this claim in mind, choose a television character from either a situation comedy, a dramatic-adventure series, or soap opera. Then, write an essay in which you analyze that character, explaining in the process why the character got your attention in the first place and what effect the character has on the commercial television audience. Somewhere in your essay you should address the question of how the character fits into your idea of the overall effect network television characters have on public consciousness.

*5. Write an analysis of one television commercial.* Your purpose is to show your readers how the commercial appeals to a particular audience, the effect of its imagery on its audience, the definition of that audience itself. At the end of your essay, address the whole issue of television advertising—its ethics and its overall effect on American society.

*6. Write an essay in which you discuss the recent changes in television technology (VCRs, large screens, potentials for taping programs, cable access, interactive television) and their implications for the future.* Be sure to focus, perhaps by emphasizing one rather than all of these technologies, so that you produce a coherent essay.

*7. Write a letter to the hypothetical producer of a television show that you think is particularly informative, entertaining, or offensive.* In the letter, explain in detail why you feel the way you do about the show and recommend changes for the better. Consider your audience as you write. Your purpose is to improve the show.

*8. Write an essay in which you reflect on your television viewing habits when you were a child.* Was your viewing supervised? In what ways? Did that supervision have a good or bad effect on you as a television consumer? Do you think that you had sufficient choice among programs? Did some shows seem to have a negative effect on you, others a more positive one? Why? What plan will you have, or do you have, for your own children's viewing habits? Give reasons for your suggested plans. Consider parents or prospective parents to be your implied audience.

*9. Write an essay in which you use your own viewing experience and some outside reading to address the question of whether cable television has qualitatively improved the range of program choices for television consumers.* Refer to specific channels and programs in developing your essay. Aim your essay at consumers of cable television. Your purpose is to help that audience decide whether cable television does indeed increase the range of viewing choice. You may make this an essay in which you attempt to persuade your audience to take some action: writing cable channel owners or Congress, for example, on the whole issue of cable access and programming.

 *10. How has a recent popular culture fad been supported by television?* Consider music videos on MTV or other music video channels, cult programs such as "Twin Peaks" or "Northern Exposure," or children's programs such as "Ninja Turtles" as possible subject matter for this essay. Your purpose in writing is to show how this fad was at least partially created by television. Your audience is those people who might have consumed the products that were sold as part of the fad.

# 12

## Perspectives on Censorship

How far does individual freedom go? Who should be
responsible for determining whether or not individual
freedoms should be limited?

### 1
### DEVELOPING A RHETORICAL APPROACH

This chapter deals with censorship. Recently, several controversies
over definitions of obscenity and pornography have caused American
society to reconsider limiting freedom of expression as it applies to
speech and the arts. Traditionally, Americans have relied on the
Constitution's First Amendment to guarantee individual freedom of
expression. However, individuals and groups have raised questions
about how much protection the First Amendment offers citizens. Some
of the readings explore censorship of particular forms of individual
expression: literature, music, and the visual arts. Other readings offer
particular viewpoints about whether or not censorship in any form is
appropriate in a democratic society. Although the readings do not cover
all aspects of the censorship theme, together they represent a wide
range of opinions and offer some possible explanations for the controversy surrounding issues related to censorship.

The readings in this chapter provide a starting point for examining
your own experiences with censorship and your opinions concerning

some of the censorship-related issues. Your responses to these readings, and those of your classmates will contribute to the development of a rhetorical community based on this topic. As you and your classmates share reactions to what these authors say, you will have opportunities to consider some of the critical questions they raise. Why do societies censor citizens? If censorship is appropriate, who is responsible for censoring? Who should set the standards for censorship? How does a society arrive at definitions of "obscenity" and "pornography"? Is it ever appropriate to limit freedom of expression?

As you and your classmates discuss and debate some of these difficult questions, and raise additional ones, you will need to narrow your own examination of the censorship theme to one question or issue that you find interesting and important enough to explore in greater detail as you develop plans for a chapter essay. You may decide to trace the history of censorship in art, or you may choose to join the debate concerning whether records, tape recordings, and compact discs should carry descriptive labels. Whatever aspect of the censorship topic you choose to explore, the rhetorical community formed with your classmates will provide a basis for your decisions about *purpose* (what you want to say in this essay and why) and *audience* (whom you want to read this essay), as well as guidance for decisions about content, organization, and style.

## 2
## . . . . . . . . . . . . . .
## GENERATING IDEAS ABOUT CENSORSHIP
## BEFORE READING

Your own experiences with censorship are a valuable source of background information. They create a foundation for responding to what the different writers are saying and contribute to the meaning you construct as you read. Your experiences represent an important contribution to the shared knowledge base you and your classmates develop around this subject and to your own sense of audience for your chapter essay.

The activities that follow provide a framework for your reading and writing by asking you to review and describe your experiences with the censorship theme.

### Probing Personal Experience

Write short, informal answers to the following questions. If you are keeping a course journal, write your answers there. Be sure your answers are written in a form that can be used in class.

*1. How do you feel about ratings for films?* Do those ratings influence your choice of which film to see? Do you believe parents use ratings to make decisions about which films they will allow their children to see? Do you believe ratings represent a form of censorship? Why or why not?

*2. Would you favor college regulations restricting public speech?* Why or why not? What experiences have you had in college classes that explain your position on this issue? What have you heard from friends at other colleges or read about in newspapers and magazines that illustrates your position?

*3. Describe your experiences at video rental stores, newsstands, and bookstores.* Do these establishments isolate or restrict magazines and films that may offend some customers? How do you feel about separating such materials from other merchandise? Do you believe keeping these materials separate makes prospective customers feel uncomfortable? Does this strategy represent a form of censorship? Do you know if there are local laws requiring retailers to isolate these materials? Do you favor such laws? Why?

*4. How much control do you have over what you are exposed to in public areas?* Consider shopping malls, subway stations, bus stops, and billboards you see daily. Have you ever seen anything in these areas that offended you? What kinds of materials offend you in public places? Why?

*5. Do you believe that definitions of pornography change from one generation to another?* Compare and contrast your own definition of pornography with your parents' and grandparents' definitions. In what ways are those definitions alike? In what ways are they different? What explains these similarities and differences?

*6. If you were responsible for deciding whether or not particular arts projects received federal funds, how would you decide?* What criteria would be most important to you? Would you fund artistic projects that involved nudity? Would you fund projects that may offend some viewers? Why or why not?

*7. Have you ever been told by parents or teachers* not *to read a particular book, see a particular film, or buy a particular tape or compact disc?* Describe an experience like this. How did you feel about being told "no"? Did you feel your actions were being censored? What did you do? Do you believe it is appropriate at times for parents or teachers to restrict what young people see or hear? Why?

## Freewriting to Capture Personal Experience

A list of topics related to censorship that you can freewrite about in short, ten-minute sessions follows. Your teacher may assign a topic or ask you to choose one yourself. If you are keeping a journal, do your freewriting there. Consider narrating an experience you had that has some connection to the freewriting topic. Writing about this personal experience could provide a starting point for reviewing ideas and opinions that have been stored in your long-term memory and for generating questions and ideas that you think should be explored. (For a detailed discussion of freewriting, see pages 103 to 104.)

> Censorship
> Pornography
> Freedom of expression
> First Amendment rights
> Obscenity
> National Endowment for the Arts
> Film ratings
> Record ratings
> Government regulation of individual expression

Freewriting is most effective if you follow this sequence: **R**eread, **F**ocus, **R**ewrite (**RFR**). (For a discussion of RFR, see page 104.)

## 3
### DEVELOPING RHETORICAL CONTEXT THROUGH GROUP ACTIVITIES

Each of the following collaborative activities asks you to work with other students in revising a freewriting. Presenting your freewriting to the group will give you a chance to hear your classmates' responses to the stories and ideas you have written about in response to the particular topic. Similarly, you will be reading and reacting to the stories and ideas your classmates have written about in their freewritings. Having this chance to interact with other writers interested in the censorship topic is an important part of your writing process, particularly your decisions about audience and purpose. As you listen to the reactions of classmates to your freewriting, you will be able to develop a better sense of how readers respond to texts and what they expect to find as they read.

These collaborative experiences will also help you evaluate and refine your ideas about censorship before developing them further, and they will help the entire class develop the shared foundation of knowledge that will constitute the classroom rhetorical community. (If you are collaborating for the first time, read the description of strategies for effective collaboration on pages 104 to 105.)

- Exchange your freewriting with a partner. Read your partner's freewriting without a pen or pencil in your hand. When you have finished reading, write a response to your partner using these guidelines: first, *summarize* what you have read. Tell your partner what you think was said in the freewriting; next, *list* any questions you have about the ideas in the freewriting. Are you confused because your partner has omitted some details? Does the connotation of a particular word trigger a particularly negative reaction? Does your partner's reasoning seem illogical? Finally, *respond* personally to what your partner has written. Did a similar experience (or a very different one) happen to you? Do you have some helpful information on an issue your partner raises? Did you find a section in the freewriting particularly powerful? Your partner then considers these personal responses, the summary, and the list of questions you provide. Together, they provide a valuable source of reader response, one that will direct your partner's planning, drafting, and reviewing processes.

After you and your partner have completed your written responses to one another's freewriting, exchange them, take a few minutes to read them, then discuss them. If you have both written on the same freewriting topic, you may discuss how the contents of the two freewritings compare and contrast. How are they alike? How do they differ? How could you benefit from information in your partner's freewriting? How could your partner benefit from information in yours? If you have written about different freewriting topics, consider possible connections between the contents of the two freewritings. The goal of this sharing is to provide you and your partner with insight into how readers respond to a text, for this response provides writers with a better sense of how to achieve writing purposes for particular readers.

- Work with a group of three or four students to draft a student policy statement on freedom of expression at your college. Use each member's freewriting as a source for this collaboratively composed statement. Begin by having group members read their freewritings aloud while the rest of the group comments and reacts. Ask one member to take notes. After all freewritings have been read, ask the note-taker to read the notes to the entire group. Then, with one group member acting as facilitator or group leader, the group should brainstorm common threads in the notes, as well as other ideas in the freewritings, that may be included in the student policy statement on freedom of expression. For example, the group may identify ideas that suggest what acts of expression may be considered inappropriate when students are in class or behaviors that may be inappropriate in public areas of the campus. The group may also identify statements in freewritings that discuss how various forms of expression should be evaluated and by whom. The group leader should provide time to discuss ideas that cause disagreement among group members, working to reach some kind of consensus before moving on to another idea.

After brainstorming and reaching consensus, the note-taker should read all of the notes aloud and the group leader should lead the group in drafting its policy statement. Return to the freewritings for examples to illustrate the group's statement. Share the statement with the entire class once it is completed, leaving some time to solicit responses.

- Working with a group of three or four students, choose a controversial video, art exhibit, piece of music, book, or movie that has been the subject of censorship debate, and compose a position paper of 3 to 4 pages in which you state a group position on its censorship. Follow the same collaborating process described above to compose your group's statement.

## 4
. . . . . . . . . . . . .
## USING READINGS TO DEVELOP
## A RHETORICAL COMMUNITY

The readings in this chapter help you and your classmates use reading while you write. Spend time sharing with classmates your interpretations and reactions to the ideas presented in this chapter's readings and your sense of audience and purpose will become clearer and your sense of control over the censorship topic will grow stronger.

The readings discuss several aspects of the censorship topic, among them what kinds of individual expression should and should not be subject to censorship, legal aspects of censorship, causes and effects of censorship, controversies arising over particular artists' creative expressions, and changing attitudes toward censorship. The information in these readings will produce different responses from you and your classmates, and your classroom sharing sessions will provide opportunities for the members of the developing rhetorical community to work toward a deeper understanding of these aspects of the chapter's theme.

Your reading will also create opportunities for you to analyze how writers make decisions about their texts with their readers and writing purposes in mind. For example, you may observe that a writer discussing legal aspects of censorship takes special care to cite the Constitution's First Amendment and to discuss its history and implications. Or you may find that one writer's use of personal experience creates a particularly effective emotional appeal in an essay on textbook writing and censorship. Your discussions with classmates about these readings will create opportunities to exchange ideas about how different strategies may be applied as you attempt to define an audience for your own essay on censorship. What kinds of personal experiences, for example, will impress different kinds of readers? What kinds of experts will readers find convincing? As you read, write about, and discuss these readings, you will decide what ideas to explore in more detail in a chapter essay.

## The Readings in This Chapter

The readings in this chapter cover several aspects of the censorship topic and have been written by academics who study censorship issues and by journalists who report on their research and on public aspects of the censorship theme. The first reading, "Pornography and Law," is from a book written by Richard S. Randall, *Freedom and Taboo*. This excerpt provides a foundation for discussions in other readings about particular forms of censorship. It provides some information about the history of censorship and the development of censorship legislation in America.

Two other readings present broad perspectives on the censorship theme. Garry Wills, a conservative journalist, presents his viewpoint on the positive aspects of "censure" in a personal essay; Irving Kristol, a college professor who describes himself as a "neoconservative," presents his case for "liberal censorship" in an essay that appeared in *The New York Times Magazine* in 1971. Although written almost twenty years apart, the two articles provide an appropriate framework for the readings on particular forms of individual expression that follow. In addition, copies of the Constitution's First Amendment and the National Council of Teachers of English's (NCTE) "Statement on Censorship" are included to provide a framework for your reading and discussions.

The rest of the readings focus on particular forms of individual expression. In "The Debate Over Placing Limits on Racist Speech Must Not Ignore the Damage It Does to Its Victims," Charles R. Lawrence III, a law professor, argues that racist speech must be regulated, even though liberal thinkers may believe such speech is protected by the Constitution's first amendment. Mary Renck Jalongo and Anne Drolett Creany, professors of education, report on their research with children's literature and censorship in an article appearing originally in an academic journal *Childhood Education*. They contrast censorship with "selection," urging educators to develop selection criteria to guide their reading choices for students and libraries. Their approach to literature and censorship contrasts with "Trials of a Textbook Writer," a personal essay by Raymond English, a researcher at the Ethics and Public Policy Center. English shares his own experiences with textbook writing as a way of presenting some censorship issues that have a bearing on what students learn in class. He argues, for example, that the pressures brought to bear on textbook writers by well-meaning activist groups may actually affect the content of individual history textbooks. Turning to other forms of individual expression, Mikal Gilmore, a journalist for *Rolling Stone* magazine, reports on music events in 1990, along the way raising issues related to censorship and the recording arts. Providing several examples of attempts to censor rock and roll music, Gilmore argues that rock music is unique because it strives to be disruptive and anti-establishment, and that rock musicians are protected by the First Amendment.

The two final articles focus more closely on visual and performing arts. Susan Brownmiller expresses her feminist argument for pornography legislation. Arguing that she is neither anti-sex nor against the First Amendment, Brownmiller believes pornography should be subject to legislation because it reflects a hatred of women and an attempt to humiliate them. Walter Berns, a college professor, explains the role of the National Endowment for the Arts (NEA) as an arbiter and perpetuator of American culture, and explores some of the critical issues affecting how the NEA fulfills its mission. Berns believes that the NEA does a better job perpetuating American culture in some areas than others; for example, he recommends eliminating visual arts funding but continuing musical arts funding.

Consider what these writers say, how they say it, and for whom. Remember, like these writers, you are using reading as a learning and writing tool. Reading gives you a better understanding not only of what the writers are saying and how they say it, but how you feel about their ideas. Your reading and reacting help you develop your own rhetorical context for writing. Your writing in response to what you read and discussion of those responses with your classmates will narrow your own area of interest and generate a reason for writing for a particular set of readers, just as the writers whose work you have read must do.

# 5
. . . . . . . . . . . . .
## READINGS ON CENSORSHIP

## CONSTITUTION OF THE UNITED STATES

### AMENDMENT 1

*Freedom of Religion, Speech, and the Press;
Rights of Assembly and Petition*

*Congress shall make no law respecting an establishment of religion, or prohibiting the free exercise thereof; or abridging the freedom of speech, or of the press; or the right of the people peaceably to assemble, and to petition the government for a redress of grievances.*

Many countries have made one religion the *established* (official) church and supported it with government funds. This amendment forbids Congress to set up or in any way provide for an established church. In addition, Congress may not pass laws limiting worship, speech, or the press, or preventing people from meeting peacefully. Congress also may not keep people from asking the government for relief from unfair treatment.

All the rights protected by this amendment have limits. For example, the guarantee of freedom of religion does not mean that the government must allow all religious practices. In the 1800's, some Mormons believed it was a man's religious duty to have more than one wife. The Supreme Court ruled that Mormons had to obey the laws forbidding that practice.


# THE STUDENTS' RIGHT TO READ
The National Council of Teachers of English


## THE RIGHT TO READ

*An open letter to the citizens of our country from the*
*National Council of Teachers of English*

Where suspicion fills the air and holds scholars in line for fear of their jobs, there can be no exercise of the free intellect. . . . A problem can no longer be pursued with impunity to its edges. Fear stalks the classroom. The teacher is no longer a stimulant to adventurous thinking; she becomes instead a pipe line for safe and sound information. A deadening dogma takes the place of free inquiry. Instruction tends to become sterile; pursuit of knowledge is discouraged; discussion often leaves off where it should begin.

> Justice William O. Douglas,
> United States Supreme Court:
> Adler v. Board of Education, 1952.


The right to read, like all rights guaranteed or implied within our constitutional tradition, can be used wisely or foolishly. In many ways, education is an effort to improve the quality of choices open to all students. But to deny the freedom of choice in fear that it may be unwisely used is to destroy the freedom itself. For this reason, we respect the right of individuals to be selective in their own reading. But for the same reason, we oppose efforts of individuals or groups to limit the freedom of choice of others or to impose their own standards or tastes upon the community at large.

The right of any individual not just to read but to read whatever he or she wants to read is basic to a democratic society. This right is based on an assumption that the educated possess judgment and understanding and can be trusted with the determination of their own actions. In effect, the reader is freed from the bonds of chance. The reader is not limited by birth, geographic location, or time, since reading allows meeting people, debating philosophies, and experiencing events far beyond the narrow confines of an individual's own existence.

## THE STUDENTS' RIGHT TO READ

### The Right to Read and the Teacher of English

For many years, American schools have been pressured to restrict or deny students access to books or periodicals deemed objectionable by some individual or group on moral, political, religious, ethnic, racial, or philosophical grounds. These pressures have mounted in recent years, and English teachers have no reason to believe they will diminish. The fight against censorship is a continuing series of skirmishes, not a pitched battle leading to a final victory over censorship.

We can safely make two statements about censorship: first, any work is potentially open to attack by someone, somewhere, sometime, for some reason; second, censorship is often arbitrary and irrational.

## A PROGRAM OF ACTION

Censorship in schools is a widespread problem. Teachers of English, librarians, and school administrators can best serve students, literature, and the profession today if they prepare now to face pressures sensibly, demonstrating on the one hand a willingness to consider the merits of any complaint and on the other the courage to defend their literature program with intelligence and vigor. The Council therefore recommends that every school undertake the following two-step program to protect the students' right to read:

> the establishment of a representative committee to consider book selection procedures and to screen complaints; and
> a vigorous campaign to establish a community atmosphere in which local citizens may be enlisted to support the freedom to read.

# RICHARD S. RANDALL ON PORNOGRAPHY AND LAW

## Pre-Reading Questions

1. What is your personal definition of pornography? What examples could you give to explain what pornography is and is not? Is pornography ever harmful? Why?

**2.** What role should the various levels of government (local, state, federal) play in determining what is and is not pornographic? Explain your answer with examples.
**3.** How did your own experiences contribute to your definition of pornography? What forces affected your views about what is and is not pornographic? Your family, friends, the media, school, or others?

## PORNOGRAPHY AND LAW
### Richard S. Randall

In Anglo-American experience, legal control of pornography has closely   1
followed the democratization of culture and the technological advances
that allowed larger and larger numbers of persons to be reached by
communications. Not until the late seventeenth century did sexual
expression unconnected with religious belief or political views become an
object of appreciable public demand for legal control. Yet it cannot be
supposed, as many libertarian writers have done, that sexual expression
qua sexual expression was previously of little or no concern or that there
was great tolerance of it. Law and government are never the only means
of limiting sexual expression; as in most areas of social life, most control
has been administered informally. It is when powerful, decisive, and (in
democracies) popular groups or forces perceive these controls to be
ineffective, as they often do in the face of major political, social,
economic, or technological change, that the formal, symbolic, but
sometimes less efficient restrictions of government are sought.

Early legal sanctions against sexual expression bear witness to this   2
relationship. Neither the common-law offense of obscene libel, nor the
Vagrancy Act of 1824 and Lord Campbell's Act of 1857 in England, nor
the various American state laws, beginning with Vermont's in 1821,
defined exactly what was to be proscribed—an unusual degree of
vagueness, considering that legal punishment followed conviction. The
terms "obscene," "indecent," "immoral," and the like were thought
self-evident or at least sufficiently clear for most persons including the
juries of peers who would decide the cases. This failure to elaborate did
not reflect a liberal social or intellectual environment or one indifferent
to control, but rather a wide consensus associated with control by
informal means. Official offenses assumed to be self-evident could only
have been built on earlier informal ones.

Under early common-law and statutory controls, offending   3
expression—that considered unsuitable for public utterance or
circulation—most often involved profanity or "indelicate" language
dealing with sexual matters, or "ideological obscenity," *themes* of trans-
gression against established morality, especially where the wrongdoing

was portrayed favorably or unpunished. The first attempt at definition emerged from the English case of *Regina v. Hicklin*,[1] in 1868, involving a pamphlet purporting to describe sexual depravity and immorality in the Roman Catholic clergy. Legal proscription depended on "whether the tendency of the matter charged as obscenity is to deprave and corrupt those whose minds are open to such immoral influences and into whose hands a publication of this sort may fall."[2] Such a finding could be based, not on the effect of the entirety, but on isolated passages. Intent and countervailing literary or social values did not matter. The *Hicklin* rule, as it came to be called, tied legal designation of obscenity to *effects* the expression *might* have on persons who were particularly susceptible, discounted by the improbability of exposure. Though skewed and imprecise by modern standards and altogether lacking in concern for the values implicit in freedom of speech, the rule did begin to move the law away from assumed self-evidence to a standard of utility. Sexual expression was proscribable for the high public good of protecting the individual (and, by implication, society) from harm. True, the reference group was the most vulnerable in the population, and the uncertain, unspecified harms of "depravity" and "corruption" might not be clear enough barriers to prevent the assertion of essentially moralistic concerns. Yet such concerns were no more than the law had already allowed and certainly no more than that on which most informal control rested.

The *Hicklin* rule prevailed in both English and American law for nearly a hundred years, and its deficiencies grew ever more clear. It did little to prevent prosecution of many nineteenth- and early twentieth-century works of literary merit. Nor could it be easily accommodated to growing constitutional interest in the value of speech. Vague terms such as "those whose minds are open to such immoral influences" were increasingly ill suited to an age in which social and moral pluralism undermined a comfortable consensus about particular sexual expression, and in which, for those very reasons, the law was asked to play an ever larger role in social control.

Although American courts had heard hundreds, even thousands, of obscenity cases by the 1950s, the Supreme Court had given almost no attention to the doctrinal or theoretical aspects of designation before its *Roth* decision in 1957.[3] In the few cases even remotely connected with sexual expression, the Court dealt with procedural questions rather than those of substance or definition. In *Roth*, it abandoned the *Hicklin* rule and recast legal designation of sexual expression.[4] Affirming the active role of law in social control, the Court said that obscenity, like libel and "fighting words," was one of the few categories of speech outside the First Amendment. Such expression was "utterly without redeeming social importance."[5] Put another way, sexual expression determined to be obscene could be legally proscribed simply as expression, without showing of a clear and present danger of harmful effect or any other proof normally associated with restriction of communication. In this "two-tier" categorical approach, the key question is whether an expression is "obscene" or not; sexual speech found obscene is proscribable, that not so found remains constitutionally protected.[6]

Answers are determined by "whether to the average person, applying [6] contemporary community standards, the dominant theme of the material taken as a whole appeals to the prurient interest," a succinct formulation that became known as the *Roth* test.[7] This was a major departure from the *Hicklin* rule. First, the hypothetical referent was not the most vulnerable individual in the population but the "average person." Second, that person must be of the "contemporary community," not that of another day, a matter the older rule had left open. Third, the communication must be judged not by isolated or selected parts but by "its dominant theme . . . taken as a whole." Finally, its effect or design must be the stimulation of "prurient interest" rather than a tendency to "deprave or corrupt."

Although the Court in fact upheld the conviction in *Roth,* the new [7] formulation was immediately recognized for what it was—a libertarian test that would narrow the scope of proscribable sexual expression. Like many reformulations, it raised almost as many questions as it answered. What, for example, was "prurient interest"? In a footnote, the Court equated it with "lustful thoughts," then cited the definition of "prurient" given in *Webster's Second Unabridged:* "Itching; longing; uneasy with desire or longing; of persons, having itching, morbid, or lascivious longing; of desire, curiosity, or propensity, lewd."[8] Though the Court said "obscenity and sex are not synonymous," it did not attempt to deal with the logical problem of defining "prurient," "obscene," "lewd," and "lascivious" as synonyms of one another. Was obscenity's being "utterly without redeeming social importance" simply a conclusion issuing from the fact of proscription, or was it another requirement of designation? Finally, the Court did not say whether the "community" whose "contemporary" standards were to be applied was the nation, the state, or the locality. Later decisions would clarify some but not all of these questions.

Although it was a major departure from *Hicklin,* the *Roth* test was [8] equally one of utility. Sexual expression was proscribable because it had a particular effect—an appeal to prurient interest. Without this effect there could be no proscription. Yet like all utility tests it must rest not only on a certain clear effect—here, prurient arousal—and agreement about its being wrong, but also on a demonstrable link between that effect and the agent at hand, that is, the particular expression under attack.

The years following *Roth* saw a surge in sexual expression of all sorts [9] and a much greater explicitness in what was portrayed. Obscenity prosecutions in response to popular demands for control increased as well. When convictions were obtained, as they frequently were, the new obscenity test encouraged appeals. As a result, much sexual or erotic representation—mainly in books, limited-circulation periodicals, and movies—came under designative scrutiny in the higher courts, in several cases the Supreme Court itself. Yet not until *Miller v. California*, in 1973, were a majority of justices able to agree on a definitional elaboration.[9] So lacking was a doctrinal consensus that Justice Harlan could observe a decade after *Roth* that "the subject of obscenity has produced a variety of views among members of the Court unmatched in any other course of Constitutional adjudication." In thirteen cases with signed opinions between 1957 and 1967, the nine justices filed fifty-five separate statements of their views.[10]

The Court was much more of one mind in application. The initial libertarian thrust of *Roth* was given full effect in a steady narrowing of the range of expression designated as obscene. In one six-year period alone, 1967–1973, thirty-one convictions were reversed. Many were disposed of per curiam, that is, through decisions without opinions or with short, sometimes cryptic, unsigned opinions.[11] In all, the Court's obscenity work in the sixteen years between *Roth* and *Miller* put it at odds with popular agencies of government—legislatures, local prosecutors, and juries.

Despite its fractionalization, the Court made several important doctrinal alterations in the basic *Roth* test. The most important were the "patent offensiveness" and "without redeeming social importance" requirements. The former meant that proscribable sexual expression, in addition to having prurient appeal, would need to affront "contemporary community standards relating to the description or representation of sexual matters."[12] Though it did not elaborate much further, the Court appeared to mean expression going "substantially beyond customary limits of candor."[13] Standing alone, of course, patent offensiveness would constitute a fairly restrictive test, but as an added element, its effect, as intended, was to narrow further the scope of designation.

A plurality opinion suggested that sexual expression could not be obscene unless it were also "utterly without redeeming social value," a matter mentioned but left in doubt in *Roth*.[14] This interpretation made the redemptive element a requirement of the test rather than merely a description of proscribed sexual expression. Although a clear majority of the justices did not endorse this addition or that of patent offensiveness, two justices who did not, Black and Douglas, found it easy to apply the requirements to reach libertarian decisions, since they opposed any regulation of sexual expression without evidence of a causal link to criminal or other harmful behavior.

Shortly after *Roth*, the Court removed so-called thematic or ideological obscenity from proscriptive designation. The New York State Board of Film Censors had refused to license *Lady Chatterley's Lover* because it portrayed adultery as a "desirable, acceptable, and proper pattern of behavior." Observing that the state had, in effect, tried to control advocacy of an idea, the Court held that portrayal of immoral behavior alone was not obscene even if shown in a favorable light.[15] The decision was something of a milestone, since depiction of immoral behavior, along with profanity and nudity, had historically been a prime target of social control. More flagrant depiction had not generally been at issue, because it was not widely produced or circulated.

This decision and the apparently additional requirements that desig- [14] nated expression be both patently offensive and without redeeming social importance led many observers and lower courts to conclude that the obscenity test was now so rigorous that only hard-core pornography would be proscribable.[16] Even so, exactly what expression would be included in this residual category was unsettled. In its several reversals of lower court findings of obscenity, the Court had declined to offer any definitive examples of what might be considered hard-core pornography or proscribable expression.

Justice Stewart, who had earlier and memorably claimed "I know it [15] when I see it" in reference to hard-core pornography, offered some illumination in *Ginzberg v. United States:*

> Such materials include photographs, both still and motion picture, with no pretense of artistic value, graphically depicting acts of sexual intercourse, including various acts of sodomy and sadism, and sometimes involving several participants in scenes of orgy-like character. They also include strips of drawings in comic-book format grossly depicting similar activities in an exaggerated fashion. There are, in addition, pamphlets and booklets, sometimes with photographic illustrations, verbally describing such activities in a bizarre manner with no attempt whatsoever to afford portrayals of character or situation and with no pretense to literary value.[17]

At odds with the hard-core pornography interpretation were several [16] other cases in which the Court seemed to say that obscenity might vary with the circumstances of the communication and the nature of its audience. The issue emerged dramatically in *Ginzberg,* in which the defendant publisher was convicted under an antiobscenity postal statute for mailing issues of two periodicals, *Eros* and *Liaison,* and a book, *The Housewife's Handbook on Selective Promiscuity.* The Court upheld the conviction, not because the materials were shown to be obscene under the *Roth* test, but because they were presented to the public in a way the Court described as "the sordid business of pandering."[18] Justice Brennan spoke for the Court:

> Where an exploitation of interests in titillation of pornography is shown with respect to material lending itself to such exploitation, through pervasive treatment or description of sexual matters, such evidence may support the determination that the material is obscene *even though in other contexts the material would escape such condemnation.*[19]

He took note of advertisements stressing lewd rather than redeeming 17
literary aspects of the publications and the attempt to get them post-
marked in such places as Intercourse and Blue Ball, Pennsylvania, and
Middlesex, New Jersey.

NOTES

1. Regina v. Hicklin [1868] L.R. 3 Q.B. 360.
2. Id. at 371.
3. Roth v. United States, Alberts v. California, decided together, 354 U.S. 476
   (1957).
4. A few lower courts had already departed from various elements of the
   *Hicklin* rule, most notably in Judge Woolsey's celebrated opinion finding
   Joyce's *Ulysses* not obscene because, among other things, the book was a
   work of literary importance and thus had to be judged as whole rather than
   by isolated passages (United States v. One Book Called "Ulysses," 5 F.
   Supp. 182 [S.D.N.Y. 1933]). For examples of other departures from the
   *Hicklin* rule, see Frederick Schauer, *The Law of Obscenity*, p. 71 n12.
5. Roth v. United States, 354 U.S. at 484–485.
6. Even on this fundamental and enduring point—that the law might be used
   to control sexual expression qua expression—the Court was not unanimous.
   Justices Douglas and Black argued, in dissent, that sexual expression (of any
   sort) should be left unregulated unless a causal link were shown to *action* of
   the kind government had the power to prevent (id. at 514). For the Court,
   Justice Brennan pointed out that the legal proscription of obscenity was
   "mirrored in the universal judgment . . . reflected in the international
   agreement of over 50 nations, in the obscenity laws of all 48 states, and in 20
   obscenity laws enacted by Congress from 1842 to 1956" (id. at 485).
7. Id. at 489.
8. Id. at 487 n.20.
9. Miller v. California, 413 U.S. 15 (1973).
10. Interstate Circuit, Inc. v. Dallas, 390 U.S. 676 (1968), at 704–705, and
    704 n.1.
11. They are cited in Paris Adult Theatre I v. Slaton, 413 U.S. 49, 82 n.8 (1973)
    (Brennan, J., dissenting).
12. "Memoirs of a Woman of Pleasure" v. Massachusetts, 383 U.S. 413, 418
    (1966).
13. See its citation of the American Law Institute's Model Penal Code,
    Jacobellis v. Ohio, 378 U.S. 184, 192 (1964) (Brennan, J., plurality
    opinion). Justice Brennan also referred to patent offensiveness synony-
    mously as "a deviation from society's standards of decency." Id.
14. "Memoirs of a Woman of Pleasure" v. Massachusetts, 383 U.S. at 418.
15. Kingsley International Pictures v. Board of Regents, 360 U.S. 684 (1959).
16. For a listing of cases on both sides, see Schauer, *Law of Obscenity*, p. 11,
    nn.73, 74.
17. Ginzberg v. United States, 383 U.S. 463, 499 n.3 (1966) (Stewart, J.,
    dissenting).

18. Id. at 467. In fact, the government admitted that the materials might not themselves be obscene. It is doubtful whether they could have been included in the emerging notion of hard-core pornography.

19. Id. at 475–476 (emphasis added).

## Post-Reading Questions

1. What does Randall mean by "informal" control of sexual expression? What experiences have you had with informal control of sexual expression? How do informal and formal control of sexual expression differ?

2. This reading is from Randall's book *Freedom and Taboo*. What readers would choose his book? How could a journalist writing a short article about pornography and the law use the information in this excerpt?

3. Why is it difficult to define terms such as *obscene, immoral,* and *indecent*? How would you define these terms? Give examples for each definition.

4. Explain the Hicklin law and its application to pornography cases. Why was this law eventually replaced?

5. Explain the Roth decision and the Roth test. What problems could arise in applying this test? Why?

6. Using your own experiences, explain how standards for sexual expression evolve. Refer to Randall's article to support your own response.

7. In your opinion, do movie ratings accurately reflect the content of movies? Explain your answer by referring to specific movies you have seen or know about.

8. Do you agree with Justice Stewart's statement about hard-core pornography ("I know it when I see it" paragraph 15)? Why or why not?

9. Summarize Randall's writing purpose in this excerpt. Does he want to persuade or inform? How do you know?

10. Write a short paragraph summarizing the main points Randall makes about laws relating to pornography. Then write a second short paragraph, describing the kind of essay in which a student could incorporate this information.

# IRVING KRISTOL ON PORNOGRAPHY, OBSCENITY, AND CENSORSHIP

## Pre-Reading Questions

1. What experiences have you had with censorship at home and at school? Describe an experience when you were told by parents or teachers that a certain film, record album or tape, or book was "off

limits." What reasons were offered for placing the item off limits? How did you feel about those reasons and about being told what you could or could not read, listen to, or see?

2. What reasons do censors have, other than control of public morality, for keeping certain books, films, or music unavailable or restricted to certain groups? Are any of these reasons acceptable to you? Why?

3. Read the first sentence of Kristol's article. Paraphrase what he is saying. Then describe an experience you had that illustrates his statement. How can his statement be related to censorship?

# PORNOGRAPHY, OBSCENITY, AND THE CASE FOR CENSORSHIP

## Irving Kristol

### I

Being frustrated is disagreeable, but the real disasters in life begin when  1 you get what you want. For almost a century now, a great many intelligent, well-meaning and articulate people—of a kind generally called liberal or intellectual, or both—have argued eloquently against any kind of censorship of art and/or entertainment. And within the past ten years, the courts and the legislatures of most Western nations have found these arguments persuasive—so persuasive that hardly a man is now alive who clearly remembers what the answers to these arguments were. Today, in the United States and other democracies, censorship has to all intents and purposes ceased to exist.

Is there a sense of triumphant exhilaration in the land? Hardly. There  2 is, on the contrary, a rapidly growing unease and disquiet. Somehow, things have not worked out as they were supposed to, and many notable civil libertarians have gone on record as saying this was not what they meant at all. They wanted a world in which *Desire Under the Elms* could be produced, or *Ulysses* published, without interference by philistine busybodies holding public office. They have got that, of course; but they have also got a world in which homosexual rape takes place on the stage, in which the public flocks during lunch hours to witness varieties of professional fornication, in which Times Square has become little more than a hideous market for the sale and distribution of printed filth that panders to all known (and some fanciful) sexual perversions.

But disagreeable as this may be, does it really matter? Might not our  3 unease and disquiet be merely a cultural hangover—a "hangup," as they say? What reason is there to think that anyone was ever corrupted by a book?

This last question, oddly enough, is asked by the very same people  4 who seem convinced that advertisements in magazines or displays of violence on television do indeed have the power to corrupt. It is also asked, incredibly enough and in all sincerity, by people—e.g., university professors and schoolteachers—whose very lives provide all the answers one could want. After all, if you believe that no one was ever corrupted by a book, you have also to believe that no one was ever improved by a book (or a play or a movie). You have to believe, in other words, that all art is morally trivial and that, consequently, all education is morally irrelevant. No one, not even a university professor, really believes that.

To be sure, it is extremely difficult, as social scientists tell us, to trace ⁵ the effects of any single book (or play or movie) on an individual reader or any class of readers. But we all know, and social scientists know it too, that the ways in which we use our minds and imaginations do shape our characters and help define us as persons. That those who certainly know this are nevertheless moved to deny it merely indicates how a dogmatic resistance to the idea of censorship can—like most dogmatism—result in a mindless insistence on the absurd.

I have used these harsh terms—"dogmatism" and "mindless"— ⁶ advisedly. I might also have added "hypocritical." For the plain fact is that none of us is a complete civil libertarian. We all believe that there is some point at which the public authorities ought to step in to limit the "self expression" of an individual or a group, even where this might be seriously intended as a form of artistic expression, and even where the artistic transaction is between consenting adults. A playwright or theatrical director might, in this crazy world of ours, find someone willing to commit suicide on the stage, as called for by the script. We would not allow that—any more than we would permit scenes of real physical torture on the stage, even if the victim were a willing masochist. And I know of no one, no matter how free in spirit, who argues that we ought to permit gladiatorial contests in Yankee Stadium, similar to those once performed in the Colosseum at Rome—even if only consenting adults were involved.

The basic point that emerges is one that Prof. Walter Berns has ⁷ powerfully argued: no society can be utterly indifferent to the ways its citizens publicly entertain themselves.* Bearbaiting and cockfighting are prohibited only in part out of compassion for the suffering animals; the main reason they were abolished was because it was felt that they debased and brutalized the citizenry who flocked to witness such spectacles. And the question we face with regard to pornography and obscenity is whether, now that they have such strong legal protection from the Supreme Court, they can or will brutalize and debase our citizenry. We are, after all, not dealing with one passing incident—one book, or one

*This is as good a place as any to express my profound indebtedness to Walter Berns's superb essay, "Pornography vs. Democracy," in the winter, 1971 issue of *The Public Interest*.

play, or one movie. We are dealing with a general tendency that is
suffusing our entire culture.

I say pornography *and* obscenity because, though they have different   8
dictionary definitions and are frequently distinguishable as "artistic"
genres, they are nevertheless in the end identical in effect. Pornography
is not objectionable simply because it arouses sexual desire or lust or
prurience in the mind of the reader or spectator; this is a silly Victorian
notion. A great many nonpornographic works—including some parts of
the Bible—excite sexual desire very successfully. What is distinctive about
pornography is that, in the words of D. H. Lawrence, it attempts "to do
dirt on [sex] . . . [It is an] insult to a vital human relationship."

In other words, pornography differs from erotic art in that its whole   9
purpose is to treat human beings obscenely, to deprive human beings of
their specifically human dimension. That is what obscenity is all about. It
is light years removed from any kind of carefree sensuality—there is no
continuum between Fielding's *Tom Jones* and the Marquis de Sade's
*Justine*. These works have quite opposite intentions. To quote Susan
Sontag: "What pornographic literature does is precisely to drive a wedge
between one's existence as a full human being and one's existence as a
sexual being—while in ordinary life a healthy person is one who prevents
such a gap from opening up." This definition occurs in an essay
*defending* pornography—Miss Sontag is a candid as well as gifted
critic—so the definition, which I accept, is neither tendentious nor
censorious.

It may well be that Western society, in the latter half of the twentieth  10
century, is experiencing a drastic change in sexual mores and sexual
relationships. We have had many such "sexual revolutions" in the
past—the bourgeois family and bourgeois ideas of sexual propriety were
themselves established in the course of a revolution against eighteenth-
century "licentiousness"—and we shall doubtless have others in the
future. It is, however, highly improbable (to put it mildly) that what we
are witnessing is the Final Revolution which will make sexual relations
utterly unproblematic, permit us to dispense with any kind of ordered
relationships between the sexes, and allow us freely to redefine the
human condition. And so long as humanity has not reached that utopia,
obscenity will remain a problem.


II


One of the reasons it will remain a problem is that obscenity is not  11
merely about sex, any more than science fiction is about science. Science
fiction, as every student of the genre knows, is a peculiar vision of power:
what it is really about is politics. And obscenity is a peculiar vision of
humanity: what it is really about is ethics and metaphysics.

Imagine a man—a well-known man, much in the public eye—in a 12
hospital ward, dying an agonizing death. He is not in control of his
bodily functions, so that his bladder and his bowels empty themselves of
their own accord. His consciousness is overwhelmed and extinguished by
pain, so that he cannot communicate with us, nor we with him. Now, it
would be, technically, the easiest thing in the world to put a television
camera in his hospital room and let the whole world witness this
spectacle. We don't do it—at least we don't do it as yet—because we
regard this as an *obscene* invasion of privacy. And what would make the
spectacle obscene is that we would be witnessing the extinguishing of
humanity in a human animal.

Sex—like death—is an activity that is both animal and human. There 13
are human sentiments and human ideals involved in this animal activity.
But when sex is public, the viewer does not see—cannot see—the
sentiments and the ideals. He can only see the animal coupling. And that
is why, when men and women make love, as we say, they prefer to be
alone—because it is only when you are alone that you can make love, as
distinct from merely copulating in an animal and casual way. And that,
too, is why those who are voyeurs, if they are not irredeemably sick, also
feel ashamed at what they are witnessing. When sex is a public spectacle,
a human relationship has been debased into a mere animal connection.

It is also worth noting that this making of sex into an obscenity is not 14
a mutual and equal transaction but rather an act of exploitation by one of
the partners—the male partner. I do not wish to get into the complicated
question as to what, if any, are the essential differences—as distinct from
conventional and cultural differences—between male and female. I do
not claim to know the answer to that. But I do know—and I take it as a
sign that has meaning—that pornography is, and always has been, a
man's work; that women rarely write pornography; and that women tend
to be indifferent consumers of pornography.* My own guess, by way of
explanation, is that a woman's sexual experience is ordinarily more
suffused with human emotion than is man's, that men are more easily
satisfied with autoerotic activities, and that men can therefore more easily
take a more "technocratic" view of sex and its pleasures. Perhaps this is
not correct. But whatever the explanation, there can be no question that
pornography is a form of "sexism," as the women's liberation movement
calls it, and that the instinct of women's liberation has been unerring in
perceiving that when pornography is perpetrated, it is perpetrated against
them, as part of a conspiracy to deprive them of their full humanity.

But even if all this is granted, it might be said—and doubtless will be 15
said—that I really ought not to be unduly concerned. Free competition

*There are, of course, a few exceptions. *L'Histoire d'O*, for instance, was written by
a woman. It is unquestionably the most *melancholy* work of pornography ever written.
And its theme is precisely the dehumanization accomplished by obscenity.

in the cultural marketplace—it is argued by people who have never otherwise had a kind word to say for laissez-faire—will automatically dispose of the problem. The present fad for pornography and obscenity, it will be asserted, is just that, a fad. It will spend itself in the course of time; people will get bored with it, will be able to take it or leave it alone in a casual way, in a "mature way," and, in sum, I am being unnecessarily distressed about the whole business. *The New York Times,* in an editorial, concludes hopefully in this vein.

> In the end . . . the insensate pursuit of the urge to shock, carried from one excess to a more abysmal one, is bound to achieve its own antidote in total boredom. When there is no lower depth to descend to, ennui will erase the problem.

I would like to be able to go along with this line of reasoning, but I 16 cannot. I think it is false, and for two reasons, the first psychological, the second political.

The basic psychological fact about pornography and obscenity is that 17 it appeals to and provokes a kind of sexual regression. The sexual pleasure one gets from pornography and obscenity is autoerotic and infantile; put bluntly, it is a masturbatory exercise of the imagination, when it is not masturbation pure and simple. Now, people who masturbate do not get bored with masturbation, just as sadists don't get bored with sadism, and voyeurs don't get bored with voyeurism.

What is at stake is civilization and humanity, nothing less. The idea 18 that "everything is permitted," as Nietzsche put it, rests on the premise of nihilism and has nihilistic implications. I will not pretend that the case against nihilism and for civilization is an easy one to make. We are here confronting the most fundamental of philosophical questions, on the deepest levels. In short, the matter of pornography and obscenity is not a trivial one, and only superficial minds can take a bland and untroubled view of it.

## III

I am already touching upon a political aspect of pornography when I 19 suggest that it is inherently and purposefully subversive of civilization and its institutions. But there is another and more specifically political aspect, which has to do with the relationship of pornography and/or obscenity to democracy, and especially to the quality of public life on which democratic government ultimately rests.

Though the phrase "the quality of life" trips easily from so many lips 20 these days, it tends to be one of those clichés with many trivial meanings and no large, serious one. Sometimes it merely refers to such externals as the enjoyment of cleaner air, cleaner water, cleaner streets. At other times it refers to the merely private enjoyment of music, painting, or literature. Rarely does it have anything to do with the way the citizen in a democracy views himself—his obligations, his intentions, his ultimate self-definition.

Instead, what I would call the "managerial" conception of democracy is the predominant opinion among political scientists, sociologists, and economists, and has, through the untiring efforts of these scholars, become the conventional journalistic opinion as well. The root idea behind this "managerial" conception is that democracy is a "political system" (as they say) which can be adequately defined in terms of—can be fully reduced to—its mechanical arrangements. Democracy is then seen as a set of rules and procedures, and *nothing but* a set of rules and procedures, whereby majority rule and minority rights are reconciled into a state of equilibrium. If everyone follows these rules and procedures, then a democracy is in working order. I think this is a fair description of the democratic idea that currently prevails in academia. One can also fairly say that it is now the liberal idea of democracy par excellence. 21

I cannot help but feel that there is something ridiculous about being this kind of a democrat, and I must further confess to having a sneaking sympathy for those of our young radicals who also find it ridiculous. The absurdity is the absurdity of idolatry—of taking the symbolic for the real, the means for the end. The purpose of democracy cannot possibly be the endless functioning of its own political machinery. The purpose of any political regime is to achieve some version of the good life and the good society. It is not at all difficult to imagine a perfectly functioning democracy which answers all questions except one—namely, why should anyone of intelligence and spirit care a fig for it? 22

There is, however, an older idea of democracy—one which was fairly common until about the beginning of this century—for which the conception of the quality of public life is absolutely crucial. This idea starts from the proposition that democracy is a form of self-government, and that if you want it to be a meritorious polity, you have to care about what kind of people govern it. Indeed, it puts the matter more strongly and declares that if you want self-government, you are only entitled to it if that "self" is worthy of governing. There is no inherent right to self-government if it means that such government is vicious, mean, squalid, and debased. Only a dogmatist and a fanatic, an idolater of democratic machinery, could approve of self-government under such conditions. 23

And because the desirability of self-government depends on the character of the people who govern, the older idea of democracy was very solicitous of the condition of this character. It was solicitous of the individual self, and felt an obligation to educate it into what used to be 24 called "republican virtue." And it was solicitous of that collective self which we call public opinion and which, in a democracy, governs us collectively. Perhaps in some respects it was nervously oversolicitous—that would not be surprising. But the main thing is that it cared, cared not merely about the machinery of democracy but about the quality of life that this machinery might generate.

And because it cared, this older idea of democracy had no problem in 25 principle with pornography and/or obscenity. It censored them—and it did so with a perfect clarity of mind and a perfectly clear conscience. It was not about to permit people capriciously to corrupt themselves. Or, to put it more precisely: in this version of democracy, the people took some care not to let themselves be governed by the more infantile and irrational parts of themselves.

I have, it may be noticed, uttered that dreadful word "censorship." 26 And I am not about to back away from it. If you think pornography and/or obscenity is a serious problem, you have to be for censorship. I'll go even further and say that if you want to prevent pornography and/or obscenity from becoming a problem, you have to be for censorship. And lest there be any misunderstanding as to what I am saying, I'll put it as bluntly as possible: if you care for the quality of life in our American democracy, then you have to be for censorship.

## Post-Reading Questions

1. Having read this entire article, explain the first sentence in terms of Kristol's thesis. How are they connected?
2. Summarize Kristol's "case for censorship." Why does he favor censorship? How do you feel about the case he makes? Why?
3. This article appeared originally in the *New York Times Magazine*. What readers would choose his article? How might they have responded to Kristol's thesis? Why?
4. Kristol wrote this article in 1971. Do you believe he would make the same argument today? Why? What changes would he make in the article to update? Why?
5. Describe the kinds of support Kristol uses to make a case for censorship. How convincing is his support? Why?
6. What plays, television shows, books, films, or videotapes would Kristol object to today? Why?
7. Analyze the questions Kristol asks in paragraph three. Why does he ask them? What would his answers be? Why doesn't he answer them in paragraph three?
8. Make a list of eight or ten words or phrases Kristol uses that reveal his personal feelings about pornography and obscenity. What connotations do these words and phrases have? How do they

contribute to a reader's understanding of Kristol's views on censorship?

9.  What changes would Kristol be required to make if this were not a personal essay but a journalistic article? How would these changes affect the content, thesis, and language choices? Why?

10. In what ways are the ideas Kristol presents in his essay still relevant today? In what ways are his ideas outdated? Why?

# GARRY WILLS ON CENSORSHIP AND CENSURESHIP

## Pre-Reading Questions

1.  Does your college have a code or set of regulations concerning freedom of expression? Would you be in favor of regulations limiting what students, teachers, and staff could and could not say inside and outside of the classroom? Why?

2.  What thesis does this essay's title "In Praise of Censure" suggest to you? What is the difference between censoring and censuring? Look up these words in a dictionary if you are unsure.

## IN PRAISE OF CENSURE
### Garry Wills

Rarely have the denouncers of censorship been so eager to start practicing it. When a sense of moral disorientation overcomes a society, people from the least expected quarters begin to ask, "Is nothing sacred?" Feminists join reactionaries to denounce pornography as demeaning to women. Rock musician Frank Zappa declares that when Tipper Gore, the wife of Senator Albert Gore from Tennessee, asked music companies to label sexually explicit material, she launched an illegal "conspiracy to extort." A *Penthouse* editorialist says that housewife Terry Rakolta, who asked sponsors to withdraw support from a sitcom called *Married . . . With Children*, is "yelling fire in a crowded theater," a formula that says her speech is not protected by the First Amendment.

But the most interesting movement to limit speech is directed at defamatory utterances against blacks, homosexuals, Jews, women or other stigmatizable groups. It took no Terry Rakolta of the left to bring about the instant firing of Jimmy the Greek and Al Campanis from sports jobs when they made racially denigrating comments. Social pressure worked far more quickly on them than on *Married . . . With Children*, which is still on the air.

The rules being considered on college campuses to punish students  3
for making racist and other defamatory remarks go beyond social and
commercial pressure to actual legal muzzling. The right-wing *Dartmouth Review* and its imitators have understandably infuriated liberals,
who are beginning to take action against them and the racist expressions
they have encouraged. The American Civil Liberties Union considered
this movement important enough to make it the principal topic at its
biennial meeting last month in Madison, Wis. Ironically, the regents of
the University of Wisconsin had passed their own rules against defama-
tion just before the ACLU members convened on the university's
campus. Nadine Strossen, of New York University School of Law, who
was defending the ACLU's traditional position on free speech, said of
Wisconsin's new rules, "You can tell how bad they are by the fact that
the regents had to make an amendment at the last minute exempting
classroom discussion! What is surprising is that Donna Shalala [chancel-
lor of the university] went along with it." So did constitutional lawyers
on the faculty.

If a similar code were drawn up with right-wing imperatives in  4
mind—one banning unpatriotic, irreligious or sexually explicit expressions on campus—the people framing Wisconsin-type rules would revert
to their libertarian pasts. In this competition to suppress, is regard for
freedom of expression just a matter of whose ox is getting gored at the
moment? Does the left just get nervous about the Christian cross when
Klansmen burn it, while the right will react only when Madonna flirts
crucifixes between her thighs?

The cries of "un-American" are as genuine and as frequent on either  5
side. Everyone is protecting the country. Zappa accuses Gore of under-
mining the moral fiber of America with the "sexual neuroses of these
vigilant ladies." He argues that she threatens our freedoms with "con-
nubial insider trading" because her husband is a Senator. Apparently her
marital status should deprive her of speaking privileges in public—an
argument Westbrook Pegler used to make against Eleanor Roosevelt.
*Penthouse* says Rakolta is taking us down the path toward fascism. It
attacks her for living in a rich suburb—the old "radical chic" argument
that rich people cannot support moral causes.

There is a basic distinction that cuts through this free-for-all over  6
freedom. It is the distinction, too often neglected, between censorship
and censure (the free expression of moral disapproval). What the
campuses are trying to do (at least those with state money) is use the
force of government to contain freedom of speech. What Donald
Wildmon, the free-lance moralist from Tupelo, Miss., does when he gets
Pepsi to cancel its Madonna ad is censure the ad by calling for a boycott.
Advocating boycotts is a form of speech protected by the First Amendment. As Nat Hentoff, journalistic custodian of the First Amendment,
says, "I would hate to see boycotts outlawed. Think what that would do

to Cesar Chavez." Or, for that matter, to Ralph Nader. If one disapproves of a social practice, whether it is racist speech or unjust hiring in lettuce fields, one is free to denounce that and to call on others to express their disapproval. Otherwise there would be no form of persuasive speech except passing a law. This would make the law coterminous with morality.

Equating morality with legality is in effect what people do when they claim that anything tolerated by law must, in the name of freedom, be approved by citizens in all their dealings with one another. As Zappa says, "Masturbation is not illegal. If it is not illegal to do it, why should it be illegal to sing about it?" He thinks this proves that Gore, who is not trying to make raunch in rock illegal, cannot even ask distributors to label it. Anything goes, as long as it's legal. The odd consequence of this argument would be a drastic narrowing of the freedom of speech. One could not call into question anything that was not against the law—including, for instance, racist speech.

A false ideal of tolerance has not only outlawed censorship but discouraged censoriousness (another word for censure). Most civilizations have expressed their moral values by mobilization of social opprobrium. That, rather than specific legislation, is what changed the treatment of minorities in films and TV over recent years. One can now draw opprobrious attention by gay bashing, as the Beastie Boys rock group found when their distributor told them to cut out remarks about "fags" for business reasons. Or by anti-Semitism, as the just disbanded rap group Public Enemy has discovered.

It is said that only the narrow-minded are intolerant or opprobrious. Most of those who limited the distribution of Martin Scorsese's movie *The Last Temptation of Christ* had not even seen the movie. So do we guarantee freedom of speech only for the broad-minded or the better educated? Can one speak only after studying whatever one has reason, from one's beliefs, to denounce? Then most of us would be doing a great deal less speaking than we do. If one has never seen any snuff movies, is that a bar to criticizing them?

Others argue that asking people not to buy lettuce is different from asking them not to buy a rocker's artistic expression. Ideas (carefully disguised) lurk somewhere in the lyrics. All the more reason to keep criticism of them free. If ideas are too important to suppress, they are also too important to ignore. The whole point of free speech is not to make ideas exempt from criticism but to expose them to it.

One of the great mistakes of liberals in recent decades has been the ceding of moral concern to right-wingers. Just because one opposes censorship, one need not be seen as agreeing with pornographers. Why should liberals, of all people, oppose Gore when she asks that labels be put on products meant for the young, to inform those entrusted by law with the care of the young? Liberals were the first to promote "healthy" television shows like *Sesame Street* and *The Electric Company*. In the 1950s and 1960s they were the leading critics of television, of its mindless violence, of the way it ravaged the attention span needed for reading. Who was keeping kids away from TV sets then? How did promoters of Big Bird let themselves be cast as champions of the Beastie Boys—not just of their *right* to perform but of their performance itself? Why should it be left to Gore to express moral disapproval of a group calling itself Dead Kennedys (sample lyric: "I kill children, I love to see them die")?

For that matter, who has been more insistent that parents should 12 "interfere" in what their children are doing, Tipper Gore or Jesse Jackson? All through the 1970s, Jackson was traveling the high schools, telling parents to turn off TVs, make the kids finish their homework, check with teachers on their performance, get to know what the children are doing. This kind of "interference" used to be called education.

Belief in the First Amendment does not pre-empt other beliefs, 13 making one a eunuch to the interplay of opinions. It is a distortion to turn "You can express any views" into the proposition "I don't care what views you express." If liberals keep equating equality with approval, they will be repeatedly forced into weak positions.

A case in point is the Corcoran Gallery's sudden cancellation of an 14 exhibit of Robert Mapplethorpe's photographs. The whole matter was needlessly confused when the director, Christina Owr-Chall, claimed she was canceling the show to *protect* it from censorship. She meant that there might be pressure to remove certain pictures—the sadomasochistic ones or those verging on kiddie porn—if the show had gone on. But she had in mind, as well, the hope of future grants from the National Endowment for the Arts, which is under criticism for the Mapplethorpe show and for another show that contained Andres Serrano's *Piss Christ*, the photograph of a crucifix in what the title says is urine. Owr-Chall is said to be yielding to censorship, when she is clearly yielding to political and financial pressure, as Pepsi yielded to commercial pressure over the Madonna ad.

What is at issue here is not government suppression but government 15 subsidy. Mapplethorpe's work is not banned, but showing it might have endangered federal grants to needy artists. The idea that what the government does not support it represses is nonsensical, as one can see by reversing the statement to read: "No one is allowed to create anything without the government's subvention." What pussycats our supposedly radical artists are. They not only want the government's permission to create their artifacts, they want federal authorities to supply the materials as well. Otherwise they feel "gagged." If they are not given government approval (and money), they want to remain avant-garde while being bankrolled by the Old Guard.

What is easily forgotten in this argument is the right of citizen 16
taxpayers. They send representatives to Washington who are answerable
for the expenditure of funds exacted from them. In general these voters
want to favor their own values if government is going to get into the
culture-subsidizing area at all (a proposition many find objectionable in
itself). Politicians, insofar as they support the arts, will tend to favor
conventional art (certainly not masochistic art). Anybody who doubts
that has no understanding of a politician's legitimate concern for his or
her constituents' approval. Besides, it is quaint for those familiar with the
politics of the art world to discover, with a shock, that there is politics in
politics.

Luckily, cancellation of the Mapplethorpe show forced some artists 17
back to the flair and cheekiness of unsubsidized art. Other results of
pressure do not turn out as well. Unfortunately, people in certain regions
were deprived of the chance to see *The Last Temptation of Christ* in the
theater. Some, no doubt, considered it a loss that they could not buy
lettuce or grapes during a Chavez boycott. Perhaps there was even a
buyer perverse enough to miss driving the unsafe cars Nader helped
pressure off the market. On the other hand, we do not get sports analysis
made by racists. These mobilizations of social opprobrium are not
examples of repression but of freedom of expression by committed
people who censured without censoring, who expressed the kinds of
belief the First Amendment guarantees. I do not, as a result, get whatever
I approve of subsidized, either by Pepsi or the government. But neither
does the law come in to silence Tipper Gore or Frank Zappa or even that
filthy rag, the *Dartmouth Review.*

## Post-Reading Questions

1. Why does Wills call college speech codes "legal muzzling" (paragraph three)? What does he mean? How does this description reflect his sense of writing purpose and his thesis?

2. How does Wills distinguish between *right wing* and *left wing* censors? Does he side with either? How do you know? Do you agree with Wills? Why?

3. Paraphrase Wills' first sentence. Evaluate it as an introductory sentence. How does Wills' choice of examples in the first paragraph relate to that first sentence? How effective are those examples? Why? How do they affect readers?

4. How does Wills distinguish between censorship and censureship? Do you agree? Do you believe one can censure without censoring? Explain your answer, using an example.

5. How does Wills see censureship as a positive social instrument? What examples does he offer to illustrate? What examples could you

add to illustrate his viewpoint? What examples could you use to reject his viewpoint?

6. What is the connection between the first and last paragraphs in Wills' essay? What writing strategy do they illustrate? How do they help support his purpose in writing?

7. What features in Wills' essay identify it as personal? How would a journalist's article on the same subject differ? Why?

8. Analyze the language Wills uses. How do his language choices provide readers with clues to his personal viewpoints? How do his language choices reflect his writing purposes?

9. What readers would find Wills' thesis most appealing? Why? What readers would reject it? Why?

10. Reread paragraphs 9, 13, and 15. How does what Wills says in these paragraphs support the interpretation that Wills' defense of censure is actually a defense of old-fashioned freedom of speech?

# CHARLES R. LAWRENCE III
# ON HATE SPEECH

## Pre-Reading Questions

1. How would you define "hate speech"? Have you ever heard such speech used? Describe situations in which you have heard or may hear people use such speech.

2. What is a civil libertarian? How does its denotation (the dictionary definition) differ from its connotation (the emotional meaning)? Have you known any people whom you would describe as civil libertarians? What were they like? In what environments would one be most likely to meet civil libertarians? Why?

3. College campuses are identified with the concept of freedom of speech. Do you believe that colleges should enact policies limiting free speech? Why? Have you ever felt that a teacher or student placed restrictions on your freedom of speech? Describe a real or hypothetical situation in which you felt your freedom of speech was limited.

## THE DEBATE OVER PLACING LIMITS ON RACIST SPEECH MUST NOT IGNORE THE DAMAGE IT DOES TO ITS VICTIMS
### Charles R. Lawrence III

I have spent the better part of my life as a dissenter. As a high school   1
student, I was threatened with suspension for my refusal to participate in a civil-defense drill, and I have been a conspicuous consumer of my First

Amendment liberties ever since. There are very strong reasons for protecting even racist speech. Perhaps the most important of these is that such protection reinforces our society's commitment to tolerance as a value, and that by protecting bad speech from government regulation, we will be forced to combat it as a community.

But I also have a deeply felt apprehension about the resurgence of 2 racial violence and the corresponding rise in the incidence of verbal and symbolic assault and harassment to which blacks and other traditionally subjugated and excluded groups are subjected. I am troubled by the way the debate has been framed in response to the recent surge of racist incidents on college and university campuses and in response to some universities' attempts to regulate harassing speech. The problem has been framed as one in which the liberty of free speech is in conflict with the elimination of racism. I believe this has placed the bigot on the moral high ground and fanned the rising flames of racism.

Above all, I am troubled that we have not listened to the real victims, 3 that we have shown so little understanding of their injury, and that we have abandoned those whose race, gender, or sexual preference continues to make them second-class citizens. It seems to me a very sad irony that the first instinct of civil libertarians has been to challenge even the smallest, most narrowly framed efforts by universities to provide black and other minority students with the protection the Constitution guarantees them.

The landmark case of *Brown v. Board of Education* is not a case that 4 we normally think of as a case about speech. But *Brown* can be broadly read as articulating the principle of equal citizenship. *Brown* held that segregated schools were inherently unequal because of the *message* that segregation conveyed—that black children were an untouchable caste, unfit to go to school with white children. If we understand the necessity of eliminating the system of signs and symbols that signal the inferiority of blacks, then we should hesitate before proclaiming that all racist speech that stops short of physical violence must be defended.

University officials who have formulated policies to respond to 5 incidents of racial harassment have been characterized in the press as "thought police," but such policies generally do nothing more than impose sanctions against intentional face-to-face insults. When racist speech takes the form of face-to-face insults, catcalls, or other assaultive speech aimed at an individual or small group of persons, it falls directly within the "fighting words" exception to First Amendment protection. The Supreme Court has held that words which "by their very utterance inflict injury or tend to incite an immediate breach of the peace" are not protected by the First Amendment.

If the purpose of the First Amendment is to foster the greatest amount 6 of speech, racial insults disserve that purpose. Assaultive racist speech functions as a preemptive strike. The invective is experienced as a blow, not as a proffered idea, and once the blow is struck, it is unlikely that a dialogue will follow. Racial insults are particularly undeserving of First Amendment protection because the perpetuator's intention is not to discover truth or initiate dialogue but to injure the victim. In most situations, members of minority groups realize that they are likely to lose if they respond to epithets by fighting and are forced to remain silent and submissive.

Courts have held that offensive speech may not be regulated in public 7 forums such as streets where the listener may avoid the speech by moving on, but the regulation of otherwise protected speech has been permitted when the speech invades the privacy of the unwilling listener's home or when the unwilling listener cannot avoid the speech. Racist posters, fliers, and graffiti in dormitories, bathrooms, and other common living spaces would seem to clearly fall within the reasoning of these cases. Minority students should not be required to remain in their rooms in order to avoid racial assault. Minimally, they should find a safe haven in their dorms and in all other common rooms that are a part of their daily routine.

I would also argue that the university's responsibility for ensuring 8 that these students receive an equal educational opportunity provides a compelling justification for regulations that ensure them safe passage in all common areas. A minority student should not have to risk becoming the target of racially assaulting speech every time he or she chooses to walk across campus. Regulating vilifying speech that cannot be anticipated or avoided would not preclude announced speeches and rallies—situations that would give minority-group members and their allies the chance to organize counterdemonstrations or avoid the speech altogether.

The most commonly advanced argument against the regulation of 9 racist speech proceeds something like this: We recognize that minority groups suffer pain and injury as the result of racist speech, but we must allow this hate mongering for the benefit of society as a whole. Freedom of speech is the lifeblood of our democratic system. It is especially important for minorities because often it is their only vehicle for rallying support for the redress of their grievances. It will be impossible to formulate a prohibition so precise that it will prevent the racist speech you want to suppress without catching in the same net all kinds of speech that it would be unconscionable for a democratic society to suppress.

Whenever we make such arguments, we are striking a balance on the 10 one hand between our concern for the continued free flow of ideas and the democratic process dependent on that flow, and, on the other, our desire to further the cause of equality. There can be no meaningful discussion of how we should reconcile our commitment to equality and our commitment to free speech until it is acknowledged that there is real harm inflicted by racist speech and that this harm is far from trivial.

To engage in a debate about the First Amendment and racist speech 11 without a full understanding of the nature and extent of that harm is to risk making the First Amendment an instrument of domination rather than a vehicle of liberation. We have not all known the experience of victimization by racist, misogynist, and homophobic speech, nor do we equally share the burden of the societal harm it inflicts. We are often quick to say that we have heard the cry of the victims when we have not.

The *Brown* case is again instructive because it speaks directly to the 12 psychic injury inflicted by racist speech by noting that the symbolic message of segregation affected "the hearts and minds" of negro children "in a way unlikely ever to be undone." Racial epithets and harassment often cause deep emotional scarring and feelings of anxiety and fear that pervade every aspect of a victim's life.

*Brown* also recognized that black children did not have an equal 13 opportunity to learn and participate in the school community if they bore the additional burden of being subjected to the humiliation and psychic assault contained in the message of segregation. University students bear an analogous burden when they are forced to live and work in an environment where at any moment they may be subjected to denigrating verbal harassment and assault. The same injury was addressed by the Supreme Court when it held that sexual harassment that creates a hostile or abusive work environment violates the ban on sex discrimination in employment of Title VII of the Civil Rights Act of 1964.

Carefully drafted university regulations would bar the use of words as 14 assault weapons and leave unregulated even the most heinous of ideas when those ideas are presented at times and places and in manners that provide an opportunity for reasoned rebuttal or escape from immediate injury. The history of the development of the right to free speech has been one of carefully evaluating the importance of free expression and its effects on other important societal interests. We have drawn the line between protected and unprotected speech before without dire results. (Courts have, for example, exempted from the protection of the First Amendment obscene speech and speech that disseminates official secrets, that defames or libels another person, or that is used to form a conspiracy or monopoly.)

Blacks and other people of color are skeptical about the argument 15 that even the most injurious speech must remain unregulated because, in an unregulated marketplace of ideas, the best ones will rise to the top and gain acceptance. Our experience tells us quite the opposite. We have seen too many demagogues elected by appealing to America's racism. We have seen too many good liberal politicians shy away from the issues that might brand them as being too closely allied with us.

Whenever we decide that racist speech must be tolerated because of 16 the importance of maintaining societal tolerance for all unpopular speech, we are asking blacks and other subordinated groups to bear the burden for the good of all. We must be careful that the ease with which we strike the balance against the regulation of racist speech is in no way influenced by the fact that the cost will be borne by others. We must be certain that those who will pay that price are fairly represented in our deliberations and that they are heard.

At the core of the argument that we should resist all government 17 regulation of speech is the ideal that the best cure for bad speech is good, that ideas that affirm equality and the worth of all individuals will ultimately prevail. This is an empty ideal unless those of us who would fight racism are vigilant and unequivocal in that fight. We must look for ways to offer assistance and support to students whose speech and political participation are chilled in a climate of racial harassment.

Civil-rights lawyers might consider suing on behalf of blacks whose 18 right to an equal education is denied by a university's failure to ensure a nondiscriminatory educational climate or conditions of employment. We must embark upon the development of a First Amendment jurisprudence grounded in the reality of our history and our contemporary experience. We must think hard about how best to launch legal attacks against the most indefensible forms of hate speech. Good lawyers can create exceptions and narrow interpretations that limit the harm of hate speech without opening the floodgates of censorship.

Everyone concerned with these issues must find ways to engage 19 actively in actions that resist and counter the racist ideas that we would have the First Amendment protect. If we fail in this, the victims of hate speech must rightly assume that we are on the oppressors' side.

## Post-Reading Questions

1. Reread paragraph one. Why does Lawrence begin his essay with a description of his own experience as a dissenter? What is Lawrence trying to establish about himself? About his point of view? How do paragraph one and two differ? Why?

2. How does Lawrence feel about college policies restricting speech? Why does he feel that way? Explain his reasons.

3. Explain Lawrence's use of the *Brown vs. Board of Education* case. Where in the essay does he refer to it? How often? Why? How does it help him achieve his writing purpose?

4. How convinced are you by Lawrence's essay? Which of his reasons do you find most convincing? Why? Which reasons do you find least convincing? Why?

5. This essay originally appeared in *The Chronicle of Higher Education*. What might Lawrence have known about his readers? How might that information have affected what he says in this essay and how he says it? Be specific as you explain these connections between readers and text.

6. What changes might Lawrence have made in what he says and how he says it if he had been asked to revise this essay for a college newspaper? What changes would you suggest? Why?

7.  What kinds of readers would react most positively to Lawrence's viewpoint on restricting free speech on college campuses? Why?

8.  Where in his essay does Lawrence discuss those whose views on this subject differ from his own? Summarize what he says about their views. How well, in your opinion, does he respond to their views? Why?

9.  Explain how Lawrence reconciles his commitment to free speech and his commitment to furthering the cause of racial equality.

10. In several places Lawrence treats this essay as a debate or argument over a well-defined issue (see especially paragraphs 10, 11, and 12). What particular rules of formal argument does Lawrence use in these and other paragraphs? How do these formalities make his essay more convincing?

# MARY RENCK JALONGO AND ANNE DROLETT CREANY ON CENSORSHIP AND CHILDREN'S BOOKS

## Pre-Reading Questions

1.  What kinds of stories did you read as a small child or enjoy having others read to you? What book titles do you remember as being your favorites? Do you think children today are reading the same books you did? Why?

2.  In your opinion, who should decide which children's books should be on school and public library shelves? How should these decisions be made? How would you decide?

3.  Do you believe there are particular issues or topics that should be "off limits" for authors writing books for pre-school children? What about authors writing fiction for elementary or high-school students? Identify specific book titles to explain your answer.

## CENSORSHIP IN CHILDREN'S LITERATURE
### Mary Renck Jalongo and
### Anne Drolett Creany

Should award-winning artist Trina Schart Hyman's (1983) version of  1 *Little Red Riding Hood* be banned because the child brings a bottle of wine to her grandmother?

Should the most popular children's book author-illustrator Tomie  2 dePaola (1975) have his Italian folktale *Strega Nona* pulled from the school library shelves because the main character practices "witchcraft" with a magic pasta pot?

Should Frank Asch's (1980) gentle story *The Last Puppy* be removed 3 from the children's collection at the public library because the first cartoon-style picture shows the last puppy being born?

Children's literature controversies like the ones raised by these 4 picture books are not unusual. But before educators assume that conservative, right-wing groups are the only ones who attempt to influence which books are purchased and circulated in libraries and schools, consider three additional objections to children's literature:

The book *Little Black Sambo* (Bannerman, 1898) was banned because 5 of its connection with racial slurs (Yuill, 1976).

Richard Scarry's books have been severely criticized by feminists for 6 their sex-role stereotypes.

During the Vietnam war era, fairytales and folktales were revised to 7 eliminate the violence. The witch in Hansel and Gretel, for example, ran away instead of being burned in the oven.

Admittedly, efforts to influence children's reading material come 8 from all directions (Zuckerman, 1986). But which practices are censorship? Which practices constitute book selection? Educators cannot smugly assume that it is always *censorship* when a group unlike themselves exerts its power and that it is always *quality control* when educators raise objections to a book. Both conservative and liberal censors have some legitimate concerns and wish to reform society (Shannon, 1989). Conservatives who want to remove books that emphasize the secular or denigrate the family are criticized for being out of pace with contemporary society. Liberals believe that neutrality toward "isms"—racism, sexism, classism, militarism, ageism and so forth—will promote social inequity; they are criticized for being "guardian angels" of the new social order (Moore & Burress, 1981; Shakford, 1978).

This article will address those standards of practice that can be used 9 to guide and inform educators as they confront the complex issues surrounding book censorship. We will: 1) differentiate between censorship and selection; 2) review historical and research trends; 3) describe the consequences of censorship and 4) suggest strategies for taking a stand on the censorship of children's literature.

## CENSORSHIP VERSUS SELECTION

Censorship is the removal, suppression or restricted circulation of 10 literary, artistic or educational material (images, ideas and/or information) on the grounds that they are morally or otherwise objectionable (Reichman, 1988). The distinction between censorship and selection is fundamentally rooted in our views of three things: the child, the book and the society at large.

## View of the Child

The printed word is one of many influences upon an individual (Gam- 11 bell, 1986). Children do not simply absorb the values presented to them via literature. Rather, children's literature confirms or fails to confirm attitudes from the larger world (Bauer, 1984).

But from the censors' points of view, childhood is a *tabula rasa*, a 12 blank slate. They want to keep the slate clean (childhood as idyllic) or perhaps emblazon it with the new social order (childhood as a vehicle for social change). Take, for example, the furor over Judy Blume's (1970) book *Are You There, God? It's Me, Margaret* which discusses menstruation. Even though this is a concern of young girls and it is not uncommon for 10-year-olds to be physically mature, many parents felt that it was inappropriate to discuss this issue in a book intended for children of this age group. To the censor, children are above all impressionable, and books are capable of corrupting them: "*Hear no evil, see no evil, speak no evil* gives rise to the fourth inevitable monkey, *Read no evil*" (Bradburn, 1988, p. 37).

A selection point of view is quite different. Adults continue to have 13 the right to object to books, but they do not insist upon removing them from the shelves for everyone else. Adults who advocate selection rather than censorship of children's books respect the child's intellectual freedom and believe that adults have an obligation to be honest with children (L'Engle, 1987).

This selection perspective does not argue that all books are equally 14 appropriate for children of all ages nor does it deny the fact that children are influenced by the things they read. Book selection invokes standards for literary quality, guidelines of nonpartisan professional groups and knowledge of child development/child psychology when rendering decisions about children's books. A selection point of view would also leave the application of those guidelines to parents and professionals.

## View of the Work

From a selection perspective, the goal is to give children access to the 15 best that literature has to offer. Mark Twain's (1884) *The Adventures of Huckleberry Finn* is a good example. Censors would advocate that it be removed because it reflects the racial stereotypes of its day. Those who view the same work from a selection perspective argue that it retains its value as quality literature in spite of conflict with modern sensibilities. They would contend that Huck Finn *should* be shared with children, but introduced with a "disclaimer" about the social context and followed by discussion.

Generally speaking, censorship tends to take a reactionary stance; to [16] take words, phrases or pictures out of context; to be essentially negative and to have book banning or labeling as its goal. Selection, on the other hand, operates from a set of standards agreed upon by the group, looks at the total work, is essentially positive and promotes quality literature (National Council of Teachers of English, 1982).

*View of Society*

From a censorship point of view, evil is lurking everywhere in society and [17] needs to be eradicated in literature. Ways of accomplishing this task are to remove books from sale, to label certain books as "controversial," to circulate lists of "objectionable" books and authors and to purge libraries (American Library Association and the American Book Publishers Council, 1972). The goal of the censor is to make moral decisions for others, to indoctrinate and limit access (National Council of Teachers of English, 1982). To censors, everyone else should be prodded or coerced into thinking as they do.

From a selection point of view, quality is elusive and needs to be [18] supported in a wide variety of forms in society. To the person applying selection standards, the purpose is to advise, educate and increase options; individual differences are respected and others can "agree to disagree" without becoming adversaries.

Fiction and nonfiction books on the topic of AIDS are a good [19] example. The censor would want this health issue ignored because the disease is usually transmitted through sexual contact. The person who operates from a set of professional guidelines would defend the right of children to have access to AIDS information as long as it is accurate and developmentally appropriate. Additionally, he or she would insist that understanding the physical and social consequences of the disease is essential to prevention.

## CENSORSHIP: HISTORY AND
## RECENT RESEARCH TRENDS

The word *censorship* originated with the office of *censor*, a Roman official [20] whose job was to uphold morality and restrict misconduct (Wynne, 1985). Censorship was noted as long ago as 389 B.C. when Plato recommended monitoring the tales of Homer and other fiction writers (Hansen, 1987). Censorship of children's literature is a relatively recent phenomenon. Prior to the 1960s, there was "complacency and consensus" about children's literature because topics such as crime, violence, death, racial conflict, social problems or sexuality were either absent or given peripheral attention in children's books (Giblin, 1986; MacLeod, 1983). Striking changes took place in American society during the 1960s as the communication environment changed from a print-dominated (book) culture to an image-dominated (television) one (Postman, 1982). Children became aware of the world at a younger age, and eventually topics once thought unsuitable for children (or even forbidden) appeared in their books (Holland, 1980a; 1980b). In the 1970s and beyond, censorship shows every sign of increasing rather than abating (Tollefson, 1987). As the trend toward a literature-based language arts curriculum takes hold nationwide in the 1990s, this scrutiny of children's books will no doubt continue.

## Research Trends

Although censorship research is basically descriptive, it does provide 21 some insight into the extent of censorship, the identity of the censors, the materials deemed offensive and the fate of challenged books. Most research on censorship is one of two types: survey data or analysis of newspaper accounts.

Surveys that investigate the extent and nature of censorship in a 22 school or library have been conducted by many individuals and organizations (Burress, 1989; U.S. National Commission on Libraries and Information Science, 1986). According to Hansen (1987), the major difficulty with questionnaires is their failure to differentiate between informal and formal complaints and the interchangeable use of terms with different meanings (e.g., *question, objection* and *complaint*). Studies that use newspaper accounts of censorship are obviously influenced by the news agency and the incidents they select for reporting (Hansen, 1987; People for the American Way, 1986). News service data have identified the most frequently challenged children's books nationwide (1982–1989) as:

- *The Adventures of Huckleberry Finn*—Mark Twain (1884)
- *The Chocolate War*—Robert Cormier (1974)
- *Go Ask Alice*—Anonymous (1976)
- *A Light in the Attic*—Shel Silverstein (1981)
- *Deenie*—Judy Blume (1973)
- *Then Again, Maybe I Won't*—Judy Blume (1971)
- *Forever*—Judy Blume (1975)

Both survey and newspaper account research suggest increases in 23 complaints about children's books. The percentage of libraries receiving complaints rose from 20 percent in 1966 to 34 percent in 1982 (Burress, 1989), and there has been a 30 to 35 percent increase in the challenge rate since 1980 (American Civil Liberties Union, 1986; People for the American Way, 1986).

Censorship research also provides information about who the cen- 24 sors are. A survey conducted by People for the American Way (1986) found that 65 percent of the objections came from parents, 21 percent from school personnel or schools and 9 percent from organized groups. Parents and teaching personnel are the most frequent objectors to materials in school libraries, whereas groups or individuals objected to materials in public libraries (Jenkinson, 1986). In 1966 parents made 48 percent of the challenges to library materials; by 1977 parents' challenges rose to 78 percent of all the objections made (Burress, 1989).

## WHAT IS CENSORABLE?

Generally speaking, books or elements of books are objectionable to 25 parents, teachers or groups for one or more of three reasons: 1) The content is considered too mature/realistic; 2) The language is profane or obscene or 3) The sexual content is considered inappropriate.

### Mature/Realistic Content

Most complaints about children's literature stem from a desire to protect 26 children from the harsh realities of life. Take, for instance, two books in which the main character dies tragically: *Where the Lillies Bloom* (Cleaver, 1969) and *Charlotte's Web* (White, 1952). Adults may feel that death and bereavement are not suitable for children, that the topic is too mature. Or, they may object to the first book in which a parent dies but not to White's book because in it a personified spider dies.

### Profane/Obscene Language

Another frequently cited objection is language, especially profanity and 27 obscenity (Green, 1990). One of the first criticisms of profanity came in 1962 from a librarian who attacked a reviewer for failing to warn her readers that a book contained the word *damn* (Darling, 1974). Currently, Paterson's *The Great Gilly Hopkins* (Paterson, 1978) and Zindel's (1968) *The Pigman* (which actually uses symbols to denote profanity) are both on censors' lists.

### Sexual Content or Theme

Another strong objection to some children's books is the presence of 28 sexual content or theme (Burress, 1989; Hansen, 1987). In some instances, parents have demanded removal of Norma Klein's (1972)

*Mom, the Wolfman and Me* for its portrayal of a single mother whose boyfriend moves in. Homosexuality is another taboo topic, if reaction to *Trying Hard To Hear You* (Scoppettone, 1978) is any indication. Nonfiction books on human sexuality have been challenged as well, such as volumes 14 and 15 of the *Childcraft Encyclopedia* (Field Experiences Educational Corporation, 1982).

## THE AFTERMATH OF CENSORSHIP

Teachers, administrators and school boards may avoid controversial books targeted by the censors to avoid conflict (Cullinan, 1986). What are the consequences for institutions, for the books themselves and for the publishing industry when a book is challenged? 29

### For Schools and Libraries

A librarian reads a book about dinosaurs at storytime. Afterwards, a mother files a complaint because the book suggests that the giant reptiles' extinction may have been attributable to drastic environmental change rather than Divine intervention. Although librarians are urged to select books according to literary standards and avoid reacting to pressure from critics (Silver, 1980), it is easy to understand why they might seek to avoid such disputes. With challenge rates hovering around 30 percent, librarians report that they frequently censor themselves rather than become confrontational with a library patron (American Civil Liberties Union, 1986; United States National Commission on Libraries and Information Sciences, 1982). 30

### For the Books Themselves

The outcome of challenges to children's books varies. Studies suggest that if parents filed a complaint, books were removed about 40 percent of the time. When the school personnel objected to a book, however, it was removed about 75 percent of the time (Jenkinson, 1986; Burress, 1989). 31

Removal is not the only response to censorship. Books are sometimes "put in the back room" so that children do not have free access to them. One librarian expressed the belief that the reshelving of books regarding human sexuality amounted to "quiet" censorship because most teens would be reluctant to request the books in person (Jenkinson, 1986). 32

In addition to removal, books may be physically altered; that is, offensive parts such as profanity may be obliterated. One famous "cover up" occurred when a librarian painted diapers on the nude baby in Sendak's *In the Night Kitchen* (Darling, 1974). Her actions created an 33 outcry among writers, illustrators, librarians and publishers of children's books who joined to fight such censorship.

### Consequences for Authors

Censorship can create an atmosphere of fear that results in "silent" 34 censorship by publishers and "formula" books from authors. Publishing houses' anxiety about controversies may prompt them to reject a manuscript or insist that it be changed before it is accepted. The crux of the matter is whether authors are traveling in the well-worn ruts of their predecessors to "play it safe," doing artistic groundbreaking work or simply trying to sell books by being sensationalistic.

What effects does censorship have on the authors of children's 35 books? Even if authors do not experience censorship in the original publication of their books, they are sometimes asked to make changes when the books are published in paperback "school editions" or in basal series (Goodman, 1988; Keresey, 1984). Barbara Cohen experienced censorship of her book *Molly's Pilgrim* (Cohen, 1983) when it was selected for inclusion in a basal reader. In journal style, she relates the negotiations that took place as editors attempted to alter the story to remove references to Molly's Jewishness and to the Bible (Cohen, 1987).

A different response to censorship by a publisher is evident in 36 controversy over *Jake and Honeybunch Go to Heaven* (Zemach, 1982). This book received mixed reviews; praise for its watercolor illustrations, doubts about its stereotyped portrayal of an all-black heaven. When three major libraries failed to order the book, the publisher went to the media with claims of censorship. In this case the tables were turned; rather than avoiding censors by producing only nonoffensive material, this publisher chose to attack library selection committees as censors (Brandehoff, 1983). Incidents such as this one suggest that the debate about children's books is here to stay—a debate that reflects America's changing vision of childhood and society.

## WHAT EDUCATORS CAN DO

Educators can take the following steps to handle the inevitable contro- 37 versies sparked by children's literature:

- *Keep current in the field.* Familiarize yourself with the differing sides of this debate (Goldstein, 1989). What elements in literature are offensive to censors of the right? The left? What happens when personal beliefs and community standards conflict? To what extent are school materials censored by the selection of administrators, librarians and teachers? Which books are you personally willing to fight for? Why? What biases do you have? How do they influence you? Maintain a file of material on censorship including newspaper clippings, reference sources and policy statements from various organizations, both partisan and nonpartisan.

- *Obtain selection criteria from national professional organizations.* Assemble support from such professional organizations as the American Library Association (1983), the Council on Interracial Books for Children (1979), the National Council of Teachers of English (1982) and the International Reading Association (Delegates Assembly, 1988). All of these groups have published policies to assist those who provide library services.
- *Communicate with parents.* Although it is tempting to take a "less said, the better" stance on children's literature controversies, open discussions about children's books can provide parents with the information needed to make informed choices about their children's reading material (Adams, 1986; White, 1974). Swibold (1982) describes the implementation of a discussion group for parents that examined changes in children's books. After advertising the event, parents and teachers read the books in question; children wrote reactions to books and adults participated in discussions together. Informed parents are less likely to become censors if they understand a book's value, the reason it was placed in the library and the appeal it has for children.
- *Evaluate books with children.* Even young children are capable of making judgments about literature. If children are taught to compare/contrast different versions of the same basic story—e.g., Galdone's (1973), Brett's (1987), Marshall's (1988) and a grocery store rack version of *The Three Bears*—they can acquire a taste for the best that literature has to offer. As children mature, we can coach them further in critical judgment skills (Shakford, 1978). We can also inform children about the issue of censorship through nonfiction books on the topic such as Monroe's (1990) *Censorship,* which is suitable for children in the intermediate grades. When children who have had such experiences become the general public, they are more likely to appreciate the distinction between selection and censorship.
- *Prepare a school policy statement.* In addition to becoming informed about censorship issues and sharing information with students and parents, educators must also prepare themselves for the challenges to children's books that will surely come (Huck, Hepler & Hickman, 1987; Palmer, 1982). Donelson (1984) makes five recommendations for dealing with censorship: 1) Develop a selection policy statement that establishes reasons for including a book in the collection (e.g., enjoyment, exploring human problems, opportunities for vicarious experiences, exposure

to different value systems and acquiring insights about the real world, past and present); 2) Form selection committees that will report to the faculty about new acquisitions; 3) Enlist community support; 4) Inform the public about classroom/library procedures and 5) Draft a policy for dealing with attempts at censorship.

- *Adopt a formal complaint procedure.* The National Council of Teachers of English (1982) guidelines for coping with censorship advise receiving objections courteously, then directing the individual to complete "The Citizen's Request for Reconsideration of a Work." This form assumes that the individual is familiar with the work in its entirety and this alone may discourage minor objections. Completed forms should be reviewed by a committee that will report findings and recommendations to the person or group with responsibility for the library.

## CONCLUSION

Censorship is an extremely complex issue. It is rooted in the universal 38 desire to shape society and promote a personal point of view. We need to be mindful that "Censors do not consider themselves as censors; they are watchdogs, guardians, vigilantes, parents, concerned citizens, or simply individuals who worry about where the world is heading. Whatever the motivation, religious, political, financial, or strictly personal, the effects on the library tend to be the same" (Mika & Shuman, 1988, p. 314). Educators must be prepared to face those groups or individuals who demand that children's literature be altered, labeled, reshelved, banned or burned. Ultimately, preserving the intellectual freedom of children is the responsibility of well-informed, caring and responsible adults.

REFERENCES

Adams, D. (1986). Literature for children: Avoiding controversy and intellectual challenge. *Top of the News, 42,* 304–308.
American Civil Liberties Union. (1986, March). *Newsletter on intellectual freedom,* pp. 1, 56.
American Library Association (1983). *Intellectual freedom manual* (2nd ed.). Chicago, IL: Author.
American Library Association and the American Book Publishers Council. (1972, January). *The freedom to read.* Chicago, IL: American Library Association.
Bauer, M. (1984). The censor within. *Top of the News, 41,* 67–71.
Bradburn, F. (1988). Preteens in the library: Middle readers' right to read. *Wilson Library Bulletin, 62(7),* 37–38, 40, 42–43.

Brandehoff, S. (1983). Jake and Honeybunch go to heaven: Children's book fans smoldering debate. *American Libraries, 14,* 130–132.

Burress, L. (1989). *Battle of the books: Literary censorship in the public schools, 1850–1985.* Metuchen, NJ: Scarecrow.

Cohen, B. (1987). Censoring the sources. *American Educator, 11,* 43–46.

Council on Interracial Books for Children (1979). *Guidelines for selecting bias-free textbooks and storybooks.* New York: Author.

Cullinan, B. (1986). Books in the classroom. *The Horn Book, 62,* 229–231.

Darling, R. (1974). Censorship—An old story. *Elementary English, 51,* 691–696.

Delegates Assembly of the International Reading Association (1988, May). *Resolution on textbook and reading program censorship.* Newark, DE: International Reading Association.

Donelson, K. (1984). What to do when the censor comes. *Elementary English, 51,* 403–409.

Gambell, T. (1986). Choosing the literature to teach. *English Quarterly, 19,* 99–107.

Giblin, J. (1986). Children's book publishing in America: 1919 to now. *Children's Literature in Education, 17,* 150–158.

Goldstein, W. (1989). *Controversial issues in schools: Dealing with the inevitable.* Bloomington, IN: Phi Delta Kappa.

Goodman, K. S. (1988). Look what they've done to Judy Blume: The "basalization" of children's literature. *New Advocate, 1*(1), 29–41.

Green, J. (1990). *The encyclopedia of censorship.* New York: Facts on File.

Hansen, E. (1987). Censorship in schools: Studies and surveys. *School Library Journal, 34,* 123–125.

Holland, I. (1980a). On being a children's book writer and accompanying dangers, part one. *The Horn Book Magazine, 56,* 34–42.

Holland, I. (1980b). On being a children's book writer and accompanying dangers, part two. *The Horn Book Magazine, 56,* 203–210.

Huck, C., Hepler, S., & Hickman, J. (1987). *Children's literature in the elementary school.* New York: Holt, Rinehart & Winston.

Jenkinson, D. (1986). The censorship iceberg: The results of a survey of challenges in school and public libraries. *School Libraries in Canada, 6*(1), 19–22, 24–30.

Keresey, G. (1984). School book club expurgation practices. *Top of the News, 40*(2), 131–138.

L'Engle, M. (1987). Subject to change without notice. *Theory into Practice, 21,* 332–336.

MacLeod, A. (1983). Censorship and children's literature. *Library Quarterly, 53,* 26–38.

Mika, J. J., & Shuman, B. A. (1988). Legal issues affecting libraries and librarians: Lesson IV: Intellectual freedom, privacy and confidentiality, problem patrons and ethics. *American Libraries, 19,* 314–317.

Mingle, P. (1984). Some thoughts on judging children's literature. *Top of the News, 40,* 423–426.

Moore, R., & Burress, L. (1981). Bait/rebait: Criticism vs. censorship: The criticizing of racism and sexism by the Council on Interracial Books for Children is not censorship. *English Journal, 70,* 14–19.

National Council of Teachers of English. (1982). *Statement on censorship and professional guidelines:* Urbana, IL: Author.

Palmer, W. (1982). What reading teachers can do before the censors come. *Journal of Reading, 25,* 310–314.

People for the American Way. (1986). *Attacks on freedom to learn: A 1985–86 report.* Raleigh, NC: Author.

Postman, N. (1982). *The disappearance of childhood.* New York: Dell.

Reichman, H. (1988). *Censorship and selection: Issues and answers for schools.* Arlington, VA: American Association of School Administrators.

Shakford, J. (1978). Dealing with Dr. Dolittle: A new approach to the "-isms." *Language Arts, 55,* 180–187.

Shannon, P. (1989). Overt and covert censorship of children's books. *New Advocate, 2*(2), 97–104.

Silver, L. (1980). Standards and free access—equal but separate. *School Library Journal, 26,* 26–28.

Swibold, G. (1982). Bringing adults to children's books: A case study. *The Reading Teacher, 35,* 460–464.

Tollefson, A. M. (1987). Censored and censured: Racine Unified School District vs. Wilson Library Association. *School Library Journal, 33*(7), 108–112.

United States National Commission on Libraries and Information Science. (1986, July). *Newsletter on Intellectual Freedom,* pp. 113–114.

White, M. (1974). Censorship—threat over children's books. *The Elementary School Journal, 75,* 2–10.

Wynne, E. (1985). The case for censorship to protect the young. *Issues in Education, 3,* 171–184.

Yuill, P. (1976). Little Black Sambo: The continuing controversy. *School Library Journal, 22,* 71–75.

Zuckerman, L. (1986). A publisher's perspective. *The Horn Book, 62,* 629–633.

**Children's Books**

Anonymous. (1976). *Go ask Alice.* New York: Avon.

Asch, F. (1980). *The last puppy.* Englewood Cliffs, NJ: Prentice Hall.

Bannerman, H. (1898). *Little Black Sambo.* London: Grant Richards.

Blume, J. (1970). *Are you there, God? It's me, Margaret.* New York: Bradbury.

Blume, J. (1971). *Then again, maybe I won't.* New York: Bradbury.

Blume, J. (1973). *Deenie.* New York: Bradbury.

Blume, J. (1975). *Forever.* New York: Bradbury.

Brett, J. (1987). *Goldilocks and the three bears.* New York: Dodd & Mead.

Cleaver, V. B. (1969). *Where the lillies bloom.* New York: Lippincott.

Cohen, B. (1983). *Molly's Pilgrim.* New York: Lothrop, Lee & Shepard.

Cormier, R. (1974). *The chocolate war.* New York: Pantheon.

dePaola, T. (1975). *Strega Nona.* Englewood Cliffs, NJ: Prentice Hall.

Field Experiences Educational Corporation (1982). *Childcraft encyclopedia* (vols. 14 & 15). Chicago, IL: Author.

Galdone, P. (1973). *The three bears.* New York: Scholastic.

Hyman, T. S., reteller. (1983). *Little Red Riding Hood.* New York: Holiday.

Klein, N. (1972). *Mom, the wolfman, and me.* New York: Pantheon.

Marshall, J. (1988). *Goldilocks and the three bears.* New York: Dial.

Monroe, J. (1990). *Censorship.* New York: Macmillan/Crestwood House.

Paterson, K. (1978). *The great Gilly Hopkins*. New York: Crowell.
Sendak, M. (1970). *In the night kitchen*. New York: Harper.
Scoppettone, S. (1978). *Trying hard to hear you*. New York: Harper.
Silverstein, S. (1981). *A light in the attic*. New York: Harper.
Twain, M. (1884). *The adventures of Huckleberry Finn*. New York: Harper.
White, E. B. (1953). *Charlotte's web*. New York: Harper.
Zemach, M. (1982). *Jake and Honeybunch go to heaven*. New York: Farrar, Straus
    & Giroux.
Zindel, P. (1968). *The pigman*. New York: Harper & Row.

## Post-Reading Questions

1. How do Jalongo and Creany introduce their subject? How effective is their strategy? What kind of reaction to the article did you have as you read the first three paragraphs? What might have caused this particular reaction?

2. Where in the article do you first sense the particular audience these authors have in mind? Define that audience. How do you know?

3. In your own words, state the authors' thesis. Is their thesis stated or implied? What is their writing purpose? How successfully do they achieve it?

4. Explain the purpose the headings serve in the article, for the writers and for readers. In what ways do they direct readers' responses?

5. How do conservative and liberal censors differ? How are they alike? What kinds of censors have you met? What were their goals?

6. Explain the difference between *censoring* and *selecting* books, as outlined by Jalongo and Creany. Do you agree with their comparison of these two concepts? Why or why not?

7. How would a teacher's attitude toward childhood affect his or her decisions about the books the students read?

8. Reread the list of books in paragraph 22. What patterns of censorship does the list suggest?

9. Describe censorship research. How is such research conducted? What kinds of information does it produce? Who would be most interested in reading the results of such research? Why?

10. Why do you think the number of complaints about children's books is rising? Do you think they will continue to rise in the future? Why?

11. Summarize Jalongo and Creany's suggestions for educators. Who else would find their suggestions useful—parents or the children themselves? Why?

12. What features of this article would you select to illustrate its academic nature? Why is this article more likely to appear in an academic journal than in an issue of *Parents* magazine? What information in this article would you recommend to a journalist writing an article on censorship and children's literature for *Parents*? Why?

# RAYMOND ENGLISH ON
# TEXTBOOK WRITING

## Pre-Reading Questions

1. How accurate are textbooks? From your own experiences, do you believe that the textbooks your teachers have used distorted facts or ideas? Has a teacher ever suggested in class that a particular textbook contained inaccuracies or distortions? Explain such an incident or the circumstances that could cause such an incident to occur.

2. In your opinion, how should an author writing an American history textbook make decisions about how much space to allocate to particular historical figures or events? Why are such decisions difficult to make?

3. List some of the reasons that objectivity is difficult to achieve when an historian attempts to describe and evaluate a past event. What part might politics play in this process? Can politics be totally avoided, even by the most neutral historian?

## TRIALS OF A TEXTBOOK WRITER
### Raymond English

In the wake of the shock of *Sputnik I* there was a surge of enthusiasm for better, more demanding education. It was an exciting moment. 1

I was a college teacher of political science who had publicly expressed concern at the political ignorance of college freshmen. Because of my outspokenness, I found myself drafted by a private educational-research organization to develop a series of social-studies textbooks. 2

For 15 years I worked on this project. But the post-*Sputnik* enthusiasm for intellectual rigor turned out to be a brief, April-day glory. By the mid Sixties, anti-intellectual influences were once more in control. I found myself under constant pressure to sacrifice scholarly standards in order to inculcate some political or social doctrine. 3

In one of our books on world history we examined the causes of the Reformation, our account being approved by a Catholic bishop and the superintendent of Lutheran schools in a big city. But objections came from a Baptist minister, who insisted that mentioning the doctrine of purgatory was equivalent to telling the children to believe it. (Query: How do you teach about Luther's objection to indulgences without mentioning purgatory?) 4

He also objected to references to "The Church" in chapters on medieval Europe. "But, Pastor," I pleaded, "you and I would not be Christians today, were it not for the Church in the Middle Ages." 5

"Ha!" he said, with flashing eyes, "*I* would!"                                    6

Then there were the passionate antisocialists, with whom my sympa-    7
thies largely lay, but who wanted me to suppress the fact that ours is and
has been a mixed economy, and to denounce "farm supports." On the
other side was the old education establishment that wanted to continue
to analyze industrialization and economic development in the terms that
Karl Marx employed after steeping himself in parliamentary reports on
conditions in British factories and mines in the 1840s—an analysis long
since discarded by most economic historians.

The 1960s and '70s brought a legion of new interferences. A history    8
book was boycotted in California (in effect it was vetoed) by two groups.
Organized Filipinos wanted a total rewriting of the account of the
annexation of the Philippines, which we analyzed in terms of the intense
imperialistic rivalries of the great powers at that time. It was the time of
the partition of Africa, of the division of China into spheres of influence,
of the takeover by European powers of Burma, Indochina, and the Spice
Islands. Japan joined the imperial scramble and took Korea and Formosa
(Taiwan).

Yet the Filipino pressure group wanted the story of the Philippines    9
told in Leninist terms: the capitalist "sugar interests" of the United
States compelled President McKinley to annex the islands in spite of a
flourishing independence movement led by Emilio Aguinaldo. I would
have been willing to mention this, although I'm opposed to loading the
average youngster with unnecessary names and complications. However,
that would not have satisfied the critics, who refused to recognize that a
failure by the United States to take responsibility would have led to a race
for Manila between the German Empire and Great Britain.

The other veto came from Zionists who opposed reference to the   10
fact that the population of Palestine before 1947 was predominantly
Arab. It is difficult to explain persisting tensions in the Middle East if
such fairly relevant statistics are suppressed.

One of the more fatuous vetoes came from a state whose committee   11
on ethnic and sex discrimination took strong exception to our account of
the beginnings of effective feminism in the 1860s and '70s. We had
pointed out that certain economic and technological advances opened
the way of emancipation to large numbers of women. Ready-made
clothes and commercially canned foods freed them from major domestic
chores; public schools took over education and much babysitting;
education and jobs opened up for more and more young women. All this
seemed too obvious to argue about; yet the committee rebuked me for
attributing the emancipation of women to technology rather than to
"character and self-assertion." I could only ask which of us was impugn-
ing the character and self-assertion of women. It was the committee that
assumed that women had been lacking in those qualities from the
Garden of Eden until the late nineteenth century.

Other dismal memories come to mind from those years. The 12 Japanese-American critic, for example, who objected to our accurate statement that there were proportionally more Japanese-Americans in executive and professional positions than any other group could boast. "Delete this!" said our critic. "It reinforces the myth of success!"

There was also the running battle with moral relativists, typified by a 13 squabble over the caption for a photograph of vandalism in a second-grade textbook. Our caption said something to the effect that everyone had to pay for this stupid behavior. "Delete 'stupid'; it implies a value judgment." To which the only response is: "Yes! It *is* a value judgment, and second-graders can appreciate it."

I must not forget some vetoes from the right. Our version of 14 American history came under fire for approving labor unions, and for recognizing the value of minimum-wage and maximum-hours laws. One stricture surprised me. In discussing the Louisiana Purchase we remarked on the fact that Jefferson went against his strict-constructionist principles in the purchase. For this we were condemned on the grounds that mentioning this fact made Jefferson "appear inconsistent." Apparently students must be taught that politicians—at least politicians like Jefferson—are "constant as the northern star."

What we need in education are fewer guilt-ridden soft hearts and 15 more intellectually tough hard heads.

## Post-Reading Questions

1. Why does English begin his personal essay with a reference to Sputnik I? What does this strategy suggest about his intended readers? What does it suggest about him?

2. Imagine that you are writing an essay on a subject of your own choosing. Imitate English's first paragraph. Write the first paragraph of your essay using his paragraph, substituting words that are appropriate to your topic.

3. Summarize English's experiences as a textbook writer. Why is he writing about those experiences in this essay? What thesis is he developing? What is his writing purpose?

4. Using one of your own textbooks, explain how its author might have reacted to English's experiences as a textbook writer. Would your textbook's author have agreed or disagreed with English? Why?

5. How does English feel about the complaints he describes in this essay? How does he reveal those feelings? Where in this essay does English reveal his personal opinions? Give some specific examples. How does this personal aspect of the essay affect your reading of it?

6. Analyze the examples or experiences English includes in his essay. How would you describe the examples he uses? In what ways are

they alike? Different? Why did he choose to include them? What effect does English intend them to have on readers?

7. Describe the way English organizes his essay. In what order does he present information? How effective is this organizational pattern? Why?

8. In your own words, state English's thesis. What sentence in his essay states or implies a thesis?

9. Imagine that you are a journalist writing about censorship issues related to education. How could you use English's essay in your article? Write a sentence or two that you would include in your article based on English's essay.

10. Do you believe teachers should use self-censorship in the classroom? Should they be discouraged from discussing their personal views on political, economical, or social issues during class discussions? Or should they be encouraged to raise these issues? Should issues discussed in class always be related to the course's subject matter? Explain your answer by referring to particular classroom experiences you have had, positive or negative.

# MIKAL GILMORE ON MUSIC AND CENSORSHIP

## Pre-Reading Questions

1. What kinds of music do you listen to? Does your family approve of your music choices? How would you feel if you were told by family members what you could and could not listen to? How do you choose the music you listen to?

2. Should compact discs, cassettes, and albums bear labels describing their contents? Do such labels represent a form of censorship? Would a record's label affect whether or not you would purchase it? Are there any kinds of music that should not be made available to minors? Why?

3. What part has rock and roll played in American life since the 1950s? What changes has it undergone? What social forces have influenced or reacted to it?

## THE YEAR IN MUSIC
### Mikal Gilmore

It may seem too good—or simply too unlikely—to believe, but 1990 has turned out to be the year in which rock & roll was reborn. 1

Well, maybe it's more accurate to say that this was the year when pop 2 partisans were forcibly reminded that rock & roll is, after all, *still* rock &

roll: a disruptive art form, viewed with rankling disdain by numerous cultural guardians and with outright animosity by many conservative moralists. Rock, of course, wasn't alone in this regard. A coalition of fundamentalists and lawmakers assailed a wide range of American artists and charged them with disseminating obscenity, subversion and blasphemy. But no other art form was threatened as frequently and as rigorously as pop music—and in the end, this atmosphere of peril may have done more to renew rock's sense of purpose and courage than any event in years.

The first indication that this was to be a contentious year came in 3 March, when *Newsweek* ran a cover story entitled "The Rap Attitude." Though the main article was ostensibly a report on the rise of bigotry and sexism in popular music in the late 1980s—and though the story made brief mention of the disturbing racial attitudes of white rock & rollers like Guns n' Roses—*Newsweek* saved its greatest disdain for rap, a music that, according to the article, amounts to little more than a "streetwise music" rife with "ugly macho boasting and joking about anybody who hangs out on a different block—cops, other races, women and homosexuals." The article proved a remarkably misrepresentative view of a complex subject. While it is true that there are some rap performers who deserve to be criticized for their misogyny and homophobia, it is also true that, by and large, rap addresses questions about race, community, self-determination, drug abuse and the tragedy of violence in intelligent and probing ways and that it does so with a degree of musical invention that no other popular form can match. *Newsweek,* though, ignored the larger picture and settled for a surprisingly alarmist view of rap and its practitioners that dismissed both as a "repulsive" culture.

The *Newsweek* article was perhaps the most scathing indictment of 4 rock-related culture by major media in over a generation, but it was only the opening salvo. That same month, one of America's most powerful religious patriarchs, Roman Catholic archbishop John Cardinal O'Connor, told a congregation at New York's Saint Patrick's Cathedral that some rock music was "a help to the devil." O'Connor seemed to have heavy metal in mind when he claimed that certain kinds of rock could induce demonic possession and drive some listeners to suicide. It wasn't the first time such a charge had been leveled. Three times parents have attempted to sue singer Ozzy Osbourne for the purported influence of his song "Suicide Solution" on the deaths of their sons (one suit was dismissed by a federal court; the other two are still pending), and at the time O'Connor made his remarks, a similar suit—charging the lethal use of subliminal messages—was being prepared in Reno, Nevada, against Judas Priest. These were grim charges—that rock could enter the souls of the young and deliver them to dark forces and darker ends—and suddenly they seemed to be granted both religious and legal plausibility.

Of course, criticisms of rock's influence are hardly new. These  5
concerns, in one form or another, have been the subject of repeated
debate, stretching back as far as Elvis Presley's first unabashedly sexy
nationwide TV appearance. In the late 1960s, as rock gathered cultural
clout and as it reflected the emerging political and sexual values of a new
generation, the argument seemed to take on a new urgency, as it did
again during the punk revolt of the late Seventies. By the mid-Eighties,
rock had acquired a new social conscience, as was evident from Live Aid,
the Amnesty International benefits and the emerging political awareness
of such artists as Bruce Springsteen. But at the peak of this development,
a new movement of moralist critics—emboldened by the Reagan administration's aim to restore conservative social values—focused instead on a
handful of songs containing explicit sexual or violent imagery and
charged that rock had grown morally corrupt and that its influence was
out of control.

The most dauntless of rock's foes was the Parents' Music Resource  6
Center (PMRC), the watchdog organization cofounded in 1985 by
Tipper Gore after she discovered that Prince was singing songs describing acts of masturbation and oral sex and that some heavy metal seemed
to extol the cause of devil worship. Though the group claims its primary
aim is simply to make parents aware of the provocative themes and raw
language that characterize much of today's rock, the PMRC has, in fact,
courted both the media and lawmakers as it has relentlessly pressured
record labels to impose rating systems on their artists. Indeed, the
PMRC has become the most effective adversary that rock & roll has ever
faced.

By early 1990 antirock sentiment had grown enough to fuel a  7
full-fledged national movement calling for the labeling of controversial
pop recordings. Spurred by the aggressive crusading of such state
representatives as Missouri's Jean Dixon and Pennsylvania's Ron Gamble, nearly twenty states were considering legislation that would require
any pop releases containing explicit language or describing or "advocating" certain sexual or violent behavior to be emblazoned with a
prominent warning sticker. The states differed a bit over which offensive
subject matter merited stickering (though Pennsylvania seemed to have
the most representative list, running the gamut from "suicide," "incest,"
"murder" and "bestiality" to "sexual activity in a violent context" and
"illegal use of drugs or alcohol," among other affronts). But nearly all
the proposed bills agreed on one matter: If a record that addressed any of
the cited disturbing themes, or that featured explicit language, was sold
*without* a warning sticker—or, in some cases, if a stickered album was
sold to a minor—the seller ran the risk of a fine or even of jail.

It was a mind-stopping development: Nearly half of the United  8
States were considering measures that, if enacted, would subject one of
the most popular (and one of the worthiest) art and entertainment forms

of our time to state regulation. In addition, the proposed legislation would have the effect of stigmatizing some of the art form's most important works, simply because of the music's willingness to express the sort of language and themes that are commonplace not only in much of today's more relevant films and literature but also in the course of modern everyday life. But then, for a zealot like Jean Dixon, stigmatizing rock-related music is perhaps precisely the point. "Rebellion is like witchcraft," said Dixon earlier this year, explaining her reprehension of the spirit of cultural and social insurrection that rock embodies for many of its fans. "That's what it is, it's like witchcraft."

And if history is any indicator, when one finds witchcraft and 9 witches, witch hunts and witch trials are not likely far behind.

It is unlikely, of course, that any of the proposed legislation would 10 have withstood ultimate constitutional scrutiny. Even so, the mainstream recording industry elected not to stand up for principle. In March, eager to ward off any further legislative action and anxious not to stir public reaction, the Recording Industry Association of America (the RIAA, the alliance of major record companies, which had capitulated to the PMRC's pressures for "voluntary labeling" in 1986) announced it was creating a uniform sticker for use by all its member companies. The bold black-and-white label would carry the warning PARENTAL ADVISORY— EXPLICIT LYRICS. What's more, the organization pledged to watch new pop releases more attentively and to make certain that any recording that might merit such a label would not end up in record stores without one. A few weeks later the PMRC—joined by several state senators, representatives of the PTA and the National Association of Recording Merchandisers (NARM, whose members include record retailers)—held a press conference in Washington, D.C., and announced that, in light of the RIAA's action, pending labeling legislation would now be dropped in thirteen states, with more likely to follow. Though both sides hoped to give the impression that a compromise had been struck, the conservative coalition had, in effect, won: It had induced the recording industry to impose a stickering system, without having to resort to the legal process and without having to face a constitutional test. And, according to Dixon's spokesman, if the industry failed to live up to its promise to police new releases, "I guarantee you there will be legislation in fifty states next year." (As it turned out, Dixon lost her bid for reelection in a Missouri primary.)

Stickers followed with a vengeance, cropping up on numerous rap 11 and heavy-metal releases—sometimes without apparent reason and sometimes over the stated protests of the recording artists. In addition, some artists were apparently pressured to change explicit or potentially controversial words or phrases, or to drop entire songs, before their recordings were released. (In the case of the pointedly violent-minded debut album by the rap group the Geto Boys, Geffen Records chose to drop the entire work.) In the end, only one major label, Virgin Records, refused to sticker its recordings, instead adorning its releases with the text of the First Amendment.

But for one conservative moralist, a Coral Gables, Florida, lawyer 12 named Jack Thompson, stickering was beside the point. Thompson is a Christian Evangelical who fancies himself a Batman-style crusader against pornography and child abuse. At the very beginning of the year, Thompson received a transcript of the lyrics to *As Nasty As They Wanna Be*, the latest album by the 2 Live Crew, a Miami group whose specialty is X-rated raps about male sexual prowess. Inflamed by the 2 Live Crew's graphic language and by what he regarded as the band's rapacious attitude toward women, Thompson launched a letter-faxing campaign to law-enforcement officials throughout Florida, urging them to take action against *As Nasty As They Wanna Be* as an obscene work. Thompson's campaign caught the attention of Florida governor Bob Martinez, who set into motion a series of actions that resulted in a federal judge officially declaring the album obscene in June—the first such ruling for a recorded work in American history. Two days later, record-store owner Charles Freeman was arrested in Fort Lauderdale after he sold a copy of the album to an undercover police officer. Within the week, three members of the 2 Live Crew—including group leader Luther "Luke" Campbell— were arrested for performing material from the album at an adults-only concert at a Broward County club.

The music community was shocked by the Broward County arrests. 13 It wasn't that music professionals particularly revered or respected the 2 Live Crew; indeed, the group had been publicly and forcefully criticized for its puerile sexist humor by numerous critics and fellow rappers. But Florida's heavy-handed response to the 2 Live Crew's relentless sex raps (which, though coarse, were also a good deal funnier and less mean-spirited than is generally admitted) amounted to a clear effort to abrogate an artist's right to free speech—an action that, if successful, could endanger the rights of numerous other Americans. There was also another concern: Why had a black rap group been singled out for an obscenity prosecution—particularly in a county in which strip shows, adult reading material and pornographic videos are readily accessible to consenting adults? "The subtext of this event," said Jon Landau, manager and producer of Bruce Springsteen, "invites the suspicion that there is a substantial racist component. This is selective prosecution at its most extreme. Therefore, until Luke's rights have been secured, discussion of the merits of his music is not really the point. The point is to make sure that we're all free to express ourselves whatever the point of view, however extreme."

By making the 2 Live Crew a central target in a potentially far- 14 reaching cultural and political battle, Thompson forced many in the music industry to recognize how much ground had been conceded to the antirock forces. In addition, Thompson also helped transform Luther Campbell into an unlikely *cause célèbre*. In late June, Springsteen granted Campbell permission to use the backing track of "Born in the U.S.A." for the 2 Live Crew's account of its troubles in Florida. The result, called "Banned in the U.S.A.," was the 2 Live Crew's most laudable moment—or at least the one instance in which the group aspired to something other than puerile scatology. In response, Thompson fired off a fax to Springsteen: "Dear Mr. Springsteen," he wrote, "I would suggest 'Raped in the USA' as your next album. . . . You're now harmful to the women and children who have bought your albums."

But the biggest drama was that of the trials. In October, a jury 15 composed of five white women and one Hispanic man convicted store owner Freeman of peddling obscenity; later that month a different jury in the same Florida county acquitted Campbell and the other 2 Live Crew members of the obscenity charges. In essence it was a split verdict—and nobody quite knew how to read its meaning. Meanwhile, in the year's other big rock trial, Judas Priest was acquitted in Reno, Nevada, of charges that subliminal messages in the band's music had led to the suicide of one youth and the attempted suicide of another—but the judge's ruling left many legal questions unresolved and made it plain to the music industry that heavy-metal recordings would likely remain subject to legal actions in the future.

In the end, none of these events settled the debate over rock's rights 16 to free speech. Certainly, there will be further calls for censorship. More arrests and more trials are also likely, and given the rightward drift of America's federal courts, it is hard to say how these conflicts will play themselves out. Still, there is hope: The tide of cultural history suggests that, as troubling as the notion may be to some, freedom of expression is a right that ultimately will not be undone. At the same time, perhaps the most frightening lesson of the Reagan era is that sometimes the tide of cultural history can be reversed.

If nothing else, all the brouhaha over censorship served to remind many 17 of us that rock still has the power to unsettle and to inflame. Of course, sometimes it provokes its critics by merely taunting them with surefire irritants like explicit sexual descriptions or rants about violence or the devil—but then sometimes the most effective (and hilarious) response to haughty disapproval is simply to become more unconscionable. At its best, though, rock & roll is a good deal more than a mere affront or a subject for argument. It is, in fact, perhaps the sole art or entertainment medium that most regularly forms an argument. That is, rock & roll itself is a disagreement with established power—a refutation of authority's unearned influence.

Not surprisingly, some of the music that did the best job of both  18
taunting *and* arguing this year came from the two camps that experienced
the greatest heat—heavy metal and rap. On the surface, these two genres
might seem to have little in common, in terms either of audience or style.
And yet both are derived from the structures of blues music, and by
keeping that form's temper fresh, rap and metal have also done a tremendous amount to revivify rock's essential incendiary spirit. In addition,
both rap and hard rock speak for and to the concerns of young and often
disenfranchised audiences—working-class whites and inner-city blacks,
who are frequently viewed with fear and suspicion by much of the American mainstream—and it is this power to articulate and stir the passions of
youthful outsiders that scares so many people about rock & roll.

In any event, as more black musicians began experimenting with hard  19
rock and more whites began making credible rap, some of the biases that
had formed unfortunate barriers between the two camps began to dissolve.
This year, the most impressive genre-shattering music came from two bands
who also had enormously wide appeal: Faith No More, an all-white,
postpunk-derived outfit that took a personalized, raplike delivery and in-
tercut it with hard-edge metallic textures; and Living Colour, whose titanic
second LP, *Time's Up*, fused punk rhythms and speed-metal leads with a
complex harmonic architecture derived from the avant-garde sensibility of
legendary jazz saxophonist Ornette Coleman. Between these two bands,
the face of modern rock was virtually overhauled this last year. In particular,
an album like *Time's Up* set new standards against which ambitious rock &
roll will be measured between now and the end of the century.

But there was also much to be valued about the hard rock that  20
elected to stay within more familiar boundaries. Indeed, heavy metal is
currently enjoying an astonishing creative and commercial peak, and as
the music of such bands as Mötley Crüe, Damn Yankees, Little Caesar,
Warrant, Winger, Slaughter, Poison, Trixter, ad infinitum, makes plain, it
is amazing how much verve and humor can still be wrung from hoary
crash-and-burn guitar riffs that frame the eternal drama of getting pissed,
getting drunk and getting laid. Of course, hard rock also has its
cutting-edge movement—composed of smart and funny bands like the
Dwarves, Tad, Fluid, Afghan Whigs, Babes in Toyland and the Seattle
brigade (which includes Soundgarden, Alice in Chains, Screaming Trees,
the late Mother Love Bone and the wondrous Mudhoney)—most of
whom play a grungy style of metal brimming with impetuous rhythms
and punk-inspired guitar-and-drum barrages that, not surprisingly, frame
the eternal drama of getting pissed, getting drunk and getting laid.
Meanwhile, some of the most enlivening and challenging rock this year
came from established thrash and Goth-rock bands like Megadeth,
Anthrax, Slayer and Danzig. In the case of Anthrax, here was a band that
was not only willing to make politically astute hard rock but also willing

to challenge the biases of its audience and of such fellow colleague-heroes as Axl Rose. "Don't even try to tell me what you think is right," the group sang in "Keep It in the Family," "when to you blacks are niggers, and Jews are kikes."

But it was rap that enjoyed more attention than any other pop genre this 21 year, and for fair reason. Despite all the swipes directed at it, rap remained committed to holding forth on some of the most disturbing concerns of the day. Records like Public Enemy's *Fear of a Black Planet,* Above the Law's *Livin' Like Hustlers,* Kid Frost's *Hispanic Causing Panic* and Ice Cube's *AmeriKKKa's Most Wanted* were works that offered tough and unflinching appraisals of a broad range of unpleasant topics—including gang violence, misogyny, racism and drug dealing—and despite the naysayers who warned that this music amounted to "ugly macho boasting" and "obscenity," all of these albums enjoyed substantial sales. Is that cause for concern? Does that mean the audience that buys rap records is an audience that likes this music because it exposes values of anger? Do people in that audience, in fact, take some of the songs on the Ice Cube, Kid Frost or Above the Law records as literal celebrations of misogyny or violence?

Obviously, precious few of the people who hear a musical account of 22 a drive-by shooting lose their repulsion toward such acts in real life, much less feel any inclination to take part in such horror. Yet this isn't to deny that one shouldn't raise hard questions about the meaning and impact of some of this music. A record like *The Geto Boys* (which, remember, Geffen found so offensive the label refused to release it) relates some truly unsettling tales about gang violence and homicidal rape, and does so from a first-person point of view that brings both the narrator and listener into the heart of modern urban horror. It may be the single most terrifying work that popular music has ever produced. Certainly, it is a record that one should take a good hard look at—indeed, any art that seems to celebrate hatred and murder is art that should be scrutinized and, when necessary, criticized. At the same time, that isn't really what *The Geto Boys* is about. Like Martin Scorsese—whose film *GoodFellas* is a deeply felt drama about contemporary gangster life—the Geto Boys and other rappers are reporting on a social reality that they know firsthand, and at times such reportage can seem ugly and morally questionable. But whereas Scorsese's work is singled out as an artistic achievement, *The Geto Boys* is roundly condemned as brutal trash. Why? Is it because the Geto Boys are talking about conditions of violence *so* modern, *so* threatening that we can't view any of it with distance? Or is it because, by telling their tales in the first person, rappers seem to be committing themselves to the worst impulses in their scenarios?

There are no simple answers to these questions. What is clear is that 23 works like *The Geto Boys* are disturbing for good reason—they're *meant* to be disturbing—and it is to our peril and discredit when we fail to examine the conditions that have made such music possible or necessary.

In any event, there was also plenty of rap this year that put forth 24
more plainly positive values about hope and community and sex,
including the music of Queen Latifah, Boogie Down Productions, A
Tribe Called Quest, M.C. Hammer and—believe it or not—New Kids on
the Block.

While M.C. Hammer's raps may seem wooden in comparison to the 25
fleet and startling vocalese of rappers like L.L. Cool J, Ice Cube and
Chuck D, it is plain that when Hammer achieves massive breakthrough
hits with songs about personal pride and the need for prayer, he is
addressing the same pressing concerns as much of the rest of the hip-hop
nation—namely, that these are difficult and scary times that we face and
that it will take openness and resourcefulness to see us through the days
ahead. (Plus, let's not ignore that Hammer's prowess as a dancer—in
fact, as rap's first great sexy showman—bespeaks its own positive values.)
In comparison, the sanitized, pop-sleek hip-hop of New Kids on the
Block may seem a little *too* positive—indeed, so affectedly wholesome
that it often appears to be the antithesis of rap's prowess and spunk. Yet
in some ways, the New Kids' overwhelming acceptance by a very young
mainstream audience only demonstrates how pervasive the textures and
rhythms of hip hop have become. The New Kids may be the acceptable
face of the most radical pop sound of today, but what their success
signifies is that rap has quickly become one of the primary edifices of
modern music. On that framework, much of the future of rock and its
culture is likely to be constructed.

Even without the din of metal and rap, there was still plenty of 26
compelling pop music made in 1990, in virtually any genre, style, age
range or nationality that one might prefer. Some of the best was made by
fresh-faced new artists enjoying their first flush of mellifluence or
inventiveness. Among such acts were Belgium's Technotronic, Holland's
Urban Dance Squad and England's D Mob, who brought an irresistible
pop sensibility to house-style dance rhythms. Other worthy first timers
included artists like the U.K.'s Beats International, Lightning Seeds,
Heart Throbs, Stone Roses, House of Love, Lisa Stansfield, Sundays,
808 State and Jesus Jones, as well as America's Chris Thomas, Lil Louis,
Deee-Lite, David Baerwald (making his first solo after the breakup of
David and David), Ernie Isley (making a lone outing from the Isley
Brothers) and Mazzy Star. There was also an impressive amount of
heartening music by long-loved veterans including Van Morrison, the
Traveling Wilburys, Prince, Rosanne Cash, Brian Eno and John Cale,
Paul Simon, Los Lobos and Robert Plant. But probably the king of the
vets, for the second year running, was Neil Young, whose *Ragged Glory*
proved that the rejuvenation begun with last year's *Freedom* wasn't a
mere fluke. Indeed, *Ragged Glory* wasn't only one of the most passionate, balls-out rock & roll guitar albums of the year, it was also one of

Young's most transcendent and affirmative works—and it stands as proof that, sometimes, rock & roll can guide and uplift a creative sensibility for a lifetime.

Perhaps the most significant work by a single artist this year came 27 from Irish-born Sinéad O'Connor. In 1987, O'Connor offered a stunning debut album, *The Lion and the Cobra,* featuring songs of embittered love-and-sex and wrought-up spirituality, sung in a fierce, feral voice as old as Gaelic pain and as modern as punk rage. Like much of the most exciting music of the last decade or so, *The Lion and the Cobra* was music that was formidable enough to win a fierce cult and yet too formidable to enter pop's mainstream. But with this year's *I Do Not Want What I Haven't Got,* O'Connor delivered an album that explored harder truths—about misplaced faith, betrayed love and murderous racism—and she managed to sing it in a soft, stunned-sounding voice that attracted one of the biggest and most surprising audiences of the year. It was the sort of success nobody could have predicted, and it showed how the barriers between the mainstream and the margins are beginning to collapse in pop.

But like most of the valuable pop journeys this year, O'Connor's 28 wasn't an easy one. During the summer, when she refused to allow the national anthem to be played at one of her performances in New Jersey, local and national media treated the event as major news. Overnight, there were calls for her to be deported back to Ireland; radio stations announced they were boycotting her music; and she was vilified by other celebrities (including Frank Sinatra) and harassed in public. Over and over, irate Americans asked the same question: What did O'Connor have against the anthem? (The answer is easy, and fairly innocent: O'Connor is opposed to nationalism of any sort and in fact refused to pose with an Irish flag for a photo session for ROLLING STONE earlier in the year.) But there was another question that wasn't asked and perhaps should have been: Namely, in a year when rock was treated as subversion by so many American lawmakers and pundits, why should a performer be forced to pay tribute to a nation that is so reluctant to stand up for the rights of its own artists?

The incident was another reminder that these are dangerous times to 29 advertise oneself as a malcontent in American pop culture. But it was also a reminder that rock's best and bravest heroes aren't about to break down when confronted by indignant authoritarians. Kicking against social repression and moral vapidity—that's an activity that, for thirty-five years now, rock & roll has managed to do better than virtually any other art or entertainment form. But at this juncture, the forces that would not only condemn but curtail or silence that impulse are formidable. If 1990 taught us anything, it is that if we value rock as a spirit of insolent liberty, then the time has come to form a bulwark against those who would gladly muzzle that spirit.

## Post-Reading Questions

1. Summarize Gilmore's definition of rock and roll (paragraph two). Do you agree with his definition? Why? What does his definition suggest about his personal view of rock and roll? Does he believe his own definition? How do you know? What language clues help readers understand his feelings?
2. Explain Gilmore's writing purposes. What is he trying to accomplish in this article? What strategies does he depend on to achieve his writing purposes? How successful is he?
3. In your own words, state Gilmore's thesis. Identify two or three sentences that state or rephrase his thesis.
4. What examples does Gilmore use to support his claim that rock and roll has been subjected to much criticism? Why might he have chosen these particular examples? How do they help him achieve his writing purposes?
5. Describe Gilmore's approach to organizing his article. What reasons might he have had to present information in the order he does?
6. What is the PMRC? What is Gilmore's opinion of it? How does he communicate that opinion to his readers?
7. Describe the kinds of readers Gilmore might have had in mind as he wrote his article. How would they react to Gilmore's views of rock and roll? Why?
8. How does Gilmore feel about censoring rock and roll? Make a list of phrases or sentences in this article that you could cite to support your analysis of his viewpoint. Do you agree with Gilmore? Why?
9. Where in this article does Gilmore describe his feelings about the individuals running the recording industry? What is his opinion? Do you agree? Why?
10. Are ratings on records the same as ratings for films? Why? Is a rating system a form of censorship? Why?

# SUSAN BROWNMILLER ON FEMINISTS AND PORNOGRAPHY

## Pre-Reading Questions

1. How would you define pornography? Is pornography harmful? If so, to whom and why? If not, why not? What experiences have you had with pornography? Have you ever been told that a magazine or movie was pornographic? How did you react? Why is *pornographic* difficult to define? Why is it difficult to control?
2. Define *informal* control of pornography. How would, for example, a bookstore manager "informally" control pornographic material? In

what ways have you experienced *informal* control of pornography? How does informal control differ from *legal* control of pornography? Do you favor legal control of pornography? Why?

3. Do you believe that men and women define pornography differently? Why?

4. Do you believe a work of art (a painting, film, or sculpture, for example) could be considered pornographic yet remain a work of art? Use your own experiences to explain your answer.


# LET'S PUT PORNOGRAPHY BACK IN THE CLOSET
## Susan Brownmiller

Free speech is one of the great foundations on which our democracy rests. I am old enough to remember the Hollywood Ten, the screenwriters who went to jail in the late 1940s because they refused to testify before a congressional committee about their political affiliations. They tried to use the First Amendment as a defense, but they went to jail because in those days there were few civil liberties lawyers around who cared to champion the First Amendment right to free speech, when the speech concerned the Communist party.

The Hollywood Ten were correct in claiming the First Amendment. Its high purpose is the protection of unpopular ideas and political dissent. In the dark, cold days of the 1950s, few civil libertarians were willing to declare themselves First Amendment absolutists. But in the brighter, though frantic, days of the 1960s, the principle of protecting unpopular political speech was gradually strengthened.

It is fair to say now that the battle has largely been won. Even the American Nazi party has found itself the beneficiary of the dedicated, tireless work of the American Civil Liberties Union. But—and please notice the quotation marks coming up—"To equate the free and robust exchange of ideas and political debate with commercial exploitation of obscene material demeans the grand conception of the First Amendment and its high purposes in the historic struggle for freedom. It is a misuse of the great guarantees of free speech and free press."

I didn't say that, although I wish I had, for I think the words are thrilling. Chief Justice Warren Burger said it in 1973, in the United States Supreme Court's majority opinion in *Miller v. California*. During the same decades that the right to political free speech was being strengthened in the courts, the nation's obscenity laws also were undergoing extensive revision.

It's amazing to recall that in 1934 the question of whether James 5
Joyce's *Ulysses* should be banned as pornographic actually went before
the Court. The battle to protect *Ulysses* as a work of literature with
redeeming social value was won. In later decades, Henry Miller's *Tropic*
books, *Lady Chatterley's Lover* and the *Memoirs of Fanny Hill* also were
adjudged not obscene. These decisions have been important to me. As
the author of *Against Our Will,* a study of the history of rape that does
contain explicit sexual material, I shudder to think how my book would
have fared if James Joyce, D. H. Lawrence, and Henry Miller hadn't
gone before me.

I am not a fan of *Chatterley* or the *Tropic* books, I should quickly 6
mention. They are not to my literary taste, nor do I think they represent
female sexuality with any degree of accuracy. But I would hardly suggest
that we ban them. Such a suggestion wouldn't get very far anyway. The
battle to protect these books is ancient history. Time does march on,
quite methodically. What, then, is unlawfully obscene, and what does the
First Amendment have to do with it?

In the Miller case of 1973 (not Henry Miller, by the way, but a porn 7
distributor who sent unsolicited stuff through the mails), the Court came
up with new guidelines that it hoped would strengthen obscenity laws by
giving more power to the states. What it did in actuality was throw
everything into confusion. It set up a three-part test by which materials
can be adjudged obscene. The materials are obscene if they depict
patently offensive, hard-core sexual conduct; lack serious scientific,
literary, artistic, or political value; and appeal to the prurient interest of
an average person—as measured by contemporary community standards.

"Patently offensive," "prurient interest," and "hard-core" are in- 8
deed words to conjure with. "Contemporary community standards" are
what we're trying to redefine. The feminist objection to pornography is
not based on prurience, which the dictionary defines as lustful, itching
desire. We are not opposed to sex and desire, with or without the itch,
and we certainly believe that explicit sexual material has its place in
literature, art, science, and education. Here we part company rather
swiftly with old-line conservatives who don't want sex education in the
high schools, for example.

No, the feminist objection to pornography is based on our belief that 9
pornography represents hatred of women, that pornography's intent is to
humiliate, degrade, and dehumanize the female body for the purpose of
erotic stimulation and pleasure. We are unalterably opposed to the presentation of the female body being stripped, bound, raped, tortured, mutilated,
and murdered in the name of commercial entertainment and free speech.

These images, which are standard pornographic fare, have nothing to 10
do with the hallowed right of political dissent. They have everything to do
with the creation of a cultural climate in which a rapist feels he is merely

giving in to a normal urge and a woman is encouraged to believe that sexual masochism is healthy, liberated fun. Justice Potter Stewart once said about hard-core pornography, "You know it when you see it," and that certainly used to be true. In the good old days, pornography looked awful. It was cheap and sleazy, and there was no mistaking it for art.

Nowadays, since the porn industry has become a multimillion dollar 11 business, visual technology has been employed in its service. Pornographic movies are skillfully filmed and edited, pornographic still shots using the newest tenets of good design artfully grace the covers of *Hustler, Penthouse,* and *Playboy,* and the public—and the courts—are sadly confused.

The Supreme Court neglected to define "hard-core" in the Miller 12 decision. This was a mistake. If "hard-core" refers only to explicit sexual intercourse, then that isn't good enough. When women or children or men—no matter how artfully—are shown tortured or terrorized in the service of sex, that's obscene. And "patently offensive," I would hope, to our "contemporary community standards."

Justice William O. Douglas wrote in his dissent to the Miller case 13 that no one is "compelled to look." This is hardly true. To buy a paper at the corner newsstand is to subject oneself to a forcible immersion in pornography, to be demeaned by an array of dehumanized, chopped-up parts of the female anatomy, packaged like cuts of meat at the supermarket. I happen to like my body and I work hard at the gym to keep it in good shape, but I am embarrassed for my body and for the bodies of all women when I see the fragmented parts of us so frivolously, and so flagrantly, displayed.

Some constitutional theorists (Justice Douglas was one) have main- 14 tained that any obscenity law is a serious abridgement of free speech. Others (and Justice Earl Warren was one) have maintained that the First Amendment was never intended to protect obscenity. We live quite compatibly with a host of free-speech abridgements. There are restraints against false and misleading advertising or statements—shouting "fire" without cause in a crowded movie theater, etc.—that do not threaten, but strengthen, our societal values. Restrictions on the public display of pornography belong in this category.

The distinction between permission to publish and permission to 15 display publicly is an essential one and one which I think consonant with First Amendment principles. Justice Burger's words which I quoted above support this without question. We are not saying "Smash the presses" or "Ban the bad ones," but simply "Get the stuff out of our sight." Let the legislatures decide—using realistic and humane contemporary community standards—what can be displayed and what cannot. The courts, after all, will be the final arbiters.

## Post-Reading Questions

1. Why does Brownmiller begin her essay with a reference to the Hollywood Ten? How does she make sure that readers of all ages will understand the reference?

2. Define a "first amendment absolutist" (paragraph two). Does Brownmiller respect such individuals? How do you know?

3. Paraphrase Justice Burger's quotation in paragraph three. Why does Brownmiller say these words are "thrilling"? What does her response to Burger's words suggest about her thesis?

4. What kinds of personal information about herself does Brownmiller include in her essay? Why?

5. Summarize the Miller case of 1973 and the Miller test (paragraph 7). Use a current situation to illustrate how this test would be applied.

6. Why are "contemporary community standards" difficult to define? Use a current situation to illustrate the difficulties you identify.

7. What is Brownmiller's writing purpose? Where in her essay is she most clear about identifying that purpose?

8. Where in her essay does Brownmiller identify and respond to those individuals whose view on pornography differs from her own? Summarize her response. How convincing is she? Why?

9. Are shoppers "compelled to look" at pornography (paragraph 13)? Use your own experiences at movie theaters or video rental places to explain your answer.

10. Summarize the feminist viewpoint on pornography as Brownmiller describes it. Do you think that viewpoint remains consistent with feminists' philosophy as you understand it? Explain.

# WALTER BERNS ON THE NATIONAL ENDOWMENT FOR THE ARTS

## Pre-Reading Questions

1. What does the term "freedom of expression" mean to you? Do you believe that any forms of expression should be subject to restrictions? Why or why not? Use your own experiences to explain your answers.

2. If you were responsible for distributing federal funds to artists, what criteria would you use to determine who to fund? What kinds of projects would you fund? How would you decide how much financial support particular projects should receive?

3. Do you believe that an artist receiving federal funding should be required to sign a non-obscenity oath? Why?

4. Have you ever felt that your individual freedom of expression was curtailed by teachers or parents?

# SAVING THE NEA
## Walter Berns

Congress and the arts community have combined to make it difficult for 1
the National Endowment for the Arts to come to a sensible (and
constitutional) resolution of the controversy concerning federal funding
of the arts. Of course, the NEA has only itself to blame for initiating the
controversy—when establishing the agency in 1965 and directing it to
fund projects with "substantial artistic and cultural significance," Congress surely did not have in mind photographs of men urinating in each
other's mouths or of a crucifix submerged in a bottle of urine and given
the title *Piss Christ*—but it is doubtful that, left to itself, the NEA would
have required grant recipients to sign "non-obscenity oaths." Nor, left to
itself, would it have made a fool of itself by rescinding the requirement
and then rescinding the rescission. For this, and all the other incidents in
what has become a nasty public dispute, Congress and the arts community are also to blame.

Congress is of the opinion that art is one thing and obscenity 2
another, and that a sensible agency can distinguish between the two. But
many a work of art and many a literary masterpiece is obscene. As I had
occasion to write a year ago when this present controversy began,
Aristophanes' *Assembly of Women* is so obscene that the English translator
of the play preferred to remain anonymous (that was a long time ago),
and Manet's *Déjeuner sur l'herbe*, now one of the Louvre's treasured
classics, was considered indecent when first exhibited in 1863. And quite
rightly so; it shows not a nude but an undressed woman—her clothes are
in a heap beside her—sharing a public picnic lunch with two fully clothed
men. Indecent, yes (at least we used to think so), but a wonderful
painting.

For its part, the arts community insists that everything produced by 3
someone claiming to be an artist is in fact a work of art: Mapplethorpe's
photograph of a bullwhip thrust into his own rectum, Holly Hughes's
giant quartz-and-steel vagina, Karen Finley's "performance art" in which
she spreads herself with chocolate while reciting lines that no newspaper
will print, as well as *Déjeuner sur l'herbe*, Giorgione's *Concert Champêtre*,
and Vuillard's *Cuisinière*. It's all art. ("It's creative, isn't it?") As a
self-styled "relatively mainstream" theatrical artist and Yale drama professor said in a recent NEA council meeting, "I'm only as free as Karen
Finley is. I'm only as free as Holly Hughes is."

Thus, thanks to Congress, the NEA was given the impossible task of 4
distinguishing between art and obscenity, and, thanks to the arts community, it is forbidden to distinguish between art and trash.

But this is not the end of its difficulties. Any attempt to distinguish 5
between art and obscenity would engage it in a legal battle with civil

libertarians. Citing a handful of recent Supreme Court decisions, they argue that the task of defining obscenity belongs to the courts alone because only the courts may inflict punishment, and, as they see it, withholding funds from an artist is no less punishment than forbidding the public display of his work. This became the at least quasi-official view when, without argument, the Independent Commission on the National Endowment for the Arts adopted it in its recent report to Congress: Congress, it said, may refuse to fund works of art, but not because it views their content as obscene, or objectionable, or "dangerous." Judgments of this sort bring the First Amendment into play, and, as one noted constitutional lawyer testified, "the First Amendment does not allow Congress to pick and choose who gets money and who doesn't."

## WHO'S TO JUDGE?

The attempt to distinguish between art and trash would run into other   6
difficulties. As the commission emphasizes, "[Congress] may insist on artistic excellence as a prerequisite for any funding," but, as it is currently organized, the NEA is manifestly incapable of making the sort of judgment this would require. At present, and contrary to the authorizing legislation, final grant-making power is exercised only nominally by the chairman (with the advice of the National Council on the Arts) and practically by the grant advisory (or peer-review) panels, which is to say, by the persons and groups ending up with the funds. As one observer put it, the NEA has allowed itself to become "an instrument for back-scratching and palm-greasing within the artistic community rather than an agency for the impartial administration of public arts appropriations."

Considering what the agency had become—"a system willfully   7
contemptuous of the public interest and the public voice [and] dedicated to the subsidy of in-group art at the expense of the taxpayers whose money it was so freely spending"—the commission might have been expected to recommend its abolition. But, as its report points out, of the 83,000 grants made by the NEA since its inception in 1966, only a "small number . . . has provoked significant controversy"; largely exempt from criticism have been its grants to symphony orchestras and museums, for example.

The controversy has to do largely with its programs in the visual and   8
performance arts, and it remains to be seen whether Congress will accept the commission's recommendations and, if so, whether they are sufficient to remedy the situation. Essentially, the commission, with a view to making the agency more responsible, recommends that the chairman's powers be made more explicit. In the words of the report, "the arts

belong to all the American people and not only those who benefit directly from the agency." It is, after all, the people's money, and someone responsible to the President and Congress, and through them to the people, should have the power to decide how it is spent.

But why not simply abolish the visual- and performance-arts pro-    9 grams? This would, of course, outrage the arts community, but, among its other advantages, it would provide no pretext for the lawyers to go to court: Congress may not be able to place restrictions on its grants to artists but there is nothing in the Constitution that requires it to make such grants in the first place. Besides, something might be gained by the abolition of these programs—for example, the funds could be redirected to education programs designed to wean children from rock to classical music, thereby providing future audiences for all those orchestras already receiving federal subsidies—and little or nothing would be lost. The commission might have learned this from Alexis de Tocqueville.

Among all the writers who have studied America, Tocqueville is   10 surely the most admired and, except on this subject of the arts, the most frequently quoted. He had a good deal to say about the arts, or, more precisely, about democracy and the arts, but none of it was calculated to please us Americans, which is probably why he is not quoted on this subject. Among other things, he suggested that we would be so busy acquiring useful things that we would have no time, no taste, and no aptitude for the arts.

Tocqueville contrasted our situation with that of the aristocratic  11 world from which he came. Aristocrats, he said, being already provided with material comforts, were free to adorn their lives with useless but beautiful things—objects, pictures, music, books—and some of them at least developed a taste for the beautiful and well crafted. The aristocratic audience for the arts was "few and fastidious," he said, but these few supported the arts, and their good taste and judgment was reflected in the artists' work. To cite merely one example, Beethoven's three Opus 59 quartets were commissioned by a Russian nobleman, Count Razumovsky, and are known even today as the Razumovsky Quartets.

But Tocqueville expected Americans to be engaged in one sort of  12 business or another and to turn to the arts, if at all, only for entertainment or relaxation on weekends. "People who spend every weekday making money and Sunday praying to God give no scope to the Muse of Comedy," he said. Here, as in everything in a democratic society, public opinion would govern what is produced or otherwise made available: at best, Fred Astaire and *My Fair Lady;* typically, television sit-coms; at worst, 2 Live Crew and Karen Finley. The point is, artists are dependent on their times and their audiences, and it was Tocqueville's judgment that our times would be prosaic and our audiences bourgeois.

Like it or not, our visual artists especially are unable to deny this sort  13 of dependence. In fact, they confirm it every time they tell us that one of the purposes of art is to shock, which means, in our case, to shock the bourgeoisie. We hear this repeatedly, and not only from the likes of Holly Hughes and Karen Finley. But to set out to shock the bourgeois public is to take one's bearings from it, to be dependent on it, in fact, to be parasitic on it: no bourgeoisie, no Holly Hughes or Karen Finley.

As it turns out, however, it is not at all easy to shock the bourgeoisie; 14 in fact, it is impossible. As Andy Warhol said, "Nothing is more bourgeois than to be afraid to look bourgeois." One way to avoid looking bourgeois is to pay high prices for Warhol's paintings of soup cans; another is to pretend to admire contemporary sculpture—for example, those oil drums welded together to resemble that huge gun that Iraq wanted to buy from the British and aim at the Israelis; still another, the tactic used by the NEA, is to fund whatever bubbles up from the arts community, which, of necessity, becomes more and more extreme. So it is that our "artists" set out to shock the bourgeoisie and succeed only in shocking some members of Congress. Tom Wolfe has a name for this: the "Boho Dance," where the artist desperately tries to stay one step ahead of the bourgeois who is struggling just as desperately to embrace him.

In this way, the bourgeois public cooperates in its own corruption; 15 indeed, it is partly to blame for it. The artist is, as I said, dependent on his audience, and the bourgeois audience has no taste for the sublime, or, in Tocqueville's words, for depictions—in painting, literature, or music—of "ideal beauty," or of human perfection, or of the gods. (Democracy, he said, will have "depopulated heaven.") What (in addition to sporting events) does this audience have a taste for? An evening spent at the movies or before the television set provides the answer: violence and sex. Thus, like our dramatists, Tom Wolfe's artists have simply understood the hidden inclinations of this audience and, in order to stay one step ahead of it, have become ever more violent and ever more lewd. By supporting the likes of Karen Finley and Holly Hughes, the NEA simply encourages the further corruption of popular culture. By saying, in effect, This is art, it encourages the further corruption of the public taste.

One does not have to be a philistine to draw this conclusion. On the 16 contrary, it is confirmed by the man generally regarded as the greatest of modern painters, Pablo Picasso. Indeed, his words provide the most telling comment on our situation:

> In art the mass of the people no longer seek consolation and exaltation, but those who are refined, rich, unoccupied . . . seek what is new, strange, original, extravagant, scandalous. I myself, since Cubism and before, have satisfied these masters and critics with all the changing oddities which have passed through my head, and the less they understood me, the more they admired me. By amusing myself with all these games, with all these

absurdities, puzzles, rebuses, arabesques, I became famous and that very quickly. And fame for a painter means sales, gains, fortunes, riches. And today, as you know, I am celebrated, I am rich. But when I am alone with myself, I have not the courage to think of myself as an artist in the great and ancient sense of the term. Giotto, Titian, Rembrandt were great painters. I am only a public entertainer who has understood his times and exploited them as best he could. . . . Mine is a bitter confession, more painful than it may appear, but it has the merit of being sincere.

Clearly, the NEA has done nothing to improve this situation. The 17 original idea was that by taking the public money and spending it for purposes that, left to itself, the public would not support, the NEA might foster a public appreciation of the arts properly so called. In a way, the NEA was to be a kind of substitute for Tocqueville's missing aristocracy; to quote from the enacting legislation, a "high civilization" requires broad cultural awareness. And it's possible that, as the commission reports, the NEA has indeed "helped to transform the cultural landscape of the United States," at least in some areas: where there were only 58 symphony orchestras and 27 opera companies in 1965, there are now 230 and 120. But only a fool or a knave could see anything "high" about the civilization being depicted in the work being subsidized under the visual-arts program, and the commission would have performed a public service by recommending its abolition. It does recommend that the NEA become a "more visible and vigorous advocate of arts education," and, assuming it has in mind education calculated to provide an audience for those orchestras and opera companies, no one can quarrel with that. Left to themselves, the teenagers now attending rock concerts and buying the works of 2 Live Crew are not likely to acquire a taste for the Razumovsky Quartets.

## Post-Reading Questions

1. How does the first paragraph create a framework for Berns' essay? What kinds of information does it contain? How does it function as an introduction?

2. In your own words, summarize the role or viewpoint of the NEA, Congress, civil libertarians, and the arts community as Berns describes them. Where in the essay does Berns introduce the viewpoint of each of these groups? Why?

3. Summarize the findings and recommendations of the Commission on the National Endowment for the Arts. What is Berns' opinion of the Commission's recommendations? How do you know?

4. Explain why funding for orchestras and museums has created less controversy than funding for the visual and performance arts. Can you give some examples of recent or current "arts" controversies?

5.  What does Berns mean in paragraph two when he accuses an artist of portraying "not a nude but an undressed woman"? Do you agree with the distinction he makes? Why?

6.  Analyze the support Berns uses to develop his thesis. What kinds of support does he use? How effective are they? Why?

7.  Why would Berns like to see an end to NEA funding of visual and performance arts programs? Do you agree with him? Why?

8.  What kinds of readers would be most likely to agree with Berns' position? Why? What readers would reject his position? Why?

9.  Reread Berns' last paragraph. What is he trying to accomplish in his conclusion? How effective is he? How would you evaluate his language choices and the evidence he uses?

10. Analyze the examples Berns uses in paragraphs 2 and 3. How are they different? How are they alike?

11. Summarize the ideas of Tocqueville and Picasso used by Berns. Why does Berns refer to them in his essay? What contribution do their ideas make to the development of his thesis?

# 6
· · · · · · · · · · · · ·
## OPTIONAL WRITING ASSIGNMENTS
## FOCUSED ON CENSORSHIP

The following list of suggestions provides contexts for your chapter essay. Whether you choose one of these options or develop one on your own, remember that you need to analyze your writing context and decide how to achieve your writing purpose for the particular readers you target. (For a review of "The Rhetorical Approach to Academic Writing," see Chapter 2.)

   *1. Write an essay describing one particular experience you or someone else close to you had related to censorship in America.*  The experience you choose should involve one of the aspects or issues related to censorship raised by one or more of the readings in this chapter. Use whatever descriptive strategies you can to help your readers (your classmates) "see" the experience as it occurred. Your purpose in narrating this experience, however, is not only to recreate it. The experience you choose must help you make a point (thesis) about censorship. You may, if your teacher agrees, compare or contrast your experience with those described in one or more of the readings in this chapter.

   *2. Imagine the high school you attended is embroiled in a controversy regarding book selection for the school library.*  Several parents have protested three or four recent library acquisitions on the grounds that they discuss subjects inappropriate for their children and the other students attending the school: teenage pregnancy, teenage suicide, and divorce. The high-school principal has requested input from recent graduates on this issue. Write a letter to the principal suitable for presentation at the next Parent Teacher Association meeting. Consider the viewpoint you will present in your letter and what your reasons are for having that viewpoint. Then consider the kinds of "proof" your "readers" (the parents and teachers concerned about this issue) require before they accept your position as one they should consider and respect. For example, what kinds of reasons and examples will they find convincing? What can you draw from the readings in this chapter to support your viewpoint? What experiences—your own and those of people you know—would persuade your readers to accept your position? Finally, consider the order in which you should present your reasons and support for those reasons. Would your letter be effective if you presented your strongest reasons first, or would it be more effective if you built up to those reasons? How will you convince your readers that you understand other viewpoints? How will you convince your readers that you have solid reasons for rejecting those viewpoints? After completing these writing plans, draft the letter.

3. *Choose one form of individual expression discussed in this chapter, perhaps the visual arts or literature.* Take a position for or against censorship laws concerning this kind of individual expression. Then drawing on your reading of the articles and essays in this chapter, your own and others' experiences, and information from some outside-of-the-classroom source or sources (your teacher may require a certain number of outside sources), write a persuasive essay convincing your readers (fellow classmates) that your position is worth respecting and considering. Remember to consider what information your readers have, how they currently feel or are likely to feel about this kind of censorship, and what kinds of questions they may ask about the reasons and evidence you present. Document any outside-of-the-classroom sources you refer to in your essay.

4. *Write an argument attacking or defending the position of the author of one of the readings in this chapter, perhaps Berns' opinion of the NEA or Lawrence's opinion of racist speech suppression.* Consider both pro and con arguments, and address what you have to say to college students who have not read the article or essay. Include a brief summary of the writer's position. For each reason you use to attack or defend the writer's position, provide detailed explanation in the form of information from other readings in this chapter and from your own and others' experiences and ideas. Include references to the article or essay itself as you explain your own position.

5. *Analyze the various opinions regarding college policies regulating what is and is not appropriate speech.* To conduct this analysis, reread those readings in this chapter that contain information related to this

issue. Then identify two or three teachers at your college whom you could interview to obtain more information about how academics feel about such policies. Finally, identify a college administrator to interview. Once you have obtained their consent, generate a list of questions to ask the teachers and the administrator. Consider what kinds of open-ended questions will produce information about the teachers' and administrator's views about appropriate and inappropriate speech. Will you, for example, ask about their views directly? Will you ask them to provide examples to demonstrate their viewpoints? Take careful notes during the interviews (or request permission to tape record). Prepare a report analyzing the various viewpoints on the issue for your classmates. Do not reveal your own opinion on this issue in the report. If two or three other students in the class are interested, consider requesting permission from your teacher to research this issue collaboratively.

6. *Conduct a survey of college student attitudes toward some issue related to the censorship theme.* If your teacher agrees, you may conduct this investigation with a group of two or three other interested students. Conduct some library research, perhaps into censorship cases in your city or into a particular area of individual expression. Then develop a questionnaire that will produce information about your survey respondents' (your subjects') beliefs about this issue. Decide which attitudes you are interested in learning more about and which individuals you are interested in surveying. Consider the ethics of conducting a survey. How will you obtain permission from the subjects? From your college, if necessary? How will you guarantee anonymity to your subjects? Then administer the survey, trying to create a representative sample of subjects. Analyze your results and report them to your classmates using this format: introduction (in which you review your reading on the particular censorship issue and explain what you were trying to learn more about and what you expected to find), method (in which you describe what you did), results (in which you present the subjects' responses), and discussion (in which you analyze the results, providing your explanation for the results and suggesting future research on this issue). Document any library sources you discuss in your research report.

7. *Using library sources, investigate censorship cases dealing with a particular form of individual expression, rock-and-roll music or photography, for example.* Or investigate one particular case that is discussed in one of this chapter's readings. Generate a list of questions your readers (your classmates) need answers to; then identify possible library sources to give you those answers. Consider whether or not to rely on articles written for specialists (journal articles) or those written for interested, non-specialist readers (newspaper and magazine articles). Once you have read and taken notes from those sources, develop a thesis for a report on the case or cases you have investigated. Will you

explain, for example, how these cases set precedents for a particular form of censorship (or lack of it), or will you persuade your classmates that this case (or these cases) demonstrates that your position regarding censorship is worth respecting? Once you have decided what point to make in your essay (your thesis), reconsider your notes and your own experiences and begin to plan a strategy for presenting your ideas to your readers. For example, decide what information from the library sources will most appropriately and effectively help you develop your thesis. Decide how you will organize your essay's contents. Will you organize information chronologically (in the order in which events occurred) or will you present your information organized by causes or effects or both? Or will you use a problem-solution format? All of this planning will help you draft an essay that will accomplish your writing purposes for your readers.

# Glossary of Rhetorical Terms

**Active reading**   a strategy in which the reader interacts with the text's ideas through summarizing, responding, analyzing, and evaluating.

**Analyzing**   a writing purpose and strategy for organizing writing in which a topic or subject is divided into parts, studied part by part, and then put back together again with a new meaning.

**Annotate**   active reading to achieve critical reading purposes. Readers highlight main ideas in a text and write marginal notes summarizing, analyzing, and responding to those ideas. These annotations then become the basis for developing personal interpretations of a text—the goal of critical reading.

**Argument**   the argumentative essay supports a proposition (thesis) with evidence (facts, examples, illustrations, logical reasoning), but also must consider possible counterarguments.

**Assumptions**   the values and ideas, stated or implied, that a writer assumes the reader will accept without supporting evidence. In general, assumptions should be kept to a minimum. Although most audiences share certain general human values—most Americans share a reverence for freedom, for example—writers should never assume that an audience shares particular values. Writers should consider the assumptions behind their theses carefully.

**Audience**   the potential readers of an essay. Some interests, traits, beliefs, and expectations usually distinguish the audience of a particular piece of writing from all the readers of a language.

**Body**   the main portion of an essay in which the thesis is supported with specific details.

**Brainstorming**   a technique for generating ideas before writing. The writer first selects a subject and freely associates ideas and experiences with it, then analyzes the relationships among the ideas and experiences.

**Cause and effect**   a thinking pattern and a strategy for organizing writing by analyzing a topic or supporting an idea (or thesis) in terms of causal relationships.

**Chronological order**   a thinking pattern and a strategy for organizing writing by arranging a topic or supporting an idea (or thesis) according to time sequence.

**Clarity**   clearness, the ability to be easily understood. Precise vocabulary, use of specific and concrete details, careful arrangement of materials and connection of thoughts all contribute clarity to an essay.

**Cliché**   an overused, trite expression: "That's a *tried and true* method."

**Coherence**   a natural and logical connection of ideas. Careful organization of thoughts before writing ensures a natural relationship of ideas. Readers expect writers to group ideas in a logical way and to use words and phrases to identify those logical connections. Use of transitional expressions, repetition, balance, parallelism, and attention to word order and punctuation highlight connections. See also *Transitional devices.*

**Colloquial language**   sentence patterns, vocabulary, and structure of everyday speech.

**Comparison**   a thinking pattern and a strategy for organizing writing in which two or more ideas and experiences are examined together to establish their similarity or difference, or the superiority or inferiority of one over the others.

**Completeness**   a sense of wholeness resulting in writing when sufficient detail to support a thesis is included. The amount of detail required to achieve completeness depends on a writer's readers and writing purpose.

**Comprehension**   an initial reading goal. Readers who comprehend are able to recognize and interpret another person's words, symbols, and signs to construct meaning as they read.

**Conclusion**   the final sentences or paragraphs of an essay, in which the writer often refers to the thesis and makes some kind of general statement about its significance.

**Concrete words**   words that appeal directly to a reader's senses: sight (*bronze, shiny*); hearing (*quiet, shrill*); smell (*musty, dank*); taste (*salty, bland*); and touch (*hard, dry*).

**Connotation**   the secondary meaning or implication of a word (often an emotional overtone) as opposed to its primary, or dictionary, definition (*denotation*).

**Contrast**   a comparison that emphasizes differences over similarities. See also *Comparison.*

**Convention**   a custom or accepted guideline. Academic writers must adhere to documentation conventions when acknowledging their sources in essays; letter writers must follow format conventions.

**Critical reading**   an active, interactive approach through which a reader moves beyond comprehension in order to develop a personal interpretation of a text. Critical reading requires summary, analysis, evaluation, and response.

**Critical writing**   academic writing in which a personal interpretation of a text is developed and supported using logical reasoning and evidence from the text itself.

**Critique**   an academic text, resulting from critical reading, in which the writer introduces, develops, and supports a personal interpretation or judgment of a text. See also *Critical writing.*

**Denotation**   the primary, or dictionary, definition of a word as opposed to its secondary meanings or implications (called *connotations*).

**Description**   writing that appeals to the senses and acquaints readers with a particular place, person, object, or group through the use of concrete words.

**Detail**   a specific physical property or subidea used to support a larger generalization. See also *Generalization.*

**Development**   the process of supporting a general idea with specific evidence. A well-developed essay—one with sufficient supporting detail—is said to have *completeness.*

**Draft**   a complete piece of writing, with introduction, body, and conclusion. A writer may compose a *first* draft, an *exploratory* draft, or a *final* draft.

**Drafting**   a writing behavior often identified as the stage at which the writer, after analyzing a writing situation and developing a rhetorical approach, composes a complete text. See also *Draft.*

**Editing**   rereading sentences, paragraphs, and words to correct errors. Editing is usually done after the final draft of a paper has been written and revised.

**Effective writing**   writing that achieves its purposes with a particular audience.

**Emotional appeal**   an attempt to influence or persuade readers by using language, examples, or stories that produce a powerful emotional response (as opposed to a rational or ethical appeal).

**Emotionally charged words**   words that arouse strong emotions in readers (*communist, saint, cheap*), frequently used in emotional appeals.

**Evidence**   the materials—facts, statistics, logical reasoning, examples, illustrations, data produced in laboratory experiments, or field research—a writer uses to support the thesis and main points in an essay.

**Example**   a specific instance of an idea or experience used to support a thesis or main idea.

**Experience**   knowledge gained through living; one of the sources for ideas in writing.

**Explaining**  a writing purpose and strategy by which an idea or topic is clarified through the use of main ideas and supporting examples.

**Fact**  a statement that can be verified by referring to recorded history, statistics, experiment, logic, or sensory experience.

**First person**  the point of view of the writer as opposed to the reader or subject: "*I* feel it would be a mistake to vote for that proposition."

**Focus**  concentration on a single main idea—in a paragraph the focus is on the idea in the topic sentence; in an essay the focus is on a particular aspect of a subject.

**Generalization**  a statement that must be supported using some kind of evidence. Generalizations are often used as *topic sentences*—to introduce the idea to be supported in a paragraph.

**Illustration**  the process of supporting a general idea with specific details. There are many ways to illustrate: by giving examples, by showing how something is done, or by tracing the reasoning behind the development of a thesis.

**Interpreting**  a writing purpose and strategy in which a subject is seen and explained in a new way.

**Introduction**  the group of sentences or paragraphs that opens an essay by providing background on the subject, defining its significance, attracting the reader's attention, or introducing the thesis.

**Irony**  a strategy in which the writer uses exaggeration or understatement to signal a difference between literal and intended meaning.

**Jargon**  special technical language; also, such language used out of context: "factor out" instead of "single out."

**Logic**  the principles of reason.

**Narration**  writing that tells a story, either for its own sake or to develop a thesis.

**Objective writing**  writing that focuses on those aspects of a subject (facts, concrete details, logical connection) that can be verified by direct observation or analysis. Objective writing emphasizes an accurate and unbiased rendering of a subject.

**Observation**  systematic attention to the sensory details of a concrete object, place, or person; one of the sources for ideas in writing.

**Opinion**  a statement of attitude or belief that, by itself, is unsubstantiated. Opinions must be supported with specific facts, details, logical reasoning, or other kinds of evidence.

**Organization**  the process of ordering and arranging main ideas and supporting evidence to produce a unified and coherent essay.

**Outline**  a plan for writing consisting of main ideas and supporting ideas. In a *sentence outline* each point is made in a complete sentence; in a *topic outline* words or phrases designate major headings.

**Paragraph**  one or more sentences forming a unit of thought. In printed matter, a new paragraph is marked by indenting the first line. In college writing, paragraphs usually contain a topic sentence or generalization developed by supporting sentences.

**Perspective** a writer's approach to or "angle" on a subject. A writer may adopt a neutral perspective on a subject, or the perspective identified with a particular group or ideology, such as a parental or conservation viewpoint. The writer's choices in terms of quantity and varieties of evidence and language (tone) often provide clues to perspective.

**Persuasive writing** writing that is intended primarily to persuade, rather than to inform or describe.

**Plagiarism** the unacknowledged use, whether intentional or unintentional, of another person's ideas, information, or words.

**Plan** an informal outline.

**Planning** a writing behavior often identified as a stage of the writing process at which a writer generates a rhetorical approach or plan for an essay. During the planning stage, writers review their own experiences with a topic, often brainstorming or freewriting to get at those ideas; generate ideas for an essay by reading, responding to reading, discussing, and researching; and evaluate and revise those ideas in terms of the particular writing situation, particularly the intended readers and the writer's purpose, but also any other factors affecting the piece being planned.

**Point of view** the stance a writer takes toward a subject, including person (first, second, or third) and involvement or distance from subject (perspective).

**Pre-writing** the planning or initial stage in the writing process. Also refers to the writing strategies, such as brainstorming and freewriting, writers use to review and recapture their experiences and responses to a particular topic or question.

**Proofreading** the final stage of the writing process involving a final check of a draft for typographical errors.

**Purpose** the writer's aim or reason for writing, including the effect of the composition on an audience and what the writer wishes to say about subject or self. Purpose is one of the aspects of a writing situation or context that determines structure and style.

**Reading context** a reading situation defined by the factors affecting the particular reader's reading process, among them the reader's experience with the kind of text being read and its subject matter and the reader's purpose.

**Reading process** the act of predicting, revising, and confirming meaning in a text in order to comprehend or interpret it.

**Reading situation** used interchangeably with *reading context.*

**Reviewing** the stage of the writing process at which a writer rereads and reshapes a draft. Reviewing behaviors include revising, editing, and proofreading.

**Revising**   a writing strategy associated with the reviewing stage of the composing process during which writers rework a draft of a paper—adding, deleting, and moving words, sentences, and paragraphs—to fit the composition's purpose and audience. When revising, writers consider organization, logic, and development of the text's contents, as well as surface features and coherence.

**Rhetoric**   the study and practice of using and shaping language to achieve writing purposes.

**Rhetorical approach**   a plan for writing developed after analyzing the needs and requirements of a particular writing situation.

**Rhetorical context**   the writing situation, including all the forces affecting what a writer must do in a piece of writing to achieve writing purposes for particular readers. Rhetorical contexts usually have no physical boundaries, yet all readers who are part of a particular rhetorical context generally share similar expectations about how texts must be written. For example, cardiologists throughout the world share expectations about how articles must be written for cardiology journals and how that writing will be evaluated. In this sense, cardiologists write within a particular rhetorical context.

**Rough draft**   an early draft of an essay, the product of planning and the basis for reviewing.

**Second person**   the point of view of the readers as opposed to the writer or the subject: "*You'll* love the new movie."

**Sensory description**   descriptive language appealing to the reader's senses, created by the use of concrete words: "He walked quietly, lifting his heels slowly from the ground to diminish the crunch of the gravel." Sensory description can also be achieved through metaphors and similes, which compare intangible qualities with physical qualities: "He walked quietly, like a cat stalking its prey."

**Skimming**   a pre-reading strategy in which a reader creates a context or framework for reading. Skimming strategies include examining a text visually, reading topic sentences, and examining additional features of a text, such as its index and table of contents.

**Structure**   the arrangement and connection of parts in a written composition; the underlying frame of ideas behind the surface arrangement of words, sentences, and paragraphs.

**Style**   the manner in which a writer expresses meaning, created by choice of language and suited to the writer's relationship with readers and approach to the subject (*perspective*).

**Subject**   the ideas and experiences on which a piece of writing is based.

**Subjective writing**   writing that focuses on attitudes and feelings that cannot be verified by reference to facts, concrete details, or logic.

Subjective writing emphasizes the expression of personal experience. See *Objective writing*.

**Summarizing**   a writing strategy used to record main points in a piece of writing without the supporting details.

**Summary**   a shortened version of part or all of a piece of writing. A summary contains only the main points in a text, usually presented in the same order as in the original, without supporting details.

**Support**   See *Evidence*.

**Thesis**   the main point or idea of an essay, from which the topic sentences of the body paragraphs derive.

**Third person**   the point of view of the subject as opposed to the writer or reader: "One should consider both sides of the issue."

**Tone**   the relationship or distance between writer and reader created by a text's language.

**Topic sentence**   the sentence that contains the main idea of a paragraph, most commonly a body paragraph. Often it begins the paragraph, but it may be placed elsewhere or implied.

**Transitional devices**   words, phrases, or other devices that relate clauses, sentences, or paragraphs to one another, including coordinating and subordinating conjunctions, transitional words and phrases, and semicolons. See also *Coherence*.

**Voice**   the character or personality of the writer in a particular piece of writing, created by the writer's language choices.

**Writing process**   a complex writing activity that involves a variety of conscious and unconscious planning, drafting, and reviewing behaviors.

**Writing situation**   the writing context, including all the forces affecting the text produced. A writer's purpose and reader are particularly powerful contextual forces; however, other factors influence the writing situation, such as deadlines and the writer's personal behaviors and experiences. When compared to *rhetorical context,* a *writing situation* is more physically bound than a rhetorical context, which often has no physical boundaries.

# Research Appendix: Using Research Tools

Incorporating research into your writing process requires management and planning more than any particular skill. Direct and control your research activities so that they fit into and develop your thesis. Chapter 4 provides an overview of research processes and some specific skills for representing the results of research in your writing. This appendix discusses the tools needed to carry out research (library tools and field-research tools such as interviewing and surveying) and documentation (acknowledgment of the sources of outside information, such as the American Psychological Association, the Modern Language Association, and *Natural Science* documentation styles). The appendix concludes with two student research papers, one of which uses MLA and the other APA documentation style.

While you work through these discussions of particular skills, keep the long and short views in mind. The long view demands that you intermittently stand back and reassess the relationship between a specific piece of information and the thesis in your essay. The short view demands that you work specific pieces of information into particular parts of your essay as coherently and accurately as possible. The first tool discussed in this appendix, a research and documentation notebook, will help you bring both the long and short views together.

## 1
### USING A RESEARCH AND DOCUMENTATION NOTEBOOK

In Chapter 4, the research notebook is described as the researcher's tool for recording in detail the entire history of an individual research investigation. This section explains how to apply the research notebook format to your own research efforts to help you manage your research.

Your notebook should be divided into four basic sections: Research Questions, Thesis, Research Plan, and Research Results. Below are brief descriptions of each section.

## Research Questions Section

In this section, list rough research questions on a topic (we use intelligence as an example) that you may choose to develop your final essay. Here are some possible research questions about intelligence: Is animal intelligence limited? In what ways is animal intelligence different from human intelligence? How do scientists study animal intelligence? Discuss your list with classmates; listen to their lists and note qualifications, disagreements, and additions. Use these notes to revise your own questions. Because these questions provide clear directions as you research, it is important that you spend some time developing specific research questions (see the "What Is Research?" section, pages 74 to 77 in Chapter 4, for a discussion of how students develop research questions).

## Thesis Section

In the second section of your notebook, develop the thesis for your chapter essay. Although you may not have narrowed your thesis before you actually conduct research, you need at least a tentative thesis, or a specific question that could lead to a thesis, to direct your research efforts. Because your thesis, your research plans, and your research questions are all interconnected, as you become more focused about one, the others become more focused as well.

For example, a student interested in animal intelligence may begin with a thesis like this: *Although animals and humans both act intelligently, they have different kinds of intelligence.* This thesis reflects the student's tentative response to research questions and helps direct the development of a research plan. As the student begins to actually put the research plan into action and generate some answers to the questions, a more sharply focused thesis may emerge: *Although animals have intelligence, it is limited by their inability to speak.*

Again, read your tentative thesis aloud to others in your class and listen to theirs as well. Use their responses to rework your thesis. Then use your thesis as a contract with yourself and your potential readers. Let it direct your research and help you use the research while you plan, write, and revise your chapter essay.

## Research Plan Section

In this section, tentatively list the kinds of information and sources you think will be useful to answer your research questions. You may begin your list with the titles of readings on intelligence in this book that you would use. Next to each reading, write a few notes explaining why each reading would be useful. Then jot down some personal experiences that may help answer your research questions, and, of course, any experiences that your classmates have shared with you. Consider plans for some field research, perhaps direct observation or interviews, to answer your research questions. Consider the kinds of library sources that may contain helpful information. Finally, include some notes in this section that tell you where you are going and why in your whole essay. These directional notes will keep you focused on answers to the questions of *why* you are including a particular piece of source information and *how* it ties in with what you have already said and what you will say in subsequent sections of your essay.

Discuss your tentative research plans with your classmates and teacher to get their feedback. Use their responses to revise and narrow your tentative research plan. You will waste a great deal of time doing unnecessary research if you do not take time to fit your research questions, in a cogent way, into your plans for your final essay. Remember, it is far more important that you limit your research to a narrow topic, a few good research questions, and specific sources for those answers than it is to compile a great deal of research that you only vaguely know how to use.

## Research Results Section

In this fourth section of your notebook, record your findings. Your findings may include some combination of data drawn from direct observation, interviews, surveys, and library research.

Notecards or annotated copies of library sources you have duplicated can serve as your first step in recording research data. Because notecards are only useful if they are accurate, you must work very carefully to record direct citations, summaries, paraphrases, and documentation information you will need to cite the source later, if you use it. It means keeping one eye on your source and one on your notecard (see pages 81 to 83 in Chapter 4 for detailed guidelines for using notecards). If you are using annotated copies of library sources instead of notecards, you should record documentation information for each duplicated article in the research results section and follow the guidelines for accuracy above.

Review your notecards and annotated copies of library sources to put more general or "boiled down" notes into your research notebook. If you have done different kinds of research—field and library research, for example—make a general plan in your notebook for using the results of those two kinds of research. Here are some questions to help you decide how to use your research results most effectively.

- Where will your field or library research appear in your essay?
- How will the two forms of research work together to support your thesis? Are some of your potential references more important than others?
- How will you ensure that the research is emphasized in the writing of your essay?
- Will you begin and end your essay with important quotations?
- What logical plan will you follow to organize the citations into your essay? Does, for example, one of your sources say the opposite of what you are arguing; does another reinforce your thesis? Where will you place these two sources to emphasize your view and diminish the opposing view?

As you record and summarize your findings in your research notebook, it is a good idea to indicate what is fact and what is opinion along with the sources of your information. Finally, to produce useful research notes, record your findings in condensed form without omitting important information.

The research notebook can help you transform library and field research into forms that are directly usable in your essay. Like an executive planning tool, it allows you to connect your research results to your thesis and plan.

## 2
. . . . . . . . . . . . . .
## USING LIBRARY RESEARCH TOOLS (GENERAL INDEXES, CITATION INDEXES, AND ABSTRACTS)

Planning a research essay is an ongoing process. At this point, we need to go back and fill in information on using library tools that is important to know every time you add research to a short essay or write a long research paper. These tools are part of your primary research; they contribute to ongoing research efforts—looking for particular pieces of information to improve the persuasiveness of your later drafts.

# Journal and Magazine Indexes

The best place to begin is the reference section of the library, which includes several useful areas when you are searching for additional sources. A quick look through journal and magazine indexes will help you identify articles that provide the exact information you need.

## What Are the Differences Between Journals and Magazines?

Before describing journal and magazine indexes, we should clarify the differences between the two sources. *Journals* are usually published for non-profit professional organizations or academic institutions; articles in journals are evaluated by experts before they are published to ensure that they adhere to professional community standards and conventions. Journal articles are carefully documented and written in technical language, using technical means of presenting findings (charts, graphs, statistics, and accurate documentation of sources). These features can make journal articles difficult to read and interpret because they are written, for the most part, with highly specialized readers in mind. Journal articles are, however, often given far more credibility (by professional readers, such as your professors) than articles in popular magazines.

*Magazines* are often written in plain language for popular audiences. They are persuasive for most general readers because they contain information obtained from experts, but communicated in less detailed and less specialized ways.

## Two Ways of Searching Indexes

Depending on the resources of your library's reference section, your search through journal and magazine indexes may be conducted using *paper* or *data base*. If your library has installed online data bases, you will be able to use a computer to identify sources and print out the publication information for those sources more quickly than you would using printed indexes. These data bases store many references that previously were available only in print form. CD ROMS (compact disc, read only memory) store vast amounts of information and reduce the amount of time necessary to retrieve information. In addition to publication information about particular sources, some college libraries subscribe to data bases that store abstracts (summaries) of articles and entire texts. Some of these data bases even store information about specific academic disciplines. The reference librarian may be able to help you conduct a computerized search that will produce a list of magazine and journal articles to fill your needs, without having to check the various indexes themselves.

## Audience Considerations in Using Journals and Magazines

Magazine indexes, such as the *Reader's Guide to Periodical Literature,* guide you to articles published in many widely circulated, profit publications. We have already pointed out that these articles are easy to read and interpret, but, because they are intended for general readers and must entertain as well as inform, they do not have as high a level of professional credibility as journals. Some of these magazines have more credibility than others, however. *Omni, Natural History, Science, Psychology Today* and others like them often include articles by professional scientists for general audiences. In the humanities, serious popular magazines, such as *Harper's, New Yorker, The Sewanee Review,* and others, have more professional credibility than fashion magazines such as *Vogue* or entertainment magazines such as *People.* General news magazines, such as *Time* and *Newsweek,* can provide general information on current issues, but they are not suitable for in-depth analysis. To decide whether or not to use a journal or magazine index, consider audience and purpose. Do you wish to convince an audience of professors and informed students? Or do you wish to address an audience of peers, informed to a degree, but not experts? Or do you want to appeal to general readers, those who may be convinced to change an opinion because of what they read in a newspaper or news magazine? None of us is an expert in everything; we all, at one point or another, function as experts and general readers, depending on the subject. Keep that fact in mind while you write.

## A Strategy for Using Journals and Magazines

This book suggests a compromise to the questions about audience discussed above. You are neither an expert (a sociologist or English teacher, for example) nor an average reader. You are a student and have read more than most average readers; also, by using this book, you have done some intensive reading in subjects about which you are writing. Given those facts, you should look for articles that function somewhere between the highly technical journal article and the oversimplified popular magazine article. Avoid superficial or sensational magazine articles. Also avoid journal articles that are too technical or complicated. Look for research reports in journals that summarize results clearly and in readable abstracts. Look for magazine articles from sources such as *Science, Omni,* or *Natural History* in the sciences or the *Atlantic* or *Harper's* in the humanities. These sources are apt to have more detailed analysis and information, without having exceedingly technical formats or styles.

The following indexes are useful sources for articles of both types:

Expert

*The Social Sciences Index*
*The Public Affairs Information Service Bulletin*
*The Humanities Index*

General

*The Reader's Guide to Periodical Literature*
  *Magazine Index*

## Using Subject Headings and Key Words

For the limited search you will be conducting, use subject headings and key words. If you are working on an essay on community in Chapter 6, for example, use key words such as *community, individual, interdependence,* or *scientific communities.* Each of the indexes listed above is organized around either subject headings, which may contain key words, or a subject index. Use these to skim entries, and select ten or twelve for possible use. Choose those that seem most directly related to your subject, most readable, and most convincing to your readers.

## Using Sources to Identify Additional Sources

You can use the references in an article to find additional sources on the same subject. After reading the article by Royte on "The Ant Man" in the community chapter, for example, look through her references to find a second article on ant communities to help you write a paper on comparisons between ant and human communities. Your research process should include opportunities for one source to lead to others; journal and magazine indexes are the tools you will most often use to make those connections.

### Citation Indexes

Another way to find articles through using authors' names as key words is to use a citation index. The *Social Science Citation Index,* for example, is a research tool that you could use if you were writing an essay on human communities. This index will enable you to find names of authors whose articles appear in this book or in outside sources that you have used. Once you have the name of an author whose work you know you will use extensively, find out how many other authors have cited this author. By looking up the names of those authors who have cited the author you have decided to use, and by skimming through the titles of their works, you may come across a useful source to add to your research. You may also find an interesting perspective on your original source that will provide you with a more thorough understanding of the issues that lie behind your thesis.

## Discipline Indexes

You may also wish to use a specific discipline index for your research. There are many specific discipline indexes in medium-sized and large libraries. If you are doing research on scientific communities from a social scientific and historical perspective, you should go to the following discipline indexes, respectively:

> *C.R.I.S.: The Combined Retrospective Index Set to Journals in Sociology* for references to journals on the sociology of science
> *C.R.I.H.: The Combined Retrospective Index Set to Journals in History* for references to journals on the history of science

## Abstracts

Once you have found the journal you are looking for, go to the abstracts publications in the appropriate discipline, also usually housed in the reference section of the library. Abstracts are brief summaries of the contents of articles that have appeared in the major journals in a particular discipline. You can skim titles of articles, find those that seem related to your subject and thesis, and read abstracts, deciding on a few articles that you may actually read in their entirety. You may use just one of those in your final essay. If you had used the discipline indexes listed above, you could follow up by consulting these collections of abstracts:

> *Historical Abstracts.* Santa Barbara, CA: ABC-Clio, 1955–
> *Sociological Abstracts.* San Diego, CA: Sociological Abstracts, 1952–

Similar publications exist in all major academic disciplines; it is up to you to find and use those abstracts that your thesis and plan require. You may need your teacher's or the reference librarian's help in narrowing down to a particular field before you search for appropriate abstract lists.

## Newspaper Indexes

Newspaper indexes provide helpful but less scholarly articles. Newspaper articles are extremely useful when you are trying to find out what happened on a particular date or what public opinion was in response to an event about which you are writing.

The most used and inclusive newspaper index is *The New York Times Index.* If you are working on an essay on community in response to readings in Chapter 6, for example, it could provide you with references to articles on scientific communities or on particular kinds of sociological research on communities that have appeared in recent science sections of the *Times*. Or you may find several articles and reviews written in response to a newspaper research report on how the communal instinct varies in different species of animals. Keep in mind that items are indexed only by subject in newspaper indexes.

This brief review of reference section items is not meant to be comprehensive. There are many more tools available. Consult your teacher and reference librarian for additional ideas. But this review does lay a path that you can follow while you look for additional sources to make an essay well-informed and convincing.

# 3
. . . . . . . . . . . . . .
# USING FIELD RESEARCH TOOLS

Many social and natural scientists use some form of field research to get information on their subjects. When scientists conduct field research, they use formal, systematic methods for collecting information. In planning an essay for a writing course, however, you do not need to follow these rigorous methods, but you do need to ensure that you are as objective as possible by employing in careful ways some of the major tools of field research. There are, in general, three kinds of field research: *direct observation, interviewing,* and *surveys* or *questionnaires*. In recording the results of any one of these three research tools, you should use the logbook technique described in Chapter 4, which will help you record data in as objective and systematic a way as possible for this general purpose. Later, when and if you take a field or laboratory science course, you will learn the more rigorous research methods of a particular science field. Your experience in this course, however, will provide you with useful general knowledge of field research methods.

Unlike library research, field research brings the researcher directly into the context within which the topic of study exists. The most direct kinds of field research—*direct observation* and *interviewing*—have the advantage of giving you first-hand information, gathered directly from the sources themselves. Because these sources are studied directly, the information you get is usually more complete and more complex than can be gained from books or elaborate statistical descriptions, where the complexities of everyday activities are usually combined into patterns of interpretations or statistical averages.

But these direct-contact kinds of field research have their limitations. It is often difficult to focus on what is significant or important in your research project when you are, as in direct-contact research, confronted with *all* the physical and psychological responses of an interview subject. In other words, direct-contact research puts a lot of strain on your interpretive abilities; it demands that you record data very carefully, that you observe or interview at least several times so that you get an accurate idea of what happens over long periods of time, and that you compare different kinds of recorded data to guard against bias in your own observations or interviews.

## Direct Observation

Direct observation requires that you give very careful attention to the processes through which you observe natural or social phenomena. In everyday life, we take what we see, feel, hear, and smell for granted. In fact, much of what you observe on the way to work or school every morning you probably forget rather quickly. Once you decide to conduct field research on a particular aspect of a subject about which you will write, however, you must find ways to ensure that you are more observant than you normally are and that you can find the appropriate language to define and describe what you observe. This requires that you think ahead of time about your subject and how it can be best observed, and about how you will record information before, during, and after your observation session. Your logbook is an indispensable tool in recording your observations, but you need to plan when and how to use it, if your observations are to produce useful results.

A brief example showing how you can use direct observation to find and organize information on the subject of women in the corporate workplace (Chapter 9) will be helpful at this point. Suppose that you have read the opening essay of this chapter, Reskin and Hartmann's "Cultural Beliefs about Gender and Work," an article explaining why it is difficult to change social attitudes toward women because of long-standing stereotypes. You decide that you want to observe women subjects as they work to find out whether they are subject to stereo-typed responses from those who work around them.

The most effective way to begin this type of direct observation research is to write a paragraph describing the purpose of your observation (how you plan to use the results of the research in your essay). Follow this first step by devising a plan for recording informa-tion while you observe. Will you begin with a general description of the context surrounding the observed behavior? Will time of day and other scenic facts be important? What types of behaviors will be significant during your observation? Why are they significant? Will you use the dual-entry format to record in your logbook—putting your in-process observations on one side of the page and your later interpretations or comments on the other? This type of pre-planning ensures that you will be able to use whatever kind of results you get.

You must avoid bias as you observe. Do not begin the observation process looking for evidence to support a particular argument. Do not, for example, begin with the assumption that women *do* suffer from stereotyped responses from other workers. Rather, begin by assuming that this may or may not be the case; then, look for evidence for both positions. Begin with a question for which you honestly want the answer; be open to recording all kinds of behavior while you observe.

You should also spend some time transferring your in-process notes into summaries and paraphrases *before* you incorporate the results of your observations into your essay. Begin this process by comparing the results of your direct observations to the rest of your essay and whatever other kinds of research you plan to use. Then, make a plan that will help you integrate your research results into your essay. Given the reading and research that you have done, what will the thesis of your essay be? What general plan will you follow as you develop that thesis? How will the results of your direct observation research fit into this plan? Once you have answers to these questions, you can summarize your direct observation research results in a way that will enable you to use them effectively in writing your essay, whatever your thesis is.

Follow these three general steps when you do direct observation research:

- Plan ahead by defining the purpose behind your research.
- Avoid bias as you observe.
- Summarize your results before including them in your essay.

## Interviews

The interview is a basic kind of field research that can either be used as your sole research tool or in combination with direct observation and library research. In fact, it may be most natural and efficient for you to consider direct observation as the base on which you build an interview plan. Suppose you have done some direct observation of pre-school children while they worked through a manual task in school. Your intention is to gather some information on children's intelligence. As you go back over the notes on that research, you may want to use interviewing as a way to find answers to these additional questions:

Who would be able to give a different and useful (to you) perspective on what you have observed?
What would you ask this person?

Perhaps you would decide to interview the pre-schoolers' teacher, posing questions such as the following:

1. How would you describe the intelligence of pre-school children?
2. To what degree does verbal ability influence your assessment of a child's intelligence?
3. Could you describe the different kinds of intelligence that you find in different students, and could you relate those kinds to particular students?
4. How does the ability to solve problems and to carry out certain assigned tasks play a role in your assessment of a student's intelligence?
5. Describe one of the most intelligent students. What are his or her most significant behavioral characteristics?

Your goal as an interviewer should be to develop a general line of questioning, and then to be flexible as you use these questions in the actual interview. Most important, though, is the direction that you give to your questions. The above questions, for example, are very carefully aimed at eliciting answers that will directly indicate whether this teacher has a multiple or universal perspective on intelligence (see the Gardner or Sternberg article in Chapter 5). Also, notice that this direction will probably not be apparent to the interview subject (in this case, the teacher). Rather, it is in the back of the interviewer's mind during the interview; this overall direction later helps the interviewer organize and interpret the results of the interview before using those results in an essay. It is important, then, for the researcher to have a plan and direction to get helpful information, but it is equally important that the plan not result in "loaded" or biased questions that may cause the person interviewed to feel restricted.

These questions also indicate that a good researcher knows how to put himself or herself in the place of the person interviewed. Each question addresses itself to an aspect of a teacher's experience from that teacher's perspective on students. Questions are neither so general as to be vague, nor are they so specific as to call forth responses that are particular to this teacher but not useful to the researcher. Also, note that the questions are "open-ended"; that is, they do not encourage yes or no responses, and allow the person being interviewed to do the talking.

Finally, these questions also avoid obvious or extreme forms of bias. The researcher has avoided loaded words—*dumb, smart,* and *clever,* for example—because they may make the teacher uncomfortable or encourage emotional or prejudiced responses. Also, the phrasing of the questions avoids giving away the perspective or attitude of the researcher. Nowhere in these questions, for example, is the researcher's stand on this issue of intelligence in young children suggested.

In summary, the key to conducting useful interviews is for you, as researcher, to keep an open mind. You must, however, have a clear general idea of your purpose in doing the interview and how you will use the information later when you write your essay. All your interview questions must focus on an aspect of your thesis.

The dual-entry format also helps you organize your interview research. Use the left side of your notebook page to note observations of what your subject says as the interview was being conducted. Some of these observation notes would be key words actually spoken by the subject; others would be brief paraphrases and summaries of what has been said. Still others would detail the subject's movements or behaviors during the interview. On this left side of the page, also add brief phrases describing your own on-the-spot reactions to what your subject says, although these kinds of reactions should never overshadow the responses of your subject.

Use the right side of the notebook later, when you review your observation notes. On this right side, record your interpretation of your subject's responses. Then, later, go back and reread these notes (perhaps using a recording of the interview, if you requested and received permission to tape it), recapturing both the details and the general importance of your interview.

Follow these steps as you use interviews as research tools:

- Be clear about the purpose of your interview before you begin.
- Have a series of logically-related questions before you begin. But use those questions in a flexible way as you interview.
- Record notes and interpretations in a dual-entry notebook.
- Have a plan for using the results of your interview before you actually use those results in your essay.
- Avoid bias in planning interview questions, in responding to answers to interview questions, and in interpreting the results of an interview.

## Surveys and Questionnaires

A survey or questionnaire is a set of questions used to find out how a particular group of people respond to an issue, event, or idea. Sometimes they are used to elicit general responses from individuals. They may, for example, be sent to television viewers or college students, or they may be administered to smaller, more specific, subsets of individuals within those groups.

The discussion that follows outlines a general process you can use to develop and check surveys and questionnaires. Surveys and questionnaires must grow naturally out of the project you have chosen to develop. They must also be aimed at a population that you feel will provide a useful response to your research question. Surveys and questionnaires must also present questions that are logically arranged, accurate, and unbiased. And, perhaps most important, these questions should be able to be interpreted without confusion. Careless mixtures of simple yes or no and open-ended questions can generate data that are impossible to use efficiently.

Suppose you were planning to write an essay on women's attitudes toward mathematics. To produce an effective survey on that subject, you need to focus on a clearly written research question, perhaps something like the following: How do women respond to mathematical problems? Such a question enables you to connect the data you gather through your survey to your background reading and personal experience.

One of the most important steps in developing an effective survey has to do with recognizing the limits you have set for yourself. A researcher using the question described above (How do women respond to mathematical problems?) has limited his research to questions of fact and description. He has not focused on interpretation of the causes behind women's responses to these problems. Rather, he will simply do a careful report describing *how* women covered by his survey responded to a particular mathematical problem. As in this case, any research question you use as the basis for a survey limits the scope of the conclusions you draw from the results of your survey. You must be aware of those self-imposed limits as you conduct your survey; otherwise, those who read your essay will think that your interpretations go further than the results of your survey warrant.

A second important step in using this research tool concerns writing the survey questions themselves. Questions should be focused on the central research topic, and should avoid producing potentially confusing data. Look at the following set of survey questions, all based on the research question "How do women respond to mathematical problems?" Are they in line with the research question?

1. Do you get nervous when presented with a mathematical problem?
2. Would you agree to do a math problem if presented with one as a game or puzzle?
3. Are you willing to work with others in solving math problems?
4. Are you a math person?
5. How well have you performed on math problems in the past?

All these questions are focused on the underlying research question. None of them would produce data unrelated to the underlying research question. But this set of questions would create problems of coherence for the researcher when he came to the point of organizing and interpreting data. Four of the five survey questions could be answered with a simple *yes* or *no,* but one (the fifth) asks for a description of a fuller kind. How, then, would the writer working with responses to these questions account for these different kinds of possible responses? Most surveys and questionnaires, to make data collection and interpretation easier, include questions demanding only yes or no, multiple choice, or true or false questions, although they may include one or two open-ended questions at the end of the survey. Then the responses of the closed-ended questions can be counted up and reported, while the open-ended responses can be examined for more complex patterns.

These five sample survey questions are also relatively unambiguous and unbiased. But several words in these questions could create bias problems. The use of the term *nervous* in question one may give away the researcher's purpose. And the word *well* in question four may bias the responses of some respondents. And what is a "math person" in question four? Surveys, in other words, should avoid ambiguous terms, unless those terms are the focus of the research project itself. Otherwise, interpretation of results may well assume a shared understanding of terms when, in actuality, the researcher and the subjects may have very different senses of what these key words mean.

One way to improve the accuracy and objectivity of your survey is to subject all survey questions to group analysis, focused on getting rid of ambiguous or slanted terms. Then, the questions can be revised and edited according to the best suggestions of different members of the group. For this reason, survey research in a writing course is often carried out as part of a group project, with three or four writers using a commonly developed survey that they can then apply in individual ways in their essays. The group work enables each writer to hear responses from others in the group to the wording of survey questions and possible bias and ambiguity. Group members may also ask one another if any questions contain words that seem to give away the researcher's intentions. A question like "Are you *afraid* to do math?" in a survey aimed at getting free and open responses to the issue of women and math anxiety may cause, because of its use of *afraid,* many interviewees to respond to the question, even the entire survey, in a less direct way.

Here are some steps you can take to ensure that you have developed a useful and unbiased survey.

- Have your project and central research question defined *before* you begin devising survey questions.

- Know *beforehand* how the population or group of people to whom you will give your survey will fit into your research project. Will the group provide a representative sample? Will they cause bias in the interpretation of survey results because of their shared values, ages, occupations, sex, or the like?
- Develop questions logically from your central research question. Arrange your questions in a sequence that is easy to follow for those who respond to the survey.
- Be sure that your survey questions are well-defined and that they can be answered with one choice, true or false, yes or no responses. Include few, if any, open-ended questions.
- Discuss with your workshop group how the data you gather from your survey can be categorized and used when you interpret your results.
- Work with a group of survey writers to check the wording of your questions for ambiguity or bias.

## 4
## WHY, WHAT, AND HOW TO DOCUMENT

### The Academic Reader's Expectations

Chapter 4 explains that academic readers expect academic writers to clearly acknowledge the source materials they have used in their articles, for reasons of honesty and courtesy and because academic readers often seek out sources mentioned in articles to read in their entirety, for their own research purposes (for a detailed discussion of this topic, review the "Why Document?" and "What Will You Be Expected to Document?" sections in Chapter 4). Also, academic readers often evaluate the arguments made and the writers themselves in terms of the sources used or cited in an academic essay.

The MLA and APA documentation systems require that a writer identify sources within the essay and in a list at the end of the essay. Failure to include the correct details in the correct place is considered unprofessional; in some cases, when students fail to provide these details about sources, it may be considered plagiarism, even when the omission is unintentional. Because most university teachers use systems such as the APA and MLA fairly regularly themselves, they are accustomed to finding documentation information in particular places within the professional texts that they read. When they are disappointed in those expectations, they are at the very least annoyed, and that annoyance can sometimes be turned into a lower grade for you. If your teacher thinks you have actually committed plagiarism, his or her response may be even more negative (for more information about avoiding plagiarism see the "How Can You Avoid Plagiarism?" and "Guidelines for Avoiding Plagiarism" sections in Chapter 4).

On a more general level, you need, even early in your academic career, to master at least the general principles behind academic documentation and the particular systems for handling that documentation. Then, you will have an advantage when you are assigned papers in your major. Before reviewing the APA and MLA guidelines for these two forms of documentation, consider what kinds of information require citations or documentation.

## What Are You Required to Document?

Any direct quotation, paraphrase, or summary of information, opinion or interpretation not your own and not considered common knowledge must be documented within an essay. In other words, anything you use from a source that represents the work of that source's writer must be identified for readers. If, for example, you are using statistics compiled by someone else, you must give that person credit for having done that work. Similarly, if you are referring to a writer's opinion about using animals for research purposes, you must let your readers know to whom that opinion belongs. This general standard applies whenever writers cite, paraphrase, or summarize ideas in a source.

## How Will Your Own and Documented Material Be Integrated?

At this point, you may be thinking that you will have to provide a citation in every sentence in your essay and that your essay will be difficult to read because the parenthetical citations will block your readers' journey through your text. This is not so.

First, many writers include an author's name in the body of the essay, thus integrating part of the required citation within the main flow of ideas. Second, some of the information in the essay will be your own ideas, opinions, and interpretations; they do not require citations. Finally, many writers write several sentences summarizing information gathered from a single source, introducing that source in the first sentence of the summary. This strategy allows a writer to delay providing the rest of the required citation until the end of the last sentence of the summary. Thus, a single paragraph may contain only one or two citations. However, this strategy works only for information summarized or paraphrased from sources. Each quotation requires a separate citation.

# 5
• • • • • • • • • • • • •
## USING APA DOCUMENTATION: THE AUTHOR-DATE SYSTEM

This section of the Research Appendix describes the APA (American Psychological Association) documentation system. APA documentation is used primarily by researchers working in social science fields such as psychology, sociology, political science, social work, and anthropology. The guidelines and examples of APA citations in this Research Appendix should suffice for most of the research assignments you are assigned as a freshman or sophomore.

If your teacher assigns a longer and more formal research paper on a social science topic, you may have to consult the *Publication Manual of the American Psychological Association* [(3rd ed.) Washington, D. C.: APA, 1983] in order to find detailed information on more specialized kinds of documentation than is covered in this appendix.

Like other documentation systems used by academic writers, the APA system provides readers with information about sources both within the body of the essay and on a separate page at the end. The following sections explain APA requirements for providing that information within the text and on a references page at the end.

## APA In-Text Documentation

Remember that all cited information, whether quoted directly, paraphrased, or summarized, *must* be documented, no matter what system you are using. When using the APA system, be sure to place the parentheses including the source information as close as possible to the place in the sentence where the cited information appears, even if that means that the majority of your citations occur within rather than at the end of your sentences. Identify authors only by their last names, except in the case of personal communications (see page 755).

APA users often do *not* include page numbers in parenthetical citations. A good general rule of thumb when using the APA system is to *supply page numbers whenever you quote directly, but omit them when paraphrasing or summarizing,* as follows:

- *As Harlow (1962) suggests* . . . (a general reference paraphrasing or summarizing the argument of one source)
- *The Royal Society Conference of Editors (1968), in discussing the metrical system, has described the problem in this way: ". . ." (p. 81)* (a direct citation)

At this point, remember that you will always need to use good judgment in deciding how many parenthetical citations to use when you are citing one source extensively. A rule of thumb is to use one citation at the end of a paragraph, if that paragraph includes summary of general information from a single source. If, however, you move from one source or one kind of information to another within the same paragraph, you must cite each source and kind of information in an independent parenthetical citation within that paragraph. *All* direct citations, however, do require a separate parenthetical citation with page numbers provided. The sample APA student research paper included in Section 9 of this appendix provides more extensive discussion of APA in-text citation conventions. Follow these specific guidelines as you use the APA system.

## Specific APA Guidelines

*1. Do not use Mr. and Mrs.* in identifying authors or sources. Use only professional titles such as Judge, Senator, Dr., or Attorney, if they are known.

*2. When citing a source by one author,* mention the author's name in the sentence and the year of publication in parentheses, or both the author's last name and year of publication in parentheses, separating name and year with a comma: *(Bennis, 1978)* or *Bennis (1978)* studied learning . . .

*3. When more than one source is written by the same author in the same year,* use **a, b,** etc. to indicate which source is being cited: *(Bennis, 1976a, 1976b, 1978).*

*4. When a source quotation is less than 40 words,* incorporate it directly within your paragraph, use quotation marks, and document, as follows: Bellis (1976) believes that in large organizations, an individual could be driven "to work toward an ultimately immoral goal without an immediate sense of personal responsibility or guilt" (p. 48). *When a source quotation is 40 words or more,* indent it five spaces from the left margin and set it off from the rest of the text as a block. Do not use quotation marks with indented quotations. Signal the end of the quotation with a period; then, skip two spaces and add the parenthetical reference, as follows:

> Whether such activity exhausts an individual to the point of numbness is questionable, but certainly the nature of the large organization makes it possible for a McNamara or an Albert Speer or an Ellsberg (while at Rand), for that matter, to work toward an ultimately immoral end without an immediate sense of personal responsibility or guilt. (Bennis, 1976, p. 48)

*5. When citing a source with two or more authors,* give the names of both authors every time the work is cited, as follows: *Cooper and Greenbaum (1986) contend that writing must now be studied from a cross-cultural perspective.* Or, *Writing must now be studied from a cross-cultural perspective (Cooper & Greenbaum, 1986).* Always put the authors' names in the order in which they appear in the source itself. Also substitute an ampersand (&) for the word "and" when identifying multiple authors in parentheses.

*6. When citing a work written by three, four, or five authors,* provide all the authors' names the first time you cite the work. Subsequent citations of the same work should use only the name of the first author, followed by *et al.,* as in this example: [First Citation] *According to Hewitt, Smith, and Kreske (1986), contrary to popular thought, there are no real opportunities to think when you are imprisoned.* (second citation) *Prison is not a good place to think (Hewitt et al., 1986).*

*7. When citing a work written by six or more authors,* give only the last name of the first author followed by *et al.* A work written by Loffer, Joffries, Denater, Bruffee, Hugger and Gorman would be cited as *(Loffer et al., 1982).*

*8. Give the full name of a corporate author* (government agency, association, private corporation, or research organization) every time it appears in the text: *The Gulf Oil Company (1984) funded study of petroleum resources is taken seriously by environmentalists and industrialists alike.* You may, however, decide to provide the abbreviated name of an organization, if it is well-known by that abbreviation: NBC for National Broadcasting Company, as in "The National Broadcasting Company (NBC) has never censored this type of show before. But, for that matter, NBC has not often presented shows that might have brought on requests for censorship."

*9. When you cite a work without a stated author,* provide your readers with a title that is shortened but just long enough to be easily found in the references list. The title "Group Therapy Goes Awry" may be shortened to "Group Therapy," as in this example: *Some experts ("Group Therapy," 1989) fear that certain therapies may produce dangerous and unexpected results.*

*10. Use the term "cited in" to let readers know that you are citing a source indirectly,* as in "Speer reports that it never occurred to him to resign even though he was aware of what his loss would do to hasten the end of Hitler's regime" (cited in Bennis, 1976, p. 49). Do not overuse indirect quotations; one or two in a paper is usually appropriate.

*11. When you cite information from an interview,* identify the subject of the interview in the text of your paper—*Frank Hubbard in an interview agreed that the mayor simply lacked enthusiasm for the issue.*— but do not provide parenthetical information in the text. The interview would not be listed in the references section of the paper.

*12. When you cite personal communication or telephone conversation,* simply include the reference within parentheses in the text of the paper: *According to J. R. Stallings, (telephone conversation, April 25, 1992)* . . . Name of correspondent (with initials), type of correspondence, and complete date should be supplied. Personal communications are *not* listed on the references list.

## References Sections

### Overall Format

APA rules require that you center and capitalize the word *references* at the top of the page on which you list all sources cited in your paper. The references section is numbered consecutively with the rest of the paper; if, for example, your text ends with page thirteen, then the references section would begin with page fourteen. If you have a notes page, it would appear immediately after the last page of your text and before the references section, as page fourteen in the example above.

APA rules require that each reference begin at the left margin with subsequent lines of the reference entry indented three spaces. Normal procedure is to double-space the entire references section; your teacher may allow you to save space by single-spacing between the lines within an entry, although you will always have to double-space between entries.

Arrange entries in alphabetical order according to the last name of the first author. If more than one reference is by the same author, provide the author's name each time and arrange the entries in chronological order of publication, as follows:

Bennis, W. (1973). The leaning ivory tower. San Francisco: Jossey-Bass.
Bennis, W. (1976). The unconscious conspiracy. New York: Amacom.

If you need to include entries with the same first author but different second or third authors, the single-author entry precedes multiple-author entries. The alphabetical order of second and third authors defines the order after the single-author reference, as follows:

Brown, J. R. (1983).
Brown, J. R., & Jones, W. (1985).
Brown, J. R., Black, J. C., & Jones, W. (1986).

When two books by the same author are published in the same year, distinguish them in your references list by using lower case letters (**a, b, c**) after the date, as follows:

```
Chomsky, N. (1976a).
Chomsky, N. (1976b).
```

Keep in mind that the student paper illustrating APA documentation that appears in Section 9 of this appendix includes a sample references section. The following list of items will provide you with the information you need to produce an accurate references section.

APA rules require that each item in your references section include the following general order of information: author(s), date, title, publication information (including name of publisher and place of publication). Each main section of information (author[s], titles, publication information) is set off from others by a period. The date of publication is always included within parentheses after the author(s)'s name(s) when using the APA system.

### Sample APA References Items

#### Books

For all books, you need to provide author's or authors' name or names, the date of publication, title, and publication information.

**One Author.**   Give the last name of the author first, followed by initials only. The date of publication follows, within parentheses, followed by a period. Underline the book title and capitalize only the first letter of the first word of the title. If there is a subtitle, capitalize the first letter of the first word only. You must also capitalize proper nouns, including those used as adjectives (*Life in England* or *Studies in English usage*). Provide the state or country of publication, if needed for clarity. Use the short title of a publishing company as long as it is intelligible, but provide full names of university presses.

```
Prelli, L. J. (1989). A rhetoric of science. Columbia,
     South Carolina: University of South Carolina Press.
```

**Two or More Authors.**   Include all names, no matter how many, with last names and initials inverted. Remember that in-text citations use a different format with multiple authors. Use commas to separate all names. Use an ampersand (&) in place of *and* before the final name in the list.

```
Cooper, C.R., & Greenbaum, S. (Eds.). (1986). Studying
     writing. Beverly Hills: Sage Publications.
```

**Edited Books.**  If you are citing an edited anthology in its entirety, use (Ed.) after the author or editor's name, as in the sample entry in the previous item. If you are citing an article in an anthology, cite the author, date of publication, and title of the article first, then provide the information on the anthology after the title of the article, introduced by *In,* as follows:

```
Chafe, W. (1986). Writing in the perspective of writing. In
    C. R. Cooper & S. Greenbaum (Eds.). Studying writing
    (pp. 12-39). Beverly Hills: Sage Publications.
```

Notice that the page numbers (in parentheses) of the article in the anthology follow the title of the anthology. Also, note that the editors' names appear in natural rather than inverted order when a specific article rather than the entire anthology is being emphasized.

## Periodicals

Supply author's name(s), date in parentheses, article title, and publication information for all articles in periodicals. These major sections of periodical entries are separated by periods.

**Professional Journals.**  Like book entries, titles of journal articles have only the first letter of the first word of titles capitalized. When citing a professional journal, add volume and page numbers to the entry. Volume numbers appear in arabic numbers and are placed immediately *after* the name of the journal. Both the name of the journal and the volume numbers are underlined, as in the following example:

```
Crosswhite, J. (1991). The dissatisfactions of rhetoric:
    Philosophy and politics in the teaching of writing.
    Rhetoric Society Quarterly, 21, 1-16.
```

Page numbers of the article appear at the end of the entry, *without* any abbreviations (*p.* or *pp.*).

**Magazines.**  When citing magazine articles, APA rules require that you provide additional information on date of publication. You do this by placing the *month* of publication after the year, in the parentheses that appear immediately after the author's name. Also, use the abbreviations *p.* or *pp.* before the page numbers, which are placed at the end of the entry.

```
Badger, J. (1992, September). A notable merge. Wordperfect:
    The Magazine, pp. 40-42, 44-45.
```

In this entry, only the page numbers on which the actual article text appears are listed; intervening pages with advertisements on them are not listed. Also, notice that the name of the magazine is followed by a comma, not a period.

## Other Sources

**Newspaper Articles.**   For all newspaper articles, supply the author's name, the title of the article, and publication information. You can omit introductory articles (*a, an, the,* etc.) in the titles of articles. Begin with the author's last name and initials. As usual with APA, follow the author's name with parentheses including the year, month, and day of publication, followed by a period. The title of the article follows the publication date, with only the first letter of the first word capitalized. The underlined name of the newspaper follows. Close each newspaper entry with page numbers, prefaced by the *p.* or *pp.* abbreviations. If the article you are citing has no author identified, simply list the title of the article first. Three sample newspaper reference entries follow:

Nicholas, J. (1992, October 30). College pays off in degree
    of family income. Arizona Republic, p. A1.
First lady, papers fuss over powder-puff tab. (1992, Octo-
    ber 30). Arizona Republic, p. A8.
Pitzl, M. J. (1992, October 30). Quayle stumps, school
    grumps. Arizona Republic, p. B1.

**Interviews.**   In a references list, it is customary to include only sources that are recoverable. Since simple conversation, oral comments or statements taken from classroom or public lectures, and interviews you conducted yourself are not considered recoverable sources, they should be cited in the text itself, but not in the references list. However, published interviews should be listed in the references list, as follows:

Ellison, J. (1984, June). [Interview with Howard Gardner].
    Psychology Today, pp. 20-24.

**Government Publications, Pamphlets, and Brochures.**   APA rules require that you begin this kind of entry with the name of the department, division, or agency responsible for the publication. Date of publication follows, in parentheses. The title of publication in normal APA form follows; the entry closes with the place and source of publication. Entries describing pamphlets and brochures should con-form as far as possible to the APA guidelines for books.

Department of Labor, Bureau of Statistics. (1990). Area
    wage survey: New Orleans, Louisiana, metropolitan area

(Bulletin 3050-36). Washington, DC: U.S. Government
   Printing Office.

### General Interest Pamphlets and Brochures

What do you do when you see a blind person? (1991). New
   York: American Foundation for the Blind.
Potter, J. C., Robinson, E. H. (1982). Parent-teacher con-
   ferencing. Washington: National Education Association.

**Films, Videos, and Television Shows.** Provide the names, roles,
and functions of the principal contributors or originators first, with their
functions in parentheses. Date in parentheses and title as usually
documented follow. Insert the words (film, video, television show) in
brackets after the title. The place and name of the distributor would
appear as the final item in the entry.

Stone, O. (Director). (1989). Born on the fourth of July.
   [Film]. Hollywood: Universal.

You can fill in similar information in the same pattern when you cite
videos or television shows. Remember that you should begin your
reference entry with the name of the person on whom your paper is
focusing; a director, for instance, if directing films is your focus, or an
actor, if acting or the star system is your paper's focus.

# 6
· · · · · · · · · · · · · ·
## USING MLA DOCUMENTATION:
## THE AUTHOR-PAGE SYSTEM

This section of the Research Appendix describes the MLA (Modern
Language Association) documentation system. MLA rules are used
primarily by writers in the humanities: history, philosophy, literature,
art history, and music, for example.

   Like other documentation systems used by academic writers, the
MLA system provides a way of giving details about sources to readers.
These details are included within the body of the essay itself and on a
separate bibliographical page at the end. Failure to include the correct
details in the correct places is considered unprofessional; when students fail to provide these details about sources, it may be considered
plagiarism, even when the omission is unintentional. In fact, many
college teachers expect students to familiarize themselves with both
the MLA and APA (the American Psychological Association, covered in
the previous section of this appendix) guidelines on their own.

Although this section of the Research Appendix covers MLA's basic requirements, some students will require more detailed information to properly document particular kinds of items. Many college writing handbooks and the *MLA Handbook for Writers of Research Papers,* 3rd edition (New York: MLA, 1988) contain such information. Your university bookstore will most likely have these books, even if they have not been specifically ordered for your class.

## MLA In-Text Documentation

The guidelines below explain how to use the MLA documentation system for citations within the essay itself. The next section explains how to compile a Works Cited and an Endnotes page at the end of the essay. Keep in mind, however, that you will need to consult the *MLA Handbook* or a writing handbook for details regarding any of the more than fifty different citation formats for different types of sources.

Below is a paragraph from a student essay on genetic manipulation. In the paragraph, the student documents materials used from one book and two magazine articles, all written by experts in the field of genetics. As you read the paragraph, take special note of what is documented and how it is done.

```
    In addition, new developments in fetal testing are
yielding results earlier than ever before, thus making in-
tervention possible. Ultrasound, a technique by which high-
frequency sound waves directed into a woman's abdomen pro-
duce a picture of the uterus and fetus, is being used as a
matter of routine by some obstetricians (Papalia and Olds
70-71). Perri Klass, a pediatrician, explains that ultra-
sound is often accompanied by amniocentesis, a procedure
consisting of drawing a sample of the fluid in which the
fetus floats while in the uterus in order to detect the
presence of genetic defects (45). The newest procedure,
however, chorionic villus sampling, which involves taking
tissue from the developing fetal sac, can yield the same
results much earlier in the pregnancy (Cowley 95).
```

An MLA citation consists of the author's last name and the page in the source where the information being cited can be found. The author's last name may be identified within the essay itself or in parentheses, as in the student sample above. When identifying the author in the sentence, use both the author's first and last name the first time the author is cited. In subsequent citations, use only the author's last name. The page number is *always* enclosed in parentheses, usually at the end of the sentence containing the cited information. No comma is used between the author's last name and the page number in the parentheses.

## Specific MLA Guidelines

*1. Do not use Mr. or Mrs.* to identify sources or authors  Use only professional titles such as Judge, Senator, Dr., or Attorney, if they are known.

*2. MLA requires that the citation fit smoothly into the text; therefore, keep citations short.* If possible, identify author in sentences, eliminating the need to include names in parentheses, as in the sample below:

```
Hubbard goes on to assert that decreases in infant death
and illness would be more easily achieved through social
and economic measures than might be possible through risky
genetic experimentation (89).
```

*3. When citing an entire work or a one-page article,* mention the author's name in the text without any page numbers or parentheses, as in the sample below:

```
Carl Leopold's article in The Scientist explains the con-
troversy surrounding the ethics of genetic research, and
calls on the scientific community to develop ethical codes
of conduct that will help define the human and environmen-
tal implications of its research.
```

*4. When more than one source is written by the same author,* indicate which source is being cited by adding a comma and a short form of the title after the author's name or by only a short form of the title if the author's name is in the body of the essay, as in the sample below:

```
With gene therapy, ''scientists are now able to arrange and
rearrange the basic building blocks of life, to maneuver
them into more functional configurations'' (Henig, ''Dr.
Anderson's Gene'' 31).
```

*5. When you cite five lines or more from a source,* type it as a block. Indent 10 spaces from the left margin; do not use quotation marks. Signal the end of the quotation with a period; then skip two spaces and add the parenthetical reference, as in the sample below:

```
Leopold captures the gist of the controversy in the follow-
ing passage:
              Today, with major environmental crises arising
              on all sides, exacerbated by the technological
```

```
consequences of science, and with commercial and
military dollars and objectives gaining in influ-
ence over the scientific community, the intellec-
tual elegance of science is being subordinated.
And so we find ourselves in our current state of
science saturation and ethics starvation. (11)
```

*6. When citing a source with two or three authors,* list each author's name in the order used on the title page, as in the sample below:

```
Ultrasound, a technique by which high-frequency sound waves
directed into a woman's abdomen produce a picture of the
uterus and fetus, is being used as a matter of routine by
some obstetricians (Papalia and Olds 70-71).
```

*7. When citing a source with four or more authors,* identify only the first author, followed by *et al.,* as in the sample below:

```
However, a single sickle-cell gene also conveys a resis-
tance to malaria; removing the sickle-cell genes would en-
tirely remove this resistance (Henig et al. 34).
```

*8. When citing the exact words of someone quoted in a source (an indirect source),* use the abbreviation *qtd. in* to indicate that you are quoting from someone else's report of a statement or conversation, as in the sample below:

```
According to Annas, ''The issue becomes not the ability of
the child to be happy, but rather our ability to be happy
with the child'' (qtd. in Cowley 94).
```

*9. When citing ideas obtained from interviews you conducted,* identify the person interviewed in the text of the essay, but use no parenthetical citation, as in the sample below:

```
Dr. Grace Noles, Chief of Pediatrics at Phoenix Suburban
Hospital, concurred with Hubbard's findings, but went on to
say that ''much more research is needed before we can
safely act on these findings.''
```

*10. When citing personal correspondence* (letters, telephone calls, conversations), cite the source in the text of your paper, providing the subject's surname in the sentence introducing the information and the rest of the source information in a parentheses, as follows: (telephone conversation, March 11, 1991).

## MLA Works Cited Sections

MLA rules require documentation both within an essay and on a separate list at the end. This list of sources is called the Works Cited section. It is a separate section that follows the last page of the essay or the Endnotes page, if one is used.

The Works Cited section lists each source referred to in the essay. These sources are listed alphabetically by the authors' last names. If a source has no author listed, the listing begins with the title of the source, inserted where it belongs alphabetically. The words *a, an,* and *the* are not considered when organizing the sources alphabetically.

What publication information must you include for each source listed in the Works Cited section? In addition to the author's name and the title of the source, you are required to provide publication details. For a book, this would include the publisher, the city of publication, and the year of publication. For a periodical article, this would include the name of the periodical, the date of publication, the page numbers, and the volume. There are over fifty different forms for listing sources in a Works Cited section. This appendix contains several examples. If you have included material requiring special documentation, you will need to consult a more detailed reference work for specifics on how to list a particular source when you are ready to prepare the Works Cited section of your essay.

Here are some general guidelines for preparing a Works Cited section:

*1. Center the words Works Cited at the top of the page.* (Do not underline them or use quotation marks to highlight the words.)

*2. List only sources you have referred to in the essay itself. (To identify sources you consulted but did not use in the essay you need to add a Works Consulted page.)* This page is organized just as the Works Cited page, alphabetically by the authors' last names, and follows the Works Cited page.

*3. Double space all entries.* The first line of each entry should begin at the left margin. Subsequent lines of an entry are indented five spaces. (Do not quadruple space between entries.) An MLA example section of a Works Cited page follows.

```
                         Works Cited
Klass, Perri. ''The Perfect Baby.'' The New York Times
     Magazine 29 Jan. 1989: 45-46.
''Lawmakers Told of Fetus Transplant.'' The Louisville
     Courier-Journal 16 Apr. 1991: A2.
Leopold, A. Carl. ''The Science Community Is Starved for
     Ethical Standards.'' The Scientist 6 Jan. 1992: 11.
```

```
Papalia, Diane E. and Sally Wendkos Olds. Human Develop-
     ment. 4th ed. New York: McGraw-Hill, 1989.
```

## Sample MLA Works Cited Items

The following are examples of Works Cited listings for some of the most commonly used sources in students' essays.

### Books

For all books you need to supply the author's name, title of the book, and publication data.

**One Author.** The last name of the author comes first, with periods after the author's name, the title, and the date. The title is underlined. Place a colon after the place of publication, a comma after the publisher, and a period at the end.

```
Sidel, Ruth. On Her Own: Growing Up in the Shadow of the
     American Dream. New York: Viking, 1990.
```

**Two or Three Authors.** When two to three authors are involved, invert the name of only the first author and follow it by a comma.

```
Kunitz, Stanley J., and Howard Haycraft. American Authors:
     1600-1900. New York: Wilson, 1938.
Roberts, William Lincoln, Thomas J. Campbell, and George
     Robert Rapp, Jr. Encyclopedia of Minerals. 2nd ed. New
     York: Van Nostrand, 1990.
```

**More Than Three Authors.** When more than three authors are involved, invert the name that appears first on the title page and follow it with a comma and et al.

```
Hubbell, Jay B., et al. Eight American Authors: A Review of
     Research and Criticism. New York: Norton, 1963.
```

**Two or More Books by the Same Author.** When citing two or more books by the same author, use the name in the first entry only. In subsequent entries, type three hyphens and a period and space twice. List the titles in alphabetical order.

```
Erdrich, Louise. Love Medicine. New York: Holt, 1984.
___. Tracks. New York: Harper, 1988.
```

**Edited Book.** When the work of the author is your focus, cite the author first.

Hearn, Lafcadio. ''Mosquitoes.'' <u>Mentor Book of Modern
    Asian Literature</u>. Ed. Dorothy Blair Shimer. New York:
    NAL, 1969. 236-38.

When the work of the editor is your focus, cite the editor first.

Shimer, Dorothy Blair, ed. <u>Mentor Book of Modern Asian Lit-
    erature</u>. New York: NAL, 1969.

**Periodicals.** For all periodicals you need to supply the author's name, title of the article, and publication data.

**Professional Journal.** For professional journals you will also need the volume number, issue number (when each issue of the journal is paged separately), year of publication, and inclusive page numbers.

Clark, Suzanne. ''Bernard Malamud in Oregon.'' <u>American
    Scholar</u> 59 (1990): 67-79.
Moskey, Stephen T. ''College Instructors as Writing Consul-
    tants.'' <u>Technical Communication</u> 30.1 (1983): 12-13.

**Magazines.** For weekly, bi-weekly, or monthly magazines, you need the complete date, instead of volume and issue numbers, as well as the page numbers.

Starbird, Ethel A. ''The Bonanza Bean Coffee.'' <u>National
    Geographic</u> Mar. 1981: 388-405.
Lacargo, Richard. ''Under Fire.'' <u>Time</u> 29 Jan. 1990: 16-21.

### Other Sources

**Newspaper Articles.** For all newspaper articles you need to supply the author's name, title of the article, and publication data. Omit any introductory article in the title. Then give the date, month, year, and page numbers, including section number if each section starts with 1. If an edition appears on the masthead, show it before the page number. If the author's name is not available, list the title of the article first.

Matthews, Jay. ''Spill Remains Poised Off California
    Beaches.'' <u>Washington Post</u> 10 Feb. 1990: 1A+.

''No Special Shield for Universities.'' Editorial. <u>New York Times</u> 11 Jan. 1990, late ed.: A22.

**Interviews.** For an interview you need to supply the name of the person interviewed, the kind of interview, and the date of the interview. (The person's title appears in the body of the essay to lend credibility and authority to the source.)

McGlaughlin, Pat. Personal interview. 15 Dec. 1991.
Safire, William. Interview. <u>Larry King Live</u>. CNN, Atlanta. 21 Feb. 1990.
Stallings, Christopher. Personal interview. 18 Oct. 1991.

**Government Documents, Pamphlets, or Brochures.** For pamphlets or brochures you need to supply as much information as is necessary to help a reader locate it. Conform as much as possible to the format used for books and periodicals, and omit whatever information is not available.

Potter, Joseph C., and Edward H. Robinson. <u>Parent-Teacher Conferencing</u>. Washington: National Education Association, 1982.
<u>What Do You Do When You See a Blind Person?</u> New York: American Foundation for the Blind.

Government documents can be treated in similar ways. An example follows:

United States Department of Labor. Bureau of Statistics. <u>Area Wage Survey: New Orleans, Louisiana, Metropolitan Area</u>. Washington: 1990.

**Films, Videos, and Television Shows.** For films you need to supply the following: title, director, producer, major performers, distributor, and year. If your paper focuses on the work of an individual, cite his or her name first.

<u>Born on the Fourth of July</u>. Dir. Oliver Stone. Prod. A. Kitman Ho and Oliver Stone. With Tom Cruise, Kyra Sedgwick, and Raymond J. Barry. Universal, 1989.
Stone, Oliver, dir. <u>Born on the Fourth of July</u>. Prod. A. Kitman Ho and Oliver Stone. With Tom Cruise, Kyra Sedgwick, and Raymond J. Barry. Universal, 1989.

You can follow similar patterns in documenting videos and television shows, filling in the slots with the information that you have on each item.

# 7
. . . . . . . . . . . . . .
## USING NATURAL AND LIFE SCIENCES DOCUMENTATION: THE NUMBER SYSTEM

## Background

Scientists outside of the social sciences—in fields such as chemistry, mathematics, physics, engineering, some areas of biology, medicine, nursing, and computer science—use the number documentation system because of its simplicity. In these fields, most professional articles are shorter than they are in the humanities and social sciences because they cover less content and are often fitted into a larger research picture in which many scientists work collectively on a particular set of experiments that are related to a more general problem or research subject. It is thus useful if articles are concise so that researchers can keep up with a large number of them and so that they can be rapidly processed by busy researchers. Short articles aimed toward simplicity need to be supported by equally simple methods of documentation.

The number system explained here is common to several science fields, but variations do exist in some fields. If you move into a science field later, you will need to check into the documentation style required by the journals in the field that you choose to enter. The following system will work for you in most general science undergraduate courses, and in your general writing courses.

Chapter 4 and other chapters in this book describe the format used by most authors of professional articles in scientific and technical fields. That format usually employs a sequence of sections headed by the terms *Introduction* (where the review of past research and the hypothesis of the experiment covered in the article are presented), *Methods* (where the methods the authors will use to study their subjects are described), *Results* (where the data drawn from the study itself are presented), and *Discussion* (where the broader implications of those results are described). We will not discuss that format in detail here. You should, however, review the information in Chapter 4 describing the format of scientific research articles, if you are planning to write a paper addressing a professional audience in one of the described fields above.

## In-Text Documentation

Many science research articles have multiple authors. As a result, scientists find it simpler and briefer to refer to numbers from a References or Works Cited list rather than to the names of several authors, especially when they refer to several articles for the same information. In the number system, sources in the References or Works Cited sections are assigned consecutive numbers that are then used in the text to refer readers to particular items in those sections. The numbers can be put in *superscript* ([1,2]), in *parentheses* (1), or they can be both *underlined and put in parentheses* (1). Superscript numbers, if they are used, are placed *after* all marks of punctuation, including periods, without spacing. Parenthetical numbers are placed *before* all marks of punctuation, with a space before the first parenthesis. Some examples follow:

```
Gould has proposed several theories.³
Michaels reached a very different conclusion (5).
Although Frederick's results are questionable,⁴ Desoto tends
     to agree with them.⁵
Sherman, in his study (9), maintains that . . .
```

When you cite more than one source in one place, simply use commas between the numbers:

```
Much recent research⁶ˑ⁷ˑ⁸ agrees that more studies must be
     conducted before any definite conclusions can be
     reached on this issue.
```

Or, if you are using parentheses, simply insert commas between the numbers within the parentheses:

```
Several researchers (3,9,12) suggest flaws in Hendrick's
     research method.
Recent research (4,9,10) has defined the problem as . . . .
```

## Reference or Works Cited Sections

Using the number system, you may use the following titles with your source list: *References, References Cited, Works Cited,* or a similar term. Number the entries in your source list using one of the following methods:

- Use the order in which you refer to sources in the text of your paper. When you mention a source more than once, use the

number originally assigned to it when you used it in the text of your paper. Usually, this is called *chronological order.*
- Number the items in alphabetical order. If you choose this method, then your textual references will *not* appear in numerical order. Usually, this is called *alphabetical order.*

*Punctuation* of entries in your source list can follow one of three possible methods:

1. You can punctuate with *parentheses*: (1), (8)
2. You can punctuate with *superscript numbers*: [9, 10]
3. You can punctuate with a *period after the number*: 1., 2.

Whichever method you choose, be consistent. When you are writing an article for a particular journal, be sure to check its masthead page to find out which of these methods it recommends.

The following hypothetical source list demonstrates formats for different kinds of sources. The references themselves are fictional to enable you to focus on the formats alone. This list uses the number-plus-period system.

## Sample References List Using the Number System

**Book with One Author.**   Use last name and initials of author. Capitalize only the first word of the title, unless it includes a proper noun. Use a semi-colon after the publisher's name. Second and subsequent lines of an entry are indented in line with the first letter of the first line of the entry. The periods following the numbers should be in line vertically.

```
1. Snaeder, F. L. Microscopic organisms. New York: Basic
   Books; 1978.
```

**Book with Two or More Authors.**   Provide names of all authors. Use semicolons between the names, regardless of the number.

```
2. Aldridge, E. D.; Michaels, K. L.; Jones, D. W. The psy-
   chopathology of speech deficiencies. Ithaca, NY: Cornell
   University Press; 1961.
```

**Corporate Author.**   Provide name of corporate body, followed by title of text, followed by place of publication and year, punctuated by usual conventions.

```
3. Center for Industrial Control. Managing the corporate
   leveling process. Annapolis, MD: The CDC Corporate
   Press; 1991.
```

**Book with Editor.** Set up like book entries without editors, except use *editor* after author's name.

4. Studebaker, J. T., editor. Micrometalic substances: fiction, fashion, or future. Cincinnati, OH: The Metals Press; 1985.

**Chapter or Selection in Edited Anthology.** Insert information on the book from which the chapter or selection is taken after the author and title information.

5. Gorney, H. P.; Koffee, J. W. Super lazer technology and the packing of unbound tissue cells. In: Reeder, S. R., ed. The lazer future. Boston: Beacon Press; 1981:153-159.

**Article in a Journal with Continuous Pagination.** Capitalize only the first letter of the title (not the subtitle) of the article. Capitalize *all* important words of the journal title. Titles of journals are usually abbreviated according to the abbreviation list appearing in the *American National Standard for Abbreviations of Titles of Periodicals,* which is probably available at your college or local library reference desk or section. Provide both the volume number and page numbers in arabic numerals immediately after the title of the journal, followed by a semicolon and the year.

6. Selopsis, A. R. Neurological damage assessment: ten problematic cases. New England Journal of Medicine. 57: 247-261; 1988.

**Article in Journal with Separate Pagination.** Place the issue number in arabic numerals in parentheses after the volume number.

7. Bendix, E. T. Meeting the EPA challenge: PCV valve efficiencies and pollution. Journal of Automotive Engineering. 11(9):19-23; 1989.

**Newspaper Article.** Author, title, and newspaper source come first; the date, with year, then month, then day is followed by a colon. After the colon, section, page number, and column number are supplied.

8. Wills, G. Where does the DNA war end? The New York Times. 1986 Sept. 25:B4 (Col. 3).

**Magazine Article.** With magazines, which are published more frequently, put the date in place of the volume number that would be used for periodicals and journals.

```
9. Whitehead, B. C. Binary thinking in the context of plu-
    ral numerality. Omni. 1987 August:38-43.
```

**Dissertation or Thesis.** Readers need to be told that the source is a graduate school research project such as a dissertation or master's thesis; this is done by placing the word *thesis* or *dissertation* at the end of the entry. The university where the research was done takes the place of the city of publication and name of publisher.

```
10. Castelani, A. D. Social networking in Micronesian spi-
     der monkeys. Amherst, MA: University of Massachusetts;
     1991. Dissertation.
```

# 8
# USING EXPLANATORY NOTES

Explanatory notes contain information about the *content* of your essay which you want to explain to your readers in greater detail but do not feel should be included in the body of your essay. Explanatory notes may also contain *bibliographic information* about the sources you used while researching your topic or writing your essay. The purpose of this additional bibliographical information is to help those readers who may wish to further their own research on the topic. These explanatory notes are identified within the body of the text in superscript and then explained on a separate page titled *Notes* after the last page of the essay and before the *Works Cited* or *References* pages. Explanatory notes are used sparingly in most undergraduate student essays; most students rarely find it necessary to include more than two or three notes in an essay. This is because the need to provide additional bibliographic information or supplemental information about an idea in a paper is a sophisticated skill, one that develops only after a scholar has studied a subject extensively. Students usually prefer to incorporate most information they consider important to their discussion directly into the flow of information presented in the essay.

Should you decide to include explanatory notes, however, you must signal their presence to your readers. This is accomplished by using the superscript number at the end of the sentence (after the period) for which you provide an explanatory note, beginning with 1. The format for explanatory notes is the same, regardless of which citation system is being used or whether the note provides supplemental information about content or a source. Here are some general guidelines for preparing the *Notes* page; these guidelines apply to both the APA and MLA styles of documentation.

1. Center the word *Notes* at the top of the page. (Do not underline it or use quotation marks.)
2. Double space all notes. Indent the first line of each note five spaces; begin subsequent lines at the left margin.
3. Identify each note using its superscript number.

## Sample Notes Page

Below is a sample *Notes* page from a professional journal article. Notice that the notes in this case provide either supplemental information about the article itself or commentary on source information that would interrupt the flow of the main discussion if it were inserted in the text, but is considered relevant by the author. In neither case would the information have fit naturally into the development of ideas in the article. Notes are also often used to acknowledge the help of other researchers, as the independent example following the sample notes page suggests.

## Notes

1. Since much of the theory informing these suggestions has focused on white, middle-class, heterosexual women, my article will be so limited. The characteristics I ascribe to this group of women I believe to be socially constructed and not due to an "essential" feminine nature.

2. I have not indicated the range or extent of the admonitions against nonsexist language in this listing. They vary from the very explicit and comprehensive NCTE *Guidelines* to a footnote in the *Chicago Manual of Style*. There, a section on "Watching for Lapses" reads, "In addition to regularizing details of style, the editor is expected to catch errors or infelicities of expression that mar an author's prose. Such matters include ... racial or sexist connotations ..." (19); the latter phrase is marked by a footnote which advises, "For useful and sensible suggestions on how to avoid sexist connotations see Casey Miller and Kate Swift, *The Handbook of Nonsexist Writing*." Other organizations have devised their own guidelines or prefer to follow guidelines issued by the Modern Language Association. The widely circulated *MLA Handbook for Writers of Research Papers* counsels readers to avoid

> statements that reflect or imply unsubstantiated generalizations about a person's age, economic class, national origin, sexual orientation,

political or religious beliefs, race or sex.... For example, conscientious writers no longer use *he* to refer to someone of unspecified sex—a doctor or an executive, say—lest readers infer that the statement can apply only to a man. To avoid this use of *he,* they recast sentences into the plural, specify sex of an individual under discussion, and occasionally, if all else fails use *he or she* or *her or him.* Careful writers also avoid designating sex with suffixes like -man and -ess and substitute nonsexist terms (police officer, flight attendant, poet, author). (34)

Although Francine Wattman Frank and Paula A. Treichler's *Language, Gender, and Professional Writing* is not official MLA policy, the book offers a wealth of information on the issue.

This notes page is from Karyn L. Hollis, "Feminism in Writing Workshops: A New Pedagogy." *College Composition and Communication* 43 (Oct. 1992): 340–348.

### Sample Acknowledgement Note

2. I would like to thank my first and second readers who gave me permission to talk about their correspondence in public and thus made this project possible.  I am indebted to Linda Brodkey whose collaboration enabled me to ground this paper in poststructuralism and language materialism. I am grateful to Frank Sullivan and Barbara Hoekje, who helped me refine my application of the linguistic method provided by Silverman and Torode. I offer my thanks to Roger Cherry, Frederick Fischer, John Gaggin, Patrick McLaurin, and Larry Roberts who read and critiqued various drafts. Finally, I would like to thank Richard Gebhardt, Paul Beauvais, and several consulting readers who "interrupted" several versions of this paper in the best sense of the word—with the aim of clarifying and enriching its points.

This note was appended to Anne M. Greenhalgh's "Voices in Response: A Postmodern Reading of Teacher Response." *College Composition and Communication* 43 (Oct. 1992): 401–410.

# 9
. . . . . . . . . . . . .
# SAMPLE STUDENT RESEARCH PAPERS USING THE HUMANITIES (MLA) AND SOCIAL SCIENCE (APA) SYSTEMS

You need to satisfy three different kinds of professional audiences when you document sources in an academic research paper. If you are writing a paper in an English, history, or language course, for example, you will probably need to use the Modern Language Association (MLA) documentation system, which is most often used in the humanities disciplines. That system is described in Section 5 of this appendix. If you are writing a paper in political science, sociology, psychology, or some other social science discipline, you need to use the American Psychological Association (APA) system. That system is described in Section 4 of this appendix. If you are writing a paper focusing on a natural science topic, you need to use the numbering documentation system that is favored by those writing in fields such as physics, biology, zoology, and chemistry. Your writing teacher may in some cases tell you which system to use for a particular paper; in other cases, you may have to consider your audience or subject matter as the defining factor in deciding which system to use.

At present, many academic fields are made up of two or more disciplines, such as biochemistry, for example, or social psychology or political anthropology. Sometimes even the traditional humanities areas are combined with the sciences, such as in biomedical ethics, or in sociolinguistics or the history of science. These new combinations can create exciting new discoveries, but they can, of course, make the research writer's job more challenging than it is when the boundaries of a field are more clearly defined. When you are writing on a topic that demands this kind of interdisciplinary research, you need to use the documentation system that either fits your *audience* (for example, you will address an audience of biology teachers even though your subject is the ethics of recent genetic research) or your *purpose* (you will emphasize scientific information drawn from zoology, although your general purpose is to persuade your readers of the desirability of an ecologically balanced perspective). In these cases, where the decision on what documentation system to use is up to you, you may wish to list the reasons behind your decision and then discuss your choice and the reasons behind it with your teacher *before* beginning your research to find out whether or not your sense of your audience and purpose is consistent with your teacher's assignment.

The following two student papers fall into the APA and MLA categories. Both papers are focused on interdisciplinary subjects where either system could have been used: the paper using the MLA system discusses the ethical (humanities) implications of a scientific subject; the paper using the APA system focuses on a survey of college students using social science research methods. In both cases, the student used the documentation system that best suited her research methods and the needs of her audience. Since the student writing on genetic research had read and interpreted existing literature on her subject, she used the MLA documentation format. This decision may have been influenced by the fact that she was addressing a general audience. In contrast, since the student writing on sleep deprivation had actually conducted social science research, she chose the APA documentation format. Her decision may also have been influenced by her intended readers: social science students and professionals; thus, the APA format seemed the logical one to use.

Since the numbering system used in the natural sciences requires only minor alterations of these two basic documentation systems, we have decided not to include a separate student paper representing this system. If you plan to use the numbering system, simply use the APA system for taking notes and recording information on sources; you should, however, transform the documentation information into the numbering system when you write your final draft. The section of this appendix that is devoted to the numbering system (Section 6) provides the specific information you need to use this system efficiently.

The following student papers have been annotated to indicate where the writers were careful to use the appropriate documentation features of the system they used. Discussions of the overall use of the appropriate system follow each paper. Reviewing and discussing these samples with your fellow students should better prepare you to use the documentation system best suited for your audiences and purposes. Ask your teacher whether you will need a title page. If you do, find out what information should appear there and whether a particular format must be used.

## Paragraph-by-Paragraph Marginal Notes, APA Student Essay

**Title Page**  The writer has included the required information on her title page: a specific title describing the paper's main focus, her name, information about the course and teacher, the date, and a running head. The running head is a shortened title, which is used to head each page in the paper and in library index citations (for published academic articles).

# A Sample Student Paper Using the APA System

Sleep Deprivation: Its Effects on GPA's
of College Students

Sheila Jones
English 102
Professor Greenberg
April 1990

Running Head: Sleep

**Abstract**   The abstract briefly summarizes the essential information in the paper, usually in the order in which it is presented in the paper. The abstract gives readers a clear sense of what the paper says.

## Abstract

A study was conducted at Jefferson Community College (JCC) in an attempt to establish a connection between students' sleep habits and their subsequent Grade Point Averages (GPA). The sample consisted of 40 JCC students, 20 male and 20 female. The sample was also broken down into age groups: half the subjects between 18 and 24 years of age, the other half 25 or older. A questionnaire was developed to generate data regarding the average amount of time students slept each night, their GPA for the last semester, the number of credit hours taken, and whether the students completed all of their courses. In addition, students' responsibilities outside of school, including jobs and family duties, were taken into consideration. The results indicate little or no connection between the students' GPA's and the amount of time they sleep each night. However, the data suggest that the students over 25 years of age tend to perform better academically than their younger counterparts.

**Paragraph 1**  Two citations provide general information on recent discoveries made by sleep researchers. These sources provide a foundation for the more specific application of sleep research to college students that follows. Because of their general nature, and because they summarize general points made in the source articles, these citations do not include page numbers.

**Paragraph 2**  This paragraph brings the discussion of sleep research into more technical, physiological areas. The paragraph begins with a reference to a general fact about the relationship between sleep and the circadian rhythms studied by psychologists; because it summarizes a general fact in the source article, it requires no page number in the reference. The middle part of this paragraph continues with summarized general information from the Nadis article; the writer assumes correctly that the reader will attribute this general information to Nadis, since no other sources are mentioned. The paragraph closes with a long, indented quotation, which is used to give readers a clear sense of the significant assertions made by one researcher (Wellborn). The citation attached to the long quotation requires a page number, as do *all* direct citations. The paragraph closes with a direct citation that is blended into the final sentence; notice how the writer's language moves smoothly into the language of the quotation without any punctuation. This makes for easier reading. Also, notice that the quotation is taken from a source that is cited in a second article, which makes the "cited in" necessary within the parentheses. This final sentence also illustrates how using the author's name in the sentence introducing a direct quotation allows for a more fluent and less technical kind of reference.

Sleep Deprivation: Its Effect
on GPAs of College Students

    The urge to sleep is one of nature's most power-
ful drives, second only to sex and hunger (Wellborn,
1987). Sleep researchers have learned that the amount
of sleep people get each night can have a profound
effect on their ability to function effectively. The
amount of sleep needed for efficient performance,
however, varies from person to person. While some
people find they cannot function on less than ten
hours of sleep, others get by quite well on only two
hours. The sleep quotient, or amount of sleep necessary to feel alert and well rested, must be determined by the individual (Sherman, 1988).

    One researcher (Nadis, 1987) links an individual's
sleep requirements to his or her circadian rhythm or
internal pacemaker located in the hypothalamus region
of the brain. The circadian rhythm is normally synchronized with the body's sleep/wake cycle and operates on a natural period of about 24 to 25 hours. A
correlation between this circadian rhythm and body
temperature has been discovered by sleep researchers.
When the body temperature reaches its low, the metabolic rate is pulled into a trough. If this trough is
reached while a person is sleeping, there's no problem. However, if one is awake when it occurs, the result can be the sudden fatigue often associated with
jet lag. This fatigue is usually accompanied by dulled
reflexes and has been cited as the cause of both minor
accidents and major catastrophes:

> Investigators of the Three Mile Island and Cher-
> nobyl nuclear disasters noted that both acci-
> dents occurred in the early-morning hours, in
> the middle of overnight shifts when workers were
> at a mental low. The Challenger-shuttle disaster
> followed an all-night discussion by exhausted
> launch officials. Pennsylvania's troubled Peach
> Bottom nuclear power plant was recently shut
> down after Nuclear Regulatory Commission inspec-
> tors found shift workers dozing. (Wellborn,
> 1987, p. 56)

**Paragraph 3** This paragraph focuses on sleep research with college students, the subject of this paper. Here, too, the references are paraphrases and summaries of general information drawn from entire articles, requiring no page numbers. Notice that a reference (Dement) is, as in the previous paragraph, cited in a second article, requiring the use of "cited in." Also, notice that one of these summary citations is drawn from two sources; both (Sweet and Nadis) sources are included in one parenthetical reference.

**Paragraphs 4 and 5** These paragraphs conclude the introduction or literature review section of this paper. They include citations to summarized information in two additional sources, both related to sleep duration and stress.

Sleep 4

According to Dr. Daniel Kripke, a sleep researcher at the University of California at San Diego, as many as 20 percent of adult Americans live in a ''constant twilight zone of sleep deprivation'' (cited in Wellborn, 1987, p. 56).

College students are often the subjects of studies conducted to determine the effects of sleep deprivation on performance. College students make good subjects because many are chronically sleep-deprived and feel tired much of the time. Dr. William Dement, Director of the Stanford University Sleep Disorders Clinic and Research Center, attributes (cited in Sweet, 1983) this chronic lack of sleep to the academic and social pressures of college life. Plus, late nights and early wake-up times make it difficult to stay awake during afternoon classes. Research has shown (Sweet, 1983) that when rats are deprived of REM (rapid eye movement) sleep, the time when most dreaming occurs, they have more difficulty learning tasks. Humans deprived of REM sleep have suffered from increased irritability and anxiety, as well as an inability to concentrate. Some researchers (Sweet, 1983; Nadis, 1987) believe that dreaming helps in learning by organizing the memory into different patterns. Therefore, they believe that sleeping before a test is more beneficial than cramming.

Research (Hicks, McTighe, & Juarez, 1986) has also shown a correlation between sleep deprivation and higher incidences of eating-related problems, suggesting that eating behaviors may be altered by reductions in REM sleep. Other research has shown a relationship between sleep duration and the level of perceived life-stress on both Type A (fast-paced and competitive) and Type B (easygoing and calm) personalities (Hicks, Grant, & Chancellor, 1986).

Given the extensive findings that sleep deprivation results in lesser performance, both in mental and physical activities, we hypothesized that students with normal sleeping patterns (seven or more hours each night) would attain higher GPA's than their counterparts who sleep less. Since we were unable to find any studies dealing with this specific relationship, we conducted an investigation at the downtown

**Paragraph 6**   Methods description is accomplished in this one, brief paragraph. Although the information presented is specific, it relates to the survey conducted by the author of the paper and does not in this case require documentation. If , however, the author were a professional psychologist and an article describing the survey and its results had been published, then the publication information for that article would have been documented.

**Paragraphs 7 and 8 and Tables**   As in many social and natural science professional articles, the writer here describes survey results in specific terms (usually numbers or percentages) and summarizes those quantitative results in a visual, in this case, in tables. When using this technique, you must be sure that the numbers and percentages in the written text are clearly related to the same qualities in the visuals. Also, it is important to have interpretations clearly developed from the quantitative data. These two paragraphs are clearly related to the tables; the conclusions drawn from the results are also clearly separated from but at the same time related to the data.

campus of Jefferson Community College to test our
hypothesis.

## Method

To test this hypothesis we developed a questionnaire to obtain data regarding age, average number of
hours spent sleeping each night, and GPA for the previous semester. Additional variables considered were
number of credit hours taken the previous semester
and whether the student had responsibilities (jobs or
family) apart from school. The questionnaire was then
administered to a convenience sample of 40 JCC students. We attempted to make the sample as representative as possible by including equal numbers of male
and female students. In addition, since JCC's population includes a large number of returning adult students, we attempted to include an equal number of
older and younger students.

## Results

As indicated in Table 1, the majority of our
sample, 88%, averaged between four and seven hours of
sleep each night. None of the subjects averaged less
than four hours of sleep per night, while only 12%
averaged more than seven hours of sleep per night.
Sixty percent of the students who averaged more than
seven hours of sleep each night had average grades
while 20% had above-average grades and 20% had below
average grades. On the other hand, of the students
whose grades were above average, 92% averaged between
four and seven hours of sleep per night. Additionally, 92% of the students whose grades were above average were over 25 years of age. In contrast, all the
students with below-average grades were between 18
and 24 years of age, while 57% of those with average
grades were between 18 and 24, and 43% were over 25
(See Table 1). This finding suggests that the age of
the students was of more significance than the amount
of sleep they received in determining their GPA.

Of those receiving four to seven hours of sleep
each night, 92% had either jobs, family responsibilities, or both, as indicated in Table 2. All of the
respondents who received more than seven hours of

**Paragraphs 9 and 10**    These two paragraphs draw conclusions directly from the survey results. The second of these paragraphs moves away from the survey into broader and more interpretive application of those results. This is acceptable in the Discussion, but not in the Results, section of an APA research paper, as long as it is clear to readers that the writer is aware of the distinction between the results of an experiment such as a survey and the broader conclusions drawn from but not confirmed by that experiment.

TABLE 1.  Average Hours Sleep/Age & GPA
Relationship

|  | 18-24 GPA < 2.0 | 25+ | 18-24 GPA 2.0-3.5 | 25+ | 18-24 GPA > 3.5 | 25+ | Total |
|---|---|---|---|---|---|---|---|
| Less than 4 hours sleep | 0 | 0 | 0 | 0 | 0 | 0 | 0 |
| Between 4-7 hours sleep | 5 | 0 | 10 | 8 | 2 | 10 | 35 |
| More than 7 hours sleep | 1 | 0 | 2 | 1 | 0 | 1 | 5 |
| Total | 6 | 0 | 12 | 9 | 2 | 11 | 40 |

TABLE 2.  Average Hours Sleep As It Relates to
GPA & Outside Responsibilities

|  | GPA* <2.0 | GPA <2.0 | GPA* 2.0-3.5 | GPA 2.0-3.5 | GPA* >3.5 | GPA >3.5 | Total |
|---|---|---|---|---|---|---|---|
| <4 hrs. | 0 | 0 | 0 | 0 | 0 | 0 | 0 |
| 4-7 hrs. | 3 | 2 | 17 | 1 | 12 | 0 | 35 |
| >7 hrs. | 1 | 0 | 3 | 0 | 1 | 0 | 5 |
| Total | 4 | 2 | 20 | 1 | 13 | 0 | 40 |

*indicates outside responsibilities

sleep per night had outside responsibilities. Of the respondents receiving only four to seven hours of sleep
each night, 49% maintained average grades while managing
outside responsibilities and 34% earned above-average
grades. Fifteen percent of the respondents had GPA's
which were below average; 40% of those had no responsibilities outside of school and averaged four to seven
hours of sleep per night. Only 25% of the respondents
with below average grades and outside responsibilities
received more than seven hours sleep each night.

                        Discussion
    While the purpose of this study was to determine
a relationship between students' GPA and the amount

9

**Paragraphs 11 and 12**   These paragraphs appropriately close the Discussion section by bringing other researchers back into the picture and by suggesting a few implications for further research. Paragraph 11 begins with a reference to another researcher who has studied one of the implication areas suggested by this survey research. This adds significance to this writer's suggested interpretations. Notice, as well, how smoothly the writer works this reference into her sentences, making the use of the parentheses unnecessary. The direct citation at the end of the paragraph again makes the necessary distinction between an author cited in a source article and an author directly cited by use of "cited in." Again, all direct quotations require page numbers.

of sleep they receive each night, the data suggest
that no significant relationship exists between these
two variables. Furthermore, the results of our
investigation suggest quite a different pattern.
While amount of sleep and responsibilities outside of
school had little effect on students' GPA's, it would
appear that age was highly significant. The pattern
suggested by the data indicates that students over 25
years of age are more likely to obtain above-average
grades, while students between 18 and 24 years old
are more likely to receive below-average grades,
regardless of amount of sleep received. The
distribution of average grades was more evenly spread
between the two age groups with the 18 to 24 year
olds only slightly outnumbering students 25 and
older.

The data generated by the present study indicate [10]
that older students perform better academically than
their younger counterparts. Since it is generally believed that intelligence does not increase significantly with age, we have concluded that older students generally have more motivation and incentive
than younger students. We would speculate that older
students take their education more seriously than do
their younger counterparts. While younger students
view their college years as a time to enjoy life and
have fun, adults returning to college after having
already faced the realities of life, regard college
as a last opportunity to better their situations.

This is consistent with the theory of sleep re- [11]
searcher Richard M. Coleman (1986) who has compared
data reported by several sleep deprivation researchers. Coleman theorizes, in Wide Awake at 3:00 A.M.,
that while the ability to perform does not change as
a result of sleep deprivation, the motivation to perform does change. Thus, increased sleepiness requires
greater incentive of the subject in order to perform
at capacity. According to sleep researcher Wilse
Webb, ''If you've got enough inner motivation and
drive, you can go that last mile. If not, when you're
so sleepy, you just give up. It's not your thinking
or memory that goes--it's your will to go on'' (cit-
edin Coleman, 1986, p.93).

**Paragraph 12**   In this paragraph, the writer identifies weaknesses in her research and suggests possible future investigations. This kind of information provides a logical way to conclude the paper, following, as it does, a discussion of findings and implications.

The instrument used for this study restricted the
data gathered regarding the average amount of sleep
of the respondents. Upon reviewing the results, we
discovered that 88% of our subjects fell into one
category, four to seven hours per night, a spread of
four hours. It is possible that if this category were
further broken down, the results might indicate a
higher correlation between students' sleep patterns
and their GPA's. Further studies are necessary before
a connection between students' sleep patterns and
their academic performance can be firmly established.

12

**References Page**   The References page is a separate page that follows the last page of the paper (or the Notes page if one is included). Usually only works cited in the paper are listed as references. The writer lists the sources in alphabetical order, doublespacing throughout and carefully using APA guidelines to format and to provide publication information about each source listed.

References

Coleman, R. (1986). Wide awake at 3:00 A.M.: By
    choice or by chance? New York: W.H. Freeman and
    Company.

Hicks, R., Grant, F., & Chancellor, C. (1986). Type
    A-B status, habitual sleep duration, and per-
    ceived level of daily life stress of college
    students. Perceptual and Motor Skills, 63,
    793-794.

Hicks, R., McTighe, S., & Juarez, M. (1986). Sleep
    duration and eating behaviors of college stu-
    dents. Perceptual and Motor Skills, 62, 25-26.

Nadis, S. (1987, February/March). Mathematics of
    sleep. Technology Review, pp. 13-14.

Sherman, C. (1988, November). The truth about a good
    night's sleep. Working Woman, p. 194.

Sweet, E. (1983, October). Sleep. Ms., p. 96.

Wellborn, S. (1987, June 15). For too many, life is
    just a snore. U.S. News and World Report, pp.
    56-57.

## Discussion of Documentation
## in "Sleep Deprivation"

This paper does a good job of following the general guidelines for writing social science research papers. Considering that this paper is intended for an audience of college students and informed generalists, the writer assembles a workable blend of articles from both technical- and general-interest journals and magazines. The general summaries avoid highly technical jargon but are sufficiently specific to be convincing. Also, the number of citations (7) is about right for a short academic research paper. The majority of citations are summaries of results of previous studies, but several direct quotations are used to lend authority to the paper's contents and to give readers the flavor of the authors themselves.

Specific documentation conventions are also efficiently used. As required by APA guidelines, summaries and paraphrases are cited without page numbers; all direct citations are cited with page numbers. This paper is perhaps strongest in the way it synthesizes the writer's words with source materials. Space and reader effort are saved in two instances when short direct quotations are incorporated into sentences in a smooth, easy-to-read manner. The paper's one long citation is not included as padding, but as a memorable example of the effects lack of sleep can have on job efficiency; the quotation itself is appropriately indented and the source accurately cited.

Again, like most social science research writers, this writer makes clear and effective use of visual material and formatting. The two tables are clearly tied in with the different sections of the paper. The scientific format—*Introduction* (literature review and problem definition), *Methods* (in this case, a survey), *Results,* and *Discussion*—is also effectively used. The sections do not repeat material; they accomplish what they are supposed to accomplish; the headings for each section are clearly marked and placed in the text in the correct places.

Like the sample student paper using the MLA system that follows, the writer of this paper strikes an effective overall balance between her sources and her own ideas. Ideas in this paper are sufficiently influenced by reading in the research and popular literature to strike readers as well-informed; yet, they do not overshadow the author's own research and interpretations. Furthermore, by also carefully observing APA conventions for citing and documenting source information and by using effectively the scientific format for her paper, this writer is able to achieve her writing purposes successfully. She convinces readers that her research and her discussion of it are worth considering and that she has mastered the conventions of academic writing.

## Paragraph-by-Paragraph Marginal Notes,
## MLA Student Essay

**Paragraph 1**   Why has this writer not cited the source of the quotation from a popular song? There are two answers to that question. First, the song lyrics are simply a lead in to the general topic of the paper; as such, readers would not be interested in following up on the source if they were to do some research on their own. Second, this quotation would be considered common knowledge because the lyrics were played repeatedly on the public media. Public or common knowledge does not require documentation.

**Paragraph 2**   The general information early in the paragraph on prospective parents' relationships with obstetricians must be documented because it has been taken from an article by an expert, but the attribution does not require a page number because it is a summary of a general point in Klass' article. The more specific information in the final sentence, however, does require a page number.

**Paragraph 3**   The opening or topic sentence is a summary of the contents of the final three sentences of the paragraph, all of which take specific information directly from a particular article. Each of the final three paragraphs requires documentation, including page numbers; the first sentence as summary of the final three does not require documentation.

# A Sample Student Paper Using the MLA System

Jones 1

Sheila Jones
Professor Greenberg
English 102
23 October, 1991

The Perfect Child: By Choice or by Chance

Looking at my children, I sometimes wonder if I 1
would have changed anything about them if given the
opportunity. I remember the lyrics to the Zager and
Evans hit song of the 60's, ''In the Year 2525,'' in
which they sing of a futuristic world where ''you'll
pick your sons and pick your daughters, too, from the
bottom of a long test tube.'' Today's newspapers and
magazines are filled with articles about new advances
in technology which lead me to wonder if we are close
to the day when Zager and Evans' prediction will become reality. New developments in fetal testing,
coupled with advances in technology, raise an ethical
question of what, if anything, should be done when
tests reveal that all is not as desired in the unborn
child.

All prospective parents want a perfect child and 2
expect their obstetrician to be able to foresee and
circumvent any possible problems in pregnancy, labor,
and delivery, according to pediatrician Perri Klass.
Klass explains that prenatal diagnosis begins, even
before there is a fetus, with genetic counseling for
prospective parents to determine whether there is a
history of genetic disease in their families. Those
who are a part of a high-risk population may desire
testing to see if they are carriers of defective
genes. For example, sickle-cell anemia is often carried by people of African ancestry, while those with
Jewish forbearers may carry the gene for Tay-Sachs
(45).

In addition, new developments in fetal testing 3
are yielding results earlier than ever before, thus
making intervention possible. Ultrasound, a technique

**Paragraph 4** This paragraph provides general commentary on the whole subject of parents' attitudes toward genetic defects. It does not require specific attribution because it is not a paraphrase of any one source. Notice, however, that the final sentence introduces two specific subjects that will require documentation in the following two paragraphs.

**Paragraph 5** This paragraph contains a direct quotation requiring the author's name and the page reference, some general paraphrase requiring the author's name but no page references, along with two summary references with author and page numbers in parentheses. The summary references come at the end of a three-sentence narrative describing the Anderson research and after a single sentence describing critical response to Anderson's work.

by which high-frequency sound waves directed into a
woman's abdomen produce a picture of the uterus and
fetus, is being used as a matter of routine by some
obstetricians (Papalia and Olds 70-71). Ultrasound is
often accompanied by amniocentesis, a procedure
consisting of drawing a sample of the fluid in which
the fetus floats while in the uterus in order to
detect the presence of genetic defects (Klass 45).
The newest procedure, however, chorionic villus
sampling, which involves taking tissue from the
developing fetal sac, can yield the same results much
earlier in the pregnancy (Cowley 95).

With the ability to detect genetic defects early
in pregnancy comes the dilemma of how to use this new
knowledge. Many prospective parents choose to abort a
less than perfect child, while others will prepare
themselves for the added responsibility of rearing a
special child. In some cases, however, other alternatives are becoming available. Among these are gene
therapy and fetal surgery.

With gene therapy, ''scientists are now able to
arrange and rearrange the basic building blocks of
life, to maneuver them into more functional configurations'' (Henig 31). Dr. W. French Anderson, chief
of molecular hematology at the National Heart, Lung,
and Blood Institute and the nation's leading genetic
surgeon, ushered in a new era in technology with his
treatment of a four-year-old girl suffering from a
rare genetic disorder. Dr. Anderson removed billions
of white blood cells from the girl and infused them
with an enzyme crucial to the immune system. The genetically altered cells were then injected back into
the girl where they began to reproduce (Henig 31).
Although this procedure has been highly touted by
some professionals, critics have contended that a
less extreme drug therapy for the child's condition
was already in existence, making the risky gene
therapy unnecessary (Henig 32). While this procedure
has, thus far, been performed only on patients currently suffering from genetic disease, similar procedures may eventually be performed on fetuses in which
genetic defects have been found.

**Paragraph 6** This paragraph describes one scholar's work on the second alternative to abortion or raising a special child, fetal surgery. It depends entirely on one researcher (Hubbard), whose views are paraphrased in the first six sentences of the paragraph. Because the author's name is mentioned in the first sentence of the paraphrase, and pronouns and transitional words are used to show that the same source is being cited, page numbers are only indicated twice, once at the end of the paraphrased information and once after a summary of several pages.

**Paragraph 7** This paragraph is a summary of one researcher's work on an additional type of fetal surgery, the fetal transplant. As a summary, it includes only the researcher's name until the final sentence, where the source article title (this is an unattributed article) and page number are given. Readers are to assume that all the general information in the paragraph comes from this one source.

Jones 3

Another controversial method of treating unborn infants shown to have defects is fetal surgery. According to Ruth Hubbard, professor of biology at Harvard University, this method sometimes involves opening the mother's abdominal cavity and womb as well as the fetus' abdomen. For example, surgery was used to repair the urinary tract of one fetus which died at birth, although the operation was pronounced successful. Hubbard adds that, for a pregnant woman, abdominal surgery has the potential to create a major trauma for both mother and child. The mother's recovery is often difficult and incomplete, since abdominal incisions do not tend to heal well when the abdominal wall is being stretched by a growing fetus. She also believes that prospective parents often accept such radical treatment without question because the scarcity of experts in this field makes it all but impossible to obtain a second opinion. When fetal screening indicates a problem, Hubbard also suggests that parents are unlikely to refuse to grant permission for a physician to intervene, even when the proposed technique is experimental (88). Furthermore, since some women have already been ordered by judges to undergo Caesarian sections when their doctors testify that the procedure is necessary for the survival of the fetus, Hubbard is concerned that prospective parents may eventually lose the right to refuse fetal therapy based on the testimony of their physician (87-90).

In addition, a fetus-to-fetus transplant was performed in May 1990 by Robert Slotnick, an obstetrician and geneticist at the University of California at Davis. In this case, tissue from an aborted fetus was transplanted into a fetus diagnosed with Hurler Syndrome, a rare and fatal disease. Slotnick hopes the transplanted tissue will produce blood cells that will manufacture an enzyme that Hurler Syndrome victims are missing. The child was born in November (1990), but Slotnick states that it will be some time before it is known if the operation was a success. Although there is a moratorium on federal funding for research using tissue from elective abortions, this venture was privately financed. Furthermore, since fetal cells can be transplanted without

6

7

**Paragraph 8** This paragraph includes direct quotations and paraphrases from several different authors, all describing problems that have been associated with genetic research and its implications for parents. Because the information and ideas cited are specific conclusions reached by different researchers, both the author and page numbers of the source articles are given. Where the direct quotation is from an indirect source, "qtd. in" is used as well.

rejection, researchers are investigating their
possible use in the treatment of other diseases
(Lawmakers A2).

    In spite of these innovations, however, there is
no guarantee that a baby will be perfect. In fact,
one of every fifty babies is born with some kind of
defect, although most are relatively minor. There is
concern that advance knowledge that a child will have
some minor flaw may influence some prospective parents to abort (Klass 46). In addition, a project to
decipher the entire human genetic code could enable
doctors to screen fetuses for traits which are not
related to disease. Dr. Paul Berg, Director of the
Beckman Center for Molecular and Genetic Medicine at
Stanford University, believes that it will soon be
possible to locate the genes associated with certain
physical traits, such as kinky hair, olive skin, and
pointy teeth (cited in Cowley 94). Prospective parents would in essence be able to select the traits
they desire in a child (Cowley 94). This could change
the definition of normal, says George Annas, a professor of health law at Boston University's School of
Medicine (cited in Cowley 94). According to Annas,
``The issue becomes not the ability of the child to
be happy but rather our ability to be happy with the
child'' (qtd. in Cowley 94). This screening for imperfections could lead to ``a sort of new-car mental-
ity,'' according to Dr. Francis Collins, a University
of Michigan geneticist who states that ``it's got to
be perfect, and if it isn't you take it back to the
lot and get a new one'' (qtd. in Cowley 98). The primary concern of the public regarding the issue of
gene therapy is that doctors will use this knowledge
to play God. The treatment of a few genetic diseases
may eventually lead to altering the genetic make-up,
causing changes in inherited gene patterns. Critics
want to limit treatment to somatic (body) cells of
those now suffering from genetic disease in order to
prohibit the genetic manipulation of eggs and sperm,
which could permanently alter the genetic make-up of
the species. Scientists would not be able to predict
the results of such irresponsible actions (Henig 34).

8

**Paragraph 9**   Direct citation of one researcher and paraphrase of information on sickle cell anemia are combined in this paragraph, which closes with an author-page reference to the source from which all the paragraph's information was taken. In this case, however, the opening sentence of the paragraph also includes an author-page citation of the same source because the sentence includes a direct quotation.

**Paragraph 10**   In this short paragraph, Hubbard is twice cited as the source of this general information concerning the reasons behind expert opposition to the use of genetic research in solving the infant death and illness problem.

**Paragraph 11**   This paragraph focuses on one long, indented quotation from a scientist who addresses the overall ethical problems facing science today. The expert's name is mentioned in the third sentence of the paragraph, after the problem has been generalized; then, the quotation is included and allowed in this case to speak for itself. This strategy should be used sparingly and only to emphasize important points in short papers. Do not pad your paper with quotations that are longer than necessary.

Jeremy Rifkin, President of the Foundation on
Economic Trends in Washington and the most visible
critic of gene therapy, states that ''by eliminating
all problem genes . . . scientists may unwittingly
eliminate some that are actually beneficial'' (qtd.
in Henig 34). Sickle cell anemia, for example, is
transmitted by a recessive gene and must be inherited
from both parents for the condition to occur in the
child. However, a single sickle-cell gene also con-
veys a resistance to malaria; removing the sickle-
cell genes would entirely remove this resistance
(Henig 34).

In spite of all this new technology, there has
not been any improvement in our country's poor record
regarding the number of infant deaths and illnesses.
According to Hubbard, social and environmental rather
than medical factors may be to blame (89). She also
believes that it is morally wrong to use our resources to promote high technology. Finally, Hubbard
argues that decreases in infant death and illness
would be more easily achieved through social and economic measures than might be possible through risky
genetic experimentation (89).

This controversy surrounding genetic research and
its potential effects on parents and unborn children
is one part of a much larger controversy that permeates every scientific field. The issue in this controversy is the ethical behavior of scientists as
they carry out and disseminate the results of their
research. A. Carl Leopold, a leading plant biologist
and ecologist, captures the heart of this controversy
in the following passage:

> Today, with major environmental crises
> arising on all sides, exacerbated by the
> technological consequences of science, and
> with commercial and military dollars and
> objectives gaining in influence over the
> scientific community, the intellectual el-
> egance of science is being subordinated.
> And so we find ourselves in our current
> state of sciences saturation and ethics
> starvation. (11)

**Paragraph 12**   This paragraph applies the ethical problem to the topic of this paper, genetic research. This is the student author's work; it requires no documentation.

**Paragraph 13**   No documentation is needed since the author is summarizing material already presented earlier and concluding with her own interpretation.

Jones 6

As Leopold suggests, the scientific community must develop ethical codes of conduct that will help define the human and environmental implications of its research. The need for such an ethical code is immediate in the area of genetic research and its social implications. When it comes to affecting parents' attitudes toward their children, moral and scientific issues are impossible to separate.

On the whole, while new developments in technology such as early fetal screening, fetal surgery, and gene therapy may offer a ray of hope for fetuses diagnosed with genetic defects, not all experts agree that this type of intervention in lives of individuals is morally correct. The fact that these technologies are also at relatively early stages of experimentation adds to these concerns about the moral implications of their effects. At this point, and perhaps always, medical professionals will have to use extreme caution as they decide whether or not to recommend the use of these technologies. As I look at my children with all their little quirks, I must admit that I would have changed nothing about them, nor would I have wanted to bear the responsibility of choosing their traits. After all, despite their imperfections, they are just right the way they are.

**Works Cited Page** The Works Cited page is a separate page that follows the last page of the paper (or the Notes page if one is included). The writer lists sources in alphabetical order, doublespacing throughout, and carefully using MLA guidelines to format and to provide complete publication information about each source listed.

Jones 7

Works Cited

Cowley, Geoffrey. ''Made to Order Babies.'' *Newsweek*
    Special Issue. 94-98.
Henig, Robin Marantz. ''Dr. Anderson's Gene Ma-
    chine.'' The New York Times Magazine 31 Mar.
    1991: 31+.
Hubbard, Ruth. ''Embryo and Gene Manipulation.''
    Society May-June 1982: 47-51.
Klass, Perri. ''The Perfect Baby?'' The New York
    Times Magazine 29 Jan. 1989: 45-46.
''Lawmakers Told of Fetus Transplant.'' The Louis-
    ville Courier-Journal 16 Apr. 1991: A2.
Leopold, A. Carl. ''The Science Community Is Starved
    for Ethical Standards.'' The Scientist 6 Jan.
    1992: 11.
Papalia, Diane E., and Sally Wendkos Olds. Human
    Development. 4th ed. New York: McGraw, 1989.

## Discussion of Documentation in "The Perfect Child"

This paper's documentation is efficient because references are accurately and clearly related to items on the Works Cited list. When the information is summarized, it is appropriately attributed to the source without page references; when information is cited directly, or when paraphrases of specific information or ideas are included, page numbers are appropriately referenced. Notice also that the writer is careful to include at least one parenthetical source in every paragraph, even when attributed information is summarized in very general ways. When cited information is more specific, or when several sources are tied together in support of summarized information, then several particular sources are cited within each paragraph. Authors and page numbers appear in parentheses immediately after any directly cited material.

In general, this paper is effectively documented because the writer has assembled a reasonable number of sources, given the relatively brief length of the paper. The sources are also combined in a logical order so that the paper reads fluently. Sources balance both the positive and the negative sides of the issue, although the writer clearly supports caution in response to the new discoveries associated with genetic research. There are several brief direct citations to add the flavor of the controversy itself, but not so many as to preclude the writer's own voice and interpretations. And, given that this assignment called for a relatively short paper, the author has appropriately avoided overusing long quotations. Only one appears, and that one comes near the end of the paper where an important general point about this controversy is attributed to an expert who writes clearly and takes the broad view. In other words, the one long quotation serves a specific and important purpose; it is not simply padding. It is also appropriately indented.

Most important, the writer of this paper has not allowed her sources to overwhelm her so that she has nothing to say, but she has assembled a sufficient number of sources to ensure that her information is accurate and that she has a good general grasp of the issue. You need to work toward achieving this balance of originality and reliance on sources in every paper you write.

## 10
· · · · · · · · · · · · ·
## A CHECKLIST OF QUESTIONS
## FOR REVIEWING DOCUMENTATION

*1. Have you chosen the appropriate documentation system—MLA, APA, or the natural science number system?* Papers on subjects related to social science fields normally use APA; papers on humanities subjects usually use the MLA system. Papers on interdisciplinary subjects should use the system best suited to the fields to which the audience of the paper belongs.

*2. Have you assembled a reasonable number of sources given the recommended length of your paper?* (Six to eight sources is usually appropriate for a five- to seven-page paper.)

*3. Have you integrated your sources into your paper in a balanced way?* Have you overused one source?

*4. Have you cited* only *those sources that you have actually used in your paper?*

*5. When you cite a source within a source have you been sure to accurately relate the source article in the Works Cited section with the names mentioned in the text?*

*6. Have you effectively balanced your sources with your own interpretations in the text of the paper?* Is your paper all quotation and paraphrase with insufficient interpretation on your part? Or is the reverse the problem?

*7. Do you have too many long quotations in a relatively short paper?* Could you cut the long quotations into shorter citations, quoted or paraphrased?

*8. Are your readers always able to tell when cited material ends and your commentary begins?*

*9. Does cited material ever break the continuity or flow of the argument in your paper?* How can you improve coherence by inserting transitional passages between cited material and your own commentary?

*10. Have you used endnotes only when providing extra information that is not directly related to your main line of argument?* Are you absolutely sure that you need to add endnotes?

# Credits

816 CREDITS

*Experience* by Robert Kubey and Mihalyi Csizkszentmihalyi. New York, Lawrence Erlbaum Associates, Inc., 1990. Reprinted with permission.

*Page 566*: Neil Postman, "Now . . . This," from *Amusing Ourselves to Death* by Neil Postman. New York, Penguin USA, 1985. Reprinted with permission.

*Page 577*: Mark Crispin Miller. "The Cosby Show," from *Watching Television*, edited by Todd Gitlin. Copyright © 1986 by Mark Crispin Miller. Reprinted by permission of Pantheon Books, A division of Random House, Inc.

*Page 584*: Eric Copage. "Prime-Time Heroes," from *The New York Times Magazine*, February 2, 1992. Copyright © 1992 by The New York Times Company. Reprinted by permission.

*Page 588*: Kiku Adatto. "The Incredible Shrinking Sound Bite," from *The New Republic*, May 28, 1990, pp. 20–23. Reprinted with permission.

*Page 597*: Kimberly Massey and Stanley J. Baran. "The VCRs and People's Control of Their Leisure Time," from *Social and Cultural Aspects of VCR Use*, edited by Julie Dobrow. New York, Lawrence Erlbaum Associates, Inc., 1990.

*Page 610*: Christine Hall Hansen and Ranald D. Hansen. "The Influence of Sex and Violence on the Appeal of Rock Music Videos," from *Communication Research*, Vol. 17, No. 2, April 1990, pp. 212–234. Reprinted by permission of Sage Publications, Inc.

*Page 632*: Edward L. Palmer. "Our Crisis in Children's Television, Our Deficiencies in Children's Education." From *Television and America's Children: A Crisis of Neglect* by Edward Palmer. Copyright © 1988 by Edward L. Palmer. Reprinted with permission of Oxford University Press, Inc.

*Page 661*: The National Council of Teachers of English. "The Student's Right to Read." Excerpted from "The Student's Right to Read." Reprinted with permission of the National Council of Teachers of English.

*Page 663*: Richard S. Randall. "Pornography and Law," from *Freedom and Taboo: Pornography and the Politics of a Self Divided* by Richard S. Randall, pp. 229–234. Berkeley, University of California Press. Copyright © the Regents of the University of California.

*Page 670*: Irving Kristol. "Pornography, Obscenity, and the Case for Censorship," from "On the Democratic Idea in America, 1972." Originally printed in *The New York Times Magazine*, March 28, 1971. Reprinted with the permission of the author.

*Page 678*: Garry Wills. "In Praise of Censure," from *Time*, September 31, 1989. Copyright 1989 Time Inc. Reprinted with permission.

*Page 683*: Charles R. Lawrence III. "The Debate over Placing Limits on Racist Speech Must Not Ignore the Damage It Does to Its Victims." Originally appeared in *The Chronicle of Higher Education*, Vol. 36, No. 8, October 25, 1989. Reprinted with permission of the author.

*Page 687*: Mary Renck Jalongo and Anne Drolett Creany. "Censorship in Children's Literature: What Every Educator Should Know," from *Childhood Education*, Vol. 67, 1991, pp. 143–148. Reprinted by permission of Mary Renck Jalongo and Anne Drolett Creany and the Association for Childhood Education International, 11141 Georgia Avenue, Suite 200, Wheaton, Md. Copyright © 1991 by the Association.

*Page 700*: Raymond English. "Trials of a Textbook Writer," from *National Review*, February 24, 1989, p. 36. © 1989 by *National Review*, Inc., 150 East 35th Street, New York, NY 10016. Reprinted by permission.

*Page 704*: Mikal Gilmore. "The Year in Music," from *Rolling Stone*, December 13–27, 1990. By Straight Arrow Publishers, Inc. 1990. All rights reserved. Reprinted by permission.

# Index of Authors and Titles